# THE CULTURAL DIVERSITY SOURCEBOOK
## Getting Real About Diversity

Edited by

Dr. Bob Abramms
Dr. George F. Simons

The *Cultural Diversity Series* includes: *The Cultural Diversity Sourcebook* ($50), *The Cultural Diversity Fieldbook* ($27), and *The Cultural Diversity Supplement: Number One* ($17.50).

Production services provided by Michele Anctil

Cover design by Eileen Klockars

Editing services by Ann Hopkins

**Available from:**

P.O. Box 134  Amherst, MA USA 01004

**1-800-736-1293**

**(413) 549-1293**

**FAX: (413) 549-3503**

# Acknowledgements & Dedication

If you are reading this book before the year 2000, it is due to the creative juices, intense energy, and fabulous organizational skills of Ann Hopkins. Her editing and proofreading brought the unruly text to heel. Amy Zuckerman, Nanci Luna Jimenez, Diane Johnson and Susan Beth Bronstein shoved us into the light of clarity as we dialogued and they insisted we follow our logic to the end—even when, at times, they didn't like what we had to say.

Our deep gratitude goes to the contributors whose work is anthologized here. Your eloquent voices touched us personally as well as professionally with the wisdom and experience you shared with us. We are pleased that you allowed yourselves to be enrolled into this diverse choir whose harmony as well as dissonance contribute to a new world symphony.

Partnering as editors and authors has exhilarated us. Keyboarding text at four in the morning, day after day—and often working till eight in the evening—casts a magic spell. Though the two of us have been friends and colleagues for years, our West Coast meetings made us kindred spirits as we "got in synch" with the issues and each other. Thanks go to Pam Fomalont who joined this early morning "Bob and George Show" for a day of brainstorming. Several source pieces and many ideas came from her files.

Later, working coast-to-coast by e-mail, phone and fax we handed drafts and comments to each other at all hours of the day and night. Hi-tech tools enabled us to work hard and efficiently as well as to support and encourage each other. We thank Gabor Lukacs, our computer wizard, who day-by-day made it easier for us to send and receive information from the far edges of the country via dissimilar platforms. His energy, interest and curiosity reminds us, too, of the countless unseen authors of software and systems who manage diversity by building a humanized interface for the future.

We dedicate this book to our own sweet partnership and all the loving partnerships we share, professionally and personally. Once more, dear reader, you hold in your hand evidence that much can be done when we bring our diverse resources and talents together.

February, 1996
Bob Abramms, Amherst, MA
George Simons, Santa Cruz, CA

# Contributors

Sharif M. Abdullah
Maya Angelou
John Balzar
Sharon Begley
Samuel Betances
Ellen Hofheimer Bettmann
Rita S. Boags
Howard Bronstein
Dale S. Brown
George Bush
John Callahan
Margaret Carlson
Tom Chappell
Jeanne Cherbeneau
Bill Clinton
Leonard Cohen
Francis Conley
Mary Cook
Ellis Cose
John Cowan
Geof Cox
Bill Day
Barbara Deane
Arlyne Diamond
Terry Dobson
Kathleen Doheny
John F. Dovidio
Barbara Ehrenreich
R. Todd Erkel
James Fallows
Pamela Fomalont
Audrey Freedman
Robert Fulghum
Sam Fulwood III
Michele Galen
Lee Gardenswartz
Richard Gaskins
Beverly Geber
Benedict Giamo
Paul Glastris
Ellen Goodman
Nikki Finke Greenberg
Jeffrey Grunberg

Philip R. Harris
Rabia Terri Harris
Cassandra Hayes
Melissa Healy
Mark Helprin
Marian Henley
Nat Hentoff
Tony Hill
Evangelina Holvino
bell hooks
Ann Hopkins
Walt Hopkins
Neil Howe
John N. Hughes-Wilson
Pico Iyer
Bailey W. Jackson
Diane Johnson
Edward W. Jones, Jr.
Richard Kahlenberg
Amy Kahn
Neal Karlen
Hank Karp
Judith H. Katz
Anne Kim
Baudouin E. J. M. Knaapen
Jerzy Kosinski
Valdis Krebs
Richard Lacayo
Jake Lamar
Dianne M. LaMountain
Eric H. F. Law
Bertram Lee
Billi Lee
Deena Levine
Elizabeth L'Hommedieu
Lente-Louise Louw
Michelle Neely Martinez
Bill Maxwell
Geoffrey Meredith
Leon McKinney
Frederick A. Miller
Richard Moran
Daniel Patrick Moynihan

Ralph Nader
Annie Nakao
Peggy Noonan
Ann Therese Palmer
Helen Pelikan
Adrian Piper
Price Pritchett
Robert B. Reich
Paul Craig Roberts
Steven V. Roberts
Everett Robinson
James O. Rodgers
Richard Rodriguez
Marlene L. Rossman
Anita Rowe
Hindy Lauer Schachter
Charles Schewe
Warren H. Schmidt
Felice N. Schwartz
Arthur Schlesinger, Jr.
Jeff Shesol
Ralph G.H. Siu
Charlene Marmer Solomon
Shelby Steele
Karen Stephenson
William Strauss
Dianne Floyd Sutton
Nancy Sutton
Elizabeth Taylor
Linda Teurfs
R. Roosevelt Thomas, Jr.
Gary B. Trudeau
Margaret Usdansky
Matthias Vandeweghe
Carmen Vazquez
Anthony Walton
Sally Walton
Cornel West
Elie Wiesel
Kenneth Woodward
Lawrence Wright
Howard Zinn

# Table of Contents

# PART 3
# GENDER ISSUES: PERVASIVE & PERSISTENT

# PART 4
# DIVERSE AMERICA: YES AND NO

# PART 9
# ALTERNATIVE MODELS AND VISIONS

# PART 10
# KEY DILEMMAS: ASSIMILATION, ACCULTURATION &
# SUBTLE DISCRIMINATION

# INTRODUCTION

# Preface

This book is part anthology, part classic articles, and part new ideas never before published. The editors are seasoned diversity consultants who collected, compiled, analyzed, and contemplated the issues of diversity in the U.S.A. today.

They acted as a combination of cultural anthropologists, investigative reporters, and detectives. They were also supported by an extensive network of colleagues, researchers, and professionals . . . people of all backgrounds and political persuasions.

What Abramms and Simons have uncovered has never before been postulated in such a clear and coherent way. Certainly not in the discipline of human resource development. Their work is a revolutionary reconceptualization of the cultural diversity field.

Each chapter of the book begins with a section of dialogue in which the authors tell how they have come to understand the issues and provides a rationale for their selection of each piece. As you think with them through this book, you will see how their conversation and study transformed their own understanding of diversity and led them to look at this field in an entirely new way. You will be delighted and engaged as you follow the trail that Abramms and Simons cut through a thicket of controversy.

# Dialogue: Introduction

*Bob Abramms*—As we introduce the readings in this book, we want our readers to know how this *Cultural Diversity Sourcebook* came about, as well as declare to them the cultural baggage we carry into the territory of diversity.

*George Simons*—We started this project because, as practitioners, we both felt a need to come to grips with the many conflicting views about cultural diversity. So we searched. We sought out interesting thinking, ideas, and experiences. Now we want to share the diverse voices we heard.

*Bob*—Diversity is misunderstood and controversial. It requires high quality focused thinking, analysis, and openness if we are to find a working consensus, or even mutual understanding of its issues.

*George*—Lots of practical literature is out there and an abundance of individuals and groups stating a point of view on issues that concern them. At the same time there's not much critical thinking about the whole picture, its directions, or its values. Diversity itself is a culture in this country and we want to examine that culture.

*Bob*—At first we expected only to edit an anthology, selecting the best of what we'd seen, and drawing ideas from a network of colleagues and associates whose perspectives we value highly. But it turned out to be much more. We researched the field extensively, collected materials for over a year, and met in Santa Cruz, CA for a week of around-the-clock brainstorming. At the end of that process, the final outline for this book took shape . . .

*George*—We've come up with some controversial points of view. But the evidence we've sifted through is compelling! A fresh perspective is needed.

*Bob*—Neither of us alone would have been so brazen as to structure this volume around the concept of "class." Halfway through our brainstorming week I looked at you, and one of us said, "All the evidence *really* points to class as a critical factor in diversity, one that is rarely addressed."

*George*—It's a radical approach. We are not glossing over the traditional factors such as race and gender which made people targeted minorities, but we want to look at these in terms of how they keep people from getting what they need to survive and succeed in this pluralistic society. We struggled with how we could navigate upstream using class as our raft, a worn concept in need of rerigging and outfitting, but one that would provide a new handle on our work and a lead line to our story.

*Bob*—It was a tough decision. After a few minutes spent weighing safer alternatives, we said "yes, class will be the main lens through which we view the landscape of diversity." Once we made our decision, commitment to this "different" perspective refreshed and motivated our work.

*George*—The result, this *Cultural Diversity Sourcebook*, invites our readers to think beyond commonly accepted boundaries. Our authors repaint the diversity landscape. Things can no longer be simply "black and white" (if you'll pardon the pun), but broader, richer, deeper, and more finely textured. "Class" is not just a new set of boxes into which to slot people, with disregard for their other differences and histories . . .

*Bob*—It's been a satisfying collaboration for both of us.

*George*—Yes, here we are, two European American men, over 45, who have been doing diversity work for a combined total of over 50 years, back before it was the slightest bit trendy or even called "diversity." But, the two of us also collected lots of ideas, reactions, and judgments on our visits to other cultures. We actually reflect a host of voices besides our own in what we say. In addition, we've made a strong effort to collect feelings and insights that are usually not heard in the "politically correct" mainstream. We have also listened to the murmurs of concern emanating from those who feel that the diversity enterprise is so fragile that backing off from any of its established principles is betrayal.

*Bob*—Perhaps it is our background that gives us deep trust in, or at least hope for, the U.S. nation and its people. Age has given us perspective on how the country has weathered challenges. We are men who came from what were once backgrounds targeted by the U.S. mainstream culture. We are both of Eastern European descent, one Jewish and one Catholic. This gives us lots of differences but much in common. The systems, fiercely prejudiced against our parents and grandparents, ultimately enabled us to achieve a great deal of success.

*George*—You and I come from rich traditions that look tragedy in the eye, complain and make noise about it, and, at the same time accept the fact that reality always short-changes our expectations. And, after all the time we need to spend saying, "ain't it awful," we are ultimately willing to step in and do something about it. On the one hand, we live in outrage at the imperfections that we see around us, while on the other we have a deep trust that things will work out. I suspect that our familial, tight-knit ethnic backgrounds provided us with a deep love and affection for human beings, strangers as well as kinfolk.

*Bob*—Perhaps that's why we are able to hold the conflicts and contradictions in this collection without despairing . . .

*George*—. . . and have chosen Leonard Cohen as our poet laureate for this volume. A big part of U.S. society feels unheard and ignored. This includes people of color, middle-class white people, and especially those of all backgrounds who are part of an economic underclass. These people are also diverse within their own racial and ethnic groups. They have divergent opinions, attitudes, values, and political philosophies. However, many of them came together as an electorate to speak quite eloquently against "business as usual." They elected a very conservative slate in the November 1994 elections. They will not be ignored.

*Bob*—And, increasingly, diversity trainers are viewed as "out of touch." We have made it our goal to present fresh perspectives that enable us to "get real" with each other, and with other stakeholders in the debate. We want organizations and managers to know the approaches to diversity that actually work and benefit their organizations, or, at least, to know what can backfire and cause more harm and resentment than good.

*George*—That's one reason we subtitled the *Sourcebook* "Getting Real About Diversity." Getting real for me means having a dialogue that rings true to the whole picture, rather than an airy notion of how we'd like things to be. It means we will speak our truth, but know it is only one of many that make up the reality in which we swim. We need our visions, but tempered with a pragmatism, and the willingness to look at what's selfish, short-sighted, raw and ugly, and what just doesn't cut it.

*Bob*—This work makes me recognize how culture-bound I have been as a white, privileged, middle-class American. I now explicitly see certain assumptions about myself as an American that I hadn't recognized before, even when dealing with diversity. My perspective is more international. We have deliberately included selections in this book that offended me when I first read them three or four years ago. Now they seem not only legitimate and valid, but unique and important.

*George*—You and I have begun to recognize—it comes out in this book—that there exists a relatively consistent U.S. culture with a vision of what the U.S. can and should be. Though we U.S. Americans have fought tooth and nail about how to achieve that vision, we accept certain values and principles by which "we the people" operate. Outsiders looking in (and we especially draw upon European perspectives) help us to see this common strain, this macro-culture amidst all the diversity found in our many micro-cultures—those sub-groups with their own values, norms, and objectives. So, we have listened to their voices here.

*Bob*—You define culture, I seem to recall, as a set of internal rules which groups create for survival, things we say to ourselves to make sense of our world and prompt ourselves to succeed in it.

*George*—Culture is whatever people, as groups, do, create and learn to live in their environment. Imagine a family, a nation, or a profession talking to each other day-in and day-out about how to survive and succeed in their niche in the world. They even stay awake nights mulling over these conversations and what to do next. When they fall asleep, their dreams organize and reinforce their experience. Cultural discussions live on in the minds of everybody who hears them, first hand, second hand, and in succeeding generations.

*Bob*—So, rules for success emerge, new ideas and spin-offs tell us about "how to do things around here."

*George*—Culture, what is talked about—and what is not—both determines the way we see and hear things, as well as sets up the filters that keep us from seeing and hearing other things. When we think, speak and act, we dip into our culture as a vocabulary, as a toolbox, even when we rebel against it. Whatever we say or create in the world is an external projection of that conversation within, whether we write a book or design an automobile . . .

*Bob*—. . . or create an Affirmative Action policy, or design a diversity training seminar.

*George*—Right. Cultures are finite, time bound, they age and die—just like the people who host them. Cultures not only blind us to certain things, they tend to reinforce themselves by repeating the same messages over and over again. Without renewal, without outsiders to shake things up, a group takes the values and practices that are working for it and overdoes them, even to the point at which they self-destruct. Diversity keeps a culture from this ever-tightening vicious noose, from hanging ourselves with our own success.

*Bob*—Today we have the chance to renew the U.S. macro-culture, the dominant culture that keeps reinserting itself into the U.S. psyche of old-timers and newcomers alike. Diversity is like a big shot of vitamins, giving us the energy to work out a new balance between the forces of cohesion, what holds us together, and the centrifugal forces of difference that drive us apart.

*George*—There's never a perfect equilibrium, but only a dynamic balance, a swaying to and fro. We teeter like a kid walking on top of a fence with arms outstretched. Too much cohesion and we have repression. Too much balkanization and we are no longer a commonwealth. Either way we fall. After a couple of decades in which U.S. Americans sought separate identities you can feel the forces for cohesion kicking back in today, to meet new survival challenges.

*Bob*—But today's dynamic environment demands constant corrections, new perspectives and new input. If we entrench ourselves in the monolithic culture against all these changes, then I think we

are doomed. Balance is also easier to achieve when you're in motion, going somewhere, when you have a future. It's like riding a bike.

*George*—Yes, today there are no corners to hide in. Millennia ago, cultures may have held still for hundreds of years, although I think even that stability may have been somewhat illusory. Inevitably populations would just exhaust their land and turn it into a desert or otherwise weaken their culture by repeating what worked until it no longer did. Either they would disappear or be invaded. This would simultaneously destroy and reinvigorate the culture.

*Bob*—In today's instantaneous global, electronic world, everybody can benefit from diversity to meet the flood of change because diversity is itself part of the flood.

*George*—Think of the tremendous cultural power wielded by the media, the print and broadcasting culture. The world can upset its cultural ecology just as easily as devastating the rain forests in Brazil. To illustrate—we stopped growing certain vegetables because they aren't viable on the market. Now, every major supermarket in California has the same tasteless tomatoes year round, and out-of-season unripe fruit from Chile and New Zealand. You can recognize the seasons not by what is available, but by what it costs. In this North American culture of uniformity . . .

*Bob*— . . . the local farmers recently made a comeback. First, in organic produce stores and eventually in the supermarkets. On one hand we have a not-so-satisfying generic produce "culture," and then diversity reasserting itself, but you get less and pay more.

*George*—Do we want the broadcast and print media to do this to people's notions of nature? Can we stop it if we don't? Has it already irrevocably done it?

*Bob*—It seems to me that any discussion of diversity needs to start by looking at how we achieve the common good of people in the U.S. Historically, our country assumes that the common good will be achieved if different groups promote their own self-interest, and give-and-take is permitted to freely occur in the political and economic "marketplaces."

*George*—It is our cultural assumption, our basic stance that if everyone is free to speak his or her mind, and individuals can proceed unhampered in their search for happiness, the good of all will be best served.

*Bob*—Balance of power and enlightened self-interest—these are the enduring ideals in the U.S. myth. (We discuss this further in our Dialogue in the "Diverse America" section.)

*George*—When, again and again, people have tried to short circuit this process, to take power, to suppress conflicts of interest, the system hasn't let them do it. We don't allow anyone, Douglas Mac-Arthur, Richard Nixon or AT&T to have too much power. As a result we have the oldest continuous standing governmental system in the world.

*Bob*—That dynamic is now reflected in the politically correct [PC] movement. It has long been obvious that a majority dominant white male culture had shaped work and political culture and set the rules for our society. If this was not yet apparent to some, our changing workforce demographics have now made it crystal clear. A reshaping of language and culture was needed if we were to respect different experiences and tap a broader knowledge base. But the PC movement does not teach diversity with a smile (See Ehrenreich article on page 288).

It tries to level the power by changing the dialogue—and it had many successes as well as created some truly silly expressions—but it overreached itself by trying to limit free expression, imposing an immoral moralism. No one likes a police state, the PC police included.

*George*—But this excess is a part of the process. I don't have a problem with attempting to limit freedom of speech sometimes—you and I do it to each other. It's a natural part of our struggle to be heard. But the point is that we're not very successful if we are equal in power. Our attempts to limit freedom in an egalitarian relationship actually call it forth. The same is true in the big picture. The system ultimately levels those who are overbearing and controlling, those who abuse it. Right now the macro-culture is eating up political correctness like a hungry Pac-Man. The remaining problem is that the larger cultural system also perpetuates the situation of those who have little voice or power.

*Bob*—People always have to fight their way in the door.

*George*—The U.S. social agenda has always been one of reluctant inclusion. When a group gets enough friction going to squeak, they get some grease.

*Bob*—It always astounds me, as you mentioned, that we live in the country with the longest standing government in the world. It has survived crises with FDR, with Nixon almost being impeached, it has and continues to have vast numbers of marginalized people, and it goes on. Still, I would like to improve the quality of our public dialogue.

*George*—Let's face it, public dialogue in the U.S. is adversarial—think of the history of unions and management. We both want a more compassionate, inclusive dialogue. But, apparently, in this culture we get there by letting our pain hang out, by complaining, by being squeaky wheels. Dialogue does not happen by deciding what's better for others to say and not say. At the moment there is a crisis of belief. We have not met our own expectations. Cohen's song reminds us "Democracy in the U.S.A." is never finished, it's always "coming," sometimes growing out of the bleakest realities. We'll only see what it looks like in the future. (See Leonard Cohen's song, "Democracy," at the end of this section)

*Bob*—Cohen's stubborn faith is an unseen, maybe unconscious, force that drives us on—not only to wait it out, but to do what we need to do. In this book, the position we take is shared by many on the political right—that debate should continue—rather than the position of many on the left, who say that because some speech has hurt others in the past, such speech should be limited in the future.

*George*—I don't think it's a position of either the right or the left—those are just convenient boxes people put each other in. Right and left have both tried to limit freedoms of speech and thought at various times with equal ineffectiveness. The right has no monopoly on being and thinking "American." Nor does the left.

*Bob*—Free speech is irrepressible here. It keeps bubbling up from below, right or left, no matter how long it takes. The truth will out, as it did in the story of the "Ludlow Massacre" (page 41).

*George*—Many women (and men who have bought into those women's point of view) fear men's speech as by nature too violent, too individualistic. If that's how the system works, they want a different system, one with a richer context of acceptance and understanding, one that automatically empathizes and foresees, one more based on personal relationships. . .

*Bob*—. . . some ethnic groups tend to be oriented this way as well.

*George*—But the question is, how much of relationship orientation can we have, or do we want, in the public realm? We know there is a positive side to relationship orientation, but at the same time we are wary of its dangers. While the U.S. system cannot be fully successful in eliminating favoritism, cronyism, nepotism, etc., it tries. Democracy, to the degree that we have it, ultimately is about getting, having, using and keeping a voice. Democracy has grown here to the degree that people have fought for and got suffrage.

*Bob*—The greatest threat to freedom of speech is that people don't speak up. That they let the media debate things for them. That the challenges are so large and so frequent that we become passive. The nation is now a theater in which there are too few actors and too many in the seats: a TV audience.

*George*—So we struggle about who has voice, and how much they have. We argue with those who would limit our voice. We try to limit the voice of those who have too much so that others can have some.

*Bob*—That's why our task as editors is to give voice to a variety of perspectives, to air contrary points of view, and to look at alternative models. Maybe, as well, to try to glue it all together by sharing what surprised us in reviewing current events affecting race, ethnicity, majority-minority, dominant and non-dominant groups, focusing wherever useful through a freshly ground lens of economic class. Most of all, we want to stir our readers into getting involved.

*George*—The "lens of class" was until recently not available to us. It was un-American to talk about class in our supposedly egalitarian society. The language of class had been largely taken over by the communist international movement, making discussion of class even more taboo in the U.S.

since the 1930s. Most in the U.S. (except for sociologists conducting research and academic debate) couldn't, wouldn't, or didn't have the vocabulary to talk about it.

There are few operative definitions of class. For example, when the government proclaims that X number of people are below the poverty line (defined by a certain income level for a certain-sized family), that is a definition of class. Such facts in hand, we can seek a new and better way to distribute the common good in a diverse society. The identities assigned in the present system, black, Caucasian, Asian-American, etc., don't necessarily lead us to what people need now.

*Bob*—Or, who they are. It is just the category they've been assigned and it perpetuates false stereotypes about who we think they are.

*George*—The distinctions we make, the "social constructs" as they are called, have real consequences that keep reinforcing themselves. That's why we propose a break. Not because "class" is necessarily the best distinction, but because it is again serviceable. For some years now, we have avoided class distinctions by using the word "diversity." It's not a bad word, but it's a bit gooey—everything sticks to it. "Diversity" has always been hard to define. When it was faddish, people packed it with whatever meanings they needed to ride the wave. Still, the word is useful if we see it as a category of activities and divide it into its constituent tasks.

The first task of diversity is achieving distributive justice. We need to ensure that all kinds of people get what they need from the common good, financially, educationally, in terms of goods and services, so that the country and its individuals are strong and healthy. This is not only fairness but enlightened self-interest, for it does me no good to have abundance in *my* life if I need to barricade myself behind 10-foot metal gates, barbed wire, security systems, and take my life in my hands simply to take a stroll in the moonlight. Women remind me that this is not new for them—they have always walked the streets at higher risk than we men.

*Bob*—We must also reduce bias and prejudice in order to be able to simply work in the same environment together. I define prejudice as using perceived group differences to stigmatize some people as less intelligent, less competent, less worthy than other groups and individuals. Getting individuals to eliminate the exclusion, the bias resulting from prejudice . . . that's diversity task number two.

*George*—We want to open the door to new public and private initiatives, to a better legislative approach, to creating a technology for dealing with poverty or the lack of access to goods and services. We need to do more to equalize the distribution of goods and services. This works at both ends, however: if someone is getting far too much, it is difficult for someone else to get what they need.

*Bob*—The overpaid and undertaxed are siphoning off resources that the organization and society need to be stable, healthy, competitive, etc. in far greater amounts than those needing social services. With the demise of Marxism touted as a worldwide solution, we can now address this issue again without being or sounding like communists.

*George*—Capitalism has to be more than simply a Darwinian, dog-eat-dog, survival of the fittest. Otherwise, it is only a caricature of itself. Ideally, capitalism is one way of achieving the common good. But in reality, we have something we call a capitalist approach which is not delivering the goods. It's certainly not working for our society to imprison an ever-increasing percentage of its population, while the underclass swells in numbers.

The third diversity task is improving people's intercultural skills. It answers questions like, "How do I deal with a specific group of people or individuals who are different from me?" "How do I communicate and negotiate with them?" "How do we get tasks done together, delegate effectively to each other?" "What do we need to know about each other to work as a team? To give good feedback?" We can't create results in the world of work unless we learn to work across differences as a team.

*Bob*—These are skills which all of our organizations need to have if they are to achieve their objectives and mission, especially in a global marketplace. Without them, how can they sensitively and effectively market to a diverse, consuming public? The American Express Financial Advisors

Benchmark Report contains some excellent examples of how organizations have sought this competence (see page 199).

*George*—That's right.

*Bob*—You know, some people tell me that diversity is a smoke screen for avoiding issues of distributive justice, real economic change, and shift of power. Power comes from having the resources to do what you need or want to do. If people don't have those resources, you can tell them how to get along with each other better, but it will not solve their basic problem. As long as we confuse economic justice with the need for intercultural communication, many African-Americans, for example, are right to worry. Such an understanding of diversity siphons off energy that should be used to meet the needs of people who've been thrust into an underclass. It's both justice and intercultural competence, not either-or . . . and justice is first.

*George*—And those people are correct to be concerned! In this book we're also going to question how well Affirmative Action works, and this can feel even more threatening. Remember that Affirmative Action created legally protected classes, but these classes are overlapping with, but not identical to, economic class. They were based on the important premise that the historical exclusion and poor treatment of women and minorities needed to be righted, that the playing field had to be leveled so that everyone could have equal access. They did exactly that for thousands of people. Equal Opportunity legislation followed to make sure that once the door was open, it would stay open, that people would be hired, promoted, etc., fairly. We went on to protect people from harassment on the basis of race and gender, etc. All of these have borne fruit and benefited our society.

*Bob*—Yes, Affirmative Action did a lot of that, but it wasn't perfect and today there is a strong call to revamp its faults and dilemmas. The AA-tree must be pruned or grafted with new more effective stock. Fewer people are willing to accept what looks to them like quota systems for hiring, admission to colleges, etc. At the same time some organizations and institutions are beginning to recognize the value that can be added by a diverse workforce. For them difference is a potential asset. Proactively hiring for variety itself is a legitimate bottom-line strategy, not a pious corporate handout. Affirmative Action was the starting point that led us there.

*George*—But it is not Affirmative Action, itself. The hope of getting the value added by diversity (our fourth diversity task) too rarely gets us to dip intentionally into the hiring pool of the poor and disadvantaged. We look for the brightest and the best, whatever group they come from. These are hard to find and recognize among the disadvantaged, given our cultural filters about abilities of the poor and their educational deficits.

*Bob*—There is still a core task of achieving justice facing all of us, government, organizations, people.

*George*—We've talked about the four diversity tasks (1) achieving justice, (2) bias reduction, (3) cultural competence and (4) diversity as value added. Later in the book we'll give our readers a more detailed look at them.

*Bob*—All of them are interrelated and affect each other. All of them are empowering. We need to discuss them separately, though, because the resources we give to each are different depending on the priorities they hold.

But, let's talk about ways we get power: people can give it to you; you can buy it; you can negotiate for it; you can seize it. Getting and having power is related to class.

*George*—This is frightening because we can define class in terms of power, too, who has it and who does not. Seeing naked power makes us feel unsafe and afraid. Unless we address it, though, the power struggle will show up in the form of violence if needs and grievances go unredressed for too long. Powerlessness and inequity in the distribution of power create violence. I won't empower others if I feel diminished by the process.

The Cold War created a balance of power. The tension frightened us. But this is not so frightening as what festered behind its walls, what it seemed to hold in check. The Cold War was like the *Portrait of Dorian Gray*, Oscar Wilde's book. Dorian Gray's debauched life never showed up on his ever-youthful face but was revealed in the ever-changing oil painting hidden in his room.

Now that the power of European communism has faltered, the facade of the Cold War has crumbled. In the power vacuum we now see conflicts all over the world that we don't have the know-how or resources to handle. Pessimistic critics like Benjamin Schwarz ("The Diversity Myth: America's Leading Export" in *Atlantic Monthly*, May 1995, pages 57–67) imply that the only way to manage diversity is for one group to dominate all others.

On one hand, Schwarz's analysis rids us of our illusions about how smoothly the integration of society has been achieved. On the other hand, we are reluctant to admit the truth about how cultural domination has operated in the U.S. and around the world. Even if Schwarz is on the money with his assessment, we don't agree that because cohesion has always been brought about by force, that this must always be so. However, Schwarz reminds us that successful pluralism is an uphill battle against great odds. It's often been an open power struggle. The violence isn't always with guns and bombs . . .

*Bob*—There's the economic violence towards people who cannot have access, maybe even the psychological access—the courage—to the means to support themselves.

*George*—Or the economic violence of people who get so much more than they should or need out of the system through exploiting others. It goes unnoticed that many older people take large social security checks even though they have no need of the system while the less well-off elderly continue to slide down in the economy. Older is fitting into the class system, too.

*Bob*—Or, on the other hand, consider the actual violence of people who enter the business called crime. Crime really is the ultimate entrepreneurial activity: you take responsibility for your actions; you assess risks. Take drug dealing—this is one of the few forms of capitalist opportunity available to marginalized and excluded people. Nothing pays so well in some neighborhoods.

*George*—That window of opportunity closes easily as well. Most people are foot soldiers. The power and the resources get funneled to the top perhaps even more quickly in this underworld than they do in society at large. Organized crime is hardly an equal-opportunity employer. It's business as usual there, too.

*Bob*—We are looking directly at this steadily growing underclass that the U.S. is creating, and we have to ask how to address and remedy it. What can we do as socially responsible business persons to enable people of different classes to coexist? Where do we get our motivation to undertake this effort? From fear of what will happen if we don't?

*George*—I've heard little discussion of the ethics of diversity. On a practical level some people are reacting to abusive training exercises and "new age" mind melts. Ethics for many has had to do with religion, but because of the separation of church and state in the U.S., our culture says spiritual values are private matters. Pragmatism reigns and we are reluctant to examine values until events force us to do so.

*Bob*—Religious values and spirituality creep and seep into the conduct of the state through the individual anyway. And these are not always mainline religions. We heard rumors of how Ronald Reagan's astrologer influenced public policy decisions and we now hear that Bill Clinton consults personal achievement gurus like Steven Covey or Tony Robbins. To this extent, the separation of church and state is a pretty porous social construct anyway. Spirituality is in our psyche; we're just not willing to take the risk of making it public.

*George*—It's a U.S. cultural value that whatever works in the market is moral, and will, at least in time, self-correct. The unseen hand will prevail. But I have trouble seeing how this is true. If the U.S. provides a wonderful market for cocaine, and drug barons in Latin America are willing to supply that market, will it self-regulate at any point soon enough to prevent awesome damage? We would like to believe that people would regulate themselves, but addiction sabotages this possibility.* This is why legalization is so hotly debated. If I can be asked to take the messiah of modern capitalism, Adam Smith (*Wealth of Nations*), on faith, surely Moses, Jesus and Mohammed, to name a few, have equally good credentials to give us principles to live by.

*Bob*—When strongly opposing moral views exist in a country, an ongoing intelligent debate should

be taking place. We should bring our whole selves to it, not leave our faith at home or hide it under a false veneer of rationalism. This debate should result from time to time in consensus or satisfying trade-offs, and in new social contracts about what will be created and what is permissible or not permissible. This is really what public discourse and law should be about.

*George*—If we could only get people to spend as much energy thinking about our national welfare as they do prosecuting, defending, or following the O. J. Simpson trial, things might be different. Public discourse and law must protect those who cannot protect themselves, whether by disadvantage, addiction, age, etc. This is based on a contract between states and between the individual and the state.

Despite the lofty language of the Constitution, social policy gets negotiated in the U.S. The parties may change, but the process remains. The "Fathers" of the Constitution (for such they were, men, mostly landholders) designed a brilliant document. They borrowed from both European theorists and the practices of Native American groups such as the Iroquois Federation—diversity was at work even then. Though the framers of the Constitution excluded various groups in its time, it became the template on which suffrage and other rights became available to our entire pluralistic nation. This is a far cry from what occurs in many other cultures. Coming to grips with the negotiated nature of the citizen's role in America can be both challenging and damaging to the immigrant or non-participant in the mainstream of society.

*Bob*—Could you elaborate?

*George*—Well, imagine coming to this country from a place where authority is handed down from ruler or is organized according to class, caste or role. Coming here, I have to learn about social contracts by experiencing this new culture. This wreaks havoc on my cultural values. My children begin to negotiate with me, rather than obey me,

---

*Anne Wilson Schaef has a lot more to say about society and its addictions related to this topic (*When Society Becomes an Addict*, 1987, Harper Collins). However, her analysis goes beyond what we are able to cover in this *Sourcebook*. See also Schaef and Diane Fassel in *The Addictive Organization* (1988, Harper Collins).

because that's what they learn at school. You see, even in the U.S., up until recently, children were to various degrees excluded from full rights, but that is changing today. The "American way" is expanding here in the U.S., not disappearing, because of diversity. Outside the U.S. people fear that it will devour them, too. "Imperialistic U.S. culture," they call it.

I have no question but that those mainstream U.S. values will endure. Call it the "melting pot," if you want. The mainline U.S. culture is not even being seriously stressed. Rather it's reinforcing itself and its values not in spite of, but because of, immigration. This immigration, legal and illegal, whether newcomers arrive from Asia, Latin America, or Eastern Europe, is based on prior knowledge of the U.S. culture. If we look at the amount of cultural information transmitted around the world today, we see that the people who come to these shores know much more about us than the Poles, Irish or the Italian immigrants knew decades ago. New immigrants are becoming Americans before they even get here.

*Bob*—Older waves of immigration came because people thought the streets were "paved with gold." They integrated, assimilated without previous knowledge of the language or culture. But we hear now that today's immigrant is less willing to buy into the notion of setting aside his or her cultural background lock, stock and barrel.

*George*—I disagree! It is part of PC dogma, and I don't think it's as true as many would like to believe. The best I would be willing to say is: Most immigrants still believe assimilation is the road to success. They want to learn the language, to become full U.S. citizens. Assimilation may be harder and slower to some degree because of greater cultural differences, and there may be more cultural conservatism and clustering because of this. On the other hand it becomes easier because of TV. To those of us born in the 1930's, in cities with thriving Polish, Italian, Irish, Czech, Latino, etc., neighborhoods, shops, clubs, churches, financial institutions and the like, the present situation seems quite normal. Assimilation may be happening even faster than before.

Earlier immigrants had their little Italies etc., but most of their children eventually moved to the suburbs and lived together. Now the old neighborhoods are gentrified and their ethnic flavor is sold at a high price in trendy boutiques and restaurants. Assimilation slowed at the color line, of course, which has for historical reasons been more resistant, as has the rural Latino population.

Oppression reinforces ethnic, racial identity, not freedom and participation. Class keeps people in their current place, especially when we use some arbitrary and indefensible notion of skin color to place people in an underclass. Race benefited European immigrants—they could be one with the macroculture by clearly not being "Negro." Even though some newcomers still use race in this way, it gets harder as many new immigrants are people of color. At the same time, interracial and interethnic partnering is on the rise. More than half of Puerto Ricans on the mainland, for example, marry people of other ethnic groups. Color is more a concept than an identifiable skin pigment (see "Who's what?: The crazy world of racial identification," page 455).

*Bob*—So we have a tempest in a melting pot because though we see differences here, outsiders can certainly see our U.S. values and mainstream approaches to life no matter who we are.

*George*—Exactly. We think different is someplace else.

*Bob*—So, we've come up with several provocative and controversial declarations:

First, "class," which one could barely speak of five or ten years ago can be rehabilitated to take a fresh look at social issues that need to be addressed. Class, equal opportunity and justice, not ethnic and racial difference will become key issues in the diversity debate.

Secondly, the values of U.S. mainstream culture and assimilation into it are alive and well. This culture itself will change as a result of assimilating newcomers and the marginalized, as it always has, but it will create for the foreseeable future an even more distinctive "U.S. culture."

Thirdly, and this is reflected in the section on issues that affect African-Americans, (starting on page 50), racism and bigotry are real, they occur, and result from three hundred years of racial prejudice and oppression. But using race and culture as the only handles for resolving these issues

11

is a dead end. These issues may be helped, but they will not be solved either by diversity training efforts or, for that matter, even by Affirmative Action. Each of these taken alone may be compounding the problem it hopes to solve. Looking at things from an exclusively black perspective is understandable, but may make the problem intractable. On the other hand, to look at people on the basis of what they need and what they can do, rather than by who society has decided they are racially, redefines the debate and provides a new entry point.

*George*—As a matter of fact, we include examples of how culture specific information about African-Americans is useless and counterproductive in the face of class dynamics.

*Bob*—It's about exclusion from power. Where power is not equal, any talk of race creates resentment and resistance.

On the other hand, we believe that gender is different in this debate—another controversial position. This is particularly true as far as how gender differences are played out in the business world. The more we frame gender as an important cultural difference, talk about issues, communication, selling styles, negotiation styles and understanding language as a cross-cultural issue, the more successful we will be at working with colleagues, bosses and subordinates of the other gender. So we have a section on this issue.

*George*—Yes, gender behavior is about cultural role, not about class. However, failure to see it as role, combined with contemporary economic trends, is quickly making it one of class. While women as a group still technically control vast amounts of money and disposable income, live longer, their edge has been slipping for over two decades now.* We also see many of them sliding into poverty, especially single women with children. This not only points to *The Feminization of Poverty* but with the growing popularity of divorce in the '60s and '70s gave rise to a whole new generation, now young adults, who grew up in poverty.

When gender and race are combined, as they always are, it becomes very complex. Gender-related issues, the situation of gay, lesbian, and bi-sexual people for example, deserve to be looked at on their own, but they also stir this up for us in a productive way. They challenge the roles we are used to.

*Bob*—That just confirms gender as a critical issue. People go berserk about homosexuality because it touches them at a very deep level. This is a justice issue, too, since gay people per capita are the targets of more violence than any other group in the population. Lesbian and gay people remind us that distributive justice involves not only not being bashed, but things like fair taxation and equal benefits, job security and removing the "lavender ceiling" to promotion. On the level of interpersonal justice it has to do with the freedom to love whom you will and to be equal members of one's own family. But it is totally different from the black justice issue. Many black people resent the confusion of the two. What I hear from black people is, in general, that gay people are good earners, not part of an underclass—there are exceptions of course.

*George*—Homophobia in the African-American community also connects uncertainties about gender roles which are undergoing their own forms of conflict. Homophobia looks different from culture to culture.

*Bob*—For most gay people, diversity needs to pay attention to the bias reduction level first, not on the economic level. Of course, you can't work exclusively on one without the other, but you can pay attention to the focal tasks as we recommend in the last section of this book (see page 476).

This *Cultural Diversity Sourcebook* airs voices that say what we are doing is not working. Our section "Diversity under Fire" (page 260) presents ideas which actually lead to another section toward the close of the book which relates to the dismantling of Affirmative Action—a hot issue in the current political climate.

---

*While women, on the average, control substantial wealth, most of this is, in fact, the result of surviving their spouses. Also, statistical averages can be misleading (see sidebar by Robert Reich, page 21). The "median" and "modal" average incomes of women have dropped dramatically, as opposed to the "mean" average income. The increase in divorce rates of our society is inextricably linked to two basic economic facts: (1) divorced men's standard of living increases, and (2) divorced women's standard of living drops by as much as two thirds.

*George*—But, much of what we're doing is working: especially those efforts that have a link to the bottom line (refer to Marlene Rossman's "The Importance of Culture in Marketing," page 315) or are integrated with mainstream organizational efforts (for example see Dale Brown's "Quality Through Equality," page 307). Are there bits and pieces that have become archaic? Yes. Are there bits and pieces we can no longer use because they are simply not doing what they were intended to do? Again, yes. But if we assume that justice will take care of the diversity issue or the cultural issues, we're crazy. Conversely, if we think understanding cultural differences and those skills will take care of justice, we are just as crazy. Many of our authors point out assumptions that have been falsely made. They encourage us to reexamine how we use our tools.

*Bob*—Politically, we're in a course correction. The contrary perspectives assembled here need to be heard even if, or especially because, they challenge the assumptions of mainstream diversity practitioners.

Two other aspects of this *Sourcebook* make it unique. First, there is a section on spirit, exploring that aspect of the American psyche which is steeped in religious tradition and as Leonard Cohen puts, it, "the spiritual hunger." We are, perhaps, the most religious nation in the world. Attendance at religious services is slipping but still substantial. Spiritual traditions are alive and new disciplines and sects proliferate. Faith and spirituality continue to have a lot to say about dealing with others, about managing diversity.

The second unique aspect of this book is that we realize that many dilemmas still exist for which we and our contributors have no answers. Some of these, like assimilation vs. acculturation, subtle discrimination, etc., are tricky. We leave it to our readers to tease out their own answers from their own resources, some of them spiritual. In this *Sourcebook* we have tried to frame those questions, pose the issues, ask good questions . . .

*George*—Or, at least contribute to the on-going dialogue.

# DEMOCRACY: A Song Written by Leonard Cohen

It's coming through a hole in the air,
from those nights in Tiananmen Square.
It's coming from the feel
that it ain't exactly real,
or it's real, but it ain't exactly there.
From the wars against disorder,
from the sirens night and day,
from the fires of the homeless,
from the ashes of the gay:
Democracy is coming to the U.S.A.

It's coming through a crack in the wall;
on a visionary flood of alcohol;
from the staggering account
of the Sermon on the Mount
which I don't pretend to understand at all.
It's coming from the silence
on the dock of the bay,
from the brave, the bold, the battered
heart of Chevrolet:
Democracy is coming to the U.S.A.

It's coming from the sorrow on the street,
the holy places where the races meet;
from the homicidal bitchin'
that goes down in every kitchen
to determine who will serve and who will eat.
From the wells of disappointment
where the women kneel to pray
for the grace of G-d in the desert here
and the desert far away:
Democracy is coming to the U. S. A.

*Sail on, sail on*
*O mighty Ship of State!*
*To the Shores of Need*
*Past the Reefs of Greed*
*Through the Squalls of Hate*
*Sail on, sail on, sail on . . .*

It's coming to America first,
the cradle of the best and of the worst.
It's here they got the range
and the machinery for change
and it's here they got the spiritual thirst.
It's here the family's broken
and it's here the lonely say
that the heart has got to open
in a fundamental way:
Democracy is coming to the U.S.A.

It's coming from the women and the men.
O baby, we'll be making love again.
We'll be going down so deep
that the river's going to weep,
and the mountain's going to shout Amen!
It's coming like the tidal flood
beneath the lunar sway,
imperial, mysterious,
in amorous array:
Democracy is coming to the U.S.A.

*Sail on, sail on*
*O mighty Ship of State!*
*To the Shores of Need*
*Past the Reefs of Greed*
*Through the Squalls of Hate*
*Sail on, sail on, sail on . . .*

I'm sentimental, if you know what I mean:
I love the country but I can't stand the scene.
And I'm neither left or right
I'm just staying home tonight,
getting lost in that hopeless little screen.
But I'm stubborn as those garbage bags
that Time cannot decay,
I'm junk but I'm still holding up
this little wild bouquet:
Democracy is coming to the U. S. A.

# Managing Diversity in Stressful Times

by George Simons, Bob Abramms, and Ann Hopkins

During the past several years, America has faced a number of significant stresses: a painful economic recession, the conflict in the Persian Gulf, a presidential election, the Los Angeles Uprising, and, consistently, violence running rampant on the streets, at home, and in the workplace. These public happenings not only stress the general public. They lay heavy pressure on both employees struggling to succeed and those people who must run diverse organizations. Managing immigrants and expatriates, as well as individuals and groups different from oneself, becomes immeasurably harder under such stresses.

Carmen Vazquez, a consulting colleague of ODT, Inc., likes to say, "None of us gets up in the morning, looks in the mirror, and says to her or himself, "I'm going to be very ethnic today." The stresses of the day, however, bring out our cultural bent. The greater the stress, the more reactive we are likely to become. Instinctively we resort to the ethnic, gender, class, etc. behaviors we were brought up with. Our native biases toward those who are different return full-blown. In a few moments we may damage years of effort and sabotage our best intentions of managing diversity.

## Economic Downturn, Diversity Downer

Economic downturn can be a major stress for inter-group relations. When the economy is booming and expertise and labor are in short supply, it is easy for an organization to see opportunity in employing people from targeted groups and encouraging immigrant labor. When recession kicks in, however, the mood shifts and we are tempted to see people who are different as a threat to the economy because they are stealing jobs from "our own." When these co-workers act like themselves or speak their own language to each other, for instance, their behavior gets blown out of proportion, becoming more of an irritant to those in the host culture and harder to accept than when the economy is thriving.

Along with downsizing and rightsizing, abetted by new computer and communications technology, comes flattening and reinventing the organization. Women and people of color who have patiently and impatiently worked their way up the ladder find out that there is no next floor to climb to. White males find their expectations frustrated. Resentments are fueled as one goes from fast-track to slow-track, and even to no-track careers. The career plateau is with us for the foreseeable future.

As lower paying jobs go abroad, worker resentments grow. Targeted groups and microcultures dig in and become reactive and resentful as well. Realizing increased vulnerability, stress increases. People try harder to be successful, to fit in, and to please in order to avoid becoming targets of the macroculture. Inevitably, they revert to their cultural background for strength and self-esteem, diminishing their willingness to learn and adapt, heightening their resentment.

Those without strong ethnic identity and ties to rely on—the situation of many white men—find their self-esteem totally devastated when threatened with joblessness. U.S. culture has told those who have joined its mainstream that "you are what you do." If you are doing nothing, then you are nothing. The dismissed white worker cannot fall back on being an oppressed Black or Chicano for solidarity and consolation, and is thus perhaps more dangerous to himself and others in such circumstances. A parent who is a woman continues to be a mother in such circumstances, but a father by inner cultural programming usually sees himself as a provider and is therefore not acceptable to himself or others if he is not providing.

## Wartime Perceptions of Others

When the nation feels its security interests threatened, people who are not fully assimilated

15

into the mainstream become suspect. This is most true when we are at war, cold or hot, with the nation from which immigrants or visitors to the U.S. have come. In this regard we do not seem to learn from history.

The American government was fresh from handing out compensation checks to Japanese-Americans interned during World War II when the Gulf War began. Once again national security became worried about the wartime behavior of persons of foreign backgrounds, in this case Arab-Americans and Arab individuals and groups living in or visiting the U.S. Oftentimes, these reactions go unrecorded in the popular press or even history books. Witness the recent "discovery" of the internment and relocation of German-Americans and Italian-Americans during W.W.II (see article from the *San Francisco Examiner* on page 187).

At the outbreak of the Gulf war, the FBI stated two security concerns. The first was the threat that some of these Arab-Americans or Arabs in America might pose, i.e., they could be involved in domestic sabotage or terrorism or be sources of information to others who were so involved. The second was that Arabs might become targets of ethnic hatred on the part of others in the U.S. whose fears and resentments had mounted during the tense weeks of war. Private organizations had in some cases acted on similar security fears. Arab anti-discrimination organizations had already before the war been complaining about the media's use of Arabs as stereotypical bad guys in films and print. Now, persons of Arab backgrounds would be even more subject to surveillance and protective action.

Managing these concerns, without violating civil rights and harassing individuals, became a major challenge to security organizations. Fortunately, the shortness of the Gulf War kept the situation from becoming full-blown and perhaps another disaster. Paradoxically, at such a time, native-born Americans as well as people of foreign descent try particularly hard to be committed citizens and good workers. Non-Americans strive to be well-behaved guests. Yet, differing cultural background drags them into misunderstanding and conflict with each other. As the "Cold War" against Iraq and Iran continued, prejudice smoldered beneath the ashes, ready to flame up with every new stress. Today, acts of terrorism such as the Oklahoma City bombing can be automatically attributed in the popular mind to Middle Eastern terrorists, until the evidence shows otherwise.

## The Stress of Political Debate

Every time an election year rolls around, it brings group interests into public debate. This is both good and bad. Elections highlight differences in order to resolve problems. They also bring out inflammatory rhetoric and heighten our identity and our passions. The debate casts issues in stark contrasts with few shades of gray. We easily slip into stereotyping and vehemently defend our prejudices. Candidates embody constituencies and positions and become objects of adulation or spite. Virtually every candidate and issue is positioned as being the "most American," reiterating and reinforcing old myths and raising fears about who is and who is not American.

Two recent examples of such stress come to mind. NAFTA, though not a ballot issue itself, became a political hot potato as candidates for office took positions on it. Anti-NAFTA propaganda subtly played on the Mexican character and the fear that jobs would be lost to Mexicans on both sides of the border. More recently, California's voters passed Proposition 187 intended to restrict services to illegal immigrants. Under the stress of this debate both sides played on ethnic fears and racist accusations. This debate was not stilled by the passage of the initiative, but continued in the struggle both for and against its implementation.

## The Criminals among Us & the Criminal in Us

America is, without question, one of the most violent civil societies in the world. The recent flood of brutal crimes has jolted us to awareness of a seamy side of American life that outsiders have long recognized. Hopefully this will stimulate examination of our national culture and its cult of the individual, of gun-toting frontier folk, of lone rangers, and of mavericks, unless our characteristically short attention span prevents it. We are shocked when, for example, people from Israel say that they would not like to live in the U.S.A. because it is too violent. Danger to life and limb to individuals is statistically higher here.

But who are the bad guys? Fear and stress make us imagine them as the "other," the swarthy, or the white devil. We often imagine that the criminal and the morally evil person has a certain profile, or "look." In film, comic books, and editorial cartoons, we use certain physical looks or disfigurations to picture them. This perpetrates bias against the visibly disabled and those whose appearance fails some cultural litmus test for being comely or handsome. Or, the female villain of our fiction portrayed as seductively beautiful, puts women in the double bind of not being okay if they meet the standards of beauty and not okay if they don't. The criminal images we carry inside us keep us from dealing with criminality in a realistic way. Better dressed "white collar" criminals are usually punished in far less severe ways than working class criminals despite the actual enormity of the injury of white collar crimes to the victims and the common good.

When, several years ago, Jeffrey Dahmer's grisly cannibalism hit the headlines, a major fast food chain called us for consulting help. Across-the-counter tension between blacks and whites in their Milwaukee stores was on the edge of violence. Normal differences in eye-contact, handling money and food and verbal pacing, which blacks and whites tolerate (perhaps at some level, even enjoy) during normal times, become irritants under stress. These differences provoked outbursts of anger and bitter complaints in a population already beset by the horror of what had taken place in their own neighborhood.

## Stress Works in Us and on Us

Stress throws us into a survival posture; we get ready to flee or fight. When we listen to ourselves, we hear the more primitive layers of our mind speak. We are more prone to make quick and simple distinctions, and, as the old saying goes, "to shoot first and ask questions later." We are driven to become more "ethnic" or more male or female. In short, we become more of what we were in the narrow confines of our family or in-group and less of what we have learned to be as mature, self-directed adults taking our place in a diverse society.

This transformation or regression can happen at any time. It doesn't require the threat of war or recession to provoke it. Typical reactions between women and men can increase friction under many kinds of stress. Even a gender sensitive man, who supports the women he works with on a day-to-day basis, can become reactive when he loses out to a woman for promotion, for example. Old negative judgments about women, their place, his suspicion about how she got what he failed to get, etc., may surface in his mind.

Poor management or lack of management can be stressful. The failed air traffic controllers strike is history now, but a look at the issues showed that paramilitary styles of management compounded a per se stressful job. The air controllers union destroyed itself by not recognizing the source of stress—they needed better management but asked for money. Today diversity can be the scapegoat for bad management. Recently a public agency called us to mediate what they described as a "major diversity incident" in one of their offices. Someone had been called a nasty name. Examining the situation, we discovered a group of workers, harassed by demanding clientele, who had been doing a daily average of four hours of overtime, unsupervised, for almost a month. Name-calling may be inexcusable; but stress resulting from bad management was the culprit here. All the diversity training in the world would not have made much difference. You can easily increase intergroup resentment by forcefully and falsely defining a problem as one caused by differences.

In this anthology we have radically reconceptualized the diversity debate beginning with what we believe to be a key theme that we will keep coming back to: the issue of CLASS. We will cover a number of additional key perspectives, including provocative and critical pieces that take issue with many common diversity approaches as currently practiced in American business today. The end of our journey will be the piece, "Getting Real: Where are we?, Where are we going?" (page 491). In the final chapter we offer a model (page 495) which should help to explain why much diversity practice is misdirected. The deeper understanding of the issues we hope we offer here should give managers, public officials, diversity trainers, as well as the general public a better handle on how we attempt to grapple with differences in our society and the multitude of factors that influence us. We are excited and optimistic. We also realize it will not be an easy journey. Leonard Cohen in "Democ-

17

racy" captures the spirit of our enthusiasm (and concern) for the future.

## About the Authors

George Simons and Bob Abramms are co-editors of this *Cultural Diversity Sourcebook*. For contact information and biographies see page 505.

Ann Hopkins, an ODT Associate, is also a teacher, psychometrist, and editor, particularly of works in philosophy, economics, and management. Her interest in diversity issues, class structures and cultural biases developed while teaching traditional and non-traditional students in the United States and writing and teaching English as a second language while resident in India.

# PART 1
# CLASS:
# <u>PREVIOUSLY UNSPEAKABLE</u>

# Dialogue: On Class

*Bob*—Our lead article in this section, "The Mighty Wedge of Class," reflects what it means to be identified, or not identified, with a particular class background, to have or not have certain privileges in the United States today.

*George*—Two things command attention here. The first is the powerful account this article gives of the permanent effect of class on an individual's personality and place in life; where she or he is placed in terms of resources, opportunities, and expectations about the future vis-à-vis the other people that this person encounters. This impact is much greater than simply how much you earn.

Secondly, it reminds us to emphasize again that, when we talk about class in the U.S., we reject Marxist assumptions about class warfare and the proletariat. We mean simply that America is being divided in terms of resources, such as money and education, and access to these important opportunities is severely limited. This needs to be recognized. All we have to do is look at the numbers.

The sidebar comments by Robert Reich, "Averages are Misleading," further clarifies how Americans may be doing better economically "on the average," while we have an ever increasing population slipping below the poverty line (see also "1.3 Million Drop into Poverty," page 29). It's amusing to see how Reich sees growing international trade making boundaries difficult to determine . . . "who's us?" versus "who's them."

*Bob*—The middle class is disappearing, leaving a nation of haves and have-nots. This is documented and supported by another sidebar, this time from the Society for Human Resource Management (SHRM) report, "Trend Toward Inequality." (Also see Bill Clinton's remarks, page 480).

*George*—And this is exactly what we're concerned about. What lies in this section will help the reader get a better sense of how profoundly class issues affect our society.

*Bob*—We are opening up a taboo topic. So, although our dialogue may be somewhat rough at first, let's begin.

*George*—We're searching for new handles in areas where the diversity enterprise has not been working, not only in dealing with hard-core exclusion of Black and Chicano populations, but also with underclass people of European and Asian descent or origins.

*Bob*—To illustrate the problematic nature of racial or ethnic differences, we've included a *USA Today* article on the invisible black middle class and the class differences between middle and upper-class blacks and poor blacks ("Success Dividing Blacks," page 30). Middle-class blacks face ongoing bias, prejudice, and discrimination. Our next section on African-Americans will document that compellingly. But poor blacks face these obstacles compounded by the disadvantage of "class"—a lack of access to resources that could leverage them out of poverty. But being part of the underclass is not exclusively a black issue. It's a pervasive (and growing) circumstance shared by other Americans of all races and ethnic backgrounds.

*George*—So the first article shows how class divides white people and the second article how it divides black people.

*Bob*—Yes. But in addition, we're looking at the results of class divisions. The *Time* article, "Time Is Not on Their Side," describes the backgrounds of classes not keyed into the macroculture's values and how their isolation reinforces alienation from those central values. Apparently Black English as it developed in Detroit, Watts, Chicago, or Mobile has similar patterns but is not linguistically connected to a common source. It developed, rather, from similar patterns of exclusion from the macroculture. The next piece in this section (page 34) offers several definitions of "class" so we can get a better handle on what exactly we're talking about . . .

*George*—As we talk, the media circus around the O.J. Simpson trial continues to stir up questions of race, class, and the fair administration of justice.

Whatever the outcome of the trial, how we think about the issues is affected by our perceptions of race and class. Beyond the trial of the man, our perceptions are on trial. We have long known that there are class distinctions in the administration of justice in this country—who is arrested, who has access to resources to defend themselves, and who is found innocent or guilty . . .

*Bob*— . . . but this case upsets them all. The rich man is black. If he is acquitted will it be because he is a rich man, or if he is found guilty will it be because he is a black man? This is a struggle between which is more relevant, class or race.

But there is more to the issue than the influence of race and class. We've also included in this section an interview with Jerzy Kosinski called, "Chance Beings" . . .

*George*—He's the writer who survived the Charles Manson massacre because he didn't show up for the party that night. He's also a holocaust survivor whose credibility has been recently impugned by some who say he made up most of his stories or took them from other people. His writing is nonetheless a powerful body of literature.

*Bob*—His interview relates homelessness to class. We are the only nation in the developed world where such numbers of people are so destitute, so impoverished that they have no place to stay. No other developed country applies so little attention and resources to this problem. The interview appeals to me because it takes a provocative, controversial and realistic perspective in saying that the U.S. culture and psyche preclude a solution. It helps us realize peculiarities unique to our culture.

*George*—And helps us reflect on those peculiarities. In terms of our definition of culture we can ask, what are the inner conversations that lead us to tolerate this level of homelessness? What are we not paying attention to?

*Bob*—What do we say to ourselves when we pass someone who is homeless and sleeping on the

---

## AVERAGES ARE MISLEADING
### by Robert B. Reich, secretary of labor in the Clinton Administration

Three weeks ago the Census Bureau reported that last year median incomes in America declined, although average incomes increased. How can that be? It means that the American who is smack in the middle is still losing ground, but there is a group of Americans at the top who are gaining so much ground so fast that the average goes up. (Beware of averages. Shaquille O'Neal and I *average* six feet tall. The average misses the interesting details. Beware of medians as well.)

What we're seeing is a gradual spread—of benefits, of income, even of employment opportunities. We now have a 5.9 percent unemployment rate—that doesn't really mean very much. If you're a college graduate, your unemployment rate is 3 percent. If you just have a high school degree, your unemployment rate is 9 percent. If you have less than a high school degree, you are higher than 12 percent. And if you are a teenage dropout in the central cities of America, it's 40, sometimes 50 percent unemployment. So what does a 5.9 percent unemployment rate mean when you have this widening disparity? . . .

My wife and I recently had to buy a new car. Now granted, I'm the labor secretary, so we went to a Big Three showroom. (We would have done it anyway.) We found a car that perfectly met our family's needs. I asked the salesperson, "Tell me honestly. Was this car actually built and assembled by American workers?" He looked at me for a long instant, trying to decide: Was I one of *those*? Or was I one of *those*? Then he looked up with a smile and said, "Which would you prefer?"

Who's us? Who's them? It's becoming very difficult to tell.

I had my hips replaced not long ago . . . and I was curious, thinking about global economics and global products. I made some inquiries, and it turns out my new hips were fabricated in France and designed in Germany. I do not even meet the domestic content requirements for being a cabinet secretary. (I'd appreciate it if you kept this in this room.) Who's us? Who's them? I don't even know who I am.

Excerpted from a speech delivered to Northeastern University, Boston MA (10/27/94)

street? What sense do we make of that as Americans? The article from *Newsweek,* "Down and Out in Washington" fills in the picture about how the homeless get dismissed. Unemployment and homelessness are gateway issues to our controversial discussions in the "Diverse America" section. In the U.S., who a man is, is defined by what he does. We find today that the largest group of unemployed people are white men between the ages of 24 and 39. So when you, as a white man, find yourself unemployed, who are you?

*George*—You have no cultural resources to fall back on, especially if you feel alienated from being a white American. This raises issues about what happens in a society when you have large numbers of unemployed people who feel their identity and dignity has been stripped from them. Throughout this book we're saying that social attention should be directed to unemployed people, regardless of race or gender.

If I were an old-time Marxist I would see this as another example of the conspiracy of the rich to exploit the divisions among the poor. We create legally protected groups and make token efforts in their behalf keeping the majority of the deprived workforce powerless, and perhaps ripe for revolution, so that the rich can get richer, etc. I reject most conspiracy theories—they drive me nuts. But often the dynamics of a situation produce the same result as if there actually were a conspiracy.

*Bob*—So we're moving away from old categories to see what moves our nation can undertake to improve things. In our section on "African-Americans" when we encounter a key question like "how can we do the right thing for blacks?," the response is: "do it for everyone!"—everyone who is part of an underclass, excluded, disenfranchised. Class is a powerful and controversial organizing scheme. For us it has become a more insightful and useful way to understand the work of diversity.

However, we must acknowledge that to most "ordinary" Americans this framework for analysis will be unusual, provocative, and probably be just beyond their level of current awareness. When we are deeply embedded in a system of cultural assumptions, to question them seems off-the-wall.

This relates to some assumptions that Ralph Nader identifies (page 40). He says the "corporatist" per-spective of U.S. media coverage is an excellent example of why certain questions get asked, and others don't—because of our deeply embedded assumptions. As another example, we've also included a piece of history from Howard Zinn (page 41). "The Ludlow Massacre," reflects, I think, how history and current dialogue about class issues has been constrained to the traditional area of politics. When the *LA Times* reviewed the book containing this piece they called it "a shotgun blast of revisionism that aims to shatter all the comfortable myths of American political discourse." (See also quote from James Baldwin on page 110.)

*George*—Cover-up is not new, though we thought it was invented a couple of presidential administrations back. But it also tells us that the class issue has been muddled by the race and gender issues and needs to emerge from their shadow. I really hope that the last thing readers of this book will think (though it may be the first thing) is, "Here's a couple of white guys taking shots against women and blacks." I think we're a couple of white guys who have unearthed evidence of a cover-up dynamic. We are not alone in suggesting that much of the diversity effort may have been a smoke screen to distance us from these issues in which poor people would have solidarity if they were not divided by race, gender, and so on.

*Bob*—Just think—if everybody used their one vote to influence social policy (even in their own enlightened self-interest) what different results we'd see in our elections. The fact that people of color were excluded from voting until the civil rights movement of the '60s is no different from those who are prevented from voting now because they lack a legal residence.

Compare this social policy (on who gets to vote) to what many European nations do. For example, they hold elections on Saturday, so people don't have to worry about taking time off work. In the U.S. those privileged people with flexible hours vote more often than people working long hours in tightly structured job situations.

Don't think this has been by accident. The framers of our constitution saw the propertied class as the only responsible citizens, and the tradition continues. The idea of a universal franchise (i.e., any citizen can vote without prior "registration") has been resisted most aggressively by the political party (the Republicans) who have the most corporate sponsorship. Conspiracy? Perhaps not. Coincidence? I think not! Another example—people in the foreign service who did not have a home they had lived in for a certain period were not eligible to vote in U.S. national elections until the 70's. Thus, until then several million people were disenfranchised.

*George*—Which raises the issue of how the U.S., its citizens and its residents are divided and counted (dealt with in "Dismantling Affirmative Action" section, page 436) and what effect this has on our political process and our diversity efforts.

*Bob*—Let's try to get beyond some of the blinders of our cultural assumptions. What's the big picture. What's really going on here? One of the most astute observers of the interrelated nature of

American crises is Sharif Abdullah. In "Critical Indicators of a Need for a Global Culture" he illustrates how the mega-crises we face often have us focus on symptoms rather than root causes. His book, *The Power of One* (from which the figures on page 45 are drawn), forces us to look into our current dilemma. He makes connections between and among the mega-crises of: diversity, leadership, economy, fulfillment, and ecology. We agree with him, that to look at diversity in isolation (as is so often done in many corporate training programs), is a flawed approach.

*George*—We conclude with the article from *Time* magazine, "In Search of a Good Name." At the end of the piece, Henry Louis Gates, Jr. articulates his concerns not for what people are called as much as about economic and social equality. Our analysis supports the same conclusion.

# The Mighty Wedge of Class: On the dissonance between middle-class packaging and a working-class core

by R. Todd Erkel (*Family Therapy Networker*)

*Although it's getting more difficult all the time, it is still possible to change classes in America. Rags to riches stories—or assembly line to corner office stories—are fewer than they once were, but they still happen. But just because people's educational and financial circumstances have changed doesn't mean their insides have. Caught between two worlds—the one they grew up in and the one they've joined—the newly middle class often feel uncomfortable, adrift, and most of all profoundly alone. This is the moving story of one man, now a middle class writer, who grew up working class, and what the transition has meant to him.*

On a Saturday evening late one May a few years ago, I stood outside a recently opened restaurant and watched as cars overflowing with hockey fans toasting Pittsburgh's first Stanley Cup championship lurched down the street.

The procession stretched as far as the eye could see along East Carson Street, the main drag running through the city's South Side. Car and truck horns honked out a victory song. Grandmothers came outside in babushkas to watch from the top of the steps. The usually quiet and purposeful regulars abandoned their stools at a dozen or so nearby family-owned bars and joined the celebration.

A decade had passed since the last shift walked out of the gates at the hulking Jones & Laughlin Steel plant that stood watch here for more than a century. For many, the hope that life would somehow return to normal ran out only recently when the mill was finally razed, its two-story corrugated shell cut into pieces and sold for scrap.

In the intervening years, the surrounding neighborhood had taken on a new blush. Young professionals, drawn by high-tech work and the lure of urban homesteading, had put a fresh face on wood and brick row houses. The neatly stenciled windows of a French restaurant stared across the street at a weathered newsstand; an art gallery cast its postmodern neon glare over an old, boarded-up saloon. As urban chic invaded a working-class community, the two cultures tried to work out a modus vivendi.

On this one night, the familiar dividing lines between the vernacular (shot-and-a-beer) and the fashionable (white wine spritzer) blurred as post-game revelers spilled out onto the sidewalk. Scanning the crowd, I spotted a face I hadn't seen since the eighth grade. Beer in hand, my old friend weaved his way through rejoicing hockey fans to get a closer look.

"Is that who I think it is?" he asked with just the right hint of disdain. I felt my stomach tighten and my victory smile fade. I'd experienced enough of these reunions to know what to expect. My college-issue wire-frames, $20 haircut, and button-down J. Crew collar confirmed what he had probably suspected all along: My aspirations had changed me; I was no longer one of his kind.

He took a slow gulp from the beer bottle and looked hard into my eyes. This was his chance to balance the scales, and he made the most of it. "Who the fuck do you think you are?" he sneered. It was a statement, not a question, and he didn't wait for a reply. The street sounds faded as I watched him disappear into the crowd.

I tried to match the face of the man I had just met with that of the kid who came to my house every Wednesday evening to watch "Lost in Space." I stood there on the curb and mourned another small death, another connection to my past severed.

I revisited the jumble of fierce resolve, nagging guilt, and painful humiliation that had churned inside me for most of the past decade, a time spent zealously reinventing myself. I experienced the familiar dissonance between my estranged parts: my middle-class packaging and my working-class core. Split in two by the mighty wedge of class, I asked myself the same question: Who am I? Where do I belong?

I remember late-summer afternoons 20 years ago, my 10-year-old self fidgeting at the supper table, having once again cleaned my plate too quickly. After a perfunctory minute or two, I would dare to break my father's rule against talking during meals and quietly ask to be excused. Bounding out the front door, I would skip every other step down to the sidewalk and tear past the neat row of squat brick houses, listening for the exhilarating sound of the wooden screen door as it rattled shut.

My friends and I would pass the rest of the evening playing whiffle ball or walking upright across the five-foot-high monkey bars. When it grew too dark to see, we would sit with our backs to a stone wall and enjoy the sweet smell of pot drifting down the street. Later, we would make plans to sleep out, walking the steep, narrow streets of the neighborhood to collect blankets and shrugs of permission from our parents. On those warm summer evenings that stretched into sleepless nights, we discovered the balm of conversation and laughter, virtues—like the warm beer and cheap cigars we stashed behind the garage—that we knew better than to drag home.

In the morning, we were awakened by the sounds of men climbing into their faded pickup trucks and trying once more to grind cold engines to life before heading off to work—as mill hands, ironworkers, railroad switchmen—long before the morning rush hour. Those men—our fathers—stood tall among the world's industrial workers and rose, with each negotiated pay increase, to a level of economic parity with many of their white-collar counterparts. They endured high school, married young, bought homes, and looked forward to a week's vacation every summer.

As their children, we figured life somehow would provide the same to us: a revolving Sears charge, a nice if not quite new car, possibly even a boat or a truck-camper like the one kept safe behind a tall fence in the back alley. As economically middle-class people in a working-class culture, we enjoyed unprecedented comfort and security.

When I decided to go to college, my mother and father offered the only advice they could: "Well," they said, "we hope you know what you're doing." But implicit in their lukewarm endorsement was the obvious truth: I didn't know—any more than they did. So, without a guidance counselor, or parents versed in the calculus of financial aid and college applications, I proceeded arbitrarily, applying to colleges whose names or looks appealed to me. I eventually settled, for no particular reason, on Penn State.

Having applied too late to attend orientation, I arrived in State College, Pennsylvania, with what I soon learned was more than a clothes problem. My credentials—an impressive grade point average and high test scores—gave my application a veneer of promise. But there was no measure for the things I didn't know, nothing to suggest I might have to learn everything about this new world of college from scratch. The system, like me, was blind to the ways in which my working-class background left me unprepared for this new world. It wasn't just poise or spending money that I lacked. Everything from my colloquial speech to my primitive social skills to my wardrobe drew a discreet line between me and my new peer group.

Adrift in this community of 60,000 not-so-kindred souls, I looked to the only place I knew of to place the blame for my ineptitude—inside, with myself. Overwhelmed by feelings of alienation and worthlessness, I quit. In retrospect, I wonder why nobody—if not my parents, then a teacher or college counselor—could have foreseen my difficult transition to college; not just from one phase of education to another, but from one set of cultural assumptions to another, one entire world to another. I wish, too, that I could have let the full extent of my alienation be known.

Even at the University of Pittsburgh, where I eventually transferred and where the presence of students from working-class backgrounds similar to mine was plain to see, the issue of class remained eerily unspoken. Though part of me knew better, I could not escape the crippling feeling that I remained alone in my bewilderment. While the university struggled with factoring the issue of race into the equation of college residents and retention of students, nobody thought to take similar precautions with working-class white students.

Quiet and hiding in the back corner of a college classroom, I began to make the connection between my feelings of shame and the working-class misgivings toward education I had long ago internalized. For while lip service is paid at every class level in America to the idea that education is the route to a better life, the reality in most working-class homes is that knowledge counts for less than good behavior. The question my parents asked every day when I came home from school was not "What new thing did you learn today?" but "Did you get into any trouble?"

The working-class experience makes the child particularly vulnerable to low self-expectations. Before I could sing the alphabet, I knew something of what it felt like to be my parents: low-achieving, poorly spoken, lacking confidence, afraid to challenge authority, reluctant to ask for help, willing to accept their situation, content to do without.

It wasn't just my parents' lack of understanding and sophistication that blocked me from a fuller view of life's possibilities, but a deep sense that failure was our fate. The message received by children whose parents have battled with the world and come away feeling defeated is that they are better off not even trying. A pervasive feeling of helplessness hangs over the working-class house like the secondhand smoke that passes silently from parent to child.

Embracing the promise of an education requires working-class children to construct an inner sense of themselves that is radically different from that of their parents, siblings, and friends, to betray their allegiance to the only source of identity and support they have ever known. At each crossroad, and with every success, I became more aware of the dichotomy—the ways in which my education simultaneously would provide me options and distance me from the life I trusted.

---

## THE TREND TOWARDS INEQUALITY

For two decades now, incomes in the United States have become more unequal—reversing a trend of increasing equality from World War II. Poverty is spreading at the same time that earnings at the top are soaring. Moreover, social mobility among income classes seems to have deteriorated. For the last quarter of the twentieth century, while our economy produces very slow growth in Gross Domestic Product (GDP) per person, intergroup competition is becoming more acute.

Studies have shown that income is highly associated with education, so one facile answer is to spread education resources liberally. Other studies indicate that family background is an essential pre-conditioning factor in educational attainment. There is no public policy answer on that one. Politically popular remedies call for reducing welfare and social services, with the nostalgic idea that Depression conditions will toughen up the poor and drive them into transforming work experiences. Another popular theme is to blame poverty on immigrants (who are, historically, the most upwardly mobile of all U.S. residents).

One thing is clear. Rising income disparity is undercutting our sense of well-being and security. It saps the typical American energy to think that there is a problem that we don't know how to "fix." Worst of all, that problem threatens the center of the American ideal—democratic equality among citizens. We were getting there after the war, and now we have lost it. This failure may lie at the heart of the sourness of public mood, even in an era of prosperity. It is certainly coloring politics.

The United States seems to be facing another round of domestic policy choices: How much can the government actually accomplish? Do we want the government to attempt it? Is there an effective role for any other institution—say, business enterprise—in accomplishing a social goal? Public discourse will focus on the proper role of government and of business, and will thrash out the tradeoffs between conflicting goals. A serious question is whether we can keep it civil.

---

HUMAN RESOURCES FORECAST 1995, © 1995 Audrey Freedman.
Each year, Audrey Freedman convenes a group of chief executives, vice presidents of human resources, academics and other human resources experts to discuss economic and management issues. UCLA sponsors the meeting, the Society for Human Resource Management circulates the report to its 60,000 members. This quote is from Mrs. Freedman's description of mid-decade human resource problems. The full report can be ordered for $25, prepaid, from Audrey Freedman & Associates, 111 Broadway, fifth floor, New York, NY 10006-1901.

A decade later, the anger I have long felt toward my parents has slowly faded. I realize now that the gifts I so desperately wanted from them (an easy self-confidence and a deep well of optimism) were not theirs to give. Instead, they handed their children a promise, visibly broken, in the hope that we might know better than they did how to make it work. In America, the illusion of free and open passage between classes is preached with religious zeal. But parents who wish for something better for their children must struggle against more than an incomplete education and economic deprivation. They must confront the truth behind the myth of making it in America: The land of opportunity is also the land of persistent class structures and struggles. And though many try, most people never rise very far from the socioeconomic level into which they are born.

Without an awareness of their experience of class discrimination, working-class kids will continue to absorb their parents' shame. They will continue to view the world—through their parents' eyes—as a malevolent force to be approached with rightful caution.

Without some explanation for the feelings present in the home, children internalize their parents' sense of powerlessness. Their unexpressed fears quietly sap the strength of the family. My middle-class friends know enough about the destructive force of class to see me as an exception: a triumph of will over environment. But we sidestep any discussion of a class system in America, afraid maybe of the feelings such awareness might stir. It's easier to assume that we now all occupy one vast, comprehensive middle class.

What I don't mention, and what others don't see, is that I often feel more lost than ever, caught between two widely separated social rungs, never sure whether I should forge ahead or fall back, uncertain whether either option really is mine. I have learned to pose in the middle-class culture, but at a price. I live most of the time on borrowed instincts, afraid to trust that part of the working class I still carry inside.

Today, my family is still wondering what on earth I will one day do for a living and uncomfortable with my willingness to expose the personal details of my life on paper where anyone might read them. They don't share my interest in what has gone before, in the past, even their own. They dismiss writing, or any kind of self-reflection, as an escape from the more pressing demands of the moment. I am engaged with the world in a way they have never known, and still don't altogether trust. Looking back, the memory of growing apart from the people and habits I know and love stirs a swirl of feelings. I still yearn to believe that my parents know what is best. The adult I've become appreciates why such knowledge eluded them. I understand more clearly the gain of my leaving their world. I'm only now willing to consider the loss.

## About the Author

R. Todd Erkel is a freelance magazine, public policy and speech writer. He has written on topics ranging from sports to international trade. His special interests include writing about class issues, land use, men's roles, and travel. Todd is co-founder of Friends of the Riverfront, a non-profit organization. He received the inaugural Clearwater Award from The Waterfront Center, a Washington, D.C.-based organization, for his work in improving public access to Pittsburgh's formerly industrial riverfront. He can be reached at: (412) 281-0482 ext. 3146; Fax: (412) 644-5512.

This article first appeared in *Family Therapy Networker* and is reprinted here with permission. To order back copies or a subscription, call 301-589-6536.

## ON VALUES:

Peggy Noonan interviews Sen. Daniel Patrick Moynihan

**Peggy Noonan:** [voice-over] I started by asking him about the optimism he felt as a young boy growing up in the '30s and '40s, an optimism this country seems to have lost. [interviewing] This is something I do not understand. We're in the middle of prosperity in this country, and yet the ebullience that you describe, it's not there. It's a hard thing to figure out.

**Sen. Daniel Patrick Moynihan:** It's a hard thing to figure out, but there are places to start, and the first is the exhaustion . . . that has come about in the course of 50 years of war and cold war. The largest event in our time is that median family income really has not grown since 1973. The cold war took a lot out of us. We can't get it in our head, and we can't dismantle its institutions in Washington. They're going to go on forever. We began with that oil shock, and something went wrong, in terms of the experience of just average-ability, average-educated workers. There's that. But there is something else also, which is that we have lost the family structure capable of disciplining young males. It is the most difficult thing in any society, and it's universally difficult. There's an African saying that it takes a whole village to raise a child, but it does at least take one male present. In our major cities, it's not unusual to have half the children born on Medicaid, which means they're paupers . . .

**Peggy Noonan:** Are you anxious about the future of the American democracy, about our ability to continue well into the next century?

**Sen. Daniel Patrick Moynihan:** I am anxious, indeed, we are going to produce a society divided along the class lines that you associate with family well-being and with a dependent population and a population resentful of the dependent population. We already see some of that. And in the end, you could have a not pretty place, and not a beautiful America. To the contrary —

**Peggy Noonan:** An America of great civil strife?

**Sen. Daniel Patrick Moynihan:** No. No. An America of great civil repression.

**Peggy Noonan:** Can you very quickly outline for me the parameters of this possible repression down the road, if current trends continue, with regard to crime, illegitimacy, the breakup of the family, et cetera? Are we going to repeal the Bill of Rights? What are we going to do?

**Sen. Daniel Patrick Moynihan:** For a long time, it has been said that if we had a constitutional convention these days, which the Constitution makes possible, you wouldn't get much of the Bill of Rights in it, and that is a mark of a society more fearful of liberty than we have been in the past, because liberty has become libertarian, it has lost its contacts with responsibility, with restraint, with measured judgments. Watch that.

**Peggy Noonan:** A future of more prisons, a future of longer sentences, a future of curfews.

**Sen. Daniel Patrick Moynihan:** Future? Did you say a future of more prisons? A future of curfews? That future has arrived. We have a million persons in prison today. "The United States has a million persons in prison? No, no, no, that's some other country, that's the Soviet Union, right?" Wrong.

*Editors Note:* In 1993, The Sentencing Project, a Washington-based public-interest group puts the rate of incarceration at 519 per 100,000 people in the US versus 368 in South Africa. It also found that America imprisons black males at a rate more than four times that of South Africa. Even though crime rates had declined 3.5% in the U.S. during the previous decade, the prison population has doubled.

# 1.3 Million More Drop Into Poverty

by Sam Fulwood III and Melissa Healy (*Los Angeles Times*)

*Economy: The officially poor total 39.3 million, Census Bureau says.*
*Middle class loses ground as the richest grow wealthier.*

WASHINGTON—Despite a growing economy, another 1.3 million people fell below the federal poverty line last year and the economic divide between rich and poor Americans continued to swell, the Census Bureau reported Thursday.

Altogether, 39.3 million Americans, or 15.1% of the population, lived in poverty in 1993, up from 14.8% in 1992 and the highest rate since 1983, when the economy was emerging from its deepest recession since World War II. The figures reveal the uneven impact of the economy's rebound as poor Americans have experienced severe setbacks and the middle class has continued to lose ground, while the nation's wealthiest 20% have grown substantially more affluent.

Bureau officials defined poverty in 1993 as an income of $14,763 for a family of four. They said that the 15.1% poverty rate was "not statistically different" from 1992, when 38 million, or 14.8%, were classified as poor. In its annual income and poverty estimates, bureau officials also said that the number of Americans without health care rose 1.1 million last year. At a time when health care reform legislation dominated the political agenda, but failed to produce a consensus, the bureau said 39.7 million Americans, or 15.3% of the population, were without health insurance sometime during the year.

California was one of three states in which the poverty rate had a "statistically significant change," rising nearly 11%. In 1993, 18.2% of Californians lived below the poverty line, compared to 16.4% in 1992, officials said. Daniel H. Weinberg, chief of the Census Bureau's Housing and Household Economic Statistics Division, seemed baffled as he tried to explain why two years after the government announced the end of the recession, the resulting recovery is not progressing according to the traditional economic pattern. Nor-mally, the poverty rate spikes the year after a recession ends and begins to decline in the second year. "This recession ended in 1991," Weinberg said. "One could expect a higher poverty rate in 1992. This (1993 rate) is unusual."

Middle-class households—60% of the population—commanded 48.2% of the nation's income in 1993, down 3% since 1988. Since 1968, the middle class has lost 9% of its share of income to the wealthiest Americans. The wealthiest 20% of Americans, meanwhile, increased their share of the nation's household income to 48.2%, up 4% since 1988. In addition to the human toll behind the statistics, political analysts noted that the economic uncertainty reflected in the findings may have a powerful impact at the polls in November

In a mid-term election that is being seen as a referendum on the Administration's economic policies, those numbers—combined with a pessimistic assessment of their economic well-being by many Americans—have created a frustrating crisis for Democratic politicians.

For example, a recent study by the Times Mirror Center for The People & The Press found that "the Clinton Administration and the economic recovery have failed to stem the tide of political cynicism. The discontent with Washington that gained momentum in the late 1980s is even greater now than it was in 1992" when Clinton was elected.

"These numbers are what lies behind the problems the Democratic Party is having with younger people and particularly with younger and less-educated blue-collar men," said Guy Molyneux, a senior analyst with Peter Hart Research, which polls largely for Democrats. "In particular, they are the ones who have lost the most ground in the last decade or more and that would also be true here. There's a lot of anger out there at government and these economic realities are underneath a lot of races that we're seeing."

Demographers said that the trends revealed in the Census Bureau's latest findings continue a longstanding trend that has seen a steady growth in disparities between rich and poor. That trend, they added, is being driven on one end by a steady increase in single-parent families, who tend to fall below the poverty line, and at the other end by two-career families in which college-educated women's earnings are bumping family incomes into higher brackets.

One expert on poverty issues noted that similar dismal figures helped undo President George Bush in 1992, in spite of strong signs that the economy was improving. "A very sizable majority was not experiencing this recovery in larger take-home pay," said Gary Burtless of the Brookings Institution. "They saw their earnings continuing to shrink and they interpreted that, rightly, as part of a very long-term trend that has reduced their living stand-

ards. Now, it's President Clinton's turn to suffer the consequences for this long-term trend."

Bureau officials cautioned that comparing the new poverty figures with those from previous years is tricky because the government made statistical adjustments to compensate for changes in the numbers of people undercounted during the 1990 census. Statisticians also discovered counting discrepancies when the bureau stopped tabulating poverty data on paper and began to use computers. Even so, officials were mystified by the jump in families living in poverty.

"They are unexpected changes and we don't have a good explanation for it," Weinberg said. In absolute numbers, the new poverty figures represent the highest number of poor people in the country since 1962, when 39.6 million—or nearly 22% of the nation's population—lived in poverty.

# Success Dividing Blacks: Growing Economic Disparity

by Margaret L. Usdansky (USA Today)

As a successful black architect, Marshall Purnell knows first hand the economic chasm that increasingly divides the black community. He tells the story of a black colleague turned down for a $15,000 business loan. The same bank had no problem giving a larger loan to the colleague's white employee.

"Who do you get mad at when it happens?" asks Purnell, of Takoma Park, Md. "That black businessman can't take that to the black community. They don't understand what his problems are. They see him as a successful businessman. But if the banker had kicked the architect or insulted his daughter, he could take that to the NAACP," Purnell says.

By almost any social or economic barometer, from homicide to teen pregnancy, blacks in the USA stood still or lost ground during the past decade, a new report on blacks shows. But the

collective portrait obscures the lesser-known world of Marshall Purnells—the first college-educated blacks to take advantage of opportunities created by the civil rights movement.

"The main question is how much fragmentation or cleavage the growing economic diversity among blacks will bring," says William O'Hare, an author of the report, "African Americans in the 1990s." What this increasing fragmentation—and isolation—will mean to the USA's 30 million blacks still is unclear.

Some experts say one result will be growing political conservatism among blacks, rising with their income. "You're not going to see people acting along racial lines any more—it will be along class lines," predicts demographer Janice Hamilton Outtz, a black Prince George's County, Md., resident who owns her own consulting business.

But Purnell, 41, despite his own isolation from poor blacks, disagrees, saying racial ties run deeper than economic ones. "If you have a family reunion and you're black," he says, "you're going to have somebody there who's poor."

Other experts say the socio-economic gap, and tensions, between blacks and other minorities will grow in the 21st century, when Hispanics are likely to replace blacks as the USA's largest minority group.

O'Hare, the Population Reference Bureau author, says he fears the result will be plummeting white sympathy for blacks. He points to support for conservative black Supreme Court nominee Clarence Thomas as evidence sympathy has already begun to wane—among some middle-class blacks as well as whites. "The black community is really torn," he says.

Carletta Aston, 47, a black management consultant in Morristown, N.J., sees the growing chasm among poor and middle-class blacks in her own life. Her children, who attended an integrated school, were taunted by poorer black children for not being "black enough." Their closest friends were middle-class whites.

"I think there is a lot of diversity in the black community," Aston says, "and one of the problems is the pressure for us to be alike—or somebody says we're not black enough." That some- body includes Whittier, Calif., orthopedic surgeon Lee Woods, 37. Like Aston, Woods grew up middle-class, in Meriden, Conn., where his family was isolated from neighborhood whites—as well as from poorer blacks in nearby housing projects.

Woods, who got his medical training in Philadelphia and Boston, makes no pretense to comfort with inner cities. "I wouldn't feel safe there," he says. But he considers black Republicans turncoats who've forgotten the bond of race. Woods worries that increasing numbers of the black middle class are growing up to share Aston's views—and will pay a high price in isolation from whites and most blacks.

"Black middle-class people need to do what the white people do," Woods says. "They need to educate themselves, to be the best they can at their professions, to have nice homes, support their families, and maintain their black consciousness by trying to help other blacks . . . .

"Being black in America is harder than being white. You just have to cope with it."

## Gap grows between rich, poor blacks
Margaret Udansky

Growth of the black middle class in the 1980s has created two black Americas, a report out today shows. The report, which examined a decade's worth of Census Bureau figures, finds a small but increasingly prosperous community of blacks who profited from civil rights—and a larger but increasingly isolated group that fell further out of the economic mainstream.

"The economic gap between rich and poor blacks is growing," the report says. "Middle-class blacks . . . may feel little in common with poor blacks." The study, "African-Americans in the 1990s," was completed by the Population Reference Bureau, a Washington research group.

The report's bright spots:
- Between 1970 and 1989, the number of black households earning at least $50,000 a year almost doubled, reaching 1.2 million, or 11.5%.
- More than a fourth of black households earned at least $25,000.

But the percentage of poor blacks continues to dwarf that of whites. Almost a third of black households earn less than $10,000, vs. less than 14% of white households.

## More blacks are affluent . . .

The percentage of black households considered affluent has more than doubled since 1970. The increase:

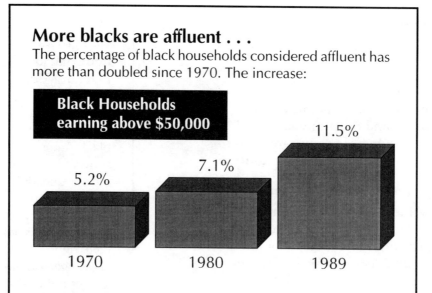

**Black Households earning above $50,000**

5.2%
1970

7.1%
1980

11.5%
1989

## . . . but still lag behind whites

Despite the strides, more black households are on the lower end of the economic scale than whites. Percentage of black and white households in various income levels:

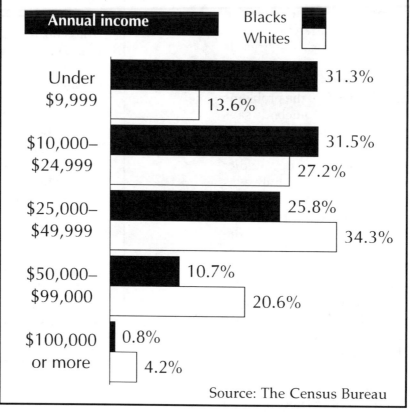

**Annual income**   Blacks   Whites

Under $9,999 — 31.3% / 13.6%

$10,000–$24,999 — 31.5% / 27.2%

$25,000–$49,999 — 25.8% / 34.3%

$50,000–$99,000 — 10.7% / 20.6%

$100,000 or more — 0.8% / 4.2%

Source: The Census Bureau

*USA Today,* 8/9/91.

# Time Is Not on Their Side: Fresh Insights Into Why Many Poor Children Do Badly in School

by Elizabeth Taylor (*TIME Magazine*)

For a child in kindergarten, the day is carefully divided into time for listening, playing, coloring, snacking and napping. Middle-class children, raised by parents who worship their watches, adapt easily to this regimen. But for many disadvantaged inner-city youngsters, the structure of the school day apparently seems totally unfamiliar. They often resist the idea that they should stop doing one thing simply because it is time to do something else.

Why are many children of the urban poor so uncomfortable in school? One explanation comes from University of Chicago Professor Dolores Norton, who is conducting a unique study of the intellectual development of children in poor families. Her conclusion: growing up in an unstructured home environment, they do not develop a sense of time that enables them to adapt well to school. "When they come to school, these children enter a world that was not created for them," says Norton, who teaches at the university's School of Social Service Administration. "Imagine yourself in a classroom with adults who speak your language, yet you are unable to interpret what they want you to do, even though you wish to please them." Not understanding the meaning of time, she asserts, is a handicap that may partly account for the poor academic performance of many inner-city children throughout their school careers.

Norton's insights come from firsthand research. For the past six years, she has been regularly videotaping, from infancy, about 40 children born to young mothers living in the most blighted, impoverished pockets of Chicago. She lets her camera roll for up to four hours at a time, capturing the ordinary rhythms and interactions of a child's life at home. Reviewing thousands of hours of tapes, Norton found that references to time were rare. Most parents hardly ever provided instructions like "Finish lunch so you can see your favorite TV program at 1:30," or even sequential statements like "First put on your socks, then your shoes." Daily routines, such as Daddy or Mommy leaving for work and regular times for bed and meals, are usually nonexistent in these cramped, dangerous quarters where even the most conscientious mothers have trouble keeping food in the cupboard and steering clear of gang violence.

Children from these homes may be able to read a clock, but that does not mean they understand time. Norton found that most of her young subjects scored lower than average on seriation tests, which measured their abilities to understand sequences of events. The less a mother had talked to her child about time over the years, the worse the youngster performed on the tests.

Other child-development experts concur with Norton's findings. Many poor children, they note, are mystified by the "time-slotted" school environment, where crayons are often taken away before the picture is finished because it is juice time. Says clinical psychologist Jeree Pawl, director of the Infant-Parent Program at San Francisco General Hospital: "The structured situation makes them feel powerless. It feels arbitrary, senseless and imposed because at home there is no predictability and rigidity." Confused youngsters may withdraw or rebel, prompting some teachers to peg these children as troublemakers or slow learners.

J. Ronald Lally, a San Francisco educational psychologist, recalls his own experiment in teaching concepts of time to low-income children in a Syracuse preschool center. "There was too much attention to time in the curriculum," says Lally, and this pitted students against teachers in a power struggle. He replaced this rigid format with a flexible curriculum in which children could set their own agendas, while teachers gradually and gently introduced concepts of time. Notes Lally: "The kids learned about time, but it wasn't connected to discipline."

Norton thinks classrooms like the one in Syracuse can teach youngsters about time and thus enhance self-discipline and turn their attention to learning. The question is whether even an ideal school can reverse the damage done by the iso-lated, timeless world into which most poor children are born.

---

## DEFINITIONS OF CLASS

**C. Wright Mills in *Power, Politics and People***

"Class" as defined . . . absorbs at least three items . . . 1) The sheerly economic and nothing else; 2) . . . the distribution of "prestige," "deference," "esteem," "honor:" in general, status; 3) the distribution of power, i.e., who can be expected to obey whom in what situations.

*On class-awareness:* "The gross facts of economic differences—in amount and in source—do not necessarily result in the awareness of these differences on the part of the participants."

**Henry Pratt Fairchild in *Dictionary of Sociology and Other Sciences***

*Class:* "A totality of persons having one or more common characteristics . . . Class may or may not signify the existence of a hierarchical scale of social power. There are age, occupational, industrial, social, ideo-politico-economic, and income classes."

*Class consciousness:* "An awareness of one's class position. Fundamentally, an awareness of the difference existing between one's class position and that of some other individual or individuals. This awareness is also generally accompanied by certain attitudes towards those occupying other class positions. These attitudes may be a feeling of superiority or inferiority towards those who occupy respectively a lower or higher rank; or a feeling of opposition or hostility where a situation of class conflict exists; or merely a feeling of aloofness or strangeness because of the difference in folkways, mores and ideologies of the different classes."

**David Jary and Julia Jary in *Sociology***

*Class:* The hierarchical distinctions that exist between individuals or groups (for example, occupational groups) within a society. In this general sense, class is an alternative general term to social stratification.

***The American College Dictionary***

*Class:* A social stratum sharing essential economic, political, or cultural characteristics and having the same social position.

# Chance Beings: An Interview With Jerzy Kosinski

*Jerzy Kosinski:* I have great respect for the homeless individual, whom I refuse to see as a victim of society and I refuse to see as a victim of his or her own self. I see the homeless person as a chance being at the mercy of forces that he or she was not able to figure out or may not be able to figure out. And if he or she cannot figure out the state of homelessness, why should he or she when the state cannot figure it out either?

Narrowing it further, if this community (one of the most affluent neighborhoods of New York City) isn't smart enough to resolve the fact that there are people who have no place to sleep, why should the homeless be smart enough to resolve their own predicaments? Are the avenues to "home" as simple as that? Clearly they are not.

*Jeffrey Grunberg:* Is the community not smart enough or is there something intentional about its desire to watch some people suffer? Is racism a part of the social problem?

*Kosinski:* I prefer to see it (I say "prefer" because maybe it is a way of wishful thinking or of wishful seeing) as a community not being smart enough, not being intelligent enough, pragmatic enough to realize the dimensions of the problem. The homeless have very little to lose and very little vested interest in the notion of order, home, and the philosophy of having in a society which is based on free enterprise. So I'd like to think that a society that allows the state of homelessness to continue (providing that the homeless person wants to have a home) is a society not smart enough to resolve the problem.

*Benedict Giamo:* What does homelessness reveal then about American Society? Or let's say the American dream?

*Kosinski:* Homeless people in my neighborhoods, whether in New Haven, where there are a great number of homeless people right outside the fortress of Yale, or here in New York, cause one to establish a new parameter. One should accept that these are a category of people who cannot afford a standard mobile home, since there is right above them a category of people who can. Homelessness then, according to this view, is a perfectly valid category of the free enterprise system. For whatever reason, this person who is homeless finds himself or herself in a mini-enterprise. This mini-enterprise is reduced to asking for help, for money, from passersby. Now had this homeless person been a foundation, this would have been considered a tax-deductible operation. If one were to make this condition tax-deductible, as with the Jewish Presence Foundation of which I am president, then this person—and the needs of this person—would and should be tax-deductible. Hence the mini-van home would serve such a purpose.

*Grunberg:* You're going to upset a lot of people if your idea takes off.

*Kosinski:* I don't know whether the mini-van home should upset people or the sight of someone who is frostbitten in the morning.

*Grunberg:* Which would bother people more?

*Kosinski:* Simply put, it is just a condition that is very prevalent today on the streets. It is a condition to be acknowledged, regardless of whether it is bothersome or not. It is certainly bothersome to the person who is frostbitten. It can also be bothersome to some individuals who pass this person by, and to assume that everyone is indifferent to someone else's misery may simply not be true. It could be safely assumed that people with homes, which in the winter are very warm, can take far less enjoyment from their well-deserved homes by seeing a homeless person sleeping at the entrance to their homes. Hence the myth of the pursuit of happiness—or the reality of it—can be infringed upon by the sight of someone who simply doesn't participate as fully in this society.

*Grunberg:* We can rest comfortably knowing that the homeless are not freezing?

*Kosinski:* Precisely. This means that some sleeplessness of my own could be reduced by the fact that the homeless are no longer frostbitten, but sleep in mini-van homes of their own which protect them from frost, attacks by dogs, drunkards, and drug addicts—or attacks by those who simply want to experience the power of their own hands or feet on someone else's flesh.

Therefore, I don't want to enter into an argument with myself or with anyone else relative to what is right or what is wrong. I'm too pragmatic for that and too philosophical. What interests me is the degree to which one can accept the state of homelessness as being a given, an inherited given perhaps, and as being unavoidable (I haven't seen it resolved, at least not in American society). And I have not been able to convince those who are in charge of wealth that they should help those who can no longer help themselves, because the notion that people should be able to help themselves is a very firm Protestant notion. You see, the first project which I embarked on in the mid-1960s involved coming up with some 400 people who were absolutely unable—not unwilling but unable—to help themselves because they were addicted to wine; they were heavy drinkers of American wine.

*Giamo:* Down on the Bowery?

*Kosinski:* Yes, the Bowery. And I tried to talk to friends of mine who would routinely donate very expensive pieces of furniture to various American museums, including the Museum of Modern Art and, in particular, the Metropolitan Museum of Art. I tried to tell them that one commode of Louis XIV, given to a tax-deductible project that could be formed for the Bowery homeless, would prove to be a truly priceless investment. The money would have been used for those who could no longer help themselves, an open project to be called "the I can no longer help myself project." As a homeless person, I therefore have to be maintained by society and should be treated no differently than those on welfare. Remember, welfare presupposes treating "well" those who no longer "fare well" by themselves. Well, I failed miserably, even with the most immediate members of my own family at the time. My late wife felt that this was not an attitude to be encouraged and that, however useful the help extended to the few hundred individuals might be, the example it would set would be derogatory—that it would, in fact, diminish the whole

ethos of work and the philosophy of achievement that is to be propagated. Therefore, it would make sense to give the same money, or possibly more, to the foundation devoted to the very opposite—helping those who can help themselves.

*Grunberg:* How did you respond to that?

*Kosinski:* I accept someone else's view the way I accept my own. We are in a country of free expression.

*Giamo:* It reminds me of a part of your novel, *The Devil Tree*, in which the protagonist, Jonathan Whalen, proposes such a Bowery project to the wife of his business partner, a wealthy financier. Of course, she shoots it down.

*Kosinski:* Exactly. This idea grew out of that period of my life, as did *Being There*. By the way, in *Being There*, the protagonist becomes homeless, but he carries no notion of home with him. (laughter)

*Giamo:* Do you think that the American ethos would accept the mini-van home for the homeless?

*Kosinski:* I'd like to think that the American ethos would acknowledge it—the Jeffersonian ethos, that is, and I think that if Jefferson were to be here, and I say this with full knowledge of Jefferson's work and his home in Monticello, that he actually would accept it. He would call it going Dutch with the American dream. And it is not an accident that this is the New Amsterdam, and it is not an accident that in Old Amsterdam provisions are made for homeless people. Therefore, if they are made in old Amsterdam, they should be made in the New Amsterdam.

*Giamo:* Would there be an emphasis on mobility with your mini-van home? As you well know, mobility is also very near and dear to the heart of American ideology.

*Kosinski:* In a country in which one-fourth of the people in American society change homes and become, however temporarily, homeless in between—on the road, if you will—that condition should be accepted as a given. I think that we must approach the situation from an entirely American point of view. I think the approach that has emerged to frame the problem of homelessness is one that has been imposed on the society. It is an imposition of the welfare state. It's also an approach to the pursuit of happiness that presupposes that the person should have a home, be stable, and all kinds of other ingredients which American reality clearly tells you is not the case. So, then, where is John Dewey and the notion of the pragmatic American self? Somehow, this has been sacrificed for so many years.

I think one should reverse it and look at the issue from the most important point of view—and that is from the point of view of the homeless themselves. How do we make the homeless condition acceptable and, hence, redeemable and remediable?

*Giamo:* Have you done any "market research" on your mini-van home proposal?

*Kosinski:* No, it's just now in a design stage of development.

*Giamo:* Any "field testing"?

*Kosinski:* No, but I'm preparing to meet with some architects who are working on this kind of unit.

*Grunberg:* By the way, is there any bathroom put into the design of the unit?

*Kosinski:* Well, I have no doubt that this could be very easily developed by some manufacturers. These things have been manufactured before. I do not have to point at the objects floating in space left by American astronauts who happened to have been homeless at the time, or am I not allowed to say this? (laughter)

*Giamo:* Basically, what you're saying is that it makes little sense to attempt small-scale, let alone large-scale, prevention, because prevention has failed and American ideology will not accept the prevention that might be needed in the cooperative ventures of both public and private sectors to resolve the social problem.

*Kosinski:* Yes, prevention has failed. But we do accept business cycles and recession and unemployment as facts of life. We do accept ruin by bad investments. We do accept crime and being shot at, and we do accept chance. Are we absolutely so deterministically minded that we no longer acknowledge that life is chancy? After all, we do take chances. Therefore, now we live in an ethos in which a homeless person should find far more understanding than in a welfare state. In other words, a person who is right now homeless in front of my home carries within himself or herself all basic American ingredients.

*Giamo:* And, whether it's valid or not, some of the homeless do tend to blame themselves for their predicaments.

*Kosinski:* Just as a businessperson might who has invested wrongly. Now if one were to be positive about it, as one should be, and pragmatic, one could improve this condition. Homelessness is very much a part of our American system and, basically, there should be nothing wrong with this condition as long as the individual is not sentenced to unnecessary suffering and punishment—since the system makes all provisions for that condition three miles away downtown in Wall Street.

*Grunberg:* Often, people seem to vacillate between feeling sorry for the homeless or being angry at them. Also, there's a great deal of energy expended in trying to determine who to blame. Is it the homeless individual's fault? Or is it society's fault?

*Kosinski:* These concerns represent non-American values injected into the American character from the outside. They came as the residue of the nineteenth century in its idealized state. And I think one can very easily turn it around. In fact, I think turning it around and improving the lot of a great number of people who now occupy the parking lots at night, and other lots to which they are not entitled, would be far easier than to act against the basic grain of American character.

*Grunberg:* So the millions of dollars, the hundreds of millions of dollars that cities are spending in their attempt to rehabilitate, rehouse, feed . . .

*Kosinski:* Work to a degree but, basically, one can also assume that persons who have been homeless carry within them (and we accept it in many other areas of life) a certain philosophy of life or certain experience which makes them, to say the least, apprehensive about ownership. I mean, here's Jerzy Kosinski who is relatively stable (with which most of my literary critics would disagree, judging by my fiction) and who doesn't want to own. Now if I don't want to own a home but prefer to rent one because of my experience of World War II (consider this an experience of homelessness, I repeat that), then why not make a provision for a certain number of people who simply may not be comfortable, or not psychologically or pragmatically equipped anymore, to deal with the state of being rehabilitated, when in fact they may prefer to remain mobile but safe?

*Giamo:* How would you distribute these mini-van homes? How would you decide who to give them to?

*Kosinski:* I would leave it flexible, as life itself. And I would say, "Here you are right now. We have no home for you. You may not want one and we are not going to ask you the standard questions. We don't have a home to give you anyway. We want to improve your lot. Now we see you as you are right now. You are without a home; we know that. We have no traditional home for you. Would you like to have one of these mini-vans?" Maybe the question shouldn't even be asked.

*Let's try again:* "Now, at this point we know that you are a vagrant. There are laws against vagrancy. We can technically arrest you and assign you a home. But, well, we don't have these homes for you either. They happen to be all used up or overcrowded or nonexistent, in case you didn't know that. Now, this means that we are basically leaving you outside of the law. We are, therefore, lawless. The state is lawless; the state should arrest you after midnight. You are a vagrant."

Now, we do have laws about vagrancy. These people should be arrested every night, but they aren't. So the state has failed. Therefore, we should acknowledge that the homeless cannot be legitimately housed, because we are unable or unwilling to do so. It is precisely under these circumstances that I am suggesting that homeless people should be provided tax-deductible, portable, mobile units which fit certain American traditions, such as being on the move.

## About the Authors

The late Jerzy Kosinski produced nine novels, two nonfiction works and numerous essays and articles. Throughout his shortened career, he was concerned with individualism, the rigors of adaptation in the face of repression, and creative problem-solving. Born in Lodz, Poland, Kosinski came to the United States in 1957. In *The Painted Bird*, he drew on his own experiences as a Jewish child in Poland during World War II. He received the National Book Award in 1969 for *Steps*, a novel that deals with the pain of adjustment to American society. The following year he received the American Academy of Arts and Letters Award for Literature.

Benedict Giamo, author of *On the Bowery: Confronting Homelessness in America* (Iowa, 1989), has an M.A. in psychology and a Ph.D. in American studies. He is assistant professor of American studies at the University of Notre Dame.

Jeffrey Grunberg is associate professor of clinical psychology at Columbia University and vice-president of social services for the Grand Central Partnership, a nonprofit organization serving the homeless in Manhattan.

# Down and Out in Washington

by Neal Karlen with Nikki Finke Greenberg (from *Newsweek*)

Jesse Carpenter froze to death last month in the federal park across the street from the White House. The 61-year-old wino had come a long way from World War II France, where he won a Bronze Star for "braving the unabated fire" of German troops while carrying wounded comrades to safety. Once back home, he had difficulty adjusting and sank into alcoholism. Finally, 22 years ago, Carpenter abandoned his wife and two children for a life on the streets.

Last week the onetime war hero was buried in Arlington National Cemetery with military honors and a 21-gun salute. Carpenter's Army record might never have been discovered if his ex-wife hadn't read newspaper accounts of the derelict's death and forwarded his Bronze Star certificate to Washington. But to the dozens of street people who found their way to the funeral, Carpenter was no less heroic in death than he had been during the war. They had known him as a gentle man, who did what he could to help the even less fortunate. He died at the feet of his buddy John Lam, a wheelchairbound derelict afflicted with Parkinson's disease. For the previous two years Carpenter had spent his days pushing Lam around town. And because local community shelters don't provide access to the handicapped, Carpenter regularly spent the nights outside with his friend.

**Invisible:** Carpenter, the attending minister eulogized, was "a child of God whom society treated as invisible." And Mitch Snyder, director of the local Community for Creative Non-Violence (CCNV), added that he provided a lesson in the facts of homeless life: "People must realize that the street people they're stepping over or refusing to look at have histories like Jesse's—that they didn't just drop down from Mars."

Invisible in life, Carpenter became a symbol in death to Washington, D.C. activists who are fighting the city government for better care for the homeless. Recently, local voters passed Initiative 17—the nation's first referendum guarantee-ing "adequate overnight shelter" to any street person who wants it. According to Mayor Marion Barry, sheltering all of Washington's 5,000 to 15,000 homeless would cost the city $60 million a year and bankrupt the local budget. "And that's just providing for current demand," warns David Rivers, director of Washington's Department of Human Services. Like other D.C. officials, Rivers fears the initiative might turn the city into a nesting ground for swarms of the nation's homeless. "We believe," he says, "that people from all over might come to the District once word gets out that we have to provide them all with a bed."

The initiative was spearheaded by CCNV, a volunteer group that feeds or shelters between 2,000 and 3,000 of Washington's homeless each day. Before November's balloting, CCNV leader Snyder staged a 51-day hunger strike to draw attention to the plight of the homeless. The initiative, argued Snyder, was a historic "first step toward a national legislative right to shelter by the 21st century." The issue, he said, was a moral imperative. "If we are going to continue calling ourselves a civilized country, people [must not] have to eat out of garbage pails or sleep in the cold because they lack a roof over their heads," Snyder contends.

Snyder's fast paid off in immediate public-relations dividends for the cause. Shortly before the election, CBS's "Sixty Minutes" and ABC's "Night-line" ran segments featuring him, and soon afterward two production companies and a Hollywood studio came dickering for the movie rights to his life story. Throughout the hunger strike, Susan Baker, the wife of White House chief of staff James Baker and a longtime advocate for the homeless, prayed at Snyder's bedside. Though reluctant to lobby her husband, she served as an intermediary when the Reagan administration finally decided to act on the Snyder situation. Snyder ended the strike when Reagan personally approved plans to help refurbish CCNV's dilapidated 1,000 bed shelter. "The president," Susan Baker told *Newsweek*, "did not want Mitch to die." . . .

Meanwhile, activists for the nation's homeless try to dispel notions that Washington-like laws will either bankrupt cities or turn them into meccas for derelicts. "A shelter is such a miserable place," says Robert Hayes, counsel for the New York-based national Coalition for the Homeless, "that nobody's going to go to a city just because he's going to get a cot." Indeed, courts in four states have already recognized the "right to shelter." In New York, expenditures for the homeless have swelled from $15 million to $200 million in the five years since such a ruling. More recently, municipalities in California, New Jersey and West Virginia have been ordered by local or state courts to provide more overnight accommodations for the needy. And next November a referendum on the issue will probably be on the ballot in St. Paul, Minn.

**'Brutalized':** Back in Washington, however, even some activists fear Mitch Snyder's plan might cause short-term warehousing of the homeless at the expense of longer-range programs aimed at helping them get back on their feet. Despite such fears, Snyder himself remains resolute: his goal is a bed for all, every night. "The longer [the homeless] live on the streets, the more time they have to get brutalized," he says. "You can't provide social services to people who are living on grates."

---

### CLASS BIAS IN MEDIA COVERAGE
#### by Ralph Nader
(from an interview with David Barsamian recorded on 9/1/94 and later broadcast on public radio in the U.S. and Canada)

*Nader observes that class bias influences what questions the media asks and he astutely observes that our cultural conditioning towards a "corporate" perspective has blinded us to what might be considered a fair distribution of the public wealth.*

"Take all the labor struggles of the last year, all the strikes, all the work stoppages, all the lockouts, and put them all together and they haven't gotten the attention that the baseball lockout and suspension has gotten. I cannot believe how many articles there are every day on the baseball strike. And to show you the corporatist twist here, there was just a poll that said 87% of the fans think that the baseball players are overpaid. The question is never asked, Do you think the owners are overprofited? The baseball players are what make baseball. When they see the owners making tons of money off television and radio and food sales and ticket sales, they're going to want their share. Even in the area of sports, the fans are growing up corporate. This business of growing up corporate is so important to discuss and talk about because it affects everyone. Children grow up in a corporate dominated society. So we never talk about what we own that we don't control. We just talk about crumbs that fall off the table of the plutocrats and the oligarchs. We own legally the public airwaves, $3 trillion in pension funds, a third of America, which are the public lands, the forests and the mines and the meadows, and we don't control any of it. The corporations control them. Some of them get it free, like gold and molybdenum. They get it on our land free, except for paying $5 an acre for the land above the mine."

---

# The Ludlow Massacre

by Howard Zinn

I was still in college studying history when I heard a song by folk-singer Woody Guthrie called "The Ludlow Massacre," a dark, intense ballad, accompanied by slow, haunting chords on his guitar. It told of women and children burned to death in a strike of miners against Rockefeller-owned coal mines in southern Colorado in 1914.

My curiosity was aroused. In none of my classes in American history, in none of the textbooks I had read, was there any mention of the Ludlow Massacre or of the Colorado coal strike. I decided to study the history of the labor movement on my own. This led me to a book, *American Labor Struggles*, written not by a historian but an English teacher named Samuel Yellen. It contained exciting accounts of some ten labor conflicts in American history, most of which were unmentioned in my courses and my textbooks. One of the chapters was on the Colorado coal strike of 1913–1914.

I was fascinated by the sheer drama of that event. It began with the shooting of a young labor organizer on the streets of Trinidad, Colorado, in the center of the mining district on a crowded Saturday night, by two detectives in the pay of Rockefeller's Colorado Fuel & Iron Corporation. The miners, mostly immigrants, speaking a dozen different languages, were living in a kind of serfdom in the mining towns where Rockefeller collected their rent, sold them their necessities, hired the police, and watched them carefully for any sign of unionization.

The killing of organizer Gerry Lippiatt sent a wave of anger through the mine towns. At a mass meeting in Trinidad, miners listened to a rousing speech by an eighty-year-old woman named Mary Jones—"Mother Jones"—an organizer for the United Mine Workers: "What would the coal in these mines and in these hills be worth unless you put your strength and muscle in to bring them.... You have collected more wealth, created more wealth than they in a thousand years of the Roman Republic, and yet you have not any."

The miners voted to strike. Evicted from their huts by the coal companies, they packed their belongings onto carts and onto their backs and walked through a mountain blizzard to tent colonies set up by the United Mine Workers. It was September 1913. There they lived for the next seven months, enduring hunger and sickness, picketing the mines to prevent strikebreakers from entering, and defending themselves against armed assaults. The Baldwin-Felts Detective Agency, hired by the Rockefellers to break the morale of the strikers, used rifles, shotguns, and a machine gun mounted on an armored car, which roved the countryside and fired into the tents where the miners lived.

They would not give up the strike, however, and the National Guard was called in by the governor. A letter from the vice president of Colorado Fuel & Iron to John D. Rockefeller, Jr., in New York explained,

> *You will be interested to know that we have been able to secure the cooperation of all the bankers of the city, who have had three or four interviews with our little cowboy governor, agreeing to back the State and lend it all funds necessary to maintain the militia and afford ample protection so our miners could return to work .... Another mighty power has been rounded up on behalf of the operators by the getting together of fourteen of the editors of the most important newspapers in the state.*

The National Guard was innocently welcomed to town by miners and their families, waving American flags, thinking that men in the uniform of the United States would protect them. But the guard went to work for the operators. They beat miners, jailed them, and escorted strikebreakers into the mines.

The strikers responded. One strikebreaker was murdered, another brutally beaten, four mine guards killed while escorting a scab. And Baldwin-Felts detective George Belcher, the killer of Lippiatt, who had been freed by a coroner's jury composed of Trinidad businessmen ("justifiable homicide"), was killed with a single rifle shot by an unseen gunman as he left a Trinidad drugstore and stopped to light a cigar.

The miners held out through the hard winter, and the mine owners decided on more drastic action. In the spring, two companies of National Guardsmen stationed themselves in the hills above the largest tent colony, housing a thousand men, women, and children, near a tiny depot called Ludlow. On the morning of April 20, 1914, they began firing machine guns into the tents. The men crawled away to draw fire and shoot back, while the women and children crouched in pits dug into the tent floors. At dusk the soldiers came down from the hills with torches, and set fire to the tents. The countryside was ablaze. The occupants fled.

The next morning, a telephone linesman, going through the charred ruins of the Ludlow colony, lifted an iron cot that covered a pit dug in the floor of one tent, and found the mangled, burned bodies of two women and eleven children. This became known as the Ludlow Massacre.

As I read about this, I wondered why this extraordinary event, so full of drama, so peopled by remarkable personalities, was never mentioned in the history books. Why was this strike, which cast a dark shadow on the Rockefeller interests and on corporate America generally, considered less important than the building by John D. Rockefeller of the Standard Oil Company, which was looked on as an important and positive event in the development of American industry?

I knew that there was no secret meeting of industrialists and historians to agree to emphasize the admirable achievements of the great corporations and ignore the bloody costs of industrialization in America. But I concluded that a certain unspoken understanding lay beneath the writing of textbooks and the teaching of history: that it would be considered bold, radical, perhaps even "communist" to emphasize class struggle in the United States, a country where the dominant ideology emphasized the oneness of the nation "We the People, in order to . . . etc., etc." and the glories of the American system.

## About the Author

Howard Zinn is a historian, author and lecturer best known for his widely read *People's History of the United States* (available from ODT at 800-736-1293). This book is a chronicle of America's grass-roots movements and of the political lives of ordinary people. Zinn has written a dozen more books on history, social movements, and politics. His many articles and essays have appeared in *Harper's*, *The Nation*, *The New Republic*, the *New York Times* and *Saturday Review*.

Zinn eloquently illuminates many subjects, such as the Constitution and the First Amendment, American law and the judicial system, U.S. foreign policy, civil disobedience, and "people's history." This passage is drawn from a chapter entitled "The Use and Abuse of History" from *Declarations of Independence* published by HarperCollins (Phone: 800-237-5534).

# Critical Indicators of a Need for Global Culture

Source materials courtesy of Sharif M. Abdullah

Culture is a set of procedures which a group of people uses to manage its survival and success in its environment. Culture allows us to go "on automatic" and not have to go through an extensive and costly data gathering and decision making exercise every time we want to act.

Groups are then joined to each other and become one culturally when they must share an environment, i.e., the set of conditions and challenges in which their life takes place. We belong to different cultures because we often live in multiple environments.

Because we are creatures in whom culture lives as a mental habit, our culture will become dysfunctional when:

1. It no longer allows us to perceive changes in our own environment.

2. It no longer responds quickly enough to changing conditions or crises in the environment for which it was designed.

3. We move from one environment to another and fail to see or make appropriate cultural adaptations.

4. We use the cultural rules of one of the groups to which we belong that were designed for one environment to act in another environment where these rules do not fit, i.e., do not meet the challenges of that new environment.

5. We fail to recognize the true extent or nature of the environment in which we are dependent for survival.

6. We fail to see how we share an environment with another group, or they fail to see how they share it with us and therefore fail to create a common culture to meet the demands of that environment.

Today, the last two of these factors seem to be the ones that are most key to our survival. All too slowly, the many groups who inhabit the "global village" are becoming aware that crises they face are mega-crises in their environment. Therefore, articulation of these crises (as Sharif M. Abdullah has provided in *The Power of One*) provides a schema to better comprehend our cultural challenge.

## MEGA-CRISIS and Their INDICATORS

The mega-crises and their indicators are represented on the chart on the following page.

This material is reproduced with permission from the Forum for Community Transformation, P.O. Box 12541, Portland OR 97212 (phone: 503-281-1813; fax: 503-249-1969). The material is copyrighted by Sharif M. Abdullah © 1991. All rights reserved. It is drawn from *The Power of One* available from the address above or order through your local bookstore (ISBN #0-9632184-0-9).

# Table One

## The Mega-Crisis

### Economy

*The "Haves" vs. "Have-nots": the growing disparity between the super-rich and the ultra-poor.*

1. Malappropriated resources;
2. Instability/collapse of global markets;
3. Gross disparities between super-rich and ultra-poor;
4. Government structures which benefit the wealthy;
5. Basic human needs unmet;
6. Growth-model economic system based on continued exploitation of rapidly depleted resources.

### Diversity

*"Them" vs. "Us": ethnicity, cultural diversity and national identity in conflict*

1. Growing ethnic and racial clashes;
2. The rapid growth of "hate groups";
3. The surfacing of long-buried cultural prejudices and animosities;
4. Extinction of cultures;
5. Growing power of "micro-nations."

### Ecology

*The Destruction of Planet Earth: the danger of ecological systems failure.*

1. Pollution (introduction of waste into the Earth's eco-system beyond its carrying capacity);
2. Overconsumption (resource depletion beyond the Earth's ability to regenerate);
3. Mechanistic approaches to the management of living systems.

### Fulfillment

*The Addictive Society: the search for personal, social and spiritual fulfillment.*

1. Crimes of violence (attempt to inject personal power into a situation of apparent powerlessness);
2. Dwindling hope;
3. Drugs and other forms of addictive behavior;
4. Spiritual, personal and societal malaise;
5. Shallow patriotism;
6. Rise in birth rate among poor.

### Leadership

*The Crisis of Global leadership: dangerous opportunity and whistling in the dark.*

1. Use of "leadership" in a vain attempt to maintain status quo;
2. Attempts to maintain "power-over" maintainers;
3. Empty symbolism and non-issues;
4. Lack of vision;
5. Militarism in all its forms; the use of force to resolve conflicts;
6. Political alienation, people removed from their "leaders";
7. System depends on complacency, acquiescence and focusing on non-issues.

Abdullah conceptualizes the interrelationship among the crises with the following figure. No one crisis dominates and all are interrelated.

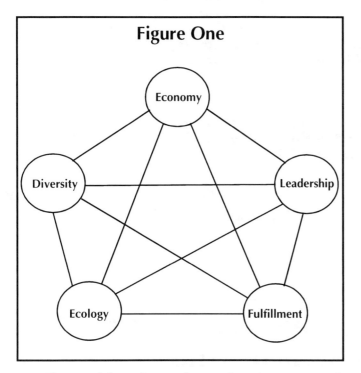

This model can be used to analyze international problems, as the figure below indicates (regarding issues of War & Peace).

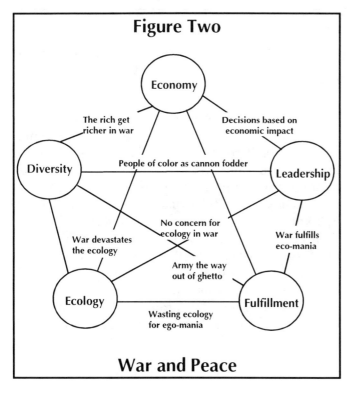

It can also help to show the interrelationship among the domestic factors that contribute to problems such as homelessness as shown below.

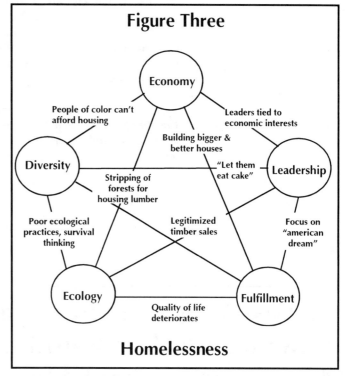

Many years ago, Chief Seattle said, "Humanity has not woven the web of life. We are but one thread within it. Whatever we do to the web, we do to ourselves. All things are bound together. All things connect. Whatever befalls the Earth befalls also the children of the Earth." This wisdom is well worth heeding today as we work to comprehend and respond to the very serious challenges we face.

## About the Author

Sharif M. Abdullah is a former practicing attorney who has worked with countless individuals and community empowerment projects. Two of his projects have received national awards for citizen empowerment and public/private cooperation. He is in increasing demand as a lecturer and facilitator for grassroots organizations, government and universities. He can be reached at the address on page 43.

"My main concern is the growing poverty and degradation of life I see around me every day. The United States seems to be writing off ever larger numbers of people—the homeless, the mentally ill, the long-term unemployed, low-wage workers, inner-city teenagers, women on welfare and their children. What I find particularly depressing is the enthusiastic part played in the writing-off process by many public intellectuals and former liberals who have persuaded themselves that poverty is caused by the moral failings of poor people.

*I fear we are in for an era of real social cruelty, conducted under the banner of national moral rearmament. An era of prisons and sermons—which, as William Blake pointed out, usually go together.*"

Katha Pollitt
Author, poet, and essayist

# In Search of a Good Name: The Debate over Whether Blacks Should Be Called African Americans Is about More Than Just a Label

by Richard Lacayo. Reported by Sylvester Monroe (*TIME Magazine*)

According to the Bible, a good name is worth more than a precious ointment—and choosing one can be just as sticky. Since December, when Jesse Jackson proposed that the group now called blacks (formerly known as Negroes, and prior to that as colored people) should adopt the designation African American, the idea has been catching on. In a recent poll conducted for *Time* by Yankelovich Clancy Shulman, 61% preferred to be called black, vs. 26% who supported African American. (Though the survey was too small to be statistically valid, it indicated that the name change has made some headway.) The name has also found favor with soul-station disk jockeys and college students, who are quick to correct those who refer to the group by any other term. Politicians, prompt as ever to respond to popular opinion, have con-

cocted their own variations. When he was elected chairman of the Democratic National Committee, Ron Brown referred to himself as an "American of African descent."

For groups, as for individuals, taking a new name is a quintessential American act, a supreme gesture of self-creation in the land where Norma Jean Baker became Marilyn Monroe, homosexuals became gays, and Esso became Exxon. But for many blacks, the choice of a word by which others will know them has a special significance. During their centuries of bondage, slaves had names that were often chosen by their masters. Booker T. Washington wrote in his autobiography *Up from Slavery* that there was one point on which former slaves were generally agreed: "that they must change their names." This process of shucking off so-called slave names, commonly in favor of names with an African or Islamic flavor, persists. Malcolm Little became Malcolm X and then Malik al-Shabazz. Cassius Clay transformed himself into Muhammad Ali. Lew Alcindor became Kareem Abdul-Jabbar. Civil rights activist Stokely Carmichael changed his name to Kwame Ture. The writer LeRoi Jones converted to Amiri Baraka.

Similarly, for more than a century the descendants of the freedmen have debated what name they should bear as a people. In every instance, a shift in appellation coincided with a new stage in the struggle for equality. In the years after the Civil War, the terms black and negro, favored by slaveholders gave way to the gentler designation colored. Early in this century, when the legal battle against Jim Crow laws was being pressed by the N.A.A.C.P., Negro returned, but with a respectful uppercase N. That gave way to black during the militant days of sit-ins and mass demonstrations during the 1960s. Blunt, proud and unequivocal, black embodied the sheer racial confidence that the civil rights movement had engendered.

Now, with a growing black middle class, the enormous expansion of political power epitomized by Jackson's presidential campaigns, and a burgeoning sympathy with the struggle against South African apartheid, yet another shift may be taking place. Jackson argues that "black tells you about skin color and what side of town you live on. African American evokes a discussion of the world." It was Ramona H. Edelin, president of the National Urban Coalition, who actually proposed the switch in December at a Chicago meeting of black leaders, including Jackson, that was held to plan a summit to set a black agenda for the next century. Edelin says she hoped that encouraging the use of African American "would establish a cultural context for the new agenda we plan to set" at the summit, scheduled for April in New Orleans.

As persuasive as the arguments in favor of a change may be, to some they represent a diversion from more important matters. "This undue concern with our name is a reflection of our powerlessness," says Cornell University professor Henry Louis Gates Jr., a leading literary theorist. "I don't really care what we call ourselves. I just want us to get economic and social equality."

◆

47

# PART 2
# AFRICAN AMERICANS:
# A UNIQUE DILEMMA

# Dialogue: On African Americans

*Bob*—Racism is alive and well, pervasive and persistent in the United States today—and at a time when Americans believe they are less racist and less prejudiced than ever before. We'll revisit this distorted perception when we discuss "Key Dilemmas" (page 398). There is a professed belief in egalitarian attitudes toward race in America. The myth belies the reality. Our collection of perspectives begins with Ed Jones, Jr. in 1973 ("What it's like to be a black manager") and moves through the 1980's ("Black managers: the dream deferred," Jones' update to his first *Harvard Business Review* article), and on to 1993 (Ellis Cose's "Rage of the Privileged"). This collection of experiences illustrates how racist behaviors haven't changed very much over time.

*George*—What these first three pieces have in common is that they focus on race, to the exclusion of gender and class. These articles narrate the experiences of successful African-American men. Therefore, it is a collection of experiences that is reflective of racial bias only—and not compounded by the additional loading of gender or class discrimination. There are some advantages to beginning with this text, but also some limitations . . .

*Bob*—It brings to mind an incident that occurred when I was conducting training for a large federal agency. My contact with this client was a senior administrator, an African-American woman who shared with me her on-going confusion at trying to identify where prejudicial attitudes and behavior were coming from.

The day before I arrived, she had found two agency colleagues from another department working at her personal computer within her private office. She asked them what they were doing there. They dismissed her concerns and continued keyboarding in her personal workspace. The behavior was outrageously rude, but before she began to throw them out of her office, she explained to me, "I had to start thinking . . . are they doing this because I'm black . . . or because I'm a woman?"

Her long-standing experience with discriminatory behavior had taught her that different approaches would work better in interrupting the discrimination depending whether it arose from racism or sexism. I was astonished to think about how exhausting it must be for African-American women to go through that kind of analysis in order to figure out how to deal with that kind of prejudice day-in and day-out . . .

*George*—An excellent contrast to the middle-class African-American male experience is, of course, bell hooks. By the way, we should probably let our readers know that she *does* spell her name in small letters.

*Bob*—bell is one of America's leading black intellectuals, and one of the most clear-eyed and penetrating analysts of culture. She is an eloquent spokesperson for people on the margins, African Americans, women, the disenfranchised, and other minorities. She is widely published and I've often found her works provocative and insightful.

In "Spending Culture" she reveals how middle-class African Americans are reluctant to address issues of class privilege. She asserts "black thinkers who may have no commitment to diverse black communities, who may regard black folks who are not of their class with contempt and disrespect, are held up in the mass media as spokespersons, even if they have never shown themselves to be concerned with [black issues]." As a middle-class white man reading bell hooks, I am often pushed to the edge of my own awareness about how *my* class background affects *my* perceptions.

*George*—Yes, the bell hooks' piece is a great article that brings us back to the issue of how complex it gets when you combine race with class (to say nothing about gender, sexual orientation, disability, etc.).

In organizing the anthology we are fully aware of how critically the construct of "race" functions in U.S. society, yet we don't think "race problems" will be "solved" simply from the vantage point of race. Race issues are so intractable given our nation's 300+ years of oppressing racial minorities, that we need another leverage point. Perhaps the way it works is the more psychological energy we throw into race, the more unmanageable the issues become.

We have chosen "class" as a fulcrum for renewing the thinking and directing resources more effectively—to remedy social injustices and lack of access to opportunity for *everybody!* The people in this country need to take a stand which says:

- We will not tolerate poverty.

- We will not have our streets littered with the homeless or schools full of children too malnourished to be educated.

- We will not accept the prejudiced targeting of individuals and groups.

- We are clear that disempowerment and disenfranchisement are an injury to us all.

- We will not waste talent, however different it looks or sounds.

- We are committed to a dignified place for everyone.

- We will not accept white collar crime any more than we accept rape and child abuse.

- We are determined to educate for the nation's needs, as well as for the individual's and the group's.

- We will not go on as we have.

*Bob*—So this is, first of all, about national resolve, not about changing terminology. It is this national resolve around class that we are after, not a shift in jargon.

*George*—A class approach does not mean that racism will disappear overnight. It doesn't mean that working on racism is not a priority. But more can be accomplished "for" people of color, by having a renewed commitment to a society accessible to all. Such a shift would serve us in responding to real social needs. This is the political challenge.

*Bob*—The next piece by Shelby Steele is brief and to the point. He asserts that most social programs were created to lessen white guilt, rather than genuinely instill African-American self-reliance.

*George*—In her book, *The Future of White Men and Other Diversity Dilemmas*, Joan Steinau Lester points out that when we feel guilty, we focus our attention on ourselves, to alleviate our pain and embarrassment, instead of directing our efforts toward the person who has been wronged or short changed. When such efforts fail—and they are set up for failure—we get resentful and blame the person wronged in the first place. Guilt is a poor policy maker.

*Bob*—We also resent carrying the sins of our ancestors. Your ancestors and mine did not create or participate in slavery in this country, but they benefited from it, and so do we. Feeling guilty gets in the way of saying, "Okay, this is the way things are. Let's get busy and change them."

*George*—As a white man, I need to say to everybody else, "I don't owe you anything. But, I am willing to be your ally and want you to be mine. If you're not ready for that, I am going to continue to clean up my life as best I can. I'll still be here, *'like that stubborn little garbage bag, that time cannot decay.'"*

*Bob*—Wow! We got off on a tangent there . . . let's get back to telling our readers about our selections . . .

*George*—Okay. Next, we have an intriguing play by Eric Law, "Band-Aid." It premiered in L.A. in April of '94 as part of an evening of short plays entitled, "Beyond the Ashes—L.A. Writers Interpret the '92 Uprising." We've included it to emphasize the frustration that minorities feel about white unawareness around race. The play is almost a refrain of "you just don't understand," "you just don't get it, do you?" It's the frustration we whites have to hear and understand, separate from the blame.

*Bob*—And "don't get it" is the blindness to the actual differences of experience caused by racial bias, the lack of access and the ongoing hurts inflicted on people of difference.

*George*—Yes, but it also stems from the unwillingness of people of difference to sometimes take care of this ignorance. Some white people have little access to the experience of African Americans and there is an apparently deliberate resistance on the part of many blacks to allow white people to have that access. In other words, "you just don't get it" may also include "I never want to be able to say that you do get it." The other side of the guilt hook is that once you declare yourself a victim, you always have someone to blame.

*Bob*—On the other hand, I think people of color use that expression because they may feel they've been explaining for a long time, but in a historical context where we as white people were, and still can be, completely oblivious to the issues. The same dynamic often operates between women and men, as well.

*George*—They *have* been explaining, and the oblivion continues, but that doesn't mean either side can stop trying.

*Bob*—As a white man I can be a better ally to people of color and do some of that explaining to other white people; as an ally to women I need similarly to do some explaining to other men. In fact, I may be in a *better* position to explain what I understand of racism to other whites than a person of color might be . . . I might be more credible and run into less defensiveness because I'm not seen as having an "ax to grind." But, nobody is off the hook for the responsibility to educate and to be educated.

There's another side to this dynamic too: African Americans are often expected to be the "resident experts," responsible for teaching whites about racism. I admire those people who choose to be professional educators and explainers . . . but we should remember that racism against blacks in particular has a particularly poignant history in the U.S., and white people are virtually born into a complicity with it. Racism is almost like a birth defect that can only be remedied by taking charge of our own lives and being committed to becoming healthy. It's a job nobody else can do for us. This leads us to Jake Lamar's "The Trouble With You People."

*George*—Yes, this piece is right-on. It's provocative critique turns some long accepted notions on their heads.

*Bob*—His experiences, whether they are with his fourth grade teacher, "Mr. Palomino," or with Mario Cuomo, help clearly portray the dynamics that play out in interracial encounters.

*George*—I wonder to what degree we can have major changes in behavior, but only slight changes

in consciousness. For example, I never expect in my lifetime to be free from reactions to black people because they are black. The imprint I got growing up still puts a charge around blackness that is triggered every time an African-American person comes into my life. My objective has been to manage my reactions in line with deeper values and commitments, which I do relatively well. So there is a big difference between how my mind automatically reacts to race and how I actually behave with people of color. The problem in all of this is the ongoing effort it takes. We like to solve problems and be done with them, and not being able to do that in this dimension of life is vexing. This reactions lingers and patience wears thin . . .

*Bob*— . . . you consciously censor the perceptions and prejudices that have originated from someplace else other than the person in front of you. But they will always come back.

*George*—Yes, I may get better at it, but it will probably always take more energy for me to deal with someone who's black than with someone who's not. Other racial and ethnic differences also take the same kind of energy to deal with, but the bigger charge created around blackness in this country remains. And, being in the diversity business, I hate to admit it—and must admit it.

*Bob*—We are always listening inside to a subconversation that's not being spoken. So, in this section, we've deliberately included some perspectives contrary to the "party line" of the mainstream diversity movement: an article by Jake Lamar from *Esquire* and one by Shelby Steele from *The American Scholar*. They help us appreciate today's African-American dilemmas. Then there's a piece by Bill Maxwell from the *St. Petersburg Times* on the self-destructive aspects of false cultural pride. This again suggests class might be more timely and productive than race as a fulcrum for change.

*George*—Earlier in this section we consciously focus on the middle class and the managerial African American. We do this because, all too often, it seems that the condition, status, and class of ghettoized or impoverished African Americans gets projected on to this middle class and the success of the black middle class is used to further dismiss the needs of underclass African Americans. Their issues need separate treatment.

Nor do we want to forget the working world of the manager, the professional and the technician to see how race still impacts them, quite apart from the issue of poverty. In these situations, race returns to the forefront. Here it can be dealt with separate from the issue of class, and much more effectively, because the class distinction between the blacks and whites is out of the way.

*Bob*—And that's why we need to stop using race to confuse and conflate the differences between blacks of different classes. Anthony Walton's "Letter to Jack" makes this even more clear. The letter comes from one of two alumni from the same university, one white and one African American, and underscores the vastly different experiences of each when they entered the world of work.

# What it's like to be a black manager

by Edward W. Jones, Jr. (*Harvard Business Review*)

*Equal job opportunity is more than putting a black man in a white man's job*

**Foreword: This author contends that most companies fail to recognize the crucial difference between recruiting blacks with executive potential and providing the much-needed organizational support to help them realize this potential. He cites his own experience in a large company to illustrate the type of lonely struggle that faces a black man in the absence of such support. Then he draws some lessons from this experience that should help management to overcome the subtle ramifications of racial differences within organizations.**

Mr. Jones is the manager of an $11-million operating unit of a major company and is responsible for the supervision of 130 employees. After six years with the company, during which he rose from trainee to area manager, he attended the Harvard Business School, where he was graduated two years ago as a Baker Scholar.

When I was graduated from a predominantly black college, I was offered a job in one of the largest corporations in America. On reporting for work, I received a motivational speech from the personnel officer and acknowledged that I agreed with his opinion: the job was going to be challenging in its own right; however, the added burden of prejudice could make it unbearable. In a tone of bravado I said, "I promise you that I won't quit; you'll have to fire me."

At the time, I did not know how important that promise would become. For I was about to begin the most trying experience of my life—the rise to middle management in a white corporation. During those years, I found myself examining my actions, strategies, and emotional stability. I found myself trying desperately to separate fact from mental fiction. I found myself enveloped in almost unbearable emotional stress and internal conflict, trying to hold the job as a constant and evaluate my personal shortcomings with respect to it. At times I would look at myself in a mirror and wonder whether I had lost my mental balance. Somehow I always managed to answer positively, if not resolutely.

I think that my experiences should prove helpful to companies that are wrestling with the problem of how to move black employees from the entry level into positions of greater responsibility. I say this because the manner in which many companies are approaching the problem indicates to me that a number of well-intentioned efforts are doomed to failure.

Failure is likely because most companies merely substitute blacks in positions formerly filled by whites and then, acting as if the corporate environment is not color-sensitive, consider their obligation over. In short, U.S. business has failed to recognize the embryonic black manager's increased chances of failure due to the potentially negative impact of racially based prejudgments. Gaining acceptance in the organization, which the embryonic white manager takes for granted, can be a serious problem for his black counterpart.

## The Job Offer

My story begins when I happened to bump into a recruiter who was talking to a friend of mine. On gathering that I was a college senior, the recruiter asked whether I had considered his company as an employer. I responded, "Are you kidding me—you don't have any black managers, do you?" He replied, "No, but that's why I'm here."

I did well in a subsequent interview procedure, and received an invitation for a company tour. Still skeptical, I accepted, feeling that I had nothing to lose. During a lunch discussion concerning the contemplated job and its requirements, I experienced my first reminder that I was black. After a strained silence, one of the executives at our table looked at me, smiled, and said, "Why is it that everyone likes Roy Campanella, but so many people dislike Jackie Robinson?"

I knew that this man was trying to be pleasant; yet I felt nothing but disgust at what seemed a ridiculous deterioration in the level of conversation. Here was the beginning of the games that I expected but dreaded playing. The question was demeaning and an insult to my intelligence. It was merely a rephrasing of the familiar patronizing comment, "One of my best friends is a negro." Most blacks recognize this type of statement as a thinly veiled attempt to hide bias. After all, if a person is unbiased, why does he make such a point of trying to prove it?

In the fragment of time between the question and my response, the tension within me grew. Were these people serious about a job offer? If so, what did they expect from me? I had no desire to be the corporate black in a glass office but I did not wish to be abrasive or ungracious if the company was sincere about its desire to have an integrated organization.

There was no way to resolve these kinds of questions at that moment, so I gathered up my courage and replied, "Roy Campanella is a great baseball player. But off the field he is not an overwhelming intellectual challenge to anyone. Jackie Robinson is great both on and off the baseball field. He is very intelligent and therefore more of a threat than Roy Campanella. In fact, I'm sure that if he wanted to, he could outperform you in your job."

There was a stunned silence around the table, and from that point on until I arrived back at the employment office, I was sure that I had ended any chances of receiving a job offer.

I was wrong. I subsequently received an outstanding salary offer from the recruiter. But I had no intention of being this company's showcase black and asked seriously, "Why do you want me to work for you? Because of my ability or because you need a black?" I was reassured that ability was the "only" criterion, and one month later, after much introspection, I accepted the offer.

## Initial Exposure

I entered the first formal training phase, in which I was the only black trainee in a department of over 8,000 employees. During this period, my tension increased as I was repeatedly called on to be the in-house expert on anything pertaining to civil rights. I was proud to be black and had many opinions about civil rights, but I did not feel qualified to give "the" black opinion. I developed the feeling that I was considered a black first and an individual second by many of the people I came into contact with. This feeling was exacerbated by the curious executive visitors to the training class who had to be introduced to everyone except me. Everyone knew my name, and I constantly had the feeling of being on stage.

The next phase of training was intended to prepare trainees for supervisory responsibilities. The tension of the trainee group had risen somewhat because of the loss of several trainees and the increased challenges facing us. In my own case, an increasing fear of failure began to impact on the other tensions that I felt from being "a speck of pepper in a sea of salt." The result of these tensions was that I began behaving with an air of bravado. I wasn't outwardly concerned or afraid, but I was inwardly terrified. This phase of training was also completed satisfactorily, at least in an official sense.

At the conclusion of the training, I received a "yes, but" type of appraisal. For example: "Mr. Jones doesn't take notes and seems to have trouble using the reference material, but he seems to be able to recall the material." This is the type of appraisal that says you've done satisfactorily, yet leaves a negative or dubious impression. I questioned the subjective inputs but dropped the matter without any vehement objections.

Prior to embarking on my first management assignment, I resolved to learn from this appraisal and to use more tact and talk less. These resolutions were re-emphasized by my adviser, who was an executive with responsibility for giving me counsel and acting as a sounding board. He also suggested that I relax my handshake and speak more softly.

## On the Job

A warm welcome awaited me in the office where I was to complete my first assignment as a supervisor. I looked forward to going to work because I felt that subjectivity in appraisals would now be replaced by objectivity. Here was a situation in which I would either meet or fail to meet clearly defined numerical objectives.

There were no serious problems for three weeks, and I started to relax and just worry about the job. But then I had a conflict in my schedule. An urgent matter had to be taken care of in the office at the same time that I had an appointment elsewhere. I wrote a note to a supervisor who worked for another manager, asking him if he would be kind enough to follow up on the matter in the office for me.

I chose that particular supervisor because he had given me an embarrassingly warm welcome to the office and insisted that I "just ask" if there was anything at all that he could do to help me. I relied on the impersonality of the note because he was out on a coffee break and I had to leave immediately. The note was short and tactfully worded, and ended by giving my advance "thanks" for the requested help. Moreover, the office norms encouraged supervisory cooperation, so the fact that we worked under different managers did not seem to be a problem.

When I returned to the office, the manager I worked for called me in. He was visibly irritated. I sat down and he said, "Ed, you're rocking the boat." He stated that the supervisor I had asked for help had complained directly to the area manager that I was ordering him around and said he wasn't about to take any nonsense from a "new kid" in the office.

In a very calm voice, I explained what I had done and why I had done it. I then asked my manager, "What did I do wrong?" He looked at me and said, "I don't know, but whatever it is cut it out. Stop rocking the boat." When I asked why the note wasn't produced to verify my statements, he said that it "wasn't available."

I left my manager's office totally perplexed. How could I correct my behavior if I didn't know what was wrong with it? I resolved that I had no choice except to be totally self-reliant, since one thing was obvious: what I had taken at face value as friendliness was potentially a fatal trap.

The feelings aroused in this incident were indicative of those I was to maintain for some time. While I felt a need for closeness, the only option open to me was self-reliance. I felt that my manager should support and defend me, but it was obvious that he was not willing to take such a stance. Worst of all, however, was my feeling of disappointment and the ensuing confusion due to my lack of guidance. I felt that if my manager was not willing to protect and defend me, he had an increased responsibility to give me guidance on how to avoid future explosions of a similar nature.

For some months I worked in that office without any additional explosions, although I was continually admonished not to "rock the boat." During a luncheon with the area manager one day, I remember, he said, "Ed, I've never seen a guy try so hard. If we tell you to tie your tie to the right, you sure try to do it. But why can't you be like Joe (another trainee the area manager supervised)? He doesn't seem to be having any problems."

## The Appraisal Incident

I directed my energies and frustrations into my work, and my supervisory section improved in every measured area of performance until it led the unit. At the end of my first six months on the job, I was slated to go on active duty to fulfill my military requirements as a lieutenant in the Army. Shortly before I left, my manager stated, "Ed, you've done a tremendous job. You write your own appraisal." I wrote the appraisal, but was told to rewrite it because "it's not good enough." I rewrote the appraisal four times before he was satisfied that I was not being too modest. As I indicated earlier, I had resolved to be as unabrasive as possible, and, even though I had met or exceeded all my objectives, I was trying not to be pompous in critiquing my own performance.

Finally, on my next to last day on the job, my manager said, "Ed, this is a fine appraisal. I don't have time to get it typed before you go, but I'll submit this appraisal just as you have written it." With that, I went into the service feeling that, finally, I had solved my problems.

Six months later, I took several days' leave from the Army to spend Christmas in the city with my family. On the afternoon of the day before Christmas, I decided to visit the personnel executive who had originally given me encouragement. So, wearing my officer's uniform, I stopped by his office.

After exchanging greetings and making small talk, I asked him if he had seen my appraisal. He answered, "yes," but when his face failed to reflect the look of satisfaction that I expected, I asked him if I could see it. The appraisal had been changed from the one that I had originally written to another "yes, but" appraisal. The numerical results said that I had met or exceeded all objectives, but under the section entitled "Development Program" the following paragraph had been inserted: "Mr. Jones's biggest problem has been overcoming his own impulsiveness. He has on occasion, early in his tour, jumped too fast with the result that he has incurred some resentment. In these cases his objectives have been good, but his method has ruffled feathers."

I asked the personnel executive to interpret my overall rating. He answered, "Well, we can run the business with people with that rating." I then asked him to explain the various ratings possible, and it became clear that I had received the lowest acceptable rating that wouldn't require the company to fire me. I could not see how this could be, since I had exceeded all my objectives. I explained how I had written my own appraisal and that this appraisal had been rewritten. The personnel officer could not offer an explanation; he recommended that I speak to my old area manager, who had had the responsibility to review and approve my appraisal, and ask him why I had been treated in that manner.

## A Bleak Christmas

I tried to sort things out on my way to see my former area manager. My head was spinning, and I was disgusted. The appraisal was not just unfair—it was overtly dishonest. I thought of standing up in righteous indignation and appealing to higher authority in the company, but I had always resisted calling attention to my blackness by asking for special concessions and wanted to avoid creating a conflict situation if at all possible. While the 15-minute walk in the cold air calmed my anger, I still hadn't decided what I was going to do when I arrived at the area manager's office.

I walked into a scene that is typical of Christmas Eve in an office. People were everywhere, and discarded gift wrappings filled the waste baskets. The area manager still had on the red Santa Claus suit. I looked around at the scene of merriment and decided that this was a poor time to "rock the boat."

The area manager greeted me warmly, exclaimed how great I looked, and offered to buy me a drink on his way home. I accepted, and with a feeling of disgust and disappointment, toasted to a Merry Christmas. I knew then that this situation was hopeless and there was little to be gained by raising a stink while we were alone. I had been naive, and there was no way to prove that the appraisal had been changed.

I was a very lonely fellow that Christmas Eve. My feelings of a lack of closeness, support, and protection were renewed and amplified. It became obvious that no matter how much I achieved, how hard I worked, or how many personal adjustments I made, this system was trying to reject me.

I didn't know which way to turn, whom to trust, or who would be willing to listen. The personnel executive had told me to expect prejudice, but when he saw that I was being treated unfairly, he sent me off on my own.

"What do they expect?" I thought. "They know that I am bound to run into prejudice; yet no one lifts a finger when I am treated unfairly. Do they expect a person to be stupid enough to come right out and say, 'Get out, blackie; we don't want your type here'? This surely wouldn't happen—such overt behavior would endanger the offending person's career."

After the Christmas Eve incident, I went off to finish the remaining time in the Army. During that period, I tossed my work problems around in my mind, trying to find the right approach. The only answer I came up with was to stand fast, do my best, ask for no special favors, and refuse to quit voluntarily.

# New Challenges

When I returned to the company, I was assigned as a supervisor in another area for five or six weeks, to do the same work as I had been doing prior to my departure for the military service. At the end of this uneventful refamiliarization period, I was reassigned as a manager in an area that had poor performance and was recognized as being one of the most difficult in the company. The fact that I would be responsible for one of three "manager units" in the area was exciting, and I looked forward to this new challenge.

I walked into my new area manager's office with a smile and an extended hand, anxious to start off on the right foot and do a good job. After shaking hands, my new boss invited me to sit down while he told me about the job. He began by saying, "I hope you don't, but I am pretty sure you are going to fall flat on your face. When you do, my job is to kick you in the butt so hard that they'll have to take us both to the hospital."

I was shocked and angry. In the first place, my pride as a man said you don't have to take that kind of talk from anyone. I fought the temptation to say something like, "If you even raise your foot, you may well go to the hospital to have it put in a cast."

As I held back the anger, he continued, "I don't know anything about your previous performance, and I don't intend to try to find out. I'm going to evaluate you strictly on your performance for me." The red lights went on in my mind. This guy was making too much of an issue about his lack of knowledge concerning my previous performance. Whom was he trying to kid? He had heard rumors and read my personnel records. I was starting off with two strikes against me. I looked at him and said, "I'll do my best."

## More Appraisal Troubles

The area's results failed to improve, and John, the area manager, was replaced by a new boss. Two weeks after Ralph arrived, he called me on the intercom and said, "Ed, John has your appraisal ready. Go down to see him in his new office. Don't worry about it; we'll talk when you get back." Ralph's words and tone of foreboding made me brace for the worst.

John ushered me into his office and began by telling me that I had been his worst problem. He then proceeded to read a list of every disagreement involving me that he was aware of. These ranged from corrective actions with clerks to resource-allocation discussions with my fellow managers. It was a strange appraisal session. John wound up crossing out half of the examples cited as I rebutted his statements. At the end of the appraisal, he turned and said, "I've tried to be fair, Ed. I've tried not to be vindictive. But if someone were to ask how you're doing, I would have to say you've got room for improvement."

Discussions with Ralph, my new boss, followed as soon as I returned to my office. He advised me not to worry, that we would work out any problems. I told him that this was fine, but I also pointed out the subjectivity and dishonesty reflected in previous and current appraisals and the circumstances surrounding them.

I was bitter that a person who had just been relieved for ineffectiveness could be allowed to have such a resounding impact on my chances in the company. My predecessor had been promoted; I had improved on his results; but here I was, back in questionable status again.

## The Turning Point

About six weeks later, Ralph called me in and said, "Ed, I hope you make it on the job. But what are you going to do if you don't."

At that moment, I felt as if the hands on the clock of life had reached 11:59. Time was running out very rapidly on me, and I saw myself against a wall, with my new boss about to deliver the coup de grace. I felt that he was an honest and very capable person, but that circumstances had combined to give him the role of executioner. It seemed from his question that he was in the process of either wrestling with his own conscience or testing me to see how much resistance, if any, I would put up when he delivered the fatal blow. After all, while I had not made an issue of my ill treatment thus far in my career, no matter how unjustly I felt I had been dealt with, he was smart enough to realize that this option was still open to me.

I looked at Ralph and any thought about trying to please him went out of my mind. Sitting up straight in my chair, I met his relaxed smile with a very stern face. "Why do you care what I do if I don't make it?" I asked coldly.

"I care about you as a person," he replied.

"It's not your job to be concerned about me as a person," I said. "Your job is to evaluate my performance results. But since you've asked, it will be rough if I am fired, because I have a family and responsibilities. However, that's not your concern. You make your decision; and when you do, I'll make my decision." With that statement I returned to my office.

Several weeks after this discussion, a vice president came around to the office to discuss objectives and job philosophy with the managers. I noted at the time that while he only spent 15 or 20 minutes with the other managers, he spent over an hour talking with me. After this visit, Ralph and I had numerous daily discussions. Then Ralph called me into his office to tell me he had written a new appraisal with an improved rating. I was thrilled. I was going to make it. Later, he told me that he was writing another appraisal, stating I not only would make it but also had promotional potential.

After Ralph had changed the first appraisal, my tensions began to decrease and my effectiveness began to increase proportionately. The looser and more confident I became, the more rapidly the results improved. My assignment under Ralph became very fulfilling, and one of the best years I've spent in the company ensued. Other assignments followed, each more challenging than the previous, and each was handled satisfactorily.

# Lessons from Experience

My point in relating these experiences is not to show that I was persecuted or treated unfairly by people in a large corporation. In fact, after talking to friends in the company who knew me during the period just described, I am convinced that many of the lack-of-tact and rock-the-boat statements were true. I am also convinced, however, that the problems I experienced were not uniquely attributable to me or my personality and that it is important for companies to understand what caused them.

The manager to whom I reported on my very first assignment made some informal notes which help illustrate my conviction:

"I discussed each case with Ed. As might be expected, there is as much to be said in his defense as against him. He isn't all wrong in any at one case. But the cumulative weight of all those unsolicited comments and complaints clearly shows that he is causing a lot of people to be unhappy, and I must see that it stops. I don't think it is a question of what he says and does, or a question of objectives. It is a question of a voice, manner, approach, method—or maybe timing. No matter what it is, he must correct whatever he does that upsets so many people."

These are not the words of a scheming bigot; they are the words of a man searching for an explanation to a phenomenon that neither he nor I understood at the time. I was not knowingly insensitive to other people or intent on antagonizing them. What this man and others failed to realize was that, being a black man in a unique position in a white company, I was extremely tense and ill at ease. Levels of sensitivity, polish, and tact which were foreign to me were now necessities of life. The world of white business presented me with an elaborate sociopolitical organization that required unfamiliar codes of behavior.

Abraham Zaleznik refers to this phenomenon in *The Human Dilemmas of Leadership*: "The anxiety experienced by the upwardly mobile individual largely comes from internal conflicts generated within his own personality. On the one hand, there is the driving and pervasive need to prove himself as assurance of his adequacy as a person; on the other hand, the standards for measuring his adequacy come from sources somewhat unfamiliar to him."

My personal pride and sense of worth were driving me to succeed. Ironically, the more determined I was to succeed, the more abrasive I became and the more critical my feedback became. This in turn impelled me to try even harder and to be even more uptight. As a result, I was vulnerable to prejudgments of inability by my peers and superiors.

### The Lens of Color

What most white people do not understand or accept is the fact that skin color has such a pervasive impact on every black person's life that it subordinates considerations of education or class. Skin color makes black people the most conspicuous minority in America, and all blacks, regardless of status, are subjected to prejudice. I personally was not as disadvantaged as many other blacks, but to some extent all blacks are products of separate schools, neighborhoods, and subcultures. In short, black and white people not only look different but also come from different environments which condition them differently and make understanding and honest communication difficult to achieve.

Many whites who find it easy to philosophically accept the fact that blacks will be rubbing shoulders with them experience antagonism when they realize that the difference between blacks and whites goes deeper than skin color. They have difficulty adjusting to the fact that blacks really are different. It is critical that companies understand this point, for it indicates the need for increased guidance to help blacks adjust to an alien set of norms and behavioral requirements.

### The Informal Organization

One of the phenomena that develops in every corporation is a set of behavioral and personal norms that facilitates communication and aids cohesiveness. Moreover, because this "informal organization" is built on white norms, it can reinforce the black-white differences just mentioned and

thus reject or destroy all but the most persistent blacks.

The informal organization operates at all levels in a corporation, and the norms become more rigid the higher one goes in the hierarchy. While this phenomenon promotes efficiency and unity, it is also restrictive and very selective. It can preclude promotion or lead to failure on the basis of "fit" rather than competence. Chester Barnard recognized the existence of the informal organization in 1938. As he stated, "This question of fitness involves such matters as education, experience, age, sex, personal distinctions, prestige, race, nationality, faith . . . "

I believe that many of the problems I encountered were problems of fit with the informal organization. My peers and supervisors were unable to perceive me as being able to perform the job that the company hired me for. Their reaction to me was disbelief. I was out of the "place" normally filled by black people in the company; and since no black person had preceded me successfully, it was easy for my antagonists to believe I was inadequate.

I am not vacillating here from my previous statement that I was probably guilty of many of the subjective shortcomings noted in my appraisals. But I do feel that the difficulties I experienced were amplified by my lack of compatibility with the informal organization. Because of it, many of the people I had problems with could not differentiate between objective ability and performance and subjective dislike for me, or discomfort with me. I was filling an unfamiliar, and therefore uncomfortable, "space" in relation to them. Even in retrospect, I cannot fully differentiate between the problems attributable to me as a person, to me as a manager, or to me as a black man.

## Toward Facilitating 'Fit'

Because of the foregoing problems, I conclude that business has an obligation to even out the odds for blacks who have executive potential. I am not saying that all blacks must be pampered and sheltered rather than challenged. Nor am I advocating the development of "chosen" managers. All managers must accept the risk of failure in order to receive the satisfactions of achievement.

I do, however, advocate a leveling out of these problems of "fit" with the informal organization that operate against black managers. Here are the elements vital to this process:

■ *Unquestionable top management involvement and commitment*—The importance of this element is underscored by my discussions with the vice president who visited me during my crisis period. He disclosed that his objective was to see whether I was really as bad as he was being told. His conclusion from the visit was that he couldn't see any insurmountable problems with me. This high-level interest was the critical variable that gave me a fair chance. I was just lucky that this man had a personal sense of fair play and a desire to ensure equitable treatment.

But chance involvement is not enough. If a company is truly committed to equal opportunity, then it must set up reasoned and well thought-out plans for involvement of top management.

■ *Direct two-way channels of communication between top management and black trainees*—Without open channels of communication, a company cannot ensure that it will recognize the need for a neutral opinion or the intercession of a disinterested party if a black trainee is having problems.

Clear channels of communication will also enable top management to provide empathetic sources of counsel to help the new black trainee combat the potentially crippling paranoia that I encountered. I didn't know whom to trust; consequently, I trusted no one. The counsel of mature and proven black executives will also help mitigate this paranoia.

■ *Appraisal of managers on their contributions to the company's equal opportunity objectives*—The entire management team must be motivated to change any deep beliefs about who does and doesn't fit with regard to color. Accordingly, companies should use the appraisal system to make the welfare of the black trainee coincident with the well-being of his superior. Such action, of course, will probably receive considerable resistance from middle and lower level management. But managers are appraised on their ability to reach other important objectives; and, more significantly, the inclusion of this area in appraisals signals to everyone involved that a company is serious. Failure to take this step signals business as usual and adds to any credibility gap between the company and black employees.

The appraisal process also motivates the trainee's superior to "school" him on the realities of the political process in the corporation. Without this information, no one can survive in an organization. After upgrading my appraisal, Ralph began this process with me. The knowledge I gained proved to be invaluable in my subsequent decision making.

■ *Avoid the temptation to create special showcase-black jobs*—They will be eyed with suspicion by the black incumbents, and the sincerity of the company will be open to question. Blacks realize that only line jobs provide the experience and reality-testing which develop the confidence required in positions of greater responsibility.

■ *Select assignments for the new black manager which are challenging, yet don't in themselves increase his chances of failure*—My assignment with John was a poor choice. He was a top-rated area manager, but had a different job orientation and was struggling to learn his new responsibilities. So naturally he would resent any inexperienced manager being assigned to him. Moreover, the fact that he had never seen a successful black manager reinforced his belief that I could not do the job.

These basic steps need not be of a permanent nature, but they should be enacted until such time as the organizational norms accept blacks at all levels and in all types of jobs. The steps will help mitigate the fact that a black person in the organizational structure must not only carry the same load as a white person but also bear the burden attributable to prejudice and the machinations of the informal organization.

## Conclusion

In relating and drawing on my own experiences, I have not been talking about trials and tribulations in an obviously bigoted company. At that time, my company employed a higher percentage of blacks than almost any other business, and this is still true today. I grant that there is still much to be done as far as the number and level of blacks in positions of authority are concerned, but I believe that my company has done better than most in the area of equal opportunity. Its positive efforts are evidenced by the progressive decision to sponsor my study at the Harvard Business School, so I would be prepared for greater levels of responsibility.

There are differences in detail and chronology, but the net effect of my experiences is similar to that of other blacks with whom I have discussed these matters. While prejudice exists in business, the U.S. norm against being prejudiced precludes an admission of guilt by the prejudiced party. Thus, in my own case, my first manager and John were more guilty of naiveté than bigotry—they could not recognize prejudice, since it would be a blow to their self-images. And this condition is prevalent in U.S. industry.

My experience points out that a moral commitment to equal opportunity is not enough. If a company fails to recognize that fantastic filters operate between the entry level and top management, this commitment is useless. Today, integration in organizations is at or near the entry level, and the threat of displacement or the discomfort of having to adjust to unfamiliar racial relationships is the greatest for lower and middle managers, for they are the people who will be most impacted by this process. Therefore, companies must take steps similar to the ones I have advocated if they hope to achieve true parity for blacks.

Equal job opportunity is more than putting a black man in a white man's job. The barriers must be removed, not just moved.

# Black managers: the dream deferred

by Edward W. Jones, Jr. (*Harvard Business Review*)

In force for a generation, equal opportunity laws have brought blacks in large numbers into corporate managerial ranks. Starting from almost total exclusion, blacks now hold positions of responsibility, with prestige and income that our parents often thought impossible. Between 1977 and 1982 alone, according to the Bureau of Labor Statistics, the proportion of minority managers rose from 3.6% to 5.2%. EEO data from 1982 show that of all "officials and managers," 4.3% were blacks (including 1.6% black females) and 20.4% were white females. The companies that led this progress deserve commendation for their efforts in recruiting, hiring, and promoting not only blacks but also other minority members and women too.

Yet in the midst of this good news there is something ominous. In conversations with black managers, I hear expressions of disappointment, dismay, frustration, and anger because they have not gained acceptance on a par with their white peers. They find their careers stymied and they are increasingly disillusioned about their chances for ultimate success. They feel at best tolerated; they often feel ignored.

A sampling of headlines from the last few years underscores these perceptions: "Black Professionals Refashion Their Careers" (*New York Times*, November 29, 1985), "Many Blacks Jump Off The Corporate Ladder: Feeling Their Rise Limited" (*Wall Street Journal*, August 2, 1984), "Progress Report on the Black Executive: The Top Spots Are Still Elusive" (*Business Week*, February 20, 1984), "They Shall Overcome: Black managers soon learn that getting through the corporate door is only the first of their problems" (*Newsweek*, May 23, 1983), "Job-Bias Alert: Roadblocks Out Of The Closet" (*Wall Street Journal*, May 17, 1982).

Little information exists about minority participation in the top rungs of America's largest companies. But two surveys of *Fortune* "1000" companies by the recruiting firm Korn Ferry International show that as of 1979 and 1985 these businesses have not made even a dent in moving minorities and women into the senior ranks. The 1979 survey of 1,708 senior executives cited three as being black, two Asian, two Hispanic, and eight female. The 1985 survey of 1,362 senior executives found four blacks, six Asians, three Hispanics, and 29 women. I think it's fair to say that this is almost no progress at all.

Equal job opportunity is more than putting a black man in a white man's job. The barriers must be removed, not just moved.

A CEO of a multibillion-dollar, multinational company framed the issue: "I'm concerned. The curve of progress has started to flatten more than it should relative to the effort we've made. I need to know how to be successful in moving up competent but diverse people who are not clones of those above them."

But not enough like him seem to be concerned. A 1983 survey of 785 business opinion leaders ranked affirmative action for minorities and women as twenty-third out of 25 human resource priorities, almost last.[1] Today, unlike the 1960s, equal opportunity is not an issue on the front burner of national or corporate concerns. For many reasons, the prevailing theme of fairness has been replaced by calls for protection of individual liberties and self-help. No one wants to listen to a bunch of complaining minorities. From many perspectives, the problem is seen as solved. It is yesteryear's issue.

My research for this article has convinced me that many of the top executives of our largest companies are committed to fairness and to promoting qualified minorities into positions of responsibility. As one white senior executive put it, "No thinking person would pick a white manager for promotion over a more qualified black manager." In most instances he's probably right. The problem is the influence of unconscious, unthinking criteria on the choice.

This article is based on three years of research, including hundreds of interviews of men, women, whites, blacks, and other minorities; of senior, middle, and junior managers; and of professionals in management, education, consulting, psychology, sociology, psychiatry, and medicine. They included more than 30 black executives, each earning at least $100,000, and more than 200 black managers, most MBAs.

My purpose here is to report on this research, to inform concerned executives of the issues as perceived by black managers. I am not trying to prove anything, only to report and to offer direct testimony on where black managers stand, the progress they have made, the problems that exist, the way blacks feel, and what seems difficult and unresolved.

## 'Color-Blind' Companies

There is a problem that the statistics don't reflect. Listen to four higher level black executives who have achieved some credibility and status in the business world:

"There was strong emphasis in the seventies for getting the right numbers of black managers. But now we're stagnating, as if the motivation was to get numbers, not create opportunity. I get the sense that companies have the numbers they think they need and now don't think anything more needs doing. Some companies are substituting numbers that represent the progress of white women and camouflaging and ignoring the lack of progress for black managers altogether. Many companies hired aggressive, self-motivated, high-achieving blacks who are now feeling deep frustration. Some have left, others stay but are fed up. Some can take more pain, others just throw up their hands and say to hell with it."

"When you work your way up, try to conform, and even job hop to other companies only to confront the same racial barriers—well, it's debilitating. I just don't want to go through that again."

"I went into corporate America to shoot for the top, just like my white classmates at business school. But the corporate expectation seemed to be that as a black I should accept something that satisfied some other need. Corporations are saying, 'We want you to be just a number in a seat representing a particular program. Stay in your place.' The psychology contract made by corporations is unfulfilled for black high achievers. We're dealing with a breach of contract."

"We can have all the credentials in the world, but that doesn't qualify us in the minds of many white people. They can train the hell out of us and we can do well, but they may still think of us as unqualified. Old biases, attitudes, and beliefs stack the cards against us."

These are typical statements black managers make in private. When you hear them over and over, you have to believe there's something very real about them. The myth is that companies are color blind. "We don't tolerate discrimination of any kind and we've instituted procedures to make that a fact," is a typical comment by a white executive. More accurately, discrimination is ever present but a taboo topic—for blacks as well as whites. If you want to move up, you don't talk about it.

When top executives talk about hiring at the lower end, it's not taboo. Often it's actually obligatory for the sake of affirmative action. But when a black middle manager thinks he (or she) has been held back by a white boss because of race, he faces a tough choice. If he remains silent, he is stigmatized by the boss's action and may find his career pigeonholed. But if he speaks up, he is liable to be marked "too sensitive, a troublemaker, not a team player" and lose in the long run even if he proves unfairness.

So highly charged is this topic in corporations that I had to guarantee all interviewees anonymity. Candor might put companies at risk of being embarrassed and careers of being ruined. One executive, noting that blacks are few in his industry, declined to fill out a questionnaire anonymously for fear he would be identified. One white consultant said he lost a great deal of business after performing a survey for a large company in which he reported that black managers were accurate when they complained of unfair treatment. "They never called me back after that," he told me, "and other companies I had dealt with for years didn't call either. The word spread that I couldn't be trusted, and I was blackballed."

## On a treadmill

Corporations and educational institutions have given thousands of black managers the background to move up to more responsible positions. The corporate door is open, but access to the upper floors is blocked. Ironically, companies that led in hiring the best prepared blacks have the worst problem because their protégés' expectations of success are proportionate to their preparation. To expand on the impressions obtained in interviews, I conducted two surveys of black MBAs. The first was a 23-page questionnaire mailed to 305 alumni of the top five graduate business schools. I received 107 back, without follow-up, for a response rate of 35%. More than 98% of the respondents believe that corporations have not achieved equal opportunity for black managers; 90% view the climate of

support as worse than for their white peers; and 84% think that considerations of race have a negative impact on ratings, pay, assignments, recognition, appraisals, and promotion. Some 98% agreed with a statement that subtle prejudice pervades their own companies, and more than half said the prejudice is overt. Less than 10% said their employers promote open discussion of racial issues.

In the survey I listed 15 words and phrases that persons I had interviewed used to describe the climate for blacks in their organizations. To elicit more information (though admittedly in an unscientific fashion: ten of the descriptions were negative and five positive), I asked respondents to select those that "best describe the organizational climate for black managers." The answers, in percentage of total respondents, were:

| | | | |
|---|---|---|---|
| Indifferent | 59% | Supportive | 15% |
| Patronizing | 41% | Positive | 11% |
| Reluctant to accept blacks | 40% | Open in its communication | 10% |
| Encouraging | 24% | Reactionary | 10% |
| Psychologically unhealthy | 21% | Negative | 7% |
| | | Untenable | 7% |
| Unfulfilling | 20% | Unwholesome | 7% |
| Whites are resentful | 20% | Trusting of blacks | 4% |

A number of respondents volunteered 18 other descriptions, of which 12 were negative. I included all 33 terms in an expanded question (contained in a shorter questionnaire) that I distributed at a meeting of some 200 black graduates of a variety of schools. I received 75 returns. Getting the most mentions were these descriptions: supportive in words only (50%), lacks positive direction (41%), has a policy of tokenism (33%), reluctant to accept blacks (33%), and indifferent (33%). The favorable descriptions that received the most mentions were encouraging (17%) and positive (15%).

It doesn't matter whether, by some impossible objective standard, these people are right or wrong; what counts is how they feel. My findings contrast sharply, by the way, with opinions offered from 1979 through 1984 by some 5,000 white managers and other professionals in the data base of

Opinion Research Corporation. Only 28% of them indicated they lack confidence in their employers' appraisal systems. In my first sample, 90% of the black MBAs declared that blacks are treated worse in appraisals than whites at the same levels.

Here are three illustrations of why black managers are frustrated and angry. First, however, a caveat. To condense into a few paragraphs events that transpired over a number of months may oversimplify them, but they do help clarify the attitude of black managers who feel rejected. The white executive who reads these accounts may think, "I'm sure there were other reasons for this. There must have been something about the person that made him unsuitable for more responsibility." But the people I interviewed and surveyed repeated the same kind of story time after time.

■ For more than ten years, John has held the number two post in his department in a large Midwestern chemical company. Some years ago, when his superior, a white, became ill, John filled in for him. After John's boss, who was a vice president, died of a heart attack two years ago, his skip-level boss, a senior vice president, named John acting department head while the company searched for a replacement. During the next 14 months, John repeatedly said he'd like the job and was qualified,. but the senior VP said they wanted to start fresh. "We want to reorient the department," he would say, or "We didn't like the way the department was run; Wally was too involved in side issues." But each candidate who came along was less qualified than John.

Finally the company lured a white executive with all the right credentials away from a prime competitor at a salary much higher than John's boss had received. It was the first time the company had brought in an outsider at such a high level. John, who is still number two in the department, is convinced that top management simply did not want a black vice president. "I've searched and searched in my mind for the reason they didn't appoint me," he said when I interviewed him. "All the excuses don't apply to me. They were always critical of my boss, but not of me. I had good ideas for the department and was excited about the prospect of running it, but they never were interested. The reason always comes down to race. They wouldn't have treated a white manager this way."

■ Then there is Ron, a bright young administrator for a financial services company in California. In his second assignment, Ron accomplished in one year what his boss had said would take him three and was rewarded with a hefty raise and a transfer to a more difficult slot. There his group again decimated the plan, achieving sales levels in 18 months that the company had predicted would take three years. Again Ron was given praise, a raise, and a transfer but no promotion.

Meanwhile, whites who had joined the company as trainees with Ron were promoted once and some of them twice. Ron was disillusioned. "My career is getting behind to the point I don't think I can catch up now," he told me. His color must have been a big factor in the way he had been treated, he claimed, because he had played according to all the rules, had outperformed his white peers, and had still come up short.

■ Bill's division was part of a company newly acquired by a large multinational enterprise located on the West Coast. Hired through a headhunter by the new parent, he was the first black manager in his division. Between the time Bill was appointed and the day he walked into his office, an executive who had opposed Bill's selection had been promoted and as a vice president was two steps above Bill as his boss's boss. Despite Bill's repeated requests, his immediate superior gave him no written objectives. But all of Bill's colleagues told him they liked his direction.

The only indication that race was even noticed was a comment from a sales manager whose performance Bill's division relied on: "I don't normally associate with blacks." Bill learned later that other managers were telling his boss that he was hard to work with and unclear in his plans. His boss did not confront Bill with these criticisms, just hinted at possible problems. Only later did Bill put them together into the indictment they really were.

After six months, out of the blue, he was put on probation. According to Bill's superior, the vice president said he "did not feel Bill could do the job" and suggested to him that Bill accept severance pay and look for other work. Bill decided to stick it out for pride's sake; he knew he could do the job. His work and educational records had proven him to be a winner.

During the following six months, his division performed ahead of plan. Bill was getting compliments from customers and colleagues. His boss assured him that he had proved his worth, and the probation would be lifted. It was. A few months later, Bill's boss finally agreed to set written objectives and scheduled a meeting with him. But when Bill walked into his superior's office, he was surprised to see the VP there too. The purpose of the meeting was not to set objectives but to place Bill back on probation, or give him severance pay, because he did not "seem to be the right man." Bill left the company and started his own business.

It's noteworthy that Bill, Ron, and John all worked for "equal opportunity employers." Are these cases unusual? Listen to the testimony of a black I interviewed, a vice president of a large insurance company: "White executives at my level say they don't see race as a factor. This is contrary to my perceptions. When I say race, I refer to what is happening to all blacks. White executives choose to see these situations as issues of personal shortcomings. They say, 'We have to look at the possibility of upward mobility of blacks on an individual basis.' But when I look at it on an individual basis, I see all blacks being treated the same way. Therefore, I come to the conclusion that black managers are being treated as a group."

## 'Colorism'

Racism is too highly charged a word for my theme. When some people think of racist they picture overt bigotry and hatred, the burning cross, the shout "nigger"—things our country has rejected by law. For black managers, what gives them a disadvantage is deep-seated attitudes that may not even be consciously held, much less manifest themselves in provable illegal behavior.

For this discussion I'll use the word colorism to mean an attitude, a predisposition to act in a certain manner because of a person's skin color. This means that people tend to act favorably toward those with skin color like theirs and unfavorably toward those with different skin color. Study after study shows that colorism exists among white Americans; whereas they generally have an automatically positive internal picture of other whites, they don't have one of blacks. It takes an effort to react positively toward blacks.[2]

A 1982 survey of Ivy League graduates, class of '57, helps explain colorism. For them "dumb" came to mind when they thought of blacks. Just 36% of the Princeton class, 47% at Yale, and 55% at Harvard agreed with the statement, "Blacks are as intelligent as whites."[3] These are graduates of three leading universities who are now approaching their 50s, the age of promotion into senior corporate positions. Though current data are unavailable, in the mid-1950s two-fifths of the American business elite were graduates of these three schools.[4]

All people possess stereotypes, which act like shorthand to avoid mental overload. We are products of all we have experienced directly or indirectly from infancy. Stereotypes will never be eliminated; the best we can do is bring people to a level of awareness to control their impact. Most of the time stereotypes are mere shadow images rooted in one's history and deep in the subconscious. But they are very powerful. For example, in controlled experiments the mere insertion of the word black into a sentence has resulted in people changing their responses to a statement.[5]

One reason for the power of stereotypes is their circularity. People seek to confirm their expectations and resist contradictory evidence, so we cling to beliefs and stereotypes become self-fulfilling.[6] If, for example, a white administrator makes a mistake, his boss is likely to tell him, "That's OK. Everybody's entitled to one goof." If, however, a black counterpart commits the same error, the boss thinks, "I knew he couldn't do it. The guy is incompetent." The stereotype reinforces itself.

While blatant bigotry is a problem in organizations, neutrality may be an even greater obstacle to blacks. While an estimated 15% of white Americans are extremely antiblack, 60% are more or less neutral and conform to socially approved behavior.[7] According to Joseph Feagin, a sociologist at the University of Texas at Austin, "Those managers and executives who are the biggest problem are not the overt racial bigots. They are people who see discrimination but remain neutral and do nothing about it. These are the people who let racially motivated behavior go unnoticed, unmentioned, or unpunished. These are the people who won't help."

Advancement in organizations obviously requires support from the top; and as they step through the maze of obstacles, aspirants try earnestly to pick up signals from those in power so they can tell which way the winds blow. Black managers feel obliged to use a color lens in interpreting those signals. A white male passed over for a choice assignment may wonder about his competence or even whether his style turned somebody off: "Was it my politics? My clothes? My laugh?" Blacks will ponder those things too, but the final question they must ask themselves is, "Was it my color?"

Of course, a decision about a promotion is a subjective thing. For blacks, colorism adds an extra layer of subjectivity. An outplacement consultant (white) who has worked for a number of the largest U.S. corporations referred to "a double standard that boils down to this: the same qualities that are rewarded in white managers become the reason the black manager is disliked and penalized." A black personnel executive explained the double standard this way: "If you're aggressive then you're arrogant, but if you're not aggressive then you're not assertive. You try to be right in the middle, and that's impossible."

Studies show that senior executives are generally taller than average. Height is thus an advantage in moving up the corporate ladder—but not necessarily if you're black. "I was interviewing with a white vice president over cocktails for an opening in his organization," recalled one black executive. "I've always had a good track record and, as you can see, I'm not very large. After a few drinks he told me that he liked me, but if I were a big black guy with large muscles, he wouldn't even consider me for the job."

The corporate posture is that there is no race problem. Perhaps in the attitude of the person at the very top that's true, but not lower down. A black VP of a large East Coast bank said, "Our president talks about adhering to equal opportunity, and every year he sends out this letter saying he's firmly committed to equal opportunity. And I believe he's serious. But as the message gets to middle managers, it's lost." Another black manager put it this way, "The general may give the orders, but it's the sergeant who decides who gets liberty and who gets KP."

At the "sergeant's" level, competition is conditioned by colorism. "It's not a conspiracy, it's an understanding," said a black personnel director at a New England-based food distribution company. "Whites don't get together and say, 'Let's do it to this black guy.' That doesn't happen. Say Joe Blow, a black manager, is vying against ten white guys for a promotion to the assistant VP level. The ten white execs will behave in such a way as to hold Joe Blow back. They'll act independently of each other, possibly without any collusion. But given the opportunity to push Joe Blow ahead or hold Joe Blow back, they'll each hold him back."

Those who seek to step into upper management are playing a new and more complicated game. The stakes are higher and the rules are often less well defined, if they exist at all. So it is here in the middle management passage where the issue of prejudice is most acute.

To get ahead, a person depends on informal networks of cooperative relationships. Friendships, help from colleagues, customers, and superiors, and developmental assignments are the keys to success. Outsiders, or people treated as outsiders (no matter how talented or well trained), rarely do as well. Black managers feel they are treated as outsiders, and because of the distance that race produces they don't receive the benefit of these networks and relationships. Few win bosses as mentors. Moreover, they rarely get the vote of confidence from superiors that helps them to move up step-by-step and allows them to learn the business. These assignments would give them the expertise, exposure, and knowledge necessary for promotion to top posts.

What senior executives would support the promotion to their peer group of somebody they envision as stupid, lazy, dishonest, or preoccupied with sex (the prevailing racial throwbacks among whites about blacks)? This attitude permeates an entire organization because the corporate climate and culture reflect the unspoken beliefs of senior executives, and middle managers, desiring to be senior executives, conform to these norms. This statement by a black middle manager, a woman, illustrates the impact that a closed circle can have on blacks' aspirations:

"A black manager who worked for me deserved a merit raise. I came to the appraisal meeting with all the necessary documentation. There were three or four 40 to 50-year-old white men arguing for their people without any documentation. I was the only one supporting my manager, and I was the only one that saw him as eligible. I was overruled just by the sheer vote of it. It turned out to be a matter of 'Joe, you did a favor for me last week, so I'll support you in getting your person in this week. You owe me one, old buddy.'

"You can try to legitimize the process by saying, 'We all got together and we went through a democratic process, so it was done fairly.' This process was democratic if by that you mean you have one vote in a group of buddies where everyone votes. But a lot of who gets what pay increase and who is put up for promotion is the underlying political buddy system. It's a matter of who believes in who, and each person's prejudices and beliefs come into play to decide the outcome."

A white consultant told me, "White managers aren't comfortable sponsoring black managers for promotion or high-visibility assignments. They fear ostracism from other whites." As a consequence, black executives are shunted into slots out of the mainstream. Here is the testimony of three of them, one from the pharmaceuticals industry, one from an insurance company, and a manufacturer:

"Too often black managers are channeled into The Relations, as I call them—the community relations, the industrial relations, the public relations, the personnel relations. These may be important functions, but they are not the gut functions that make the business grow or bring in revenues. And they're not the jobs that prepare an executive to be a CEO."

"The higher you go, the greater the acceptance of blacks for limited purposes, such as for all those programs that reach out to communities for various projects, the velvet ghetto jobs. And you become an expert on blacks. At my company, if an issue has anything to do with blacks, they come and ask me. On black purchasing they ask me. Hell, I don't have anything to do with purchasing, but because I'm black they think I ought to know something about it."

"White managers don't want to include black managers in the mainstream activities in corporations. Even blacks who have line responsibilities, to the extent that they can be pushed aside, are being pushed aside. They ask you to take a position of visible prominence not slated to the bottom line and give you financial rewards rather than leadership. It's all for outside appearance. But money doesn't relieve a poverty of satisfaction and spirit."

## Pressure to Conform

"Business needs black executives with the courage and insight to help us understand issues involving equal opportunity," John deButts, former CEO of AT&T, once said. "They must tell us what we need to know, not just what they think we want to hear." But black managers are often afraid to risk their careers by speaking their minds.

In most organizations, conformity is an unwritten rule. If you don't conform, you can't be trusted—especially for higher positions. Black managers try to conform to the corporate values regarding race, and female managers, the values regarding women. If race is "not an issue," acceptance means you are expected to pretend race is not an issue. "A lot of black managers," one black executive told me, "are afraid that if they stand up and take an active role in some black concern, even though they believe it's the right issue, people will say, 'Oh, he's black and just standing up for blacks as any black would.'"

Moreover, some white managers become defensive if prejudice is mentioned. After all, it's un-American to be prejudiced, and who wants to be un-American? So white and black managers, fearful of confronting the issue, take part in a charade. "There is often less than total candor between blacks and whites at any level, and the higher up you go the more that is true," says psychiatrist Price Cobbs. "There is mutual patronizing and misreading, making blacks and whites unable to exchange ideas and express their feelings."

At each step up the organizational pyramid, of course, there are fewer positions. But the slots for minority members are even more limited. This creates an additional game—king (or queen) of the little hill—in which minority members and women compete against each other for the tiny number of near-top jobs available to them. And the first one who gets to the top of this smaller hill is sorely tempted to fend off rather than help, other minority players.

Attempts by black managers to convince white superiors they are trustworthy, safe, and therefore acceptable manifest themselves in different ways. One black executive explained, "It might take the form of a manager not wanting a black secretary—not so much because he thinks the individual is unqualified, but because he's concerned about how his superiors and peers might perceive them. 'Hey,' they might say, 'that's a black operation over there, so it can't be too effective.'"

Here are some true stories that illustrate running a gauntlet:

■ Al, who aspired to the lower rungs of senior management, had to fill a vacancy in his organization. The most qualified candidate was another black manager, George. Al's company was an "equal opportunity employer," but he worried that if he promoted George he would be perceived as favoring blacks and therefore would be unacceptable as an executive. So he promoted a less qualified white candidate. George initiated a suit for discrimination, the company settled, and Al resigned.

■ Bob was an ambitious person who changed employers when passed over for promotion. After a year at his new job, he saw that white managers he thought to be inferior performers were being promoted above him. Actually, many of the company's black managers were becoming vocal about a perceived pattern of favoritism toward white managers, who were faring better on appraisals, assignments, promotions, and pay. So that his superiors would see him in a positive light, Bob didn't associate openly with other black managers but he privately encouraged their efforts to speak up. They should be the "bad guys" while he played the "good guy" in the hope that at least one black might be the first to crack the color barrier at a high level.

In meetings with black managers, senior executives would say that they recognized that blacks were not moving up fast enough, but it takes time and the blacks should not be too pushy. Bob told the white executives, "I don't see why you're even meeting with those guys. They're a bunch of complainers." Two months later, Bob was the first black to be promoted to the executive level.

■ Charlie, a junior executive, did not wear race on his sleeve but was straightforward and honest on the subject. One day several lower level black managers sought his advice on correcting what they saw as a pattern of discrimination stunting their careers. Charlie concluded that senior man-

agement ought to know about their concerns, and he agreed to arrange a meeting with top officers. Two days before the meeting the president took Charlie aside in the executive dining room and said, "Charlie, I'm disappointed that you met with those people. I thought we could trust you."

■ Ellen, a politically astute black manager, noted that promotions for black managers in her organization diminished coincident with an increase in promotions for white females. Ellen skewed promotions in favor of white females and was a regular participant in meetings about women's issues. She would not promote black males because they were "undependable." Ellen was surprised when a white male declined a promotion because the black male who trained him "was more deserving."

The twist that colorism puts on the maneuvering of ambitious managers is not a new phenomenon. Jews and Italians (among Irish, and other ethnic newcomers in America) have tried to pass as less Jewish or less Italian than their Jewish or Italian colleagues. Obviously it is more difficult for blacks to overcome white executives' feelings about color, but they, like whites, will use what tactics they can to get ahead. But for blacks it's more than merely changing roles like changing hats. Adopting a white value system often means unconsciously devaluing other blacks—and ultimately themselves.

## Race & sex

Another phenomenon that black managers are talking about is "substituting the lesser evil." In their evident push to demonstrate progress toward equal opportunity, some companies are promoting white women in lieu of black men and women. Many of the black managers I interviewed mentioned this phenomenon. Of all the complex interracial issues, certainly the most controversial is the combination of race and sex. The white male-black female, black male-white female relationships are very sensitive matters. Here the most primitive feelings interact, and the stereotypes come boiling to the surface.

At higher levels of organizations, white women have problems in achieving acceptance that in some ways are like those of blacks. Even so, race poses the bigger barrier.[8] According to Price Cobbs, the psychiatrist, "There will be far more white

## Harlem

What happens to a dream deferred?

Does it dry up
like a raisin in the sun?
Or fester like a sore—
And then run ?
Does it stink like rotten meat?
Or crust and sugar over—
like a syrupy sweet?

Maybe it just sags
like a heavy load.

*Or does it explode?*

From Selected Poems of Langston Hughes
(New York: Alfred A. Knopf, Inc.)
Copyright 1951 by Langston Hughes
Reprinted by permission of the publisher

women in the old boys' club before there are large numbers of blacks—men or women."

Since white women comprise 40% of the U.S. population, compared with blacks' 12%, they naturally should move into positions of power in greater numbers than blacks. What seems to be happening, however, is the movement upward of white women at the expense of blacks—men and women. Black managers are concluding that senior executives who are uncomfortable promoting blacks into positions of trust and confidence—those positions that lead to the top jobs—feel less reluctant to promote white females to these posts. "It's as if there is a mind-set that says, 'We have a couple of women near the executive suite—we've done our job,' and they dismiss competent blacks," one black executive said. "It's corporate apartheid," said another.

If the comfort level is a big factor in an invitation to enter the executive suite, it is understandable that white women will get there before blacks. After all, the mothers, wives, and daughters of top officers are white women, and they deal with white women all their lives—but only rarely with black men and women. And they are likely to view white women as being more from their own social class than black men and women. Stereotypes no doubt

play a role here too. One study indicates that the higher the white male rises in the corporate hierarchy, the less likely he is to hold negative stereotypes about women but the more likely he is to hold negative stereotypes about blacks.[9]

Black women, of course, seemingly have to overcome issues of both race and sex. But these combined drawbacks may cause less resistance than that experienced by black men. A study of biracial groups concluded that black women are not perceived in the same sexual role as white women or in the same racial role as black men. Within a social context, black females are more readily accepted in roles of influence than black males. The author of the study reasoned that white society has historically allowed more assertive behavior from black women than black men because black women are considered to be less dangerous.[10]

If personal comfort levels are a main criterion for advancement, black women are less threatening and therefore more acceptable to white male executives and so will advance faster and farther than black men. Recently *Fortune* magazine found that "the figures for black men tell a disturbing story. From 1976 to 1984, black men lost ground relative to both white women and black women."[11]

### Balancing act

Most black managers feel that to satisfy the values and expectations of the white corporate hierarchy they must run a gauntlet of contradictory pressures. Running the gauntlet means smarting from the pain of prejudice even as white colleagues deny that your reality of race has any impact. It means maintaining excellent performance even when recognition is withheld.

It means being smart but not too smart. Being strong but not too strong. Being confident but not egotistical to the point of alienation. Being the butt of prejudice and not being unpleasant or abrasive. Being intelligent but not arrogant. Being honest but not paranoid. Being confident yet modest. It means seeking the trust and respect of fellow blacks and acceptance by whites. Speaking out on issues affecting blacks but not being perceived as a self-appointed missionary or a unifaceted manager expert only on black subjects. Being courageous but not too courageous in areas threatening to whites.

It means being a person who is black but not losing one's individuality by submersion into a class of "all blacks," as perceived by whites. Defining one's self while not contradicting the myriad definitions imposed by white colleagues. Being accepted as a leader for whites and not being seen as an Uncle Tom by blacks. Being a person who is black but also a person who is an authentic human being.

Some black managers are becoming psychological contortionists, struggling to play by the rules of this game. Feelings of self-worth and self-esteem are vital ingredients of mental health. High-achieving black managers are particularly vulnerable to depression if they strive for what white peers attain only to find that the objects of their desire are withheld. The knowledge that these goals should be attainable because of educational preparation and intellectual capability makes the conflict sharper and black managers that much more vulnerable to depression. According to Price Cobbs, the level of outrage and indignation among black managers exceeds that of black Americans who are unemployed. Another psychiatrist I talked to adds: "Those black managers in the potentially greatest psychological trouble are the ones who try to deny their ethnicity by trying to be least black—in effect, trying to be white psychologically."

According to Abraham Zaleznik, a social psychologist at the Harvard Business School, if companies promote only those blacks "who are going along with the values of others, they are eliminating those blacks who have more courage, leadership potential, and a better sense of self worked out. This would be tragic because it would attack the very basis of building self-esteem based on an individual's unique capabilities."

## Where to From Here?

The picture of frustration and pain that I have drawn is the reality for many, but certainly not all, black managers. I have stressed what is the predominant condition. Most black managers are convinced that their best is never seen as good enough, even when their best is better than the best of white colleagues. The barrier facing black managers is no less real than a closed door. But in the minds of many of their superiors, if people can't make it on their own, it must be their own fault.

I am not talking about the disadvantaged but about high achievers, those blacks who are most integrated into the fabric of our country's white oriented culture. Yet because of colorism many of these best qualified managers are seen as unqualified "affirmative action hires." (Even so, affirmative action should not be a distasteful term—though it is in Washington these days. Its objective is to ensure that all qualified persons compete on a level playing field.)

What will be the outcome if many of America's best educated and best prepared blacks are not allowed to succeed, and if our country's leaders, including those in corporations, no longer care about this issue? Everyone may agree that "a mind is a terrible thing to waste," but are we not contradicting ourselves if we make waste matter of some of our best black managerial minds or relegate them to the scrap heap of human potential? How hypocritical will we appear in America if "equal opportunity" becomes primarily a white female slogan and the law is used to construct a system akin to corporate apartheid in which the positions of power and authority are nearly all held by whites? What will today's black managers say to their children if one day they ask, "Why don't I have the opportunity you had, and what did you try to do about it?"

Just as one cannot be a little bit pregnant, corporations cannot have a little bit of equal opportunity. There is unlimited opportunity, based on uniform rules, or equal opportunity does not exist. If, at a certain higher level, opportunity appears to peak because no blacks have ever been at such a level, blacks and whites may perceive that blacks could never—and therefore should never—be promoted there. They don't satisfy the "prototype" for an executive at that level, and therefore, among those who are competing for advancement, they are less appealing as candidates than their white competitors.

So their effectiveness as managers, even in their present roles, becomes an issue. Such a perception combines with ego adjustments of whites working for blacks (whites who may never have been subordinate to a black person before) to make effective leadership by a black much more difficult. Who wants to work for someone not seen as a winner? Or someone with a questionable future?

Will black managers ever be allowed to move up the organization and succeed in the old-fashioned way, by earning it? They must be allowed to fail as well as succeed. In other words, they must be treated the same as white managers.

The first step is to accept how deeply rooted our feelings are about race and color, then remove the taboo from candor on racial realities. We must open up communication and not deny or pretend corporations cannot manage attitudes, but they can manage behavior with accountability, rewards, and punishment, as in all other important areas of concern. What gets measured in business gets done, what is not measured is ignored.

The commitment must come from the top down—that of course is obvious. But more than sincerity is needed from the board of directors down through the management structure: commitment, example, and follow-through. Unless the CEO influences the corporate culture to counter the buddy system by compelling all managers to focus on competence and performance rather than comfort and fit, the in-place majority will merely perpetuate itself and the culture will continue to default to traditional racial etiquette and attitudes.

Equal opportunity will not be achieved by promoting one or two high-profile, "most acceptable" blacks into the executive suite, putting a black on a board of directors, or bringing in one or two "name" blacks from outside and bypassing middle management. A fair chance means that black managers can move ahead and still be genuine, that they don't have a psychological gauntlet imposed on them. Fairness means that successful black managers can be role models. A fair chance means that there can be black division heads of marketing, production, and strategic planning, as well as urban affairs and community relations. It also means that black executives can become part of the headquarters elite and report directly to the CEO, not only as vice presidents but as senior and executive vice presidents. It means black executives can be CEOs.

Where do we go from here? The answer lies in our vision for America: whether we want a land of opportunity for all Americans based on individual dignity and respect, or a land of advantage and disadvantage based on skin color. Whether we want a nation where competence and character will be the criteria for leadership, or whether color will ordain that Americans stay in a place determined in the minds and by the values of others. Senior corporate executives can help decide the outcome. Where do they choose to go from here?

## References

1. Survey conducted in 1983 by Sirota and Alper Associates, New York.

2. See Faye Crosby, Steven Bromely, and Leonard Saxe, "Recent Unobtrusive Studies of Black and White Discrimination & Prejudice: A Literature Review," *Psychological Bulletin*, vol. 87, no. 3, 1980, p.546.

3. *Wall Street Journal*, May 21, 1982.

4. Suzanne Keller, *Beyond the Ruling Class: Strategic Elites in Modern Society* (New York: Random, 1953), p.202.

5. William E. Sedlacek and Glenwood C. Brooks, Jr., "Measuring Racial Attitudes in a Situational Context," *Psychological Reports*, vol. 27, 1970, p.971.

6. Mark Snyder, "Self-Fulfilling Stereotypes," *Psychology Today*, July 1982, p.60.

7. Tom Pettigrew, "The Mental Impact," in *Impacts of Racism On White Americans*, ed. Benjamin P. Bowser and Raymond G. Hunt (Beverly Hills, Calif.: Sage, 1981), p.116.

8. John Fernandez, *Racism and Sexism in Corporate Life* (Lexington, Mass: Lexington Books, D.C. Heath, 1981), p.80.

9. Kathryn Adams, "Aspects of Social Context As Determinants of Black Women's Resistance to Challenges," *Journal of Social Issues*, vol. 39, no. 3, 1983, p.69.

10. Anne B. Fisher, "Good News, Bad News, and an Invisible Ceiling," *Fortune*, September 16, 1985, p.29.

11. See Alexander Thomas and Samuel Sillen, *Racism and Psychiatry* (Secaucus, N.J.: Citadel, 1972), p.49.

## About the Author

In July–August 1973, *HBR* published Edward Jones's personal account, "What it's like to be a black manager." At the time he was a division manager at New York Telephone Company. A decade later, *HBR* asked Jones to assess the progress of black managers in U.S. corporations. This article is the result.

From New York Telephone Jones moved to AT&T where he oversaw nationwide strategic planning for media markets and initiated the company's satellite strategy. In 1984 Jones formed Corporate Organizational Dynamics, Inc., a consulting firm specializing in organizational effectiveness. He is now writing a book titled *Managing the Dynamics of Difference*.

# Rage of the Privileged

by Ellis Cose (*Newsweek*)

*Though they struggle to hold their anger in check, even the most successful blacks find themselves haunted by racial demons.*

I was studying rage, I told my host, an eminently successful corporate lawyer. Specifically, I was looking into the anger of middle-class blacks—into why people who seemingly had so much to celebrate were filled with resentment and rage. "Well, I can tell you why I'm angry," he began, launching into a long tale about his compensation package. Despite the millions he had brought into the firm the year before, his partners were balking at giving him his due. "They want you to do well, but not that well," he grumbled. The more he talked, the more agitated he became. What I had originally thought would be a five-minute conversation stretched on for nearly an hour as this normally restrained and unfailingly gracious man vented long-buried feelings.

Much more was on his mind than the fact that his partners were still "fumbling with my compensation." One source of immense resentment was an encounter of a few days previous, when he had arrived at the office earlier than usual and entered the elevator along with a young white man. They got off at the same floor. No secretaries or receptionists were yet in place. As my friend turned toward the locked outer office doors, his elevator mate blocked his way and asked, "May I help you?" My friend shook his head and attempted to circle around his would-be helper, but the young man stepped in front of him and demanded in a loud and decidedly colder tone, "May I help you?" At this, the older man fixed him with a stare, spat out his name and identified himself as a partner, whereupon his inquisitor quickly stepped aside.

My friend's initial impulse was to put the incident behind him. Yet he had found himself growing angrier and angrier at the young associate's temerity. After all, he had been dressed much better than the associate. His clients paid the younger man's salary. The only thing that could have conceivably stirred the associate's suspicions was race: "Because of his color, he felt he had the right to check me out."

He paused in his narration and shook his head. "Here I am, a black man who has done all the things I was supposed to do," he said, and proceeded to tick off precisely what he had done: gone to Harvard, labored for years to make his mark in an elite law firm, married a highly motivated woman who herself had an advanced degree and a lucrative career. He and his wife were in the process of raising three exemplary children. Yet he was far from fulfilled.

"Had I been given a fair shot, who knows where I would be?" he sighed. Moreover, despite his own clear achievements, he was concerned for his children. With so many black men in jail or beaten down by society, whom would his daughters marry? With prejudice still such a force, who could ensure their success? As for himself, he said, he had come to terms with reality. He no longer expected praise, honor, or acceptance from his white colleagues, or from the white world at large. "Just make sure my money is at the top of the line. I can go to my own people for acceptance."

I was certain he did not mean what he said. If acceptance was not important to him, the perceived lack of it would not have caused him such pain. I was certain as well that his distress was not atypical. Again and again, as I spoke with blacks who have every accouterment of success, I heard a plaintive declaration—always followed by various versions of an unchanging and urgently put question. "I have done everything I was supposed to do. I have stayed out of trouble with the law, gone to the right schools, and worked myself nearly to death. What more do they want? Why in God's name won't they accept me as a full human being? Why am I pigeonholed in a 'black job'? Why am I constantly treated as if I were a drug addict, a thief, or a thug? Why am I still not allowed to aspire to the same things every white person in America takes as a birthright? Why, when I most want to be seen, am I suddenly rendered invisible?"

That well-to-do blacks should have any gripes at all undoubtedly strikes many as strange. The civil rights revolution, after all, not only killed Jim Crow but brought blacks more money, more latitude and more access to power than enjoyed by any previous generation of African-Americans. Some blacks in this new era of opportunity have amassed fortunes that would put Croesus to shame. If ever there was a time to celebrate the achievements of the color-blind society, now should be that time.

Yet, instead of celebrating, much of America's black privileged class claims to be in excruciating pain. Donald McHenry, former U.S. permanent representative to the United Nations, told me that though he felt no sense of estrangement himself, he witnessed it often in other blacks who had done exceptionally well: "It's sort of the in talk, the in joke, within the club, an acknowledgment of and not an acceptance . . . of the effect of race on one's life, on where one lives, on the kinds of jobs that one has available." Dorothy Gilliam, a columnist for *The Washington Post*, expressed a similar thought in much stronger terms. "You feel the rage of people, [of] your group . . . just being the dogs of society."

Ulric Haynes, dean of the Hofstra University School of Business and a former corporate executive who served as President Carter's ambassador to Algeria, has given up hope that racial parity will arrive in this—or even in the next—millennium. "During our lifetimes, my children's lifetimes, my grandchildren's lifetimes, I expect that race will . . . matter. And perhaps race will always matter, given the historical circumstances under which we came to this country." That makes Haynes angry. "Not for myself. I'm over the hill," he says. "I'm angry for the deception that this [racial prejudice] has

perpetrated on my children and grandchildren." Though his children have traveled the world and received an elite education, they "in a very real sense are not the children of privilege. They are dysfunctional, because I didn't prepare them, in all the years we lived overseas, to deal with the climate of racism they are encountering right now."

Even many Americans who acknowledge Haynes' distress will be disinclined to care. For one thing, few Americans of any color are as well-fixed as Haynes. For another, the problems of the black middle class pale by comparison with those of the underclass. Yet, formidable as the difficulties of the so-called underclass are, the nation cannot afford to use the plight of the poor as an excuse for blinding itself to the difficulties of the black upwardly mobile. For though the problems of the two classes are not altogether the same, they are in some respects linked. And one must at least consider the possibility that a nation which embitters those struggling hardest to believe in it and work within its established systems is seriously undermining any effort to provide would-be hustlers and dope dealers with an attractive alternative to the streets.

> There's an air of frustration [among young black managers] that's just as high now as it was 30 years ago. . . . They have an even worse problem [than I did] because they've got M.B.A.s from Harvard. They did all the things that you're supposed to do . . . and things are supposed to happen.
>
> *Darwin Davis*
> *Sr. Vice president, Equitable Life Assurance Society*

Why would people who have enjoyed all the fruits of the civil rights revolution—who have Ivy League educations, high-paying jobs, and comfortable homes—be consumed with anger? To answer that question is to go a long way toward explaining why quotas and affirmative action remain such polarizing issues; why black and white Americans continue to see race in such starkly different terms; and why solving America's racial problems is infinitely more complicated than cleaning up the nation's urban ghettos and educating the inhabitants—even assuming the will, wisdom, and resources to accomplish such a task.

It is to understand, among other things, what a black financial manager feels upon being told that a client is uncomfortable with his handling an account, or what a black professor goes through upon being asked whether she is really qualified

73

to teach. For many black professionals, these are not so much isolated incidents as insistent and galling reminders that whatever they may accomplish in life, race remains their most salient feature as far as much of America is concerned.

# The Dozen Demons

What is it exactly that blacks spend so much time coping with? For lack of a better phrase, let's call them the dozen demons. This is not to say that they affect blacks only, or that there are only twelve, or that all black Americans encounter every one. Still, you're not likely to find a bet more certain than this: that any random gathering of black American professionals, asked what ails them, will eventually end up describing, in one guise or another, the following items.

> I think it's very difficult once we have achieved, and we have good educations, and we know we're good . . . to run up against this brick wall. . . . Nobody wants to be perceived as being a victim of racism or prejudice. It hurts. It hurts deeply.
>
> Ella Louise Bell
> Assistant Professor, Sloan School of Management, MIT

1. *Inability to fit in:* During the mid 1980s, I had lunch in the Harvard Club in Manhattan with a news-room recruiter from *The New York Times*. The lunch was primarily social, but my companion was also seeking help in identifying black, Hispanic, and Asian-American journalists he could lure to the *Times*.

   As we talked, it became clear that he was focusing on such things as speech, manners, dress, and educational pedigree. He had in mind, apparently, a certain button-down sort, an intellectual, non-threatening, quiet-spoken type—something of a cross between William F. Buckley Jr. and Bill Cosby. Someone who might be expected to have his own membership at the Harvard or Yale Club. That most whites at the *Times* fit no such stereotype seemed not to have occurred to him. I suggested, rather gingerly, that perhaps he needed to expand his definition of a "Times person."

   Even as I made the argument, I knew that it was unpersuasive. Not because he dis-

agreed—he did not offer much of a rebuttal—but because he and many similarly placed executives almost instinctively screened minority candidates according to criteria they did not apply to whites. The practice has nothing to do with malice. It stems more from an unexamined assumption that whites, purely because they are white, are likely to fit in, while blacks and other minority group members are not.

2. *Lack of respect:* Ron Brown, a psychologist and specialist in interracial relations, notes that black professionals—like the corporate lawyer cited above—constantly have to prove they are worthy of respect. He recalls being in a car with a black general and several other blacks near a military base in Biloxi, Mississippi. As they approached the gates to the base, the general said, "Don't worry," and flashed his two-star badge. The guard replied, "No sir," and demanded to see some identification. "And you could just tell from the back he [the general] was rocking with rage . . . These little incidents boil over [into fury] where you should feel . . . pride."

   Knowing that race can undermine status, African-Americans frequently take aggressive countermeasures in order to avoid embarrassment. One woman, a Harvard-educated lawyer, carries a Bally bag when going to certain exclusive shops. Like a sorceress warding off evil with a wand, she holds the bag in front of her to rebuff racial assumptions, in the hope that the clerk will take it as proof that she is fit to enter.

3. *Low expectations:* Shortly after I was appointed editorial board chairman of the *New York Daily News*, I was visited by a black employee who had worked at the paper for some time. More was on his mind than a simple desire to make my acquaintance. He had also come to talk about how his career was

blocked, how the deck was stacked against him—how, in fact, it was stacked against any black person who worked there. His frustration and anger I easily understood. But what struck me as well was that his expectations left him absolutely no room to grow. He believed so strongly that the white men at the *Daily News* were out to stymie black achievement that he had no option but failure, whatever the reality of the situation.

Even those who refuse to internalize the expectation of failure are often left with nagging doubts, with a feeling, as journalist Joseph Boyce puts it, "that no matter what you do in life, there are very few venues in which you can really be sure that you've exhausted your potential. Your achievement is defined by your color and its limitation. And even if in reality you've met your fullest potential, there's an aggravating, lingering doubt . . . because you're never sure. And that makes you angry."

> We treat white folks like children. We're selective in our terminology. . . . We waste a lot of time that ought to be devoted to candor.
>
> *Basil Paterson*
> *Lawyer and former vice chairman of the*
> *Democratic National Committee*

4.  **Shattered hopes:** Of the executives sociologist Sharon Collins met while doing her research, one black senior manager stood out. He was such a corporate politician, she recalls, that he could "hardly say anything without putting it in terms of what's good for the company." Yet, as he neared the end of an illustrious career, he had noticed that colleagues were passing him by, and he had reluctantly concluded that racial discrimination was the only explanation that made sense. That realization left him profoundly disillusioned. "He knows the final threshold is there, and he's losing hope that he can cross it," says Collins.

An associate in a prominent law firm experienced a similar disappointment after two years of trying desperately to succeed. The lawyer is Mexican-American, but insists his experience was also typical of the firm's black associates—none of whom ever got a shot at any big assignments. This discontent, he makes plain, was felt by all the nonwhite lawyers. He remembers one in particular, a black woman who graduated with honors from Yale. All her peers thought she was headed for the stars. Yet when associates were ranked by the firm, she was never included in the first tier but at the top of the second.

If he had been alone in his frustration, he says, one could reject his complaint as no more than a case of sour grapes. "But the fact that all of us were having the same kinds of feelings" means something more systemic was at work. He acknowledges that many whites had similar feelings, that in the intensely competitive environment of a top law firm, no one is guaranteed an easy time. But the sense of abandonment, he contends, was exacerbated for nonwhites. He finally quit in disgust and became a public defender. By his count, every minority group member who entered the firm with him ended up leaving, having concluded that nonwhites—barring the spectacularly odd exception—were not destined to make it in that world.

5.  **Faint praise:** For a year and a half during the early 1980s, I was a resident fellow at the National Research Council—National Academy of Sciences, an august Washington institution that evaluates scientific research. One afternoon, I mentioned to a white colleague who was also a close friend that it was a shame the NRC had so few blacks on staff. She replied, "Yes, it's too bad there aren't more blacks like you."

I was stunned enough by her comment to ask her what she meant. She answered, in effect, that there were so few really intelligent blacks around who could meet the standards of the NRC. I, of course, was a wonderful exception. Her words, I'm sure, were meant as a compliment, but they angered me, for I took her meaning to be that blacks (present company excluded) simply didn't have the intellect to hang out with the likes of her.

6. *Coping fatigue:* When Armetta Parker took a job as a public relations professional at a large manufacturing company, she assumed that she was on her way to big-time corporate success. A bright, energetic woman then in her early thirties, Parker had left a good position at a public utility in Detroit to get on the Fortune 100 fast track.

Corporate headquarters was in a town of nearly forty thousand people, but only a few hundred black families lived there, and she met virtually no black singles her own age. Though she expected a certain amount of social isolation, "I didn't expect to get the opportunity to take a really hard look at me, at what was important to me and what wasn't." She had to face the fact that success, in that kind of corporate environment, meant a great deal of work and no social life, and that it also required a great deal of faith in people who found it difficult to recognize competence in blacks.

Nonetheless, Parker did extremely well, at least initially. Her first year at the company, she made it into "The Book"—the firm's roster of those who had been identified as people on the fast track. But eventually she realized that "I was never going to be vice president of public affairs [at that company]." Moreover, "even if they gave it to me, I didn't want it. The price was too high." Part of that price would have been accepting the fact that her race was not seen as an asset but as something she had to overcome.

After six years she left. A large portion of her ambition for a corporate career had vanished. She had realized that "good corporate jobs can be corporate handcuffs. You have to decide how high of a price you're willing to pay."

Dave Johnson, a former IBM executive who retired last year after 29 years of service, agrees. "Corporate America's culture will force you to retire real quick," he says. Johnson now runs his own consulting business in Baltimore and spends much of his time helping younger black managers cope with corporate frustrations.

7. *Pigeonholing:* Once upon a time one would never have thought of appointing a black city editor, a big-city newspaper executive told me. Now one could not think of not seriously considering—and even favoring—a black person for the job.

The executive was making several points. One was about himself and his fellow editors, about how they had matured to the extent that they valued all managerial talent—even in blacks. He was also acknowledging that blacks had become so central to the city's political, economic, and social life that a black city editor had definite advantages, strictly as a function of race. His third point, I'm sure, was wholly unintended but clearly implied: that it was still possible, even for the most enlightened management, to classify jobs by color. And logic dictates that if certain managerial tasks are best handled by blacks, others are best left to whites.

What this logic has meant in terms of the larger corporate world is that black executives have landed, out of all proportion to their numbers, in community relations and public affairs, or in slots where their only relevant expertise concerns blacks and other minorities.

> People can't even discuss their anger. In our survey of black journalists we found that about a third were afraid to talk about racial issues. They feared it would damage their chances for advancement.
>
> *Dorothy Gilliam*
> *President, National Association of Black Journalists*

8. *Identity troubles:* The man was on the verge of retiring from his position as personnel vice president for one of America's largest companies. He had acquired the requisite symbols of success: a huge office, a generous compensation package, a summer home away from home. But he had paid a price. He had decided

along the way, he said matter-of-factly, that he could no longer afford to be black.

I was so surprised by the man's statement that I sat silent for several seconds before asking him to explain. Clearly he had done nothing to alter his dark brown complexion. What he had altered, he told me, was the way he allowed himself to be perceived. Early in his career, he had been moderately outspoken about what he saw as racism within and outside his former corporation. He had learned, however, that his modest attempts at advocacy got him typecast as an undesirable. So when he changed jobs, he decided to disassociate himself from any hint of a racial agenda. The strategy had clearly furthered his career, even though other blacks in the company labeled him an Uncle Tom. He was aware of his reputation, and pained by what the others thought, but he had seen no other way to thrive. He noted as well, with evident pride, that he had not abandoned his race. He had quietly made it his business to cultivate a few young blacks in the corporation and bring their careers along; and he could point to some who were doing very well and would have been doing considerably worse without his intervention. His achievements brought him enough pleasure to balance out the distress of not being "black."

9. **Self-censorship and silence:** Many blacks find their voices stilled when sensitive racial issues are raised. They are painfully aware, as New York politician Basil Paterson puts it, that "whites don't want you to be angry."

A big-city police officer once shared with me his frustration at waiting nineteen years to make detective. In those days before affirmative action, he had watched, one year after another, as less qualified whites were promoted over him. Each year he had swallowed his disappointment, twisted his face into a smile, and congratulated his white friends as he hid his rage—so determined was he to avoid being categorized as a race-obsessed troublemaker.

He had endured other affronts in silence, including a vicious beating by a group of white cops while carrying out a plainclothes assign-

ment. As an undercover officer working within a militant black organization, he had been given a code word to whisper to a fellow officer if the need arose. When he was being brutalized, he had screamed out the word and discovered it to be worthless. His injuries had required surgery and more than thirty stitches. When he was asked by his superior to identify those who had beat him, he feigned ignorance; it seems a fellow officer had preceded his commander and bluntly passed along the message that it was safer to keep quiet.

Even though he made detective years ago, and even though, on the side (and on his own time), he managed to become a successful businessman and an exemplary member of the upwardly striving middle class, he says the anger still simmers within him. He worries that someday it will come pouring out, that some luckless white person will tick him off and he will explode, with tragic results. Knowing him, I don't believe he will ever reach that point. But I accept his fear that he could blow up as a measure of the intensity of his feelings, and of the terrible cost of having to hold them in.

10. **Mendacity:** Even more damaging than self-imposed silence are the lies that seem an integral part of America's approach to race. Many of the lies are simple self-deception, as when corporate executives claim their companies are utterly color-blind. Some stem from unwillingness to acknowledge racial bias, as when people who have no intention of voting for a candidate of another race tell pollsters that they will. And many are lies of business, social, or political convenience, as was the case with Massachusetts Senator Edward Brooke in the early 1970s.

At the time, Brooke was the highest-ranking black politician in America. His name was routinely trotted out as a vice presidential possibility, though everyone involved knew the exercise was a farce. According to received wisdom, America was not ready to accept a black on the ticket, but Brooke's name seemed to appear on virtually everyone's list. During one such period of vice presidential hype, I interviewed Brooke for a newspaper profile.

After asking the standard questions, I could no longer contain my curiosity. Wasn't he tired, I asked, of the charade of having his name bandied about when no one intended to select him? He nodded wearily and said yes, he was.

To me, his response spoke volumes, probably much more than he'd intended. But I took it as his agreement that lies of political convenience are not merely a nuisance for those interested in the truth but a source of profound disgust and cynicism for those on whose behalf the lies are supposedly told.

11. *Collective guilt:* Political scientist James Q. Wilson has argued that the "best way to reduce racism . . . is to reduce the black crime rate."

There is much wrong with that way of thinking, but probably the most pernicious is that it makes hard-working, honest black people responsible for the acts of unregenerate crooks—which is not very different from defining the entire race by the behavior of its criminal class.

Law-abiding blacks generally find such presumptions galling—and point out that well-behaved whites rarely have to answer for the sins of white criminals. Until white middle-class people accept responsibility for "poor white trash," says Ulric Haynes, "I'm not willing to accept the burden of my black brethren who behave outrageously . . . although I am concerned. And I will demonstrate my concern." Yet, rejecting the "burden" of (or blame for) misbehaving blacks is not always an option.

In the mid 1980s, I was unceremoniously tossed out of Cafe Royale, a restaurant that catered to yuppies in San Francisco, on the orders of a maitre d' who apparently took me for someone who had caused trouble on a previous occasion. I sued the restaurant and eventually collected a few thousand dollars from its insurance company. But that seemed cold consolation for the humiliation of being dismissed by an exalted waiter who would not suffer the inconvenience of distinguishing one black person from another.

12. *Exclusion from the club:* Many African-Americans who have made huge efforts to get the right education, master the right accent, and dress in the proper clothes still find that certain doors never seem to open, that there are private clubs—in both a real and a symbolic sense—they cannot join.

In 1990, in testimony before the U.S. Senate Judiciary Committee, Darwin Davis, senior vice president of the Equitable Life Assurance Society, told of the frustrations he and some of his black friends had experienced in trying to join a country club. "I have openly approached fellow executives about memberships. Several times, they have said, 'My club has openings; it should be no problem. I'll get back to you.' Generally, one of two things happens. They are too embarrassed to talk to me or they come right out and tell me they were shocked when they made inquiries about bringing in a black. Some have even said they were told to get out of the club if they didn't like the situation as it is."

Two years after his testimony, Davis told me his obsession with private clubs sprang in part from concerns about his children. Several years before, he had visited a club as a guest and happened to chance upon a white executive he knew. As they were talking, he noticed the man wave at someone on the practice range. It turned out that he had brought his son down to take a lesson from the club pro. Davis was suddenly struck by a depressing thought. "Damn!" he said to himself. "This is

> *Think of how much a black person has to sell of himself to try to get race not to matter. . . . You have to ignore the insults. You have to ignore the natural loyalties. You have to ignore your past. In a sense, you have to just about deny yourself.*
>
> *Sharon Collins*
> *Sociologist, University of Illinois, Chicago*

being perpetrated all over again . . . I have a son the same age as his. And when my son grows up he's going to go through the I same crap I'm going through if I don't do something about this. His son is learning how to . . . socialize, get lessons, and do business at a country club." His own son (who is now an Equitable agent), Davis concluded, would "never ever be able to have the same advantages or even an equal footing."

## The Road From Here

When the lawyer fuming over his compensation package declares that he will "go to my own people for acceptance," he is not only expressing solidarity with other members of his race, he is also conceding defeat. He is saying that he is giving up hope that many of his white colleagues will ever see him as one of them. His white peers would of course be shocked to discover that he finds his workplace a hostile environment and that he feels a need to protect himself from them emotionally. What, they would wonder, can be his problem?

Administrators watching black students huddled together on many college campuses often ask essentially the same question: Why can't they join "the mainstream"?

> I am not one of those who look upon [affirmative action] as a stigma. I personally don't because I figure I have done my work. I've tried to prepare myself, and all I'm asking for is a fair shot. So, if affirmative action gives me a fair shot, fine.
>
> Donald McHenry
> Former U.S. ambassador to the United Nations

Whites often take such behavior as a manifestation of irrational anti-white prejudice. But in most cases, it is perhaps better understood as a retreat from a "mainstream" many blacks have come to feel is an irredeemably unwelcoming place. Some people would say that blacks who feel that way are flat-out wrong, that for African-Americans who are willing to meet whites halfway, race no longer has to matter, at least not all that much.

Yet pretending (or convincing ourselves) that race no longer matters (or wouldn't if minorities stopped demanding special treatment) is not quite the same as making it not matter. Creating a color-blind society on a foundation saturated with racism requires something more than simply pro-

claiming that the age of brotherhood has arrived. Somehow, as America went from a country concerned about denial of civil rights to one obsessed with "reverse racism" and "quotas" that discriminate against white males, some important steps were missed. Among other things, we neglected as a nation to make any serious attempt to understand why, if racial conditions were improving so much, legions of those who should be celebrating were instead singing the blues.

In many respects, that is not at all remarkable. For the United States clearly has more pressing problems than the complaints of affluent blacks unwilling to accept a few race-related inconveniences. And don't whites have problems too? Don't struggling whites—even if they are male—deserve a little sympathy? Isn't there an inequality of compassion here? Life is rough for a lot of people, not all of whom are black. So why, given the advantages at least some African-Americans conspicuously enjoy, should whites feel any consternation (much less, guilt) whatsoever?

To an increasing number of whites, that question seems less and less outrageous. And that may not be entirely bad. It would probably be healthier for all concerned if the current dialogue about racial justice focused much less on issues of guilt and victimization. Making someone feel sorry for you, after all, is somewhat different from getting them to recognize you as an equal—or even as a human being. At best, pity provides a foundation for charity, or for what is perceived as charity—for which one is expected to be appropriately grateful, even if what is offered is not what one needs or feels one deserves.

It may very well be that the civil rights debate has been so distorted by strategies designed to engender guilt that many whites, as a form of self-defense, have come to define any act of decency toward blacks as an act of expiation. If an end to such strategies—and indeed an end to white guilt—would result in a more intelligent dialogue, I, for one, am all for wiping the slate clean. Let us decide, from here on out, that no one need feel guilty about the sins of the past. The problem is certainly not that people do not feel guilty enough; it is that so many are in denial. And though denial may be a great way to avoid an unpleasant reality, avoidance is not a good substitute for changing that reality. Nor, more to the point, will it do much to narrow the huge chasm that separates so many blacks and whites.

The racial gap will never be completely closed—not as long as blacks and whites in America live fundamentally different lives. But we can nonetheless take our hands away from our eyes and recognize, at the very least, that exhorting blacks to escape the ghetto then psychologically battering those who succeed is a sure prescription for bitterness. Honest dialogue may not be a solu-

tion. But it is certainly preferable to censorship that passes for civility.

## About the Author

Ellis Cose, contributing editor at *Newsweek* magazine, writes on urban, black, and energy issues. A graduate of the University of Illinois (B.A.) and George Washington University (M.A.), he has reported for the *Chicago Sun Times*, the *Detroit Free Press*, and served as President of the Institute for Journalism Education. His previous book, *Energy and the Urban Crisis*, was published while he was Director of Energy Policy Studies at the Joint Center for Political Studies.

# Spending Culture: Marketing the Black Underclass
by bell hooks

At the end of *class*, Paul Fussell's playful book on the serious issue of social status, there is a discussion of a category outside the conventional structures entitled "The X Way Out." Folks who exist in category X, he reports, "earn X-personhood by a strenuous effort of discovery in which curiosity and originality are indispensable." They want to escape class. Describing the kind of people who are Xs, Fussell comments:

> The old-fashioned term Bohemians gives some idea; so does the term the talented. Some Xs are intellectual, but a lot are not: they are actors, musicians, artists, sport stars, "celebrities," well-to-do former hippies, confirmed residers abroad, and the more gifted journalists . . . They tend to be self-employed, doing what social scientists call autonomous work . . . X people are independent-minded, free of anxious regard for popular shibboleths, loose in carriage and demeanor. They adore the work they do . . . Being an X person is like having much of the freedom

> and some of the power of a top-out-of-sight or upper class person, but without the money. X category is a sort of unmonied aristocracy.

Even though I grew up in a Southern black working-class household, I longed to be among this X group. Radicalized by black liberation struggle and feminist movement, my effort to make that longing compatible with revolution began in college. It was there that I was subjected to the indoctrination that would prepare me to be an acceptable member of the middle class. Then, as now, I was fundamentally anti-bourgeois. To me this does not mean that I do not like beautiful things or desire material well-being. It means that I do not sit around longing to be rich, and that I believe hedonistic materialism to be a central aspect of an imperialist colonialism that perpetuates and maintains white supremacist capitalist patriarchy. Since this is the ideological framework that breeds domination and a culture of repression, a repudiation of the ethic of materialism is central to any transformation of our society. While I do not believe that any of us really exists in a category outside class, in that free space of X I do believe that those of us who repudiate domination must be willing to divest of class elitism. And it would be useful if progressive folks who oppose domination in all its forms, but who manage to accumulate material plenty or wealth, would share their understanding of ways this status informs their commitment to radical social change and their political allegiances, publicly naming the means by which they hold that class privilege in ways that do not exploit or impinge on the freedom and welfare of others.

Lately, when I find myself among groups of black academics or intellectuals where I raise the issue of class, suggesting that we need to spend more time talking about class differences among black people, I find a refusal to deal with this issue. Most are unwilling to acknowledge that class positionality shapes our perspectives and standpoints. This refusal seems to be rooted in a history of class privilege wherein privileged black folks, writers, artists, intellectuals, and academics have been able to set the agenda for any public discourse on black culture. That agenda has rarely included a willingness to problematize the issue of class. Among these groups of black folks there is a tacit assumption that we all long to be upper-class and, if at all possible, rich. Throughout my years in college and graduate school, black professors were among those committed to policing and punishing in the interest of maintaining privileged-class values. My twenty years of working as a professor in the academy have not altered this perception. I still find that most black academics, whether they identify themselves as conservative, liberal, or radical, religiously uphold privileged-class values in the manner and style in which they teach, in their habits of being, in mundane matters like dress, language, decor, and so on. Increasingly, I find these same attitudes in the world of black cultural production outside academic settings. These values tend to be coupled with the particular crass opportunism that has come to be socially acceptable, a sign that one is not so naive or stupid to actually believe that there could be any need to repudiate capitalism or the ethic of materialism.

To a grave extent, the commodification of blackness has created the space for an intensification of opportunistic materialism and longing—for privileged class status among black folks in all classes. Yet when the chips are down it is usually the black folks who already have some degree of class privilege who are most able to exploit for individual gain the market in blackness as commodity. Ironically, however, the sign of blackness in much of this cultural marketplace is synonymous with that of the underclass, so that individuals from backgrounds of privilege must either pretend to be "down" or create artwork from the standpoint either of what could be called "darky nostalgia" or the overseer's vision of blackness. When I recently commented to several black women scholars doing work in feminist literary criticism that I thought it was useful to talk about ways the shifting class positionality of writers such as Alice Walker and Toni Morrison inform their writing, style, content, and construction of characters they responded hostilely, as though my suggestion that we talk about the way in which privileged-class status shapes black perspectives was in some way meant to suggest these writers were not "black," were not "authorities." That was my intent. Since I do not believe in monolithic constructions of blackness and am not a nationalist, I want to call attention to the real and concrete ways class is central to contemporary constructions of black identity. It not only determines the way blackness is commodified and the way our sense of it shapes political standpoint. These differences in no way negate a politics of solidarity that seeks to end racist exploitation and oppression while simultaneously creating a context for black liberation and self determination; however, they do make it clear that this united front must be forged in struggle, and does not emerge solely because of shared racial identity.

To confront class in black life in the United States means that we must deconstruct the notion of an essential binding blackness and be able to examine critically ways in which the desire to be accepted into privileged-class groups within mainstream society undermines and destroys commitment to a politics of cultural transformation that consistently critiques domination. Such a critique would necessarily include the challenge to end class elitism and call for a replacing of the ethic of individualism with a vision of communalism. In his *Reconstructing Memory*, Fred Lee Hord calls attention to the way his students at a predominantly black institution make it clear that they are interested in achieving material success, "that if black communal struggle is in conflict with the pursuit of that dream, there will be no struggle." Like Hord, I believe that black experience has been and continues to be one of internal colonialism, and that "the cultural repression of American colonial education serves to distort." I would add that the contemporary commodification of blackness has become a dynamic part of that system of cultural repression. Opportunistic longings for fame, wealth, and power now lead many black critical thinkers, writers, academics and intellectuals to participate in the production and marketing of black culture in ways that are complicit with the existing oppressive structure. That complicity begins with the equation of black capitalism with black self-determination.

The global failings of socialism have made it easier for individuals within the United States to reject visions of communalism or of participatory economics that would redistribute this society's resources in more just and democratic ways, just as it makes it easy for folks who want to be seen as progressive to embrace a socialist vision even as their habits of being affirm class elitism, and passive acceptance of domination and oppression. In keeping with the way class biases frame discussions of blackness, privileged African American critics are more than willing to discuss the nihilism, the pervasive hopelessness of the underclass, while they ignore the intense nihilism of many black folks who have always known material privilege yet who have no sense of agency, no conviction that can make meaningful changes in the existing social structure. Their nihilism does not lead to self-destruction in the classic sense; it may simply lead to a symbolic murder of the self that longs to end domination so they can be born again as hard-core opportunists eager to make it within the existing system. Academics are among this group. I confront that hard-core cynicism whenever I raise issues of class. My critical comments about the way class divisions among black people are creating a climate of fascism and repression tend to be regarded by cynics as merely an expression of envy and longing. Evidently many black folks, especially the bourgeoisie, find it difficult to believe that we are not all eagerly embracing an American dream of wealth and power, that some of us might prefer to live simply in safe, comfortable, multiethnic neighborhoods rather than in mansions or huge houses, that some of us have no desire to be well-paid tokens at ruling-class white

institutions, or that there might even exist for us aspects of black life and experience that we hold sacred and are not eager to commodify and sell to captive colonized imaginations. I say this because several times when I have tried at academic conferences to talk in a more complex way about class, I have been treated as though I am speaking about this only because I have not really "made it." And on several occasions, individual black women have regarded me with patronizing contempt, as though I, who am a well-paid member of the professional-managerial academic class, have no right to express concern about black folks of all classes uncritically embracing an ethic of materialism. In both instances, the individuals in question came from privileged class backgrounds. They assume that I have made it and that my individual success strips me of any authority to speak about the dilemmas of those who are poor and destitute, especially if what I am saying contradicts the prevailing bourgeois black discourse.

One dimension of making it for many black critics, academics, and intellectuals is the assertion of control over the discourse and circulation of ideas about black culture. When their viewpoints are informed by class biases, there is little recourse for contestation since they have greater access to the white-dominated mass media. A consequence of this is that there is no progressive space for black thinkers to engage in debate and dissent. Concurrently, black thinkers who may have no commitment to diverse black communities, who may regard black folks who are not of their class with contempt and disrespect, are held up in the mass media as spokespersons even if they have never shown themselves to be at all concerned with a critical pedagogy that seeks to address black audiences as well as other folks.

The commodification of blackness strips away that component of cultural genealogy that links living memory and history in ways that subvert and undermine the status quo. When the discourse of blackness is in no way connected to an effort to promote collective black self-determination it becomes simply another resource appropriated by the colonizer. It then becomes possible for white supremacist culture to be perpetuated and maintained even as it appears to become inclusive. To distract us from the fact that no attempt to radicalize consciousness through cultural production would be tolerated, the colonizer finds it useful to create a structure of representation meant to suggest that racist domination is no longer a norm, that all blacks can get ahead if they are just smart enough and work hard. Those individual black folks who are either privileged by birth or by assimilation become the primary symbols used to suggest that the American dream is intact, that it can be fulfilled. This holds true in all academic circles and all arenas of cultural production. No matter the extent to which Spike Lee calls attention to injustice. The fact that he, while still young, can become rich in America leads many folks to ignore the attempts he makes at social critique (when the issue is racism) and to see him only as an evidence that the existing system is working. And since his agenda is to succeed within that system as much as possible, he must work it by reproducing conservative and even stereotypical images of blackness so as not to alienate that crossover audience. Lee's work cannot be revolutionary and generate wealth at the same time. Yet it is in his class interest to make it seem as though he, and his work, embody the "throw-down ghetto" blackness that is the desired product. Not only must his middle-class origin be downplayed; so must his newfound wealth. Similarly, when Allen and Albert Hughes, young biracial males from a privileged class background, make the film *Menace II Society* fictively highlighting not the communities they live in but the world of the black underclass, audiences oppose critique by insisting that the brutal, dehumanizing images of black family life that are portrayed are real. They refuse to see that while there may be aspects of the fictional reality portrayed in the film that are familiar, the film is not documentary. It is not offering a view of daily life; it is a fiction. The refusal to see that the class positionality of the filmmakers informs those aspects of black underclass life they choose to display is rooted in denial not only of class differences but of a conservative politics of representation in mainstream cinema that makes it easier to offer a vision of black underclass brutality than of any other aspect of that community's daily life.

Privileged black folks who are pimping black culture for their own opportunistic gain tend to focus on racism as though it is the great equalizing factor. For example, when a materially successful black person tells the story of how no cab will stop for the person because of color, the speaker claims unity with the masses of black folks who are daily assaulted by white supremacy. Yet this assertion of shared victimhood obscures the fact that this racial assault is mediated by the reality of class privilege. However hurt or even damaged the individual may be by a failure to acquire a taxi immediately, that individual is likely to be more allied with the class interests of individuals who share similar status (including whites) than with the needs of those black folks whom racist economic aggression render destitute, who do not even have the luxury to consider taking a taxi. The issue is, of course, audience. Since all black folks encounter some form of racial discrimination or aggression every day, we do not need stories like this to remind us that racism is widespread. Non-black folks, especially whites, most want to insist that class power and material privilege free individual black folks from the stereotypes associated with the black poor and, as a consequence, from the pain of racial assault. They and colonized black folks who live in denial are the audience that must be convinced that race matters. Black bourgeois opportunists, who are a rising social class both in the academy and in other spheres of cultural production, are unwittingly creating a division where, "within class, race matters." This was made evident in the *Newsweek* cover story, "The Hidden Rage of Successful Blacks." Most of the black folks interviewed seemed most angry that they are not treated as equals by whites who share their class. There was less rage directed at the systemic white supremacy that assaults the lives of all black folks, but in particular those who are poor, destitute, or uneducated. It might help convince mainstream society that racism and racist assault daily inform interpersonal dynamics in this society if black individuals from privileged classes would publicly acknowledge the ways we are hurt. But such acknowledgments might only render invisible class privilege, as well as the extent to which it can be effectively used to mediate our daily lives so that we can avoid racist assault in ways that materially disadvantaged individuals cannot. Those black individuals, myself included, who work and/or live in predominantly white settings, where liberalism structures social decorum, do not confront fierce, unmediated, white racist assault. This lived experience has had the potentially dangerous impact of creating in some of us a mind set that denies the impact of white supremacy, its assaultive nature. It is not surprising that black folks in these settings are more positive about racial integration, cultural mixing, and border crossing than folks who live in the midst of intense racial apartheid.

By denying or ignoring the myriad ways class positionality informs perspective and standpoint, individual black folks who enjoy class privilege are not challenged to interrogate the ways class biases shape their representations of black life. Why, for example, does so much contemporary African American literature highlight the circumstances and condition of underclass black life in the South and in big cities when it is usually written by folks whose experiences are just the opposite? The point of raising this question is not to censor but rather to urge critical thought about a cultural marketplace wherein blackness is commodified in such a way that fictive accounts of underclass black life in whatever setting may be more lauded, more marketable, than other visions because mainstream conservative white audiences desire these images. As rapper Dr. Dre calls it, "People in the suburbs, they can't go to the ghetto so they like to hear about what's goin' on. Everybody wants to be down." The desire to be "down" has promoted a conservative appropriation of specific aspects of underclass black life, whose reality is dehumanized via a process of commodification wherein no correlation is made between mainstream hedonistic consumerism and the reproduction of a social system that perpetuates and maintains an underclass.

Without a sustained critique of class power and class divisions among black folks, what is represented in the mass media, in cultural production, will merely reflect the biases and standpoints of a privileged few. If that few have not decolonized their minds and choose to make no connection between the discourse of blackness and the need to be engaged in an ongoing struggle for black self-determination, there will be few places where progressive visions can emerge and gain a hearing. Coming from a working-class background into the academy and other arenas of cultural production, I am always conscious of a dearth of perspectives from individuals who do not have a bourgeois mind-set. It grieves me to observe the contempt and utter uninterest black individuals from privileged classes often show in their interactions with disadvantaged black folks or their allies in struggle, especially if they have built their careers focusing on "blackness," mining the lives of the poor and disadvantaged for resources. It angers me when

that group uses its class or power and its concomitant conservative politics to silence, censor or delegitimize counter-hegemonic perspectives on blackness.

Irrespective of class background or current class positionality, progressive black individuals whose politics include a commitment to black self-determination and liberation must be vigilant when we do our work. Those of us who speak, write, and act in ways other than from privileged class locations must self-interrogate constantly so that we do not unwittingly become complicit in maintaining existing exploitative and oppressive structures. None of us should be ashamed to speak about our class power, or lack of it. Overcoming fear (even the fear of being immodest) and acting courageously to bring issues of class as well as radical standpoints into the discourse of blackness is a gesture of militant defiance, one that runs counter to the bourgeois insistence that we think of money in particular, and class in general, as a private matter. Progressive black folks who work to live simply because we respect the earth's resources, who repudiate the ethic of materialism and embrace communalism must gain a public voice. Those of us who are still working to mix the vision of autonomy evoked by X category with our dedication to ending domination in all its forms, who cherish openness, honesty, radical will, creativity, and free speech, and do not long to have power over others, or to build nations (or even academic empires), are working to project an alternative politics of representation—working to free the black image so it is not enslaved to any exploitative or oppressive agenda.

## About the Author

bell hooks is Distinguished Professor of English at City College in New York. She is the author of many books, most recently *Teaching to Transgress: Education as the Practice of Freedom*, available from Routledge. bell hooks is one of America's leading black intellectuals, is also one of our most clear-eyed and penetrating analysts of culture. Her commitment has been to share the culture of the margin, of women, of the disenfranchised, of racial and other minorities. Raising her powerful voice against racism and other forms of oppression in the United States, hooks unlocks the politics of representation and the meaning of that politics for, and in, our lives.

hooks affirms a vision of intellectual and political engagement, foreseeing the possibility of active, critical participation in movements for radical social change. This essay is taken from her 1994 book, *Outlaw Culture*. *Outlaw Culture* speaks clearly and strongly for the need to connect the production of knowledge with transformative democratic values. Her book is available from Routledge, 29 West 35th Street, New York, NY 10001; Phone 212-244-3336.

---

## WHAT EXACTLY IS WHITE GUILT, AND HOW DOES IT WORK IN AMERICAN LIFE?
by Shelby Steele (*The American Scholar*)

*Why white guilt doesn't help—*
*Shelby Steele says it's about selfishness, not compassion*

I think white guilt, in its broad sense, springs from a knowledge of ill-gotten advantage. More precisely, it comes from the juxtaposition of this knowledge with the inevitable gratitude one feels for being white rather than black in America. Given the moral instincts of human beings, it is all but impossible to enjoy an ill-gotten advantage, much less to feel at least secretly grateful for it, without consciously or unconsciously experiencing guilt.

The knowledge of this advantage is powerful because of the element of fear that guilt always carries, the fear of what the guilty knowledge says about us. The fear for the self that is buried in all guilt is a pressure toward selfishness. It can lead us to put our own need for innocence above our concern or the problem that made us feel guilt in the first place. But this fear for the self does not only inspire selfishness; it also becomes a pressure to escape the guilt-inducing situation.

Escapist racial policies—policies where institutions favor black entitlement over black development because of a preoccupation with their own innocence—have, I believe, a dispiriting effect on blacks. Such policies have the effect of transforming whites from victimizers into patronizers and keeping blacks where they have always been—dependent on the largesse of whites.

Effective racial policies can only come from the sort of white guilt where fear for the self is contained, so that genuine concern can ultimately emerge. The test for this healthy guilt is simply a heartfelt feeling of concern without any compromise of one's highest values and principles. One could, for example, advocate social policies that attack poverty rather than black poverty and policies that instill values that make for self-reliance.

Selfish white guilt is really self-importance. Nothing diminishes a black more than this sort of guilt in a white, which to my mind amounts to a sort of moral colonialism. We used to say in the 1960s that at least in the South you knew where you stood. I always thought this was a little foolish, since I didn't like where I stood there. But I think one of the things we meant by this—at the time—was that the South had little investment in its racial innocence and that this was very liberating in an ironical sort of way. It meant there would be no entangling complications with white need. It gave us back ourselves. The selfishly guilty white person is drawn to what blacks least like in themselves—their suffering, victimization, and dependency. This is no good for anyone—black or white.

---

Shelby Steele's work has appeared in *Harper's, New York Times Magazine, Commentary,* the *Washington Post,* and *American Scholar,* among many other publications. He won a National Magazine Award in 1989, and one of his essays on race was chosen for The Best American Essays 1989. Steele is a professor of English at San Jose State University in California. He is the author of *The Content of Our Character,* available from HarperCollins (1-800-237-5534).

# BAND-AID
# A Play by Eric H. F. Law

## CHARACTERS

**WHITE WOMAN:**
A community organizer, of good intentions, needy. She thinks of herself as a liberated woman.

**MAN OF COLOR:**
College educated, middle class, angry. He has no patience for the same old games.

*The play takes place in April, 1993 in Los Angeles. The action is set in the context of an interracial harmony conference.*

# BAND-AID

*(Los Angeles. One year after the 1992 riot. It is break time at an interracial harmony conference. MAN OF COLOR is in the hallway dabbing a white napkin on his forehead in front of a mirror. WHITE WOMAN enters.)*

**WHITE WOMAN**
Wasn't that wonderful? Those kids were so cute and talented.

**MAN OF COLOR**
Excuse me.

**WHITE WOMAN**
I love the costumes and the drums. I mean I never knew Koreans had drums.

**MAN OF COLOR**
I'm sorry I . . .

**WHITE WOMAN**
I always believed there are a lot of commonalities between the Koreans and African Americans. If only we did more of these kinds of events, we wouldn't have had the riot . . .

**MAN OF COLOR**
I'm . . .

**WHITE WOMAN**
I mean "civil unrest" a year ago. Don't you think so?

**MAN OF COLOR**
I'm not in the mood to talk!

**WHITE WOMAN**
I beg your pardon?

**MAN OF COLOR**
Go talk to someone else!

**WHITE WOMAN**
Are you not feeling well?

**MAN OF COLOR**
No, I just . . .

**WHITE WOMAN**
*(Notices the blood-stain on his white napkin.)* You're bleeding!

**MAN OF COLOR**
It's nothing.

**WHITE WOMAN**
Let me take a look.

**MAN OF COLOR**
It's really . . .

**WHITE WOMAN**
Oh, you got a cut. Let me see what I have. *(She searches through her pocket book and pulls out a first-aid kit.)* Here, let me put this on it.

**MAN OF COLOR**
You always carry a first-aid kit around with you?

**WHITE WOMAN**
Earthquake preparation. You never know when the Big One's going to hit. (*She finds a BAND-AID and tears it open.*) What happened to you?

**MAN OF COLOR**
The TV camera.

**WHITE WOMAN**
TV camera?

**MAN OF COLOR**
It attacked me.

**WHITE WOMAN**
You're very creative.

**MAN OF COLOR**
I was sitting next to the camera and someone tripped over the cable and the camera landed on my head.

**WHITE WOMAN**
(*She puts the Band-Aid on him.*) There.

**MAN OF COLOR**
(*He turns and looks into the mirror.*) You wouldn't have one of those clear Band-Aids, would you?

**WHITE WOMAN**
What's wrong with . . .

**MAN OF COLOR**
No, it's just . . .

**WHITE WOMAN**
Men have come a long way, I tell you.

**MAN OF COLOR**
I beg your pardon?

**WHITE WOMAN**
Ten years ago, men didn't care about how they looked with a Band-Aid on their face.

**MAN OF COLOR**
I'm not . . .

**WHITE WOMAN**
To them, a Band-Aid was just a Band-Aid.

**MAN OF COLOR**
I don't mean . . .

**WHITE WOMAN**
You don't have to explain. I guess women's liberation has liberated men too.

**MAN OF COLOR**
It has nothing to do with . . .

**WHITE WOMAN**
You can care about the way you look. That's all right with me.

**MAN OF COLOR**
It's not all right.

**WHITE WOMAN**
It's all right. You can . . .

**MAN OF COLOR**
This Band-Aid doesn't match my skin! I thought I'd never have to wear one of these so called "flesh-colored" Band-Aids again when they came out with the clear ones.

**WHITE WOMAN**
Too bad. It'll have to do for now. Just be a good boy and . . .

**MAN OF COLOR**
Don't call me boy!

**WHITE WOMAN**
(*Silence.*) I'm sorry. I didn't mean to . . .

**MAN OF COLOR**
I'm sorry. I over reacted.

**WHITE WOMAN**
So.

**MAN OF COLOR**
So.

**WHITE WOMAN**
How do you like the program so far?

**MAN OF COLOR**
I don't want to talk about it.

**WHITE WOMAN**
Come on. I want to hear what you think.

**MAN OF COLOR**
I'm only here because my university sponsors this thing.

**WHITE WOMAN**
I'm on the planning committee; if we did something wrong, . . .

**MAN OF COLOR**
I don't . . .

**WHITE WOMAN**
You've got to tell us so we can . . .

**MAN OF COLOR**
Why is the burden always on us?!

**WHITE WOMAN**
Burden!?

**MAN OF COLOR**
Why is it always our responsibility to teach you? Why can't you figure it out by yourselves?

**WHITE WOMAN**
All I wanted was your reaction to the program! What's wrong with you?

**MAN OF COLOR**
Of course, there is always something wrong with people of color.

**WHITE WOMAN**
I didn't . . .

**MAN OF COLOR**
It's always our fault, isn't it?

**WHITE WOMAN**
I think you have a problem with your anger.

**MAN OF COLOR**
I think you have a problem dealing with people of color.

**WHITE WOMAN**
This *is* an interracial harmony conference.

**MAN OF COLOR**
You think having Korean dancers and tacos and Gospel choirs is going to create interracial harmony?

**WHITE WOMAN**
We're supposed to find common ground. Why dwell on things that divide? . . .

**MAN OF COLOR**
You just don't get it, do you?

**WHITE WOMAN**
Get what?

**MAN OF COLOR**
You're white and I'm a person of color.

**WHITE WOMAN**
Why is everything "racial" to you?

**MAN OF COLOR**
Because they are!

**WHITE WOMAN**
No, they're not. We're both human beings. Can we start from there?

**MAN OF COLOR**
When you say, "We're both human beings," aren't you saying I should be like you?

**WHITE WOMAN**
No, I . . .

**MAN OF COLOR**
Then, what do you mean?

**WHITE WOMAN**
It means exactly that—we are all human beings. If we respect each other, we'll be able to live together in harmony.

**MAN OF COLOR**
Of course, but there's a price to pay.

**WHITE WOMAN**
Of course, nothing comes easily.

**MAN OF COLOR**
I mean for people of color.

**WHITE WOMAN**
You're thinking "racial" again.

**MAN OF COLOR**
I have to. If I don't, I'll get hurt.

**WHITE WOMAN**
Get hurt by whom?

**MAN OF COLOR**
You. No, I don't mean "you." I mean people like . . . You know what I mean.

**WHITE WOMAN**
No, I don't know what you . . .

**MAN OF COLOR**
I've been in the same job for too long. Whites with less credentials and less experience pass right by me. They get the promotions and that's what hurts.

**WHITE WOMAN**
I can understand that.

**MAN OF COLOR**
How can you under- . . .

**WHITE WOMAN**
That's no different from growing up as a woman in a male dominated society.

**MAN OF COLOR**
No, it . . .

**WHITE WOMAN**
As a woman, I have to watch every step I take. Every corner I turn, I may be attacked by powerful men. And I don't mean just physically. Women have to fight every step of the way to get to where we are.

**MAN OF COLOR**
Yeah, when you fight, you win. When people of color fight back, we get killed.

**WHITE WOMAN**
That's not . . .

**MAN OF COLOR**
Martin Luther King.

**WHITE WOMAN**
Yeah, but . . .

**MAN OF COLOR**
Malcolm X.

**WHITE WOMAN**
But you have made great strides.

**MAN OF COLOR**
We changed a few laws; that's about it. What good are the laws when a person of color can't get justice even with solid proof—like a *video tape*!?

**WHITE WOMAN**
That's over. Can't we move on?

**MAN OF COLOR**
It may be over for you. For me, it's a . . .

**WHITE WOMAN**
Look at you—a person of color working in a prestigious university (*looks at his badge*) as the director of the Multi-Cultural Center. Thirty years ago, this could not have happened.

**MAN OF COLOR**
Thirty years ago, there was no multi-cultural anything.

**WHITE WOMAN**
You should be proud.

**MAN OF COLOR**
Yeah, but . . .

**WHITE WOMAN**
If there were more educated people like you, we wouldn't be dealing with this racial stuff. I really believe that education is the solution.

**MAN OF COLOR**
May I remind you that you are dealing with racial stuff even with educated me.

**WHITE WOMAN**
Yeah, but I can talk to you.

**MAN OF COLOR**
You mean you can't talk to other people of color with less degrees, with less expensive clothes, or with less use of the proper English language?

**WHITE WOMAN**
All I'm saying is that you're educated, you've made it and you're a great example of . . .

**MAN OF COLOR**
You just don't get it, do you?

**WHITE WOMAN**
What don't I get this time?

**MAN OF COLOR**
You're thinking like a white person.

**WHITE WOMAN**
Just what does that mean?

**MAN OF COLOR**
You white people all think alike.

**WHITE WOMAN**
You're being . . .

**MAN OF COLOR**
It's true. You're all racists and don't even know it.

**WHITE WOMAN**
Not all whites are . . .

**MAN OF COLOR**
Have you read the history of North America?

**WHITE WOMAN**
It's not fair to those of us who really tried to . . .

**MAN OF COLOR**
Who murdered the Native American Indians and stole their land? Who kidnapped Africans and forced them to be slaves? Who locked up the Chinese on Angel Island? Who put the Japanese Americans in concentration camps? Who . . .

**WHITE WOMAN**
I don't have to take responsibility for what white people did in the past!

**MAN OF COLOR**
If you enjoy the privileges of being white, then you should take the resp- . . .

**WHITE WOMAN**
Privileges?

**MAN OF COLOR**

Like you can go to court and believe you can have a fair chance of winning! You can count on the color of your skin not to work against you when you apply for a loan! You can go into the store and buy flesh color Band-Aids that match your skin!

**WHITE WOMAN**

For your information, my father marched in Selma with Martin Luther King. I was taught to be in solidarity with the poor and the minorities ever since I was a child. I had made a conscious decision to work in the ghettos. I live in South Central.

**MAN OF COLOR**

So?

**WHITE WOMAN**

I have given up my privileges to be in solidarity with you.

**MAN OF COLOR**

That doesn't mean . . .

**WHITE WOMAN**

And how can you dismiss me as just another white?

**MAN OF COLOR**

What do you want from me?

**WHITE WOMAN**

I'm not one of them!

**MAN OF COLOR**

What do you want from me?

**WHITE WOMAN**

I'm not a racist!

**MAN OF COLOR**

You might choose to live in South Central today. But tomorrow, if you choose, you can move back to your lily-white neighborhood. You have a choice. That's why you're white, and I'm a person of color.

**WHITE WOMAN**

(She covers her eyes with her hands.) Deal with me.

**MAN OF COLOR**

What are you doing?

**WHITE WOMAN**

Deal with me, I can't see.

**MAN OF COLOR**

This is exactly the problem I have with people like you!

**WHITE WOMAN**

Deal with me.

**MAN OF COLOR**

You're not blind!

**WHITE WOMAN**

I can't see the color of your . . .

**MAN OF COLOR**

Open your eyes! You're just pretending to be blind!

**WHITE WOMAN**

Why won't you deal with me when I don't care about the color of your skin? (Silence.) Goddammit! Deal with me! Deal with me!

**MAN OF COLOR**

You see this Band-Aid?

**WHITE WOMAN**

(She opens her eyes.) Band-Aid!

**MAN OF COLOR**

All my efforts of trying to make it in this country are like putting on Band-Aids—one at a time. You see, when we get hurt in your world, we put on a white Band-Aid. The next time we get hurt, we put on another one and another one and another one. Pretty soon we are covered with Band-Aids. Then one day, you look in the mirror and you suddenly see how ridiculous you look. So I painfully peeled these white Band-Aids off one at a time reviewing all the old wounds. They never healed. This interracial harmony conference, forced integration, busing, affirmative action and my goddamn job are nothing but Band-Aids. (He hands the Band-Aid to her.) But, no thanks; I'd rather bleed.

**THE END**

90

> ## Discussion Questions
>
> 1. What was the woman's approach to racial issues?
>    Why didn't it work with the man?
>
> 2. What was it that made the man angry?
>
> 3. What was the man's perception of racial issues? How was it different from the woman's?
>
> 4. Have you encountered a similar situation before? Where and when? How did this kind of situation make you feel?
>
> 5. What could they have done differently that would make this encounter more productive in terms of mutual understanding?
>
> 6. Get in touch with the image of the BAND-AID as a negative image for approaching racial issues. What would be an alternative image that would help us approach racial issues positively?

## About the Author

Eric H. F. Law is a partner of Diversity Dynamics, which provides culturally sensitive consulting and training services to maximize workplace relations. Eric specializes in developing innovative training tools, processes and workshops that help clients explore diversity in its practical, theoretical and spiritual dimensions. He is the author of the book, *The Wolf Shall Dwell With The Lamb—a Spirituality for Leadership in a Multi-Cultural Community*, published by Chalice Press, St. Louis (800-366-3383).

His forth-coming book, *Developing Intercultural Sensitivity for Health-Care Professionals* published by the American Occupational Therapy Association, Inc., will be released in spring of 1996. He can be reached at: Diversity Dynamics, 3175 South Hoover Street, Box 357, Los Angeles, CA 90007; Phone: 213-656-0436.

# A RESPONSE TO "BAND-AID"
## by Diane J. Johnson

Upon first reading "Band-Aid," I was intrigued by the metaphorical use of a simple first-aid article to illustrate the complex issues related to interracial relations. Eric H. F. Law successfully presents the notion that many interventions aimed at creating racial harmony are well-intentioned. However, most times they are merely short-term. Often they are naive and ultimately, ineffectual methods of dealing with racism within American society.

As an African-American woman who has thought long and hard on issues related to human understanding of race, class, gender and other social identities, I found "Band-Aid" compelling. Both the characters and the dialogue reflect views often shared by individuals attempting to deal with the intricate dynamics of understanding race, class and privilege. Strangely enough, I found myself wincing as I read further along into the play. The dialogue seemed almost stereotypical in its portrayal of two people on opposite sides of both the gender and color line. The particular perspectives and orientations they represented seemed too neat and predictable. Maybe my discomfort comes from realizing that the conversation between the White Woman and the Man of Color in the play mirrors far too many "real life" conversations. It is terribly frustrating (and sad as well) that white people can be so unconscious of what they do not know. Doesn't the white woman perceive her condescension and racism from the very beginning, evidenced from the first line out of her mouth, "those kids are so talented and cute . . . " The dialogue Law uses emphasizes extreme perspectives, almost to the point of caricature, to make the point that racial understanding can be extremely elusive.

Although Band-Aid was conceived to illustrate the complexity of race and gender issues, the play does not provide me with a deeper, more complex insight into the perspectives of two people grappling with those issues. The insistence of the White Woman character to "deal with her" embodies the myopia that many privileged members of society hold. Her closing her eyes and pretending that color does not make a difference reflects a common naiveté. Feminist poet and social activist, Audre Lorde, comments on this rationalization in her seminal essay, "Age, Race, Class and Sex: Women Redefining Difference" (*Sister Outsider*, Crossing Press): "too often, we pour the energy needed for recognizing and exploring difference into *pretending those differences are insurmountable barriers, or they do not exist at all.*" (emphasis mine). The White Woman character seems to think that by starting from the point of "we're both human beings" that racial understanding is a natural conclusion.

However, the acceptance that we are all human beings does not provide significant context to inter-racial and cross gender relationships. We need to incorporate the diverse aspects of socio-economic, political, cultural, institutional and personal experiences to have a realistic dialogue about race. Hopefully, this anthology, *The Cultural Diversity Sourcebook*, will begin this critical process.

As I completed reading the play I thought how much more engaging the dialogue would have been had the two characters been a woman of mixed heritage and a working class white man or a Japanese woman and a Latino male and a white woman. Those combinations of characters would have more fully illustrated the multiple dimensions of race in Los Angeles and America. As a vehicle to begin a conversation about race, and eventually, gender, class and privilege, "Band-Aid," only barely begins to examine the complex and intricate layers that are part of a critical conversation within American society.

Diane J. Johnson is President of Mmapeu Consulting, a national consulting firm that specializes in organizational development, program planning and diversity initiatives. Her decade of work with both for-profit and not-for-profit organizations provides her with an integrated perspective of organizational diversity work. She is also author of *PROUD SISTERS, The Wisdom and Wit of African-American Women*. She can be reached at: Mmapeu Consulting, 183 Bridge Street, Suite 2R, Northampton, MA 01060-2404; Phone: 413-586-5905.

# The Problem With You People

by Jake Lamar (*Esquire*)

*You scorn us, you imitate us, you blame us, you indulge us, you throw up your hands, you tell us you have all the answers—now shut up and listen*

I'm concerned about the state of white America. It's not just the major problems plaguing the white community that worry me—the breakdown of the white family, the growing white underclass, the rampant social pathology—but the more subtle convolutions of white consciousness. In Caucasian-American habitats across the country, from the bowling alleys to the boardrooms, from trailer park to yacht club, a malaise is thickening. I'm writing in an attempt to fathom the white experience.

Pardon me for generalizing about whites and whiteness, but turnabout is fair play. I've grown up hearing whites expound on "the Negro question" and "the race problem." I've encountered many a white pundit who, when not offering me prescriptions for curing one "black dilemma" or another, has expected me to serve as a spokesman for my race, to intuit the views of thirty million African-Americans of varying social, economic, educational, and religious backgrounds and boil them down into a single comprehensive and generic "black view." And it's not just me. Any time a black cultural figure comes to the fore—director Spike Lee, playwright August Wilson, actor Eddie Murphy, for example—whites expect him somehow to encompass in his person and work all the hopes and aspirations of "his people."

So these days, I'm inclined to abstract the folks on the other side of the racial equation. At times I might address "you" while implying "you people." Sometimes "you" might mean "some of you people" or "most of you people, but not necessarily you." As in, how come I haven't heard you stand up and speak out against Guns N' Roses? You'll probably find this hard to get used to.

You may not want to face the hard truths of the matter, but America is on the brink of a white-identity meltdown. Your people, who are accustomed to defining great masses of other citizens by the fact that we are not you—that is, nonwhite—confront the specter of an America in which the mainstream has been altered beyond recognition.

The notion of the mainstream is crucial to understanding today's white crisis. The desperate yearning to be considered normal, part of some standard Disneyfied American citizenry, runs deep in white consciousness. I've witnessed the poignant efforts of young whites striving to conform to the vague tenets of the mainstream, taking crushingly dull jobs, settling down with the least challenging of spouses, dreaming of the perfect family, groping for an illusory sense of security. The quest for conformity can be fraught with doubt, and doubt is anathema to the mainstream. To reaffirm your conventionality, you must constantly tell yourself what you are not.

This need for reassurance has led in recent years to an obsession with the people whom you mainstreamers consider most unlike you: the infamous underclass. The underclass—you needn't even say *black* anymore; it's a code word—is a handy Dumpster for all your problems. You mainstreamers may live far beyond your means, piling up thousands of dollars of debt on credit, skimping on your tax returns. But when it comes time to tally the ills of the country, you bemoan "the pathology of the underclass." And as your less scrupulous colleagues avoid taking responsibility for the stunning perfidy of your investment bankers and the profligacy of your S&L operators, you return blithely to the conviction that all those awful *urban*—another code word—problems persist because of anonymous blacks who are "afraid of a hard day's work." And then there's that story you like to tell about the woman on welfare—she *must* be black—who used her food stamps to buy alcohol . . .

Today, things are falling apart for the mainstream. The grim statistics needn't be rehearsed here: the large number of whites who have lost their jobs, defaulted on their loans, been forced to seek government handouts. There has been a disturbing increase in white rage. While whites grow ever more hysterical about "black crime," criminal acts that are traditionally Caucasian American—white-on-white violence, if you will—are on the rise. The spectacle of white males walking into post offices or cafeterias and shooting everyone in sight has become almost common. And as America's superpower status recedes as rapidly as its economy, you have become more vociferous in your attacks on nonwhites, not just the underclass but all the others who have threatened your world order.

The current world situation doesn't look promising for all the talk of the end of the Cold War and the victory of market capitalism. Your tribes seem unable to keep the peace among yourselves—the Yugoslavians are killing each other like animals, the Soviet republics are reverting to atavistic loyalties, and radical nationalists are popping up all over the place. Given your bloody past, one can't help but wonder: Can you be trusted to run a country in a civilized manner?

You probably think none of this has anything to do with you, so let me narrow my focus a bit. As one of the children of the civil-rights movement assigned with integrating society, I've spent a good deal of time among the sort of white people you know. These are the whites who pride themselves on their fair-mindedness and lack of prejudice, the well-intentioned "color blind." Like the rest of white America, they are struggling with pesky nonwhites who refuse to stay in their place. The color-blind are just more reluctant to admit it.

Your feelings toward nonwhites in general and black Americans in particular are more tangled than those of some other mainstreamers. You appropriate the clothes, philosophies, and art of other cultures, sometimes out of sincere interest, more often to make a fashion statement.

You think Jonathan Demme is a hip filmmaker because his films are populated on the margins by "authentic" blacks singing the music of our people. Perhaps you enjoy the fact that the Rolling Stones, like countless other rock bands, tours with black backup singers—in your gut, you believe that proximity to blackness confers a soulfulness. There is a subterranean but direct lineage from Norman Mailer in the late Fifties hailing "the Negro hipster" who lives on the edge of danger to today's white rappers contorting their faces and flailing their arms about in absurd attempts at street credibility.

When it comes to art produced by African-Americans, you laud "the gritty urban drama" of the new black directors, groove to the antiwhite lyrics of NWA and Ice Cube, and dress in the latest inner-city-inspired fashions on sale at your local malls. You like your blacks badass and hostile, as long as we're available in a CD format.

You like reading books and articles about impoverished blacks, preferably those written by white journalists who have braved pilgrimages into the urban wilderness. You respond to the earnest piety of Alex Kotlowitz's best-selling *There Are No Children Here*, his tale of humanity amid grinding poverty and despair, and feel vaguely edified as you peruse this genre of ghetto pastorale. Or you shake your head sadly as you read the tough-love philosophizing of Joe Klein and Pete Hamill, and ask along with them, "What can be done?" before quickly answering your own question: "Not much, really." When solutions are offered, they are along the lines of "We need to get more blacks into the mainstream." In other words, we should become more like you.

I remember well my first righteous white liberal. It was the fall of 1970, my first day of fourth grade at a racially mixed, lower-middle-class parochial school in the Bronx. My new teacher—I'll call him Mr. Palomino—fancied himself a rebel. He wanted to create an "open" classroom. He also wanted to be my buddy, but there was something strained and clammy about his overtures. I'd been taught by two nuns and one female lay teacher in the previous three years and had encountered a wide range of Catholic authority figures. But I'd never met one who looked at me with Mr. Palomino's clinical gaze. Did this zealous reformer view me as some sort of anthropological specimen?

Mr. Palomino marveled one day when I put out a one-boy newspaper with sports, comics, and a national news section. Pulling me aside, he asked, "Where do you get your ideas?" I sensed not admiration but mystification in his voice, and a trace of disbelief that I might actually have created the paper on my own. Mr. Palomino seemed amazed that I might be a reasonably bright kid. I knew he was trying to "get through" to me, but his awkward, patronizing manner made me want to keep him out.

"I don't know where I get my ideas," I replied. I could tell Mr. Palomino didn't appreciate my answer. He probed a little further. I shrugged and gave more vague answers. Finally, the teacher gave up and walked away, clearly disappointed.

The weirdness between us increased. Mr. Palomino stopped calling on me in class, even if I was the only student raising my hand. He began grading my homework more harshly and punishing me for minor transgressions like not finishing my milk at lunchtime. Over the years I've often wondered about him, about why he turned hostile toward me when I didn't respond to his unctuous chumminess. Was it that I wasn't grateful enough?

In the sixth grade, I transferred to the sort of reform-minded "secular humanist" private school whose nonregimented atmosphere Mr. Palomino had tried to imitate. I went on to Harvard and a job at *Time* magazine, lived in once-segregated neighborhoods, and along the way met a lot of you who, despite your studious liberalism, just couldn't keep from being condescendingly caste-conscious. I saw that you might, for instance, go out of your way to address the black woman who empties your office wastebaskets in the evenings by her first name. "Well, hello . . . *Janet*. How are you tonight . . . *Janet?* Thank you so much . . . *Janet.*" I'm not suggesting that this was an unkind gesture. What always rankled was the excessive magnanimity in your voices, a tone, an emphasis that indicated that you were congratulating yourselves for knowing the cleaning woman's name, and the implication that Janet should be thankful for such a small courtesy.

Yet dealing with the help is often easier for you than knowing what to make of blacks who inhabit the mainstream. After Clarence Thomas was nominated to the Supreme Court last summer, but before the start of his confirmation hearings, a curious argument commenced between your liberal and conservative pundits. The liberals kept demanding that Thomas "remember where he came from." The conservative mandarins responded that Judge Thomas had "never forgotten where he came from." In this particular debate, political ideology—not to mention actual judicial achievement—became beside the point. The Left was demanding humility and the Right was saying, "Don't worry, he's humble."

When Thomas finally took the stand in the first, pre-Anita Hill phase of his confirmation hearings,

he not only remembered where he came from, he obsessed on it—his roots, in fact, were all he wanted to talk about. Instead of discussing judicial philosophy, Thomas couldn't help becoming choked up about his ascent from poverty. Instead of defending his actions as chairman of the Equal Employment Opportunity Commission, Thomas spoke, misty-eyed, about staring out the window of his office at the EEOC, watching busloads of black criminals on their way to jail. "There but for the grace of God go I," he remembered thinking. Some of you who loathed the judge's politics still gave Thomas points for this oozy gratitude.

Perhaps there was something innately appealing to a lot of you about Thomas's relationship with John Danforth, the Missouri senator who was usually described as the judge's "patron." Wasn't there something inspirational about the way Danforth was always hovering, speaking for Thomas, singing his praises, defending him against his critics with a paternal protectiveness? A political Huck-and-Jim camaraderie.

During the second phase of Thomas's hearings, after the Anita Hill scandal exploded, liberal and conservative whites agreed on one thing: how wonderful it was to see so many black professionals paraded across the TV screen. You praised the African-Americans who testified for and against Thomas or Hill for being "dignified." In characterizing the witnesses, your media commentators consistently used that favorite adjective of whites who are surprised to discover the existence of intelligent blacks: *articulate.* Across the political spectrum, you spoke in amazed tones about the brainy buppies, as if you had stumbled upon some new species of American citizen: the black mainstreamer. What a pleasant surprise it was to you!

Even your most excruciatingly high-minded leaders can be befuddled by a face-to-face encounter with a mainstream black. One afternoon in 1988, when I was working at *Time* magazine, I attended a luncheon for your political icon Mario Cuomo. Several correspondents escorted the governor into the *Time* corporate dining room, where about twenty staffers awaited him. We stood in a sort of receiving line as Cuomo shook each journalist's hand and made chitchat. When he got to me, the governor said, "Ah, you must be the softball player."

I had no idea what the governor was talking about. It had been at least ten years since I'd touched a softball. As a kid, I'd been a clumsy athlete; as far as I was concerned, one of the best things about adulthood was that it had no gym requirement. "No, that's not me," I told Cuomo.

Uncertainty flashed in the governor's enormous eyes. Evidently, one of the *Time* reporters had mentioned a softball player to him, and Cuomo had assumed that I, the only African-American in the receiving line, had to be the jock. As a righteous white liberal, Cuomo knew he'd just made a classic faux pas. He stared at me blankly seemingly at a most uncharacteristic loss for words. A white reporter, one who'd spent some time with Cuomo before, stepped forward. "Actually, Governor, maybe you were thinking of me. We talked once about basketball."

Cuomo tried to recover. "Yes, of course," he said, acknowledging the reporter, then turning back to me. "I was talking about what a wonderful sport basketball is, how it creates synergy." Cuomo stopped short, wondering perhaps if now he'd really blundered into cultural-cliché territory, talking to a black journalist about basketball. The governor muttered something else about synergy before quickly turning away and moving on down the receiving line.

Mario knows rhetorical correctness; real people can be harder to handle.

I know what you're probably thinking: Why pick on the liberals? We're on your side. Why make everything racial? We're not the racists!

Strange the way you often consider "racial" and "racist" synonymous terms. When an African-American points out the racial attitudes of well-intentioned bourgeois whites, you get riled up and defensive, taking any observation as an accusation of racism. And since whites like you consider yourselves so thoroughly unbiased, utterly free of anything so heinous as a racist thought, nothing in your thinking can have a racial aspect at all. This allows you to make easy calls against the real racists—David Duke, say—while rarely questioning anything racial in your own politically enlight-

ened sphere. You suffer from liberal cognitive dissonance. You consider yourself most astute on race issues, yet you cannot acknowledge presumptions you make solely on the basis of race. You steadfastly refuse to confront the mystery of your own manners.

So what can you do? You folks love grand prescriptions, pithy cure-all pronouncements. It seems to be part of your nature to abhor a conundrum. Instead of any sweeping solutions, however, I will submit just one leading question: Aren't you all still feeling just the least bit guilty?

Perhaps that's why you embrace every moderate-to-conservative black thinker who comes along—every Shelby Steele, Glenn Loury, or Thomas Sowell. It's comforting to be told, *by a black person*, that racial problems are not really your responsibility anymore. Doesn't guilt lead to modest proposals like the one made not too long ago by columnist Charles Krauthammer?—he suggested that the government pay reparations to us for slavery and be done with it. And doesn't an emphasis on black "moral decay" and "pathology" make it easier for you to justify doing nothing? I wonder whether your "black problem" has less to do with solutions and more to do with absolution.

## About the Author

Jake Lamar was born in 1961 and grew up in New York City. After graduating from Harvard in 1983, he took a job writing for *Time* Magazine. He left *Time* six years later to write his first book, *Bourgeois Blues* (Simon & Schuster, 1991). Lamar has taught creative writing and American literature at the University of Michigan, and his articles have appeared in The *New York Times*, *Esquire*, and *Details*. His novel, titled *The Last Integrationist*, will be published by Crown in 1996. A recipient of the Lyndhurst Prize, he currently lives in Paris, where he is working on his next book.

# Assumptions and Behaviors that Block/Facilitate Relations Between Blacks and Whites

by Bertram Lee and Warren H. Schmidt

## Assumptions That Block Authentic Relations

### Assumptions Whites Make

- Color is unimportant in interpersonal relations.
- Blacks will always welcome and appreciate inclusion in white society.
- Open recognition of color may embarrass blacks.
- Blacks are trying to use whites.
- Blacks can be stereotyped.
- White society is superior to black society.
- "Liberal" whites are free of racism.
- All blacks are alike in their attitudes and behavior.
- Blacks are oversensitive.
- Blacks must be controlled.

### Assumptions Blacks Make

- All whites are alike.
- There are no "brothers" among whites.
- Whites have all the power.
- Whites are united in their attitude toward blacks.
- Whites are always trying to use blacks.
- All whites are racists.
- Whites are not really trying to understand the situation of the blacks.
- Whites have got to deal on black terms.
- Silence is the sign of hostility.
- Whites cannot and will not change except by force.
- The only way to gain attention is through confrontation.
- All whites are deceptive.
- All whites will let you down in the "crunch."

# Assumptions that Facilitate Authentic Relations

## Assumptions Whites Make

- People count as individuals.
- Blacks are human, with individual feelings, aspirations, and attitudes.
- Blacks have a heritage of which they are proud.
- Interdependence is needed between whites and blacks.
- Blacks are angry.
- Whites cannot fully understand what it means to be black.
- Whiteness/blackness is a real difference but not the basis on which to determine behavior.
- Most blacks can handle whites' authentic behavior and feelings.
- Blacks want a responsible society.
- Blacks are capable of managerial maturity.
- I may be part of the problem.

## Assumptions Blacks Make

- Openness is healthy.
- Interdependence is needed between blacks and whites.
- People count as individuals.
- Negotiation and collaboration are possible strategies.
- Whites are human beings and, whether they should or not, do have their own hang-ups.
- Some whites "get it."

# Behaviors That Block Authentic Relations

## Behaviors of Whites

- Interruptions.
- Condescending behavior.
- Offering help when not needed or wanted.
- Avoidance of contact (eye-to-eye and physical).
- Verbal focus on black behavior rather than white behavior.
- Insisting on playing games according to white rules.
- Showing annoyance at black behavior that differs from their own.
- Expression of too-easy acceptance and friendship.
- Talking about, rather than to, blacks who are present.

## Behaviors of Blacks

- Confrontation too early and too harshly.
- Rejection of honest expressions of acceptance and friendship.
- Pushing whites into such a defensive posture that learning and reexamination is impossible.
- Failing to keep a commitment and then offering no explanation.
- "In-group" joking, laughing at whites in black culture language.
- Giving answers blacks think whites want to hear.
- Using confrontation as the primary relationship style.
- Isolationism.

# Behaviors That Facilitate Authentic Relations

## Behaviors of Whites

- Directness and openness in expressing feelings.
- Assisting other white brothers to understand and confront feelings.
- Supporting self-initiated moves of black people.
- Listening without interrupting.
- Staying with and working through difficult confrontations.
- Demonstration of interest in learning about black perceptions, culture, etc.
- Taking a risk (e.g., being first to confront the differences).
- Assuming responsibility for examining one's motives.

## Behaviors of Blacks

- Showing interest in understanding white's point of view.
- Acknowledging that there are some committed whites.
- Acting as if "we have some power," and don't need to prove it.
- Allowing whites to experience unaware areas of racism.
- Openness.
- Expression of real feelings.
- Dealing with whites where they are.
- Meeting whites halfway.
- Treating whites on one-to-one basis.
- Telling it like it is.
- Realistic goal-sharing.
- Showing pride in their heritage.

In conclusion, blacks *and* whites must get rid of the reactives and focus on the proactives for meaningful relations.

## About the Authors

This analysis was created by Bertram Lee (an African-American) and Warren H. Schmidt (a white American) during a National Training Laboratory in Bethel, Maine where both were co-trainers in a T-group in the 1960's.

# An Interview with Shelby Steele

from *On Values: Talking with Peggy Noonan*

*Shelby Steele:* I remember the community that I grew up in, which was a very poor black community, and most people were married and most of my friends had two parents who worked, and there was considerable stability—but the other side of that was that we lived behind a wall of segregation, and I can remember that period also with an abiding pain and frustration. And I wonder in many ways about the peace that was on the surface, that was visible on the surface in that era; the coherence that we had seemed to me the result of an awful lot of repression. A lot of the conflicts that we now struggle with and that confuse us so much were repressed. So there was a down side to that era, and I remember that time very painfully. I couldn't go places, I couldn't do things, I couldn't know certain people. I wouldn't come into a restaurant like this. I never ate in a restaurant till I was 18. We had a lot of picnics and I realize why now.

*Peggy Noonan:* Because you couldn't go to local restaurants?

*Shelby Steele:* You couldn't go to local restaurants at all, and you could not do a lot—you couldn't—if you took a car trip, you had to go to the black community and find some persons who'd let you stay in their home. You couldn't go to a motel, you couldn't do a lot of things. So I don't look back on it longingly, because I remember the pain of it, and the resentment of it, and the distinct sense that everybody was lying, and that they were living falsely and dishonestly, and that I was paying the price, and my people were paying the price. And it's not good to do that to a human being, it really marks people in ways they never ever really get over . . .

*Peggy Noonan:* What do you mean by living dishonestly?

*Shelby Steele:* They were pretending that they had a decent life and a decent society, but they were killing me. I'd have some white friends I met at the

YMCA. They'd go make money by caddying at the golf course. I'd go to the golf course and the man would let us stand around all morning before he got up the nerve to tell us they didn't let niggers on the course to caddy. Well, what kind of life is he living? It's that—what Du Bois called the double vision—Wright, Richard Wright, also called it something similar to that, the second vision that blacks have of the underbelly of American life, the side that was just implacably evil, that had no problem doing that to other human beings. And it's taken a lot of growth and struggle to put that in perspective.

*Peggy Noonan:* Shelby, the big historical event that occurred between your childhood and right now was the American civil rights movement. I don't know too many people who would disagree with that.

*Shelby Steele:* Mm-hmm.

*Peggy Noonan:* What did it change?

*Shelby Steele:* I think it changed everything. America's self-conception prior to that movement, when we had—we were an industrial giant, we had won two world wars, we had a period of postwar prosperity that was unheard of in human societies, and we thought very highly of ourselves, our self-esteem was up, you might say.

*Peggy Noonan:* And for good reason.

*Shelby Steele:* And for good reason, for good reason. And I think the civil rights movement sort of hit like a heart attack. [W]e didn't really know where it came from, given that self-conception and all the repression that had preceded that moment in history. But suddenly, America had an awful lot to be ashamed of. America was really confronted with its shame, with the fact that it had oppressed this large group of its own citizens for three centuries, for the most base of reasons. And so here is, on the one hand, this great society, and on the other hand, this recognition, suddenly, admission, really, that America had perpetrated evil, and that a part of its greatness was the result of its practice of evil. And we've never gotten over that yet. We are still, I believe, in the throes of negotiating a new conception of America that is more inclusive, that is more mature, that accepts what was great about us, what was really rotten about us.

*Peggy Noonan:* Who hasn't gotten over it?

*Shelby Steele:* [Our] society. [I]t's really only been a quarter of a century, and the shame was of far greater proportions than people admit. And it's just taken—I mean, all of the things, the turmoil that we're in now, and the right and the left, and political correctness and so forth, it seems to me, is the negotiation of that. Who are we, as a people? How can we redeem ourselves? I think, in many ways, we've become a society preoccupied with redemption as a result of the civil rights movement. Our social policy really is—has a great deal more to do with redeeming America than with actually solving social problems. [M]y feeling is that most of the social policy regarding race, gender and ethnicity since 1964 has really been focused around this need to redeem, this need for America to prove to itself that it is a country that is not evil, that it is better than its record demonstrates for those three centuries. And I think most of our social policy, for the most part, has really been about the redemption of white America. I think affirmative action is a good example of that. I think multiculturalism, diversity, all of these—these reformist ideas that come from—pretty much from the American left—

*Peggy Noonan:* Yeah.

*Shelby Steele:*—are really ideas by which white America is saying, "We're going to redeem ourselves. We're better than what we—than what our victims are saying we are. Our victims are screaming constantly that we're racist, that we're sexist, that we're materialistic, we're militaristic, we're shallow. No, we're going to say that we're compassionate, we are caring, we are concerned, and so forth." And so we put into place all kinds of social policies that, in effect, demonstrate that, I think very, very mistakenly. You know, I think we had—I think America had a chance in 1964 to really, honestly begin to make up for what it had done. Simple logic tells you that if you have completely defeated and dehumanized a people for three centuries, the thing that they need most of all is development. They need to be developed, primarily educationally, up to a point where they

are, in fact, equal. Not where they're . . . claiming to be equal, but [where] they are, in fact, equal by any standard measure. You also must not discriminate against them. That's what I think we should have done at that moment. I think we did not do that—

*Peggy Noonan:* And instead we got manipulated into—

*Shelby Steele:* I think what happened is that it was the left in America—

*Peggy Noonan:* The political left.

*Shelby Steele:*—yeah, and I don't mean to get too mired in politics here, but it was the left in America that really brought the civil rights movement into being, that made it happen, that made America change, that made America recognize what it had done wrong. And the left did that by upholding principle, democratic principles, and reasoning from those principles, by saying that every individual in the society has a right to life, liberty and the pursuit of happiness, without regard to color. So the civil rights movement that was . . . a democratic movement, and Martin Luther King . . . [was] like a founding father. It was a second democratic revolution.

But instantly, after they sort of won that moral victory in the mid-'60s, the left sort of took its victory almost as a mandate to begin the process of engineering for us the kind of society that would have the look of a society that had never practiced oppression. So we get these ideas like multiculturalism and diversity . . . what would America look like if we'd never had racism or sexism? And so right away we begin to pursue those—what I call ideas of the good, through engineering. And in order to engineer, you have to be willing to bend principles, to bend standards, in order to prefer certain people, so that you can reach this image of the good, diversity or whatever.

[W]hat I think has happened is that we've made it virtuous to step over standards, to step over principles, to take a relativistic attitude toward the principles that undergird our democratic society. And so we are eroding democracy . . . [We're] Balkanizing people and saying to them . . . that your greatest advantage in American society is for you to go back inside your race, gender and ethnic group and pursue the entitlements that are due that group because of redress. In the name of the good, we are Balkanizing our society, rather than integrating it. [T]hen we wonder why the groups can't get along. Well, there's no incentive to get along. More is due me as a black than as an American citizen. And so my incentive is to be black, against your white.

*Peggy Noonan:* And then I claim, "Well, more is due to me as a woman than as an American citizen."

*Shelby Steele:* Right, right.

*Peggy Noonan:* "I deserve a little more than you, don't you think? Women have been subjugated longer and worse than you guys."

*Shelby Steele:* Well, of course, and then we come out and we compare our wounds, and I say that "Women don't know anything about oppression. Let me tell you what slavery—" and we go back and forth. And my feeling is, is that absolutely nothing is due you as a woman, and nothing is due me as a black. All my rights are due to me as a citizen of the United States, as an individual, as they are due you, and they ought to be exactly the same. And when they're not, we're in trouble, and that redress for past wrongs is never an excuse for violating the freedom of the individual.

*Peggy Noonan:* Down here on the ground, regular people, working-class people, middle-class people in America, have they changed so much in the past 30 years? They don't marry like they used to, and they don't stay married like they used to. They have illegitimate children at an extraordinary rate. When you and I were kids, the national illegitimacy rate was 5 percent. The national rate now is something over 30 percent, and it is rising, it shows no signs of going down.

*Shelby Steele:* Right.

*Peggy Noonan:* I know this is a long question, but is there some connection between these big political currents up here and what is happening, what has been happening on the ground down here for the past 30 years?

*Shelby Steele:* I think there's an absolute and direct connection. [L]ooking back at the mid-'60s for a moment, when certainly the left became driven by the idea of redemption, and the idea that we had to engineer toward redemption, we had to create

the society that looked non-oppressive. In order to engineer, you have to bend standards, bend rules, have preferences. In other words, you have to take on an attitude of relativism toward everything. So then you say, "Well, it's not for me to judge if she's 14 and she has a baby. I have no right to judge that anymore." That's relative to her circumstance as a what, a dweller of the ghetto or whatever. And so what relativism began to do is to erode those values. And so my culture is as good as your culture. If I'm pregnant at 14, that's as good as you being pregnant and married at 28. It's all relative and we use relativism to redeem ourselves from our history of oppression. And so it got all interwoven, interconnected, and in the process, you no longer have the right to tell me anything, and I don't have the right to tell you anything. And—

*Peggy Noonan:* But isn't this all another form of a big lie that none of us acknowledge?

*Shelby Steele:* Yes.

*Peggy Noonan:* I look around sometimes and I think, you know, most of us adults, we have a pretty strong, at least, intuitive sense of the difference between right and wrong, and we know that a 14 year-old girl should, first of all, not be sleeping with her boyfriend, second of all, she shouldn't be conceiving a baby, third of all, she should not be having a baby out of wedlock. We know that. We don't say it because we want to be nonjudgmental, open-minded, easygoing people, we don't want to look like hypocrites.

*Shelby Steele:* We don't want to be racist.

*Peggy Noonan:* All right, we don't want to be racist, yes, that is part of it.

*Shelby Steele:* And so the point I keep trying to make when I talk to people is that people are more interested in not being racist than they are concerned about that 14 year-old girl who's pregnant.

*Peggy Noonan:* They're more interested in the pose than in her reality.

*Shelby Steele:* Guilt causes self-preoccupation, not preoccupation with the person who's causing the guilt, who's suffering, and so America has very selfishly been preoccupied with its own innocence, and has utterly—because if that girl was your own child . . .

*Peggy Noonan:* You would care, and you would judge—

*Shelby Steele:*—and you would make it clear to her, and you would so forth and so on. But when it's blacks in the ghetto, well, maybe it's their culture, maybe it's a manifestation of their—their suffering and their legacy of slavery, and it's not for me—

*Peggy Noonan:* To judge.

*Shelby Steele:*—to judge. And in fact, it is virtuous not for me to judge, because in not judging, I demonstrate the fact that I am not a racist, that I am a liberal person.

*Peggy Noonan:* What is the way out?

*Shelby Steele:* The way out is for us to stop being so preoccupied with our own innocence. What we should have learned from the civil rights movement is that we're not innocent, and it's not realistic to expect that we are innocent, that nobody is innocent, that no society is innocent, that we're flawed, imperfect people.

*Peggy Noonan:* By innocence you mean blameless, sinless?

*Shelby Steele:* Right . . . America has committed sins. America has been racist. But the answer is not to then adopt relativism and say anything blacks do is fine, because I want to make sure that everybody sees me not to be racist. The answer is to assert values, is to say, "I don't care whether you're black or whether you're white or brown or whatever, it is not a healthy thing in the modern world for you to have a child at the age of 14." And to assert that value, and to put incentives in place that reinforce that value. Until we do that, we are simply writing those people off.

*Peggy Noonan:* Shelby, you are tough on liberals and the left, and you sometimes, as you have been talking in our conversation here today, I've heard some things that have made my—my little conservative heart very happy. And yet I sense that you are possibly not about to sign up with Bill Bennett and Dan Quayle anytime soon. Am I correct?

*Shelby Steele:* Right. Yes.

*Peggy Noonan:* Why?

*Shelby Steele:* One of the problems that the right has, and it's a difficulty for them, is that where were they, back in the early '60s, when the left stood for principle? And it was their standing for principle that finally led to greater freedom for many Americans. So they have a problem. It's—in other words, their stand for principle today is convenient . . . They were not standing for principle when I was a kid and lived in a segregated society and went to segregated schools and so forth. It was fine then. And my feeling is that they did not—that they have not yet really confronted that shame that came to the fore in the '60s. And their problem is a problem not of whether they're right or wrong, their problem is a problem of credibility.

## About the Contributors to this Interview

Shelby Steele's work has appeared in *Harper's, New York Times Magazine, Commentary,* the *Washington Post,* and *American Scholar,* among many other publications. He won a *National Magazine* Award in 1989, and one of his essays on race was chosen for The Best American Essays 1989. Steele is a professor of English at San Jose State University in California. He is the author of *The Content of Our Character,* available from HarperCollins (1-800-237-5534).

Peggy Noonan was a Special Assistant to President Ronald Reagan from 1984 to 1986; in 1988 she was chief speechwriter to Vice President George Bush during his first campaign for the presidency. In 1989 she completed the bestseller *What I Saw at the Revolution—A Political Life in the Reagan Years* (Random House, 1990). Her journalism and essays have appeared in *Time, Newsweek, The New York Times, The Washington Post, Harper's, Forbes, Mirabella, Harper's Bazaar,* and *The Washington Monthly.* She has recently published *Life, Liberty and the Pursuit of Happiness* (Random House, 1994).

# False Cultural Pride Is Self-Destructive

by Bill Maxwell (*St. Petersburg Times*)

Many of my white acquaintances are dismayed when I tell them that black people generally consider me, along with other blacks like me, to be a poor role model for young black males.

Why? Because I'm one of an increasing number of black professionals who reject the pseudo-negritude that is literally killing the souls of black folks everywhere.

What is pseudo-negritude? It is false consciousness of and false pride in the cultural and physical aspects of the African heritage.

Negritude itself—genuine consciousness of and pride in one's blackness—is desirable. In fact, it undergirds every positive aspect of black-American society. By genuine I mean, for example, realistically assessing our heritage, actively making our own personal behavior a shining example of the positive and publicly rejecting self-destructive behavior.

Pseudo-negritude, on the other hand, often embraces unwholesome sacred cows, unsavory personalities and self-defeating behavior. One unwholesome sacred cow (and one of the most harmful) is the belief that black people shouldn't openly criticize one another's negative traits—unless, of course, the person under attack is a so-called Uncle Tom, as I'm often called.

This refusal to criticize has resulted in a dangerous cult of silence that tacitly condones criminality and was the subject of a recent *Washington Post* column. In it, William Raspberry discussed the Rev. Jesse Jackson's eulogy of Launice Janae Smith, a 4-year-old killed by a stray bullet fired into the playground where she played. Jackson wants black people to start informing on black criminals, to stop believing that to turn in a black thug is to betray one's people. "It's like seeing your apartment building in flames and not telling anybody about it because the landlord is black, the tenants are black and the guys who set the fire are black," Jackson said. "Some people think they're being disloyal to the race if they tell it. No: They will burn the race up unless they tell it . . . We've got to stop indicating that if blacks kill blacks, it's kind of all right. We've got to tell it."

Pseudo-negritude also has produced what many call the "soul patrol," a network of influential, mostly urban Afro-centrists and their followers who have determined what other black people should say and think.

Their major goal, like the "blacker-than-thou" crowd of the 1960s and 1970s is to produce a monolithic culture, one in which all black people must vote, for instance, for a political candidate because he or she is black. The soul patrollers fear and, therefore, condemn individuality.

Only the truly courageous challenge the Afro-centrists.

For this reason, I applaud an action taken recently by KACE-FM, a private black-owned radio station in Los Angeles. The station, which plays rap and rhythm and blues, stopped playing several rap songs. Program director Rich Guzman said the station would no longer play "socially irresponsible music" that "glorifies drug use, is sexually explicit, encourages violence or denigrates women . . . We took a good hard look at the sad state of our community . . . and we decided to get back to the basics of what we are licensed to do, which is to serve our community."

Several years ago, I wrote a column arguing that rap music is an accurate reflection of one part of African-American culture. I stand by that argument.

Even so-called "gansta" rap reflects a real side (the dark side) of black culture. But, like the executives of KACE-FM, I reject the behavior praised in hip-hop and that which is depicted in today's crop of stupid sitcoms.

And for this stance, along with others, such as believing that black people should learn to write and speak standard English and should behave appropriately in public places, I'm demonized and have become a poor role model for our young males.

If this were simply the belief of youngsters, I could write it off as ignorance or inexperience. Sadly, however, parents—many in responsible positions—agree with the children, or seem to do so by their silence.

Real cultural pride, real negritude, is selective. Our role models—the Arthur Ashes, Bill Cosbys, Mike Espys, August Wilsons, Colin Powells, Louis Sullivans—should be shining examples of what honest, hard work can produce. But precious few young black males have heard these giants.

I see nothing of value in pseudo-negritude, which produces silence on the likes of L. L. Cool J or Snoop Doggy Dogg, two crotch-tuggers whose repertoires consist of calling black women "bitches" and "ho's.' Gladly, I reject this part of black culture.

## About the Author

Bill Maxwell is a syndicated columnist who writes for the *St. Petersburg (FL) Times*.

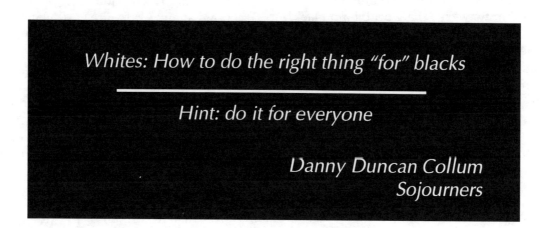

*Whites: How to do the right thing "for" blacks*

*Hint: do it for everyone*

*Danny Duncan Collum*
*Sojourners*

# Letter to Jack

by Anthony Walton '82 (*Notre Dame Magazine*)

Dear Jack:

Late one afternoon last summer, we sat for several hours in your car in front of my house talking about several recent racially-based attacks by whites upon blacks in Maine towns. These attacks, unexpected and out of character for the state, set you to reading and thinking about what Gunnar Myrdal called the American Dilemma: the inability of the United States to live up to its stated creeds and goals, a failure that has resulted in a never-ending conflict.

You had been reading several disturbing books—*The Fire Next Time, Faces at the Bottom of the Well, Chain Reaction, Two Nations, The Promised Land*—and while much of this bad news wasn't really news to you, having grown up in Chicago, you seemed surprised and mystified, even dismayed, by the depth of alienation you were discovering in black Americans. In particular, you found strange the claim of one writer, Andrew Hacker, that blacks never, ever, feel at home in the land of their birth. You said this couldn't possibly be true and asked me if I thought it was.

Jack, I am an Illinoisan of African descent by way of Mississippi; you are an Illinoisan too, Irish and Catholic. We're both from the suburbs of Chicago, we both went to Notre Dame, and we both went on to obtain advanced degrees. We both come from ambitious families who didn't settle for what their respective societies had planned for them, your grandfather blazing the trail out of Irish slums of Chicago for your family, my father, from the cotton fields of Mississippi, for mine. We have much in common and are, at times, frighteningly alike. But then there is this thing that permeates the world around us, that drives so much of what we discuss and how we see the world: I am black, and you are white.

Sometimes I wonder how we can keep this from coming between us. In our workaday friendship it isn't much of an issue, but the fact that we so often end up discussing it is indicative, to me, that racial matters are a bigger issue in our lives—in our nation's life if not our own—than we might wish to admit. Racism is, in fact, *the* American issue, on which the country will succeed or fail, because so much else is linked to it. But the country seems to move further and further from any true understanding.

I want to tell you a story. I was in Miami recently, working as a consultant for a large foundation there, the only black person in my particular group of seven or eight people. Let me be clear: The people I was working with were consummately professional in our dealings, and more than kind; I was enjoying my stay immensely, and my employers had even arranged for me to have a penthouse suite at a swanky hotel on Biscayne Bay. We conducted our business meetings in the same hotel, and this is where, on my fourth morning there, something happened that I will probably never get over. It may illustrate, a little, some of the alienation I'm talking about.

Each morning at 9 we met in a conference room, outside of which there was a buffet with toast, Danish, muffins, orange juice and coffee. On the morning in question, having already arrived in the meeting room, I stepped back out into the foyer for one last cup of coffee before convening the meeting. While I was pouring my cream and sugar, a security guard (black) came upon me and said menacingly, "Are you a guest at this hotel?" My instinct was to resist. After all, I was a paying guest, I was clothed in business attire (which made it quite irksome to watch whites in torn T-shirts and flip-flops stroll in and out unmolested) and I had been walking around in plain sight of the hotel staff for several days. Why this intimidation, now?

I said to the guard, with what I hoped was equal menace, "Why are you asking me?"

He said, "It's my job."

I said again, "Why are you asking *me*? What am I doing that would make you think I am not a guest?" We had reached a standoff and the guard went for his walkie-talkie. I looked back at the door to my conference room and figured at any second one of my colleagues would come out to look for me. I pulled the penthouse key from my pocket and cursed the guard as he walked off.

I tell you this, Jack, because I want to point out some of the nuances that are indicative of how we live, racially speaking, today, and how damaging they are. My altercation with the guard, whom I understand is basically trying to feed his family, is the least of the troubling issues. What's really disturbing me in retrospect is how that incident colored the rest of my interaction with the whites I was working with. *They had absolutely nothing to do with what had just happened*, but I wonder if they noticed how distant I had suddenly become when I walked back into the room. Jack, I was so angry I couldn't see straight for several hours. I didn't want to take it out on these people, but I couldn't help it. They became implicated in the mess. Perhaps that's my failing, but I learned from that incident how shadows are cast upon the most innocuous of exchanges.

On the plane going home, I was even more dismayed to realize that the guard was, in fact, doing his job, a job defined from high within that particular corporation. I had been in Miami, where fear of crime against tourists is endemic, and the most efficient way of maintaining control is to roust

> A young African American alumnus writes to a white friend and fellow alumnus about the many things they have in common and the one thing that determines their differing views of the world: "I am black, and you are white."

all suspicious characters (though I was pained to think of myself as suspicious). I began to think, darkly, that the treatment I received was what the majority wanted and endorsed. I acutely understood the old joke: What do you call a black man with a Ph.D.? Nigger.

I'm asking you to imagine it, Jack—having to be apprehensive every time you're in a new place. The reason blacks always and forever feel different is because the determination of that difference by others is always hanging in the air. It may be malicious, waiting for a hostile opponent to call you "nigger"; it may be the innocent, even well-meaning "jokes" meant to make everyone "comfortable"; or it may be the going-out-of-the-way to welcome blacks in social or business situations. The effect is largely the same. The black person is reminded of his otherness, his difference, his stigma, and it's exhausting, an invention of whites to preserve advantage. Whites have a power, Jack, real and practiced, and they know it; a power to attempt to insult, to humiliate and stigmatize a black at any moment. It is the only social power some whites have, their own lives being otherwise full of degradation and humiliation.

The simplest disagreement between a black and a white can ignite, at any moment, into a racially tinged conflagration fraught with danger for all concerned. What wears you down, Jack, is this unending peril coupled with the gratuitous and petty assaults on your person and character. This is what causes many African-Americans to turn inward and regard themselves as a group apart. It also causes them to give up on the possibility of real community. I think most black children leave their parents' home for school full of hope and fellow feeling, and then are worn down, some quicker than others, by what they experience in the world. This applies as much to Evanston as to Cabrini Green.

Many blacks just give up on the wider society. This is, I think, one of the key psychological factors inhibiting black progress out of the ghettos and rural backwaters, but it can also work on the most credentialed and assimilated blacks. If I perceive, in a silly example, that a waiter is ignoring me or in some other way disdaining me, do I assume that he's busy or that he's racist? You'll say, Jack, that I shouldn't jump to conclusions, but how do I overlook all the previous slights and humiliations? Why should I give him the benefit of the doubt?

Why do I have to act in a saintly way that is not required of him?

You begin to see the prison we Americans are in because of racism: The waiter can't have a bad day, at least not with me, because of all the bad days I've had at the hands of whites in the past.

I'll tell you another story. When I was a kid, my parents would rent a cabin on Lake Michigan in the Upper Peninsula of Michigan, near the town of Escanaba. Each vacation generally passed pleasantly. But as I've gotten older, something that happened there has taken on a symbolic meaning for me.

That summer I was about 10, and there were several families staying in cabins down the road from us who were from the Chicago suburb of Villa Park. I didn't know what Villa Park meant then—working-class Slavs, Italians, Irish from the city escaping urban decline, i.e., blacks—but these people would have a bonfire every night and roast hot dogs and marshmallows and sing camp songs and enjoy the beach. One night they invited my brother and sister and me, and we went to the bonfire and sat for about 45 minutes, then decided we were cold and wanted to go inside (I also seem to remember some nightly Canadian radio show that we had discovered and didn't want to miss). When we thanked the parents for having us and turned to leave, one of the kids blurted out, "See? You make us invite them, and they don't want to come anyway."

Through the years, this incident has played over and over in my mind, and it is illustrative of what I think the problem is. I don't really know what was driving that little boy's frustration with us—perhaps he just wanted us to stay and become friends—but as a grown man I know what "them" means. It means me. It means my family, my relatives, black people, people with dark skin. And the fact of that dark skin, in opposition to those with other skin, trumps all other aspects of my personality, my *self*.

My version of that evening in Escanaba now goes something like this: We were the only black family in the vicinity, and in a well-meaning gesture, the other families didn't want it to seem as though they were ignoring us. We accepted their politeness out of reciprocal politeness, but then our good manners, because of the racial shadow, were seen as a rejection, while their courtesy was seen as patronizing. This is what the shadow of racism does to everything in American life, Jack; it charges everything with a meaning that may or may not be accurate and poisons the most banal of social exchanges. It leads to the current national situation where blacks are discussed only, *exist* only, in terms of the problems they present for whites.

This estrangement, in both the public and private spheres, is what scares me the most. I suppose the fact that you and I are aware of these issues is itself reason for hope, but it seems to me in the last several years Americans are increasingly unwilling to listen, to *hear* each other, while contemplating these issues. It's as if it is too much effort to see one another clearly, to talk to each other with precision. We lack a vocabulary. The words we use have been bandied so much that they are drained of common meaning. They have one meaning for the speaker and a quite different, often contradictory, code for the listener.

A black says, "Affirmative action." A white says, "Reverse discrimination." Someone else says, "Quotas."

Or a black says, "Slavery." A white says, "I wasn't born then." Someone else says, "Ancient history."

This lack of a common language forces ethnic groups to compete as it were, on an exchange of grievances in which each individual claim cancels all others. These denials preclude any agreement on a common history from which a relevant discussion can be based, and in the clamor, truth is lost.

So blacks worry that what they view as their historic claim on restitution and justice will be lost if they acknowledge any grievances of whites, while whites feel that they have done their part—or, increasingly, that they had nothing to do with the things that blacks are complaining about in the first place. It's over. Who cares any more?

This denial of history's legacy is disturbing. I understand that whites are very tired of all this; that is the blindness of privilege, in this case racial privilege. One could say whites don't care, but I think it's more accurate to say that they don't care *enough*. Racism and its aftereffects don't affect whites existentially, only as an external inconvenience and annoyances—crime, taxes, calls to conscience—not life-altering complication. When the annoyances get too clamorous, they respond with force: Hire more cops, cut welfare, build prisons. But they seem simultaneously to expect some kind

of mercy—a magical absolution—to swoop down and end all this. It is, tragically, a mercy that whites as a group have never been willing to grant.

Again we pay the price of historical ignorance. Americans do not have any sense of how much racism has cost the country, morally, spiritually and economically, and so they misunderstand what it will take to ameliorate it. We can't even speak of healing, because the country has never been whole. Is it possible for us, all of us, given the foregoing, to forge a new vision of this country and each other?

Perhaps the problem is that it is in the interest of some to remember and in the interest of others to forget. The immense suffering and dislocations of Africans on this continent are not a myth; to cite and recount them is not to make excuses. Jack, this refusal to confront history is another reason why blacks feel alienated, because we have our own versions of things, our own memories, which seem to be constantly disputed, ignored and disparaged.

We have our own cultural windows through which we view the world. Our experience has forced us to. You and I, because you are white and I am black, can observe the same event, analyze the same pattern of facts, and draw very different conclusions. Consider the recent New York City shooting of a black undercover policeman by a white patrolman who mistook him for a criminal. Was it a tragic mistake or racist haste? Our social realities force us to be aware of different nuances, perhaps even force us to frame different contexts.

It's interesting to look at the experiences of your tribe, American-Irish Catholics, in comparison with those of American blacks. Daniel Patrick Moynihan and Nathan Glazer have described life in 19th-century Irish-American slums like this: "Drunkenness, crime, corruption, discrimination, family disorganization, juvenile delinquency were the routine of that era." In the hundred years since then, Irish Catholics have become the single most successful ethnic group in the country while significant numbers of blacks fall further and further behind. Why is that, Jack? Simple industry on the part of the Irish? Black incompetence? Or is it because, whatever else blacks do—become spiritual WASPs or street criminals—they cannot become white?

When your ancestors arrived in Boston, New York, Chicago, they had a very hard time but they did get a chance. So did the Germans, Italians,

Slavs, Scandinavians and others who came to America. There were blacks in Boston, New York and Chicago then too, and there are many more now, but millions of them have still not gotten a chance at the full possibilities of American life, partially because groups like Irish Catholics have seen them as a threat and suppressed them ruthlessly.

I think of an article I read last year in which an Irish woman in the Mount Greenwood neighborhood of Chicago—a consciously segregated all-white Irish enclave—told a reporter who asked for comment on the unabashed disdain of blacks the reporter was discovering there: "You don't have to keep bringing up that they were slaves." That struck me. Why? Were blacks not slaves? Is it not relevant anymore? Does she not want to think of it? While I was contemplating this woman's desire to deny blacks their history, it also occurred to me that there is no group on this planet that clings more vociferously to the past, to a sense of cosmic injustice and tragic destiny, even while living in places like Lexington, Bronxville and Kenilworth, than Irish Catholics. So why must black history be denied?

Something I've learned from our talks, Jack, is that whites have their own myths and ways of seeing themselves, their own narratives of suffering and success, which often do not leave much room for other, competing, concerns. The suffering in the old country and the ideal of boot-strapping one's way out of the American ghettos are what these stories celebrate, and the mythopoeticization of the stories leads to the "blacks-are-slackers" mind set that infects much of the country. "We did it, why can't they?"

A kind of psychological double knot is applied, involving the invocation of white suffering and then, in turn-of-the-century immigrant groups, the cry of "but-we-weren't-here-anyway." This leads to an interesting point: Just as whites need to learn more about blacks, blacks need to understand better white legends and perceptions, and how they shape what happens in our society.

In *The New Republic* last summer, Fred Barnes wrote, "I'm waiting for a politician to say that white racism is one part of the problem, but there's another part, an internal problem in the black community—crime, gangs, illegitimacy, welfare dependency—that blacks must confront aggressively." This statement, besides being obvious, is

true; but were I able to speak with Mr. Barnes on this subject, I would have a question for him: Where do "white racism" and "internal black problems" intersect? Might they be connected? To paraphrase Reinhold Neibuhr, can immoral behavior by blacks be separated from immoral society? Are whites not privileged in our society, and doesn't that privilege work in ways damaging to others?

Jack, some will say that I'm making excuses, but I would say I'm merely describing. It's amusing to me that there is such a fervor over multiculturalism and Afro-centrism and the like these days, because whites—after years and years and years of sending signals, overt and implicit, that blacks are not welcome in American society—seem surprised that some blacks would want to separate themselves from it. Historically, in every possible legal, cultural and social way they could, whites have obstructed, undermined and oppressed blacks. Whites lock us out, Jack, then chastise us for not coming in. They deign to bring us in, then they complain that we don't know how to act, or are ungrateful. They castigate us for not meeting standards they themselves have never met, and they ignore the fact that the problems facing blacks are the same problems their forebears faced, but without the handicaps imposed on us. And whites couldn't have transcended without the very government they vilify and accuse of throwing money away on blacks. Didn't the GI Bill, VA mortgages, college loans, Social Security, the Interstate Highway program, military spending *et al* greatly help whites rise?

When have whites, even grudgingly, accepted blacks as a group? Why have they designed and acceded to a system that can have only one outcome, then act astonished when that outcome occurs? That brings us to the saddest part of all. I think that large numbers of blacks are giving up, turning their backs on any kind of transformative future, settling instead for a kind of internal exile, a permanent state of alienation.

Much of the way the black and white people of the United States have interacted in the last 50 years has been predicated on the forbearance of the blacks—being more Christian, more forgiving, more patient, in good hope—than whites. I don't think large numbers of blacks are concerned with being "better" anymore, Jack, particularly the youth. They're just angry. There comes a time when calm waiting begins to look like begging.

So we retreat. And attack. The time of innocence is past. We lost a tremendous opportunity in this country after the Civil War, and much of our current racial quagmire can be traced to that failure. Americans, black and white, fumbled another chance in the time of Martin Luther King, Jr., and now whites are beginning to shake loose of any feeling or notion of responsibility, or involvement even, in what has happened.

This is to be expected. Being white in America carries its own burdens, and it would take a poet or a saint to see and embrace how blacks and whites are stuck to each other down through history. I suspect that whites want to be free of this, of us, blacks, and in the current climate that means putting us out of mind. Blacks demand to be remembered and seem to be destined to assume various mythological roles in the national theater, Teirisias, Siren, Minotaur. I think of De Tocqueville: If we cannot be equals, we are doomed to be enemies.

I've painted a bleak picture, Jack, and I hope I'm not saying more, as the Quakers put it, than that which is true. I think I'm speaking the truth, as I see it, because I'm speaking to you, whom I treasure and have nothing to gain from exaggeration. I don't think that our relationship, or any of the millions like it in the country, invalidates anything that I've said. Instead, our friendship only points to the tragic irony of the American dilemma.

I have to struggle always to remember that a significant number of whites have been very, very good to me, a number of others haven't been so good, but the same could be said of blacks in my life. I have begun to think that the best advice is to not view humans as anything other than individuals who have the capacity, either way, to continually surprise you.

When we walk out of our private lives, however, we are in a world that is trapped in a false way of seeing people; we are, literally, doomed to our groups, our tribes, and these groups have a way of ending up in conflict. The problem, my friend, is that every single person has to find some way of living through the smoky illusions of race and group, these untruths and lies that fester and pass from generation to generation until they make us actors in a script we didn't write, don't believe, and have no desire to see. Thurgood Marshall said, "We can run from each other, but we cannot escape each other."

If we cannot find some way to live together peacefully, the alternative can be seen around the world—in Africa, in India, in the Middle East, in Northern Ireland, in Yugoslavia—in short, to commence drawing lines. And when that happens, my buddy, no matter how much we love Notre Dame, jazz, Irish poets, football or each other, you are going to be over there and I am going to be over here. And what then?

## About the Author

Anthony Walton's essays and articles have appeared in journals ranging from *The New York Times* and *Reader's Digest* to *Poetry Ireland*. He lives in Brunswick, Maine.

*The American Negro has the great advantage of having never believed that collection of myths to which white Americans cling: that their ancestors were all freedom-loving heroes, that they were born in the greatest country the world has ever seen, or that Americans are invincible in battle and wise in peace, that Americans have always dealt honorably with Mexicans and Indians and all other neighbors or inferiors, that American men are the world's most direct and virile, that American women are pure.*

from James Baldwin
*The Fire Next Time*

# PART 3
# GENDER ISSUES:
# PERVASIVE & PERSISTENT

# Dialogue: Gender

*Bob*—This section, George, begins with your article from the *International Management Development Review*, though I'm a little uncomfortable with its title: "The Ultimate Cultural Difference."

*George*—Well, for some years now I have operated on the theory that the first, most pervasive difference we carry with us, the one with the most consequences, and thus "the ultimate cultural difference" is that of gender. Even though another form of difference, e.g., race, may be focal for us, gender is usually at play in it as well. Because of our gender, at every stage of our lives we are perceived and treated differently. Even the biases and prejudices others have toward us are different . . .

This different treatment shapes the internal cultural environment of our minds. Gender is the difference that we normally use to learn about all other differences. There really is a male culture and a female culture which in many of their features transcend ethnic and racial differences, even though these features express themselves in many and sometimes contradictory ways. When we address gender successfully, most of the other differences of culture can be much easier to manage . . .

*Bob*— . . . because?

*George*—Gender is the toughest to deal with. It's the difference most closely tied to our identity, especially at a time when social roles are changing. We are most threatened when our gender is questioned or jeopardized. Our response to gender issues is passionate and powerful. You can see this in terms of how loaded some people's reactions are to gays and lesbians. Sexual orientation is a gender issue that touches this nerve.

*Bob*—Yes, I explored that connection in an article I wrote nearly 15 years ago entitled "Managing a Diverse Workforce: Teaching MBA's about Gay/Lesbian Issues in Management."[1] The social forces at work that reinforce sexism and sex role stereotyping are exactly the same forces that fuel heterosexism and homophobia.

*George*—Gender issues are often perceived as women's issues. I assert that this is narrow and simplistic thinking. Men can learn from their own experience of gender as well. For example, U.S. men have a history of being identified with what they do. They need to grow to a greater awareness of who they are, beyond their work-identity, if they are to grapple with the prospect of being "downsized" out of a job and needing to create a new livelihood.

This is further confounded (or enriched, depending upon your tolerance for ambiguity) by race. For example, perhaps white men can learn from the long experience of black men, about how to cope with their roles being undermined both at home and at work.[2] Black men, as a consequence of individual and institutional racism, have long needed to find an identity different from the "job-related" identity available to white men who had far better access to employment.

Perhaps black men can learn from white men and reacquire dignity without sexism, and with the support of black women. Black women have been the matriarchal heads-of-households for so long (all traceable to the nation's history with slavery), that black women will have to learn new skills to be better allies to black men. Sexism cuts both ways on both sides of the color line, though differently in different cultures.

Gender also raises the question of diversity as value added. Since we have now a vast number of women immigrating into workplace cultures designed by and for men, how do we empower both men and women to employ their gender-developed skills to be globally effective and competitive, to have a successful, peaceful (or at least creatively conflicted) workplace?

*Bob*—Imagine if a mass immigration took place from Albania to the U.S., so that over a period of

---

[1]*EXCHANGE: The Organizational Behavior Teaching Journal;* 1983, Volume VIII, Number 1.

[2]See Ali, Shahrazad, *The Blackman's Guide to Understanding the Blackwoman;* Civilized Publications, 2019 S. 7th St., Philadelphia, PA 19148, 1990.

30 years, 50 percent of the employees in the U.S. were Albanians. They think, act, walk and talk differently from those already there. The arrival of so many women in the workplace is a culture shock of similarly massive proportions. Role changes have led some men to feel particularly threatened, especially at work, their traditional domain. I'll never forget the Montreal Massacre by the disaffected student who thought women were taking his deserved place in the engineering program. On December 6, 1989 he opened fire on a classroom of women students, screaming, "You're all a bunch of feminists!"

*George*—These aberrations do show that the gender issue is there, even though the vast majority of men are not violent, are not abusers. But I want to go back to your metaphor of the Albanians because at least for white men like you and me, I think it's more like an invasion of British . . .

*Bob*— . . . because they talk the same language?

*George*— . . . yes. Because women *seem* to talk the same language and we *think* we know them. But what they're liable to do, believe, value, and how they'll handle information will come as a total surprise. If they were Albanians, we'd probably recognize and accept that they're really different because they're Albanians and cut them some slack. Coming from the mainstream U.S. culture, we could hardly be racist about the British since they're supposed to be like us, we tend to admire them, we've inherited their systems of government, etc., and we blind ourselves to the differences. With women, we men have the same feeling, "We men can't imagine how our wives, our girlfriends, our sisters or our mothers could be so different from us when they show up in the workforce!?"

*Bob*—So the point you make is that we need transcultural competencies for gender, too. We don't know how to deal with each other in our changing roles, especially on the job.

*George*—Especially there. Lack of these competencies, starting with the inability to recognize difference, turns this into injustice and bias in the way both women and men treat each other. Women competing at work are coming from behind. Those who do poorly are falling into a new disadvantaged class. Women define it as an issue of power, basically their lack of power in the public and workplace arenas.

*Bob*—If we men really have all this power why are we so reluctant to share it?

*George*—Probably because we don't experience the power, usually being in a power struggle ourselves. Most men feel themselves in a one down situation with other men, and competing with women confuses the issue all the more. It's been one of the goals of the men's movement to give men identity and self-esteem so that they don't have to try to get it by having power over someone else.

I have a friend whom I would describe as a men's medicine man. Gordon (Gordon Clay, National Men's Resource Center, 415-457-3389) drives around the country with a van full of books on men's issues, about everything from basic men's health to relationships. He offers men books to read and sits around talking with them. One of his aims is to heal what he calls "the father wound." I would best describe this as an attempt to recover or perhaps create an integral masculine culture, a place where men are sure of, and comfortable with, our manhood and don't need to go looking for it every day.

It's called "the father wound" because it hurts whenever our fathers can't pass on manhood to us as they would have liked, and we compound the hurt by blaming them for it and running to our mothers for help. The feminist agenda for "fixing" men is neither helpful nor empowering. Men's anger toward women is often a misdirected frustration at not getting something we want from them—something they could never give in the first place. The problem is that we simply keep looking in the wrong place. Women can't give masculinity. When women clutch on to their boy children to prevent them from becoming like their fathers they are perpetrating a recipe for disaster.

Let me get personal. Despite the fact that I've been committed to sharing power with women in the workplace for years, I often don't feel particularly "powerful" working with women. I hear this from other men, too. They say, "What is this power women keep thinking we have . . . I don't feel I have it!"

*Bob*—Now a feminist critique would assert that you don't *feel* it because you've *always* had it . . .

*George*—Perhaps. Perhaps. I do my best to "empower" the women I work with, and it's hardly ever enough. It's both a moral commitment and a practical decision for the future of my world as I see it. I am most happy when I see the women I am associated with as friends and colleagues whose successes I celebrate and whose frustrations I can share.

*Bob*—How can men be men? How can women be women? This leads us to the Felice Schwartz article that caused such furor when it appeared in *The Harvard Business Review* in 1989. It was the first time a prominent theorist proposed that women should be treated on the opportunity track in a way that reflects and accommodates their biological differences, namely that women bear children and are often the primary care-givers (at least initially). I remember taking in all the media debates, the talk shows, the front page stories and magazine features.

Then, I went back to reread the original article to look at what kicked off the controversy. I found Schwartz's "New Facts of Life" to be very practical, pragmatic, respectful and full of common sense. It simply proposes an alternative option to competing and achieving on the male track. I think it's excellent. But the widespread adverse reaction indicates our inability to come to grips with the fact that women are different and may need accommodation of the rules or systems that work for men. Women deserve the choice . . .

*George*—Key for me, here is the fact that some men also choose not to enter a competitive way of life. So while Felice Schwartz may be arguing for a broader range of freedom of choice for women, I would say we should argue that this same freedom should be more culturally available to everyone. But then, who supports those alternative lifestyles? Many women are willing to be single working moms, but balk against supporting a man and a child. Down deep many of the old gender role distinctions are still very operative.

*Bob*—This is a corollary to the "Question & Answer"—"How to do the right thing 'for' blacks." To which we answered, "Do it for everybody!" How do we do the right thing for women? Do it

for everybody. Allow a career-secondary path for men who choose to have their primary emphasis be on the circle of their family—or develop an entirely new model . . .

*George*— . . . if you can find the freedom and resources to do so. Women want in on men's turf, to be full fledged workers, professionals, etc., but men don't want in on women's turf; it's still too culturally forbidden for most. There are two other challenges here. The first we can't deal with here at length. It's the question of how in a time of declining earnings any of us, women or men, can afford, or will be inclined to, take the path of the career-secondary route that Schwartz proposes. Here's the reality-check message: Some of us do have to do things that we don't like to do, or don't want to do, in order to survive, regardless of gender.

*Bob*—In the heyday of yuppiedom it looked like a woman "could have it all" and it was assumed that men already "had it all." Now the Generation X crowd is wondering if there's much left to have.

*George*—That relates to the second challenge which also helps us "get real" about class. Some people are simply better positioned than others. Because of the class they now belong to, they can take advantage of situations where "we do it for everybody," so that inequities creep back in or even show up at the start. This is why level-the-playing-field strategies are still needed, even if they are totally unlike the Affirmative Action ones we have now.

*Bob*—Part of getting real, too, is realizing that we live in economies with fluctuating shortages, with winners and losers. To be winners we have sought out cheap resources, using women in sweatshops, exploiting immigrant men, or moving manufacturing off shore. Today we have a high-tech off-shore labor force. We can pipe data electronically to Malaysia, for example, for overnight processing and get it back by opening time the next day.

*George*—This approach to the economy persists like our commitment to the internal combustion engine or the IBM computer. Since we have vast numbers of these fossil-fuel-burning engines driving around, they exclude other options as *the* way to get there or get the job done. If we had made the decision a long time ago to develop a technology to use hydrogen from water as a fuel source, and had stuck with it, we probably would have cheaper and cleaner road transportation today. Success kills innovation. We have so many IBM PC's and clones out there that it's a gargantuan economic effort to move to a more efficient operating system though technically such is readily available.

*Bob*—Now, I'm not sure I'm following you. How does that relate to gender?

*George*—Well—we're stuck today in a workplace that's becoming more stressed. One that has no obvious alternatives. It's out of control, living a life of its own, like a runaway train. So redefining how we want to participate looks impossible against the odds. I'll put it another way: what ever happened to the housewife? Where I live, there's an advertisement in the paper every day for hiring a housewife, someone who will come in to cook, clean, pay the bills and do all the things once relegated to the role of supportive housewife to the full time husband. But today all couples need a housewife . . .

*Bob*— . . . to fill the traditional role.

*George*—Exactly, but the traditional is going, going, gone. Today it takes two people working full time to maintain the standard of living that previously was maintained by one person for an entire family. So the loss of the housewife, or simply not having one (whether you are a man or a woman) is indeed a class issue, but also an issue that packs a charge of explosive resentment into the framework of gender, at least among heterosexuals.

Many women feel oppressed if they perform both roles (homemaking and working); feel guilty if they perform only one; or feel angry that they themselves have no one in the support role. Men can be angry if the women are not performing either one of the two roles, or moving back and forth between roles.

*Bob*—And the bottom line is that even in relationships where both heterosexual partners' spouses believe themselves to be in egalitarian (50%-50%) partnerships, the women do 85% of those things that were traditional household chores of the wife. So although I may pitch in and make my contribution of 15%, I perceive myself as a hero when I do because of men's historical lack of participation in

"maintaining the hearth." Even a modest contribution feels like equal sharing to men.

*George*—There's another side to this. Probably 60% of the 85% of the things which are perceived as part of the traditional role of the wife, I as a single man living on my own just wouldn't do. That's why it looks so ratty around here. [*Both Bob and George chuckle.*] But I think there's some truth to that.

*Bob*—We wouldn't clean up that much and we wouldn't care. There's a biological basis for that: our olfactory nerves are not as sensitive as women's [refer to *Male & Female Realities* by Joe Tanenbaum, 1990, p.41, available from 1-800-736-1293].

*George*—Also, men used to do nearly a hundred percent of what women are now demanding as their right—meaningful work outside the home. The fact that women are doing what used to be men's work hasn't lessened the burden on men: they still have to work just as hard, given our economic climate. But the inclusion (or invasion, if you think back to our Albanian metaphor) of women may be making the workplace more stressful for men. Dealing with difference, while exciting and productive, always takes more energy.

If men en masse decided to become full-time homemakers and dads, and invaded woman's turf, you would hear a different tune. Those few who have become househusbands tell both of some great satisfactions and some hair-raising stories.

*Bob*—None of which are particularly different from mom's parenting experiences, by the way . . .

*George*—The point is that we are developing new roles and new relationships to meet changing circumstances.

*Bob*—I used to think it was like a cultural exchange program where each side thinks that they are being sent to Siberia while they believe their partners are cruising the Caribbean. But, now the grass isn't much greener on either side of the fence. We're in it together.

*George*—So this gender issue is an extremely powerful one and in the best interests of both sides to resolve amicably. If we remember the immigrant model, then we see that women are usually immigrating into a field where men have been dominant. A field where men have set the rules, decided what the objectives of the organization were, and determined the style of competition. Women have acculturated successfully (at least at the entry levels) and learned *in spite of* the fact that men have not often shared the rules with them.

*Bob*—The next item is from a recent *Newsweek* magazine . . . about the physiological differences between men's and women's brains. Every time a new cover story appears it's as though news is happening for the first time. This always astonishes me.

*George*—There may be a new technology to empirically support that there are substantial differences . . .

*Bob*—But this concept has been with us (or those of us that have followed the field) for twenty years. Historically, "scientific" differences in brain or biological functioning have been used to demean, dismiss, and oppress women. With the women's movement making giant strides in the '60's and '70s we spend all our energy imagining that the sexes were equal. During the '70's a husband and wife team of researchers and writers, Jo Durden-Smith and Diane de Simone, wrote provocative think pieces that appeared in a variety of journals that eventually culminated in a definitive piece of work in the early 1980s *Sex and the Brain* (Little Brown, 1984). This work outraged feminists who were invested in wishful thinking about how the sexes were pretty much the same. Well, the *Newsweek* piece is the most recent in a long string of evidence that we're not the same; that biological differences hold sway over our behavior, feelings, and thinking patterns.

*George*—However, it's not just physiology. Our problem is psychology and politics. Why else would we commit such resources to do this kind of research? Why does the energy go in this direction? If you admit physiological differences, does it score points for your side? It does if difference means deviation from a male standard. I hear it coming from both sides. What happens when we point out that men live shorter lives than women? That women have it better or take better care of themselves? That men self-destruct? That more resources and research have to be channeled to exploring the health effects of stress in the workplace? If we want an ongoing war between the sexes, there is plenty of ammunition available.

U.S. Americans, both women and men, in the past believed our individual inalienable right is to be someone else tomorrow if we so choose. For us to forgo this is insufferable. In the '80s many women I knew chose new names for themselves. I don't hear much of that any more. In the '90s world of limits, we seem to feel more trapped in our identities and need to come to terms with them.

We are also less optimistic about change despite the fact that there may be better tools to do it with. I am reminded of a cartoon I recently saw. A snail is riding on a turtle. In one panel the snail is obviously scared out of its wits and is yelling "Whoaaaa!" to the turtle. In the next, it's shouting "Yeeh Hawh" and enjoying the ride. Cognitive science has the potential to revolutionize how we live and work together, but we may be too invested in the present pop psychology and politics to change. Research on gender differences is available from many perspectives, many of which challenge existing doctrine. Let's use it to benefit each other, not to trap each other.

Researchers include Carol Gilligan, Robin Lakoff and Deborah Tannen, just to mention a few who have been popularized. It's also a matter of perception, as illustrated by writings like John Gray's (*Men Are from Mars, Women Are from Venus*) becoming best sellers. Despite his somewhat simplistic approach to gender issues, many couples find his advice quite useful. In the *Hagar the Horrible* cartoon we assume that Helga is proving her point, but analysis from a man's perspective shows just the opposite (page 134).

*Bob*—Now, to continue this section, let's note that we have an interview from Frances Conley, the surgeon who filed sexual harassment charges against the Stanford Medical School. It's powerful testimony about how pervasive and how disempowering sexist behavior can be.

*George*—The Frances Conley article, like the Anita Hill-Clarence Thomas debate, raises the question, "Why do women wait so long to speak out?" and the other question, "Why don't men hear us?" Many women are waiting less now and more men are listening, but it still leaves us with the big question of how we redefine public and private life.

*Bob*—We assume and take so much for granted about the way we see the world. One way to discover our sexist assumptions is to reverse our gender roles. That's why the first two *MAXINE* cartoons (pages 136 and 142) by Marian Henley are so provocative. They're only funny if you can begin to stretch your way out of the box of "sexist assumptions" which we all carry around, and have for thousands of years. But let's get back the workplace.

*George*—Well, we've used an interview of mine to examine some of the workplace gender dynamics. It doesn't offer direct solutions, but helps us to look in some better places for our answers, e.g., in the role models men have for dealing with women, in the double binds women fall into, and in the demise of affection in the workplace.

*Bob*—To close this section we have an excellent piece from Barbara Ehrenreich, that I think re-establishes a common sense perspective on accepting and understanding gender differences, how gender does impact things, and yet can be used in a more constructive way.

# The Ultimate Cultural Difference—And How to Bridge It

by George F. Simons (*International Management Development Review*)

*Sushi in Paris, barbecue in Kyoto, couscous in Dallas. Today it can be hard to recognize where you are. Managers in multinational environments are challenged by the exotic and the foreign in numerous ways. Expertly versed in the styles, mannerisms, and personalities of other cultures, Dr. Simons detects "potential misunderstandings simmering" in many a manager's office.*

First there are national characteristics in the way people do business. While negotiating, the French have a predilection for seeking broad agreement about principles before attacking detail. The Americans across the table are frustrated as they seek to tie off one small item at a time in order to create a "deal." Both the French and the Americans, however, are likely to be deep in detailed discussion before their Japanese counterparts would be satisfied that the proper preliminaries had been celebrated. But what if the negotiation is between Morihara Sakamuru who got his MBA at Harvard, Frank Adams who grew up in Brussels, and Jean-Paul Martin who lives in Nairobi. Personal experience and gender differences may belie what we presume to be other people's cultural style.

Despite unprecedented numbers of women in the workplace, and their presence in the ranks of management, despite an international woman's movement and the proliferation of women's concerns in the media for decades, despite radical modernization in many societies, men and women in almost all situations are still:

- Talked to and talked about differently
- Touched and approached differently
- Dressed and dealt with through role assumptions and expectations that are significantly different.

Check your own experience. This disparate treatment is due to habit unconsciously learned and practiced. It is so deep-rooted that even insistent egalitarians, whose sons have dolls and whose daughters scrimmage at football, constantly treat boys and girls differently without even knowing it.

Everyone knows that women are more poorly paid, less frequently promoted, and are allowed less time to speak at meetings. Management studies have shown that they are given less useful feedback on their performance, assigned domestic duties in the workplace and so on. Yet, the public complaints and private distresses of women do not disappear when aired, legislated, and financed, because they are only symptoms of more deeply entrenched cultural and linguistic dynamics.

This article is not a campaign for changing sex roles or altering masculinity and femininity. It will end with *vive la difference*. To celebrate and profit from that difference, you must first explore why the sexes both understand and fail to understand each other from kindergarten to the boardroom.

## Different languages

Separate and unequal treatment that men and women experience throughout life, irrevocably divides them into two separate cultures with distinctive languages. These languages are always spoken in our minds, and are usually expressed verbally as well. The grammar and vocabulary of our spoken and written language reflect different thinking patterns and unequal levels of power and confidence in men and women. We are inclined to think of ourselves first as Dutch or British or Chinese and then as men and women, when in fact we are male and female first, then Greek or Brazilian or Japanese.

If you have never shuffled back to your office after encountering the opposite sex, shaken your head and muttered, "I don't think we speak the same language," you are an exception to the rule. You were, of course, right.

Though both of you communicate with the same language, what you intend to say and what you actually say can be worlds apart.

Male and female realities are different.[1] What we say and do, what we feel and want, what our work means to us, even in seemingly identical

---

[1] An excellent resource is *Male & Female Realities* by Joe Tanenbaum, available from 1-800-736-1293.

business matters, often throws us into conflict with one another. For example:

- In strategic planning he chooses a high-risk strategy, she a low-risk

- She thinks he does not tell her enough about the project; he does not tell her certain things because he does not think she needs to know

- She finds a piece of advertising copy insulting; he finds it humorous

- At meetings he finds her either too slow to participate or too stridently aggressive; she finds it impossible to speak and be heard, and feels constantly interrupted

- As the deadline approaches both find each other's emotional states irrational and a nuisance.

Employees receive cultural briefings on how to behave in Beijing or Riyadh, but is anyone briefed on the way to live and work with the other sex? Though we are prepared for assignments abroad at professional language institutes, we are not trained in man-talk or women-talk.

> *We prepare for assignments abroad at professional language institutes but we are not trained in man-talk or woman-talk.*

On the streets abroad, or in company boardrooms, we expect to find a different culture. Alien attitudes and behavior may annoy and unnerve us. At the outset we may have preconceptions of foreigners, but eventually, if we have any business sense at all, we learn to understand, accept and work in other cultures. We learn how others express themselves and their sense of time and courtesy. We begin to understand their customs and habits that may be alien to our culture. We also teach about ourselves, and simultaneously about who we are!

## Blaming the Other

This does not apply to the cultural and linguistic peculiarities created by gender. We assume that men and women from the same place should understand each other and behave as we expect them to behave. When they do not, we withdraw and blame them. "'Just like a woman!" or, "Stupid, insensitive man!" Anger, frustration and resentment become the currency between the sexes, instead of curiosity, creative exploration, fresh possibilities and realistic commitments.

Both researchers and lay people disagree about the differences between men and women. We cannot deny how biology affects us, but we struggle with the implications which culture has drawn from biology. Feminists not only demand social and economic change but also make it clear that a patriarchal culture alienates and oppresses both women and men. Some feminists see greater benefit for their own sex in denying or playing down differences between the sexes. To assume equality may be a better strategy than fighting for it. Some people believe that maintaining distinct sexual differences and playing at sexual politics gives them a tactical advantage. Some simply accept their privilege or plight automatically. Everyone plays the game in one way or another.

Frontiers between men and women are not identical in every culture. Women and men treat each other differently in different environments. Nor are gender differences consistent or predictable for all individuals. In a culture with a very high masculinity index a man may express very little machismo. Gender differences are not right or wrong, better or worse. Deny them and they only cause more of the misunderstanding and conflict.

What keeps gender issues from being seen and dealt with? Very few people try to calculate the cost that male-female conflict adds to business. Admitting that men and women may not understand each other nearly as well as we assume, opens a Pandora's box in both our business and personal lives.

Several simple insights and skills can make a great difference in how men and women understand each other and work together productively:

- Men and women together constitute a cross-cultural situation

- Neither is right or wrong, they simply have certain differences and speak different languages

- Every individual is unique within the context of his or her sexual and national, racial, and corporate culture

- Gender and personal differences are corporate assets that can make the enterprise more creative and productive if conflict is handled well.

We can take advantage of gender differences instead of condemning, denying, avoiding, or trying to change each other. To work and live together successfully, men and women must learn to be clear that expectations about each other are not commitments. An expectation is how we believe another person should think, feel or act. "She should know not to disturb me with such a trivial question," or, "He should acknowledge my contribution on this project." Either we do not communicate this inner demand to the other person, or, if we do, we fail to gain an agreeable response. We then begin to feel upset or blame the other person.

## Not Seeing Eye-to-Eye

To illustrate this point further: I expect my female associate or subordinate to behave according to standards which I believe are obvious. "I shouldn't need to tell her about it unless something goes wrong," I say to myself. She on the other hand, expects regular feedback from me and says to herself, "I shouldn't have to ask for it. Maybe he dislikes me or thinks I'm not competent: why is he so standoffish!" Both of us become annoyed because we feel that the other "should have known better."

Acknowledging that there is a difference between expectations and commitments helps us to spell out our expectations so that we can agree about what we should give and receive from one another. To do this, one must ask questions that encourage the other person to paint a full picture of what he or she understands and means to communicate to us. We frequently question the reason behind decisions and our curiosity is often understood as "I don't believe you," "Defend yourself," or "Show me your reasons and I will tell you why they are wrong." Questions which ask for opinions without appearing to attack the other person are:

- What does . . . mean to you?

- What do you say to yourself about. . . ?

- How do you picture the situation?

- What do you see as the pros and cons of . . . ?

There are many more questions that can be used to understand people who are different from ourselves. Since unspoken languages play a major role in how we communicate, body language and tone of voice must convey interest rather than aggression.

On the other hand, even if the other person does not ask such questions, we can respond as if they did, if we share fuller, more descriptive pictures of how we ourselves see, interpret and talk to ourselves about the issue at hand. We can voice our own opinions in such a way that we tell the listener that we are contributing our own experience and offering our ideas, rather than dictating opinions. For example:

- Here's how I see . . .

- Here's what happened to me that leads me to think . . .

- I imagine that if . . .

- Some of the constraints are . . .

It is important not to present one's opinions as the only valid representation of reality. When men start to speak for themselves this way, we reduce the linguistic power distance which separates us as men and women. By not assuming that our personal or gender viewpoints represent the absolute truth, we involve the points of view of others and gain a better picture. Combining our insights enables us to make clear agreements.

We have a native reluctance to request and promise things because we do not know what the future will bring, nor can we read the other person's mind. Each commitment puts us at risk to want what we ask for or to fulfill our pledge, and to know what steps to take if this becomes difficult or impossible. As we never understand one another perfectly, all requests and promises are in danger of being broken at some point. Instead of feeling upset when this occurs, question the person carefully, elicit reasonable answers and this will enable you to deal with the other person as well as your own feelings. You can then make a new commitment if needed.

## Coping Strategies

Understanding how to elicit information from each other, a use of clear language, the ability to apologize, gather information and start again when we fail, reduces the risk and lessens the reluctance to make commitments.

Will these methods take more time than our normal ways of dealing with each other? Yes. Can our business afford this time? Absolutely! If we subtract the time used in these methods from the time wasted in misunderstandings, avoidance, bickerings, false starts and "doing it wrong" the spreadsheet is in our favor.

## Bridging the Gap

Why all the fuss about men and women? Does it boil down to better communications? Yes and no—recognizing the cross-cultural nature of gender collaboration as an issue in its own right alerts us to the true nature of the inexplicable gaps and failures we encounter in our attempts to understand and work with people of whatever sex, corporation or nationality. *Vive la difference!* Learn the skills and attitudes to bridge gender differences and you will have mastered what it takes to communicate and negotiate with almost everyone.

## About the Author

Dr. George Simons specializes in training people to communicate, negotiate, and to manage cultural and gender diversity. He has consulted and conducted seminars in over 25 countries to clients such as Ahmdahl, Apple, Colgate, Digital Equipment, Mobil, Pepsico, Procter & Gamble, Shell, and Whirlpool. He is founder of GSI and a trainer associated with ODT, Inc.

# Management Women and the New Facts of Life

by Felice N. Schwartz (*Harvard Business Review*)

The cost of employing women in management is greater than the cost of employing men. This is a jarring statement, partly because it is true, but mostly because it is something people are reluctant to talk about. A new study by one multinational corporation shows that the rate of turnover in management positions is 2 1/2 times higher among top-performing women than it is among men. A large producer of consumer goods reports that one half of the women who take maternity leave return to their jobs late or not at all. And we know that women also have a greater tendency to plateau or to interrupt their careers in ways that limit their growth and development. But we have become so sensitive to charges of sexism and so afraid of confrontation, even litigation, that we rarely say what we know to be true. Unfortunately, our bottled-up awareness leaks out in misleading metaphors (''glass ceiling'' is one notable example), veiled hostility, lowered expectations, distrust, and reluctant adherence to Equal Employment Opportunity requirements.

> Two facts matter to business: only women have babies and only men make rules.

Career interruptions, plateauing, and turnover are expensive. The money corporations invest in recruitment, training, and development is less likely to produce top executives among women than among men, and the invaluable company experience that developing executives acquire at every level as they move up through management ranks is more often lost.

The studies just mentioned are only the first of many, I'm quite sure. Demographic realities are going to force corporations all across the country to analyze the cost of employing women in managerial positions, and what they will discover is that women cost more.

But here is another startling truth: The greater cost of employing women is not a function of inescapable gender differences. Women *are* different from men, but what increases their cost to the corporation is principally the clash of their perceptions, attitudes, and behavior with those of men, which is to say, with the policies and practices of male-led corporations.

It is terribly important that employers draw the right conclusions from the studies now being done. The studies will be useless—or worse, harmful—if all they teach us is that women are expensive to employ. What we need to learn is how to reduce that expense, how to stop throwing away the investments we make in talented women, how to become more responsive to the needs of the women that corporations *must* employ if they are to have the best and the brightest of all those now entering the work force.

The gender differences relevant to business fall into two categories: Those related to maternity and those related to the differing traditions and expectations of the sexes. Maternity is biological rather than cultural. We can't alter it, but we can dramatically reduce its impact on the workplace and in many cases eliminate its negative effect on employee development. We can accomplish this by addressing the second set of differences, those between male and female socialization. Today, these differences exaggerate the real costs of maternity and can turn a relatively slight disruption in work schedule into a serious business problem and a career derailment for individual women. If we are to overcome the cost differential between male and female employees, we need to address the issues that arise when female socialization meets the male corporate culture and masculine rules of career development issues of behavior and style, of expectation, of stereotypes and preconceptions, of sexual tension and harassment, of female mentoring, lateral mobility, relocation, compensation, and early identification of top performers.

The one immutable, enduring difference between men and women is maternity. Maternity is not simply childbirth but a continuum that begins with an awareness of the ticking of the biological clock, proceeds to the anticipation of motherhood, includes pregnancy, childbirth, physical recuperation, psychological adjustment, and continues on to nursing, bonding, and child rearing. Not all women choose to become mothers, of course, and among those who do, the process varies from case to case depending on the health of the mother and baby, the values of the parents, and the availability, cost, and quality of child care.

> *Women who compete like men are considered unfeminine. Women who emphasize family are considered uncommitted.*

In past centuries, the biological fact of maternity shaped the traditional roles of the sexes. Women performed the home-centered functions that related to the bearing and nurturing of children. Men did the work that required great physical strength. Over time, however, family size contracted, the community assumed greater responsibility for the care and education of children, packaged foods and household technology reduced the work load in the home, and technology eliminated much of the need for muscle power at the workplace. Today, in the developed world, the only role still uniquely gender related is childbearing. Yet men and women are still socialized to perform their traditional roles.

Men and women may or may not have some innate psychological disposition toward these traditional roles—men to be aggressive, competitive, self-reliant, risk taking; women to be supportive, nurturing, intuitive, sensitive, communicative—but certainly both men and women are capable of the full range of behavior. Indeed, the male and female roles have already begun to expand and merge. In the decades ahead, as the socialization of boys and girls and the experience and expectations of young men and women grow steadily more androgynous, the differences in workplace behavior will continue to fade. At the moment, however, we are still plagued by disparities in perception and behavior that make the integration of men and women in the workplace unnecessarily difficult and expensive.

Let me illustrate with a few broadbrush generalizations. Of course, these are only stereotypes, but I think they help to exemplify the kinds of preconceptions that can muddy the corporate waters.

Men continue to perceive women as the rearers of their children so they find it understandable, indeed appropriate, that women should renounce their careers to raise families. Edmund Pratt, CEO of Pfizer, once asked me in all sincerity, "Why would any woman choose to be a chief financial officer rather than a full-time mother?" By condoning and taking pleasure in women's traditional behavior, men reinforce it. Not only do they see parenting as fundamentally female, they see a career as fundamentally male—either an unbroken series of promotions and advancements toward CEOdom or stagnation and disappointment. This attitude serves to legitimize a woman's choice to extend maternity leave and even, for those who can afford it, to leave employment altogether for several years. By the same token, men who might want to take a leave after the birth of a child know that management will see such behavior as a lack of career commitment, even when company policy permits parental leave for men.

Women also bring counterproductive expectations and perceptions to the workplace. Ironically, although the feminist movement was an expression of women's quest for freedom from their home based lives, most women were remarkably free already. They had many responsibilities, but they were autonomous and could be entrepreneurial in how and when they carried them out. And once their children grew up and left home, they were essentially free to do what they wanted with their lives. Women's traditional role also included freedom from responsibility for the financial support of their families. Many of us were socialized from girlhood to expect our husbands to take care of us, while our brothers were socialized from an equally early age to complete their educations, pursue careers, climb the ladder of success, and provide dependable financial support for their families. To the extent that this tradition of freedom lingers subliminally, women tend to bring to their employment a sense that they can choose to change jobs or careers at will, take time off, or reduce their hours.

Finally, women's traditional role encouraged particular attention to the quality and substance of what they did, specifically to the physical, psychological, and intellectual development of their children. This traditional focus may explain women's continuing tendency to search for more than monetary reward—intrinsic significance, social importance, meaning—in what they do. This too makes them more likely than men to leave the corporation in search of other values.

The misleading metaphor of the glass ceiling suggests an invisible barrier constructed by corporate leaders to impede the upward mobility of women beyond the middle levels. A more appropriate metaphor, I believe, is the kind of cross-sectional diagram used in geology. The barriers to women's leadership occur when potentially counterproductive layers of influence on women—maternity, tradition, socialization—meet management strata pervaded by the largely unconscious preconceptions, stereotypes, and expectations of men. Such interfaces do not exist for men and tend to be impermeable for women.

One result of these gender differences has been to convince some executives that women are simply not suited to top management. Other executives feel helpless. If they see even a few of their valued female employees fail to return to work from maternity leave on schedule or see one of their most promising women plateau in her career after the birth of a child, they begin to fear there is nothing they can do to infuse women with new energy and enthusiasm and persuade them to stay. At the same time, they know there is nothing they can do to stem the tide of women into management ranks.

Another result is to place every working woman on a continuum that runs from total dedication to career at one end to a balance between career and family at the other. What women discover is that the male corporate culture sees both extremes as unacceptable. Women who want the flexibility to balance their families and their careers are not adequately committed to the organization. Women who perform as aggressively and competi-

> *It is absurd to put a woman down for having the very qualities that would send a man to the top.*

tively as men are abrasive and unfeminine. But the fact is, business needs all the talented women it can get. Moreover, as I will explain, the women I call career-primary and those I call career-and-family each have particular value to the corporation.

Women in the corporation are about to move from a buyer's to a seller's market. The sudden, startling recognition that 80% of new entrants in the work force over the next decade will be women, minorities, and immigrants has stimulated a mushrooming incentive to "value diversity."

Women are no longer simply an enticing pool of occasional creative talent, a thorn in the side of the EEO officer, or a source of frustration to corporate leaders truly puzzled by the slowness of their upward trickle into executive positions. A real demographic change is taking place. The era of sudden population growth of the 1950s and 1960s is over. The birth rate has dropped about 40%, from a high of 25.3 live births per 1,000 population in 1957, at the peak of the baby boom, to a stable low of a little more than 15 per 1,000 over the last 16 years, and there is no indication of a return to a higher rate. The tidal wave of baby boomers that swelled the recruitment pool to overflowing seems to have been a one-time phenomenon. For 20 years, employers had the pick of a very large crop and were able to choose males almost exclusively for the executive track. But if future population remains fairly stable while the economy continues to expand, and if the new information society simultaneously creates a greater need for creative, educated managers, then the gap between supply and demand will grow dramatically and, with it, the competition for managerial talent.

The decrease in numbers has even greater implications if we look at the traditional source of corporate recruitment for leadership positions—white males from the top 10% of the country's best universities. Over the past decade, the increase in the number of women graduating from leading universities has been much greater than the increase in the total number of graduates, and these women are well represented in the top 10% of their classes.

The trend extends into business and professional programs as well. In the old days, virtually all MBAs were male. I remember addressing a meeting at the Harvard Business School as recently as the mid–1970s and looking out at a sea of exclusively male faces. Today about 25% of that audience would be women. The pool of male MBAs from which corporations have traditionally drawn their leaders has shrunk significantly.

Of course, this reduction does not have to mean a shortage of talent. The top 10% is at least as smart as it always was—smarter, probably, since it's now drawn from a broader segment of the population. But it now consists increasingly of women. Companies that are determined to recruit the same number of men as before will have to dig much deeper into the male pool, while their competitors will have the opportunity to pick the best people from both the male and female graduates.

Under these circumstances, there is no question that the management ranks of business will include increasing numbers of women. There remains, however, the question of how these women will succeed—how long they will stay, how high they will climb, how completely they will fulfill their promise and potential, and what kind of return the corporation will realize on its investment in their training and development.

There is, ample business reason for finding ways to make sure that as many of these women as possible will succeed. The first step in this process is to recognize that women are not all alike. Like men, they are individuals with differing talents, priorities, and motivations. For the sake of simplicity, let me focus on the two women I referred to earlier: what I call the career-primary woman and the career-and-family woman.

Like many men, some women put their careers first. They are ready to make the same trade-offs traditionally made by the men who seek leadership positions. They make a career decision to put in extra hours, to make sacrifices in their personal lives, to make the most of every opportunity for professional development. For women, of course, this decision also requires that they remain single or at least childless or, if they do have children, that they be satisfied to have others raise them. Some 90% of executive men but only 35% of executive women have children by the age of 40. The automatic association of all women with babies is clearly unjustified.

The secret to dealing with such women is to recognize them early, accept them, and clear artificial barriers from their path to the top. After all, the best of these women are among the best managerial talent you will ever see. And career-primary women have another important value to the company that men and other women lack. They can act as role models and mentors to younger women who put their careers first. Since upwardly mobile career-primary women still have few role models to motivate and inspire them, a company with women in its top echelon has a significant advantage in the competition for executive talent.

Men at the top of the organization—most of them over 55, with wives who tend to be traditional—often find career women "masculine" and difficult to accept as colleagues. Such men miss the point, which is not that these women are just like men but that they are just like the best men in the organization. And there is such a shortage of the best people that gender cannot be allowed to matter. It is clearly counterproductive to disparage in a woman with executive talent the very qualities that are most critical to the business and that might carry a man to the CEO's office.

Clearing a path to the top for career-primary women has four requirements:

1.  Identify them early.

2.  Give them the same opportunity you give to talented men to grow and develop and contribute to company profitability. Give them client and customer responsibility. Expect them to travel and relocate, to make the same commitment to the company as men aspiring to leadership positions.

3.  Accept them as valued members of your management team. Include them in every kind of communication. Listen to them.

4.  Recognize that the business environment is more difficult and stressful for them than for their male peers. They are always a minority, often the only woman. The male perception of talented, ambitious women is at best ambivalent, a mixture of admiration, resentment, confusion, competitiveness, attraction, skepticism, anxiety, pride, and animosity. Women can never feel secure about how they should dress and act, whether they should speak out or grin and bear it when they encounter dis-

crimination, stereotyping, sexual harassment, and paternalism. Social interaction and travel with male colleagues and with male clients can be charged. As they move up, the normal increase in pressure and responsibility is compounded for women because they are women.

Stereotypical language and sexist day-to-day behavior do take their toll on women's career development. Few male executives realize how common it is to call women by their first names while men in the same group are greeted with surnames, how frequently female executives are assumed by men to be secretaries, how often women are excluded from all-male social events where business is being transacted. With notable exceptions, men are still generally more comfortable with other men, and as a result women miss many of the career and business opportunities that arise over lunch, on the golf course, or in the locker room.

The majority of women, however, are what I call career-and-family women, women who want to pursue serious careers while participating actively in the rearing of children. These women are a precious resource that has yet to be mined. Many of them are talented and creative. Most of them are

> A policy that forces women to choose between family and career cuts hugely into profits and competitive advantage.

willing to trade some career growth and compensation for freedom from the constant pressure to work long hours and weekends.

Most companies today are ambivalent at best about the career-and-family women in their management ranks. They would prefer that all employees were willing to give their all to the company. They believe it is in their best interests for all managers to compete for the top positions so the company will have the largest possible pool from which to draw its leaders.

"If you have both talent and motivation," many employers seem to say, "we want to move you up. If you haven't got that motivation, if you want less pressure and greater flexibility, then you can leave and make room for a new generation." These companies lose on two counts. First, they

fail to amortize the investment they made in the early training and experience of management women who find themselves committed to family as well as to career. Second, they fail to recognize what these women could do for their middle management.

The ranks of middle managers are filled with people on their way up and people who have stalled. Many of them have simply reached their limits, achieved career growth commensurate with or exceeding their capabilities, and they cause problems because their performance is mediocre but they still want to move ahead. The career-and-family woman is willing to trade off the pressures and demands that go with promotion for the freedom to spend more time with her children. She's very smart, she's talented, she's committed to her career, and she's satisfied to stay at the middle level, at least during the early child-rearing years. Compare her with some of the people you have there now.

Consider a typical example, a woman who decides in college on a business career and enters management at age 22. For nine years, the company invests in her career as she gains experience and skills and steadily improves her performance. But at 31, just as the investment begins to pay off in earnest, she decides to have a baby. Can the company afford to let her go home, take another job, or go into business for herself? The common perception now is yes, the corporation can afford to lose her unless, after six or eight weeks or even three months of disability and maternity leave, she returns to work on a full-time schedule with the same vigor, commitment, and ambition that she showed before.

But what if she doesn't? What if she wants or needs to go on leave for six months or a year or, heaven forbid, five years? In this worst-case scenario, she works full-time from age 22 to 31 and from 36 to 65, a total of 38 years as opposed to the typical male's 43 years. That's not a huge difference. Moreover, my typical example is willing to work part-time while her children are young, if only her employer will give her the opportunity. There are two rewards for companies responsive to this need: higher retention of their best people and greatly improved performance and satisfaction in their middle management.

The high-performing career-and-family woman can be a major player in your company. She can give you a significant business advantage as the competition for able people escalates. Sometimes too, if you can hold on to her, she will switch gears in mid-life and reenter the competition for the top. The price you must pay to retain these women is threefold: you must plan for and manage maternity, you must provide the flexibility that will allow them to be maximally productive, and you must take an active role in helping to make family supports and high-quality, affordable child care available to all women.

The key to managing maternity is to recognize the value of high-performing women and the urgent need to retain them and keep them productive. The first step must be a genuine partnership between the woman and her boss. I know this partnership can seem difficult to forge. One of my own senior executives came to me recently to discuss plans for her maternity leave and subsequent return to work. She knew she wanted to come back. I wanted to make certain that she would. Still, we had a somewhat awkward conversation, because I knew that no woman can predict with certainty when she will be able to return to work or under what conditions. Physical problems can lengthen her leave. So can a demanding infant, a difficult family or personal adjustment, or problems with child care.

I still don't know when this valuable executive will be back on the job full-time, and her absence creates some genuine problems for our organization. But I do know that I can't simply replace her years of experience with a new recruit. Since our conversation, I also know that she wants to come back, and that she *will* come back part-time at first unless I make it impossible for her by, for example, setting an arbitrary date for her full-time return or resignation. In turn, she knows that the organization wants and needs her and, more to the point, that it will be responsive to her needs in terms of working hours and child-care arrangements.

In having this kind of conversation it's important to ask concrete questions that will help to move the discussion from uncertainty and anxiety to some level of predictability. Questions can touch on everything from family income and energy level to child care arrangements and career commitment. Of course you want your star manager to return to work as soon as possible, but you want her to return permanently and productively. Her

downtime on the job is a drain on her energies and a waste of your money.

For all the women who want to combine career and family—the women who want to participate actively in the rearing of their children and who also want to pursue their careers seriously—the key to retention is to provide the flexibility and family supports they need in order to function effectively.

Time spent in the office increases productivity if it is time well spent, but the fact that most women continue to take the primary responsibility for child care is a cause of distraction, diversion, anxiety, and absenteeism—to say nothing of the persistent guilt experienced by all working mothers. A great many women, perhaps most of all women who have always performed at the highest levels, are also frustrated by a sense that while their children are babies they cannot function at their best either at home or at work.

In its simplest form, flexibility is the freedom to take time off—a couple of hours, a day, a week—or to do some work at home and some at the office, an arrangement that communication technology makes increasingly feasible. At the complex end of the spectrum are alternative work schedules that permit the woman to work less than full-time and her employer to reap the benefits of her experience and, with careful planning, the top level of her abilities.

Part-time employment is the single greatest inducement to getting women back on the job expeditiously and the provision women themselves most desire. A part-time return to work enables them to maintain responsibility for critical aspects of their jobs, keeps them in touch with the changes constantly occurring at the workplace and in the job itself, reduces stress and fatigue, often eliminates the need for paid maternity leave by permitting a return to the office as soon as disability leave is over, and, not least, can greatly enhance company loyalty. The part-time solution works particularly well when a work load can be reduced for one individual in a department or when a full-time job can be broken down by skill levels and apportioned to two individuals at different levels of skill and pay.

I believe, however, that shared employment is the most promising and will be the most widespread form of flexible scheduling in the future. It is feasible at every level of the corporation except at the pinnacle, for both the short and the long term. It involves two people taking responsibility for one job.

Two red lights flash on as soon as most executives hear the words "job sharing": continuity and client-customer contact. The answer to the continuity question is to place responsibility entirely on the two individuals sharing the job to discuss everything that transpires—thoroughly, daily, and on their own time. The answer to the problem of client-customer contact is yes, job sharing requires reeducation and a period of adjustment. But as both client and supervisor will quickly come to appreciate, two contacts means that the customer has continuous access to the company's representative, without interruptions for vacation, travel, or sick leave. The two people holding the job can simply cover for each other, and the uninterrupted, full-time coverage they provide together can be a stipulation of their arrangement.

Flexibility is costly in numerous ways. It requires more supervisory time to coordinate and manage, more office space, and somewhat greater benefits costs (though these can be contained with flexible benefits plans, prorated benefits, and, in two-paycheck families, elimination of duplicate benefits). But the advantages of reduced turnover and the greater productivity that results from higher energy levels and greater focus can outweigh the costs.

A few hints:

- Provide flexibility selectively. I'm not suggesting private arrangements subject to the suspicion of favoritism but rather a policy that makes flexible work schedules available only to high performers.

- Make it clear that in most instances (but not all) the rates of advancement and pay will be appropriately lower for those who take time off or who work part-time than for those who work full-time. Most career-and-family women are entirely willing to make that trade-off.

- Discuss costs as well as benefits. Be willing to risk accusations of bias. Insist, for example, that half time is half of whatever time it takes to do the job, not merely half of 35 or 40 hours.

The woman who is eager to get home to her child has a powerful incentive to use her time effectively at the office and to carry with her reading and other work that can be done at home. The talented professional who wants to have it all can be a high performer by carefully ordering her priorities and by focusing on objectives rather than on the legendary 15-hour day. By the time professional women have their first babies—at an average age of 31—they have already had nine years to work long hours at a desk, to travel, and to relocate. In the case of high performers, the need for flexibility coincides with what has gradually become the goal-oriented nature of responsibility.

Family supports—in addition to maternity leave and flexibility—include the provision of parental leave for men, support for two-career and single-parent families during relocation, and flexible benefits. But the primary ingredient is child care. The capacity of working mothers to function effectively and without interruption depends on the availability of good, affordable child care. Now that women make up almost half the work force and the growing percentage of managers, the decision to become involved in the personal lives of employees is no longer a philosophical question but a practical one. To make matters worse, the quality of child care has almost no relation to

> *Incredibly, very few companies have ever studied the costs and statistics of maternity leave.*

technology, inventiveness, or profitability but is more or less a pure function of the quality of child care personnel and the ratio of adults to children. These costs are irreducible. Only by joining hands with government and the public sector can corporations hope to create the vast quantity and variety of child care that their employees need.

Until quite recently, the response of corporations to women has been largely symbolic and cosmetic, motivated in large part by the will to avoid litigation and legal penalties. In some cases, companies were also moved by a genuine sense of fairness and a vague discomfort and frustration at the absence of women above the middle of the corporate pyramid. The actions they took were mostly quick, easy, and highly visible child care information services, a three-month parental leave available to men as well as women, a woman appointed to the board of directors.

When I first began to discuss these issues 26 years ago, I was sometimes able to get an appointment with the assistant to the assistant in personnel, but it was only a courtesy. Over the past decade, I have met with the CEOs of many large corporations, and I've watched them become involved with ideas they had never previously thought much about. Until recently, however, the shelf life of that enhanced awareness was always short. Given pressing, short-term concerns, women were not a front-burner issue. In the past few months, I have seen yet another change. Some CEOs and top management groups now take the initiative. They call and ask us to show them how to shift gears from a responsive to a proactive approach to recruiting, developing, and retaining women.

I think this change is more probably a response to business needs—to concern for the quality of future profits and managerial talent—than to uneasiness about legal requirements, sympathy with the demands of women and minorities, or the desire to do what is right and fair. The nature of such business motivation varies. Some companies want to move women to higher positions as role models for those below them and as beacons for talented young recruits. Some want to achieve a favorable image with employees, customers, clients, and stockholders. These are all legitimate motives. But I think the companies that stand to gain most are motivated as well by a desire to capture competitive advantage in an era when talent and competence will be in increasingly short supply. These companies are now ready to stop being defensive about their experience with women and to ask incisive questions without preconceptions.

Even so, incredibly, I don't know of more than one or two companies that have looked into their own records to study the absolutely critical issue of maternity leave—how many women took it, when and whether they returned, and how this behavior correlated with their rank, tenure, age, and performance. The unique drawback to the employment of women is the physical reality of maternity and the particular socializing influence maternity has had. Yet to make women equal to men in the workplace we have chosen on the whole not to discuss this single most significant difference between them. Unless we do, we cannot evaluate the cost of recruiting, developing, and moving women up.

Now that interest is replacing indifference, there are four steps every company can take to examine its own experience with women:

1. Gather quantitative data on the company's experience with management-level women regarding turnover rates, occurrence of and return from maternity leave, and organizational level attained in relation to tenure and performance.

2. Correlate this data with factors such as age, marital status, and presence and age of children, and attempt to identify and analyze why women respond the way they do.

3. Gather qualitative data on the experience of women in your company and on how women are perceived by both sexes.

4. Conduct a cost-benefit analysis of the return on your investment in high-performing women. Factor in the cost to the company of women's negative reactions to negative experience, as well as the probable cost of corrective measures and policies. If women's value to your company is greater than the cost to recruit, train, and develop them—and of course I believe it will be—then you will want to do everything you can to retain them.

We have come a tremendous distance since the days when the prevailing male wisdom saw women as lacking the kind of intelligence that would allow them to succeed in business. For decades, even women themselves have harbored an unspoken belief that they couldn't make it because they couldn't be just like men, and nothing else would do. But now that women have shown themselves the equal of men in every area of organizational activity, now that they have demonstrated that they can be stars in every field of endeavor, now we can all venture to examine the fact that women and men are different.

On balance, employing women is more costly than employing men. Women can acknowledge this fact today because they know that their value to employers exceeds the additional cost and because they know that changing attitudes can reduce the additional cost dramatically. Women in management are no longer an idiosyncrasy of the arts and education. They have always matched men in natural ability. Within a very few years, they will equal men in numbers as well in every area of economic activity.

The demographic motivation to recruit and develop women is compelling. But an older question remains: Is society better for the change? Women's exit from the home and entry into the work force has certainly created problems—an urgent need for good, affordable child care; troubling questions about the kind of parenting children need; the costs and difficulties of diversity in the workplace; the stress and fatigue of combining work and family responsibilities. Wouldn't we all be happier if we could turn back the clock to an age when men were in the workplace and women in the home, when male and female roles were clearly differentiated and complementary?

Nostalgia, anxiety, and discouragement will urge many to say yes, but my answer is emphatically no. Two fundamental benefits that were un-

attainable in the past are now within our reach. For the individual, freedom of choice—in this case the freedom to choose career, family, or a combination of the two. For the corporation, access to the most gifted individuals in the country. These benefits are neither self-indulgent nor insubstantial. Freedom of choice and self-realization are too deeply American to be cast aside for some wistful vision of the past. And access to our most talented human resources is not a luxury in this age of explosive international competition but rather the barest minimum that prudence and national self-preservation require.

## About the Author

Felice Schwartz is president and founder of Catalyst, a not-for-profit research and advisory organization that works with corporations to foster the career and leadership development of women.

---

*"I've been conducting a study with my partner and husband, the social psychologist and futurist David Loye, of a statistical analysis of data from 89 countries, which confirms my hypothesis that the way a society structures the relations between the female and male halves of humanity is of central social, political, and economic importance. The study shows that in many contexts gender equity or inequity is as good a predictor of quality of life as gross domestic product—and in some cases better."*

Riane Eisler
Author of international bestseller,
*The Chalice and the Blade: Our History, Our Future*

# Gray Matters

by Sharon Begley, with Andrew Murr and Adam Rogers (*Newsweek*)

Of course men and women are different. *Boy*, are they different. In every sphere of life, it seems, the sexes act, react or perform differently. Toys? A little girl daintily sets up her dolls, plastic cups and saucers, while her brother assembles his Legos into a gun—and ambushes the tea party. Navigating? The female tourist turns her map every which way but right, trying to find the way back to that charming bistro, while her boyfriend charges ahead, remembering every tricky turn without fail. Relationships? With spooky intuition, women's acute senses pick up subtle tones of voice and facial expressions; men are insensitive clods who can't tell a sad face until it drenches them in tears. Cognition? Females excel at language, like finding just the right words to make their husbands feel like worms; males can't verbalize even one good excuse for stumbling home at 2 a.m.

Stereotypes? Maybe—but as generalizations they have a large enough kernel of truth that scientists, like everyone else, suspect there's *something* going on here. As Simon LeVay, the Salk Institute neuroscientist who in 1991 discovered structural differences between the brains of gay and straight men, put it recently, "There are differences in the mental lives of men and women."

The mind, of course, is just what the brain does for a living. So if LeVay is right, those mental differences must arise from differences in that gelatinous three-pound blob. For a decade neuroscientists have been discovering evidence of differences. Although the findings are tentative and ambiguous, at the end of the day, relaxing over beers at a neuroscience conclave, most specialists agree that women's and men's brains differ slightly in structure. But the studies have been frustratingly silent on whether the anatomical differences in their brains make men and women think differently. But now—drumroll, please— thanks to an array of new imaging machines that are revolutionizing neuroscience, researchers are beginning to glimpse differences in how men's and women's brains actually function.

With new technologies like functional magnetic resonance imaging (FMRI) and positron emission tomography (PET), researchers catch brains in the very act of cogitating, feeling or remembering. Already this year researchers have reported that men and women use different clumps of neurons when they take a first step toward reading and when their brains are "idling." And, coming soon to a research journal near you, provocative studies will report that women engage more of their brains than men when they think sad thoughts—but, possibly, less of their brains when they solve SAT math problems. "Now that we actually have functional brain data, we're getting lots of new insights," says Richard Haier, professor of pediatrics and neurology at the University of California, Irvine, and leader of the SAT study. "Even at this early point we have data to support the idea that men and women in general have brains that work differently." The latest studies:

**Make Your Mind a Blank:** To compare male and female brains at work, subjects were instructed to think of . . . nothing. In January scientists led by Ruben Gur of the University of Pennsylvania reported a PET study of 37 men and 24 women, mostly recruited by ads in local papers. Each volunteer got an injection of radioactive glucose. Glucose is brain food; active regions of the brain use more glucose than quiescent areas and so emit radioactivity, which PET detects. For 30 minutes a volunteer lay in a quiet, dimly lit room with eyes open and head in a tunnel with detectors embedded in the walls. Each volunteer was told to relax, without "exerting mental effort"—while PET read his or her mind.

In men's idling brains, the action was in the temporal-limbic system. This primitive region controls highly unsubtle expressions of emotion, such as fighting. It is often dubbed the "reptilian" brain. In most of the women's supposedly idling brains, the neurons were buzzing in the posterior cingulate gyrus, an evolutionarily newer addition to mammals' brains. Not even the researchers are sure what all of this shows. For one thing, 13 men and four women showed activity more like the other sex's. But the real problem is that "thinking of nothing" is nearly impossible. Volunteer (and co-researcher) Lyn Mozley admits that "some of the time I was probably thinking, 'When is this going to be over?'" What the PET scans may actually be showing is that, when told to think of nothing, men fixate on sex and football, while women weave together strings of words. But if, in men, the pilot light is always on in neurons that control aggression and action, it may explain why they're more violence-prone than women.

**I say tomahto . . . .** Last month researchers announced that men and women use different parts of their brains to figure out rhymes. Sally Shaywitz, her husband, Bennett Shaywitz, and colleagues at Yale University weren't looking for the brain's poetry center; rather, sounding out is the first step in reading, so rhyming was meant as a proxy for that skill. The 19 men and 19 women volunteers had to determine whether pairs of nonsense words (lete and jete, loke and jote), when flashed on a screen, rhymed. A volunteer lay in an FMRI machine, which is a four-foot-long tube containing a detector that pinpoints active brain regions.

In all 19 men, one region in the left inferior frontal gyrus (that's behind the left eyebrow) lit up like Las Vegas. So far, so good: for more than a century scientists have known that the left brain controls language. But in 11 of the 19 women, that area plus one behind the right eyebrow lit up. The right side of the brain is the seat of emotion. Perhaps women are more felicitous with language because they draw on feelings (right brain) as well as reason (left brain) when they use words. The Yale team made one more intriguing find. In eight of the women—42 percent—the brain worked like the men's. "That some of the women's brains looked like the men's is true of all these sex studies," says neuropsychologist Melissa Hines of UCLA. "Girls play with boys' toys more than boys play with girls', for instance. Males for whatever reason are more exclusively channeled into one way of behaving"—and, possibly, thinking.

**Let X be an integer . . . :** At Irvine, Haier PET-scanned 22 male and 22 female student volunteers while they did SAT math problems. Half the men and half the women had SAT math scores above 700, the other half scored 540 or so. Accord-

ing to his unpublished results, which he previewed at a science meeting last summer, in gifted men the temporal lobes were on overdrive compared with the average men. (The temporal lobes are behind the ears.) Ability seemed to correlate with effort. But in the 700-club women, the temporal lobes showed little activity, and there was a hint that the women didn't use their brain any more intensely than the average women. "There was a suggestion that women who did better [in math] might be using their brain more efficiently than women who did average," says Haier. "The men and women performed equally well. They just seemed to use the brain differently to do it." "Different," in other words, does not mean "better."

**No hard feelings:** Last year Penn's Ruben Gur and his wife, neuroscientist Raquel Gur, enlisted PET in the aid of an old stereotype: that men can't read emotions on people's faces. (The pair got into the field of sex differences when they were struck by their own temperamental differences. He is more intrigued by numbers and details, she likes to work with people; he reacts to a setback by taking a deep breath and moving on, she analyzes it.) They and their colleagues asked volunteers to judge whether male and female faces showed happiness or sadness. Both sexes were almost infallible at recognizing happiness. But sadness was a different story. Women picked out a sad face 90 percent of the time, on men and women, but men had more trouble. They recognized sadness on men's faces 90 percent of the time—that is, they did as well as the women—but were right only 70 percent of the time when judging sadness on women's faces.

Well, of course. Evolutionarily speaking, it makes sense that a man would have to be hypervigilant about men's faces; otherwise he would miss the first hint that another guy is going to punch him. Being oblivious to a woman's emotions won't get him much worse than a night on the sofa. The Gurs may even have stumbled on why women can't understand why men find it so hard to be sensitive to emotions. According to the PET scans, women's brains didn't have to work as hard to excel at judging emotion. Women's limbic system, the part of the brain that controls emotion, was less active than the limbic system of men doing worse. That is, the men's brains were working overtime to figure out the faces. But the extra effort didn't do them much good.

**Sad, so sad:** The little boy in black standing at his father's funeral, the happily married woman hearing her husband demand a divorce . . . 10 women and 10 men called up these and other sad memories while psychiatrist Mark George of the National Institute of Mental Health and colleagues PET-scanned them. In both sexes, the front of the limbic system glowed with activity. But in women, the active area was eight times as big as it was in the men. That difference in intensity might explain why women are twice as likely as men to suffer major depression, say the scientists. In depression, the limbic system is unresponsive and almost lethargic; "perhaps hyperactivity during normal bouts of sadness" made these circuits unresponsive, George speculates.

The brain-imaging studies are the latest, and the highest-tech, periscope into sex differences in the brain. Yet no matter how "scientific" it gets, this research serves as ammunition in society's endless gender wars. When Raquel Gur gave a talk to M.D.-Ph.D. students in Illinois about sex differences in brains, a group of women asked her to stop publicizing the work: they were afraid women would lose 20 years of gains if word got out that the sexes aren't the same. They had good reason to worry. Among the choicer passages from recent pop-science books: Male brains "are not so easily distracted by superfluous information." "A woman may be less able to separate emotion from reason." And "the male brain is a tidier affair," as Anne Moir and David Jessel write in their 1991 book "Brain Sex." The subject of sex differences in the brain attracts almost as much inflammatory rhetoric as the "science" of racial differences in IQ.

Even before scientists caught images of the brain thinking or emoting, there were hints that men's brains and women's differed. As long ago as 1880, English surgeon James Crichton-Browne reported slight differences in the brain anatomy of men and women—a slightly larger [bundle] of neurons *here* in one sex, and *there* in the other. But by far the most frequent finding through the years has been that the [group] of nerve cells through which the left side of the brain talks and listens to the right—it's called the corpus callosum—is larger in women than in men. In perhaps the best study of this kind, in 1991 UCLA neuroendocrinologists Roger Gorski and Laura Allen examined 146 brains from cadavers and found that the back part of women's callosum is up to 23 percent bigger than men's.

This brought neuroscientists as close as they ever get to jumping up and down in public. It fit their cherished idea that, in male brains, the right and the left side barely know what the other is doing, while in women there's practically nonstop left-right neural chitchat. If women's brains are paragons of holism, while men's are a house divided, it could explain findings both serious and curious. Women's language ability better survives a left-brain stroke—perhaps because they tap the language capacity of the right brain. Women tend to have better language skills—perhaps because the emotional right brain enriches their left-brain vocabulary. And women have better intuition—perhaps because they are in touch with the left brain's rationality and the right's emotions simultaneously.

There is just one problem with these tidy explanations. A bigger corpus callosum matters only if it has more neurons, the cells that carry communications. After all, fat phone cables carry more conversations only if they contain more wires. But despite years of searching, scientists cannot say for sure that women's corpus callosum has more neurons.

The quest for other anatomical differences has been only a little more successful. In rats, biologists have found 15 regions that differ in size between males and females. Finding such differences in humans has been much tougher. But in November, at the annual meeting of the Society for Neuroscience, Sandra Witelson of McMaster University in Ontario reported results from a study of nine autopsied brains. (She gets them from people with terminal cancer who bequeath their brains to science.) Women, despite having smaller brains (on average) than men because their whole bodies are smaller, have more neurons. The extra 11 percent are all crammed into two layers of the cerebral cortex whose job is to understand language and recognize melodies and tone of voice.

Neuroscientists know of only one force that can prune and stimulate, kill and nourish the brain's [bundles] of neurons: sex hormones. Before birth, a fetus's brain is bathed in sex hormones—different ones, in different amounts, depending on whether the fetus is male or female. Ethics prevents scientists from experimenting to see how a fetus's brain would change if its hormone exposure changed. But nature has no such compunctions. Girls with a rare birth defect called CAH, which made them churn out high levels of the male hormone testosterone as fetuses, score better than the average female on spatial tests. (The extra testosterone exposure also masculinizes their genitals.) As girls, they prefer cars and trucks and other toys that boys usually grab. Other girls were exposed to male-like levels of testosterone before birth when their mothers took the hormone DES to prevent miscarriages. As children, the DES girls did better than their normal sisters on rotating a figure in space and other tasks at which boys outdo girls. Finally, boys with a syndrome that makes them insensitive to testosterone are better at language than their unaffected brothers. But they are less adept at spatial tasks—the typical female intellectual pattern. Hormonal effects, wrote psychologist Doreen Kimura of the University of Western Ontario in 1992, "appear to extend to all known behaviors in which males and females differ . . . [such as] problem solving, aggression and the tendency to engage in rough-and-tumble play."

Are these hormonal effects present at birth, or do they result from how a child is raised? The feminized boys (whose cognitive abilities resemble women's) and the CAH girls (minds like boys) are not physically normal. Their parents know they are different, and likely treat them differently from their sisters and brothers. Perhaps even more crucial, the hormonally abnormal girls might identify, psychologically, not with girls but with boys, aping their behavior and preferences. Similarly, the feminized boys might identify with girls. So if the girls play like tomboys and do better in math than normal girls, and the boys have superior language tasks compared with their normal brothers, it is impossible to tell whether the reason is hormones alone or life's experiences, too. Only Hines's DES girls are pure products of prebirth hormones: they looked like ordinary little girls, so people treated them as girls and they saw themselves as female. Their male-like cognitive function is the only one ever found that cannot be easily explained away as the result of nurture.

Hines's work has been seized as proof that biology is destiny, but other research undermines that dogma. For one thing, the overlap between men's and women's scores on just about every psychological test is huge. Any randomly chosen woman might do better at a "male" skill than a man, and vice versa. "This [overlap] is also true of brain structures," says UCLA's Gorski. More important, the nature-nurture dichotomy is simplistic. Nurture affects nature; experience, that is, affects biology. The brain is so malleable that rats raised in a cage filled with toys and mazes grow more connections between their neurons than rats raised in a bare cage. Also in rats, mothers sense their sons' testosterone and lick them more than daughters; that causes more nerve cells at the base of the tail to grow. The human brain is malleable, too: in people whose hands were amputated, scientists reported last year, the part of the brain that once registered feelings from the missing hand vanishes.

Is it farfetched to wonder whether parts of girls' brains grow or shrink, while different parts of boys' expand or shrivel, because they were told not to worry their pretty heads about math, or because they started amassing Legos from birth, or because . . . well, because of the vastly different experiences boys and girls have? "Surely the more complex social interactions among humans also sculpt the developing nervous system," argues psychologist Marc Breedlove of UC, Berkeley. "The studies provide no evidence favoring either nature or nurture." But, he adds, "there's one thing I know that testosterone does to masculinize [men's] brains. It causes them to be born with a penis. And everybody treats the baby differently [than they do a girl]. I'm sure that affects the development of the brain. Is that a biological effect or a social effect? It's both."

The recent PET scans and FMRIs are silent "on how the brains of men and women get to be different," says Irvine's Richard Haier. The scans probe adults, whose brains are the products of years of living, feeling, thinking and experiencing. Children have not yet been scanned in the service of science. But in studies of fetal brains (from miscarriages) and newborns' (from stillbirths), "none of the sex differences in [the brain] have been reliably detected," says Breedlove.

The powerful new techniques of brain imaging are just beginning to be [targeted to] the age-old question of what makes the sexes different. As the answers trickle in, they will surely challenge our cherished notions of what makes us think, act and feel as we do—and as members of the opposite sex do not. But if the first tantalizing findings are any clue, the research will show that our identities as men and women are creations of both nature and nurture. And that no matter what nature deals us, it is we—our choices, our sense of identity, our experiences in life—who make ourselves what we are.

◆

## COMMENTARY ON HAGAR THE HORRIBLE

Much contemporary psychology and feminist propaganda promote the belief that men can't express feelings. Some men, like Hagar, meet this accusation with a healthy grunt of dismissal. Other "more sensitive men" have internalized this accusation and allowed their self-esteem as men to diminish.

Fortunately, both the men's movement and some perceptive therapists and health care practitioners are beginning to recognize that both what and how men feel is different from what and how women feel. For example, poet and patriarch Robert Bly points to grief as one of the most overlooked and poignant of men's emotions, a feeling that men themselves rarely experience fully until they share it with each other. Culture has dictated that women and men show affection and anger differently. (See Simons, George and Deborah Weissman, *Men and Women, Partners at Work*, available from ODT, Box 134, Amherst MA 01004, 1993, pages 44–45.)

Hopefully, as men, and in particular European-American men, are included in the reach of diversity efforts, more respect for men's feelings will emerge. That men's feelings are generally misunderstood now does not mean that their emotional range and forms of expression are adequate to the changing culture of life and work. They, like the women who have entered new environments, are challenged to acculturate and broaden their emotional skills to succeed.

# Walking Out on the Boys

Elizabeth L'Hommedieu interviews Dr. Frances Conley (*TIME Magazine*)

*Dr. Frances Conley, tired of being called "honey" by male surgeons, resigned from the Stanford medical school. Last week a professor there was charged with sexual harassment.*

**Q:** *After 16 years as a professor at Stanford, you resigned abruptly, charging what you called "gender insensitivity" on the part of male colleagues. Most people interpreted that to mean sexual harassment. Were you sexually harassed?*

**A:** I am not talking about sexual harassment. I think harassment is too volatile a term. Sexism is one way of describing it. It is a pervasive attitude problem. The examples I can give will seem trivial, but they are real, and they do affect a person who has a professional life. If I am in an operating room, I have to be in control of the team that is working with me. That control is established because people respect who I am and what I can do. If a man walks into the operating room and says, "How's it going, honey?", what happens to my control? It disappears because every woman who is working in that room with me has also been called "honey" by this same guy, and it means all of a sudden I don't have the status of a surgeon in control of the case being done. I have suddenly become a fellow "honey."

**Q:** *Surely there is more to it than being called "honey." Are there any other examples?*

**A:** When I was younger I would be repeatedly asked to bed by fellow doctors. This would always happen in front of an audience. It was always done for effect. Another common example is that if I have a disagreement with my male counterparts, I generally tend to get the label of being "difficult" because I am suffering from PMS syndrome or because I am "on the rag." That is a gender-identification problem. You can't say that to a male counterpart who disagrees with you. These men tend to use the female image and those things that are perceived by society as making women inferior, i.e., the fact that we are different biologically, and they make that the focus of their dealing with me. I define that as sexism. It is not sexual harassment.

I have had male doctors run their hands up my leg, never in an operating room, but in meetings. It is always done for an audience. Two months ago, I stood up to leave a meeting of all men and me, and as I stood up one of them said to me, "Gee, I can see the shape of your breasts, even through your white coat." I am sorry, but to me that is not right.

**Q:** *Why wouldn't men do this to you simply because you are an attractive woman?*

**A:** I have analyzed it, and I believe it's because they cannot see me as a peer. They have to establish a relationship that makes me inferior to them. The one they can immediately grab onto is a sexual relationship where the man is supposed to be dominant and the woman subservient.

**Q:** *You've said twice now that these sexist remarks are made in front of an audience. Why would that be?*

**A:** They have to show their peers that they do not accept this woman as an equal.

**Q:** You have been a surgeon for 25 years. Why did you tolerate this kind of treatment for so long?

**A:** In order for a female to get taken into the club, which is necessary in order to get cases and to get trained, you have to become a member. I decided that I would go along because I wanted to get to where I wanted to be. I really wanted to be a neurosurgeon. I thought I could be a good neurosurgeon. Had I made an issue of some of the things that were happening during the time that I was a resident, I wouldn't have gotten to where I am.

**Q:** *How pervasive do you think this kind of treatment of female doctors is?*

**A:** The vast majority of men that I have worked with—and there have been a lot of them—are wonderful, warm, supportive human beings who make me feel good about me when I am with them. It is just a few bad apples, but those bad apples can make you feel pretty small.

*Q: Are all the "bad apples" concentrated in the Stanford neurosurgery department?*

*A:* No, they are not. I would say they are much more concentrated in the surgery department across all specialties rather than in, say, pediatric medicine or anesthesia.

*Q: What do you think you have accomplished by resigning?*

*A:* First, I will be able to rebuild myself and regain my self-dignity. When I resigned, I had not intended to make a statement. As it turned out, I did, because I wrote a letter to a local newspaper, and that does make a statement. Many media people said, "You are so naive." I really had not anticipated the reaction to the editorial I wrote. I have been amazed. It is like an abscess that has been festering for years. It's been getting bigger and bigger. What I did was throw a scalpel at it and opened it. Now there is pus running all over the floor. What I have done, I hope, is help others open up a dialogue about this. If we can get men and women to start talking to one another about what gender insensitivity means, then we will have accomplished a great deal.

*Q: The day after you resigned, you attended a student-faculty senate meeting at which one student described a teacher's using a sex doll to "spice up" a lecture, and another student said her breasts had been fondled. This must have struck a chord with you.*

*A:* I think the thing that hit me the most was realizing that these were medical students complaining, and they are having these kinds of problems in their learning place, where they are supposed to be free to learn and to train to become professionals. This is a pervasive, global problem for women who are trying to get into professional careers. I think the reason it is coming out is because of the critical numbers. Since close to 50% of Stanford's medical classes can be women, when you do something in a class that is sexist in nature, you're offending not four people but 40.

*Q: Stanford President Donald Kennedy has just brought disciplinary charges of sexual harassment and professional misconduct against a male cardiology professor. The charges are based on complaints that two female medical students filed with the university several months prior to your resignation. Do you think your resignation played a part in the university's decision to take action?*

## Maxine  **By Marian Henley**

*A:* No. I do not believe that my situation influenced this decision. I know nothing about this case. I have enough faith in the people who run the university to feel that they are doing what is right regardless of whether or not I have made a flap. I do not think that Kennedy or any other people would have taken my resignation into account.

*Q: You have said that the structure of medicine was set up for men by men. How do you think medicine would differ were it to be set up by women?*

*A:* It would be far less dictatorial. It would be management by committee—by teamwork. Uniformly, my operating room is a team, and I believe this to be true of most women's O.R.s. The people who work with me are respected, professional, and do a job. We are all doing a job to reach a common goal, and that is to take good care of that patient. I think the nurses feel as if they have tremendous self-worth when they are in my O.R. There are lots of pleases and lots of thank yous. My operating room is a happy environment.

*Q: Where does Stanford president Donald Kennedy stand on all this?*

*A:* I have spoken with Kennedy, and I think he is very supportive. I am not sure he was aware that the gender-relationship problems were quite as significant as they are, and I think he has been most surprised by that. I know he has been getting an earful, because I have been getting copies of many letters that have been sent to him.

*Q: You have said that with so many more females in medical schools across the country, their environments must change. What steps would you suggest?*

*A:* One is to raise the level of consciousness about this type of behavior so that the consciousness is ongoing. The second is to be sure that the appointments that are made to executive positions are made with a great deal of care as to what that person's feelings are and how they relate not only to women but also to minorities, nurses and secretaries. It has to be an environment where people are respected for being people—where every person has self-worth and dignity. There would also be value in having more women in higher administrative positions in medical schools, where the decisions are being made.

*Q: What has been your husband's reaction to your resignation?*

*A:* He has been very supportive of it, primarily because he has been very aware of my unhappiness. He, too, has been flabbergasted by the supportive response and feels that it should have come out a long time ago.

*Q: How has he handled all your private complaints over the years?*

*A:* He has always let me be a very independent person, and that has been terribly important for me so that I could develop as a professional the way I wanted to. I think at times he has been distressed by my complaints. He will occasionally make sniping comments at people who he thinks have been demeaning to me, but he hasn't wanted to jeopardize that which I have done. He has been very careful not to be actively entered into the situation, but he has always been phenomenally supportive of me.

◆

# Gender Issues in the Workplace
an interview with George F. Simons

*Q: What should a male manager be careful of in managing a female subordinate?*

*A:* No matter how far we've come, we must keep in mind that men and women grew up in different cultures. In every society, men and women are treated differently from the moment of birth. They are talked to and talked about differently. Consequently, men and women literally speak a different language even though both might talk in English.

Men as managers need to know that women are not crazy, but different, when they show up with different meanings and values and procedures that seem "off-the-wall" from a male perspective. They can start looking for value that women's differences add, especially in a diverse global environment where we now need the personal skills in which women have traditionally excelled. This is good news for women who have had second thoughts and hesitations about the pressures exerted on them to become more like men to succeed in business.

The action words that many men use are all about sports and war. As a matter of course they say things like, "When in doubt, punt," and talk about the "top brass" and "biting the bullet." Men brought up in such a world get daily reinforcement from each other in the language they use. The fact that a woman has a good knowledge of "man-talk" does not keep her from experiencing it as aggressive, negative, or unnecessarily limiting. Many organizational women must function in a world of strong male paradigms and it can keep many of them on-edge, uncomfortable, frustrated and angry.

Overall, men need to be more sensitive to these differences in how women think and talk. Listening to each other's metaphors can broaden both sexes' workplace vocabulary and give us more ways to speak to each other.

Because many men still take their workplace context for granted, they don't trust women who "don't speak the language," or "don't play by the rules," or who are "out to change the rules." Women, in fact, often don't know the rules—and men, no matter how obvious these things seem, must learn to believe women when they say this.

*Q: What should a woman be aware of in managing a male subordinate?*

*A:* Things have improved greatly in this area, but even today, for some men, working for a woman is an intolerable blow to the male ego. Men need to be empowered to do this, probably by other men. A woman identified as an affirmative action appointee—in the job just because she's a woman—will find it hard to "earn her stripes" in men's eyes and get their respect. The concept of "chain of command" actually serves men here. Other male allies can help by respecting and communicating a woman's qualifications and legitimacy. She may have to strategize with other men on how to get this support at the outset.

A woman manager should also realize that many men don't ask for task help from a man, let alone a woman, unless they are in very deep trouble. Men usually want to appear as if they are in charge and know what they are doing. Women who manage men have to be on the lookout for such "quiet" breakdowns. They should be aware, too, that men also hide their stress, so it's easy for a woman manager to unknowingly overload a male subordinate with work.

*Q: What should a woman manager be careful of in dealing with a male boss?*

*A:* Many men were brought up to take care of women, to do the tough jobs for them, to protect them from the harshness of life. They may unconsciously fear women's emotions. Today especially, the negative reactions of women and other protected classes to traditional male behavior can be vexing. Men may be reluctant to give hard critical feedback when it is needed for fear that a woman will react emotionally or that she will see criticism as a sexist attack. It's a double bind. Without good feedback, the woman may continue to do a poor job and not identify the improvements she needs to make. Consequently, many woman managers need to ask for and insist on critical feedback from male bosses.

Physically protective and possessive gestures, such as a man's putting his arm around a woman when introducing her have largely disappeared from today's management scene because of sexual harassment fears engendered by almost any kind of touching in the workplace. However men may still be inclined to other verbal and non-verbal behaviors that give the impression: 'This is my kid.' It may be up to the women managers themselves to alert their male bosses and colleagues that certain things they do, although well-meant, are not supportive, especially in front of others.

Women managers must learn the meaning and function of male vocabulary as it is used in the organization. On the other hand they must be careful about how much male language they import into their own vocabulary. What they do use may not sound the same when it comes out of their mouths. It may get them written off instead of listened to. Learning to interpret the nuances of "man-talk" is far more important than trying to talk like men. Women in such situations are indeed like immigrants who learn the words of a new language but not the subtleties of meaning or the appropriate contexts in which to speak them.

Women in the workplace may have to reassess how openly they should speak about personal matters, family and friends, etc., around men when they are first on the job. Until men recognize women for their abilities, such talk leads some men to write off women who use it as "gossips" or as not being "real players." They think that women are wasting time, can't separate work from the rest of their lives, and above all don't understand business when they use such terms.

*Q: What should a man be careful of in interacting with a woman boss?*

*A:* Many men lack good social models for dealing with women in the workplace. To fill this gap, they tend to take models from their earlier experiences. Depending on a man's upbringing, this may or may not be very useful. He may have only two powerful female roles to call on, mother and teacher. When the boss is a woman he may unconsciously begin to treat her as if she is one of these. If she is seen as the teacher whom he resented and put up with, or the mother he went to for nurture or, conversely, avoided because he disliked her possessiveness, he may behave inappropriately toward the woman boss. He may keep her at a distance and not inform her about what is going on. He may expect more nurturing than she is willing to give. There can be even worse consequences if men use other inappropriate female models men may have, e.g., girl friend, big sister, etc.

Many women managers tell us that they are often infuriated when men "walk on eggs" around them or "take care of them." They want men to be direct and open, to ask questions and give prompt feedback, though it may be hard to take, particularly at first. Both sexes must continually put themselves in each other's shoes. This requires knowing more of what the other person is really like. Constantly remind yourself to search this out as well as to remind others very specifically of what you need from them. We are different, and keeping ourselves alert to how differences manifest themselves is hard, particularly when people would like to gloss over them.

*Q: How can a manager of either sex deal with gender hostility between two subordinates?*

*A:* Every manager must possess a thorough knowledge of federal and state law as well as organizational policies and regulations regarding sexual harassment. Beyond that, a manager's most important asset in a conflict of this sort is having his or her own gender issues straight, so when he or she must act on others' gender issues, it doesn't trigger unmanageable defenses or lead to political side-taking in defense of one's own kind.

There are many things which law and corporate policy do not cover adequately. For such cases, the manager should have acquired the skills to be a facilitator and mediator, able to listen and reflect, to help the parties resolve their grievance with each other.

*Q: How should a manager deal with a subordinate who flirts with opposite sex co-workers?*

*A:* Once again one must first be aware of and address the legal liabilities that flirting entails. Above and beyond the legal framework we may have a corporate policy to guide us. Corporate policy usually echoes the legal framework and may be even more specific and restricting than the law.

Unfortunately, the legal aspects of securing a human and gender-friendly workplace have come to dominate the discussion of this issue today. The law exists to protect our rights. The paradox is that in many respects the legal climate hamstrings our ability to have a humanly warm environment and kills supportive affection in the workplace.

Let's be sensitive for a moment to what is not addressed in this law-dominated climate. For example, if you don't meet your true love in the workplace, where are you going to find him or her? Many of us spend most of our time at work or commuting to and fro. Secondly, when you put men and women or even persons of the same sex together, some sexual dynamics are always present. Bonding along affectional orientation lines is bound to occur whether we like it or not.

Flirting—and we're not talking about heavy "coming on" or "hitting on" someone here—used to be an emotional outlet which kept things friendly between the sexes without its getting too serious. Can we reinvent flirting to fit our changing gender realities and work in the present climate? Flirting as we knew it in past generations relied for the most part on established sex roles. When we don't know what to say, even today, we fall back on these old roles. Many women, however, have learned, over the past quarter century of the present wave of the women's movement, to resist these old habits and not to respond to related signals coming from men. And men's narrow work focus has become even more narrow in reaction to women's pulling back from gender camaraderie.

We don't know much about how to relate to the other sex in a way that's free of sex-role stereotyping, or even in a gender respectful way, despite the fact that many people believe they're successful at it. What can we do safely with each other? Where does a manager have to draw the line? How can people still enjoy each other in their wholeness (including gender and affectional orientation) without stepping over the line, especially when zero tolerance of harassment is the rule of the day?

In this climate a manager's first responsibility is to make sure that people's behavior is not creating productivity problems or offending coworkers. When forced to become gender police, few of us have energy and time to envision and encourage a positive interpersonal climate in the face of so many obstacles.

*Q: How should a manager deal with office romance?*

*A:* For most managers, this question is really, "What does the company culture say about this?" There are companies that like to see people getting together personally as well as professionally, but most firms saw problems in this even before sexual harassment became the big threat it is today.

When a couple starts seeing one another, everyone in the office knows it. Co-workers start treating the couple as a single entity. Problems of confidentiality arise. As the manager, you may have to call these people in and talk to them in a friendly way, saying, "Here's what you need to know about what is legal and what causes problems. Here's how our company culture deals with romance. Here are the risks, challenges and problems you are going to face. Here's what you can do and what you must avoid." This is an unpleasant task and most of us would prefer that it not be in our job description. It feels like prying.

◆

# Making Sense of la Différence

by Barbara Ehrenreich (*TIME Magazine*)

Few areas of science are as littered with intellectual rubbish as the study of innate mental differences between the sexes. In the 19th century, biologists held that a woman's brain was too small for intellect but large enough for household chores. When the tiny-brain theory bit the dust (elephants, after all, have bigger brains than men), scientists began a long, fruitless attempt to locate the biological basis of male superiority in various brain lobes and chromosomes. By the 1960s sociobiologists were asserting that natural selection, operating throughout the long human prehistory of hunting and gathering, had predisposed males to leadership and exploration and females to crouching around the campfire with the kids.

Recent studies suggest there may be some real differences after all. And why not? We have different hormones and body parts; it would be odd if our brains were 100% unisex. The question, as ever: What do these differences augur for our social roles, in particular the division of power and opportunity between the sexes?

Don't look to the Flintstones for an answer. However human beings whiled away their first 100,000 years or so, few of us today make a living tracking down mammoths or digging up tasty roots. Much of our genetic legacy of sex differences has already been rendered moot by that uniquely human invention: technology. Military prowess no longer depends on superior musculature or those bursts of hormones that prime the body for combat at ax range. As for exploration, women—with their lower body weight and oxygen consumption—may be the more "natural" astronauts.

But suppose the feminists' worst-case scenario turns out to be true, and males really are better, on average, at certain mathematical tasks. If this tempts you to shunt all the girls back to home ec, you probably need remedial work in the statistics of "averages" yourself. Just as some women are taller and stronger than some men, some are swifter at abstract algebra. Many of the pioneers in the field of X-ray crystallography—which involves three-dimensional visualization and heavy doses of math—were female, including biophysicist Rosalind Franklin whose work was indispensable to the discovery of the double-helical structure of DNA.

Then there is the problem that haunts all studies of "innate" sex differences: the possibility that the observed differences are really the result of lingering cultural factors. Girls' academic achievement, for example, as well as apparent aptitude and self-esteem, usually takes a nose dive at puberty. Unless nature has selected for smart girls and dumb women, something is going very wrong at about the middle-school level. Part of the problem may be that males, having been the dominant sex for a few millenniums, still tend to prefer females who make them feel stronger and smarter. Any girl who is bright enough to solve a quadratic equation is smart enough to bat her eyelashes and pretend that she can't.

Teachers too may play a larger role than nature in differentiating between the sexes. Studies show they tend to favor boys by calling on them more often and pushing them harder. Myra and David Sadker, professors of education at American University, have found that girls do better when teachers are sensitized to gender bias and refrain from sexist language, such as the use of "man" to mean all of us. Single-sex classes in math and science can also boost female performance by eliminating favoritism and male disapproval of female achievement.

The success of such simple educational reforms only underscores the basic social issue: Given that there may be real innate mental differences between the sexes, what are we going to do about them? A female advantage in reading emotions could be interpreted to mean that males should be barred from psychiatry—or that they need more coaching. A male advantage in math could be used to confine girls to essays and sonnets—or the decision could be made to compensate by putting more effort into girls' math education. In effect, we already compensate for boys' apparent handicap in verbal skills by making reading the centerpiece of grade-school education.

We are cultural animals, and these are ultimately cultural decisions. In fact, the whole discussion of innate sexual differences is itself heavily shaped by cultural factors. Why, for example, is the study of innate differences such a sexy, well-funded topic right now, which happens to be a time of organized feminist challenge to the ancient sexual division of power? Why do the media tend to get excited when scientists find an area of difference and ignore the many reputable studies that come up with no differences at all?

However science eventually defines it, *la différence* can be amplified or minimized by human cultural arrangements: the choice is up to us, and not our genes.

## About the Author

Barbara Ehrenreich is the author of *The Worst Years of Our Lives: Irreverent Notes from a Decade of Greed* (Pantheon, 1990), *Fear of Falling: The Inner Life of the Middle Class,* and *The Hearts of Man: American Dreams and the Flight from Commitment* (Doubleday, 1983). Ehrenreich's first novel is *Kipper's Game* (Harper Collins, 1994). In addition to her work for *Time* Magazine, Ehrenreich writes a biweekly column for *The Guardian* in the U.K. Her new book, a collection of essays entitled *The Snarling Citizen,* is published by Farrar, Straus & Giroux.

## Maxine    By Marian Henley

142

# PART 4
# DIVERSE AMERICA:
# YES AND NO

# Dialogue: Diverse America

*George*—This section is called Diverse America. It attempts to provide a helicopter view of the cultural landscape of the U.S., focusing in particular on how we do diversity and the myths that seem to undergird our efforts. Our perspective has been enriched by our recent work with European clients who, attempting to come to grips with diversity, provide us with new perspectives. Most of these are branches of American corporations overseas with a mandate to deal with diversity. Exporting this effort has brought us face-to-face with what is peculiarly American about the diversity effort, how that fits into U.S. culture and is distinguished from what is going on in other parts of the world.

Take the issue of cross-cultural learning as an example. Generally in the U.S., verbal stereotyping and jokes about cultural characteristics of other people (because of our spirit of individualism and the unequal distribution of power) have become taboo. This is contrary to the way many Europeans, living largely in monocultures, acquaint themselves with other cultures. In Europe, ethnic humor, teasing and verbal stereotyping are common. Within certain bounds this can often generate a dialogue of discovery instead of giving offense. One of the best selling books on diversity in Europe begins with a multi-ethnic joke about the difference between heaven and hell. The joke explains that the difference between heaven and hell lies in the fact that in heaven, the chefs are French, the car mechanics are German, the police are British, the organizers are Swiss, and the lovers are Italian while in hell the chefs are British, the car mechanics are French, the police are German, the organizers are Italian, and the lovers are Swiss.

In the sidebar we've enclosed the joke in a short drama about a European man attending a diversity training program conducted by an American women. Notice not only how the joke stereotypes the various European groups, but also the subtle negative reactions of both the joke-teller and the American trainer to each other. These are some of the dynamics of difference we are talking about.

I first heard this old joke when I started working in Europe almost thirty years ago. It places each European group in a very traditional stereotype. If you take away most of the power imbalance that characterizes intergroup relations in the U.S. diversity dialogue, then bring the stereotypes to the surface with humor, affectionate teasing and other forms of discussion, you can come up with a possible way of learning and knowing.

Europeans, by and large, abhor and fear what they see as the crude hypersensitivity of the U.S. diversity scene. What we describe as awareness and sensitivity have not been the culturally adaptive or functional behavior for them as it has for us. For U.S.-Americans ethnic humor reinforces divisions and avoiding it creates respect where we fear none exists. For Europeans, the divisions are already very clear, mutually accepted and not in need of defense.

Humor is like a French pig snuffling out truffles. The ridiculous beast of humor is used to signal where the cultural conflict—and hence the learning—can lie. Laughs are created by the incongruous meeting of what we expect next and what we receive. A good ethnic joke confirms our stereotype, makes us consciously think about it, and if you're aware of the stereotype, challenges its ridiculous simplicity at the same time. It is also used to affectionately tease others. In a European business or social context you are expected to be sophisticated enough to go through this entire cycle, and not be afraid that the stereotype is the last word on the subject, as our trainer from the U.S. did in the sidebar.

This process of learning from stereotypes is not new. Europeans have been at it for a long time and for that reason we've included a chart (page 146) called "A Short Description of the People Found in Europe and Their Characteristics," which we have extracted and translated from prints of the original, an oil painting dating back to the beginning of the 18th century, now found in the Vienna Volksmuseum.

Compare this with the postcard and poster (pages 160–161), now in at least its third edition, commonly found in tourist shops and airport ki-

---

## SCENE

Coffee break at the first European diversity training program at the XYZ Corporation. A four-star hotel meeting room. Table with carafes of coffee and juice. Real silverware and napkins. Cookies/biscuits.

**Dramatis Personae**

Baudouin: Highly successful male European sales manager in an American owned corporation

Nancy: U.S.-based internal diversity trainer doing her first European gig.

*B:* Quite interesting what you were saying earlier about understanding differences. I think you'll find things a bit different here. We Europeans understand each other rather well. We've had a lot of history to learn from.

*N:* Well there's a lot to do to stay competitive in the European Community. I think . . .

*B:* Yes, the European Union poses some interesting challenges in the legal domain, but we do know the differences that divide us.—Can I pour you some more coffee?

*N:* Oh no, I'm used to decaf. One's enough for me.

*B:* Decaf?

*N:* Yes, you know, without caffeine.

*B:* Oh yes. Well, as I was saying, our differences are rather apparent. Let me put it this way: you know the difference between heaven and hell, don't you?

*N:* No, I'm not sure what you mean . . .

*B:* Well, in heaven, the chefs are French, the car mechanics German, the police British, the organizers are Swiss, and the lovers are Italian. In hell . . .

*N:* I don't think we should stereotype . . .

*[Baudouin touching her hand to keep her attention. Nancy draws back as if shocked by static electricity, then listens politely, with visibly pained resignation as Baudouin continues.]*

But listen . . . *[continuing his story]* . . . in hell, the chefs are British, the car mechanics are French, the police are German, the organizers are Italian, and—the lovers are Swiss. *[He laughs]*

*N:* *[Turning sideways to B. and detaching herself from the conversation.]*

I think it's time we got back to work.

*[Then in a voice loud enough to be heard throughout the room,]*

Time to work, everybody, break's over.

*[The participants continue chatting with each other as though they had not heard her.]*

---

osks all over Europe which describes "The Perfect European" in the European community. Not surprisingly, you can correlate some of the stereotypes in the contemporary postcard with those that existed several centuries ago in the chart of the Volksmuseum tableau.

What does this comparison tell us? It helps us to see how American we are and how American our diversity efforts are. Europeans encounter us as Americans with American values, even if we are Black, Latino or Asian, or hyphenated ethnics of some sort. So we have also included in this section the article "Innocents Abroad" (page 156) which addresses how American culture continually reinforces itself. While many things may change on the surface, some very fundamental cultural characteristics reinforce themselves. What we may see as an attempt to move from the melting pot to the

# A Short Description of the Peoples Found in Europe and Their Characteristics

| Name | Spaniard | Frenchman | Italian | German | Briton | Swede | Pole | Hungarian | Russian | Turk or Greek |
|---|---|---|---|---|---|---|---|---|---|---|
| Behaviors | Arrogant | Frivolous | Reserved | Openhearted | Good appearance | Big and strong | Coarse | Faithless | Malicious | Like April weather |
| Nature and characteristics | Marvelous | Good spirited & talkative | Jealous | Very good | Charming | Cruel | Very wild | The cruelest | Quite Hungarian | A quick devil |
| Intellect | Smart and wise | Farsighted | Astute | Witty | Annoying | Stubborn | Poorly attentive | Even less | None at all | Superficially open |
| Expression of the characteristics | Manly | Childish | However you please | Well balanced | Feminine | Unknowable | Mediocre | Bloodthirsty | Infinitely coarse | Tender |
| Sciences | Learned in letters | In the affairs of war | In spiritual authority | In worldly authority | Worldly wise | In liberal arts | In different languages | In the Latin language | In the Greek language | In political falsehood |
| How they dress | Respectable | Inconsistent | Crazy | Imitate everything | French fashions | Leather | Long coats | Colorful | In furs | After the fashion of women |
| Vices | Arrogance | Cheating | Lecherous | Wasteful | Restless | Superstitious | Loudmouth | Treacherous | Quite treacherous | Even more treacherous |
| What they love | Praise and fame | War | Gold | Drink | Sensuality | Rich food | Titles | Turmoil | Brawling | Their own body |
| Diseases | Constipation | Genetic | Plague | Gout | Consumption | Dropsy | Hernia | Fright | Coughing | From weakness |
| Their land | Fruitful | Well worked | Pleasing and sensual | Good | Fruitful | Mountainous | Forested | Rich in produce and gold | Full of ice | Charming |
| Virtues in war | Very courageous | Deceitful | Foresight | Unconquerable | Heroic at sea | Without failure | Immovable | Cold-heartedness | Wearying | Quite lazy |
| Worship | The very best | Good | Somewhat better | Even more pious | Changeable as the moon | Zealous faith | Believes all kinds of things | Not boring | A schismatic | Also one |
| Recognize as their ruler | A monarch | A king | A patriarch | An emperor | Now this, now that | Liberal rule | An elected one | An unconquerable one | A freebooter | A tyrant |
| Have a surplus of | Fruit | Goods | Wine | Grain | Bogs | Mines | Fur pieces | Everything | Swarms of bees | In things that are tender and soft |
| How they pass the time | With games | In deception | Discussing the latest news | By drinking | With work | By drinking | Quarreling | Criticizing and complaining | By sleeping | From wounds |
| Compared with the animals | An elephant | A fox | A fox | A lion | A horse | An ox | A bear | A wolf | A donkey | A cat |
| Their life's end | In bed | In war | In the cloister | In wine | In water | On the earth | In the stable | By the sabre | In snow | Through deceit |

Tables of Peoples—Stiermark, Early 18th Century—A Short Description of the Peoples Found in Europe and Their Characteristics—Vienna, Austrian Museum for Folk Art—Wolfrum Art Publishers, Vienna salad bowl in our diversity effort, Europeans are seeing as part of the fuel that puts the fire to the melting pot.

*Bob*—Let's start to identify some of these myths of U.S. culture.

*George*—All right. What are the powerful themes, myths and driving values in American culture? First, the myth of the new frontier. America, for many immigrants from Europe, was the promised land. Religious groups emigrating from Europe to North America saw themselves as a present-day "Chosen People." This was the land given them by God where they would be free from servitude. It became their "Manifest Destiny" to conquer and possess, "from sea to shining sea." To educate, civilize and evangelize the peoples found there became the "White Man's Burden." Out of this emerged what I would call "public religion," i.e., values that are cut loose from their religious origins and traditions, but which live on in the culture and psyche of the macroculture. You could compare it to how Shinto pervades public life in Japan, where religious rituals have become expressions not of faith, but of national identity.

*Bob*—The mentality of conquering the frontier was strongly based in religion?

*George*—Yes, and we need to remember these religious and quasi-religious roots, especially when we get into the section on spirituality (see "Spirit Section" beginning on page 326). While America has declared the separation of church and state to guarantee a non-partial government, U.S. Americans are among the most religious of peoples in their private lives. As a result, we have a tension, perhaps we could even say a myth, which denies the religiosity of the American enterprise.

From this "manifest destiny" of the people is born the myth of the missionary responsibility. So many U.S. Americans feel the need to export, if not religion, then democracy around the world. Exporting diversity (our present effort to realize democracy) is another corollary to this myth. Remember Cohen's words, "Democracy is coming to the USA."

*Bob*—But missionary zeal seems a little different, if we talk about marketing products instead of exporting democracy.

*George*—I think so. Marketers hold a "get real" perspective that diversity practitioners could benefit from looking at. The success of marketing is measured by the bottom line. This indicates whether marketers have reached, or failed to reach, a culture. Sales of products or services are a form of quick feedback.

A similar religious fervor is evident in the born-again entrepreneur and salesperson that comes out of the United States. Revival type sales meetings, complete with confessions and testimony are today's echoes of R. H. Tawney's analysis of *Religion and the Rise of Capitalism*. No nation embodies the religious nature of capitalism as overtly as the United States.

Many missionaries in the period of European expansion were quite diversity conscious for their own time. Starting with Christopher Columbus, such missionaries are categorically and uncritically chucked into a garbage pail marked "White Trash" by today's p.c. sanitary engineers. Yet, alongside the "believe or die" type of missionaries, there were countless others who lived lives of service for the health and welfare of native peoples and colonists alike. Some researched, documented and preserved native history and traditions.

They also know about acculturation: Jesuits of the 15th and 16th centuries who lived as Brahmins in India, Mandarins in China, and advisor-ambassadors in Shogun courts of Japan. Today's Mormons have amassed amazing amounts of cultural information for their globe-hopping missionaries and make it available for business people and others interested in cross-cultural studies.[1]

Missionaries are cultural agents, as are we all. We can't cross cultural boundaries without causing change, without making transactions in the cultural marketplace. Long before Europeans displaced them, Native American groups were made war on, displaced and colonized each other. They exhausted their ecology, and did all the bad things that we have learned to do more efficiently with modern technology. Perhaps it is the missionary's virtue that he or she consciously knows that the cultural objectives of his or her activity involve

---

[1] An inexpensive series of "Culturegrams" documenting customs and values of nearly every country in the world is available from Intercultural Press: P.O. Box 700, Yarmouth, Maine 04096; Phone 207-846-5168; Fax: 207-846-5181

changing the belief and behavior of the target group, whereas many of us, even interculturalists and ecologists and media folk, would like to believe that we don't have an agenda.

*Bob*—Then all those gurus of personal achievement: Dale Carnegie, Napoleon Hill, Earl Nightingale all the way to Og Mandino, Werner Erhart, Marianne Williamson and Tony Robbins are of the same genre?

*George*—Effectively they are preachers talking about individual salvation and the rights and responsibilities of the saved, i.e., reinforcing and developing the public religion and assimilating all takers to its standards. This is neither good or bad in itself. It just is. It's U.S. culture.

*Bob*—And you would say the U.S. "religion" of individual achievement has a few blind spots when it comes to social justice or responsibility toward the common good?

*George*—Insiders don't call them blind spots. The myth tells them how justice and the common good can be achieved. If people behaved correctly—e.g., if welfare moms took responsibility by having fewer babies and getting a job—these problems wouldn't exist—so runs the myth.

*Bob*—Oh, this is a variant of another U.S. myth that success is available to all. We're told as young people that even if you come from a log cabin in a poor backwater of Illinois you can be President of the United States. So the myth prevails that we have a classless society that allows anyone to come from the bottom, pull themselves up by the bootstraps, achieve wealth, fame, success—and make it to the top.

*George*—This myth motivates some people . . . not a bad thing. It also makes everyone who wants to run for high public office write a campaign biography to make sure that the electorate knows that they have the right "folksy" background. Campaign advertising positions the candidate as a "true American" who rose from the bottom, descended from penniless immigrants (Kennedy) or the poor of the land (Truman). Recently we heard Clarence Thomas' sound bites on this . . . But remember there's only been one "Honest Abe" and it's been said that his opponents gave him that name in irony because he was so shifty. Throughout the history of the United States, though, people have

probably moved from one class to another with more ease and more quickly than in many parts of the world. That's what makes the myth believable.

*Bob*—The myth is part of the culture that worked for many people as a motivator, but the truth is that most of us need personal and societal supports to really succeed. Many people lack these supports.

*George*—Incidentally, when I say "myth," I don't mean something bad or untrue. A myth is simply a story line that a group of people commonly believe and use as a model for how reality should be. It undergirds culture by stories of how to survive and succeed. It works for the group that creates it, but maybe not for others. Scientists have myths, too, they just think of them as "givens" about reality. Fortunately, we have a politically and ethnically diverse society that keeps questioning each myth with other myths.

Some of our myths appeal abroad and take root in other parts of the world. But they often clash with the values and the environment of the people to whom they're sent. Latin America adored U.S. democracy and tried to emulate it for almost two centuries—Simon Bolivar, et al. Emulation of the U.S. still continues in fits and starts. For many Latin Americans the ideal is now tarnished, as our interactions with Latin countries lead them to see us as the oppressor, not a model for them to emulate. You don't have to love the U.S. to love [beisbol] any more.

*Bob*—U.S. myths notwithstanding, we are not a classless society. We possess macrocultural values of equality, justice, and fairness which are espoused even when they're not practiced. If you have faith in the American system and if you apply yourself, things will work out. The consensus around this belief is at best questioned a bit from time to time, for example, by Generation X, who don't seem to consciously operate on that principle—yet. (See "The New Generation Gap," page 162.)

*George*—They probably will, in their own way. [*George reaches to take a bill out of his wallet*] You only need to look at the dollar bill to get a summary of the cultural myths. It's the only money I know of that says "In God we trust." Then we have the motto "novus ordo seculorum," "a new order of things." The U.S. was founded as a nation on the belief of the positive value of change. Then here at the apex of the pyramid is the eye of God. It says "annuit coeptis"—God has given thumbs-up to our enterprise. "Annuit" means "given the nod." (It's nice that Latin verbs are non-sexist. You don't need a stated subject for the verb so it could mean "he or she has given the nod.") So you hear echoes of manifest destiny, the religious mythology reflected on the basic unit of currency in the country where "money is God." If so, money should be able to liberate us from race and ethnicity and, ultimately, class. But in recent years the dollar just doesn't buy what it used to.

*Bob*—Another feature of the U.S. psyche is the obsession with individuality. It says you're responsible for making it on your own; it values individual freedom at all costs. These assumptions differ certainly from those in other cultures. A further trait of the U.S. culture, and one which presents a dilemma in the diversity field, is the habit we have of supporting the underdog. Often this is seen as patronizing or offensive by microcultures in the U.S. The sidebar from Nat Hentoff, "Free Speech vs. Political Correctness," (page 171) illustrates how under the guise of supporting the underdog we diminish him or her, or take away challenge and responsibility in ways that trigger anger and rejection.

*George*—Acculturating to U.S. values is like learning how to swim. There are two ways to do it: someone takes you out and throws you in the water to thrash about until you learn how, or someone works with you to overcome fear of water, then shows you step by step how to float and propel yourself. In fact, the latter is what almost always happens.

The myth says you do it the first way. My dad told me this happened to him and threatened to throw me in. "Sink or swim"—that's our cultural paradox. That is what the immigrant must do, theoretically. Actually, there is family support, government assistance, and volunteer help (we also have a tradition of "barn raising" to call on). We maintain the old mythical way at the belief level, but also provide encouragement, support and understanding on the action level. No wonder we're a bit schizophrenic. Think of how many parents you know who feel like they should help their kids and at the same time believe the best way to do that is to throw them out on their own . . .

*Bob*— . . . so they get used to the water. Why don't you say something about the U.S. cultural bias against being culturally competent? Are we simply arrogant?

*George*—It may look that way. We're certainly as ethnocentric as anybody else in the world, but it goes deeper than that. I think the bias in the U.S. macroculture of being "doers" not "thinkers" evolves from the Yankee frontier challenge. We took a heritage of just-get-the-job-done British pragmatism as a virtue for survival in the wilderness. Since we left them, the British have made a national virtue of "muddling through," to the exasperation of, say, the French who want finely-tuned intellectual agreement before committing to action.

*Bob*—When people talk about Anglophone versus Francophone differences in Canada, you'll hear a joke about this cultural difference. They say "if you ask a Frenchman the time, he'll tell you how to build a watch." Francophones discuss the larger picture . . .

*George*— . . . It's important for the French to root their thinking. By the way, you just used humor like the Europeans do, to promote a cultural learning. Many Francophones like to sink an intellectual pole deep into the earth, their way of grounding a well-defined mental form so that they can bring it into a "perfect" product in reality. We "Anglos" just crank it out—and it often shows up in poor quality. But, if we need to, we keep on fixing it till it's good enough, which for us means "perfect." Think of all those "recalls" in the U.S. auto industry. This accounts for the popularity of Tom Peters' admonition, "Ready, Fire, Aim."

Don't make too much of this, however. It's another case of myth versus reality. Remember that the American Colonies had already outstripped the British Motherland in educational institutions and opportunities before the Revolution of 1776, and our university system today, despite its cracks, its lowering of standards, etc., is still a world-class accomplishment. We can turn out world-class products when we have to, or want to.

But let's go back to the so-called U.S. bias against cultural competency . . . Now some U.S. companies are beginning to see the need for cultural skills. I happen to speak four languages rather fluently, simply because words have been a life-long love of mine. I put a lot of energy and effort into language studies and had opportunities to travel and live abroad that reinforced my skills as I went along. This ability makes me somewhat suspicious to other Americans—even though I am from a working-class immigrant family (I share the myth even if I'm not running for political office) and as middle-class a guy as you can get. But I'm peculiar because I deliberately *learned* languages. If I spoke broken Polish, Hungarian or German because I'd learned them at home, I'd be excused (this facility would be expected to disappear in the next generation). Yet, while the global economy is heating up and Americans need to communicate clearly to work with other peoples, the attitude still prevails that we're okay speaking only English and don't need to learn all that fancy cultural stuff.

*Bob*—The attitude is, "let everyone else speak English."

*George*—Yes. Let everyone else deal with us on our terms. Overcoming that mind set and achieving cultural competence is the third important challenge of diversity. We also resist because U.S.-Americans have the "Don't tell me what to do" attitude as part of our culture. Once we find something practical or pragmatic, though, we'll do it. Also Generation X, described in the article "The New Generation Gap," takes pragmatism to a whole new dimension. Perhaps the X-ers will even learn a few languages, but not in the education system as we have it. Many of the diversity values that political correctness tried to instill are being rejected because people feel imposed upon—dealt with in an autocratic and authoritarian fashion.

*Bob*—Autocratic in what way?

*George*—In the sense that a self-proclaimed, politically correct elite tries to impose its values on everybody else in what is seen as a coercive un-American way.

*Bob*—It makes sense then that perhaps what is not explicitly stated, for example in the "White, Male & Worried" article (page 167), in this section is that there is not only fear in the traditional workforce but resentment about the way white men are being talked about and dealt with.

*George*—Affirmative Action accomplished a great deal, but now is up against a brick wall. It is no longer culturally acceptable to many U.S. people, not just white men. The reason is that the macroculture holds dear both being fair and being perceived as fair, and many people have decided that Affirmative Action is not fair. People who do not qualify for its benefits see reverse discrimination at work, which is not fair. They see themselves paying reparations for a previous war while those on the other side see themselves as the victims and the others as benefiting from ill-gotten gains. So the question becomes "How much?" "How long?" No country has endured paying reparations or victimization for very long without revolting.

You can see this in the media dramatization of the debate. "White, Male & Worried" was a cover story for *U.S. News & World Report*. The cover included the line: "Does Affirmative Action mean that no *white men need apply?*" in red against a white background in letters four times as large as the title of the article. This is all exaggerated media hype . . .

*Bob*—What would you say to a person who believes that the reason for resistance to, and rebellion against, Affirmative Action (AA) is because at last the AA system *is* having a real impact. The most qualified people *are* getting the jobs and the competition for the white men is getting tougher. AA is touching a nerve because people are not getting jobs or being promoted because there are more qualified people in the game as a result of Affirmative Action.

*George*—By-and-large, you are referring to the experience of white men, but black men also can feel resentment over white women edging them out in jobs.

The way I see it, AA may have put more many competent people on the workplace playing field, but the changing demographics force the issue even more. Now there are just more non-traditional workers in the game. I think the angst, the resentments, are acute now because of industry and economic trends. When downsizing, rightsizing and outsourcing are the fad, the competition is tougher for everybody. Fewer will make the cut. AA is just a very visible and vulnerable target in an economy that is fiercely competitive and of questionable health even as the Dow Jones Index climbs to unthinkable heights.

*Bob*—As long as the economic pie seemed to be growing, Affirmative Action could be carried out with little or no backlash. But the pie hasn't grown for the average worker since the late 1960's, though Reaganomics and other political propaganda was able to maintain the illusion through the heyday of the Yuppie years of the 1980s. The trickle-down economics were actually an upward flood. Most Americans have less buying power and a lower standard-of-living than the previous generation. The fewer rich are outrageously wealthy.

*George*—Equal opportunity becomes problematical when work itself is being redefined and pundits predict "the end of the job." Even an AA policy that produced jobs equitably for all disadvantaged groups might still put those groups at a disadvantage.

*Bob*—I'm not following you.

*George*—Our industries and enterprises are becoming more entrepreneurial, more team, more matrix oriented. The world of the "boss" and the "worker bee" is over. But instead of training AA candidates to be entrepreneurial, it trains them to think in terms of their right to hold a job.

*Bob*— . . . as opposed to creating value. We're conditioning AA candidates to have certain expectations . . .

*George*— . . . expectations and values about work that may be out of date. Think of Civil Service, the Post Office. Affirmative Action was strongly implemented here. It successfully put minorities and women into bureaucracies where jobs were jobs. Federal agencies grew enormously and much social benefit did accrue to people from formerly excluded classes—at a time when the affluence of society appeared to support it. This is not true today. Trying to get a traditional job is a bit like scrambling for deck chairs on the Titanic. What we built through AA now makes reengineering and reinventing government so difficult—and so necessary. AA tells job candidates . . .

*Bob*— . . . you deserve a seat; it's your birthright. But you need to know that the ship is not very seaworthy! You may have to pry up a few deck planks to fashion your own raft to get where you want to go.

*George*—A woman, for example, at this point comes into an organization whether she is an "AA candidate" or not. She gets the job, is perhaps promoted. Suddenly the organization flattens. Who then will be let go? The organization may make valiant efforts to find a rationale other than "last in, first out" to decide. They know the traditional fashion of layoffs would strongly affect women and other protected groups.

Now, no matter who I am, the competition for jobs and advancement is so much greater because the number of positions and their responsibilities have changed. The ladder is not as high as before. There are fewer rungs to success but they are farther apart. There may be no place to go. The glass ceiling is right over my head, even for white men. Diversity as value added (now and in the future) will include redefining work successfully. Identifying ways to help people support themselves in how to do meaningful work in this culture is the new challenge. Using a more sophisticated concept of class rather than race and gender as an entitlement may open the doors to support talent wherever it is found. AA can't fix the economy.

*Bob*—And, there will always be resentment and jockeying at the dividing lines, e.g., the person who earns just a bit too much to qualify for help.

*George*—We will have to be extremely careful to continue to reduce bias and prejudice, though focusing on class should help. But we can already see that there are many expectations that will not be realized, whether they're expectations of white men, black people, women . . .

*Bob*—There may only be crumbs left in that pie pan.

*George*—I think to bake a better or bigger pie we have to recognize what's happening. Downsizing in some organizations is almost at the point of anorexia. People are stressed out doing what used to be two or three jobs. Cutting jobs is a business trend, which is not likely to change tomorrow or the next day. It just leaves us with these burning issues about who "gets the goodies" in the society.

*Bob*—Which is really why the rest of the articles in this section relate to the sensitivities of diverse America. We couldn't include everybody, but there is a rich sampling.

# The More Things Change

by George F. Simons

Maybe because I'm a man . . . Maybe because I'm white . . . Maybe because I'm getting older . . . Maybe because I work outside the country much of the time . . . Maybe because my father kissed me whenever I left home . . . Maybe because of all these things, I am forced to believe that the traditionally dominant White Anglo-Saxon Protestant (WASP) Culture is not only alive, but thriving in America today, especially among people who are not WASPs. Such values as stringent sexual ethics, individual salvation (whether spiritual or economic), future oriented idealism and xenophobia are energetically promoted by the politically correct and the politically incorrigible. (I'm one of these.) Let's look at some of these values in detail.

> There was a time when I used to believe with Diogenes the Cynic that "I am a citizen of the world," and I used to strut about feeling that a "blade of grass is always a blade of grass, whether in one country or another." Now I feel that each blade of grass has its spot on earth from where it draws its life, its strength; and so is man rooted to the land from where he draws his faith, together with his life.
>
> Das Gurcharan
> "Local Memoirs of a Global Manager,"
> in *Harvard Business Review*, March–April, 1993

behavior that was created by Puritans for Puritans. Be warm, be affectionate, be close to the people you enjoy working with every day, and you may soon be in court, because someone's Puritan ethic has been upset, just watching you do "dirty" things, i.e., just being in your presence when you do things that offend their sensibilities. The workplace is becoming a very unfriendly, impersonal place for many of us.

## The Puritan Sexual Ethic: Alive and Well

The Puritan sexual ethic dominates the workplace. "Nobody touches anybody," is now policy in many U.S. workplaces. We Eastern European-, Latino-, Black-, Mediterranean- and other hyphenated Americans are now held to a standard of

This, from the Puritan perspective, however, is exactly as it should be. Work is pain. Today's Puritan, like her or his New England forbears, believes it should be difficult, unpleasant, a way of disciplining the flesh and working out one's salvation. So, we have workplaces that are not only smoke and fragrance-free, but so affection-free and so unpleasant that many of us do as little as we can. Much of the energy, excitement, joy, and creativity that could characterize our work if we were turned on to the earthiness, of ourselves and each other, is drained out of us. There's a strong urge in us to get "down where the iguanas play," as Dory Previn used to sing it. That's probably why a lot of people in this culture take pottery classes. They have permission to throw mud around and be creative, but it still looks like work.

## Cultures: Strength Is Weakness

The French say, "Plus ça change, plus de la même chose." "The more things change, the more they remain the same." It sounds cynical to our progressivist ears. It is not. It is a profound Gallic insight into how culture actually works. The deepest unconscious values of our origins continue to work themselves out in our everyday desires and deeds. As a result we at once reproduce our culture in the world of artifacts, social structures, laws, and art, and at the same time reinforce these core values in ourselves and in each other. U.S. Americans produce more of what is U.S. American, just as sure as rabbits produce bunnies and the ever more litigious U.S. legal climate produces more lawyers.

Perhaps no image so captures the ability of a culture to self-destruct than that of the fu-fu bird (also known to schoolboys throughout the British Commonwealth as the "ousalum bird"). This legendary creature was a philosophical paradigm that grade school boys of my generation talked about. The image is simple but powerful: The fu-fu is a winged creature that flies around in ever tighter circles until it finally flies up its own arse and disappears. Cultures are like this. We overuse our strengths, our cultural formulae for success and survival, do the same stuff over and over until those very strengths become our Achilles' heel. Too many of us have lost the cultural wisdom we had as nine-year-olds.

## Individual Salvation & Individualism

In America, salvation is individual: you make it on your own. Of course, few of us really do, but this Puritan belief is the cornerstone of America's secular creed. Because we are U.S. individualists, we want to believe that we can pull ourselves up by our own bootstraps (the sure sign of God's favor), and we resist any attempt on the part of others to know us, classify us, or compare us to anyone else. We are surprised (and sometimes deeply offended) when they try. Anyone who says, "Just like an American!" is accused of stereotyping, and can never be (politically) correct.

This is U.S. ethnocentricity coming out. Our many hyphenated identities, African-American, Jewish-American, Italian-American, etc., help us preserve the illusion that we have somehow escaped the norms and values of the general culture, the power of the group. Yet, clutching our fading ethnicity to our individualistic hearts, we reassure ourselves that we belong somewhere.

True, each of us is in some way unique. Each of us is also a lot more like the rest of our neighbors than we will comfortably admit. But if we believe we are unlike any others, how can we or would we want to get close to them, or why would we want to? I have no intention of erasing histories of our past, nor do I want to minimize any of the differences we have or conflicts we must still resolve. Still, I would like to heretically suggest that we are very much more alike than different.

Two colleagues of mine who are intensely involved in diversity work recently told me of kindred experiences. One was an African-American man, who just returned from a consulting assignment in Africa. The other was a Chinese-American woman who a summer ago vacationed in China with her Chinese-born parents who had emigrated in their thirties. Both my colleagues were shocked and devastated to learn from their hosts how thoroughly U.S. American they themselves were. If you want to find out what an U.S. American looks like, go abroad for a while, then look in the mirror. You don't have to have been in the USA for very long for this to begin to happen.

It comes as no surprise to anyone who has read a history book, that our first Puritan settlers could be bigots. They came to these shores to guarantee religious freedom for themselves, not for others. However, the principles that brought them here outlived the early colonists' narrowness to become a part of U.S. culture and philosophy. Freedom of religion, freedom of assembly, and freedom of speech are still values that every new group fights for (at least for themselves) and eventually should obtain in our system if it is true to itself. The last paragraph began with a bad premise: we read history books. We Puritan-Americans are focused on the future, not the past, on social transformation not preservation, despite our diversity delvings and eco-concerns.

History, tradition, and ritual are taboo to "the American way." At the moment of history in which they arrived on these shores, Puritans were seeking to escape the oppression of these elements of life. To make a new start then, U.S. Americans must be pure of the earthiness of such things.

Newcomers must abjure "the old country" and not have garlic on their breath. The Puritans and their cultural descendants saw themselves as bold innovators, striking off to a new promised land, seizing opportunity as God-given, making the future as they went along. Today, we U.S. Americans see ourselves as distinguished by what we have chosen, not by what we have inherited or have in common with others. This makes us strange among the nations of the earth. It also puts feminists, activists, liberals, libertarians, the far left and the far right in the same cultural bed, whether or not they can sleep together.

Many of today's intergroup struggles are about extending individual salvation, the rights of the individual, the rights that every white U.S. man is assumed to enjoy (though, at best, only a minority of them actually do) to the other sex, and to every race, ethnicity, belief, and sexual orientation.

## Meanwhile, Back in the Melting Pot

The recently created "salad bowl" image of the diverse U.S. culture is just as much a pragmatic U.S. artifact as the "melting pot" philosophy that it was created to replace. Despite the wishful thinking, this country remains as playwright Israël Zangwill described it generations ago as "God's Crucible, the great Melting Pot where all the races . . . are melting and reforming . . . Left, right and middle each cry out in their own way, 'Into the crucible with you all! God is making the American.'"

If you don't believe Zangwill, ask someone who has decided to become a U.S. American. Countless new immigrants to this country understand that their new rights are based on these values very well, and they consciously choose them. Newcomers not only contribute to the flavor of the stew, they reinforce the culture of the nation because in wanting to be citizens they tend to embrace new values without the subtleties that come of experience in the land.

Though it may not promise as much any more, The Promised Land of the early settlers is still the promised land of Lady Liberty's "teeming masses" today. It's why so many come. For those of us for whom being here is a birthright and not a victory, this promise may seem somewhat faint and far away.

Whether we like it or not, something in us is at least unconsciously struggling to become more U.S. American. This does not keep us from having the vision of the salad bowl which preserves more of the distinctiveness of the variety in the mix of ingredients. Perhaps we can in some way become a more balanced meal of both stew and salad in the various dimensions of our lives, but the old stewpot is a reminder that we are part of something greater than ourselves. Despite ourselves, our culture marches on in four quarter time, as Leonard Cohen sings:

> From the wars against disorder, from the sirens night and day,
>
> from the fires of the homeless, from the ashes of the gay:
>
> Democracy is coming to the U. S. A.[1]

---

[1]From his 1994 album: *Future*, available from Sony Music Corporation.

## AMERICA THRIVES ON CHAOS
by James Fallows

In *More Like Us: Making America Great Again,* I argue that America's mythic promise—the freedom for each of us to make of ourselves whatever we choose—is yielding to an increasingly rigid class and social structure more reminiscent of the stratified societies of Europe and Asia. The culprit is the rise over the last century of intelligence testing, school tracking, entrance exams, degree snobbery, credentialism, and professionalization—all elements of a new meritocracy that effectively pigeonholes Americans and limits their potential from an early age.

But equating future success with some kind of innate, measurable "intelligence" or "ability" is neither necessary nor natural. And what's more, it is fundamentally at odds with what I call the "peculiar genius" of America: A vision of people always in motion, able to make something different of themselves, ready for second changes until the day they die.

This vision starts with the act of immigration—choosing to become an American—and continues through the choices and changes that make American life so different from Japanese or Italian life. People go away to college; they come back home; they go west to California to get a new start; they move east to Manhattan to try to make the big time; they move to Vermont or their parents' religions or values or class; they rediscover their ethnicity three or four generations after their immigrant ancestors arrived. They go to night school; they have nose jobs; they change their names.

If that sounds chaotic, well, that's exactly the point. After three years of living in and reporting from Asia's relatively rigid and structured societies, I have a newfound perspective on—and affection for   good old American disorganization.

Japan is strong because each person knows his place. America is strong when people do not know their proper places and are free to invent new roles for themselves . . .

---

Excerpted from *More Like Us: Making America Great Again,* by James Fallows, Houghton Mifflin Co., 1989.
Reprinted with permission.

# Innocents Abroad
# (Yes, Virginia, There Is a US American Culture)
by George F. Simons & Baudouin E.J.M. Knaapen

**M**any *US Americans are highly adverse to being labeled or stereotyped in any way.* This very statement may turn people off, whether they agree or disagree, because it is a generalization about us. Paradoxically, resistance to this statement tends to substantiate it. We insist on thinking of ourselves as individuals who are free to choose our own labels, Chicano, Polish-American, African-American or Black, etc.

Many Europeans have less difficulty, it seems, identifying US Americans than we ourselves do. The *Amis*, as the Germans call us, look and work and behave in relatively definable and predictable ways. Just for the fun of it, and to get an outsider's feel of ourselves, let's use that word to describe ourselves throughout this article. Whether female or male, black or white, you can spot an Ami, as the French say, *dans un coup d'oeil*, at a glance. In the experience of many Europeans there is a distinct, definable Ami Culture, despite the rainbow of ways in which we feel that we exist. They experience our "Ami-ness," not our diversity.

If the first paragraph of this article didn't make you nervous as an Ami, the second one might have. But before you take offense and move on to someone else's column, I challenge you to explore our US diversity enterprise from an uncommon perspective, seeing it as it looks to many non-Amis—particularly in Europe.

There are two reasons to do this: first, outside perspectives are helpful because they can empower us to see things which have become transparent to us because they are so familiar, i.e., things that are so much a part of the culture that we don't notice them any more; secondly, and perhaps more importantly, because many US corporations are beginning to export their diversity efforts and need to do so with sensitivity. US corporations are insisting that their European and Asian divisions, affiliates, and subsidiaries "manage diversity," and are often uncritically promoting domestic models

that may be inappropriate in an overseas setting. There is a particular danger in doing this in Eastern Europe where eagerness to learn from the West creates an eagerness to accept new ways often uncritically.

Many Europeans will be quick to tell us that they have been managing diversity a lot longer than we have. Here lies a critical distinction that if not recognized will damage the dialogue between us. When European business people talk about managing diversity, they are usually talking about managing interactions *between* relatively stable, identifiable cultural groups. They are largely concerned with doing business and working effectively with partners who are different from themselves.

When Ami businesspeople talk about managing diversity, they are usually talking about managing the tensions between acculturation and assimilation of groups *within* the US population and how these affect the workforce and the marketplace. They are looking for inclusion, conflict reduction and productivity.

The fact that many Western European enterprises have been successful throughout the continent and beyond may be taken as evidence that they have passed the test of managing a daunting diversity of languages, cultures, markets and regulations. This needs to be acknowledged from the Amis.

The term "diversity" itself is new to Europe and is only beginning to achieve common currency in the business world. European business schools and training organizations have concentrated on developing what they call the "Euromanager" and focused on international and global management skills. US diversity practice has moved from a legal basis of equity concerns and "leveling the playing field" to an ideal of utilizing all available human resources to improve the creativity and productivity of the enterprise and the nation. How well this is actually achieved remains to be seen.

Perhaps most shocking to the ears of US diversity practitioners is the opinion held by many Europeans that diversity efforts *à la americaine* are just another step in the continuing process of homogenizing US culture. Many Amis are deeply worried that "diversity" and "multiculturalism" have gone too far in unnecessarily underlining differences and promoting social and workplace rifts. Others argue the contrary, that diversity efforts have not even begun to reach their goals. Both may be right—along with those Europeans who see US diversity efforts making Amis more like Amis.

To many European eyes our national debate about diversity looks like more bubbling and stewing in the same old melting pot in which, as Israël Zangwill observed generations ago, "God is making the American." Diversity programs throw more wood into the stove. They are today's efforts in the continual shaping and peculiarizing of US culture. Diversity programs are an important part of the current process for assimilating newcomers and excluded groups into a mainstream.

Put in less provocative and more academic terms, diversity is an US cultural artifact, a new set of corollaries and applications emerging from existing US cultural premises about who we are and how we should be as a nation. This is a wholly proper thing for us to be doing in our own context, though it seems contrary to how many of us tend to feel and profess about our diversity work. Diversity work is the US creating its now and future culture. Europeans who believe this is so are rightfully nervous. Even well-intended efforts to export US diversity programs can easily turn out to be thinly disguised cultural colonialism, unconscious attempts to make Belgians, Germans and Italians more like Amis rather than to address the real diversity challenges of Europe.

Let's look at some of these challenges to see how our US organizations might contribute to our European partners' efforts, by sharing our diversity experience in a sensitive and judicious way, at the same time paying attention to how various Europeans might receive our ideas.

- **US Management Practice.** As exported and exercised overseas, this itself is a diversity issue, perhaps the prime one that many European affiliates face on a day to day basis. The domination of US models and procedures is high on the list of diversity issues that need to be addressed, and is perhaps the greatest challenge that most US HQ's and expatriate managers, including diversity specialists and trainers, have to overcome. Different groups of Europeans respond to US management initiatives differently, adding another dimension to their own diversity challenges.

- **Equity and Equal Opportunity.** Discrimination and harassment against women and other historically excluded workers is as real in European enterprises as it is in the US, despite an historically wider net of social protection enjoyed by many European workers. Women's roles and levels of participation, for example, are quite different in the various EU countries and different again in Eastern Europe and their issues must be addressed differently. We can give some impetus to the effort toward greater inclusion in our European affiliates but we cannot define it for them.

There is also considerable denial that discrimination and harassment are issues. This denial ties in with Europeans' all too recent history of collaboration and acquiescence in discriminatory ethnic and racial policies both at home and in colonies abroad.

Europeans are also loathe to being dragged into the morass of legislation and litigation that they see in the US where the courts seem to be the ground on which our diversity efforts are ultimately played out. They insist that there must be another way.

Masculinity and femininity tend to be more highly defined than in the US and many Europeans would like to cherish gender diversity while pursuing appropriate levels of equity. To them, gender diversity in the US is making a melting pot of the sexes, too. Many of them would prefer to say, *"Vive la différence!"*

- **Prejudice and Stereotypes.** Racial, ethnic and regional stereotypes are alive and well in Europe, and Europeans can be challenged to take a fresh look at them. They would like to do so without becoming victims of the kind of humorless and inflexible political correctness that can accompany US diversity programs.

Western Europe would like to believe that its forces of ethnic and religious strife are under control rather than just masked by prosperity. These forces are unfortunately still available as powerful tools to demagogues as demonstrated by events in the former Yugoslavia. Even as Northern Ireland winds down, the political reemergence of a xenophobic Radical Right and their success in recent elections, e.g., in Belgium and Austria, are further evidence that all is not well.

- **Fear of Cultural Loss.** Europe is rich in national, regional, ethnic, and linguistic diversity and would like to remain so. It would like to reinforce this creative resource and take advantage of the indigenous characteristics of its peoples. Its indigenous minorities are struggling for survival. Europe fears the US melting pot whose consequences, in their view, include the destruction of culture (or, as some cynically put it, "the lack of culture"), the disintegration of education and language as well as the loss of personal privacy.

A first, indispensable diversity skill is to learn a second language fluently enough to use it in ordinary circumstances. By continental standards, no Ami who has not or cannot at least become reasonably fluent in a second language should ever be considered for management or especially for diversity work in an overseas setting.

The US has been undergoing a de-Eurofication from the time of its origins, which, if anything, has rapidly picked up speed in the new era of multiculturalism. US diversity efforts inimical to Euro-American values are rightly suspect in European minds.

When today's US management gurus talk about "culture change" as a necessary component of reengineering and rightsizing, etc., many a European hears this in a way that his or her US colleagues fail to appreciate, as a direct attack on general culture and values. They are less inclined to compartmentalize organizational practice and separate it from the rest of life.

- **Becoming an Employer of Choice.** Population distribution, the aging of much of Europe, migration and other factors, while differing from factors in the US, will be increasingly important to organizations who wish to attract, retain and benefit from the full potential of the best available employees. In this area European affiliates will have to do their own homework and HR planning. Priorities set in the US can at best serve as suggestions for some avenues that could be explored.

- **Marketing to the EU and to the World.** Growth and success of Western European organizations, both within the boundaries of the European Union and beyond, means increasing diversity of markets and customer needs. Here is one of the most immediately fruitful areas for a dialogue between Europeans and Amis involved in international regional trade. In this respect both sides have much to learn from each other. The challenge is to listen and debate the issues productively. It is very important for participants in the discussion to possess transcultural communication skills.

Diversity competence is generally accepted as a competitive advantage on both sides of the Atlantic. Some recurring obstacles to US driven diversity initiatives in Europe include:

- The US diversity initiative does not appear to be connected with the workplace world that Europeans see. Much of the US effort has been fueled by the pain of exclusion felt by a large numbers of workers. Those dynamics are of different proportions and are dealt with differently in various European nations.

- Amis are often seen as preaching empowerment and equality but not practicing it when it comes to their European subsidiaries and subordinates. "They force us to adopt their models instead of empowering us to empower our employees in ways that work here," is the complaint of many euro-managers in US-held companies.

This is a cultural issue which results in a lack of trust. Amis, too quick to stereotype diverse Europeans as hopelessly caught in

158

hierarchy and traditional working relationships, can feel that US management models that are imposed lock, stock, and barrel bring salvation. We don't trust our partners abroad to do it on their own and quickly enough to meet our expectations. We want it "yesterday," and we want individuals to be independent and responsible in getting it done, whatever the feelings of their colleagues about this may be.

Nothing could be further from the truth. This Ami perception is not the European's reality. Numerous European companies have clearly demonstrated that they are capable of successful restructuring, total quality and empowerment initiatives. They empower themselves to do these things in a culturally appropriate way. We see ourselves selling made-in-the-USA management styles as the products they obviously need. They see themselves as consumers weighing US products for value and quality, deciding if and when to buy them, and then, how to use them. Of course, if they are part of a US held or managed organization, this choice can become much more difficult.

- While Amis speak of "managing diversity," Europeans generally see the task in terms of "integrating diversity." Some are also beginning to use this and related terms (e.g., *gérer diversité, das multikulturelle Management*). Both terms are likely to put us at odds with each other. "Managing" to many Europeans smacks of what they fear is the US tendency to forcefully control everything and everybody. This, we would like to believe, is the opposite of our intentions.

"Integrating diversity," a favorite French phrase, on the other hand, has overtones of civil rights and smacks of assimilation to many Amis. This is exactly what the French do not mean or, at least not what they intend to do. They are speaking rather of the balancing and coordinating of diverse activities and skills from a central perspective to reach a specific business objective.

The Amis and Europeans both fear that the other will be so seduced by their respective hidden cultural values as to thwart the success of the diversity effort to which we are both committed. On the other hand, these hidden values need to be and can be examined as part of the ongoing diversity effort.

- Finally, perhaps the chief obstacle coming from the US side is the simple ignorance which too many managers and, in particular, diversity managers have of both the general and management cultures of Europe. Unfortunately, U.S. diversity managers are often chosen because they already represent and specialize in historically excluded segments of the workforce.

This is not an accusation. It is just an acknowledgment of the fact that too few Amis have the day-to-day experience of living, communicating and working in cultures outside the US and appreciating the European challenges and problems. There is an isolationist and moralistic streak in US culture. When combined with the normal ethnocentricity found in any group of people, it makes us appear arrogant and insensitive to our overseas partners despite our best intentions.

In sum, discussions with our European colleagues about US diversity are hard to conduct without our slipping into what they feel is "intellectual colonialism." There may be reasons for Ami owned or led organizations to do diversity abroad, but they are not the same reasons that give rise to the effort in the US. Different history, different proportions, and different social and political dynamics are always in an interplay. This also means that different results will emerge from transferring our technology as it is and they may not be what the US is looking for. Europeans feel best when they are addressing their own agenda, even though that can stimulated by the US experience. And indeed, there is diversity within diversity in Europe. Some people even feel that calling US folks "Amis" is an ethnic slur.

## About the Authors

Dr. George F. Simons is Principal of George Simons International, a Santa Cruz, CA consulting and training firm specializing in Gender and Cultural Diversity. He may be reached at 408-426-9608 (phone) and at 408-457-8590 (fax).

Baudouin E.J.M. Knaapen, Partner in Knaapen-Kok Consult in Nieuwegein, The Netherlands, can be reached by phone at +31-3402-56868.

Readers interested in the theme of Diversity in US organizations abroad are invited to continue the discussion of this topic by electronic mail-GSINTGS@AOL.COM

# The New Generation Gap

by Neil Howe and William Strauss (*Atlantic Monthly*)

A new generation gap reflecting two different world views is emerging today. In the late 1960s the fight was mainly between twenty-year olds and the fifty-plus crowd. Today it's mainly between young people and the thirty to forty-year-olds. Each time, the same conspicuous generation has been involved. Each time, that generation has claimed the moral and cultural high ground, casting itself as the apex of civilization and its age-bracket adversaries as soul-dead, progress-blocking philistines. The first time around, the members of that generation attacked their elders; now they're targeting their juniors.

We're talking about Baby Boomers. Born from 1943 to 1960, today's 69 million Boomers range in age from thirty-two to forty-nine. The younger antagonists are less well known: America's thirteenth generation (or "thirteeners"), born from 1961 to 1981, ranging in age from eleven to thirty-one, and sometimes also labeled "Generation X." The old generation gap of the late 1960s and early 1970s featured an incendiary war between college kids and the reigning leaders of great public institutions. Back then the moralizing aggressors were on the younger side. And back then Americans in their thirties and early forties (the "Silent Generation," born from 1925 to 1942) stood in between as mentors and mediators. The new generation gap of the 1990s is different. It features a smoldering mutual disdain between Americans now reaching mid-life and those born just after them. This time the moralizing aggressors are on the older side. And this time no generation stands in between.

What separates the collective personalities of Boomers and Thirteeners? First, look at today's mainline media, a hotbed of forty-year-old thinking. Notice how, in Boomers' hands, 1990s America is becoming a somber land obsessed with values, back-to-basics movements, ethical rectitude, political correctness, harsh punishments, and a yearning for the simple life. Now look again—and notice a countermood popping up in college towns, in big cities, on Fox and cable TV, and in various ethnic side currents. It's a cone of physical frenzy and spiritual numbness, a revelry of pop, a pursuit of high-tech, guiltless fun. A generation weaned on minimal expectations and gifted in the game of life is now avoiding meaning in a cumbersome society that, as they see it, offers them little. Already Thirteeners blame Boomers for much that has gone wrong in their world, a tendency that is sure to grow once Boomers move fully into positions of political leadership.

"Something strange is going on in the hearts of baby boomers," announced *American Demographics* magazine in a recent article heralding the 1990s. Around the same time, *Good Housekeeping* took a full-page in *The New York Times* to run an ad inspired by the Boomer marketing guru Faith Popcorn. The ad welcomed America to "the Decency Decade, the years when the good guys finally win. . . . It will be a very good decade for the Earth, as New Traditionalists lead an unstoppable environmental juggernaut that will change and inspire corporate America, and let us all live healthier, more decent lives," when consumers will "look for what is real, what is honest, what is quality, what is valued, what is important."

How can this be? How can a generation that came of age amid the libidinous euphoria of People's Park now be forming neighborhood associations to push "alcoholics, drug dealers, and wing nuts" out of Berkeley parks and out of their lives?

Over the past five decades, as Boomers have charted their life's voyage, they have consistently aged in a manner unlike what anyone, themselves included, ever expected. They began as the most indulged children of this century, basking in intensely child-focused households and communities. To most middle-class youths, poverty, disease, and crime were invisible—or, at worst, temporary nuisances that would soon succumb to the inexorable advance of affluence. With the outer world looking fine, the inner world became the point of youthful focus. In 1965 *Time* magazine declared that teenagers were "on the fringe of a golden era"—and, two years later, described collegians as cheerful idealists who would "lay out blight-proof, smog-free cities, enrich the underdeveloped world, and, no doubt, write finis to poverty and war."

Hardly. Over the next several years Boomers discovered that they were never meant to be doers and builders like their parents. Instead, finding their parents' constructions in need of a major spiritual overhaul, even creative destruction, they triggered a youth-focused "Consciousness Revolution." Beginning in the late 1960s the generation gap became a full-fledged age war between the Boomers and the GI Generation.

This GI-Boomer age war paralleled the Vietnam shooting war. It crested in 1969, along with draft calls and casualties. A couple of years later—after Ohio's National Guardsmen killed four Kent State students, after student opinion turned solidly against the war, and after Congress amended the Constitution to allow eighteen-year-olds to vote—Boomers began heeding the Beatles' simple words of wisdom: "let it be." The generation gap began to ease, in its outward forms at least, replaced by a grinding pessimism and a gray Boomer drizzle of sex, drugs, unemployment, and a sour (if less confrontational) mood on campus. In the 1970s the GI-versus-Boom clash had a quiet denouement that has proved over time to be at least as consequential as the Boomers' angry demonstrations. No pact was signed, no speeches were made, but something of a deal was struck. On the one hand, Boomers said nothing as GIs then on the brink of retirement proceeded to channel a growing portion of the nation's public resources (over a period from the post–Vietnam peace dividend to the post–Cold War peace dividend) toward their own "entitlements." On the other hand, GIs did not object as Boomers asserted control of the culture.

Along the way, the word "yuppie"—a term of derision among others, of self-mocking humor among Boomers—labeled a generation of supposedly sold-out ex-hippies. Introduced in 1981, the word referred to "young upwardly mobile professionals," a group that included only about one out of every twenty Boomers. But a much larger proportion fit the subjective definition: self-immersed, impatient for personal satisfaction, weak in civic instincts.

Notwithstanding their affluent reputation through the 1980s, Boomers, especially those born in the middle to late 1950s, have not prospered. Debt is a big problem: *U.S. News & World Report* says that roughly one fourth of all professional and managerial Boomers are "nebbies" (negative-equity Boomers) teetering on the edge of personal bankruptcy. Yet amid these financial problems, polls show, Boomers overwhelmingly consider their careers better, their personal freedoms greater, and their lives more meaningful than those of their parents. The American Dream lives on for them in the form of a finely tuned inner life.

Although 1990s-edition Boomers are no throwback to the 1960s, they see themselves as they did then (and always have): as the embodiment of moral wisdom. Addressing America's unresolved social issues, from crime and homelessness to health and education, Boomers are far more inclined than other generations to believe, with Jeffrey Bell, that "the setting of society's standards is, in the final analysis, what politics is all about." Whatever the problem, the Boomers' solution could not be more different from that of their parents at a like age. Their call is not for the white-coated scientist but for the black-cloaked preacher. A generation that came of age in an era of "Is God Dead?" is immersing itself in spiritual movements of all kinds, from evangelical fundamentalism to New Age humanism, from transcendentalism to ESP. The leaders among Boomer blacks, once known for the Afro cut and the black-power salute, are bypassing the rusty machinery of civil-rights legislation pioneered by their elders and are preaching a strict new standard of group pride, family integrity, and community loyalty.

On both sides of the political spectrum Boomer politicians advocate stark, no-pain, no-gain "cures"—like the Oregon Plan for Medicaid triage, or Dan Quayle's demand that limits be placed on jury awards for "pain and suffering," or Al Gore's call for stiff energy taxes, or Massachusetts Governor William Weld's notion that a ten year prison sentence should mean 10.0 years behind bars, or Bill Clinton's proposal that "we ought to have boot camp for first-time nonviolent offenders." Boomer editorialists adamantly reject dickering with foreign tyrants, compromise on the deficit, mercy for S&L violators, welfare for anybody who doesn't work for it. It is in the shadow of such a generation that Thirteeners are coming of age.

As they shield their eyes with Ray-Ban Way-farer sunglasses and their ears with Model Walk-men, today's teens and twenties present to Boomer eyes a splintered image of brassy looks and smooth manner, of kids growing up too tough to be cute, of kids more comfortable shopping or playing than working or studying. Ads target them as beasts of pleasure and pain who have trouble understanding words longer than one syllable, sentences longer than three words.

On the job, Thirteeners are the reckless bicycle messengers, pizza drivers, yard workers, Wal-Mart shelf-stockers, health care trainees, and miscellaneous scavengers, hustlers, and Mcjobbers in the low-wage/low-benefit service economy. They're the wandering nomads of the temp world, directionless slackers, habitual nonvoters. In school they're a group of staggering diversity—not just in ethnicity but also in attitude, performance, and rewards. After graduation they're the ones with big loans who were supposed to graduate into jobs and move out of the house but didn't, and who seem to get poorer the longer they've been away from home—unlike their parents at that age, who seemed to get richer. In inner cities Thirteeners are the unmarried teen mothers and unconcerned teen fathers, the Crips and Bloods, the innocent hip-hoppers grown weary of watching white Boomers cross the street to avoid them. In suburbs they're the kids at the mall, kids buying family groceries for busy moms and dads, kids in mutual-protection circles of friends, girding against an adolescent world far more dangerous than anything their parents fear, kids struggling to unlink sex from disease and death.

When they look into the future, they see a much bleaker vision than any of today's older generations ever saw in their own youth. Polls show that Thirteeners believe it will be much harder for them to get ahead than it was for their parents—and that they are overwhelmingly pessimistic about the long-term fate of their generation and nation.

They were among the first babies people took pills not to have. During the 1967 Summer of Love they were the kindergartners who paid the price for America's new divorce epidemic. In 1970 they were fourth-graders trying to learn arithmetic amid the chaos of open classrooms and New Math curricula. In 1973 they were the bell-bottomed sixth-graders who got their first real-life civics lesson watching the Watergate hearings on TV. Through the late 1970s they were the teenage mall-hoppers who spawned the Valley Girls and other flagrantly non-Boomer youth trends. In 1979 they were the graduating seniors of Carter-era malaise who registered record-low SAT scores and record-high crime and drug-abuse rates. When they were small, the nation was riding high. When they reached adolescence, national confidence weakened, and community and family life splintered. Older people focused less on the future, planned less for it, and invested less in it.

The pop culture conveyed to little kids and (by 1980) gave teenagers a recurring message from the adult world: that they weren't wanted, and weren't even liked, by the grown-ups around them. Taxpayers revolted against school funding, and landlords and neighborhoods that had once smiled on young Boomers started banning children. From the late 1960s until the early 1980s America's pre-adolescents grasped what nurture they could through the most virulently anti-child period in modern American history. Ugly new phrases ("latchkey child," "throwaway child," and later "boomerang child") joined the sad new lexicon of youth. When Thirteeners were ready to enter the adult labor force, the politicians pushed every policy lever conceivable—tax codes, entitlements, public debt, unfunded liabilities, labor laws, hiring practices—to tilt the economic playing field away from the young and toward the old. The results were predictable.

Older people have prospered, Boomers have barely held their own, and Thirteeners have fallen off a cliff. Polls show that most teenagers (of both sexes) expect to be earning $30,000 or more by age thirty, but in 1990 the U.S. Census Bureau reported that among Americans aged twenty-five to twenty-nine there were eight with total annual incomes of under $30,000 for every one making more than $30,000.

Welcome, Thirteeners to American contemporary life. While older age brackets are getting richer, yours is getting poorer. Today more young adults are living with their parents than at any other time since the Great Depression. When you marry, you and your spouse will both work—not for Boomerish self-fulfillment but because you need to just to make ends meet. If you want children, you'll have to defy statistics showing that since 1973 the median real income has fallen by 30 percent for families with children which are headed by persons under thirty. Your generation, in fact, has a weaker middle class than any other generation born in this century

Everywhere they look, Thirteeners see the workplace system rigged against them. As they view it, the families, schools, and training programs that could have prepared them for worthwhile careers have been allowed to rot, but the institutions that safeguard the occupational livelihood of mature workers have been maintained with full vigor.

Like warriors on the eve of battle, Thirteeners face their future with a mixture of bravado and fatalism. Squared off competitively against one another, this melange of scared city kids, suburban slackers, hung immigrants, desperate grads, and shameless hustlers is collectively coming to realize that America rewards only a select set of winners with its Dream—and that America cares little about its anonymous losers. The Thirteener finds himself essentially alone. Between his relative poverty and the affluence he desires, he sees an enormous obstacle: those Boomers.

A quarter century ago kids called older people names. These days, the reverse is true. For the past decade Thirteeners have been bombarded with study after story after column about how dumb, greedy, and just plain bad they supposedly are.

Amidst this barrage, Thirteeners have become (in elders' eyes) a symbol of an America in decline. Back in the 1970s social scientists looked at the American experience over the preceding half century and observed that each new generation, compared with the last, traveled another step upward on the Maslovian scale of human purpose, away from concrete needs and toward higher, more spiritual aspirations. Those due to arrive after the Boomers, they expected, would be even more cerebral, more learned, more idealistic, than any who came before. No chance—especially once Boomers started to sit in judgment and churn out condemnatory reports on the fitness of their generational successor. In the classroom Boomers instruct the young in "emotional literacy"; in the military they delouse the young with "core values" training; on campus they drill the young in the vocabulary of "political correctness." The object is not to get them to understand—that would be asking too much—but to get them to behave.

To date Thirteeners have seldom either rebutted their elders' accusations or pressed their own counter charges. Polls show them mostly agreeing that, yes, Boomer kids probably were a better lot, listened to better music, pursued better causes, and generally had better times on campus. So, they figure, why fight a rap they can't beat? And besides, why waste time and energy arguing? But among friends they talk frankly about how to maneuver in a world full of self-righteous ideologues.

Every phase and arena of life has been fine, even terrific, when Boomers entered it—and a wasteland when they left. A child's world was endlessly sunny in the 1950s, scarred by family chaos in the 1970s. Most movies and TV shows were fine for adolescents in the 1960s, unfit in the 1980s. Young-adult sex meant free love in the 1970s, AIDS in the 1990s. Boomers might prefer to think of their generation as the leaders of social progress, but the facts show otherwise.

Thirteeners fume when they hear Boomers taking credit for things they didn't do (starting the civil-rights movement, inventing rock-and-roll, stopping the Vietnam War) and for having been the most creative, idealistic, morally conscious youth in the history of America, if not the world. Even among Thirteeners who admire what young people did back in the sixties, workaholic, values-fixated Boomers are an object lesson in what not to become in their thirties and forties. What Thirteeners want from Boomers is an apology mixed in with a little generational humility. Something like: "Hey, guys, we're sorry we ruined everything for you. Maybe we're not such a super-duper generation, and maybe we can learn something from you." Like two neighbors separated by a spite fence, Boomers and Thirteeners have grown accustomed to an uneasy adjacency.

If history tells us that the Boom-Thirteenth quarrel will worsen over the coming decade, it also suggests when and how this new generation gap could resolve itself. Once Boomers start entering old age, they will ease their attacks on Thirteeners. Once they see their values focus taking firm root in American institutions—and once their hopes are fixed on a new and more optimistic (post–Thirteenth) generation—Boomers will lose interest in the quarrel. As they enter mid-life, Thirteeners will likewise tire of goading Boomers. They will quit trying to argue about Boomer goals and will focus their attention on how to achieve their own goals practically, with no more hurt than is absolutely necessary.

The key to a favorable resolution of the Boom-Thirteenth clash may lie in one of its inherent causes. To find this cause, visit America's hospital nurseries or day-care centers or primary-school classrooms, grades K through 5. It's the fledgling "Millennial Generation" of Jessica McClure and Baby M, of Jebbie Bush and Al Gore III, whose birth years will ultimately reach from 1982 or so to sometime around 2000. Recall that one big reason Boomers are so intent on policing Thirteener behavior is to clear and clean the path for these Babies on Board to grow up as the smartest, best-behaved, most civic-minded kids in the history of humankind—or, at a minimum, a whole lot better than Thirteeners. And while Thirteeners would hardly put it the same way, they, too, are eager to reseed the desert that was their youth and help the nation treat the next round of kids to a happier start in life.

Two decades from now Boomers entering old age may well see in their grown Millennial children an effective instrument for saving the world, while Thirteeners entering mid-life will shower kindnesses on a younger generation that is getting a better deal out of life (though maybe a bit less fun) than they ever got at a like age. Study after story after column will laud these "best damn kids in the world" as heralding a resurgent American greatness. And, for a while at least, no one will talk about a generation gap.

## Editor's Note

Limitations of space require us to provide an edited version of this article which first appeared in the December 1992 issue of *The Atlantic Monthly*. This abbreviated version omits the author's identification and discussion of two additional generations, The Missionary Generation (those born from 1860 to 1882) and the Lost Generation (those born from 1883 to 1900). These reflect characteristics and antagonisms similar to the Boomers and Thirteeners and may provide some basis for predicting what could happen in the decades ahead.

---

### FIGHTING FOR A PLACE

"Looking back over the years, it has often struck me how the world of boxing has reflected the world I live in. The parade of world champions has matched the waves of immigrants arriving on these shores and the rise of oppressed people fighting for their rightful place in U.S. society.

"I can remember when they were German, then Irish, then Italian, then Black. Now I watch the Golden Gloves tournaments and see lots of Latinos and people from the Caribbean and Asia, and what worries me, still too many black Americans.

"I don't know if the newcomers will become the heavyweight champions like those in past generations—some of them seem so small. But this I do know, they are not just fighting for a purse. They are fighting for acceptance, and for a place in the American Dream for themselves and their families and for the people they love. You can see it in the discipline, the passion and the determination with which they throw their punches and the fancy footwork needed to avoid the blows coming their way.

"I have to remind myself of this the next time one of these people sounds loud, abrasive, pushy, foreign or elusive to me."

Overheard in a conversation.

# White, Male, and Worried

by Michele Galen with Ann Therese Palmer (*Business Week*)

Last April, Doug Tennant lost his job as a long-term contract employee for Pacific Gas & Electric Co. in Tracy, Calif. He says he was the first one in his three-person unit to be laid off. He claims the others—a black woman and a man of Indian descent—were kept on even though he was more qualified. Tennant, who is white, blames PG&E's push for a more diverse workplace. "I feel like I'm losing out," he says. PG&E says his race and sex had nothing to do with his departure.

Marilyn Moats Kennedy, a Chicago based career counselor, recently got a plaintive letter from a white male who wanted a job hauling baggage for United Airlines Co. It seemed that all the candidates who were having any luck were women and minorities. "How am I going to get on with the airlines?" the man wrote. "Wrong pigment, wrong plumbing."

He hasn't selected any colleges yet, but Curt Harms is concerned about the impact of diversity on his chances for acceptance. "I'm worried," says Harms, a 15-year-old sophomore from Lake Bluff, Ill., who is white. "If there's a candidate who has grades and credentials exactly the same as mine, these days it's more likely they'll take that person over me, if the person is a minority or a woman. There's nothing I can do."

Peek inside any corporate boardroom, or take a look at the senior managers of most top corporations, and it's hard to see what Harms, Tennant, and others like them are complaining about: It's still a white man's world.

But in a growing minority of companies—especially those aggressively pushing diversity programs—some white males are coming to a different conclusion. They're feeling frustrated, resentful, and most of all, afraid. There's a sense that, be it on the job or at home, the rules are changing faster than they can keep up. "Race and gender have become factors for white men, much the way they have been for other groups," says Thomas Kochman, a professor at the University of Illinois-Chicago who consults with companies on white male issues. "The worm is turning, and they don't like it."

The phenomenon Kochman and others are talking about is far from universal in Corporate America. In fact, most white males don't feel particularly threatened or haven't noticed such changes where they work. But then, the impact of diversity programs, even in the companies that have them, is still limited. "Sadly, we find a lot of these diversity programs hang out there by themselves and don't loop back into a coherent management development program," says Jeffrey A. Sonnenfeld, director of the Center for Leadership & Career Studies at Emory University. "The programs often are window-dressing."

**Open Season.** But in such companies as AT&T, DuPont, and Motorola, where diversity is becoming more than just a buzzword, the emotional landscape for white males is changing. There, white men must compete against people they may not have taken all

> As companies hire and promote more women and minorities, they feel a backlash from some white males

that seriously as rivals—mainly women, blacks, Hispanics, and Asians. White males also say that the diversity programs often make them feel threatened or attacked. "In the diversity group I was in, there were some understandable reprisals against white males and, implicitly, the company," says John L. Mason, vice-president for recruiting and equal employment at Monsanto Co. "The reprisals discounted all the good things white males have done."

Even in companies where diversity programs are new or haven't made much impact, white males are feeling pressure. Often for the first time in their lives, they're worrying about their future opportunities because of widespread layoffs and corporate restructurings. Outside the corporation, white men are feeling threatened because of racial and gender tensions that have been intensifying in recent years. "'White male' is what I call the newest swear word in America," says Harris Sussman, president of Workways, a strategic consulting firm in Cambridge, Mass. "We all know that's not a compliment."

No matter what company they're in, white males must face a sobering new reality: With a more diverse population entering the work force, white men are slowly becoming a minority. From 1983 to 1993, the percentage of white, male professionals and managers in the work force dropped from 55% to 47%, while the same group of white women jumped from 37% to 42%. The diversification of the workplace will only pick up. Through the year 2005, the Labor Dept. estimates that half of all labor force entrants will be women, and more than one-third will be Hispanics, African Americans, and those of other races.

All this is driving what some diversity experts and executives call a white, male backlash. So far, it has occurred mostly in companies experiencing the greatest flux, where some men blame their stalled careers on racial or gender differences. "When everybody is working and happy, diversity is just talk over the water cooler," says one laid-off, white, male executive who attributes his 18-month job hunt to employers who "earmark" jobs for female and minority candidates. "But when it impacts you directly, you become kind of angry."

**Quandary.** At the heart of the issue for many white males is the question of merit—that in the rush for a more diverse workplace, they will lose out to less qualified workers. Most white men claim they have no problem with promoting or hiring women and minorities if they are the best people for the job. It's another story when two candidates are of equal merit. In that case, if the company picks a woman or minority, some white men are quick to cry reverse discrimination—even though the law lets companies take race into account in employment decisions to remedy past discrimination.

The shifting dynamics of the work force have placed managers, many of whom are white males themselves, in a moral quandary. In their efforts to make their companies more diverse, they are certain to hire or promote women and minorities over other white males. That is sure to lead to anger from those who are passed over. In the extreme,

productivity could suffer as white males flee to more old-line competitors. Yet if these managers fail to embrace diversity, they not only perpetuate past injustices but risk leaving their companies less globally competitive.

Many white, male managers say that those pressures become even harder to bear when they, rather than senior executives, are blamed for a litany of past wrongs committed by white men. "I'm certainly not part of the power structure," says James Gault, a systems engineer with American Telephone & Telegraph Co. in New Jersey. "But compared to blacks and women, I am."

Complicating such issues is the split between what many white men say they believe and what they actually feel: They recognize intellectually that they're still calling the shots and getting most of the promotions. But that does little to assuage fears that the pendulum will swing too far. "White males are like the firstborn in the family, the ones who have had the best love of both parents and never quite forgave the second child for being born," says Kochman, the University of Illinois professor. "We're dealing here with a sense of entitlements."

For companies committed to a corporate culture that embraces groups besides white males, all this raises two dilemmas: First, how to ensure a diverse work force without antagonizing either white males, whose support is critical for change, or women and minorities, who may resent efforts to win over white males; and second, how to reverse historical discrimination without creating new forms of it.

The experience at Rochester Telephone Corp. shows how tough those tasks can be. Until recently, white males criticized the company's diversity efforts as affirmative action under a different name—something they say doesn't affect them. The predominately white unions refused to support the initiative. "It was very divisive," says Robert Flavin, president of Local 11709 of the Communications Workers of America. "The minorities had an open door to the president."

Now, Michael O. Thomas, who is black, is trying to change all that. Hired last summer as Rochester's corporate director of staffing and diversity, Thomas expanded the definition of diversity to cover job sharing, career planning, and other employee concerns as well as race and gender. To oversee those efforts, he and members of an internal Diversity Council, already comprising a cross section of the company, hired a diversity manager—who happened to be a white female—and eliminated the minority-run diversity department. He also refocused the council's mission to make it more inclusive and help set an agenda. Thomas says his efforts have drawn mixed reactions from minorities, some of whom worry he's ignoring their problems. Thomas is determined to prove them wrong. His approach is already winning over labor. "The old program didn't have anything to do with our members. Now it does," says Flavin.

**Tokenism Charges.** While Rochester's diversity program isn't focusing on white males, some of the most aggressive employers on the diversity front are realizing that winning over white male employees requires special efforts—and is crucial to their programs' success. AT&T and Motorola Inc. are hiring consultants to lead seminars that help white males handle anxieties over their changing status. CoreStates Financial Corp. is forming a white men's support group similar to those in place for people of color as well as gays, lesbians, and bisexuals. For all male employees, DuPont Co. is creating a "Men's Forum." "White males are feeling left out," says Bernard Scales, DuPont's manager of diversity, who is black. "They are questioning from the sidelines: What is going on? What is the company doing? What is it that women and people of color are trying to tell them?'

Managers who ignore such issues risk inflaming dissension and hurting morale and productivity. At some companies, white middle managers are filing internal complaints about unfair treatment. At NutraSweet Co., CEO Robert E. Flynn says evidence of white, male resistance surfaced in two similar incidents in recent months: White men picked white males for key positions—without posting the jobs for females, minorities, and others. Both jobs were reopened so that a broad range of candidates could apply. In one case, the initial candidate got the job, but some of the women and minorities who were interviewed got promoted as well. The other case is pending. "There is a backlash," Flynn says. "There is some uneasiness about how aggressive we are in terms of diversity."

All too often, say many women and minorities, that uneasiness is expressed in the kind of behavior they have long had to put up with from white men. Women complain that some white, male managers try to undermine their credibility by doing such

things as attributing their rise to tokenism. "When a female or minority or some combination is appointed to a particularly prestigious job, there's always the comment that the reason they were selected is that they were a woman or minority. That's one of the statements white males still aren't afraid to make in public," says Sara Kelsey, vice-president and assistant general counsel at Chemical Bank in New York. "I find those remarks very irritating because the men make it sound like that's the only reason."

**Orgy of Blame.** Rather than address such behavior, white males say too many diversity programs just encourage women and minorities to vent their anger. Ken E. Richardson, a white male, attended a week-long diversity program in the spring of 1992. An administrator with the Licking County (Ohio) Sheriff's office, he was one of five white males in a racially and sexually diverse group of 30. Having lived in a mixed neighborhood and abroad, Richardson says he has always respected cultural and racial differences. But in the training session, he says he was blamed "for everything from slavery to the glass ceiling." The instructors—a white female and two black males—seemed to "feed into the white-male-bashing," he says. "I became bitter and remain so."

Despite the risk that some programs will alienate men like Richardson, even such white, male bastions as the oil industry are pushing diversity initiatives. For Amoco CEO H. Laurance Fuller, managing diversity is a "business imperative." He says women and minorities account for 40% of his work force though they remain disproportionately in lower-ranked jobs; one of every six employees is not a U. S. citizen. Last fall Fuller established a Diversity Advisory Council, which he chairs. Its mission is to create an environment in which Amoco Corp.'s increasingly diverse work force can reach its full potential

The council is finalizing a long-term action plan, but some white, male middle managers are already worried. From time to time, they've questioned Fuller—himself white—about the consequences of diversity on their careers. "I reply that they have nothing to fear but more and better competition, which can only enhance Amoco's prosperity and their own," Fuller says.

For now, such reassurance is all the attention some white males at Amoco seem to want. Last summer, the company accepted a consultant's suggestion to hold a focus group solely for white, male middle managers. It was intended to get them to express their concerns, says Jim Fair, Amoco's director of media relations who attended the workshop. But some men didn't think they needed the seminar. "Are you trying to get me to be upset?" Fair reports one manager asked the moderator. Others objected to being singled out. Fair said the men agreed that a more valuable experience would be sessions with different people together.

**Surprising Conclusions.** AT&T has embraced just such an approach, partly through a course called "White Males: The Label, the Dilemma." Led by consultant Sussman, the course presents the future work force, then asks white men how they feel about being labeled a minority. The women and minorities in the class react to the white males' views or challenge their conclusions. Beate Sykes, an AT&T diversity counselor, sought out the course in response to requests by white men "to do something for them."

The intensity of the one-day seminar surprised some of the white men who attended. "I didn't realize how much other white men felt attacked and how oblivious" they were to the benefits that their race and gender bestowed, says James Gault, the systems engineer. "They felt everything was equal now." Other attendees say the seminar changed their self-image. "I never thought of myself as a white male," says Lee Arpin, a development manager. "In a lot of cases, we have privileges we don't appreciate."

Minorities left the seminar with insights into white men. David Clanton, a software designer who is black, says the class made him "more empathetic" to white males because it showed how deeply felt their concerns were, just like other groups. He learned that white men don't like being lumped together or blamed for "something their fathers and grandfathers might have done." The class also helped him feel more comfortable with white male colleagues who seemed to be "more to my way of thinking than I would have expected." Not all AT&T employees view the company's attention to white men favorably. On Nov. 5, Sussman was the key speaker at a mandatory, all-day conference sponsored by an affirmative action committee at an AT&T division in northern New Jersey. The occasion drew some complaints from women and minorities, who wanted to know why an affirmative action workshop should devote any time at all to white men. One minority employee was so incensed that the worker didn't attend.

Other companies with diversity programs are reaching out to white males. Corning Inc. has made a big diversity push since 1987 and, among other things, now requires all employees to attend race and gender sensitivity training. The result, says Gail O. Baity, manager of strategic corporate education, is that "white males are asking questions like 'The demographics show there will be fewer white males entering the work force. Will we be in the minority?' Or they're asking about parity. 'You have all these programs focused on women and color. What about me?'"

> White, male employees "have nothing to fear but more and better competition."
>
> —Laurance Fuller
> CEO, Amoco Corp.

**Core Requirements.** In response, Corning has made a special effort to share employment statistics to correct a misperception of trends. "White males still predominate within the company and still hold the predominant positions of authority," Baity says. Corning also is trying to make the advancement process more objective by identifying core competencies for various jobs. When an employee gets a certain post, Corning can then point to the fulfillment of the core competencies as a valid reason why he or she deserved it. Ultimately, Corning expects managers to assemble a diverse talent pool for any opening, then select the best person.

That's an approach more companies are likely to take as women and minorities continue to make strides. Companies will also find that diversity programs to encourage those trends are in their interest. The programs are in their customers' interests as well: They help to promote employees who, given their rich backgrounds, are not only qualified but more sensitive to the diverse cultures of the markets they serve. "There's not too many white faces in Indonesia," says NutraSweet's Flynn, who is pushing to raise the company's foreign revenues.

But companies must walk a fine line: If they pay only lip service to diversity, they risk losing or alienating women and minorities, an increasingly important sector of the talent pool. If they push diversity too hard without taking stock of the fears of their white, male employees, they risk losing white males or their backing. To be sure, the transition from a corporate culture dominated by white males to one that embraces all employees equally will not take place without a degree of tension. But if companies are to compete in the changing marketplace, and if they are to treat all employees with equal respect, diversity is essential. And so, too, is the proper training for all involved.

## About the Authors

By Michele Galen in New York with Ann Therese Palmer in Chicago and bureau reports.

---

### FREE SPEECH VS. POLITICAL CORRECTNESS
by Nat Hentoff

A vigorous dissent from political orthodoxy on campus was made by a black Harvard Law School student during a debate on whether the law school should start punishing speech. A white student got up and said that the codes are necessary because without them black students would be driven away from colleges and thereby deprived of the equal opportunity to get an education.

The black student rose and said that the white student had a hell of a nerve to assume that he—in the face of racist speech—would pack up his books and go home. He'd been all too familiar with that kind of speech all his life, and he had never felt the need to run away from it. He'd handled it before, and he could again.

The black student then looked at his white colleague and said that it was condescending to say that blacks have to be "protected" from racist speech. "It is more racist and insulting," he emphasized, "to say that to me than to call me a nigger."

---

# Burdens on Asian-Americans

by Anne Kim (*Los Angeles Times*)

I am an American. I've spent a large portion of my life trying to convince people of this, so I'll say it again: I am an American. A-M-E-R-I-C-A-N. Yes, I'll admit my parents are Korean immigrants, but I was born—and made in the USA.

Everyone assumes Americans come in only two flavors, chocolate and vanilla. Even if you arrived from Tanzania or Iceland two hours ago, you get the benefit of the doubt. But if you're of a different variety—vaguely Asian or slightly Hispanic people automatically label you "fresh off the boat," even if your family helped welcome the Mayflower.

Even the supposedly sensitive people act as if you were less than a real American, or at least less than a real person. For one thing, I've noticed that certain people bow when they're introduced to me. One professor who did this also swore I had an "unusual" accent, though he's the one who "warshes" dishes and "wrastles" hogs and whose vowels are as flat as the Kansas prairie.

Some folks wonder how long I've been in the States, and some folks ask outright if I speak English. The considerate ones speak loudly and clearly, just in case. When this happens, the temptation is terrible to rattle off something unintelligible—but preferably obscene—in pidgin French or ancient Greek. (I can recite the first 10 lines of The Iliad in perfect dactylic hexameter.) So far, I haven't had the guts.

People also act very disappointed if I don't live up to stereotype. My last skirmish with this kind of idiocy happened only last week during, strangely enough, a blood drive. After asking the usual questions about malaria and yellow jaundice, the nurse (named Cookie) asked if I were good in math. I said no, and she said, "Really? Too bad. You're [Asians are] supposed to be."

I wanted to hit her, but Cookie was holding a large needle. Another attitude that seems especially prevalent is the mail-order-bride mentality. Occasionally when I'm with my boyfriend—who is as Anglo as you can get—total strangers walk up and ask him where I'm from, if I speak English, blah-blah-blah. The next time someone does that, I'm going to have him reply, "Oh yes. Glad you asked. Bought her from a catalog, for $4.99. Postage and handling extra, of course, but quite a bargain, nonetheless."

The same mentality is responsible for a certain class of male that seems to think Asian women are easy to please, utterly subservient and desperately clamoring for Anglo husbands.

Two such individuals have crossed my path in the past year alone. One of them was a fellow whose last name coincides with that of a well-known Walt Disney character. During lunch in the dorm cafeteria, he casually sauntered over and said (this is true), "Hello. Me see you here very long-time. Me think you very pretty." He then said, "I don't like American girls. I only like Asian women." So solly to disappoint you, Romeo.

The second fellow was a middle-aged convenience store clerk from Springfield, Mo., whose pick-up line was 20 Questions. "Are you Chinese?" No. "Are you Taiwanese?" No. "Are you Mongolian, Cambodian, Laotian, Filipino, Japanese, Hawaiian?" No, no, no, no, no.

Second-class treatment like this has made a lot of American-born Asians and Hispanics ashamed of their heritage in a way that other Americans aren't. In fact there's a heavy burden on us to deny all ethnicity and to prove we're just like everyone else, i.e., real Americans.

My little brother takes pride in the fact that he can't pronounce his Korean name at all. Years of teasing have squelched any sort of pride, and he refuses to hang around with Asians. Culturally, the boy is mush—a messy mix of MTV and McDonald's.

So why is it that Europeans can indulge in ethnic eccentricities such as corned beef and green beer without losing their identities as Americans? Why is it that a local Oktoberfest turns everyone else into de facto Germans, but Asian festivals attract nothing but condescending gawkers? It's unfair. Tell me, where are you from?

◆

**U.S. attitudes toward and treatment of Native Americans can be traced from the earliest days of the new republic through the third quarter of the last century in policy statements, personal reflections, and commentary:**

. . . [The] gradual extension of our settlements will as certainly cause the savage, as the wolf, to retire; both being beasts of prey, tho' they differ in shape.

George Washington, 1783

If it be the design of Providence to extirpate these savages in order to make room for cultivators of the earth, it seems not improbable that rum be the appointed means. It has already annihilated all the tribes who formerly inhabited the sea-coast.

*The Autobiography of Benjamin Franklin,* 1791

. . . [Senator Henry Clay said] . . . that it was impossible to civilize Indians. . . . He believed they were destined to extinction, and, although he would never use or countenance inhumanity towards them, he did not think them, as a race, worth preserving.

Memoirs of John Quincy Adams (a cabinet meeting, 1825)

Next to the case of the black race within our bosom, that of the red on our borders is the problem most baffling to the policy of our country.

James Madison, 1826

From whichever side we consider the destinies of the aborigines of North America, their calamities seem irredeemable: if they continue barbarous, they are forced to retire; if they attempt to civilize themselves, the contact of a more civilized community subjects them to oppression and destitution. They perish if they continue to wander from waste to waste, and if they attempt to settle, they still perish.

Alexis de Toqueville, *Democracy in America,* 1835

We must act with vindictive earnestness against the Sioux, even to their extermination, men, women, and children.

Gen. William Tecumseh Sherman, 1866

The American people need the country the Indians now occupy; many of our people are out of employment; the masses need some new excitement . . . An Indian war would do no harm, for it must come, sooner or later.

*The Bismark* [Dakota Territory] *Tribune,* June 17, 1874

# Recognizing Sexual Orientation Is Fair and Not Costly

by Michelle Neely Martinez (*HR Magazine*)

For HR professionals, extending employment policies to individuals based on their sexual orientation raises employment concerns in the areas of hiring and promotion, extension of health care and other benefits, and the potential for increased liability.

To understand these employment concerns and make some decisions based on this diversity and fair employment issue, HR professionals must first look within their organizations and determine how sexual orientation is perceived, how it affects productivity and possibly compensation, and how it could affect the costs of benefits programs.

## Negative Attitudes

For many top managers, the fear of extending fair employment to gays and lesbians is based on claims that serious moral and societal problems will result from this recognition—the same claims made when equal opportunity employment was sought for African-Americans and women.

In a 1987 *Wall Street Journal* survey, 66 percent of CEOs from major companies said they would be reluctant to put a homosexual on a management committee. In general, attitudes have not changed dramatically.

> Because most gay and lesbian employees fear being exposed, they go through a battle every day to keep that personal information secret.

One reason attitudes have not changed is that controversy exists over whether sexual orientation that deviates from the societal norm is an innate characteristic or whether it is a matter of choice. And for many individuals, homosexuality goes against their basic religious beliefs. In either case, however, a precedent exists for granting protec-

tions in these areas—the Civil Rights Act of 1964 protects both race and gender, which are innate characteristics, and religion, which is a matter of choice.

Another reason attitudes have not shifted is that many managers believe gays and lesbians do not exist in their workplaces. Mark Kaplan, partner of Philadelphia-based Kaplan and Associates, a firm specializing in sexual orientation issues, said: "If there are not openly gay people in the workplace, you have to ask yourself why. If you have 5,000 employees, for example, you have at least several hundred gay and lesbian employees."

Kaplan's estimate is supported by Alfred Kinsey's 1948 study which suggests that about 10 percent of the U.S. population is gay or lesbian. Newer studies give a percentage range of from 6 percent to 10 percent of the total population.

## A Productivity Issue

Recognizing differences such as that of sexual orientation is really a productivity issue, said Kaplan, because "gay and lesbian employees use a lot of time and stress trying to conceal a big part of their identity."

He believes it is also a productivity issue for straight employees who know and love someone who is gay or lesbian. Their productivity suffers when those employees are subjected to a homophobic environment or must endure office jokes slurring gays and lesbians.

Because most gay and lesbian employees fear being exposed, they go through a battle every day to keep that personal information secret. Kaplan believes that most gay and lesbian employees are in an "avoiding" stage, meaning they avoid conversations or situations that may expose their personal activities and involvements.

Reprinted with the permission of *HRMagazine* published by the Society for Human Resource Management, Alexandria, VA.

"The reality is that it is appropriate and normal for people who work together to know something about each other," he said.

When providing awareness training for organizations, Kaplan uses an exercise to illustrate this point. He asks training participants to think about their two closest co-workers and what they know about these two people. For example, he asks participants to list where they vacation and where they live or to describe their families or political views. It's a way to illustrate how personal life influences the office in a way that usually helps individuals get to know one another, and therefore, work better with one another.

But because discrimination based on sexual orientation is still legal in most of the country, gays and lesbians tend not to share their lives with co-workers.

A gay vice president who runs a multimillion-dollar department of a major office-equipment maker in Chicago, told *Fortune* magazine, "I'd like to be the CEO of this company." But he believes that if his sexual orientation becomes known, his chance will be blown. He brings women to company social functions, and his lover does not call him at the office. What bothers him most is that he has no way of knowing how scared he should be of what others would think if they discovered his sexual orientation.

## Helping Companies Act

The real goal for consultants like Kaplan is to help companies act, usually by implementing a nondiscrimination policy that includes sexual orientation, before a gay or lesbian employee speaks up. Kaplan usually works with an organization's diversity manager or task force to see how sexual orientation fits in with the organization's other diversity issues.

"Straight people tend not to know much about gays and lesbians, so we first work with the diversity team discussing how gay and lesbian issues are similar to and different from gender and race issues," said Kaplan. "We work with the diversity manager or task force to get them up to speed, because if they do not know how to deal with the issue, the silence continues."

Next, Kaplan prefers to work with managers. Then, if possible, he conducts focus groups of gay and lesbian employees to gather data. He believes that managers can often be the real culprits to workplace intolerance.

"Managers have to educate themselves about gays and lesbians and understand their own attitudes toward the group," he said. "They must understand that not everyone is heterosexual, and they must understand their responsibility as a manager to make the work environment positive so all employees can succeed. For example, if they hear negative remarks, managers really have to confront the problem. It is their responsibility."

"This struggle for gay and lesbians to conceal their personal lives also hinders their networking and mentoring experiences, because those relationships are based on trust," said Kaplan.

*Many HR professionals believe that it is easier to attract and retain talented employees if the organization is recognized for its diversity.*

Some companies such as AT&T, Sun Microsystems Inc., Digital Equipment Co., Levi Strauss & Co. and US West Communications support or at least recognize gay and lesbian employees and the groups they have formed in an effort to network and to share concerns specific to sexual orientation. The groups are most important for support, but also work to demystify homosexuality, to encourage workplace tolerance, usually by promoting diversity training, and to lobby for the same benefits that heterosexuals have. Many of the high-tech firms in the Silicon Valley are leading a trend to prohibit discrimination on the basis of sexual orientation, although social prejudice against gays and lesbians is decreasing slowly.

Many HR professionals believe that it is easier to attract and retain talented employees if the organization is recognized for its diversity. Russ Campanello, vice president of human resources for Lotus Development Corp. based in Cambridge, Mass., said that his organization is full of technical talent that came to the company because of its reputation for diversity.

## Benefits as an Equity Issue

For gay and lesbian employees, extending benefits such as health care, relocation expenses, bereavement leave and family leave to include their partners is important. In many companies, such benefits are from 30 percent to 40 percent of total salary. Organizations that have extended some or all of these benefits to gay and lesbian employees believe that benefits are an equity-in-compensation issue.

In July 1990, the American Federation of Teachers extended bereavement leave for employees on the death of a domestic partner along with all other relationships generally noted in the contracts. In November 1991, the AFL-CIO extended fringe benefits to all persons living in a household as a family. Pacific Gas & Electric (San Francisco), Legal Services Corp. (Des Moines), Mt. Sinai Hospital (New York) and the D.C. Nurses Association (D.C.) are examples of other organizations that offer "soft cost" benefits such as bereavement, sick and parenting or dependent-care leave to employees with domestic partners.

A pioneer in diversity issues, San Francisco-based Levi Strauss .& Co. has offered domestic-partner benefits (same or opposite sex) since mid–1992. Reese Smith, director of employee benefits at Levi said he had originally made a proposal in 1982 to extend the benefits, but the first response from management was that they did not want additional costs.

"From my view it was cost-related," said Reese, "but once we did an analysis, we found that the cost was not a reason not to extend benefits."

Extending benefits was not discussed again until 1991 when a lesbian employee asked Reese to consider extending benefits. This time, Reese went to the senior HR committee to talk about benefits.

Reese said: "We (the committee) couldn't agree on what to do or how to proceed, so I said 'let's revisit the issue in six months.' We didn't know much more six months later, except in the interim, we learned that all employees at our Texas plant were receiving additional benefits because in that state, there is no waiting period for common-law

marriage. Half of our employees live there, yet employees in other areas did not have the extensive benefits, so the issue evolved into one that included geographic discrimination."

"We then went to the senior management group and asked if they would entertain a proposal on extending benefits," said Reese. "That is when senior management said same-sex partners must get benefits so the policies would be fair and equal."

So far, less than 1 percent of Levi employees have signed up for domestic-partner benefits. And that does not mean enrollment, explains Reese. "Some employees want to enroll and some want to just say that they have a partner in case the partner needs benefits," he said. "Slightly more than 50 percent are female employees signing up their male partners. About 40 percent have been male/male relationships."

However, Reese points out, if senior management won't buy into the benefit plan, you have a losing battle. The biggest excuse used is that AIDS will drive up benefit costs. "Every HR manager knows that smoking, heart disease, cancer—not AIDS—are what drives up costs," he said.

Reese can't remember when differences in sexual orientation were accepted at Levi. "I've been here for 16 years, my boss for 22 years, and we can't remember when sexual orientation was not part of the culture. A lot of things that are debated in other companies are not an issue with us. I'm amazed at companies that don't look at how life really is instead of maintaining an 1890s perception of life."

> *Enrollment is less than 1 percent and that's what was expected.*

## Costs Are Not Outrageous

Lotus Development Corp., which has offered benefits to same-sex partners since September 1991, believes that the extension of benefits is also the concept of equal pay for equal work as well as recognizing the nontraditional family, said Diane Duval, the company's benefits manager.

Like Levi Strauss & Co., Lotus is a self-insured organization that also has not experienced a negative financial impact by extending benefits to same-sex partners in permanent, exclusive arrangements. Enrollment is less than 1 percent and that's what was expected, explained Duval.

"When you look at the size of the gay and lesbian work group in your organization, then at how many are in permanent exclusive arrangements with a same-sex partner, and how many are with someone who doesn't have benefits already, the numbers are small," said Duval.

When an organization is self-insured, it may have much more leverage in securing these benefits than a fully insured employer, because more liability is on the employer, explained Duval. "But even when a company is self-insured, it really comes down to a lot of negotiations."

Bessie Williamson, insurance administrator for the multicultural employer American Friends Service Committee, a Philadelphia-based international organization with a mission of peace and social justice, says her organization offers domestic-partner benefits (same or opposite sex) through John Hancock Insurance. An organization with approximately 350 employees, American Friends extended the benefits to domestic partners in January 1987.

Since the plan's implementation, costs have not increased, and less than 1 percent of employees have signed up for domestic-partner benefits.

Williamson's advice to HR professionals is, "If you have a plan that includes sexual orientation, that is a good start." To educate employees and help reduce prejudices, her organization holds ongoing discussions and holds a conference on gay and lesbian issues that serves as an outreach to employees.

## Proposed Law

Though there is no federal fair employment law based on sexual orientation, H.R. 1430 and S. 574 seek to amend Title VII of the Civil Rights Act of 1964 by adding "affectional or sexual orientation" to the classes protected by this act. Some HR professionals believe that the proposed law creates another protected class of individuals that could expose employers to jury trials and punitive and compensatory damage.

If such legislation were enacted, would not the very definition of spouse be in question? Will all benefits—COBRA benefits, family leave, bereavement leave policies, health and life insurance—be expanded? HR professionals are concerned about potential liability, because so many questions are left unanswered; the legal impact of this legislation is far from clear.

For employers who believe in fair employment and basic workplace rights of minority groups, implementing diversity training that includes sexual orientation is a first step. Establishing a fair employment policy that includes sexual orientation is the most important step an organization can take to recognize and to value the differences in employees.

## About the Author

Michelle Neely Martinez is senior editor for *HRMagazine*, the official publication of the Society for Human Resource Management (SHRM). SHRM has been a leader and innovator in diversity in the human resource industry. SHRM has had a long-standing commitment to outreach and inclusion of a variety of opinions and perspectives, both in terms of editorial content for its magazine, as well as for speakers at its national conference.

In 1993 SHRM formally announced its Diversity Initiative focusing on: (1) educating members on issues of diversity, (2) examining and influencing the composition of the membership and volunteer leadership, and (3) looking at diversity issues internally on the SHRM staff. A bimonthly newsletter, *Mosaics*, is distributed to all SHRM members.

SHRM also offers a complete catalog of outstanding diversity resources available by calling 1-800-444-5006 (fax: 612-885-5588). SHRM members are eligible for discounts on the many products offered including the video series, "The Workplace Kaleidoscope."

For information regarding SHRM membership, as well as listings of conference and special events, contact them at: Society for Human Resource Management, 606 North Washington St., Alexandria VA 22314; Phone: 703-548-3440; Fax: 703-836-0367.

# Making Our Society Safe for Differences

An Interview with Samuel Betances

*Q: Dr. Betances, people are talking a lot about cultural diversity. Do you think that this is an important issue in education?*

A: Cultural diversity is critical in education because we as educators have a responsibility to change the meaning of what is involved in being an American citizen. Our country has increasing numbers of people from all over the world. Some have just arrived, others have been here a long time, and still others were uprooted from their homes and have come as refugees. Some are American Indians who have been denied their sovereignty. Still others (e.g., Mexican Americans) were conquered and forced to become part of the United States.

We live in a society where many people have found success. But many are on the other side and need to be brought into the mainstream of opportunity. In that sense multicultural education and an acceptance of cultural diversity are wonderful opportunities for making our society safe for differences.

*Q: What do you mean by a society that is "safe for differences"?*

A: I mean the ability of people to respect others and the ways they are not like us. For example, if I don't speak English very well, my teachers must help me learn English without making me feel that my Spanish is an impurity—something evil or unpatriotic—that I must purge from myself. By respecting me for what I bring and empowering me with what I need, I am made to feel a part of the society rather than somebody who is incomplete.

Differences are all around us: sexual preference, gender, religion, or class. We need to understand and appreciate that we have to be able to become full human beings who are happy with ourselves and collaborators with other citizens so we can make the society productive. We all need to pay taxes rather than live off other people's taxes. We best ensure the health, safety, and security of our society when we learn to respect each other and ourselves.

You know, if I am not happy with the color of my skin, I am not going to be happy with the color of yours. If I feel incomplete because I am monolingual, I may become envious of someone who is bilingual. To the degree that we do not fully appreciate differences, we become threatened by diversity and want others to assimilate to our view of what is correct or normal.

*Q: You talk often and with conviction about what it was like growing up in poverty. How poor were you?*

A: Growing up, my family was so poor, somebody broke into our little apartment and didn't take anything. You may think you're a victim when robbers take your TV and VCR, and indeed you are. But you are a real victim when somebody ransacks through all of your family's possessions and doesn't take anything.

*Q: In your own life you have had to make accommodations and adaptations. Are you still threatened by cultural differences?*

A: As a youngster in Downtown Chicago, I had to learn to check things out. For example, before going into a restaurant, I used to make sure that Hispanics or black people were accepted there. I could not be sure that I would be welcome. Today, I still go through these "psychological somersaults"—that is, in feeling uneasy as I wonder at times whether I will be welcome in certain places. I wish that I didn't still carry this burden of insecurity. I wish that I were confident enough just to be myself and embrace and accept others. My own insecurities may cause me at times to misinterpret the meanings behind some of the looks that I get from others. My insecurities come from rejection, which sometimes causes me to reject myself even before people reject me! One of the worst things about racism, stereotyping, and the belittling of one group by another is that the victims often flee when no one is chasing them. Although I am on my way to doing away with that practice in myself, I am not there yet. But I feel that speaking out will help me come out of my own closet of insecurities and will help others too.

*Q: Are you suggesting that these insecurities, and the memories of what caused them, stay with us for a long time?*

*A:* Yes. And because we still feel the pain, we may try to protect our children and the next generation (through words and behaviors) from injuries to which they may not be so vulnerable. I may tell my children to be on the lookout for this or that when, in fact, society may no longer be as threatening as it was when I was growing up. We need to stop feeling paranoid without reason. But we also need to realize how evil and demeaning racism and discrimination are. Their effects last a lot longer in the psyche than most of us think.

*Q: How do you interpret the differences that exist among groups?*

*A:* Differences among people are wonderful facts of life. Problems emerge because of the meaning we attach to such differences as skin color, gender, age, or sexual orientation. The diversity agenda must be concerned with making sure that people understand that differences are okay. We must not send a message that to become successful in our society, women have to act like men, African Americans need to straighten their hair, or Hispanics have to forget Spanish. We have to use diversity as a process of discovery and acceptance, of celebration of differences rather than thinking of differences as problems.

*Q: How can education help facilitate this process of discovery?*

*A:* Education universalizes the human spirit. You cannot be universalized if you are only in one world, the world of your ethnic group, the world of your neighborhood, the world of your religion, or the world of your family. Our lives are enhanced when we understand and appreciate many worlds. Diversity is the key to the universalization process of education. Students are given access to many different points of view. They are able to extend their knowledge. Diversity also empowers those who have experienced rejection or been denied access to get their fair share.

*Q: You are often called on by corporate leaders to help create a positive environment for workplace diversity. What do you tell them about multicultural issues?*

*A:* If corporate leaders don't understand that it's in our collective best interest to address these issues, the nation will be impoverished and we'll make a mockery out of democracy.

We won't achieve social justice, we won't be able to make the kind of winning teams—whether in education, business, politics, religion, or other areas of public service—that will enable us to have the quality of life that's healthy in a heterogeneous society like ours.

I'm proud of the fact that my mission to make total quality management really work makes sense to corporate leaders.

*Q: What do you tell them?*

*A:* First, I tell them that without total quality respect—without TQR—TQM [Total Quality Management] won't work. I tell them if you don't hire those of us who speak two languages, bring passion to the job, have a sense of humor, and appreciate diversity, you won't penetrate important markets. I tell them that they need to embrace diversity for the bottom line.

When I do my best work, the audiences I address come to see diversity as a plus instead of a minus. People walk away knowing that the issue of diversity isn't about taking a Black person to lunch or being kind to an Asian or saying "hola" to an Hispanic.

It's about making it possible for all of us to make larger contributions to society than the ones we've been allowed to make in the past.

*Q: Humor is a salient feature in your work, as you've mentioned. Why do you use it to get your points across?*

*A:* Because humor is the "sugar that makes the medicine go down." With humor, we laugh together, so we have a common experience that we can't deny. It's a way of showing you're human and that you're willing to reduce the level of authority so that you can be inclusive; and it lets others identify with you, as well. It creates bonds among workshop participants, audience members, or students, and helps release tension. It also promotes understanding by exposing apparent contradictions not easily revealed or readily accepted when presented through a didactic lecture.

Once you have done that, you have a better chance for communication and understanding. Humor can help us learn tolerance and respect and make our society safe. Without humor, you'll cause injury when you challenge people to be better.

*Q: Can you give an example of how you use humor to improve understanding between races?*

*A:* My Puerto Rican heritage allows me to heighten consciousness of the media's use of scripts that recycle debilitating stereotypes of Puerto Ricans. For example, I tell my students that West Side Story couldn't have been written by a Puerto Rican.

"Why?" they ask.

"Because you can't call for Maria at three o'clock in the morning in a Puerto Rican neighborhood and have only one window open!"

*Q: Yes. Certainly not something most people would think of! On another subject, what books have you found particularly helpful in learning about the experiences of ethnic groups in the United States?*

*A:* One of the most fascinating books I have read is *The Ethnic Myth: Race, Ethnicity, and Class in America*, by Stephen Steinberg (Beacon Press, 1981). It is a wonderfully informative comparison of the experiences of the Italians, Irish, Jews, and other immigrants to the United States. An excellent, sometimes angry account of the Mexican American/Chicano experiences is Rudolfo Acuna's *Occupied America: A History of Chicanos*, Third edition (Harper and Row, 1988).

Another highly readable book is *Affirming Diversity: The Sociopolitical Context of Multicultural Education*, by Sonia Nieto (Longman, 1992).

I also like Mary White's *The Japanese Educational Challenge: A Commitment to Children* (The Free Press, 1987). She points out that one ethnic group cannot always be a model for another. Another

interesting account of Asian Americans is Ronald Takaki's *Strangers from a Different Shore: A History of Asian Americans* (Little, Brown and Company, 1989). I learned from Takaki that the label *model minority* serves to cover up the pain and struggles of individual groups of Filipinos, Koreans, Japanese, and East Indians. When we learn about the experiences of other ethnic groups, we can form coalitions of interest rather than coalitions of color to overcome the effects of prejudice. *Racism and Sexism: An Integrated Study*, by Paula S. Rothenberg (The St. Martin's Press, 1988) is another excellent book.

These stories help us to express our own joys and frustrations by citing examples drawn from others' experiences and to universalize our spirits and visions. We need to prepare for the twenty-first century by focusing on processes that create a new cultural vision of what we are and what we must become to make America healthier and freer—a place where we can learn about each other with passion and concern. Differences are always going to be with us. We must prepare for the art of embracing the diversity that is all around us.

## About the Interviewee

Dr. Samuel Betances is a professor of Sociology at Northeastern Illinois University where he has taught for the past twenty years. He earned his Masters and Doctorate at Harvard University. He has lectured and published extensively in areas related to diversity, social change, gender and race relations, demographic changes and the impact of the global economy on group relations in the USA.

He is a very much sought after and celebrated speaker and consultant. Dr. Betances has consulted with city officials, educational policy makers, community leaders and business managers. He has a distinguished record as a motivational keynote speaker and consultant with such major Fortune 500 companies as AT & T, Xerox, McDonald's, Merrill Lynch, and Inland Steel. He can be reached at Souder, Betances and Associates, Inc., Pacific Suite, 5448 N. Kimball Avenue, Chicago, IL 60625, Phone: (312) 463-6374, Fax: (312) 463-0429.

# Sensitivity Toward European Americans: Diversity Within Diversity

published by *Resisting Defamation* (Fourth Edition, 1996)

This article was initiated in San Jose by members of over sixty families from diverse neighborhoods. One of its purposes is to combat slurs and stereotypes expressed against Americans of European origins. It also serves as an outline for a one-hour seminar, "Sensitivity Toward European Americans: Diversity Within Diversity." The seminar begins with the presenter drawing an outline of Europe, from the Ural Mountains to Iceland, on a chalk board and marking three lines:

- The line showing the limits of the Asian Arab and African Berber Muslim invasions, slave-takings, and colonizations for 700 years in Southern Europe (1200 to 500 years ago).

- The line showing the limits of the Asian Mongolian invasions, slave-takings, and colonizations for 550 years in Eastern and Central Europe (750 to 200 years ago).

- The line showing the limits of the Asian Turkish Muslim invasions, slave-takings, and colonizations for 500 years in Central Europe (600 to 100 years ago).

The frequent invasions, imperial oppressions, ethnic genocides, cultural genocides, rapes, and immense slave-takings that accompanied these three major, centuries-long colonizations explain the diversity of nations and tribes that provide such a rich texture to the great European diaspora.

There are four principal stereotypes that demean and degrade European Americans, and five principal reasons for determining certain words and phrases to be slurs against European Americans.

At the end of this article readers will be better

informed about the complex, richly-textured, and ancient ethnic and cultural diversity of European Americans.

## Section One: Negative Stereotypes About European Americans

❶ The first negative stereotype is that Americans of European origin are not a diverse ethnic group. This is the Homogeneous Whites stereotype.

### Analysis and Rebuttal

The great diaspora of indigenous Europeans to North America began 503 years ago in 1492. Since then, millions of Europeans have migrated here and now tens of millions of diverse European Americans live in the United States.

European Americans are diverse in religion. Some follow no religion at all.

European Americans are diverse in country of origin. They come from Iceland, Hungary, Spain, Portugal, Greece, Ukraine, Armenia, Croatia, Russia, Norway, and other European countries. (see Table 2)

European Americans are diverse in home country language. There are over fifty indigenous languages and dialects in Europe. Only a relatively few Europeans speak English as a native language.

European Americans are diverse in how long they or their families have lived in North America. Some families have been here for hundreds of years, but most European American families have either a grandparent or parent who immigrated here.

Europeans Americans are diverse in wealth. In fact, over half of all the people in the U.S. who live below the poverty line are European Americans.

European Americans are diverse in race. Much of Spain, Italy, and Sicily was occupied by Asian Arab and African Berber soldiers and colonists for up to 700 years. Europe was repeatedly invaded and colonized by Mongols and Turks from Asia for hundreds of years. Consequently, European Americans have ancestors from all three major races.

However, most European Americans share a commitment to community, values, morality, education, and government that has been shaped by 3000 years of history, culture, and the arts.

One example of European American diversity is Irish Americans. Immigrating here for the past 300 years, the Irish faced enormous challenges in gaining legal acceptance and civil rights. For example, South Carolina passed a law excluding Irish immigrants in 1698, and Maryland passed a similar law in 1715.

The Irish were often confronted by hostility in the U.S. For example, in 1834 there was an anti-Irish riot in Massachusetts during which a convent was burned. There was a major riot against Irish immigrants in Boston in 1837, and there were anti-Irish riots in Philadelphia in 1844 in which three churches were burned, 30 Irish immigrants were killed, and 200 families lost their homes to fire.

Irish immigrants often had to face employment and housing discrimination. Many times, employers and landlords would post signs telling Irish immigrants that they were not welcome. The most frequently displayed sign said: "Irish and dogs need not apply." Irish Americans had to fight for legal acceptance and civil rights.

Portuguese Americans, Scottish Americans, Italian Americans, German Americans, Polish Americans, Russian Americans, Armenian Americans, Greek Americans, and many others have similar stories to tell about their own diversity and their own hardships during the great European diaspora, all of which goes to disprove the Homogeneous Whites stereotype.

❷ **The second negative stereotype is that European Americans are somehow more racist or especially racist when compared to other ethnic groups. This is the White Racism stereotype.**

## Analysis and Rebuttal

A leading spokesperson for the White Racism stereotype is Professor Mari Matsuda who has taught law in Hawaii, Michigan, and California.

In an August 1989 article in *The University of Michigan Law Review,* she argues that European Americans are either supporters of "hate propaganda" by groups like the KKK or "are drawn into unwilling complacency with the Klan." She denies any other possibility.

The bulk of her article is a recital of false or mostly false horror stories of alleged racist actions by European Americans, but none by other groups. Consequently, this stereotype is also known as Matsuda's Libel to experts in understanding hate speech and writing.

A local example of this stereotype was voiced in public discourse in 1991 and 1992 by Anastasia Steinberg, Hate Crimes Coordinator for Santa Clara County District Attorney George Kennedy. Ms. Steinberg stated the stereotype as follows:

*The profile of the hate criminal is the white male between 19 and 26.*

She became so thoroughly identified with this defamatory stereotype that her profile statement has become known to hate speech experts as Steinberg's Lie. It was publicly discredited by a Japanese-American Deputy Police Chief of San Jose in September 1992 when he disclosed the actual statistics for local hate crime suspects.

In summary, there were 85 hate crimes in San Jose with a total of 91 suspects in 1991. Contradicting Steinberg's Lie, only 22 of the suspects were European Americans for a share of only 24% overall. This is a strong contrast with the fact that European Americans make up about 45% of San Jose's population.

Contrary to the outrageous and malicious promotion of the White Racism stereotype, Americans of European origins are warm-hearted, generous, and diverse.

❸ **The third negative stereotype is that European Americans are never victims of hate speech or hate crimes. This is the Victimless Majority stereotype.**

## Analysis and Rebuttal

This stereotype is promoted by malicious people who argue, directly or indirectly, that members of most European American ethnic groups cannot be victimized by hate speech or hate crimes. Consequently, this stereotype is known as the Victimless Majority stereotype.

However, we know from the San Jose Police Department that there were 27 European American victims out of the total 90 hate crime victims in San Jose in 1991. European Americans provided 30% of all hate crime victims in San Jose in 1991.

At least four young European or European American men were murdered in 1990 in the Bay Area in racially-motivated murders.

Professor Mari Matsuda promoted an extremist version of this stereotype in her August 1989 article. While urging protection for non-European Americans, she claimed that "the harm and hurt" of being called a "white devil" is much less for a young European American child than "the harm and hurt" to a young non-European American child slapped with a similar slur.

Another version of this stereotype is known as Hirschhaut's Lie. *The San Jose Mercury News* on January 29, 1991, quoted political activist Richard S. Hirschhaut as saying:

*No minority group in San Francisco should be allowed to become fair game for the bigots and haters among us.*

This is a clear statement that, in his view, members of European American ethnic and cultural groups (non-minority groups) are never victims of hate crimes.

The argument that European Americans cannot be or are not victimized by hate speech and hate crimes is a pathological denial of the truth. European American children and adults are frequently victimized by hate speech and hate crimes.

❹ **The fourth negative stereotype is that European Americans lack the right of self-designation and the right to an ethnic voice. This is the Passive Ethnicity stereotype.**

## Analysis and Rebuttal

Americans of diverse European origins do have the right to decide what label will be applied to them. Daily newspapers often seek to decide for them, resulting in confusing and demeaning descriptions like white, Anglo, Caucasian, and non-Hispanic white.

European Americans have the right to speak out of their ethnic voices, just like all other ethnic groups. European Americans are rarely allowed to do so, but it is an established right inherent in every ethnic group.

European Americans have at least three levels of voices. First, they have their American voice with which they talk about matters of community-wide concern. European Americans are usually comfortable with this voice.

Second, they have their European American voice (or their multicultural voice) with which they talk about matters of special concern on the multicultural level like voting rights, college admissions, redistricting, health care, and other community issues. Most European Americans do not use this voice confidently, but it is a necessary voice in the public arena. In fact, European Americans have the duty to speak out when European Americans suffer from racially-motivated murder, malicious prosecution, hate speech, and discrimination.

Third, they have their religious, cultural, ethnic, or national origin voices with which they talk about matters of concern in those areas of discourse. For example, they could talk about matters of concern to Catholics or Protestants, or about matters affecting Irish Americans or Greek Americans. Most European Americans understand this voice, but they rarely use it.

## EDITORS' NOTE

We have found this submission to be one of the most intriguing and provocative pieces we have collected. When we first read the statement, "However, most European Americans share a commitment to community, values, morality, education, and government that has been shaped by 3000 years of history, culture, and the arts" and "Americans of European origins are warm-hearted, generous, and diverse," we were taken aback. Was the implication of these statements that peoples of other backgrounds (by omission) are less committed to community, values, morality, etc. and that the qualities of being warm-hearted and generous are not as common among any other branch of the human family? Was this a cover for some insidious form of prejudice that was only *appearing* to take racial pride in white ethnicity? Why would it generate resentment among a non-white ethnic group to allow a white ethnic group the same power of self-definition that non-whites desire? We have fallen victim to a fallacy of logic that says: "whites cannot be victimized." Discussing this together, the editors identified what is perhaps an unspoken diversity issue that affects how we live and work together: justifiable pride in one's heritage and self-esteem.

When people show pride and self-esteem it brings out a kind of negative reaction in others. Some of us are old enough to remember when Muhammed Ali first said "I am the greatest!" Much furor ensued both in the media and in private discussions. It took many of us several years to see that this was a man feeling good about himself and saying it. It took us longer to see that what he said was also an antidote to messages that he (and, no doubt, countless other black youngsters) had internalized for generations. Many of us *still* find it hard to see either of these points. Today, according to one study of schoolchildren, young European-American women showed a significantly lower level of self-esteem than African-American women of the same age. Perhaps they have been getting all too well the message not only that they don't stack up as members of their gender, but that ethnic pride is not for them. It is a question that deserves more study.

How can so many U.S. Americans get over resistance to people different from themselves enjoying who they are? In this multicultural nation, taking pride in one's heritage cannot be a zero sum game. Your taking pride ought not diminish my right to do the same thing, or make my heritage any less precious. Pride in your heritage should rather remind and empower me to do likewise. Too often we feel bad about ourselves, or even attacked, when someone from another group expresses their happiness and joy in their heritage. This brings out the worst in us: envy, mean-spirited competition and schadenfreude (taking pleasure when something goes wrong). Some deep uncertainty about our own worth and identity pleads for attention so we can better learn to enjoy both ourselves and our diverse neighbors. Perhaps such statements of ethnic pride are made more because we would like to believe them, than because we actually are convinced to the core that they are true.

Many of the European ancestors of today's population hid their identities and customs, suppressed their language and values to become Americans. Though this is done consciously in the first and second generations, in the third it perhaps shows up only as a dissonant chord in one's psyche. Though the California State Commission on Self-Esteem has been scrapped, diversity practitioners and teachers throughout the nation have the continuing challenge of working with this dynamic of envy that seems to arise around the expression of ethnic pride.

# Table 1: Slurs Against Americans of European Origin

There are five criteria that may be used to determine that a label or phrase is a slur against European Americans:

1. Does it smother the ancient, complex, and richly textured ethnic and cultural diversity of European Americans?

2. Does it violate the right of European Americans to designate themselves?

3. Is it well-understood in the European American community, or in the perpetrator's community, to be demeaning or insulting?

4. Does it mock or degrade the name of a European country or tribe by transforming the name into a defamatory usage?

5. Does it dehumanize and target European Americans with the name of an animal or insect?

| | | | |
|---|---|---|---|
| acting white | frenchie | Irish (as synonym for anger) | swamp Yankee |
| Anglo | frog | | typical American |
| Archie Bunker | | jar-head | |
| arkie | gabacho/gabacha | jerry | vanilla |
| | gaijin | Jew (as verb) | vandal |
| bak guai | gentile | | visigoth |
| barbarian | gnome (of Zürich) | kraut | |
| big-nose | good old boy | | WASP/Wasp |
| Blanco/Blanca | goy | Lao wai | Welch/Welsh (as verb) |
| blue-haired | goyim | lily-white | westerner |
| bohunk | goyish | limey | white |
| bolillo | gringo/gringa | | white acting |
| bubba | guerito/guerita | mayonnaise | white boy |
| bugger | guero/guera | mick | white culture |
| burrito | guinea | | white devil |
| Byzantine | gusano/gusana | nativist | white eyes |
| | gwei luo | non-Hispanic white | white female |
| canuck | gyp | | white girl |
| Caucasian | | ofay | white male |
| cracker | hakujin | okie | white trash |
| | haoli/haole | opie | whitebread |
| dago | harp | | white-eyes |
| dead white male | hayseed | paddy | white-guys |
| dominant culture | heathen | pagan | whitemale |
| donkey | heinie | pale | whitewashed |
| dumb blonde | Heinz 57 | paleface | whitey |
| Dutch (as synonym for trouble) | heretic | patsy | wigger |
| | hick | peckerwood | wog |
| Dutch courage | hillbilly | polack | wonder bread |
| Dutch treat | honky | portagee | wop |
| DWEM/DWEAM | hooligan | potatohead | wretched refuse |
| | huddled masses | preppie | |
| egg | Hun | | Yankee dog |
| eurotrash | hunky (as noun) | redneck | yid |
| | | round-eyes | yokel |
| fair-haired | ice people | round eye scum | |
| fig newton | infidel | rube | |
| fish eyes | | Scot (as in scot-free) | |
| | | scotch (as synonym for cheap or as verb) | |
| | | shiksa | |

185

# Table 2: European-Californians by Country of Origin

The diversity of European Americans is often smothered in print and electronic media. In Northern California, writers and newscasters usually suppress all mention of European American ethnic, national origin, and cultural diversity.

However, the 1990 census shows that European Americans claim descent from at least twenty-seven countries. For example, you will note below that 104,783 California residents claim descent from Austria or 0.4% of all Californians. 5,635 Santa Clara County residents or 0.4% similarly claim descent from Austria.

| National Origin | Statewide | | Santa Clara Co. | |
|---|---|---|---|---|
| | # | % | # | % |
| Austria | 104,783 | 0.4% | 5,635 | 0.4% |
| Belgium | 31,591 | 0.1% | 2,127 | 0.1% |
| Czechoslavakia | 124,056 | 0.4% | 6,561 | 0.4% |
| Denmark | 262,101 | 0.9% | 14,551 | 1.0% |
| Netherlands | 591,618 | 2.0% | 25,481 | 1.7% |
| England | 3,646,656 | 12.3% | 190,930 | 12.7% |
| Finland | 64,302 | 0.2% | 3,625 | 0.2% |
| France | 1,034,708 | 3.5% | 51,626 | 3.4% |
| German | 4,940,252 | 16.6% | 249,421 | 16.7% |
| Greece | 125,792 | 0.4% | 7,342 | 0.5% |
| Hungary | 159,121 | 0.5% | 7,468 | 0.5% |
| Ireland | 3,431,047 | 11.5% | 168,162 | 11.2% |
| Italy | 1,448,432 | 4.9% | 102,233 | 6.8% |
| Lithuania | 63,871 | 0.2% | 3,756 | 0.3% |
| Norway | 411,282 | 1.4% | 22,184 | 1.5% |
| Poland | 578,256 | 1.9% | 30,532 | 2.0% |
| Portugal | 356,495 | 1.2% | 37,187 | 2.5% |
| Romania | 57,417 | 0.2% | 2,440 | 0.2% |
| Russia | 447,591 | 1.5% | 18,159 | 1.2% |
| Scotch-Irish | 546,496 | 1.8% | 25,887 | 1.7% |
| Scotland | 646,674 | 2.2% | 34,677 | 2.3% |
| Slovak | 101,328 | 0.3% | 6,213 | 0.4% |
| Sweden | 587,772 | 2.0% | 31,320 | 2.1% |
| Switzerland | 140,351 | 0.5% | 9,197 | 0.6% |
| Ukraine | 56,211 | 0.2% | 3,359 | 0.2% |
| Welsh | 238,134 | 0.8% | 11,817 | 0.8% |
| Yugoslavia | 69,535 | 0.2% | 4,876 | 0.3% |

# Italians: The 'Other' Internees

by Annie Nakao (*San Francisco Examiner*)

One enemy alien was 97-year-old Placido Abono, who had 100 grandchildren and great-grandchildren. Others were Giuseppe and Rosalie DiMaggio, parents of baseball's "Yankee Clipper." Still another was Neno Aiello's beloved Auntie Frances, a 68-year old Sicilian widow who'd raised him from childhood in the Delta town of Pittsburg. "She had to leave, a lot of people did . . . there wasn't anybody in town who left that I didn't know," said Aiello.

They lived in disparate neighborhoods from Pittsburg to Monterey Bay to San Francisco's North Beach. But when the bombs fell on Pearl Harbor, many foreign-born Italians and Germans—like 110,000 Japanese immigrants and their American-born children—were uprooted from their communities in the hysteria following the outbreak of World War II. Unlike the Japanese, alien residents of Italian and German descent did not undergo massive internment in wartime camps. But thousands were forced to relocate from coastal areas under military orders following Pearl Harbor, while thousands of others were interned as potentially dangerous aliens.

In all, about 10,000 foreign-born Californians—Japanese, Italian and German—were evacuated from the West Coast in February of 1942. In Pittsburg alone, 1,400 people had to move.

While the Japanese internment has since become a rallying point for constitutional freedom, few know the story of other civilians caught in wartime hysteria. Now an exhibit sponsored by the American Italian Historical Association, called "Una Storia Segreta" ("A Secret Story"), will document the Italian relocation.

For many Italian Americans, the exhibit, which runs through March 27 at Fort Mason in San Francisco, unveils a part of their history told only in classified documents and the painful memories of those who wished to forget. "There are an enormous number of Italian Americans in this country, who do not know anything about this," said Lawrence DiStasi, project director for the association. "That was because old people did not want to talk about this." DiStasi, 56, was one of those who knew nothing of the Italian wartime evacuation until he heard stories about it 10 years ago. "It was astonishing to me," said DiStasi.

At the outbreak of World War II, Italians, then the last large immigrant group to come to the United States, were probably the least assimilated. In 1940, only half of the 100,922 foreign-born Italians in California were naturalized, according to Stephen Fox, a Humbold State University History Professor who in 1990 wrote, "The Unknown Internment: An Oral History of the Relocation of Italian Americans during World War II."

Like all immigrants, the newcomers were too occupied surviving and raising families to apply for citizenship. Not speaking English, many felt they could not possibly past the test. Some who came from poor villages in Sicily were not even literate in Italian.

The lack of citizenship became a key factor used to determine loyalty in the days after Pearl Harbor, as was any perceived support of the Mussolini government. Those suspected of even remotely advocating fascism were arrested and in some cases interned. An estimated 3,500 Italian immigrants were arrested—among them journalists, teachers, and community leaders. About 228 were actually interned.

Far more Germans were targeted. An estimated 11,000 were detained or interned, Fox said. Thousands of others were ordered from homes or businesses in coastal areas decreed off-limits to foreigners. The actual number is not known, Rose Scherini, curator of the exhibit, and others say, because the military kept few records.

"People did it on their own, usually moving a few miles away," said Scherini. For example, many of those from Pittsburg moved to farm camps in Brentwood or Oakley. Another 3,000 had to leave Monterey. The evacuations idled 75 percent of Monterey Bay's small boat fleet. Those who stayed still had to observe a 9 p.m. to 6 a.m. daily curfew and travel restrictions—they could not travel more than 5 miles from home and work.

Families were divided and indignities suffered. Fox's book recounts how one family had to have a police escort to go to the dentist because they had to cross through an unapproved zone. One San Jose man couldn't report after getting a draft notice because he couldn't drive to the Army's office in Monterey—it was beyond the 5-mile radius from his home.

In Pittsburg, many of whose earliest settlers immigrated from the tiny village of Isollo delle Demini in Sicily, virtually every family was affected.

Though Aiello's immediate family was safe from evacuation—both his parents were citizens—the loss of his aunt, other relatives and neighbors changed their lives. "People became so frightened that they were even afraid of a knock on the door," said Aiello, who was 13 at the time. "You never knew who it might be and who might be taken away."

The DiMaggios were not relocated but Giuseppe DiMaggio couldn't work out of Fisherman's Wharf or eat at his son Joe's restaurant, Fox wrote in his book. "It was very traumatic for individual families," Scherini said. "It stigmatized them."

Even more disruptive were the long-standing quarrels between those who had admired Mussolini and those who did not. "It created a situation where people were informing on each other," said DiStasi. "There was a lot of suspicion and antagonism." Fear was so widespread that posters advised against the speaking of Italian. "Don't speak the enemy's language," they said.

## Logistical Reason

Unlike the case of the Japanese, though, the initial rush to relocate Italian and German aliens never escalated to full-scale internment due to political and logistical reasons, Fox believes.

For one, it was easier to lock up 110,000 Japanese instead of 11 million Italian and Germans scattered across the country. Besides, full-scale internment might have meant the internment of San Francisco Mayor Angelo Rossi and New York Mayor Fiorello La Guardia.

"I think it was just a huge embarrassment—there were little old ladies whose sons were killed at Pearl Harbor, who were being relocated . . . people were raising hell because the parents of Joe DiMaggio would have to be interned," Fox said. Others believe bigotry fed the drive to intern the Japanese. Indeed, Italian and German immigrants had not faced similar virulent racism.

In any case, the relocation orders were reversed six months later and by Columbus Day, 1942, Italian aliens were no longer classified as "enemies." But the legacy of the experience persists, said DiStasi. Though generational differences are a factor, DiStasi said the trauma of being labeled disloyal drove some Italian American families to assimilation, often to the detriment of their culture. "Large numbers of Italian Americans remain in a kind of ethnic shadow to this day, most without knowing why," he said.

## Japanese Payments Criticized

More recently, the financial compensation given to Japanese American internees has sparked some criticism among other internees. "Frankly, they're not thrilled that the Japanese are getting money for their experiences," said Fox. Still others, acknowledging that the suffering of the Japanese internees was far greater, just want their story told.

"People of Italian ancestry aren't looking for financial remuneration—they're just looking for an apology," said Aiello. "These people's civil rights were infringed upon. People need to know that it occurred."

# Crossed Wires

by Kathleen Doheny (*Los Angeles Times*)

*Puzzled by your partner's logic—or lack of it? It could just be that your brains work differently.*

Hanging up a few pictures seemed easy enough. But only when Cathy Pitt and her fiancée, Bill Kapsalis, stood with nails and hammer in hands did they realize how differently they approached this basic task. Her plan was to eyeball the wall and pound in nails where she thought the Ansel Adams photographs would look best. He wanted to use a tape measure and to find the stud in the wall to be sure the photos would be straight and secure.

The Great Computer Hunt was further evidence that the West Hills couple looks at the world from different perspectives. Bill's plan was to buy a family computer, with features to please Cathy and him, along with her sons—Michael, 10, and Ryan, 8. "I made a chart," he says. There were columns for the amount of memory, whether the computer was expandable, whether it had CD drive and other data. He photocopied the chart and filled in the data on a fresh copy as he looked at more than 10 models.

Cathy's reaction to the chart? "She laughed," Bill says. Then she threw up her hands and left the decision to him.

These scenarios sound all too familiar to San Diego therapist Rebecca Cutter, who not only has lived and researched them but has written about them in her new book, "When Opposites Attract" (Dutton). Her subtitle says it all: "Right Brain/Left Brain Relationships and How to Make Them Work."

Differences such as those experienced by Pitt and Kapsalis, Cutter contends, are not always due to gender, as couples often believe, but to basic "brain wiring." A partner who is right-brain dominant, valuing intuition and emotions, sees the world differently from one who is left-brain dominant, valuing logic and familiar routines.

Everyone exhibits behaviors that are both right-brain and left-brain, but some people fall closer to one end of the continuum than to the middle. When a very left-brain dominant person hooks up with a very right-brain partner, different views of the world—and the relationship—are inevitable, Cutter says.

While the lefty balances the checkbook to the penny, her right-brained partner estimates the balance—or doesn't worry about it at all. A right-brainer often wants to spend leisure time partying, while a left-brainer often prefers to devote the time to her hobby.

The differences, while daunting, don't have to doom a relationship, Cutter says, a self-described right-brainer happily married to computer specialist Rick Johnson, who she says leans to the left. Some critics say Cutter is oversimplifying the problem, but she contends that making an effort to understand how an oppositely wired partner thinks and feels can go a long way toward relationship harmony.

For starters, she suggests each partner ask the other: "What's it like being in a relationship with me?" Often, a left-brain dominant person will say to the right-brain dominant partner: "You are not predictable. You're off the wall. You hurt me in ways you don't know."

One source of hurt feelings, Cutter has found during counseling sessions, springs from the sense of failure a left-brainer can feel when a right-brainer is always pressing to know her feelings—instantly.

A right-brain dominant person is likely to respond, "You're not romantic enough. You're boring. Sometimes I feel alone. You become preoccupied." The incredible ability of a left-brainer to focus on a single task and to be very practical can leave a right-brain spouse feeling isolated and unloved, Cutter explains.

Like many other therapists, Cutter began thinking about brain dominance differences two decades ago. In the early '80s, she happened upon a paperback written for the spouses of engineers and computer programmers, aimed at helping them understand their "logical" partners. "It was gender-biased," Cutter says. "All the partners were female, all the computer scientists were male."

The more couples she counseled, the more she began to believe that brain wiring differences sparked many disputes. When she noticed the patterns in both straight and gay relationships—and then married a left-brainer—she was convinced. Of course, gender differences can be at the root of many disagreements, she says. But she thinks they have gotten too much blame.

Brain-wiring differences often surface during arguments, Cutter says. A right-brainer spews out all her feelings, looking for a thread or a connection that might solve the argument. A left-brainer prefers to sit and think things through before talking. The left-brainer feels bombarded; the right-brainer feels ignored.

Gift-giving occasions can be ticklish too. For their first Valentine's Day together, Cutter's beloved presented her with road flares. Cathy Pitt had hoped for a piece of jewelry on the first Christmas she shared with Kapsalis. But on Christmas morn, it was a VCR she unwrapped.

"I was grateful for the VCR, because we did need one," she says. So she thanked him and added that jewelry wouldn't have been a bad present either. Cutter suggests couples look beyond what seem like unromantic motives.

The road flares, she knows now, reflected Johnson's love and a genuine concern for her safety. After some thought, Pitt decided that the VCR represented "his desire to spend more time with me—to sit and watch movies at my place."

Respecting each other's thought processes can often lead to compromise. Cutter has gone through the same picture-hanging experience as Pitt. Today, she and her mate would do things differently, she says. "He would listen to my input," she says. "And I would not make fun of him." When the couple assembled a set of bunk beds, Pitt was content to measure just one post. But Kapsalis persuaded her to measure all four. In their newly-wed days, she recalls, her spouse would be likely to say something like, " 'OK, this picture should be hung 27 and 22/23 inches from that one'—and I would be rolling on the floor."

For her part, Cutter no longer gives her husband presents like the South American poncho, a gift she considered exotic but he obviously did not.

It has hung in the closet for several years. As she puts it now: "He's not Juan Valdez."

Gradually, as one partner understands where the other is coming from, they might even exhibit uncharacteristic behaviors. After "The Year of the Road Flares," Cutter received a garden hose—wrapped around crystal wine glasses. Cathy Pitt recently received a ring.

Some couples learn to value input from their opposite partner. Steve Parks, a hospital publications editor, has been married for six years to Kathy, a compensation and benefits administrator at another hospital. When they searched for a day-care center for their daughter, Trina, now 20 months, he says both approaches proved valuable.

"I went from gut feeling," he says. As they toured the centers, he took note of how happy the children seemed and whether he got a warm feeling from the place. "My wife got references, checked them, called around. She went unannounced one day (to visit)."

While other therapists call Cutter's approach oversimplified, they also say she is making some valid points. "She is certainly picking up on a critical area of misunderstanding among couples—that is, a fundamental difference in wiring," says Steven Goldstein, a psychologist at Kaiser Permanente in Woodland Hills who specializes in brief psychotherapy and has read Cutter's book.

What Cutter calls hemispherical differences Goldstein sometimes considers temperamental differences. Arguing styles, in his view, are temperamental differences. One partner likes to mull things over; another wants to discuss everything out loud immediately. Arguing over which approach is best, Goldstein says, is like trying to answer the question: "Which is better, to be a zebra or a tiger?"

Save the arguments, he tells couples, over solvable concerns like whether to buy a house or a condo. With temperamental differences, he says, the fight can go on and on—"because there is really no problem to be resolved." The solution, he says, is to respect the differences.

Cutter's views beg the question: Wouldn't it be simpler if right-brainers paired up with right-brainers and the lefties did the same? In some ways, sure. When two right-brainers hook up, Cutter says, "it's probably the easiest relationship to be in for connectedness and companionship." But it is also "like two kids at home without a parent," she says, especially if neither wants to take responsibility for finances and other logical, left-brain tasks.

Two left-brainers often lack passion and spontaneity. "From the outside it could look like a cold relationship, but not to them." But it's when op-posites hook up, Cutter says, that the real sparks often fly. "The chemistry comes from being very different."

◆

---

## ARE YOU RIGHT OR LEFT?

Everyone uses both the right and left hemispheres of the brain. But under certain situations, the right hemisphere (involved in intuition and emotions) will be dominant over the left (involved in facts and logic) or vice-versa.

Over time, some people tend to become more left-brain or right-brain dominant, while others remain flexible, exhibiting left-brain or right-brain dominance as situations dictate.

In her book *When Opposites Attract,* San Diego therapist Rebecca Cutter includes a quiz to help determine how you're wired. Here are three questions from that quiz:

A. I am good at remembering names.

B. I have trouble remembering names.

A. I speak in monitored, carefully thought-out phrases.

B. I speak spontaneously, not thinking about what I'm saying.

A. I am told that I am very predictable.

B. I am told that I am often unpredictable.

Results: If you answered quickly, you are more likely to be right-brain dominant, according to Cutter. If you gave it some thought before answering, you are more likely left-brain dominant.

If all your answers are A, you tend to be left-brain dominant.

If all your answers are B, you tend to be right-brain dominant.

If you could answer yes to both A and B, depending on the situation, it might indicate that you fall somewhere in the middle of the continuum.

Source: *When Opposites Attract: Right Brain/Left Brain Relationships and How to Make Them Work* (Dutton 1994).

# Human Family

by Maya Angelou

I note the obvious differences
in the human family.
Some of us are serious,
some thrive on comedy.

Some declare their lives are lived
as true profundity,
and others claim they really live
the real reality.

The variety of our skin tones
can confuse, bemuse, delight,
brown and pink and beige and purple,
tan and blue and white.

I've sailed upon the seven seas
and stopped in every land,
I've seen the wonders of the world,
not yet one common man.

I know ten thousand women
called Jane and Mary Jane,
but I've not seen any two
who really were the same.

Mirror twins are different
although their features jibe,
and lovers think quite different thoughts
while lying side by side.

We love and lose in China,
we weep on England's moors,
and laugh and moan in Guinea,
and thrive on Spanish shores.

From *I Shall Not Be Moved* by Maya Angelou. Copyright © 1990 by Maya Angelou.
Reprinted with permission of Random House, Inc.

We seek success in Finland,
are born and die in Maine.
In minor ways we differ,
in major we're the same.

I note the obvious differences
between each sort and type,
but we are more alike, my friends,
than we are unalike.

We are more alike, my friends,
than we are unalike.

We are more alike, my friends,
than we are unalike.

## About the Author

Maya Angelou is the author of the best-seller, *I Know Why the Caged Bird Sings.* In the sixties, at the request of Dr. Martin Luther King, Jr., she became the Northern Coordinator for the Southern Christian Leadership Conference, and in 1975 Maya Angelou received the *Ladies' Home Journal* Woman of the Year Award in Communications. She has received numerous honorary degrees and was appointed by President Jimmy Carter to the National Commission on the Observance of International Women's Year. Maya Angelou is currently Reynolds Professor at Wake Forest University, Winston-Salem, North Carolina.

# PART 5
# BEST PRACTICES

# Dialogue: Best Practices

*George*—One way to get practical about what diversity can offer your organization is to see what others are doing successfully in this field. What are comparable companies or agencies doing to empower people, contribute to the bottom line and make the workplace better—whether or not they've had a course on "Diversity," or even use the word. In this section we talk about best practices, look for successes and give examples of interventions that have made a concrete difference.

*Bob*—Yes, quite often organizations discover they already have diversity experts in-house. Often these are people who don't have a college degree. The belief that expertise and credibility requires initials after one's name illustrates the pervasiveness of class-based assumptions and keeps us from tapping all the available talent.

Here's a specific example. I did a diversity diagnosis at a large Boston-area hospital not too long ago. During the interviews, I discovered through anecdotes that there were several people who consistently got high performance results from a diverse workforce. These "diversity-competent" managers could have served as coaches and role models for others less experienced. They were working with people at the bottom end of the wage scale in ways that were creative, enterprising, humane, and dramatically productive for the organization.

The results were everywhere. Mentally retarded and legally blind individuals couriered material and documents about the hospital and were extremely effective at it. People with physical and mental disabilities served on a kitchen crew that had higher morale and esprit de corps than I've seen anywhere else in my career as a consultant. A former drug-addict working in the kitchen told me about how his manager had taken him from sleeping under a highway overpass, to pride in being self-sufficient. As I listened, I felt that I was in the presence of a "miracle" the manager had worked. He was a missionary reaching out to bring high-risk candidates into his operation. I was not surprised to find that the best diversity managers also had strongly grounded spiritual values and beliefs that nourished their commitment to reach

out to others (see the section on Spirit later for other examples of applications to diversity, page 326).

What an experience, talking to these remarkable managers and their employees about their approaches! It taught me that whenever possible the entree for diversity should be through people inside who are really savvy, rather than from providing models, speakers, or training programs coming from outside. If this sounds paternalistic to you, too bad; these people were making a difference.

*George*—It sounds less like paternalism than recognition of the fact that often people who are not at all politically correct are getting diversity to work. It's much better than a diversity effort that tries to fix people who are already doing a good job, rather than learning from *them*. That's at the micro level.

At the macro or systems level we want to look at the characteristics of organizations that have succeeded in the entire area of diversity. The benchmark studies of this show that it's not giveaway programs that make a diversity effort succeed but accountability for diversity tasks. Posters, tee shirts, seed money for affinity groups can all help, but putting diversity on somebody's job description is the royal road to results.

*Bob*—The American Express Financial Advisors Report to Benchmark Partners is probably the single most impressive piece in this section. It synthesizes the best of what 32 top firms have done to effectively implement diversity efforts. Few organizations can afford to undertake a benchmarking project like this, but any organization can pick up a lot of useful tips and suggestions from the results that American Express Financial Advisors have generously shared here. We've put the report first, since it's so comprehensive.

*George*—On one hand, don't forget that best practices also includes initiatives which individuals have taken to carry a diversity mandate to their everyday job situations. For example, the manager who initiates an after-hours ESL (English as a Second Language) course. Those countless efforts which can't begin to get recorded here are what may be keeping our organizations afloat despite the turbulent times. On the other hand, the material in this section enables us to take a closer look at some particularly productive efforts from a systems perspective.

*Bob*—Yes, for example, your piece on "Teaching Language and Culture" (page 214). One best practice is to have the organization teach its culture to all its members in an explicit fashion. Newcomers (whether they are women, people of color, or white males) are often without a clue as to the real rules and messages that things operate by.

*George*—The advantage for the "old guard" in disclosing their "ways to really get things done around here" is to boost everyone's performance . . . It also enables old and new people to connect with each other.

*Bob*—This article explains why it is important to address the task of "learning the ropes" explicitly. Such efforts would not normally be *called* a "diversity program," but something like "New employee orientation—how to succeed at XYZ company."

*George*— . . . and you wouldn't be getting "backlash" about that either. I personally resent the word "backlash." It's a condemnatory and gratuitous dismissal of dissent. The article, "Majority Supports Steps to Diversity," from the *LA Times* shows: first, that diversity is pretty well accepted in U.S. workplaces; and secondly, there are some major disparities between what different groups see or feel is fair. When dissent on either side of an issue is not listened to seriously, we are asking for trouble. We'll come back to integrating some of these disparate points of view in the "Key Dilemmas" section toward the end of our anthology (page 398).

*Bob*—We've added Dianne Sutton's "Managing Your Starship: Multicultural Management for the 21st Century" (page 221). This piece is included here because it's *fun* to read! Especially for those "Trekkies" out there.

*George*—I'm one of them. I have to say, at least to the other Trekkies reading this—if you'll tolerate this short tangential excursion into Federation Space, Bob . . . Captain Kirk's blue-collar, make-it-work-with-whom-you've-got multiculturalism in the crew of the original Enterprise (the first Star Trek TV series) has sadly disappeared in the Second and Third Generations. Captains Picard, and now Janeway, manage a pale assimilated crew whose set of values reflects the coming to power of the Yuppie generation. Real diversity, vision, tragedy, humor and pathos are in scarce supply. The baddies are generally aliens out there or the failures of political correctness on the part of the crew. Other Star Trek spin-offs like Babylon VI are the equivalent of B-movies on TV. Well, I guess you can see where my sympathies lie. The real-world multicultural challenge is still much more like Kirk's universe than any of the others. There may have been moments when it was sexist and offered ethnic stereotypes but it was way ahead of its time.

*Bob*—Hopefully we won't have to wait till warp speed intergalactic travel is an everyday event to see the benefits of effective cross-cultural teamwork described so well in this article.

*George*—That can start right now if you transport yourself to "Getting the Best Results from a Diversity Action Council" on page 225. This piece offers practical, down-to-earth recommendations for organizations taking their first steps in exploring how to approach the topic.

*Bob*—"The Byword is Flexible" (page 227)—You and I could actually have a discussion using only the titles of the articles themselves! Mary Cook's *Management Review* article clearly points out that the workforce *is* diverse and that flexible jobs, schedules, benefits, etc., are all appropriate responses that help both companies and individuals match up needs that may, in fact, change over time. Similar flexibility is needed for "Team Building to Break Down Cultural Barriers." Lee Gardenswartz and Anita Rowe offer simple tips and principles for diverse teams.

*George*—Organizations often have unrealistic expectations as they undertake diversity initiatives. Rita Boags's review of the "Successful Implementation of Cultural Diversity Programs" tells of lessons learned from the firing line of organizations trying to move forward.

*Bob*—It's especially valuable because it reveals failures and shortcomings. This is one area where a professional consultant is invaluable. An experienced consultant can provide a reality check on what's viable.

*George*—I like the piece, "Developing Multicultural Organizations," by Bailey Jackson & Evangelina Holvino. It presents a cohesive model for looking at diversity efforts along a continuum, presenting the differences in skills taught for each step along the way. Oftentimes, in my experience as a consultant, I have seen organizations implement an effort that is mismatched to where they sit on the continuum. Knowing where your organization is enables movement to the next appropriate step.

I also like the section on "Change Agent Assumptions and Values." It's consistent with the model we propose at the conclusion of the book (see page 491).

*Bob*—While a congressional committee debates how to count Americans in the next census, "A More Accurate Way to Measure Diversity" offers a concrete data-based procedure for analyzing how employees move up the corporate pipeline. This approach provides a rich perspective as well as tips about what to do when some individuals or groups get "stuck" in the pipeline.

*George*—In "The Challenge to Diversity" Tom Chappell highlights dilemmas organizations face in balancing competing needs and issues as they try to develop best practices. The article demonstrates how seemingly opposing points of view can be integrated to produce real bottom-line results.

*Bob*—We close with Dianne LaMountain's "Organizations Touchy About Class." So often we think dealing with diversity effectively means that we must be *doing something!*

*George*—When you have difficult diversity issues within an organization, numerous factors are required to do anything well.

*Bob*—A war story to illustrate: a division of a large international computer manufacturer was under fierce competitive pressure to increase profitability or face its U.S.-based operation being transferred overseas. I was retained to do diagnostic interviews to help them decide where to begin a major diversity initiative. The result of my focus group sessions—a recommendation to drop the diversity effort. There were too many other critical issues needing to be addressed related to core business issues. Any diversity "program" would have been seen as "fiddling while Rome burned."

*George*—Dianne LaMountain's report about her client's unwillingness to deal with "Class" may in fact turn out to be a "best practice." If the timing, support, resources, and credibility are not present . . . the best thing to do may be to do nothing at the moment. Reports of "false starts" with diversity programs are far too common. These anecdotes serve as a word of caution.

# Diversity: Report to Benchmark Partners
by American Express Financial Advisors

## Why Diversity Is Important
### Diversity will help us get there

Diversity will help us get there.
On our collective journey toward our regional and divisional goals,
diversity adds texture, flavor, fiber and strength to our strategies.
Alternately a road, a vehicle, a map, and the added enrichment along the way,
diversity helps us get where we want to go.

Diversity is important
because, to survive, our company must reflect and serve the real market—
and the real market is diverse.

Diversity is important
because large, unclaimed markets lie in diverse areas,
and these offer us the opportunities for growth and learning.

Diversity is important
because it enriches our entire company and each of us personally,
helping move American Express Financial Advisors toward its Best Place to Work goal.

Diversity is important
because it helps us choose creation and innovation
over repetition and stagnation.

Diversity is important
because it becomes an asset,
helping American Express Financial Advisors attract the best people—
and develop new clients.

—*Pamela Hill Nettleton*

Acknowledgments: It is important to note that without the support of our senior executive office, the resources needed to effectively complete this project could not have been available. Many people gave generously of their time and knowledge to make this project possible. The Home Office employees, Field Force personnel and Consultants who made up the project team were integrally involved at every step of the way. Our sincere appreciation for their contributions.

*Richard Gaskins*, Project Manager.

## Executive Summary

### Our Vision

Here at American Express Financial Advisors, we recognize that embracing and achieving true diversity among our work force and our clientele is an evolutionary process, presenting demanding challenges and unequaled opportunities for organizational and personal growth.

We are committed to creating an environment that supports our company values, to reflecting our larger market—and our community—which is diverse.

We believe that understanding and valuing the differences among people will maximize our growth at American Express Financial Advisors.

We want to make American Express Financial Advisors a place where the individual differences between people can be valued mutually by each other and the company in a process supporting the company goals within the framework of People, Service and Profitability.

Understanding that diversity is a growing concern among responsible American organizations and companies, we elected to undertake a detailed and comprehensive approach to enhancing diversity within American Express Financial Advisors.

> *A diversity benchmarking team make-up must represent the change it wants to create.*
>
> American Express Financial Advisors Diversity
> Benchmark Team

Diversity within individual companies enhances diversity for us all. When one organization succeeds at enhancing diversity, the immediate and larger community benefits.

## Rationale for Benchmarking Diversity

We selected and interviewed other companies "best in class" who are taking this journey with us. Calling them "benchmark partners," we collected their experiences and share our gathered information in this document. American Express Financial Advisors has recognized the importance of internal and external benchmarking diversity by dovetailing it with our 1994 reorganization effort. In designing a diversity enhancement effort for American Express Financial Advisors, we wanted to do it right the first time, to benefit from the experience of other organizations, to avoid reinventing the wheel.

Selected projects and teams within American Express Financial Advisors were concerned with diversity efforts, but in-house expertise in this area was limited. The company recognizes the business need for ensuring the acquisition, development

and retention of a diverse talent pool to meet the changing competitive environment.

Using this benchmarking study, American Express Financial Advisors seeks to improve upon present diversity efforts and to learn about best practices implementations, while avoiding the pitfalls identified by others. In working with benchmark partners, we set as a goal the establishment of long-term relationships with other firms regarding the sharing of our learnings on diversity enhancement efforts.

This project represented the first opportunity for American Express Financial Advisors to benchmark a specific work process for ourselves and for other companies. This gave us a chance to gain benchmarking experience; at the same time, it gave us the opportunity to capture the steps of the benchmarking process so we could effectively replicate it in other areas of opportunity, such as technology and organizational structure.

## Key Best Practices

Detailed information gathered from our benchmark partners follows, but four success factors for enhancing diversity kept resurfacing from various organizations during our discussions. We named these factors "key best practices":

- Building knowledge and skill training for enhancing diversity

- Providing information and resources to assist in the process

- Possessing top-down/bottom-up leadership influence for support

- Establishing incentives and accountability to support initiatives.

## Resulting Action Plan

Building on the detailed information from our benchmark partners, we created an action plan for our diversity efforts at American Express Financial

Advisors. We outlined a step-by-step process toward diversity goals which anticipates common obstacles—in a way, reaping the benefits from our benchmark partners' experiences.

We developed action steps (such as "Definition of diversity will be understood by all American Express Financial Advisors personnel and validated by an attitude survey" and "Establish diversity incentives for division vice presidents"), attached timetables to them, and assigned implementers responsible for meeting each deadline and each goal.

A simplified "road map" reflecting anticipated obstacles and planned responses was created, and has become the document most frequently referred to internally during diversity effort discussions.

## Overview: Selecting Our Benchmark Partners

For our benchmark partners, we selected companies which had characteristics in common with American Express Financial Advisors. We wanted benchmark partners who:

- Were best in their class
- Had complex relationships with multiple business units
- Had well-deserved reputations as leading-edge companies
- Generally had "good press"
- Were national in nature, for the most part
- Had a diversity team or effort of some sort in place.

We narrowed our initial list of 75 companies to 23, through a committee review process. We interviewed each of the final 23 companies over the telephone, and selected seven to visit in on-site interviews. Nine additional companies were added, and interviewed with expanded questions aimed at validating our preliminary recommendations and augmenting the original interviews, resulting in a total of 32 companies being interviewed.

## Deciding What to Ask

During interviews with our benchmark partners, we focused our questions on seven strategic areas: Organizational Readiness; Attraction/Sourcing; Orientation; Training; Retention Strategies; Career Development; General Information. We elected to focus our questions on the "people systems" within companies—the areas that directly effected and were affected by diversity efforts. Our specific questions were written by committee.[1]

## Conducting Our Interviews

Through committee assignment, using benchmarking criteria, specific critical factor questions were developed relating to each of the seven areas, such as training questions for a broad topic area and management training questions for a sub-topic area.

These questions were tested during our first interview. After a review of that interview, additional questions asking for more detail on selected critical factors were developed, such as course offerings, hours, cost, course design and instructor profile. Those became the questions and sub-questions used in all remaining interviews. Each benchmark partner received at least two telephone calls to complete the interview. For those selected for site visits, an average of three telephone sessions were completed, covering higher level critical factors, such as performance indicators, product focus, and the "who, what, when and how" of their diversity efforts.

## Undertaking Benchmarking

The benchmarking project was initiated by the American Express Financial Advisors Best Place To Work Diversity Council and the American Express Financial Advisors 1994 Design Team in their efforts to identify effective diversity enhancement activities in the future shaping of American Express

[1]For a list of the specific questions asked, see the original full-length version of this report. It is available from Richard Gaskins, American Express Financial Advisors, IDS tower 10, Minneapolis MN 55440; Phone: 612-671-8171; Fax: 617-671-5384.

Financial Advisors. We began our benchmarking implementation process in February 1992 after identifying a project champion, project manager, and project consultant within our executive staff. The project was completed February 1993.

We articulated a project mission, drafted guiding principles and wrote project strategies. We named our anticipated primary and secondary benefits, and created a stakeholders' requirements assessment. A complete copy of this plan is available upon request. The benchmark process had four phases: planning and organization, collecting and analyzing information, summarizing findings and making recommendations. Steps, key to each phase, were followed.

---

*We elected to focus our questions on the "people systems" within companies—the areas that directly effected and were affected by diversity efforts.*

—Steven Kumagai
American Express Financial Advisors Senior Vice President and Associate General Sales Manager

---

## Phase I: Planning and Organization

We first identified our benchmarking topic area to be field force diversity, vs. the Home Office and Field Force and provided our stakeholders with a project plan listing the benchmarking topic areas and attached completion dates to each aspect of the plan. A benchmarking team was formed by: a) defining the roles, responsibilities, necessary skills and time commitments, and b) selecting members to make up a cross-functional team, ensuring joint efforts from both the field and the home office. The team was trained in key benchmarking processes and principles by using consultants and in-house personnel. We then completed an internal assessment to validate benchmarking sub-topic areas, defining specifically what would be benchmarked; identified and selected benchmark partners; conducted benchmark interviewing training; created our list of initial benchmark interview questions; developed interview materials, including an interview form, matrix and telephone log; and gathered feedback on all these steps from the stakeholders.

## Phase II: Collecting and Analyzing Information

For this second phase we contacted the identified benchmark partners to gauge their interest, and sent them a briefing package that included an introductory memo and questionnaire. This was followed with a phone call, which scheduled a subsequent interview of approximately an hour and a half with interested companies to discuss initial questions. We developed follow-up questions requesting more detail from our benchmark partner when appropriate, followed by thank you letters to each benchmark partner. We summarized our findings on forms and matrices, then met in core groups to debrief and to create a list of benchmark partners to visit on-site. A second stage of interviews with a pared-down list of benchmark partners followed. A summary of our findings in a preliminary report to the stakeholders concluded this phase.

## Phase III: Summarizing Findings

We created a summary findings report and presentation, including what the best-practices companies are doing and which corrective processes and programs need to be developed internally, then organized our findings into a report to share with benchmark partners.

## Phase IV: Making Recommendations

The group created a "road map" of recommendations and strategies for enhancing field force diversity within American Express Financial Advisors and a strategic alignment of potential recommendations.

## Strategic Alignment Process

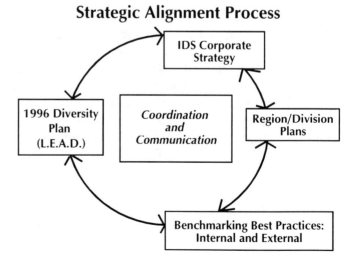

We developed a detailed action plan and communicated all recommendations to stakeholders.

# Prescriptions

Over and over again, certain "prescriptions" for the successful enhancement of diversity within an organization were given by our benchmark partners: accept diversity as a management and strategic planning opportunity; assess diversity-related needs and concerns and develop action plans with support to address and resolve them; provide diversity awareness, training and education to support desired goals and objectives; be willing to revamp policies, systems and practices as needed to enhance diversity; provide for and assure necessary reinforcement and accountability in diversity areas.

# Strengths

As we identified the strengths of our benchmark partners, we aligned our findings with our own 1996 diversity business strategy, which groups such strengths into four categories we call "LEAD": Leadership (more visible commitment, information and training), Environment (support systems and practices), Acquisition (targeted recruiting) and Delivery (programs that reinforce key measures of success).

Our benchmark partners' strengths are listed below.

## American Express Financial Advisors 1996 Diversity Business Strategy

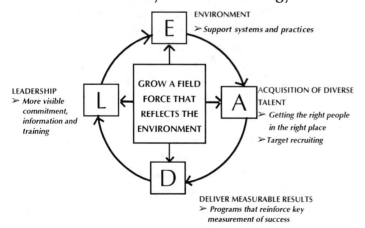

## Leadership

- Perceiving the CEO as the champion of diversity

- Encouraging continuously a strong push/pull philosophy of supporting diversity enhancements from leadership

- Mandating a formal management development and education program, interwoven with principles of diversity

- Establishing goals at the corporate level and implementing them at the local level

## Environment

- Understanding that diversity is a long-term evolutionary process and needs to be a systemic change, rather than a program

- Requiring management to support company diversity posture

- Determining regional and divisional diversity strategies and goals at the field, rather than corporate levels

- Treating diversity as something separate from an EEO or Affirmative Action Program

- Defining diversity as broad, global and inclusive of the total workforce

- Focusing on diversity hiring as being hiring the "best minds"

- Tying diversity explicitly into company values, philosophy, management principles, competitive advantage and total quality management

- Tracking diversity concerns through attitude surveys, focus group meetings, special committees and appraisal feedback

- Proactively addressing backlash from workforce individuals who feel excluded from diversity enhancement efforts by utilizing workshops and broader diversity definitions

## Acquisition

- Providing divisions with funds and support for maintaining or creating local market presence inclusive of diverse areas

- Extensively using a variety of sourcing for diversity hiring

- Using college intern programs as a method to meet and eventually hire diverse population candidates

- Using bilingual literature to support recruitment efforts

- Providing candidates with brochures describing company position on diversity

- Describing diversity posture and goals in annual reports and other prominent publications

### Delivery

- Utilizing an incentive compensation and reward system to support diversity initiatives

- Incorporating diversity principles and measurements into performance appraisal systems, rather than treating them separately

- Moving from a decentralized to centralized guidance of diversity enhancements for consistency in message and cost reasons

- Holding management accountable for supporting and meeting the goals of diversity

## Acknowledged Gaps

Along with strengths and accomplishments come challenges and obstacles. Our benchmark partners were well aware of existing gaps in their efforts to enhance diversity. One of those gaps is the ongoing struggle of many companies to justify diversity from a profitability standpoint. Some companies are working toward establishing this case, but definitive results are not yet available. Many of our benchmark partners were able to identify areas needing improvement and attention: proving a business case for diversity; demonstrating visible management commitment to diversity; bringing awareness training to each level of the company; expanding diversity training among recruiters; raising the low readiness level among division management for initiating diversity enhancement efforts; and monitoring and evaluating diversity efforts more extensively.

## Key Management Challenges

Our benchmark partners also identified diversity enhancement challenges specific to management:

- Motivating field management to take on key diversity enhancement initiatives

- Reducing management fear of litigation around diversity

- Balancing the perceived short-term high cost of diversity enhancements with the long-term benefit of keeping financial obligations manageable

- Controlling employee turnover, diverse employees and others

- Educating the workforce to understand that diversity goes beyond gender and people of color

- Avoiding backlash from white males

- Continuing effective communication of enhancements and support needed

## Key Learnings from Our Benchmark Process

Along with the learnings that came from benchmarking, we also gained knowledge about the benchmarking process itself. As we attempt further benchmarking on other matters of concern, we will be guided by these learnings:

### Success Factors to Achieve

- Obtain active top executive support to champion the benchmarking effort; this unlocks barriers to obtaining cooperation and information. Positioning requests as having the support (or as having come from) the CEO or a member of senior management almost guarantees a quicker, more thorough response.

- Include the clients and stakeholders in determining areas to benchmark and in selecting benchmark partners. It is critically important to get their ownership in order to manage their expectations when they later request additional information or the inclusion of another company.

- Establish a formal client/stakeholder link representative on the core team who has the responsibility of keeping his or her group updated.

- Periodically and strategically formally "spoon feed" clients and stakeholders information to increase their readiness level for efficiently processing eventual recommendations.

- Involve the total benchmark team in an opportunity to brainstorm, to develop outcome thinking strategy, and to frame their concerns.

- Be very careful of releasing preliminary findings, because the conclusions change as additional information is gathered.

- Assign benchmark interviewers strategically to internal interviewees, aligning them, where possible, based on personality and politics.

- Organize the benchmark team around the key processes and assign one member to be responsible for each process. This works better than a committee, and allows the captain to use additional resources where appropriate.

- Involve field people in the team from the beginning through the development of recommendations.

## Pitfalls to Avoid

- Limiting the benchmarking team to people at the same level, with the same politics, from only the field or only the home office, or who are performing the same function—"silo thinking." Results not truly representational of the organization may occur.

- Beginning benchmarking work without training each member of the team in the principles of benchmarking and benchmarking interviewing. Late new members must also be trained.

- Expecting untrained staff to be persuasive and persistent enough over the telephone to be effective in identifying final contacts at benchmarking partner organizations.

- Including only "liberals" or "conservatives" on the benchmarking team.

- Avoiding the selection of team members who are known to question the validity of your topic. Actually, these team members may bring valuable input to your team and will certainly put the team's key learnings to the acid test.

- Underestimating the importance of using a facilitator with benchmarking expertise, at least at initial benchmarking team meetings. Too many people with strong opinions on an issue (such as diversity) left in a room alone together with no facilitator can "raise a lot of blood pressure" without significantly advancing a project's progress.

- Using the entire team to write the summary findings. This is the path of unrealistic expectations. Limit this writing team to a maximum of four people.

- Deciding to use too many similar companies as benchmark partners.

- Assuming that benchmarking clients and stakeholders are at the same readiness level as the benchmarking team when it comes to understanding challenges, pitfalls, reports and recommendations.

## Codes of Conduct in Working With Benchmark Partners

- Do not ask for statistics, information and policies from benchmark partners that you are not willing to share yourself.

- Check with the legal department before deciding what internal information will be shared outside the company.

- Provide a benchmark findings report that will be of value to benchmark partners.

- Use only the designated benchmark contacts when interviewing and corresponding.

## Potential Outcomes

- After the benchmarking project is completed, core team members who have enjoyed their active role in impacting and changing corporate culture may wish to extend their involvement in benchmarking efforts.

- After the final report is completed and accepted, the role of the project manager moves to positioning the benchmarking results effectively to accelerate organizational learning, to make learning continuous, and to coordinate communication with top executives.

# Best Practices Highlights

This list of best practices culled from our benchmark partners follows the American Express Financial Advisors 1996 diversity strategy of grouping diversity efforts into four "LEAD" categories: Leadership, Environment, Acquisition and Delivery. If specific information would be of interest to you, contact us and we will obtain the source organization's approval to release the details.

## Leadership—
## Commitment, Approach, Training

- Top management put diversity in the forefront of corporate posture and communicate their personal commitment regularly and forcefully.

- Senior Management have regular dinners six times a year focusing on diversity championing.

- A management learnings lab for working with divisional people to strengthen their people management skills is utilized.

- A continuous training process for all managers, with a minimum annual hours commitment, is provided. Incorporated into the management development courses are diversity principles and diversity skill development.

- Diversity training is required of all managers and the monitoring and control is decentralized.

- A top-down commitment to work and family programs is present and clear. The mission states: "We will be mindful of ways to help our employees fulfill their family responsibilities." The company resolves problems that, for the diverse employee, often feel quite major—in resolving these, recruitment and retention are supported.

- Diversity training is mandatory for all employees, and each business unit goes through training as a group. One of the most important components of the training is to create long-term diversity goals for the units. Training is not viewed as a stand-alone item. Business units develop "task teams" that go back to areas and continue work started in the training.

- Diversity is approached from the top down.

- Awareness training is offered in one-day and two- or three-day workshops for all employees and managers, respectively.

- A Senior Management coordinator was established, with the objective of promoting and marketing to clients and advisors with diverse backgrounds.

## Environment—
## Networks, Support, Philosophy, Definitions, Concerns

- Management bonus pay is tied to diversity improvement criteria.

- The company has a diversity center.

- A newsletter preparing management to conduct business in the global age is published and circulated. This provides an excellent communication vehicle and keeps opportunities of diversity in front of all employees.

- A question and answer brochure on diversity was published and distributed. This helps employees understand the inclusive nature of a broad definition of diversity, communicates the extent of company commitment to diversity, provides examples of how to handle selected situations and answers questions typically asked.

- Each company division has a work life council made up of representatives of that division. The council reports to a division executive and sends representatives to a regional and corporate council. This provides needs and issues feedback to divisional, regional and corporate levels. The concept is similar to American Express Financial Advisors Best Place To Work councils, with the exception that they are cross-functional and down to the division level.

- Guiding principles for diversity are provided to management and employees. This is a simple communication that provides a rationale for supporting diversity.

- A national day care referral service for employees is provided.

- A glossy brochure describing diversity at the company is provided. The purpose is to describe company commitment to diversity as well as to reflect the diversity profile of the employee population. The brochure is used for recruiting and for positive employee relations.

- Diversity is defined from an inclusive perspective as "all the various characteristics that make one individual different from another." This definition is a method of preventing employees from feeling excluded in efforts to enhance diversity within the company.

- Model diversity letters for executives and managers to send to their subordinates reflecting the company's posture and initiatives are provided annually. This expedites communication, making it easy, consistent and likely to actually get done.

- Sales brochures are printed in a second language to assist representatives in the sales process.

- A corporate philosophy embracing pluralism as a definition of diversity was adopted. It is inclusive of all employees, shows diversity is not a program with a start and finish, but an ongoing process that will change the makeup of the company.

- A one-day awareness program about the value of human diversity is provided to all employees.

- Employee resource groups meet with the human resource vice president quarterly to provide input. The company uses the meetings for sources of input on diverse population concerns and needs.

- Recognizing that the attention paid to diverse employee groups could leave white males feeling a little left out, a workshop was developed to help them adjust to the changes they face.

- A child development center is provided for all employees at headquarters for mildly ill children, allowing the parent to still come to work.

- Diversity is on the agenda for every quarterly sales meeting. This keeps diversity in front of employees and has begun to be considered a business issue like any other business issue.

- Business units prepare an "organizational audit" each year that includes several indicators, i.e., financial performance, diversity measures and other "people management" indicators.

- Diversity efforts (including training programs and the use of diversity consultants) are managed at the local level and coordinated through headquarters to reduce inefficiencies and expense. Business units must justify using a program or consultant outside of those approved by headquarters.

- The definition of diversity is very broad.

- Diversity is seen as a process, a change of culture.

- A diversity department was established, consisting of complaint management, EEO/Affirmative Action compliance programs, monitoring external requirements like internal ones, diversity administration and development.

- Managers and a company diversity center address diversity issues raised by clients.

- Employee networks are an important piece in diversity efforts. Networks are organized across all regions and for international, regional and local chapters. Human Resources meets regularly with repre- sentatives of all groups. No management advisers are part of the group. Groups assist in client marketing and recruiting efforts.

- Sales literature applications, contracts and commercials are available in Spanish.

- In any diversity activity, the white-maleism issue was addressed immediately. White males should not feel left out.

- Diversity is incorporated as a "business goal" with a top to bottom approach, getting a high degree of commitment from Senior Management.

- Marketing strategies were established to take advantage of local diverse cultures and regions.

- A centralized program is used.

- Support systems for advisors with diverse backgrounds are offered.

- It is a corporate-wide objective to have diversity a part of the corporate culture.

- The company sponsors a program to increase national awareness of the diversity issue. Every employee is required to go through these sessions, which include lecture and videotapes.

- In working with core groups, a means of relational amnesty is provided so people can "test" reactions to problems in a safe, non-threatening environment.

- Organizational diversity is linked with total quality management in an organizational approach to make both processes more successful.

- The overriding principle is inclusion and involvement—no one stands outside of diversity.

- There should be a centralized strategy, even with decentralized implementation.

- Division office employees are tied to home office employee groups as charter members of a group. These employees receive the same information as home office employees and have an opportunity to participate in activities or provide input.

- A skills inventory is used to quickly find employees who can give input on a given subject due to personal, professional or educational interest. The inventory was revised once a year with employee-provided information. A skills inventory may be useful to locate field force members who are able to share information on a given topic.

## Acquisition—
### Recruitment, Community Relationships, College Relationships

- College relationships supporting minority recruitment are exemplary and the corpo-

ration has specific dollars allocated for this purpose.

- Community involvement is done on a consistent basis.

- A separate diversity program for managers is provided, focusing on hiring and retention.

- A retreat is sponsored between faculty members and employees to help raise awareness of diversity issues. This enhanced the company's relationship for recruiting purposes and created presence in the community.

- Recruiting sources:
  * Colleges are selected based on the diversity of the student body
  * Intern programs are offered
  * Intern programs include matching a person at a higher level and similar interests with an intern for six months
  * Employees recruit at their alma mater
  * National conventions
  * National advertising
  * Press recognition for diversity efforts.

- Continuous, extensive training in recruiting is provided.

- The company is just beginning a Hispanic high school science competition program. Once the winners are chosen, they will be followed through their college years. Throughout that time, the company will offer internships and other incentives to keep students interested in the company, with the ultimate objective of the student coming to work for them once they graduate from college.

## Delivery—
### Incentives, Rewards for Executives, Delivery of Enhancements, Promotion/Advancement Programs, Retention, Awards

- A clearing house for complaints and grievances on the basis of conflict resolution is established. This is used before problems reach the Legal Department, and even then it is on a need-to-know basis, information-sharing only.

- Corrective measures type of intervention is used to train and enhance future promotion potential for women of color, although future job availability is not promised.

- A people management responsibilities performance appraisal system has diversity principles incorporated into it. This makes diversity measurement a part of regular management performance appraisal, rather than keeping it separate.

- The top 235 corporate officers are appraised on how well they meet pluralism-related criteria through a pluralism performance menu. The purpose is to ensure that the officers demonstrate what they have done.

- Employee resource groups are asked to provide lists of diverse candidates who they think are ready for advancement within the company. The intent is to develop a pluralistic mix from the bottom up.

- An awards program was developed for diversity management. This award acts as an incentive and recognition for employees who promote diversity initiatives at a local level. The award is considered to be very prestigious within the company and keeps diversity in front of the employees.

- Management-level bonus criteria include diversity efforts. Managers must show expertise or growth in all areas to get 100% of the bonus. The evaluation doesn't focus only on numbers, but also on environment, attitude, turnover, etc. Expectations are set up front, so there are no surprises at review time.

- Qualitative and quantitative diversity measurements are tied to compensation.

- A women of color program provides outbound, financial and overall corporate picture training. No promotion guarantees are given.

- A development support network of black employees discusses problems, develops action plans and holds employees accountable for implementing the action plan and reporting on the results.

- Success regarding achievement of diversity goals is recognized and rewarded, and quarterly goals regarding retention are monitored.

- A monitoring or tracking system for people employed with diverse backgrounds is used.

- Mentorship programs are in place for minority recruits.

- Organizational awards are tracked to see who is getting them, why they get them, and how the results improve the organization.

- Succession planning is used to identify management subordinates who show talent for moving to a higher level position in the company. Succession planning is also used to monitor the progression of minorities and women into greater levels of responsibilities.

- A handbook is provided, describing the parameters of a mentoring program. Each business unit interested in developing a mentoring program is free to do so and uses the handbook to develop it. This may become a training-the-trainer type of tool.

- Tracking systems are used to monitor parity and goal attainment of business units.

- Career flowcharts are provided to all employees. The chart clearly illustrates how one can make upward progression in a given career. This tool can be used to understand how one can move from A to B, or to decide that management or home office employment is a better career choice. Offering options to retain talent is a better alternative than losing it.

> The overriding principle is inclusion and involvement—no one stands outside of diversity.

# Parameters We Learned as a Basis for American Express Financial Advisors Diversity Plan Development

- The definition of diversity must expand to become more inclusive and less exclusive.

- Diversity leadership must come from field force regional/divisional management.

- Diversity strategies must align with existing business strategies and goals.

- Divisions must build diversity strategy within their business plans.

- Company diversity posture must receive division support.

- Field management must adopt a long-term perspective of diversity.

- Diversity committees are needed on the regional and divisional levels.

# Conclusion

## Outcomes

From our diversity benchmarking efforts, we experienced the following deliverables: an action plan of steps, responsibilities, roles and deadlines toward enhancing diversity; a road map of how we will proceed and what our likely challenges and obstacles will be; a developing communication process aimed at transmitting information to key executives for implementation; an internal assessment of our diversity activities; identified relevant best practices of other companies; and an outline of a successful benchmarking process that can be replicated in other areas within the company.

## Benefits

- A snapshot of our readiness level for taking on diversity enhancement efforts.

- A head-start on diversity change in functional areas, stimulated by careful communication of selected key learnings.

- Knowledge of the gaps between what our practices are and what those are of the best practices companies.

- The creation of permanent corporate diversity advocates out of temporary benchmarking team members.

- Increased support from senior executives to implement diversity enhancements.

- An understanding of the critical forces needed to motivate diversity enhancement.

- Alignment between benchmarking process recommendations and our business objectives and plans.

◆

# APPENDIX 1:
# Interview Results

Through telephone and site interviews with our benchmark partners, we gathered responses to our questions. A synopsis of those responses follows; for a complete listing of all information gathered, contact Richard Gaskins (612) 671-8171.

*Organizational Readiness:* What is your definition of diversity in your organization? Diversity definitions ranged from none to the perhaps traditional definition of "race, gender and disability" to recently developed definitions embracing literally all dimensions of and all differences between any persons. Aspects of diversity included: race, gender, age, physical ability, physical appearance, nationality, cultural heritage, personal background, functional experience, position in the organization, mental and physical challenges, family responsibilities, sexual orientation, military experience, educational background, style differences, economic status, thinking patterns, political backgrounds, city/state/region of residence, IQ level, smoking preference, weight, marital status, nontraditional job, religion, white collar, language, blue collar and height. Others qualify "anyone whose lifestyle doesn't quite mirror the traditional family" as being diverse. Whichever specific categories were included, diversity is generally defined as understanding, respecting, valuing and accommodating human and cultural differences.

*Diversity is defined in a variety of ways:* all the ways people differ that impact performance; creating an environment where everyone can achieve their maximum potential; an ethnic and sexual mix; "pluralism"—promoting mutual respect, acceptance, teamwork and productivity among people who are diverse; all-encompassing; each member of the organization is diverse in some way; full utilization of the workforce; getting the most out of each employee; providing a safe environment for differences; allowing each employee to contribute to their greatest potential; not excluding white males; in some companies the word "diversity" is avoided and not used; the definition is not static, is constantly modified and aligns easily with Total Quality Management; the definition is not specific; and different answers would be given by different people.

---

*In discussing whether to drive diversity programs from the bottom or the top, companies stress that culture cannot be changed without direction and commitment from top management.*

—William J. McKinney
American Express Financial Advisors, Vice President Field Management Support

*Many companies stressed that, to them, diversity is not a program, but a process—a part of the way they do business. "Program" implies a start and a finish, but enhancing diversity is evolutionary, ongoing and the methods to achieving maximum potential must be continually reexamined.*

---

*An editorial note:* While each of our benchmark partners had in common their desire to approach diversity with sensitivity and respect, they differ in the vocabulary they use discussing this issue. Some companies say "African American," others say "Black." Some say "minorities," others say "persons of color." Even the use of the term "diversity" varies from company to company, from the traditional ("diversity" meaning minorities) to an all-inclusive use across all boundaries. The terms may differ—and you'll see the terms they used accurately reflected in our information here—but the desire to use inoffensive language is the same. At American Express Financial Advisors, we have made our own choices, and use this language in our introduction to each section.

# APPENDIX 2

## Diversity Benchmarking Process

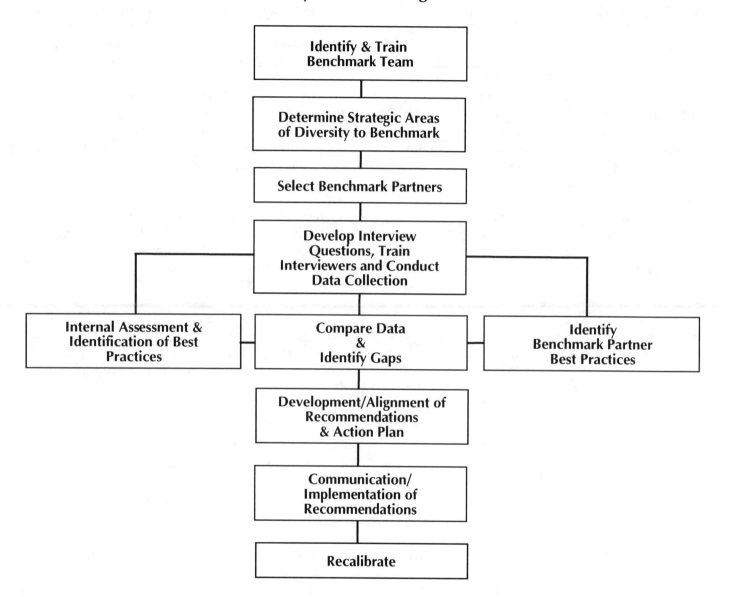

# American Express Financial Advisors
# Proposed Definition of Diversity

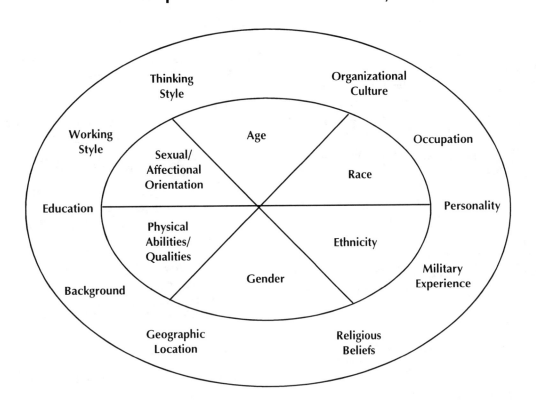

## Our Benchmark Partners—

We offered our benchmark partners anonymity in exchange for their participation in this process, and so we do not attribute any specific data to any one particular benchmark partner. However, we do wish to recognize the significant time, effort and cooperation each of these respected organizations devoted to assisting us in our process. Our sincere appreciation to:

Aetna Life & Casualty Company

Allstate Insurance Companies

Apple Computers, Inc.

AT&T (American Telephone & Telegraph)

Avon Products, Inc.

Burger King Corporation

Digital Equipment Corporation

Dreyfus Corporation

Dupont

Environmental Protection Agency

Federal Express Corporation

Ford Motor Company

General Mills, Inc.

Grand Metropolitan Pillsbury

Hughes Aircraft Company

IBM (International Business Machines)

Johnson & Johnson

Kidder, Peabody Group, Inc.

Martin Marietta Corporation

Merck & Co., Inc.

Merrill Lynch & Co., Inc.

Motorola, Inc.

Nordstrom, Inc.

Northern States Power Company

Philip Morris Companies, Inc.

Piper Jaffray, Inc.

Proctor and Gamble Company

Prudential Insurance Co. of America

TRW

TRW Space and Defense

US West, Inc.

Xerox Corporation

# Teaching Language and Culture

by George F. Simons

The teaching of languages, whether it is English as a second language (ESL) or languages for U.S. managers and workers going abroad, has surged with the growing awareness of the global and diverse nature of workplaces and markets.

Language textbooks and teachers have always had something to say about the culture that corresponds to the language they are teaching. In the past the focus was often on art, history, literature, and everyday mores and transactions. This might be enough for the casual tourist, but not enough for a learner to really become effective in another culture. Consequently, many language schools today are adding courses in cultural diversity to their curricula. Such courses, however specialized they become, must answer three basic questions:

- *What is culture and how does it work?*

- *Who has a culture?*

- *How is learning a language affected by culture?*

## What is culture and how does it work?

Culture is a form of internal programming that we can best describe as:

*A set of mental formulae for survival and success,*

*developed by a specific group of people,*

*stored as unconscious instructions in the mind, and*

*sometimes heard as conversations with oneself in the conscious mind.*

In other words, our culture is always at work to help us interpret reality and to know how to act. It's us talking to ourselves. Much of this takes place in the background of our minds. We usually don't notice it, though on occasion we hear echoes of voices from our past.

## Who has a culture?

Any group of people who must succeed and survive in a given environment creates a culture. We develop best procedures from our common experiences of reality and our successes and failures in dealing with it. Then, we hand these on to others, sometimes explicitly, sometimes just by living them out. Nature writer Barry Lopez (1990) puts it this way in one of his children's books:

*The stories people tell have a way of taking care of them. If stories come to you, care for them and learn to give them away where they are needed. Sometimes a person needs a story more than food to stay alive. That is why we put these stories in each other's memory. This is how people care for themselves.*

Whoever has a culture also develops language that reflects and expresses that culture. Here are some common groups we belong to that develop their own ways of thinking (internal talking) and speaking about things:

- Nations, racial and regional groups, families

- Men and women

- Age, class, and educational groups

- Public and private organizations

- Professions, trades, work teams

- Social, sports, or hobby groups

The average person lives and works in several or even many cultures and usually has some cross-cultural skills to draw on. Moving from one to the other she or he already speaks several "languages" even if all of them are in the same native tongue.

Women and men in the same culture may have strong differences in speech patterns. Different word forms and levels of politeness may be found in some languages, but even in English, the sexes have different vocabularies due to their socially assigned roles and differing perceptions. Linguists such as Robin Lakoff (1975) and Deborah Tannen

(1990, 1994) have noticed such things as tag questions, and indirect ways of saying things that make women's speech different from men's.

# How is learning a language affected by culture?

Culture and language are survival tools. They are shortcuts to getting things done. They are always working together. When we listen to others, for example, we create interpretations or expectations in our minds at lightening speed. While others speak, we are guessing what will come next and then checking the accuracy of our guesses against what they actually say. This is why:

- We often "hear" but don't get the message, because we chose interpretations that fit our own cultural expectations.

- Speaking a second language is hard work when we first start to do it. We can't anticipate what others will say as well as a native speaker can. So we try to listen to every word first, translate these words into our native tongue, and then form an interpretation.

- Many jokes are funny, because the punch line is not what we expected. We laugh at the incongruity. Conversely, thigh-slappers from another culture may not strike us as funny at all, because the punch line had nothing to do with our expectations as listeners, or there may be humor throughout a story and we are disappointed waiting for the strong punch line which *our* culture expects.

Thus learning a language is not just mastering new words, accents, and grammar. It demands internalizing a set of expectations about how life is or should be for the group with which one wishes to communicate. Knowing just the language doesn't tell you anything about what a person from another culture will say next, or whether they are making sense, or telling the truth, or meaning the same thing you mean with the same words. Social interaction with the imagination, feelings, and beliefs of the speaker becomes essential if one is to gain more than a technical or literary competence in a language.

If we learn a language without learning a culture, we may know words and phrases but do not know what to say, when, how, or to whom. Cultural diversity taught to language learners must impart culturally specific answers to the questions below, or, at least, arm them with the questions as investigative tools:

- *What am I allowed to speak about, or ask about?* What is impolite or polite? How intimate may I become? What may I reveal about myself, my feelings, my wishes? May I ask about your family, your work, etc.? What feelings may I show, e.g., as a man or woman?

- *Whom may I ask about certain things?* E.g., may I dispute with the professor? May I ask the boss for a favor or must I send a friend?

- *When may I speak?* When is it my turn? When may I interrupt, or may I at all? May I speak while others are speaking or must I wait my turn? What is the signal that I can speak, interrupt, start a new topic?

- *How directly or indirectly must I speak?* How loudly or how softly? How formally or informally?

In reality, the questions are interrelated and often being asked at the same time. Language students, even before immersion in their target culture, need to explore and practice answering these type of questions in role plays, games, and exercises that deal with explicit cultural differences while the new language is being learned.

When it comes to designing a language curriculum, an overview of cultural diversity may be useful as a separate introductory course, but diversity must be an integral and daily part of teaching language skills. Language competence and cultural competence are in fact one and the same. The truly competent language teacher may turn out to be the most effective cultural diversity trainer. It is also hard to imagine an effective teacher or trainer of diversity, even outside the realm of language teaching, who has not mastered a second language. Fluency in another language should be one criterion used in the selection of competent diversity consultants and trainers, even where the intervention itself may not require its use.

## References

Lakoff, Robin, *Language and Woman's Place*, NY, Harper and Row, 1975.

Lopez, Barry, *Crow and Weasel*, North Point Press, Berkeley, CA, 1990

Tannen, Deborah, *You Just Don't Understand: Women and Men in Conversation*, NY, William Morrow, 1990.

_____. *Talking from 9 to 5*, William Morrow, 1994.

How about efforts to equalize opportunities for women?

Answer: Only 16% of respondents were in the backlash category of saying America is going overboard. Another 31% said they want more effort. And 48% were in the middle, saying enough is being done now. The poll found that female and black respondents were more eager to speed up the process, while whites and men were more

# Majority Support Steps to Diversity in the Workplace, *Times* Poll Finds

by John Balzar (*Los Angeles Times*)

*Employment: Despite reports of friction, most back efforts toward equal opportunity. More than 80% say race relations at the office are good.*

You are black, Latino, female. These are grand days of opportunity in the American work force. Well, maybe not so grand. And white males trying to climb the career ladder? Your timing is rotten. But you still hold all the best jobs, don't you?

"The only sin which we never forgive in each other," said Ralph Waldo Emerson, "is difference of opinion."

For a generation, Americans worked under a loose-knit addendum to our social contract called "affirmative action." Now affirmative action has evolved into "diversity." Not only are we claiming that we want to pry open the doors of opportunity, but we are all being asked to appreciate our racial, gender and cultural differences. The ensuing social friction showers us with hot sparks: Million-dollar legal judgments for workplace harassment. Demands and boycotts; counter-demands and backlash. Income disparities by color and gender. Anger met by rage.

Sometimes it's enough to make us ask: Is diversity a great American flop?

Actually, no.

In a national survey of 987 American workers conducted last summer, the *Los Angeles Times* Poll found more agreement over workplace diversity than news headlines might suggest. And the poll found that a large majority either supports current efforts or is willing to do more to push toward equality of opportunity. When asked, 83% of respondents said race relations were good to excellent at their place of employment, and this included 52% of African Americans surveyed. Among blacks, 46% said they had suffered discrimination on the job in the last five years. An equal number said they had not. As for workplace relations between men and women, 88% of the respondents said things were good to excellent, including 91% of the women. Only 18% of the women surveyed said they had been subjected to gender discrimination in the workplace during the last five years, versus 10% of the men.

Have we gone too far in the quest for diversity?

In the poll, 30% of respondents said the nation has gone overboard with attempts to guarantee minorities a fair shake in the workplace, but 26% said more effort is needed. And 39% put themselves in the middle, agreeing that enough is being done. Blacks and whites, however, view America differently: 66% of blacks want more aggressive efforts, while only 19% of whites want to go faster.

216

likely to say they are content with the pace of diversity efforts. In this regard, polls are tricky. Reword the questions slightly and the numbers can shift. And people respond differently to the same questions depending on their race and culture.

In a recent lecture on racism, Houston attorney Xavier Lemond explained: "White people look at discrimination from an individual point of view. White people come up to me and say: 'My parents taught me never to be prejudiced—look at our maid, Suzie, she's like one of the family.' . . . Blacks look at discrimination from a societal point of view—whoever does it to the least of my brethren does it to me."

Still, at the very time when America depicts itself—and is depicted abroad—as a country divided, a large majority of Americans seem to support workplace diversity. And even in the polarized politics of the 1990s, 57% of respondents who describe themselves as politically conservative say they favor current efforts to guarantee fairness in the workplace—or want even more done.

In interviews conducted across the nation, a common theme emerged: Americans regard diversity differently than other social movements. Yes, it touches our lives and ambitions as directly as any matter of public policy. The goal itself reflects a remarkable turn of human events, a society striving to make good on the high-minded promise of justice sounded in its Constitution and Declaration of Independence. But diversity lacks the exultation that has sustained America through other struggles. Few workers among us rejoice at being part of a noble cause. No leader stands up to inspire us, no martyr lays down sacrifices we can follow, no call to action is lofty enough to be recorded in Bartlett's *Familiar Quotations*.

Instead, the process of diversity is bureaucratic, its vernacular legalistic, its victims and beneficiaries often dehumanized as mere fine print in this new social contract. Our politicians and business managers cling to a stubborn contradiction: Diversity is not a matter of quotas, oh no. But how else can progress be measured except to count the numbers?

For the worse, and for the better, diversity has altered our concepts of merit. And it comes at a time when the nature of employment itself is undergoing broad change.

So we confront diversity as a personal matter. We are not crusading. We are coping. We drink society's medicine, and we decide ourselves if it comes from a glass half full or half empty.

Dale Robinson sells cars in Denver. He strides confidently on the lot. He is the only African American at the dealership. Shoppers, he says, "expect to see a guy in a tie who is white. And if they see a black guy, it can create more anxiety. Even black customers have a tendency not to want to deal with black salesmen." Angry? Sometimes. Hurt? Yes. Resigned? Hardly. He said he learned the trade from an African American who humiliated him and made his life miserable. "He taught me the guy who takes the most makes the most." He taught the young man to cope.

So Robinson teams up with a white salesman sometimes. The partner softens the buyer and then Robinson is introduced into the deal as the supposed "floor manager." It's the old good-guy, bad-guy routine. But because Robinson is introduced as someone with power over the deal, he is given respect. "As soon as they perceive me as someone who can give them what they want, color isn't an issue anymore."

Sometimes prejudice explodes in his face, and a manager or customer utters a racist jape. That only hardens his resolve. "If a guy comes in and treats me like—and calls me a lowlife . . . that's the guy I'm going to make all my money on. I go to the bank and say: 'I've got $3,000 of that guy's money in my pocket.' "

Robinson's circumstance falls short of the American ideal. But he measures progress. It's a job, not a life, he said. "I took a lot of abuse to get where I am in car sales. I look at it victoriously at the end of the month when I get my paycheck."

Onetime Los Angeles area gang member Anna Gill now works in Houston. A Latina, she perhaps typifies the incomplete but incremental progress America has made. In moving from one job to another, she has gone from hopelessness to hope. That itself is a great distance. But Gill feels it is further still from hope to reality.

She remembers her job as a fund-raiser at New Orleans Children's Hospital. "It was very chauvinistic and racist. When they hired a young white male, younger than me, I had to train him. I said, that was it. I knew what his salary was. It was more than mine. I knew where his job was going, which was higher than mine. They didn't really believe in me. They saw my race, they didn't see me." Now she is an alumni fund-raiser at the University of Houston. And she says she has hope because of a supervisor who is committed to having a diverse work force, to promoting minorities. "We're moving ahead," Gill said. "But not fast enough . . . . Racism is here forever, in one form or another, I'm sorry to say."

Because workplace diversity is so personal, our feelings are often ambivalent, sometimes contradictory. If asked, we're apt to say anything, including the truth. Around the nation, any number of companies congratulate one another for progress in diversifying work forces, and their efforts are held up as examples in their communities. But a good number of these companies would rather leave it there. Big firms like the Bank of America in Los Angeles and Corning Glass in New York, and smaller ones like Quark Inc. in Denver, all refused requests by *The Times* to explore their diversity programs firsthand.

An exception is the Atlanta Marriott Marquis Hotel. Come over and you'll see all kinds of diversity, a manager offered. No tally sheet was necessary. Not only could you see diversity at the hotel, you could feel it.

David Hill lost both of his legs to a land mine in Vietnam. He started his career at the Marriott as a furniture repair specialist. From his wheelchair, he could easily refinish wood. But to advance, he needed a way to operate a sewing machine so he could repair upholstery too. Hill and his supervisor put their heads together. For less than 50 cents, they devised what Hill calls his "foot"—a simple rod and wooden block that enables him to operate the sewing machine. "I'm very happy," he says, rolling through the lobby to his job.

Steven Griffieth has the skeletal disease scoliosis. He had been a custodian when he joined the hotel staff as a trainee two years ago through a program sponsored by Goodwill Industries. His small, frail body was not up to that job. Today he is guest services coordinator. "I really didn't have any idea I would get that far," he said. Diversity is personal, but its actualization is not. Griffieth nods to the computer at his desk. "I didn't have a lot of experience dealing with technical equipment. But I enjoyed people. I look at some of the associates I work with who have college degrees and see myself here without a degree. And they're anxious to help me and educate me."

Maybe it helps that the hotel's human resources director did not come from a university business school but up from the ranks of waitresses. And if it matters—and it probably does in a story about diversity—Hill and Griffieth are African Americans.

*The Times* Poll asked Americans their views of diversity training at the workplace—a phenomenon that has swept across businesses nationwide. Sixty-two percent of respondents said they believe that these sessions are worthwhile in raising sensitivities to race and gender differences.

One company that offers such consultation and training is Gamma Vision of Seattle. For a round-table discussion, it gathered workers and managers from two of its public-works clients, Puget Power and Pierce County Transit. The purpose: to explore views on diversity. On some points, these front-line employees shared a consensus. As practiced at the workplace today, diversity can shape conduct but not always attitudes. "Some people's minds will never change. But you can at least let them know certain kinds of behavior are not acceptable at the workplace," said Stephanie Ostmann, a human-resources trainer for the transit system. They also agreed that progress was being made, but not secured.

"We're downsizing . . . And we're going to end up losing a lot of the people we worked really hard to move into the crafts," said Barbara Revo, manager of labor relations for the power company. In her frustration, she joined in a conversation about technology and diversity. Maybe that's the answer to all our prejudice. Put everybody behind a computer screen at home. Filter our contact with each other until everyone assumes the digitalized shape of their software program. "You couldn't tell a person's color, you wouldn't know whether they were tall or short or fat or thin," she remarked.

That offered little consolation to bus driver Ronda Barfield. "I don't think any time soon we're going to find a computer to drive the buses." So like millions of other Americans, Barfield copes. She is a beneficiary of this epic struggle for justice. Only within her lifetime have women gained the peacetime opportunity to operate buses in Pierce County. But she is still its victim. Each day as the shifts change, drivers gather to gossip and gripe at the dispatch center. "The lobby experience," they call it. And the male-dominated culture of the past clings to its traditions: The banter is raw and salacious. Barfield avoids the dispatch lobby and sits alone in her car each day until one minute before her shift begins. "For some reason, I personally happen to be the topic of conversation. The less they see me, the less they talk about me."

## Contributors

*Times* researchers Doug Conner in Seattle, Lianne Hart in Houston, Ann Rovin in Denver and Edith Stanley in Atlanta contributed to this story.

## How Americans View Diversity Efforts

A national survey of 987 working Americans found that many believe efforts to promote fairness for minorities are adequate. But there are many discrepancies between how various groups view such efforts.

### MAJOR GAPS IN WHAT THEY SEE

• **Believe more effort is needed to guarantee racial minorities fairness in the workplace:**

Whites 19%
Blacks 66%

• **Have been discriminated against in the workplace because of race or ethnic background in last five years:**

Whites 11%
Blacks 46%

• **Believe race relations at their workplace are good or excellent:**

Whites 87%
Blacks 52%

• **Believe more effort is needed these days to guarantee that women get fair treatment in the workplace:**

Men 26%
Women 38%

(Numbers do not add up to 100% because all responses are not shown.)

Source: *Los Angeles Times* Poll taken July 23–26, 1994. Margin of error is 4 percentage points.

## TAKING THE DIVERSITY INITIATIVE

A diversity initiative is a systemic approach to a culture change that will take many years. According to Sally J. Walton of Global Perspectives, Santa Cruz, CA, here are some things you can do:

1. Collect information on the diversity of your organization.

2. Discuss your findings with your colleagues.

3. Identify barriers to diversity within your group and determine strategies to overcome them.

4. Gather information about what other organizations do to support diversity in the workplace. Discuss with your group how to meet their needs and support their efforts to enhance the diversity of the group.

5. Brainstorm with members of your department, unit, or, if small, the whole company, on ideas for a diversity initiative.

6. Develop an action plan for valuing differences.

7. Include your organization's diversity commitment statement in all publications.

8. Invite members of diverse groups to present or facilitate workshops and programs.

9. Incorporate and integrate a diversity philosophy into your training curriculum and presentations.

10. Practice group meeting maintenance skills so that all opinions can be heard.

11. Dedicate a portion of each meeting to the issue of valuing differences in the workplace to raise awareness.

12. Build alliances with local universities and colleges, and offer a mentoring program to HRD students from diverse backgrounds or disciplines.

13. Document your efforts and results.

14. Focus on process improvement rather than "fixing" the situation in your company overnight.

# Managing Your Starship: Multicultural Management for the Twenty First Century

by Dianne Floyd Sutton

In 1966 the Starship Enterprise set out on its five year mission with an unusual crew on the bridge. Captain Kirk, Mr. Spock, Lt. Uhura, Ensign Sulu and Chekov represented every color and creed in the human spectrum, and one race not even from earth. It was a minor miracle for television—to show a Black woman and an Asian in positions of managerial responsibility. Now, less than twenty-five years later it has become a commonplace corporate reality. No one notices the "miracle" of interracial presence in the StarTrek reruns anymore. So it is little wonder that no one notices the even more miraculous management achievement of Captain Kirk. Captain Kirk is a multi-cultural manager and—at least on television—a very successful one.

I would like to take a closer look at Captain Kirk's management style.

Perhaps the best place to begin is with one of Captain Kirk's ancestors, Tiberius J. Kirk. Until recently only a few scholars have known anything about the Starship Captain's great-great grandfather. He spent his professional life working for an import-export enterprise, Star Shipping Lines.

Tiberius Kirk rose quickly to middle management. In May 1955 he was at the peak of his career, running the Star Shipping Line's regional office in Newark, New Jersey. Kirk was generally thought of as a good though unimaginative manager. He had a crew of six working directly with him in the office. Indirectly the regional warehouse and dockside operations of the company employed more than four hundred.

Kirk's four principal subordinates were white and male. The youngest was twenty-four; the oldest, fifty-seven. Each was married with a wife and children at home. The most senior was three years away from mandatory retirement. Kirk didn't relish losing his accumulated experience though clearly a sixty year old couldn't be as vigorous as a younger man.

Sally Hudson, age 22, was Kirk's secretary. She was the only woman in the office, but she would be leaving in a month to get married. Tiberius was already advertising for her replacement in the "Help Wanted—Female" section of the paper. He was not looking forward to training a new girl. It had taken Sally eight months to master the complex routines that sometimes involved the custom regulations of four countries. Still, Kirk knew that he couldn't really depend on a married woman who was thinking of children.

The final member of Mr. Kirk's staff was a Black man, Arbus Howard Jones. Jones was highly valued for his contribution to the office and, privately, his co-workers thought him a credit to his race. He had worked for Star Shipping Lines for twenty-five years and never finished the week with unprocessed paperwork. Tiberius Kirk never knew that a large part of Jones' effectiveness came from his personal system for cross-referencing Bills of Lading. Jones' system cut almost an hour off the average processing time for each completed shipment. It could have saved the company forty thousand dollars a year if it had been used in all offices.

At the office, everyone called Arbus, "Howard." It sounded more normal.

This description of the 1955 office of Tiberius J. Kirk offends nearly everyone who reads it. It is a cliche: white male management, transient female clerical support, and a token Negro—unrecognized for his real competence and more "white" in his behavior than is consistent with dignity in 1990. But, cliche or not, it is an accurate sketch of most offices well into the 1980's.

In many ways, the regional office of Star Shipping Lanes was not a bad place to work. The people who worked there knew what was expected of them. Within those limits they also knew how to treat one another. In many ways because of this, the office functioned well. Many managers miss those "good old days." They know that something fundamental has changed but can't say exactly what it is. They only know that it is more difficult now for both managers and workers to know how to act at the office.

I think that the key point is that Tiberius J. Kirk had a mono-cultural (one culture) workplace. Today, most managers don't.

The kind of "culture" that I am talking about is exactly what the *American Heritage Dictionary* describes. It says:

culture, n. . . .

5. The totality of socially transmitted behavior patterns, arts, beliefs, institutions, and all other products of human thought characteristic of a community or population.

6. A style of social and artistic expression peculiar to a society or class.

In the sense of the "style of social . . . expression," there was only one culture at Star Shipping Lines in 1955; white, male, European, and "in the Prime of life." I don't claim that this is the culture of everyone who worked there, but when the employees of Tiberius J. Kirk came to work, they left their personal culture at the door. Successful "Negroes" were chameleons. Perhaps they were leaders and role models in their family, church, and community—but never at the office. Women could be successful—but only by making it explicit that they would never let family or children interfere with their career in a way that a man would not. At the office everyone was white, male, European, and definitely not "over the hill." At the very least their managers, including Tiberius J. Kirk, could depend on them to act that way.

Now, this seems outrageous.

In 1965, Captain Kirk's great-great grandfather retired, and since then many workplaces have become multicultural. Of course the first things that we think of are changes that have come from Equal Employment Opportunity and Affirmative Employment. They have changed the demographics of almost every workplace in America. Equal Employment Opportunity is the law, and Affirmative Employment sets goals for hiring and promoting minority groups and women . . . but the multi-cultural workplace is not the same as the workplace of Equal Employment Opportunity and Affirmative Employment.

It is important to remember that Equal Employment Opportunity and Affirmative Employment started as products of mono-cultural thinking. In most discussions there remains an unspoken assumption that bringing non-white, non-European, non-male workers into the mono-cultural office will have little or no affect on the way people relate to one another at work. This is simply not true.

For one thing, the number of "non-traditional" workers in the labor pool is larger than anyone anticipated. Many more non-traditional workers are coming. In Workforce 2000, the Hudson Institute uses U.S. Department of Labor data to project that more than 80% of new workers in the year 2000 will be non-white, women or immigrants. The number of young workers will decline. The average worker will be much older. Multi-culturalism is the keynote of this emerging labor pool. We may not yet have the diversity of the bridge of the Starship Enterprise, but that is where we are heading.

Multi-culturalism brings new management problems. The old "common sense assumptions" have become "discredited stereotypes." In many ways it really is harder to know what to expect at work.

Today, Tiberius Kirk could not assume that Sally Hudson would be leaving when she married or if she became pregnant. Within broad limits, Kirk would simply have to adjust to her new family ties, pregnancy, and the demands of a dependent child. If Kirk was planning to retire his senior clerk at age sixty so that he could promote a younger man, it simply wouldn't work. You can bet that Arbus Howard Jones would choose for himself what he was called.

True, there are laws to enforce these points—but I think the real change has gone far beyond the law. Sally Judson demands that her cultural identity as a nurturing parent be acknowledged. Arbus Jones insists on the intrinsic worth of the cultural history that gave him his name. Although managers may avoid recognizing these cultural perspectives and subvert the law, they will pay for doing so in a real business sense.

It is no longer tacitly accepted that a single "work culture" overrides the employee's personal culture. Ignore the personal culture of your employees and they will know it. Your business efficiency will suffer from their resentment. Meanwhile your more sensitive competitors will reap the benefit of not having to train a replacement for Sally Hudson. They will implement the improvements suggested by an Arbus Jones who knows that his idea will be valued and considered seriously.

The key insight in a multi-cultural management is simply this: when people come together to work, they do not stop being the people they are at home. They never did. Now—partly due to changes in law, and partly due to increasing numbers—they are even less willing to pretend.

But let's get back to Captain Kirk and the bridge of Starship Enterprise.

Captain Kirk is a multi-cultural manager. He has to be. Dr. McCoy is from the State of Georgia in what used to be the United States. He has the prickly personal honor of a "southern gentleman" and is quick to react with outrage at anything he sees an as affront to his sense of dignity. Lt. Uhura—whose name is the Swahili word for freedom—grew up in Africa. Lt. Commander Scott ("Scotty") may have a Scottish brogue, but he is the true spiritual brother of every competent blue collar worker who ever came up through the ranks to management. Ensign Chekhov is a Russian chauvinist who seldom misses a chance to explain how a Russian invented the airplane, radio, and the impulse engine. Ensign Sulu's family tree includes people from many parts of the orient and as such he is heir to the oldest human cultural tradition. (The Chinese really did have some justification for referring to Caucasian traders like Marco Polo as "hairy white barbarians.") And Mr. Spock is . . . well, Mr. Spock is Mr. Spock—someone whose cultural background is ultimately unknowable.

Mr. Spock should remind us that any summary of cultural heritage is likely to hide as much as it reveals.

The challenge to Captain Kirk is to get his crew to bring their full abilities to bear on the work before them. This is a survival issue for the Enterprise—much as it is for any business.

How does he do it?

First, Captain Kirk is clear about his mission and he makes sure that it is clear to everyone who works with him. He is also clear that "seeking out new worlds" has nothing to do with what language his crew members learned at birth, how long their hair is (when it doesn't get caught in the machinery), or how they decorate their cabin. Kirk does not allow himself or anyone else to act as if the goal of the Enterprise is to have everyone conform to a stereotype.

Next, Captain Kirk pays attention to the differences among his crew members and he respects them.

When Mr. Spock states that the probability is "point nine three" that evacuating the colonists from Rigel Nine will fatally infect members of the Enterprise crew with their plague, Kirk does not tell Mr. Spock that he is an inhuman calculating machine. When Dr. McCoy says: "You can't just leave them down there to die, Jim. Let me get some of the colonists into sick bay, so I can try to find an anti-toxin," Kirk does not tell McCoy that he is a bleeding heart who is completely ignoring the danger to the Enterprise. Captain Kirk—the multicultural manager—is aware of the personality and cultural background of his subordinates. Spock and McCoy have both made important points. If Kirk insists that his crew conform to a single cultural style in all their expression, he will not only alienate a substantial portion of his crew, but—much worse—he may never hear anything at all from many of his subordinates.

Captain Kirk also insists that the members of his crew respect each other. It is never acceptable for one crew member to insult another. Russian, Georgian, Black, Female, or Vulcan . . . any crew member who attacks another on that basis is wrong. It is the act of making the attack that is important. Kirk knows that he cannot change the personal prejudices of his crew, but he can and does insist that those prejudices are not expressed in any work context. No doubt Captain Kirk does not accept new crew members who cannot communicate around their cultural bias.

Finally, Captain Kirk knows that he has blind spots. I am sure that Kirk spends some of his off duty hours on "continuing education for Starship Captains." No doubt this includes studying the different ways that people in the Federation think. Still, when Spock acts outside the patterns that Kirk is used to, Kirk has to consider the possibility that Spock is acting in a way that is perfectly normal, but based on cultural values unknown to Kirk. Kirk knows that the attitudes of his crew will surprise him from time to time. When it happens, he makes an extra effort to discover the crew member's point of view before he assumes that the crew member is behaving irrationally or committing a breach of discipline.

There is really nothing about the management style of Starship Captain James T. Kirk that is unknown to managers of the late twentieth century. Kirk focuses on organizational goals, listens and communicates well, and enforces mutual respect among his subordinates. Nonetheless, Captain Kirk benefits from a multi-cultural perspective.

He knows that:

- The workplace is the common meeting place for many cultures.

- People with different cultures act differently and may offend one another in complete ignorance of the offense that they offer.

- It is not workable to pretend that everyone is from the same culture.

- It is not workable to base standards of performance on the stereotypes of a particular culture.

- If we want to manage from a multicultural perspective, then there are some things that we can do.

- Recognize that differences (cultural, gender, sexual orientation, age, etc.) do exist.

- Learn about other cultures.

- Learn about our own cultural background and style. Understand our personal cultural conditioning.

- Respect and be sensitive to individual differences and cultures.

- Root out stereotypes and set and communicate the goals for our organization.

- Explain the rules for workplace behavior. Demand that workers respect one another on the job.

- Hold people accountable after explaining the rules.

- Aspire to flexibility.

It is a short list, but hard to master. Multi-cultural management is more a way of thinking about the workplace than it is a list of things-to-do.

We can only guess what the Starfleet Academy taught Captain Kirk about managing a multi-cultural workforce, but I believe that we are going to have to learn those lessons much sooner than most people think. Managers with a mono-cultural perspective will not be employable in the twenty-first century.

They certainly will never command a Starship.

## About the Author

Dianne Floyd Sutton is the founder and president of Sutton Enterprises, a human resource development organization that provides public and private sector clients with training and consulting services. Since 1987, she has developed and delivered courses on management and supervisory development, interpersonal communication skills, employee development skills, Equal Employment Opportunity (EEO) law, Affirmative Employment (AE) programs and racial, ethnic, gender and disability sensitivity.

Ms. Sutton serves on the Executive Board of the Training Officers Conference in Washington, D.C. She is a member of the National Association of Negro Women, The American Society for Training and Development, The World Future Society and the DC chapter of The Society of Professionals in Dispute Resolution. She has received commendations from the Hispanic American Cultural Effort (HACE) at USDA and many Native American groups for her pioneering efforts in EEO training. She can be reached at: Sutton Enterprises, 5702 Colorado Avenue, NW #800, Washington, DC 20011, Phone: (202) 723-6870; Fax: (202) 723-6840.

# Getting the Best Results from a Diversity Action Council

by James O. Rodgers (*Managing Diversity Newsletter*)

Implementing a diversity strategy should be approached in the same manner as implementing any initiative or corporate culture change. When embarking on a diversity strategy, it is useful to establish a steering committee or Diversity Action Council (DAC) that will direct the activity and monitor the progress of the initiative. To be successful, this council must have the full support of the executive team. It needs to show some results early. And, most importantly, it must be seen as a strategic committee made up of respected, credible, and talented people. The following are ways to ensure the best use of the committee members' time and effort:

1. Name the committee in a way that signals action. The name "Diversity Action Council" or "Valuing Differences Action Committee" signals that specific actions will be forthcoming from this group.

2. Choose the steering committee members carefully to ensure maximum success. The makeup of the DAC is critical to the overall success of the council as well as their effectiveness in implementing a diversity strategy. In addition to an appropriate mix of representatives from ethnic, gender, age, and function groups, the right mix of skills and influence are needed. Consider equipping the DAC with the following types of people:

   *Inventor—one who sees and can articulate the "big picture."*

   *Entrepreneur—one who presents the pros and cons; who encourages efficiency and effectiveness.*

   *Integrator—one who knows how to forge alliances and understands the strategic connection.*

   *Expert—one who has the technical knowledge and skills regarding the new strategy.*

   *Manager—one who is predisposed to get the job done.*

   *Sponsor—one who can ensure top level support and access to resources.*

   *Observer—one who can provide impartial facilitation to the process as needed (such as a shadow consultant).*

   The challenge, of course, is to find these types in as many different kinds of people as possible. It is not really that hard. You may just have to look a little harder. How can they be approached? What are the options?

3. Clearly define the leadership. Which approaches are more likely to work here? The DAC must have strong leadership. There should be only one chair, preferably a high level manager who can ensure that the resources (financial and organizational) will be available when needed.

4. Ensure the DAC understands the Diversity Vision and their own role and responsibility in making it happen. To be effective, each member must know where he/she personally stands on the issue of diversity. A training/education session that explores the fundamentals of diversity should be conducted soon after convening the council so that each member can discover the role he/she can play to make the strategy effective. There are a number of tools and exercises available to help in this process.

5. Provide a clear focus and clear objective. The DAC needs to be bonded by a common goal. All members of the DAC need to understand diversity well enough to implement the changes necessary. Of course, along with clear responsibility you must give the group clear authority to take actions that will support the

implementation of a diversity strategy. The members must all know who they are meeting and what can be expected to come out of their efforts. Unfortunately, many steering committees flounder and committee members lose interest long before objectives are met.

6. Structure early meetings to ensure members become fully engaged and excited about their work. Careful planning of the meeting agendas around certain themes helps build the momentum you need and avoids the tendency to become "just another meeting." Early agendas should focus around these topics:

### 1st Meeting

Context. Why is diversity on the agenda? Why does it make sense for the company to explore this issue? How important is it?

### 2nd Meeting

Content. What are some of the things we may be doing differently as a result of this effort? What are the new expectations?

### 3rd Meeting

Awareness and Team Building (2–3 day event). What are the behaviors and attitudes that may be challenged by this effort? How do labeling and stereotyping affect the types of decisions we are making? Can we do a better job of working together? Most importantly, how can the DAC serve as a model of how a diverse team can address a complex issue with speed and come up with better-than-expected solutions?

### 4th Meeting

Strategic Implementation. Who from the inside (sponsors) and outside (consultants) can provide support to the organization? Who needs to be trained and when? When do we give feedback to executives? How do we "loudly" communicate the elements of the diversity strategy to all employees?

7. Involve the DAC in early data gathering efforts. The first step in implementing a diversity strategy is to better understand where the organization is now. Some activities that will begin the process of successfully managing diversity include:

Interview and educate executives on the strategic approach of diversity and on why it is imperative to have diversity as a part of the company's strategic planning process.

Identify elements of the culture and the "real rules" of success at your company (through surveys and interviews).

Conduct focus groups to identify and confirm how people feel about issues of diversity and to discover exactly what the key diversity issues really are.

## About the Author

James O. Rodgers is president and senior consultant of J. O. Rodgers and Associates, Inc. and a proponent of The Strategic Approach to Diversity. For more information, contact Mr. Rodgers at 4319 Covington Highway, Suite 201, Decatur, GA 30035; (404) 289-1300 or 1-800-549-5681.

## Editors Note

Another excellent source of information is *How to Develop a Diversity Committee*, recently published by the American Association of Retired Persons. Based on a case study of the city of San Diego, CA, the report presents a 16-step process for anyone to follow. For a free copy, contact AARP, Workforce Programs Department, 601 E Street, N.W., Washington, DC 20049; Phone: 202-434-2090.

---

*Our pride in our own cultural identities is not an end in itself, but the home from which we travel in order to meet others.*

Catharine R. Stimpson
From remarks to AAUP Annual Meeting (1991)

# The Byword is 'Flexible'

by Mary Cook (*Management Review*)

The byword for companies in the 1990s is flexible. Flexible benefits, flexible work schedules, flexible jobs and flexible work arrangements will be common. Job sharing is gaining popularity with young mothers and workers who want more time with their families. Formal job sharing programs are offered by only 16 percent of U.S. companies, but that figure is growing, according to a survey by the American Society for Personnel Administration. The Quaker Oats Co. and Levi Strauss & Co. are just two firms offering job sharing opportunities.

Home work is another important issue. Forty-seven years ago the U.S. government imposed a ban on home work to stop the widespread exploitation of immigrant and child laborers. This past January, new Labor Department regulations went into effect allowing some home work in the garment industry. Americans are now free to make gloves, mittens, embroideries, buttons, buckles, handkerchiefs and certain kinds of jewelry in their homes for commercial firms. Single mothers in particular have gained a potential source of income that won't entail childcare or travel costs. Unions have fought the idea of home work for years and are sure to challenge this new decision.

Organized labor is concerned that home work will grow beyond the garment industry. Unions are concerned about the millions of potential home-workers in such industries as telecommunications and information processing. It is easier for unions to recruit and organize members who work in offices and factories than when they are working out of their individual homes and apartments.

Today the home-based workforce is one of the fastest-growing components of the U.S. labor market. The Labor Department estimates the number of home workers at about 5 million and expects that figure to rise by more than 15 million by the mid 1990s. Corporate giants J.C. Penney, The Travelers Corp., Pacific Bell and even IBM now agree that there are advantages to having some employees work at home at least part of the time. Many managers believe it helps them recruit and retain employees as well as cut utility and office space leasing costs.

The largest area of job growth in America today is in the temporary help area. A flexible workforce lets firms boost productivity in busy times and prevents layoffs and bad publicity in slack periods. Companies that have downsized now frequently turn to temporary workers rather than gear back up to the bloated payrolls that led to the cutbacks. Small companies use temps when they can't afford full-time workers. So, America's shadow labor force, another 25 million temporary, part-time and self employed contract labor workers, make up the nation's growing contingent labor force. Contingent workers fill one out of every four American jobs today, and by the year 2000, the Bureau of Labor Statistics estimates the number will grow by more than 80 percent. The most interesting element of this part-time phenomenon is that most part timers are managers, white collar professionals, lawyers and accountants.

Alternative sources of workers also include retired, older workers who want to continue working and disabled workers who previously have not been able to hold jobs. More than 87,000 of America's most severely disabled adults were placed in jobs in 1985, earning about $400 million and saving taxpayers that amount in other aid, according to the U.S. Department of Health and Human Services. Of nearly 36 million disabled Americans, about 4 million are considered developmentally disabled. Many of these people are able to hold low-skilled jobs.

◆

# Developing Multicultural Organizations

by Bailey W. Jackson and Evangelina Holvino

## New Views of Social Change

The recent resurgence of racism and of other forms of social injustice in our cities and towns, colleges and universities, and offices and plants, has renewed interest and generated new insights into both past and present social dynamics. At least five important learnings can be attributed to these renewed concerns:

- The individual consciousness-raising strategy has had only limited success in significantly improving the workplace environment for those recently given access, such as women, racial minorities, or handicapped persons.

- Lasting social justice change in the workplace requires a direct and comprehensive effort focused on the organization as a system. This system must be developed so that it can provide support for the enhancement and use of social diversity in the workplace.

- Traditional organization development efforts have not made the kind of impact on social oppression in the workplace that its founders had hoped.

- A number of recent demographic analyses tell us that our national and global populations are undergoing dramatic demographic changes. Based on information that challenges assumptions of an eternal White male workforce, many organizations have begun to develop new recruitment, development and incentive programs that appeal to a workforce with a wide range of cultural values, needs and goals.

- Evidence is beginning to show that there is a direct relationship between the quantity and quality of the product or service an organization delivers and the ability of that organization to provide a just working environment for all its employees.

Multicultural Organization Development presently includes a fairly broad range of visions, definitions, assumptions, strategies, techniques, terminologies, goals and objectives. They include people working under such titles as Managing Diversity, Affirmative Action, Equal Employment Opportunity, racism and sexism awareness training and cross-cultural training. From these areas of concern, four themes appear as they define their goals:

- social and cultural representation of perspectives, world views, life styles, language and management styles;

- valuing and capitalizing on differences as a means toward effectiveness and growth; promoting the full use of available human resources in achieving its mission, internal operations and external interface with the environment;

- eliminating racism and sexism; and

- diversity of stakeholders, involving members of all cultural groups as equal partners in the enterprise and reflecting a commitment to the empowerment of all people.

## A Definition of a Multicultural Organization

These themes have been integrated by Jackson and Hardiman (1981) into the following definition, which may also serve as a guide for multicultural organization development practitioners.

A multicultural organization:

- reflects the contributions and interests of diverse cultural and social groups in its mission, operations, and product or service;

- acts on a commitment to eradicate all forms of social oppression within the organization;

- includes the members of diverse social and cultural groups as full participants, especially in decisions that shape the organization; and

- follows through on broader external social responsibilities including support of efforts to eliminate all forms of social oppression and to educate others in multicultural perspectives.

# Levels in Multicultural Development

Jackson and Hardiman (1981) have developed a model that describes three levels and six stages in the multicultural development process. The stages are sequential. Experiencing the learnings and limitations of each stage contributes to the ability of the organization to move to the next stage. An organization may demonstrate indicators of one, some, or all of the stages in its separate divisions or departments.

# Level One

### Stage One: The Exclusionary Organization

The Exclusionary Organization is devoted to maintaining dominance of one group over other groups based on race, gender, culture, or other social identity characteristics. Familiar manifestations of such organizations are exclusionary membership policies and hiring practices.

### Stage Two: The Club

The Club describes the organization that stops short of explicitly advocating anything like White male supremacy, but does seek to establish and maintain the privilege of those who have traditionally held social power. This is done by developing and maintaining missions, policies, norms and procedures seen as "correct" from their perspective. The Club allows a limited number of members from oppressed groups such as women and racial minorities, provided that they have the "right" perspective and credentials.

# Level Two

### Stage Three: The Compliance Organization

The Compliance Organization is committed to removing some of the discrimination inherent in the "club" by providing access to women and minorities. However, it seeks to accomplish this objective without disturbing the structure, mission and culture of the organization. The organization is careful not to create "too many waves" or to offend or challenge its employees' or customers' racist, sexist, or anti-semitic attitudes or behaviors.

The compliance organization usually attempts to change its organizational racial and gender profile by actively recruiting and hiring more racial minorities and women at the bottom of the organization. On occasion, it will hire or promote "token" racial minorities or women into management positions, usually staff positions. When the exception is made to place a woman, racial minority, or member of any other oppressed social group in a line position, this person must be a "team player" and a "qualified" applicant. A "qualified team player" does not openly challenge the organization's mission and practices, and is usually 150% competent to do the job.

### Stage Four: The Affirmative Action Organization

The Affirmative Action Organization is also committed to eliminating the discriminatory practices and inherent "riggedness" of The Club by actively recruiting and promoting women, racial minorities and members of other social groups typically denied access to our organizations. Moreover, the affirmative action organization takes an active role in supporting the growth and development of these new employees and initiating programs that increase their chances of success and mobility. All employees are encouraged to think and behave in a non-oppressive manner and the organization may conduct racism and sexism awareness programs toward this end.

This organization's view of diversity also includes the disabled, Latinos, Asians/Asian American-Pacific Islanders, Native Americans, the elderly, and other socially oppressed groups.

Although the affirmative action organization is committed to increasing access for members of diverse groups and increasing the chances that they will succeed by removing those hostile attitudes and behaviors, all members of this organization are still required to conform to the norms and practices derived from the dominant group's world view.

# Level Three

## Stage Five: The Redefining Organization

The Redefining Organization is a system in transition. This organization is not satisfied with being just "anti-racist" or "anti-sexist." It is committed to examining all of its activities for their impact on all members' ability to participate in and contribute to the growth and success of the organization.

The redefining organization begins to question the limitations of the cultural perspective as it is manifest in its mission, structure, management, technology, psycho-social dynamics and product or service. It seeks to explore the significance and potential benefits of a diverse multicultural workforce. This organization actively engages in visioning, planning and problem-solving activities directed toward the realization of a multicultural organization.

The redefining organization is committed to developing and implementing policies and practices that distribute power among all of the diverse groups in the organization. The redefining organization searches for alternative modes of organizing that guarantee the inclusion, participation and empowerment of all its members.

## Table One: Three Dimensions of Organization Change

| | Exclusionary | The Club | Compliance | Affirmative Action | Redefining | Multicultural |
|---|---|---|---|---|---|---|
| **Target of Change** | —— | Upper level management or members of oppressed groups | Personnel and other systems and mechanisms | System:<br>• structures<br>• rewards<br>• relationships<br>• climate | System:<br>• mission<br>• values<br>• structures | System and environment |
| **Interventions** | —— | Management training<br><br>Support and Consciousness Raising groups | EEO audits<br><br>EEO training, goal setting and action planning<br><br>"Minority" training | Performance appraisal systems<br><br>Racism and "isms"<br><br>Career development programs | Visioning and strategic planning<br><br>Skills for managing differences<br><br>MC team building | Ecological planning<br><br>MC autonomous teams and self-management systems |
| **Skills** | —— | Confronting and interrupting offensive behavior | Law and policy analysis<br><br>Education<br><br>Bargaining | MCOD systems diagnosis<br><br>Intergroup relations | Value clarification<br><br>Conflict management skills | Synergistic problem solving<br><br>Alternative work structures |

### Stage Six: The Multicultural Organization

The multicultural organization reflects the contributions and interests of diverse cultural and social groups in all of its facets; it acts on a commitment to eradicate social oppression in all forms within the organization; the multicultural organization includes the members of diverse cultural and social groups as full participants, especially in decisions that shape the organization; and it follows through on broader external social responsibilities, including support of efforts to eliminate all forms of social oppression and to educate others in multicultural perspectives.

# Applications

Multicultural Organization Development is the process of assisting an organization in moving from its present level and stage of development to become a fully multicultural organization. It uses organization change technology and principles to help eliminate or diminish the negative impact of an organization's monocultural characteristics and to develop and strengthen the multicultural characteristics of each stage.

The role of the Multicultural Organization Development change agent is:

- to assist in assessing the present stage of multicultural development;

- to help organization members make choices about the level they want to achieve;

- to assist in change efforts within the context of organizational goals and limitations; and

- to help organization members envision and assess risk and possibilities in becoming a fully multicultural organization.

The Multicultural Organization Development model can assist internal and external change agents to diagnose and plan for social change in organizations. For example, Table 1 presents three specific dimensions of organization change to be considered in Multicultural Organization Development efforts: target of change, appropriate interventions, and skills needed at each stage of the change effort.

# Target of Change

As we move from a monocultural to a nondiscriminatory and later to a multicultural level in multicultural organization development, the strategy for organizational change shifts from targeting change at the individual level, to targeting change at the systems level, to targeting change at the interface between organization and environment.

An effective intervention at the Club Stage is to increase awareness of racism and sexism through educational and training programs (an individual level intervention). Establishing mechanisms that tie rewards to support for the affirmative action agenda is an effective intervention in the affirmative action organization (a systems level intervention). An appropriate strategy in the multicultural stage is to align internal mechanisms, mission, relations with the environment and the multicultural agenda of an organization (a macro-systems level intervention).

# Interventions

The further we move in the continuum towards developing a multicultural organization the greater the need to use innovative strategies and new forms of intervening with organizations (racism and sexism workshops alone will not do). An example is the use of the action research model to set up multiracial-multigender diagnostic teams which are representative of the diversity encountered in the organization. The task of the teams is to diagnose, problem solve, develop action plans, and to support the implementation and evaluation of affirmative action change goals. The intervention is usually facilitated by an outside consultant (Alderfer, et al, 1980).

In the redefining and multicultural stages, interventions should stress working in diverse teams to develop multicultural visions and goals, design and implement alternative organization structures, and develop strategic plans which consider the impact of the socio-political environment on the organization. Interventions which are relevant at this multicultural stage, but are not so commonly used in multicultural change efforts are:

• *Ecological diagnosis and planning:*

Focusing attention on internal dynamics and planning within the context of critical external events and boundaries related to the mission of the organization (Brown and Covey, 1986).

• *Alternative work structures:*

Implementing flat structures and other forms of organizing work which increase participation, control and ownership of all organizational members. These include matrix and parallel organizations (Stein and Kanter, 1980); worker councils and cooperatives (Bernstein, 1980); autonomous work groups (Trist, 1977); action learning groups (Morgan and Ramirez, 1983).

• *Ideological negotiations:*

Resolving conflicts of interests among organization members by directly or indirectly addressing value and ideological differences (Brown and Brown, 1983).

• *Strategic management:*

Aligning the components of an organization, its mission and strategies, its structures, and human resources—technically, politically and culturally—to achieve organizational effectiveness (Tichy, 1983).

• *Multicultural team building:*

Addressing task and relationship issues by paying special attention to cultural differences (Halverston, 1986).

## Skills

The knowledge, skills and attitudes needed to implement change also vary according to different levels and stages of multicultural change. Change agents working in monocultural organizations need thorough knowledge of EEO/AA guidelines and discrimination practices; at the multicultural stage they need to know about and be able to work with alternative cultural systems. Appropriate skills for a monocultural organization include bargaining, negotiation and the coercive use of power. In a multicultural organization conflict management skills need to include synergistic problem solving, value clarification, consensus building and

other collaborative strategies for managing differences.

## Roles and Strategies

The roles and strategies of change agents also vary according to the stage in the multicultural development process. For example, during the initial stages of development from "monocultural" to "nondiscriminatory," the change agent plays different roles: provocateur and politico in the exclusionary and club stages; evaluator and action researcher in the affirmative action stage. When the organization is at the redefining or multicultural stages, the change agent functions more as a collaborator and committed participant, who explores, experiments and problem solves in multi-disciplinary change teams.

## Diagnostic Clues

Different stages in the multicultural development model suggest specific diagnostic indicators to help assess the organizational stage in the multicultural development process. For example, what is the status of members of socially oppressed groups in the organization? Are they treated as tokens (club stage), invited guests (compliance stage) or as legitimate members of the organization with diverse cultural perspectives (multicultural stage)?

Another important diagnostic dimension is the learning climate in the organization. Compliance stage organizations often find themselves "reinventing the wheel" or complaining about "how we tried that before and it did not work." At this stage processes and mechanisms must be developed to institutionalize changes. In the affirmative action stage, members show a mixture of confusion and insights about the dynamics of social oppression and change in organizations; they often feel puzzled and conflicted about the degree of "progress" they have achieved in becoming "multicultural." In this case, collective mechanisms for increasing organizational learning need to be developed—the nondiscriminatory practices and gains made so far must be maintained. In the redefining stage, organization members sometimes feel frustrated and "at the end" of their learning capacity. Change agents can help redefine the learning task in terms of a new stage of multicultural development so that members can redirect their energy and celebrate their accomplishments.

## Conditions Which Support Change

Different stages of multicultural development suggest different conditions which support change. Conditions that support change in the monocultural stages tend to be external environmental demands, such as political decisions, litigation, or legislative decrees. On the other hand, conditions that support change in the multicultural stages are more encompassing: paradigm shifts, alternative world views, commitment from top management, interracial coalitions, a critical mass of organizational members with a change agenda, and world-wide socio-political changes.

## Values and Assumptions

In multicultural organization development, attention must be paid to the fit between the change agent values and the multicultural organization development change process. In addition to being clear about the possibilities and the stages in mul-

ticultural organizational change, we must also be clear about the values we bring to the change process. We have found that the different assumptions and values change agents hold about the nature of society and the need for change greatly influence how multicultural organization development is defined and implemented. Different assumptions reflect different visions, which in turn define possibilities and challenges in the multicultural change effort. An example of such different sets of assumptions and their impact is discussed and summarized in Table 2.

## Change Agent Assumptions

Consider a change agent who believes that society is basically harmonious, where people have basically similar interests, and that though in need of reform, society is basically good and sane. Change is viewed as a slow, evolutionary process in which modifications are gradually introduced; their effectiveness and appropriateness are assessed through time. Values this change agent holds dear are basic individual rights, reward for the "best person," efficiency, and economic survival. A change agent with this world view is likely

| Table Two: Change Agent Assumptions | | | |
|---|---|---|---|
| | **Monocultural** | **Non-discriminatory** | **Multicultural** |
| **Nature of Society** | Harmonious<br><br>Similar interests<br><br>Needs to improve but basically OK | | Conflict<br><br>Different Interests<br><br>Oppressive; Alienating; Needs Radical Change |
| **Oppression Liberation Model** | Dominance<br><br>Assimilation | Desegregation<br><br>Integregation | Pluralism<br><br>Diversity |
| **Self Interest in Change** | Survival and social acceptability | Adaptation and full use of human resources | Equity; Empowerment; Collective Growth |
| **Values and Ideology** | Basic rights of individual<br><br>Best person is rewarded<br><br>Efficiency and economic survival | | Interdependence<br><br>Ecological survival<br><br>Development of human and societal potential |

to hold the nondiscriminatory level of multicultural organization development as the vision of the future, since this type of organization embodies individualistic values and guarantees equal opportunities for all. This change agent will define the organizational change goal as: to integrate members of diverse groups in order to better use their resources, increase organizational effectiveness, and contribute to a better society.

On the other hand, consider a change agent who believes that society is basically alienating and depriving for many members. Conflict of interests have not been adequately resolved, and fundamental changes are needed to address the problems that threaten the survival of humanity. Values this change agent holds dear are: interdependence, equitable distribution of resources, ecological and global survival, and the realization of human potential. This change agent is likely to see the need for a new and different type of organization, representative of· different cultural models in the world, with new and perhaps unexplored structures which support equitable distribution of resources and the self-realization of all its members. For this change agent, the vision of a multicultural organization implies a paradigm shift; it involves having a radically different vision of an organization from the hierarchical profit and product centered view which is now dominant in our society. The organizational change goal in this case is: to transform the organization in order to enhance human diversity, social justice, and the realization of a humane society.

## Summary

Multicultural organization development can make important contributions to increasing organizational productivity and quality of work life. It can also serve to bridge the gap between work and the organizing activity, social change and the socially responsible organizations of the future.

## References

Alderfer, C. P., C. J. Alderfer, L. Tucker, and R. Tucker. 1980. "Diagnosing Race Relations in Management." *Journal of Applied Behavioral Science* 16:2, 135–166.

Bernstein, P. 1980. *Workplace Democratization*. New Brunswick: Transaction Books.

Burrell, G. and G. Morgan. 1979. "Organizational Microcosms and Ideological Negotiations." In *Bargaining Inside Organizations*, ed. M. Bazerman and R. Lewicki. Beverly Hills: Sage.

Brown, L. D. and J. G. Covey. 1986. "OD in Social Change Organizations: Some Implications." Forthcoming in *Readings in Organizational Development*, ed. W. Sikes and J. Gant. Greenwich: VAI Press.

Halverston, C. 1986. "Managing Intercultural Differences in Work Groups." OD Network 1986 Conference Proceedings; ed. R. Donleavey. New York: OD Network.

Jackson, B. and R. Hardiman. 1981. "Organizational Stages of Multicultural Awareness." Unpublished paper.

Morgan, G. and R. Ramirez. 1983. "Action Learning: A Holographic Metaphor for Guiding Social Change." *Human Relations* 37:1, 1–28.

Stein, B. and R. M. Kanter. 1980. "Building the Parallel Organization: Creating Mechanisms for Permanent Quality of" *Journal of Applied Behavioral Science* 16:3, 371–388.

Tichy, N. 1983. *Managing Strategic Change*. New York: Wiley.

Trist, E. L. 197. "Collaboration in Work Settings: A Personal Perspectivew." *Journal of Applied Behavioral Science* 11:3, 268–278.

## About the Authors

Dr. Bailey W. Jackson is at the School of Education of the University of Massachusetts at Amherst. His consulting firm, New Perspectives, Inc. can be reached at 45 Kingman Road, Amherst, MA 01002-1590; Phone: 413-549-4141; Fax: 413-549-3876.

Dr. Evangelina Holvino is an organization development facilitator and consultant who has been working in the United States, Southeast Asia, West Africa, Latin America and the Caribbean since 1979 to promote change for social justice in the workplace. Evangelina is committed to and specializes in the complex issues of social diversity and how they relate to staff and organization development in the overall context of social change. She makes presentations on issues of race, gender, and class in organizations and is a research associate with the Gaston Institute for Latino Community Development and Public Policy. She can be reached at Chaos Consultants, P.O. Box 737, Brattleboro, VT 05302-0737; Phone: 802-257-5218; Fax: 802-257-2729.

# Team Building to Break Down Cultural Barriers

by Lee Gardenswartz and Anita Rowe

Effective team building is always a challenge. It becomes even more complicated in a culturally diverse work environment where norms, values, traditions, and priorities may seem foreign and out of synch with one another.

But take heart. In any work group, the best team building happens by design, not by osmosis. There are a number of things that can be done to foster cohesion and cooperation in a multicultural work group.

## 1. Encourage Shared Values

For any group to function well as a team, there must be a commonly shared set of assumptions, expectations, and priorities. Some examples of an organization's values might be:

- Our hospital is a venerable, respected institution.

- At our store, no effort at customer satisfaction is too great.

- Our company is an industry leader with innovative products.

When the company's values are shared, each group member has a common purpose. Instilling your team with shared values is the best way to overcome bickering within a culturally diverse work group. For example, on a softball team, the goal is to play well and possibly win the game. The cultural origin of the players is irrelevant when the top priority is to catch the ball, hit the ball, and play the game well. The same thing happens in a work group. If the group shares the value of providing excellent customer service, then each member of the group will be appreciated for contributing to the end goal. Cultural differences become irrelevant when each player has his eye on the ball.

## 2. Get Input On The Group's Objectives

Values may define the heart and soul of a work group, but goals and objectives give these values their vitality—they are its life blood. The only way to get "buy in" is to get everyone's input in determining these goals and objectives. Doing this effectively requires cultural sensitivity. Imagine you are having a strategy meeting with your multi-cultural work group. You need to understand different perspectives. In the dominant American culture, it is savvy to speak up at meetings and "throw your two cents in." However, there are many cultures where this is not so. Sometimes giving input could be construed as diminishing an authority figure who by virtue of position is considered to have the answers.

## 3. Reward Excellence

But do so in a way that feels like a reward. While working with organizations over the past dozen years, we discovered that in the dominant American culture a super achiever's exceptional performance is often spotlighted. The theory holds that this attention both validates the individual and motivates others. Calling attention to high performers through awards, announcements, and pictures on bulletin boards works—in some cases. It can also embarrass and intimidate.

In some cultures, this kind of attention would be an affront to the person. It is important to acknowledge excellence. Recognition reinforces continued high performance. However, do so in a way that the individual appreciates. Maybe a very quiet "thank you" or a simple nod of the head and a smile when looking at a report or a product, would be the real reward.

## 4. Avoid Lip Service

Paying lip-service to valuing differences is easy. The hard part is making it come alive in the work group. Don't waste time defining values if you aren't going to make them operational. Do not ask for participation if you do not plan to act on the information. Do not talk about treating people with dignity if you really don't care enough to learn the nuances of cultural diversity. You can't fool people and trying only erodes trust. Above all, "walk your talk" as Tom Peters says.

### 5. Acknowledge Cultural Conflicts

Conflict is normal and natural in any work group. But seldom do we stop to realize in a diverse team that the conflict is often a result of cultural differences rather than personal ones. One boss we know complained because an employee took time off to take his wife to a routine doctor's appointment. The boss couldn't understand why the wife didn't go to the doctor by herself. The boss felt the employee was using this as an excuse to get time off work.

During a conversation with the employee, the boss learned that in the staff member's culture, taking care of family was top priority and that his role as husband demanded he take his wife to a doctor's appointment. Finding a resolution where the employee gets his work done and can still fulfill his family obligation is the best way to deal with cultural conflicts like these.

### 6. Become Fluent In The "Cultural Software"

It is human nature to ascribe meaning to actions. The problem with doing this in a culturally diverse work group is that you may be wrong. Managers may interpret silence in meetings or not volunteering for extra projects as a lack of initiative. However, an employee may feel he is showing that boss proper respect by not speaking up and challenging his boss in that meeting. A manager from a foreign culture may think Americans are loud and aggressive. On the other hand, we may define speaking up as being industrious and a sign of a real go-getter.

The caveat here is to make certain you know the "cultural software" or rules by which your employees are operating. The natural inclination is to use one's own culture as the yardstick by which all other actions are judged—but the

probable inaccuracy of messages and stereotypes that result are almost always harmful and destructive.

One business manager we know was frustrated at her bookkeeper. The manager had just completed some payroll tax paperwork on an employee who was leaving the company and asked the bookkeeper if it was done correctly. The bookkeeper responded with silence and a blank stare.

The manager had never done that particular computation before and was anxious to have the bookkeeper's input. Finally, after much coaxing, the bookkeeper showed the manager where she had made an error. What the manager didn't understand was that in the bookkeeper's culture it was unacceptable to challenge authority by telling a supervisor, "you've got that wrong." Work groups can accommodate differences, but not until we know what they are and understand them. Make sure that you interpret behaviors correctly and sensitively.

Beyond exploring these six steps to intercultural team building, there is one other noteworthy item. Any leader or manager is a role model. Good, bad, or indifferent, the medium is the message and you are the medium. If you want a cohesive group and you want to minimize cultural differences among those from different backgrounds, realize that the group will get its message and take its cue from you.

Leadership starts at the top . . . so does tolerance, treating people with dignity, and valuing differences. A leader or manager genuinely committed to respecting diversity can show the way and help an entire organization reap the rewards.

## About the Authors

Lee Gardenswartz, Ph.D. and Anita Rowe, Ph.D. specialize in the "human side of management" for a variety of regional and national clients, helping them manage change, handle stress, build productive and cohesive work teams and create inter-cultural understanding and harmony in the workplace. Gardenswartz and Rowe recently authored *Managing Diversity: A Complete Desk Reference and Planning Guide* (Business One Irwin,

1993) which won the book of the year award from the Society for Human Resource Managers (SHRM).

Anita and Lee have lectured widely, giving keynote speeches, facilitating team building retreats and teaching seminars across the country. Gardenswartz and Rowe can be reached at: 12658 W. Washington Boulevard, Suite 105, Los Angeles, CA 90066. Phone: (310) 823-2466; Fax: (310) 823-3923.

# Successful Implementation of Cultural Diversity Programs: Headaches, Heartaches and Breakthroughs

by Rita S. Boags

This article shares the lessons learned, from my experiences and those of others, in designing educational interventions for Cultural Diversity Programs. Much personal investment and professional pride over the last 15 years have gone into the design and execution of such programs and produced a wide assortment of results which include many headaches (back to the drawing boards), heartaches (real disappointments in myself and others) and breakthroughs (finding an answer which solves a puzzle or explains a particular result). This article examines what has worked, what has not worked and why, and those new strategies that make up more effective intervention models.

## The Primary Problem With Most of Our Interventions

A successful intervention achieves the *expected outcome* through the implementation of a program designed to achieve a specified result. The major difficulties with interventions start here. Fundamentally, what we want to have happen as a result of a program effort is frequently out of line with the program we design or with the resources provided.

For example, consultants are increasingly asked to do Cultural Awareness Training for management. The usual request is for a training seminar or workshop to address the issues of diversity. The hope is that the new awareness of diversity and its complexities will result in some measure of behavioral change, which will positively impact the minority and female population who report to the newly aware manager. This does not become an unreasonable request until one looks at the resources provided to achieve those results. The time allotted for the training ranges anywhere from a two hour session for 20 to 30 participants, to two days for 150 people.

When sponsors are asked what they expect from Awareness Training sessions, they give a long list of desired results. A partial list, particularly when the audience is management, is for managers to become more:

- open, friendly and inclusive toward members of minority groups (and cease claiming that everyone is treated the same)

- sensitive to, and aware of, the possible differences in motivation, values and work ethics between themselves and their subordinates (make inquiries and not assume)

- aware of differences when making performance evaluations (and cease interpreting differences as deficiencies)

- willing to value the diversity of a different gender, age groups, culture, etc. (and see it as potential added value)
- pro-active toward hiring and promoting people of different cultures (learn to put substance over style)
- in touch with their stereotypes so they can let go of them.

Putting just this short list of results into place would require that participants make a substantial number of radical behavioral changes, changes which are usually sought in vain since these outcomes are not consistent with the usual designs of the intervention or the resources provided to implement the design. The typical design of "Cultural Diversity Awareness Training" lacks the firepower

to deliver even one of the results listed above. Predictably, the aftermath of such training sessions is that things proceed as before. Both trainers and sponsors are disappointed, the participants are frustrated. Typically, the trainers want to find fault with the participants, claiming that "they aren't ready," "they are too resistant," etc. Sponsors may blame their consultants. The fault lies usually with an all encompassing design and limited resources, rather than with the participants, or the consultants.

A major challenge for our firm is to work within the available resources, but change the expectations for the outcome of any given program so that they are consistent with a reasonable outcome. Remember that if you only have two hours to spend on a program to teach an elephant to dance, you cannot deliver the elephant dancing in forma-

## The Three Tiers Model of Diversity

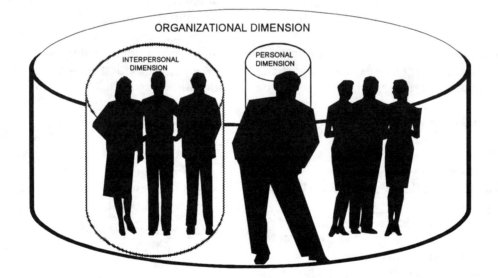

*Personal Tier*—Our personal, private world; the sum total of an individual's history and Life Span

*Interpersonal Tier*—Patterns of relationship and communication: inclusion and exclusion of individuals and groups

*Organizational Tier*—The culture, environment, processes and practices of organization of which we are a part

tion. Everyone is better served by a program that heightens interest and awareness that the elephant exists who can dance and lets us know what it will take to accomplish the goal. It will take many more passes to understand what you might want to do with a dancing elephant and then train it to follow suit. (Belasco, 1990)

This logic of program design is based upon a model credited to Dr. Price Cobbs (1994), which demonstrates the dimensions of change necessary to transform the behavior of individuals in a multicultural workplace. His three-tiered approach to the design and execution of Diversity programs seeks to impact individuals within an organizational context. Training is designed to address behavior at the Personal/internal level, Interpersonal/between people level and the Organizational/cultural-environmental levels. Based on this model, a Cultural Diversity Awareness Seminar of any length will not deliver the goods. The seminar or workshop is a beginning, an introductory phase of a comprehensive, long-term, and multi faceted intervention.

# Heartaches

What has been tried before and did not work breaks down into five main categories.

1. **Attempting to design and carry out an intervention when the training objectives appeared to be unreasonable, unsound or unworkable.** As mentioned, this always leads to disappointment and personal feelings of inadequacy. At times, it has cost me a contract with the sponsoring organization. If an alternative design or course of action cannot be negotiated with the sponsoring party at the inception of the program, then some other firm should take on the task.

2. **Not knowing the needs and capabilities of the training populations.** About five years ago a colleague and I got the bright idea that providing follow-up to our Introductory Diversity Seminars might be a way to get our management participants to move from Awareness to Action. We began to provide goal-setting sessions designed to pursue a limited number of action items. The most critical steps for

management to take, especially in the eyes of their subordinates were:

- Provide candid and accurate feedback to subordinates about job performance;

- Develop people on the job through coaching and mentoring;

- Offer career development and planning activities;

- Correct poor performance when it occurs;

- Build work teams from a multi-cultural base rather than a unilateral one;

- Empower the workforce so that they can learn to be more responsible and responsive.

We thought these follow-on ideas and tips would yield results that would also help us build in a level of accountability. What we did not take into account was that many of the managers and supervisors had little capability or facility for implementing these steps. These steps were fundamentally built upon Interpersonal skills, which were the very skills that managers in a technical environment were not expected to have, had not been taught, or evaluated upon. There was no sound reason to expect that managers or supervisors would make the effort to implement these steps. This is particularly true with a multi-cultural workforce, where self-doubt about how to manage across lines of difference and anxiety about interactions are at high levels. We had based our interventions upon Assumptions of what a manager or supervisor should know. Now we gather data prior to implementing a program. Focus groups have proved most helpful in flushing out the issues, concerns, fears, and needs of seminar participants and the people you wish for them to impact.

3. **Doing a Seminar only, or operating in a piecemeal fashion, without the support of the leadership of the organization, including a tie-in to overall organizational goals, and setting concrete action steps or building in accountability, sets the stage for failure.** The Diversity effort is put into a vacuum where the overall results for Diversity effectiveness rest

solely on a training effort which is not sufficient. Or, the training effort is an isolated, singular event mode, which is axed if the effort falls out of priority status. Either effort is bound for minimal success.

This kind of strategy reflects the "spray and pray" philosophy of intervention. It's a training philosophy that has little strategic organizational value, but it may provide some education and insight to a scattering of individuals.

A better strategy, however, is to offer a single course or seminar to a division or department. This concentrates the effect of spray and pray. Individuals are then more likely to have a common ground to rally around and may end up doing something as a group activity.

4. **Not listening to or hearing our participants. For years (about 10 or more) our clients have asked for concrete skills-based training to help them to become more competent in the arena of Diversity.** A number of colleagues and I have balked at this request. It feels like spoon-feeding or helping them to be lazy. We want them "to engage their intellect" in coming up with solutions themselves. The intent behind an Awareness training design is for the workshop activities to lead to soul-searching, then to a discovery of undesirable behavior, and ultimately to a replacement with more appropriate or desirable behavior. Many of our participants never get to this last step since they cannot make this translation from awareness to concrete actions. They have neither learned the art of introspection nor developed an ability to problem-solve in the human relations arena.

It took much soul-searching on our parts to come up with a way to translate this thorn in our sides to a more useful and pragmatic training design. A most recent example took place over the last three months. We assisted an organization in the food services industry to make their own Diversity Training video. The company sponsors could not find in the market the exact concrete examples that their people could relate to. They used their own data and created vignettes that everyone in their system could understand. The video has met with a great reception among workshop participants, who can now see exactly what poor service looks like from a multi-cultural perspective and take concrete actions to correct the problems as depicted.

5. **Using personal experiences in the Diversity Seminar setting and working from a relational format with managers.** This format, used to establish rapport with seminar participants, has brought some highly negative reactions from management. Feedback on evaluation sheets has included comments such as "unprofessional," "too personal" and "stuck on herself." This format, however, is very necessary and can be highly successful when used in Career Development seminars, particularly for an audience of minority women.

White male managers frequently complain that their issues are not heard by minority or female workshop trainers. One way we have corrected this is to team-teach in a cross-gender, cross-racial pair. This provides an "interpreter" of experiences and viewpoints who will be identified as one "of us" rather than a "them."

## Headaches

Going back to the drawing board and improving the content and delivery of training programs has been triggered by four major changes in design strategy.

1. **Built in self-auditing processes**

   Better program designs, leading to more successful interventions, can be created by monitoring or auditing the process through formal assessments of the training population, evaluations of the program's impact and evaluations by the participants. Following a program, changes in the way an organization operates are monitored and evaluated.

   Several examples will illustrate the value of measurement in creating successful interventions. Prior to implementing the pilot program for a mentoring project at a large, global, established manufacturing firm, we conducted a survey of potential portages and their bosses.

## Success Criteria of High Potentials

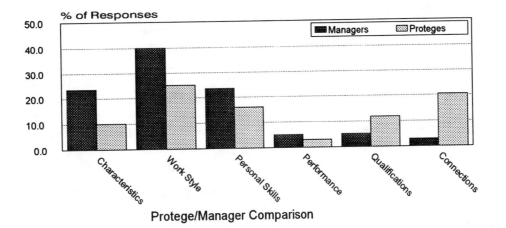

We used a focus group format which included a written questionnaire. We asked a series of questions designed to uncover attitudes and practices around mentoring, development, and diversity.

An analysis and comparison of the data from protégés and their bosses showed us clearly why women and minorities were not more successful in this company. We uncovered a fundamental communication gap between managers and their protected class subordinates, who were focusing on the wrong things. They did not know the unwritten, culture-specific criteria by which they were being evaluated. Consequently, they did not work those issues with their bosses or members of upper management and were not perceived as "high fliers."

That discovery from the preliminary study changed the way we designed and implemented that and other programs, i.e., Career and Leadership Development. The success of the Training design is predicated upon certain assumptions about your seminar or workshop participants. When you can discover the essential needs of your population and design to those needs, rather than suppositions, you achieve a much higher probability of success. In the example cited above, the preliminary

measurements kept the design team from flying blind, or addressing the wrong issues.

## 2. Failure and limited success

Though difficult and painful to get negative feedback from your training participants, it is essential to understand and incorporate the messages if you are going to be more successful. It is always important to know and meet the needs of your training audience. If you cannot meet those needs, or if you view them as counterproductive, the participants should be told.

An issue that frequently comes up in Diversity Seminars results from a request by management participants for a formula for relating to each individual ethnic, gender or age group. If we provided such a formula, how would it be used? Can a group of relatively unsophisticated managers and supervisors remember that much detail? Could they call upon it in their everyday conversations? Would it help the relationships with their culturally diverse subordinates evolve into a more natural form?

The conventional practice would be to let the participants know why the formula, which can be viewed as just a more sophisticated listing of cultural stereotypes, will not be provided. Instead, we offer alternative courses of action

241

and discuss the relative benefits. We believe that participants will benefit on many levels when they gather their own data about different groups and bridge the communication gap first hand. While this is a noble goal, what happens when the participants are too reluctant or feel too threatened to bridge the gap themselves? We can provide cognitive maps, or a mental picture by which individuals might carry out a successful dialogue. We can role-play their most feared interactions and help them walk away with a practical solution.

### 3. Continuing to ask why and look for a better design

No matter how successful a program is, it can always be refined and made better. I am always looking for ways to make changes that would either speed up, reinforce or enhance the learning process by using more attractive means of learning new information.

For example, the case study technique has much time-honored educational value. But for people in the aerospace community, the usual written format for presenting case studies may be perceived as dull and lacking in real challenge. We know that the engineering and technical professionals are visually oriented and enjoy manipulating symbols. We therefore joined forces with a computer programming company and developed *The Organization Game*. We took common case study scenarios which negatively affect women and minority group members and translated them into a computer game format using the journey of variously shaped symbols through a series of grids and barriers.

The game was projected on a large screen while the seminar participants, protégés and their mentors, responded to questions about the experiences and frustrations faced by women and minorities in their organization. The sharing of various viewpoints and interpretations of the story line, as a part of the seminar process, gave the participants a first-hand experience in discovering what true diversity is about. The participants learned

**The Computer Screen from *The Organization Game* (1990)**

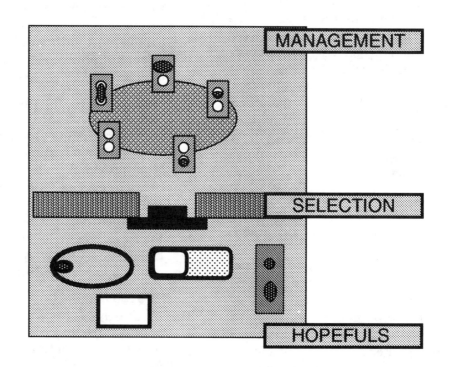

about critical organizational practices and developed career strategies in a very short time span, while having fun together.

### 4. Client input

The best ideas for changes in training designs have come from clients. In order to bypass the denial expected from a group of vice-presidents in a highly successful financial firm, the president suggested that we conduct each of our Diversity and Sensitivity Training sessions with the most representative group within an organization. This meant that not only was it necessary to provide diversity within each workshop across race, gender, and generations but to include diversity across levels. The end result was that vice-presidents, managers, sales representatives, analysts, mail clerks, cafeteria workers, etc. had an opportunity to spend two unobstructed days together exploring diversity in all of its aspects.

The design was a spectacular success, after much initial fear and reluctance on all parts of the organization. A wonderful by-product of the design was the breaking down of barriers that existed across levels and building a more cohesive workforce that had experienced communicating across levels.

My own resistance to having clients make significant input into the design and implementation of programs was resolved when one of my projects was sponsored by a Team rather than an individual. The use of design teams, standard practice in this global chemical firm, included representatives of our eventual customers and target groups, human resources personnel, and the consultants. They helped put the goals of the program and strategies of the training team into clearer perspective. Most importantly for the Diversity Program consultants, it forced an appreciation for the partnerships which can lead to far greater measures of success and satisfaction for those who work in the field.

## Breakthroughs

The *Systems Model* has grown in favor over the years and become a design strategy used by many

writers and change consultants for explaining the effects of change strategies in organizations. Training, particularly diversity training, desires to produce far-reaching change. In order to do this, the intervention is best served when it is viewed as a part of a totality rather than a singular event, as in the Three Tiers Model.

This means then that from the inception of the outcome in the designer's mind, he or she must consider the critical components of the system which hold a particular behavior in place. These components must then be included as a part of the training design and program. The most frequently stated goal of Awareness Training is to change attitudes of managers towards their female or minority employees. In order to do that successfully, we need to go far beyond a simple prejudice reduction exercise, or completing a Stereotype Inventory. We need to know what sustains those attitudes in an organization, how they get played out on a daily basis in the participant's behavior patterns, what would induce the participants to want to make the desired changes, and then do the required work to change. This is the kind of knowledge that goes into a Systems approach to program design, making it a more difficult design challenge for the trainer and the sponsor alike. Use of the model makes the design process a more comprehensive and complex one, and makes the execution more precise and less global. The outcomes will be smaller, but with more lasting, measurable results. Currently, a Systems approach is used in our designs, whether it is a one-time only workshop or a comprehensive program.

An examination of one of our most successful projects will serve as an example. Several times a year a Southern California aerospace firm conducts seminars for its protected class employees. These seminars are implemented by divisions, under the sponsorship of its Affirmative Action Committees. It is up to the Committee coordinator and the consultant to work out the details of the program for that year, with the only proviso being that the program address issues of upward mobility of women and minorities.

The 1990 year's first offering was entitled Empowerment Strategies in a Multicultural Environment. The company and division leadership had gone on record as saying that it wanted more empowered employees, particularly among women and minorities. To this end, it had distributed hundreds of copies of William Byham's book, *ZAPP: The Lightning of Empowerment.*

Our biggest initial stumbling block from a design standpoint was that no one, including the seminar sponsors, knew exactly what the company meant by the term empowerment. Furthermore, it was not clear how the concept translated into one's behavior in the workplace. Additionally, no one knew what the lower level managers were taught to look for, encourage, and reward in their subordinates. We knew we must include in our seminar leaders who could speak authoritatively about empowerment from the company's perspective.

The seminar was conducted with the principal consultant and five co-faculty. These were company officers who were proponents of the idea and who could define empowerment from their personal and division's vantage point. A recently-named female vice-president was a part of the faculty team and provided a wonderful role model of empowerment for the group.

A series of follow-up activities to the seminar was designed to produce measurable results in this scientifically oriented culture. They included an empowerment project; a joint seminar with each participant's boss to achieve alignment on current, day-to-day issues of empowerment; and a forum for ongoing group support and networking. These follow-ups have become a standard component for programs designed to teach leadership and empowerment skills.

## The Systems Approach Applied to Cultural Diversity Programs

Six fundamental concepts which our firm builds into each training package or intervention provide a greater probability of producing the desired result for participants and the organization. Presenting this set of concepts to the organization's sponsors and to selected participants enables them to understand and appreciate the specific content of a seminar and the context from which it is offered. The following concepts define the current approach:

1. Managing change

2. Paradigm shifts and change

3. Re-defining self and sources of self-esteem

4. Tools to enable individual success

5. Creation of a receptive environment for new behavior

6. Accountability for results.

## How Each Part Contributes to the Success of Program

### 1. Managing Change

An underlying assumption of every training program, or intervention, is the recommendation for change. We assume that everyone takes that as a given, but we sometimes forget to lay out what that process entails and how challenging it is for some. White male managers, or males in general, may view the call for change inherent in Cultural Diversity training programs as alarming or threatening. Responding to the programs with resistance (passive or active), denial of the issues, or attack upon the instructor is a natural way for them to respond to change which is viewed as threatening.

Jaffe and Scott (1988) have outlined an excellent four step process which is easily conceptualized and grasped. Introducing the process within the context of the seminar provides instructor and participants a way to understand transitional behavior and use it for self-understanding. Rather than viewing the variety of responses to change as annoyances to be side-stepped, we have made them part of the educational content.

### 2. Paradigm shifts and change

Introducing the concepts of Paradigm Shifts is a useful teaching model. It allows for the orderly exploration of old, unproductive methods of managing one's workforce or career, and for creating something which is new, unknown, and perhaps subconsciously unwanted. Exercises based upon Paradigm shifts, especially when used in conjunction with visual aids (CSC, 1992), allow for concrete ways to talk about what is mostly invisible and difficult to conceptualize. The majority of mid-level managers and supervisors have received little human behavior training or much, if any, management training. The framework of Paradigms helps to explain their anxiety and therefore resistance about making the transition between the known and the unknown, the old and the new.

### 3. Re-defining self and sources of self-esteem

The behavior observed in so much of our Cultural Diversity training for managers was resistance to the information, to the issues, and to the recommendations. To break through this resistance we asked, "What drives the resistance to implementing a truly multicultural workforce?" "Why are people holding back from the establishment of a more productive organization?"

The answer to these questions came from observing managerial responses to other company initiatives, particularly those involving greater employee empowerment through flattening of organizations and the greater utilization of teams. The resistance here was not so obvious, but the impact was just as powerful.

It was clear that the two sets of recommendations were related. Giving up power to one's subordinates is perceived as an attack upon one's self-esteem; this is particularly true if one has always defined oneself on the basis of the amount of power one could exert personally in the organization. By extolling empowerment, the training department and the company are seen as destroying the whole inner world of the manager, or employee, who is being asked to change.

According to Senge (1990) helping participants to re-define themselves within a new paradigm and finding new sources of self-esteem helps to lessen the individual's tenacious grip on the past.

### 4. Tools to enable individual success

Frequently our training programs make recommendations for new behavior that many of our participants are unwilling to attempt. This is particularly true when these recommendations involve cross-cultural communications of an open and candid nature; managing performance through coaching and feedback; building a cross-cultural team; or becoming

pro-active in including culturally different groups.

The cumulative impact of other courses and seminars is frequently seen in our diversity seminars. When upper level managers are serving as mentors in a mentoring program, they function much better when their involvement has included a course on Coaching and Counseling employees. Protégés in similar programs do better when their participation includes seminars on career development or personal efficacy.

Currently we operate from a very simple principle in our training courses: we teach the skills and behavior that we believe people need in order to be successful. We teach through example, case studies, role playing, and where possible through actual involvement. The best diversity workshops are those in which the participants are diverse and the design includes activities which enable many opportunities for cross-cultural dialogue. This reduces fear and opens channels of communication for further development after the workshop is completed.

### 5. Creation of a receptive environment for new behavior

The best and most successful programs are those that intervene from a multiplicity of sources. This intervention must be well-orchestrated and not haphazard. When some form of strategic planning is in place there is an orderly process to the change efforts.

A frequent example of a company's attempt to make changes in the complexion of the leadership is to recruit senior level women and minorities from other companies or civil service organizations. This tactic will work only if the organization is pre-disposed to be receptive and the indigenous groups are supportive.

One of our most far-sighted and best examples of creating a receptive environment occurred three years ago when a group president of an aerospace firm decided that it was time for his organization to meet the issues of diversity head on. His strategic plan was simple and straightforward. By 1993 he wanted to have

245

one minority and one woman as a part of the nine member team which ran the divisions in his business unit of 9000 people. He wanted candidates to be groomed from within to move into those positions and he wanted the organization to support them. Fundamental to the success of the candidates was that they be perceived as "qualified" from a technical and internal standpoint. He hired a consulting firm to design and implement that strategy. Cultural Diversity seminars were conducted starting with himself and his executive team and delivered systematically down through the divisional ranks.

Simultaneously, Leadership Seminars were offered to identified High Potential minority and female candidates. A process of *Individual Development Planning* was initiated which required the collaboration of the candidates and their bosses in a long-term developmental plan. The Human Resources department coordinated this work with the succession planning effort of the organization. This assured that job assignments were made to provide those in the grooming process with the relevant set of required work experiences.

Five years after the start of this project, a number of individuals are now in place. They are well-respected by their organizations and accepted by their constituencies. Carrying out this simple, well-thought out strategic plan for diversity in this organization required a high degree of coordination and cooperation from many sources, and it produced the desired results.

### 6. Accountability for results

People are more likely to take action when their actions lead to something concrete, and when someone is around to take notice. The training programs designed by this firm always have a project that its participants are asked to design, and where possible execute. Frequently those projects have a concrete product as the end result which serves to display their talents and gain them positive visibility.

In one of our programs, *Corporate Champions*, participants were asked to *create* and *innovate*: to become champions of a new product, process, need or improvement in the company. These projects are a concrete application of the information gained in training sessions and seminars. What gets applied gets understood, learned and owned.

Accountable end results provide a way to measure the impact of training and put the sponsors of the program in a positive light with their organization's leadership.

## Summary

The design and execution of successful programs in the Cultural Diversity arena are complex. The issues are not simple, and the level of change desired requires changes within many levels of an individual and an organization. To design and implement successful programs, we must take these interacting forces into account. For this firm, that means using a systems approach which is comprehensive and multi-faceted.

### References

Asman, David. Ed. *Adding Value through Synergy*. (Doubleday/Currency, 1990).

Barker, Joel A. *Future Edge: Discovering the new paradigms of success*. (William Morrow & Co., 1992).

Belasco, J. A. *Teaching the Elephant to Dance: Empowering change in your organization*. (Crown Publishers, Inc., 1990).

Block, R. "Empowering Employees," *Training and Development Journal*, April, 1987, Pp. 34–39.

Boags, R. and Simeon, O. T. *The Organization Game*. (Los Angeles, 1990).

Byham, William C. et al. *ZAPP! The Lightning of Empowerment*. (DDI Press, 1989).

Cobbs, Price M. "The Three Tiers Framework for Understanding Issues of Diversity" from *Valuing Diversity in the 1990's*. (Pacific Management Systems Workshops, San Francisco, CA, 1994).

Cobbs, P. M. "Valuing Diversity: The Myth and the Challenge," *The State of Black America, 1989* (National Urban League, Pp. 151–159).

Computer Systems Corporation. *Paradigm Shifts*. (Multi-media visual aid). (Pacific Palisades, CA, 1992).

Jaffe, D. T. and Scott, D. S. "Survive and Thrive in Times of Change," *Training and Development Journal*, April, 1988, Pp. 24–27.

Pfeffer, Jeffrey. *Competitive Advantage Through People: Unleashing the power of the workforce.* (Harvard University Press, 1994).

Senge, Peter M. *The Fifth Discipline: The art and practice of the learning organization.* (Doubleday/Currency, 1990).

## About the Author

Dr. Rita Boags is a Licensed Clinical Psychologist whose practice centers around human potential development and organizational consulting. Her experience in education, psychotherapy, and organizations enables her to create unique program offerings in the areas of Cultural Diversity, Mentoring, Leadership Development and Team Building.

Dr. Boags has implemented programs for a variety of organizations including Hughes Aircraft Company, TRW, Inc., First Interstate Bancorp, E. I. DuPont de Nemours & Co., Digital Equipment Corporation, XEROX Corporation, the City of Pasadena, California State University at Northridge, the Bonneville Power Administration, TRANSAMERICA Life Companies, Glendale Federal Bank, ICI Americas Inc., Fannie Mae, and the World Bank. She can be reached at P.O. Box 2497, Castro Valley, CA 94546-0497. Phone: (510) 581-2946; Fax: (510) 581-6112.

# A More Accurate Way to Measure Diversity

by Karen Stephenson and Valdis Krebs (*Personnel Journal*)

Just because a company hires minorities and women doesn't mean that it's doing a good job of promoting them. With the assistance of a computer program that diagrams work networks, HR can identify why some employees aren't moving up the corporate pipeline.

Affirmative action and equal employment opportunities may have helped corporate America do a better job of hiring women and minorities. They haven't, however, helped U.S. companies do a better job of promoting these individuals into the upper ranks of their organizations. For example, although women and minorities constitute 65% of the total work force, women occupy only 3% of the top jobs, and minorities hold about 2%.

A typical rationale used to explain these low percentages is that women and minorities are in the pipeline for promotions. The problem, however, is that these individuals have been in the corporate pipeline for some time, and they still aren't being promoted. By solving only half of the problem, many businesses have created another problem—frequent, voluntary turnover of the targeted groups. Once these individuals leave, corporations reinitiate a costly and never-ending cycle of recruiting to comply with EEO goals.

Why this senseless cycle? Why can't corporations hold on to these talented people in the first place? Why aren't women and minorities integrated meaningfully into the corporate culture? Many companies implement training programs on managing and valuing diversity to help their organizations become more sensitive to diversity issues. Although these programs serve an important purpose, they may not solve diversity problems. The reason? HR professionals often have few clues to the extent of the effectiveness of these programs.

A lack of measurement tools has forced firms to estimate the effectiveness of their diversity efforts by looking at the boxes that employees occupy on the organizational chart. This approach can be deceiving, however, because companies that are successful at hiring women and minorities often aren't successful at promoting them. Fortunately, new ways to measure the real work environment for women and people of color are being developed. X-rating your organization is one such way to do this. This method, which involves using a computer to diagram formal and informal networks and relationships between employees, allows HR professionals to see what previously was invisible.

This technology is the basis for Redondo Beach, California-based TRW Space & Electronics Group's Measuring Organizational Diversity (MOD) program. "It's amazing what it can reveal to managers who think everything is wonderful," says Belinda Ross, diversity consultant at TRW. "The analogy to an X-ray is perfect. You can feel healthy and fine, yet the diagnostic reveals areas for intervention and leverage." MOD allows the company to view how its human resources are utilized. And seeing how the organization is helps TRW plan for how it should be.

Diverse departments aren't always what they appear to be. Rather than argue that the pipeline is blocked, it's easier to demonstrate how the X-ray process works in revealing how the pipeline in an organization becomes blocked and what HR professionals can do to clear it. Figures 1 through 4 are different snapshots of the same managers and professionals in a financial-services company. Each figure depicts a network based on work and social interactions in the office. The data are real and are derived from the organization's hierarchy and from surveys administered to employees. The lines drawn connecting individuals with each other represent two-way communications/relationships. The density of the lines denotes the intensity of each relationship, with the darker lines denoting the relationships of higher intensity.

Figure 1 is the standard organization chart of a department of 16 employees in a division of 238 employees. The chart has been modified to indicate the gender and ethnicity of the employees. The top executive is a Caucasian male; his administrative assistant is a woman of color. Of the executive's five direct reports, three are male managers, one of whom is a male of color. There are two Caucasian female managers. Reporting to the managers on the organization chart are nine professionals, two of whom are male. Of those two, one is a male of color, the other Caucasian. Of the seven women professionals, three are Caucasian, four are women of color.

If you were to draw this organization chart as a prescribed or flat network rather than a vertical hierarchy, all the linkages would be the same, except that the executive would be at the center of this network. The conversion from hierarchy to network reveals an interesting pair of assumptions. The goal in hierarchies is to get to the top, whereas the goal in networks is to get to the center—to be in the thick of things. The prescribed network is equivalent to the formal hierarchy in that the person on top of the hierarchy now appears at the center of the network. Although decisions radiate outward from the center to the managers and professionals on the periphery, that doesn't mean that the executive in the center of the prescribed network is at the center of other critical networks within the organization.

Figure 2 shows how work gets done in the department. To form this network employees were asked with whom they interact or work to get their jobs done in the department. This network is different from the organization chart in several ways. First, the bulk of the work flows through a Caucasian female manager. Second, all managers are working with their professional subordinates except one Caucasian male manager. There is no link connecting this manager to one of his subordinates, who is a woman of color.

Figure 3 shows the informal communication network in this department. This network was determined by surveying employees regarding their involvement in the rumor mill. It reveals whom employees talk to if they really want to find out what's going on in the organization. This illustration reveals that the Caucasian woman manager through whom most of the work flows isn't in the thick of things in the informal network. Perhaps she's too busy doing her work and the work of others to hobnob by the watercooler. In any event, she talks mostly to other women of equal or lower rank in the organization.

The Caucasian male executive talks mostly with a Caucasian male manager in one of the work groups. Perhaps this is his source for what's going on in the organization, or he is grooming this individual as his replacement. This same manager isn't speaking informally to any of his subordinates, who are women. Instead, his informal ties mostly are with his boss and the other men in the organization.

Figure 4 illustrates this department's support relationships—who informs whom on what it takes to succeed in the organization. In this type of network informal mentoring relationships are evident. For example, the Caucasian woman manager through whom most of the work flows isn't in the thick of things here either. She's integrated in the work networks but is isolated socially. In all probability, she may grow frustrated and leave. What will happen to the work flow in that department if she goes?

Earlier we suggested that the executive was training an heir apparent. Certainly these two Caucasian males are connected strongly in both the support and informal networks. On closer inspec-

tion, these strong nonwork connections overshadow the actual working relationship.

Relatively isolated are a male professional of color and a male manager of color. They're unique in their work groups because they're the only ones who are of a particular gender and ethnic mix. Perhaps they feel that they have no one to turn to who is like them and who can advise them.

What's interesting about this department is that, by the numbers, it's exemplary in terms of EEO compliance. The work force is composed of

## Prescribed Network (Figure 1)

Below is a diagram of the reporting relationships between 16 people who work in the same department. These relationships have been illustrated in the form of a prescribed network instead of a hierarchy to point out an important difference between the two. In a hierarchy, the goal is to get to the top. In a prescribed network, the goal is to get to the center—to be in the thick of things. In a prescribed network, decisions radiate outward from the executive at the center to the managers and professionals on the periphery. As you'll see in Figures 2 through 4, just because the executive is at the center of the network doesn't mean that he's at the center of the other critical networks.

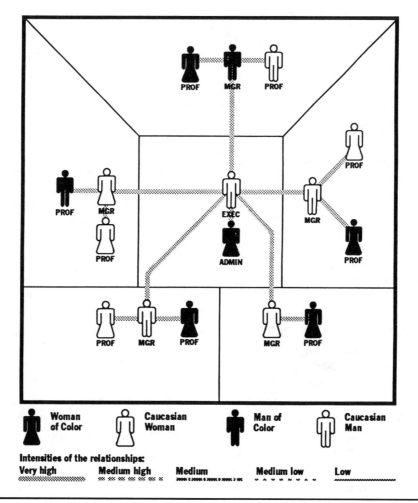

approximately 40% men and 60% women. The racial/ethnic mix is 56% white and 44% people of color. However, if you were the executive of this department, what would you think if you saw these diagrams? No matter what the numbers indicate, women and minorities aren't being integrated into the workplace in this example. Many of these employees will leave. How can an executive head off this potential disaster?

Baselining and benchmarking your organization can improve diversity efforts. To measure diversity, HR professionals usually look at the number of women and minorities throughout the organization. If a great disparity of women and minorities are found between two adjacent management levels in the hierarchy, then a glass ceiling exists between these two levels. This invisible barrier prevents these individuals from advancing beyond the lower level. It's fairly easy to locate the glass ceiling in an organization.

The more-difficult assignment is to determine what keeps this obstruction in place despite recent efforts to remove it. Obviously, many firms have been chasing after windmills by not looking deep enough into the problem. As we have seen in the glass-ceiling example, subtle forms of discrimination creep into social behavior. This behavior sets up exclusionary hurdles that are difficult to overcome because they're difficult to see.

From the diagrams, we saw that generally there are two types of work relationships in the workplace—formal and informal. These ties can either be strong or weak. Using these two critical dimensions, you can develop a framework for organizing business relationships. When co-workers have both strong formal and informal ties, they're well-integrated both inside and outside the formal hierarchy. When they have strong formal and weak informal ties, their relationship may be all business.

There's nothing wrong with this scenario. Not everyone can be the best of friends at work. However, the lack of social ties between people who frequently work together could be a sign of exclusion in the organization. As illustrated in Figures 2 and 3, the Caucasian female manager has good working relationships, but weak informal links with most of her department. Weak formal and strong informal ties generally represent clubs, softball teams and links outside the hierarchy. These informal ties can be instrumental in making work

go smoothly when new work responsibilities emerge, or cross-functional goals need to be achieved. Finally, weak formal and weak informal ties may represent the relative isolation of a new hire.

Using this framework, diagnosing your organization is a relatively easy procedure for monitoring change and the effective use of all of your human resources. Diagnosing occurs in three general phases:

*Phase 1:* Baseline the environment for women and people of color by measuring both the formal and informal organization.

*Phase 2:* Apply training or other interventions to address the problems found in Phase 1.

*Phase 3:* Take annual measures to see if the environment is improving and if the interventions are having their intended effects.

There are four measures by which to evaluate the formal and informal organization. By using them, an organization can track its progress. These measures include:

1. *Demographics:* Determine the percentage of the population of the designated target groups by organizational level, line and staff.

2. *Turnover:* Determine the percentage of the voluntary turnover for women, minorities and Caucasian males. Is there a difference among these groups? What's the cost of the difference?

The next two measures are calculated from survey data that can be administered yearly or as needed. The survey is constructed around questions that are designed to elicit responses about inclusion and access to work relationships and social ties.

3. *Inclusion:* This measures how central (or in the thick of things) a particular person or group is in the organization. From this measure we can see the level of inclusion of women and people of color in key networks and information flows. Typical survey questions that reveal inclusion may include the following: With whom do you interface to get your job done? With whom do you discuss what is going on in the organization?

4. *Access:* This measures how easily members of targeted groups can get access to the decision-

## Work Network (Figure 2)

The diagram below shows how work gets done in the department. To form this network, employees were asked with whom they interact or work to get their jobs done. This network is different from the prescribed network in figure 1 in several ways. First, you'll notice almost immediately that the bulk of the work in this department flows through a Caucasian female manager. She has ties with 10 other people in the department. As indicated by the darker colors, many of these ties are strong. It's also important to note that all managers are working with their professional subordinates, except one Caucasian male manager. There's no link connecting this manager to a woman of color.

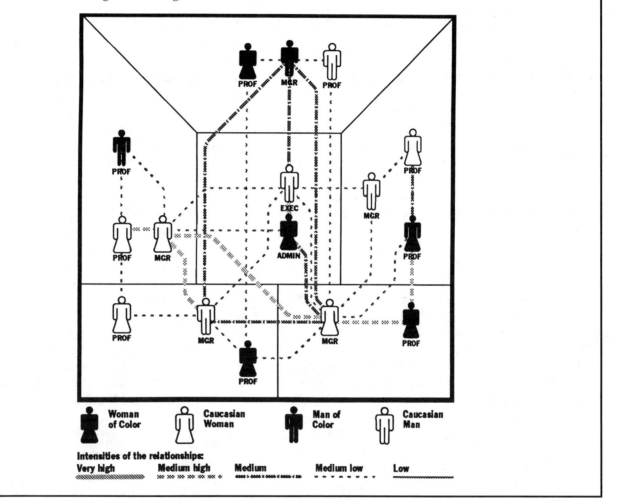

making core in their organization. It also reveals how visible members of targeted groups are to this influential decision-making group. Typical survey questions that reveal access may include the following: With whom do you discuss your new ideas and innovations? With whom do you discuss what it takes to succeed in the organization?

These measures of the informal organization usually are leading indicators of the movement

of members of targeted groups up the management ladder. As the environment of the organization moves towards greater inclusion, you start to see a larger percentage of women and people of color in organizational levels in which they previously were rare participants.

Surveys can determine formal and informal networks between employees. The survey population is chosen by determining which organizational groups—a department, a work team or the whole organization—need to be studied. After the scope of the survey has been determined, a survey roster is generated from employee data from the HRIS. When studying a large population, such as a company that has more than 500 employees, an organizationwide scan of the firm can be generated from a random sample of the employees. This is done by aggregating individual responses into designated groups. These groups can be defined by whatever demographics are available on the HRIS.

For instance, you can look at the relationships between marketing, sales, engineering and manufacturing or the ties among Caucasian males, Caucasian females, minority males and minority females, or the networks of older, long-term employees and younger, short-term employees. Many combinations are possible. You can slice your organization by whatever data are available on all employees. Common groupings are by any combination of race, gender, age, service, disabled status, department, project team or organization level. Smaller populations of employees (20 to 500 individuals) can be surveyed by taking a complete census of the population.

To capture all of the relationships within the focus population, you must achieve a complete census or close to it. If some individuals don't take the survey, then their network ties can be estimated from all the other responses. However, all key individuals in the survey population should take the survey for ultimate accuracy. Key individuals are defined as the top management in the group being studied, their liaisons and influential employees. A complete census gives you a detailed look at the organizational dynamics of the firm.

All survey responses are confidential. Completed survey forms aren't shared with anyone. The survey data are used only in aggregate to determine the relationships and networks within the organization. To ensure confidentiality of individual responses, the survey should be administered by a trained person in human resources or a contracted specialist from the outside.

There are ethical considerations. From the outset, it's important to understand the purpose and objective of the study. Will the results be seen by management only or shared openly with all employees? Employees usually are curious to see how their organization really works. Will the output be group or individual networks and measures? The decision should be made at the beginning and

properly communicated to the surveyed population. Once expectations are set, managers and employees find the output constructive and interesting.

These network measures give us a complete view of the organizational system from both a formal and informal perspective. By including the informal facets of organizational life, you get a much better feel for the real dynamics of the organization. This is an as-is picture of behavior and emergent structure in the corporation. From this X-ray, you can diagnose the real environment for women and minorities. Training and other interventions can be planned from this feedback. After the training and intervention have been completed and given time to set in the organization, another X-ray can be taken to verify improvements and look for the next intervention (if needed).

All network diagrams and measures are generated on the basis of matching survey responses. A relationship line is drawn between person A and person B if and only if A and B agree on their relationship. This prevents certain individuals from overstating their connections or importance in the organization. The data are analyzed using a proprietary software tool called InFlow. Simulations and what-if analysis can be performed by interacting with the diagrams on the computer screen. This provides a better understanding of the as-is situation along with aiding in the design of the future should-be organization.

X-rays can reveal diversity problems that HR isn't aware of. An executive at a Fortune 500 firm had his department X-rayed recently. He was both pleased and shocked at what the images revealed:

1. Most work groups in the organization were working with each other and with other departments as expected. The emphasis on cross-functional communication and collaboration, under the TQM cultural-change effort, seemed to be working.

2. Although the company had many women and minorities in its work force and a few in management, the company still had a glass ceiling. The department seemed to be run by a dominant coalition of Caucasian and African-American males, with the executive right in the thick of things. Although the highest-ranking woman manager was hooked into this dominant coalition, she wasn't a full member

## Information Network (Figure 3)

Below is a diagram of the informal communication network (or grapevine) in the department. This network reveals whom employees talk to if they really want to find out what's going on in the organization. In this diagram, the Caucasian female manager through whom most of the work flows isn't in the thick of things in the informal network. The Caucasian male executive talks mostly to a Caucasian male manager in one of the work groups. Perhaps he's grooming this individual as his replacement. This manager isn't speaking informally to any of his subordinates, who are women. His informal ties are with his boss and the other Caucasian men in the organization.

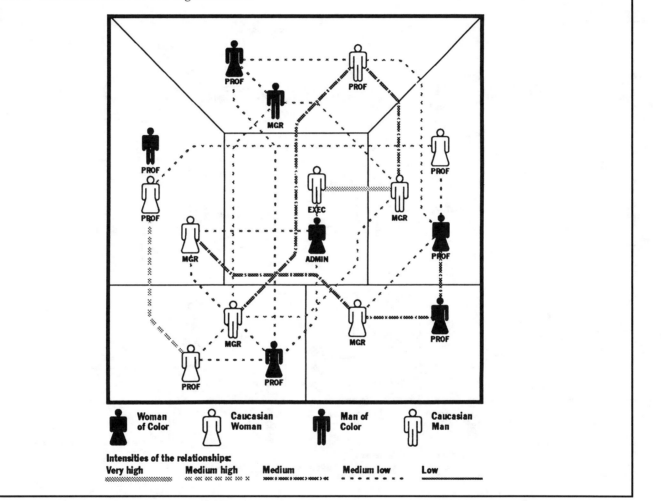

of the clique. It also was interesting to note that her informal networks mostly were with men, and she had no informal networks with any member of her ethnic group.

3. Parts of the department were isolated. They were out of the loop in critical information flows. These work groups all appeared to be located in distant buildings on the company's campus.

4. The executive had few links into the organization. Although he had seven people reporting to him directly, his information routes to and from the rest of the organization went mostly through four individuals who controlled 92% of his information.

5. A disgruntled employee was at the center of many informal communication flows in a critical work group.

## Support Network (Figure 4)

This diagram illustrates the department's support relationships. In this network, informal mentoring relationships are evident (who informs whom on what it takes to succeed in the organization). The Caucasian female manager through whom most of the work flows isn't in the thick of things here, either. She's integrated into the work networks but is socially isolated. Here again, the executive and the Caucasian manager are connected strongly. Their support and informal networks overshadow their working relationship. Relatively isolated are a male manager of color and a male professional of color. Perhaps they feel that they have no one to turn to who is like them and can help them.

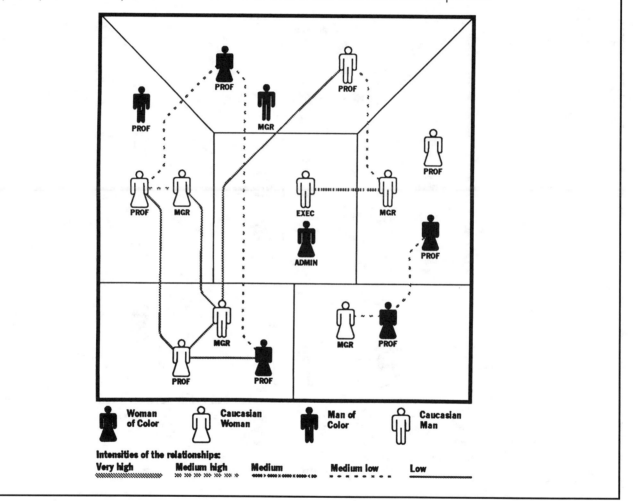

The executive was troubled—particularly about the problems with diversity management. "How could this be?" he asked. "We have great EEO/AAP numbers." He spent many hours reviewing the various diagrams and then sat down with his direct reports to review all parts of the department. The managers asked many questions while images of their work groups were projected onto a screen from the computer. They were shown many views of their organization as they probed deeper to understand the true dynamics of their work environment. After some deliberation and discussions with these key people, the Fortune 500 executive called in the company's internal diversity consultant to discuss possible interventions for his organization. After a few sessions, they came up with the following interventions:

1. Establish task forces and special project teams under strict diversity guidelines. (This allowed qualified women and minorities to exhibit their

skills and to form ties with others from various parts of the organization.)

2. Send managers of the department to the company's Managing Diverse Work Teams training. It was especially important to send the managers who appeared to avoid informal contact with diverse others.

3. Co-locate employees who are isolated from critical information with those whom they work and interact with frequently. Design offices and locate employees according to workflow.

4. Break the stranglehold of information that a few subordinates have on the executive by adopting the popular method of creating informal networks, MBWA (management by wandering around), discussed by Tom Peters and Robert Waterman in their bestseller, *In Search of Excellence*. The executive made a special point to establish ties with women and minorities throughout the organization. This change achieved two objectives: The executive received better information more quickly, and women and minorities were given access to the top of the hierarchy, which will help break the glass ceiling.

Later this company began to encourage employee support networks, some of which already had begun informally. These networks were seen as a way for employees to feel more of a sense of community with others like themselves in the organization, while also piggybacking on the excellent access and inclusion that a few members of the group enjoyed. Through these and other initiatives, the organization is moving beyond compliance and more fully utilizing the diverse talent in the organization.

Diagnosing and baselining your organization allow you to measure what you manage, and, therefore, better manage what you measure. You may compare various parts of your organization with each other. This allows you to see where you need to focus your attention. You can compare organizational units with themselves over time. Are they getting better? Are the interventions working? You also can compare your firm with other enterprises. How are you doing in your industry or in your region? How do you measure up in terms of Best Practices or World Class organizations?

Just as companies compare results of salary surveys and employee-opinion surveys, so can you benchmark on the environment for your diverse work force. Will you become a preferred employer? Are you using your entire work force effectively? Or are you inhibiting full participation (and therefore full productivity) of a large segment of your work force inadvertently? Management guru Tom Peters has said that Japanese management's difficulty in dealing with cultural differences may prove to be its major weakness in the next century. Homogeneous societies, such as Japan, will not be able to compete with countries and companies that use their diverse talent fully. Any corporation that can use diverse information sources effectively and efficiently will have the upper hand.

## About the Authors

Karen Stephenson is president of the Human Resources Roundtable (HARRT) at the Anderson Graduate School of Management at the University of California, Los Angeles.

Valdis Krebs is president of Krebs & Associates, a management-consulting firm in Simi Valley, California.

# The Challenge to Diversity

by Tom Chappell

Even at Tom's of Maine where I, the co-founder and CEO, was eager to have a more diverse company, we decided, four years after I sent the word that the company had to hire more women, that the company wasn't working hard enough toward this goal of diversity. The board had already amended the Mission and Beliefs statements with a commitment to "competence." Now it wanted to put our commitment to diversity in writing. Echoing Saint Paul, we drafted this for the Beliefs Statement:

- We believe that people bring different gifts and perspectives to the team and that a strong team is founded on a variety of gifts.

To the Mission Statement, the board added the goal:

- To honor and seek a diversity of gifts and perspectives in our work together.

When we brought these amendments to the company at large, the employees bought the Beliefs Statement on diversity but balked at the Mission version. Seek was a red flag. The implied initiative to look far and wide for new talents bothered them. "Why can't you honor and encourage the gifts that are here rather than think you have to go outside the company to find them?" someone asked. The resentment was wide and strong.

They had a point. After all, according to the Statement of Beliefs, employees at Tom's are supposed to believe "that human beings and nature are worthy of our respect." Wasn't the board's eagerness to go outside the company to fill jobs evidence of its lack of recognition of the abilities of its current employees? The board, however, defended its more explicit commitment to diversity by pointing out that because of our commitment to respecting human beings, we had to nurture diversity. In an effort to encourage creativity and high performance, Tom's was trying to get away from the traditional business practices of treating employees as interchangeable "tools" (or as Kant might put it, as "means" rather than "ends in themselves"—worthy for what they are and not for their utility). It followed that if the kind of high performance we were after could be better found in an employee not yet working at Tom's, then we wanted to hire her.

Equal opportunity efforts, whether pure window dressing or a genuine desire for diversity, have provoked a backlash across the country. White males especially feel that they're being displaced and, worse, sometimes by job candidates who are not as experienced or well trained as they. Cries of reverse discrimination have been heard by businesspeople and executives around the country as well as in the federal courts (which are no less confused as to what to do about the issue).

We listened to our employees, talked through their resentment, and this is what we heard: The company was not doing enough to affirm the "gifts" that it already had. Top management had to work harder to reach out to learn more about the skills of its existing employees and explore ways for people to contribute more to the team. The board, however, refused to yield on its determination to find the best employees possible, even if it required going outside the company. While understanding fears of the unknown and of outsiders and the defensiveness among the employees, the company could not veer from its ambition to be the very best at what it did, even if that meant looking for talent outside the company or outside of Maine. It was the only time since the Mission was initiated that the Tom's of Maine board had used its authority. But the board did agree to rewrite the new statement on diversity for the Mission, to accommodate the justifiable concern among employees that they might be overlooked. The Mission now reads:

- To recognize, encourage, and seek a diversity of gifts and perspectives in our work life.

The company has already begun efforts to take advantage of the obvious gift of current employees and to try to flush out the latent skills of others. Professional growth is now a top priority at Tom's; we've surveyed employees and management about the kinds of training and courses they want. The community life department has already begun publishing a list of programs and courses within a fifty-mile radius of Kennebunk. In-house, we've begun working with our management to help them become better leaders, particularly with an eye to the guiding principles of the Mission.

When a job opens up at Tom's of Maine, our employees are encouraged to apply. But they are also aware that no job will be filled until the opening is advertised in the local press as well as in newspapers outside Maine and all the best candidates have been interviewed. For every job, it is open season. The only advantage our employees have is that, if the choice is between two finalists equally qualified for a job and one is a Tom's of Maine employee, the Tom's person will get the job. Otherwise, hiring from within is bound only to increase the homogeneity of any company. This also holds for new management positions that open up—no executive working for the company has an automatic lock on the job. They have to apply like anyone else. I don't leave the executive search outside the company entirely in the hands of a recruiter either; these jobs are also posted at Tom's of Maine. To reach outside may not be the kindest or friendliest practice, but it is the one that best serves our goals of diversity and competence.

Tom's of Maine does not seek to hire women or ethnics or people of color because that is the law, or even because it is fashionable or "politically correct." We are seeking diversity because it is good for the company, profitable for the company. Diversity heightens the value of interdependence in the company. The more we talk to each other, the better our ideas and solutions are. The more different our own people are, the broader our perspective will be. The more differences we are put in touch with, the more progress we will make as people, managers, and company.

## About the Author

Tom Chappell is president of Tom's of Maine, Inc., a leading manufacturer of natural personal care products.

# ORGANIZATIONS TOUCHY
## ABOUT DEALING WITH DIVERSITY OF CLASS
by Dianne M. LaMountain

While I knew, both in theory and from personal experience, that class was a diversity issue, its real significance was brought home with one particular consulting assignment. The client, a large public agency, initiated a diversity intervention with a one day "diversity awareness" seminar for everyone in the organization. The training stressed the wide range of diversity that can affect working relationships. These included race, sex, age, ethnic heritage, communication style, family background, religion, geographic roots, etc. The focus was on differences in perception, differences in how we communicate, and assumptions made about each other. The training was conducted with vertical slices of the organization so that representatives of all levels in the hierarchy were present at most sessions. During the sessions, participants seemed to focus on race and gender as the two main diversity issues they were concerned about. At the end of each session, given their increased awareness, participants were asked to return to work and watch for examples of how diversity issues played out in their workgroup. They were also told there would be a follow-up questionnaire sent out which would help determine the next appropriate step in the intervention.

After three months a questionnaire was distributed asking all employees to list the diversity issues they felt were having the most impact in the organization, with specific examples where possible. The issue most often cited as having adverse impact on organizational effectiveness by those responding was no longer race or gender—it was class! Those at the lower end of the hierarchy reported that top management perceived themselves to be "better than" both lower level employees and clients and acted in a "condescending" and "classist" manner. Examples included patronizing interactions with lower level employees, disapproving comments about clients' lifestyles and a perceived bias in decisions made about clients' eligibility for services. Many staff expressed the belief that managers who were making service delivery decisions were judging clients without understanding the environment or motivation affecting client decisions and behaviors. They also felt management was often making decisions for staff "for their own good" and "in their own best interest." (A majority of the responses received were from the lower levels in the organizational hierarchy.)

When the agency's H.R. person was given the results of the survey, the decision was made to keep the results quiet and discontinue diversity intervention for the foreseeable future. While the organization appeared ready and willing to deal with other diversity issues, the issue of class was "taboo!" It has been almost two years and the issue remains in limbo!

Dianne M. LaMountain
Senior Associate, ODT Inc.
(Diversity Consulting Firm)

# PART 6
# DIVERSITY UNDER FIRE

# Dialogue: Diversity Under Fire

*Bob*—Our objective in this section is to respect, recognize, validate, appreciate and incorporate perspectives that may challenge current practice or run contrary to dogmatic politically correct (p.c.) thinking.

*George*—We've collected insightful articles that express strong dissent—some from people who are frustrated and angry. We want to approach these views positively and productively. This material is a counterpoint, and perhaps a corrective, to those well-intended diversity initiatives that have gone astray.

Diversity initiatives sometimes seem to saw down the legs of a chair to make it level. As a result the chair, though now stable, may not be as tall as we want. We need to listen to stuff that's hard to hear, and learn to constructively interpret negative feedback, so that we can build up the short leg rather than shortening the long ones.

*Bob*—The first thing we have to do is just hear what the dissenter says. In this country there is a cultural bias against feeling or saying anything negative, probably because, as we have mentioned elsewhere, our self-esteem is so low and we feel so vulnerable.

*George*—Yes, we aren't trying to put diversity advocates on the defensive with these articles. On the contrary, we are trying to break through defensive walls already built around diversity training and consulting. The interventions we now have work for some people and not for others. We want to know why.

*Bob*—In our lead article (page 263) Hank Karp talks about things that don't work and proposes measures that could make diversity efforts more effective overall.

*George*—You hear people say that "diversity is for everybody." However, too many still complain that this is only rhetoric. Grandiose promises and visions of benefits are not coming true. Perhaps these plusses may show up sometime in the future, but right now they are just wishful thinking. When that happens diversity training looks like hype and damages its own credibility.

When reading this section people need to keep in mind that we are not attacking everybody's work here. Diversity training is not monolithic. It is a vastly fractionalized field with hundreds of perspectives, options, and assumptions. We want to get beyond the standard approaches and allow more of this variety to challenge us.

*Bob*—People ought to leave a diversity training session able to apply something of what they've learned right away. It shouldn't always feel like delayed gratification. You know, be in pain now so you can work together more effectively later.

*George*—That reinforces what I've been saying ("The more things change," page 152) about how Puritan assumptions, in this case, delayed gratification, run rampant in the political correctness movement. I'm not saying that delayed gratification is wrong—no pain, no gain, and all that—just acknowledging that right now it's better if you have the pain and I get the gain! [*both laugh*]

*Bob*—Some people's limits for being pushed around by diversity or p.c. dogmatism have been reached and now they're starting to speak up. We all know the famous ones, e.g., Arthur Schlesinger ("The Cult of Ethnicity," page 268) and George Bush in his noted anti-p.c. address at the University of Michigan (page 272). But we're also starting to hear from everyday people who are not really thrilled with the p.c. prescriptions for how to speak and hold hands—or not hold hands.

*George*—I think we will be surprised by how many so-called "dead white males" aren't dead yet and are going to get involved in this. They've been passive heirs of the dominant power structure and guiding philosophy of many social institutions. Unconsciously and involuntarily, a bit like the prince in the tale of "The Prince and the Pauper," they have been forced to lay down their pretensions for awhile. But now chastened, they will be powerful competitors for our attention.

Actually this "chastening" has happened to U.S. men in general. Feminism challenged male domination and made us aware of it. Now the men's movement seeks to consciously redefine male roles, to live out masculinity without patriarchy. I expect masculinity to be stronger and better for the experience. Even the so-called generation of "soft" men are aware that they are missing something in their experience as men that they want to rediscover. So too, with diversity thinking and policy. Schlesinger wires us to the male polarity of diversity. He and so many others can become legitimate partners in the dialogue after being aroused, as it were, from the culture-induced coma of belonging to the dominant group. What he, like us, took for granted, he will now have to understand, and negotiate. The words of Admiral Yamamoto spoken shortly after Pearl Harbor come to mind, "I fear we have awakened a sleeping giant."

Let me switch topics here . . .

Today I can't, try as I might, talk about philosophers, poets and historical events or make literary allusions to the classics and expect instant understanding and resonance. I can't assume that everybody has the same educational background or canon of studies I've had. There's still freshness available from the old as well as the new ideas, but I've got to sell the old ones on their own merits if I am to preserve what is truly valuable about them from the p.c.-bookburners. This is actually an enjoyable endeavor, speaking to critical minds and hearts. Unfortunately, too many students seem to be at least as uncritical in accepting p.c. dogma today as we were in swallowing the Western canon in my college years. I expect they'll get over their gullibility as we have.

*Bob*—Maybe this is a tribute to the success of diversity. It's being taken seriously enough to be opposed by those who have been too long silent. Another way this gets voiced is in cartoons and other forms of humor. Take the Shesol cartoon about "Politically-Correct Man" as an example. It shows the excesses of policing language.

*George*—We've included humor in this anthology, especially cartoons, because that's how Americans often best express their disgruntlement with political and social practices. In fact, today is the 100th anniversary of the first comic strip in the U.S. Watch how fast a timely cartoon or joke makes the round of an average office and is copied and faxed and found all over the e-mail networks.

*Bob*—Mark Helprin's "Diversity is not a virtue" from the *Wall Street Journal* is more serious in format. His critique is based on an analysis of individual rights versus group rights. When he refers to the U.S. as a free-market economy, it's also helpful to understand that (as far as I can see) the U.S. is committed to capitalism for entrepreneurs and workers at the bottom of the socio-economic ladder. But corporate "welfare-ism" is certainly at a peak frenzy, and with international trade ruled by GATT and the World Bank, we are in a dangerously similar predicament to the socialist centrally planned state he decries. But Helprin does accurately portray the trend towards the fascism of the left (also see the sidebar by Howard Bronstein in the Future section—page 502).

*George*—Maybe it feels that way in the U.S. because we're not "up-front" about connections between business and government. U.S. business doesn't benefit from the conscious alliance of government, banks and enterprise, as say in Germany and Japan. Our system and our culture condemn such connections as hindrances to freedom. Yet, somehow those connections must to some degree happen if we are to be competitive, so instead of an open system we have an informal "old-boy" network.

*Bob*—On the other hand, there is a serious counterpoint to this argument made in the 1950's bestseller by C. Wright Mills, *The Power Elite* (Oxford University Press). In that book Mills asserts that there *is* a very powerful alliance at work in the U.S.; however it's covert—a cabal or shadow government, not accountable to citizen input. Certainly, this theme has been proposed again and again over the last 40 years.

*George*—My bias is against conspiracy theories, but highly in favor of watchdogging power. You can't replace Harry Truman's supervision of W.W.II military spending with a bureaucracy and expect it to work. It seems like the Lone Rangers of today are the outsiders, like Ralph Nader.

But back to my point: another element to consider when we think of Helprin's analysis is that the U.S. bent towards individualism is not primarily values-based. That is, it is not consciously chosen. Our

261

orientation towards individualism arises out of the idiosyncrasies of our culture.

*Bob*—A theme running through current critiques is the balkanization of interests and the loss of concern for the common good. The cartoon from the *Hartford Courant*, "Bosnia-Herzego USA," pretty much sums it up.

*George*—Powerful, but not at all funny.

*Bob*—I like the trilogy of pieces that begin with John Cowan's "The Diverse Workforce." The OD Network brought out these pieces and has a commitment to publishing articles that lead to intelligent conversations about current business issues. One thing is true for sure: to speak out about what's on your mind, especially if it's a critique of party-line p.c.-assumptions is getting harder and harder to do, especially in "enlightened" (i.e., progressive) business circles. Two responses with counterpoints follow his story about Gramma Liza Feeney Cowan.

Then, Leon McKinney (page 276) relates his first-hand experience of working at McDonnell Douglas, where the company was simultaneously downsizing and investing in diversity training. The latter in direct defiance of the company's critical bottom-line concerns. As we mentioned in the dialogue for the "Best Practices" section (page 196), inappropriate investment in misplaced diversity efforts is not an isolated event and contributes to diversity's spotty reputation.

*George*—The fact that the quality of diversity initiatives is erratic shouldn't surprise us, though. Anything that begins to pay off, diversity included, can become someone's vested cash cow. Someone will always see a social trend as a way to make a fast buck, or further their personal vested interests.

This is a tragic theme of human history: an idealistic revolution falling prey to the same vices it sought to replace. Whether we are watching works of Shakespeare or the ancient Greek playwrights,

well-written and acted tragedies are powerfully cathartic. We identify our human nature on stage. It could happen to us. Crichton's novel *Disclosure* was instantly condemned by lots of p.c. folks. It reminds me of how portrayals of uncelibate priests, greedy ministers and gay rabbis in books and film were defensively and severely condemned by religious folk a generation ago. Defensiveness, it seems to me, is a sign of fragility. When p.c. can laugh at p.c., it will have accomplished its best work.

*Bob*—Actually, that was how p.c. began. It was used in jest by cutting-edge feminists to laugh at themselves. When p.c.-trends invaded the general culture, the humor was lost and p.c. became transformed into a way of punishing people whose language or behavior strayed from "party line" opinions. We're closing this section with a piece by an individual who can see both perspectives . . .

*George*— . . . besides being my favorite social commentator . . .

*Bob*—Barbara Ehrenreich is articulate and realistic, identifies and provides strategies, rather than parroting an ideology.

*George*—Her piece fits with my philosophy that in diversity training you are most effective if you can keep it light and palatable. Then, in a context of openness to learning you can invite a discussion of the more serious issues in a way that is not so emotionally loaded. Some of the things that come up in diversity work *are* hard issues to deal with, so it helps if you can laugh at yourself and some of your predicaments. Make human connections and the exchange of ideas and ideology will follow. This is one of the reasons why games for diversity training are so important. If we're too grim on the issues, we're not open to learning anything.*

*Bob*—Ehrenreich says both sides should lighten up.

---

*See page 507 for resources developed by GSI.

# Where Diversity Training Goes Wrong

by Hank Karp and Nancy Sutton (*Training Magazine*)

*Finger-pointing, white-male bashing, language-policing—they're just some of the ways to kill a good idea.*

Since the Civil Rights Act of 1964, enlightened organizations have been concerned with fairness in the workplace. That's when terms like equal-employment opportunity and affirmative action entered the business lexicon, and corporate human-resources departments took on the job of ensuring compliance with these laws.

In 1987 the Hudson Institute's report *Workforce 2000* made diversity a household word in companies across the country. The report predicted that before the turn of the century, the work force would become more female and ethnic. Many businesses are convinced they must prepare employees for the change. Hence, diversity training. Lots of it.

These training programs usually are dominated by one of two basic approaches: increasing awareness of policy or increasing sensitivity to the concerns of people in different groups than one's own.

Programs dealing with policy focus almost entirely on legal issues concerning diversity. They are designed to inform managers (primarily) about equal-employment-opportunity laws and their applications, as well as affirmative-action rules. The point of such training is to demonstrate the company's commitment to equal opportunity and ensure that managers understand why they must comply with company policy regarding diversity.

The second approach focuses on increasing the trainee's sensitivity to diversity. Often, these programs try to heighten the individual's awareness of what it's like to be misunderstood, undervalued and stereotyped at work.

The prevailing attitudes and work styles in most U.S. companies are still predominantly dictated—whether consciously or unconsciously—by white males. Consequently, a great deal of awareness training is designed specifically to sensitize the SWAM (straight, white American male) manager to the changing complexion of the work force, and to help him develop more "appropriate" and creative ways of working with his subordinates.

These diversity programs often share seven characteristics. Together, the elements add up to a deeply flawed approach. Obviously, some diversity programs do not have these seven characteristics. However, enough of them do to justify making the point that there is a different way to come at diversity training—we call it a pragmatic approach—that will avoid some of the problems that have been associated with diversity programs in general.

Here are the seven characteristics, coupled with a more pragmatic way of dealing with the problems that each one poses:

1. **The trainers are usually women or ethnic minorities.** The current tendency is to avoid having white males do diversity training. The thinking is that female or minority trainers are more effective because they likely have first-hand experience with discrimination.

   There is no question that it is useful to have a minority trainer conduct diversity training; after all, she has a perspective that comes from personal experience. If you want a group of SWAM managers to learn about what it's like to be a female member of a SWAM-dominated group, it's reasonable to have a female conduct the training.

   But single-minded adherence to this approach tends to ignore the group that's being trained. While it is important that a diversity trainer be able to create and share an empathic connection to a disadvantaged group, it's every bit as important for the trainer to connect with the trainees. The ideal would be to conduct diversity training with a two-person team, one trainer presenting a minority point of view and the other reflecting the participant group.

Naturally, it's not always possible to provide two trainers for every program. But it is essential that whoever the trainer is, he is extremely sensitive to a point of view he does not naturally understand.

This limited point of view is a problem for every trainer, even though it isn't often acknowledged. In conventional diversity-training courses, the trainer is supposed to be the expert in the field and, in theory, has conquered her own prejudices. The tendency is to look at the trainer as the model who will show us the way.

A more pragmatic approach is to recognize that no one can be entirely free of prejudice.

> If one is a SWAM (straight, white American male), then one is an oppressor, by definition, and needs to change.

Just as the SWAM trainer, while expert in technique and well-intentioned, may not be completely aware of the impact of some of his statements on female trainees, so the African-American female trainer may not be totally empathic with the Hispanic men in the class.

This is just fine. Trainers who acknowledge their own shortcomings increase their credibility as well as that of the program.

2. **The emphasis is on sensitizing the white male manager.** Many programs focus on increasing the white male manager's awareness of diversity and changing his attitudes about it. The philosophy seems to be that everyone else is OK; all we need to do is overhaul the SWAM.

A common assumption is that the SWAM manager needs diversity training most, since he'll have to do most of the attitude adjustment in the face of coming demographic changes. It is highly likely that the training groups will be composed mostly of SWAMs.

However, any demographic change in an organization is going to affect *everybody* in the organization, not just one particular segment. What's more, despite opinions and some anecdotes to the contrary, we've heard of no research indicating that any one ethnic or gender group is more sensitive to diversity needs than any other. In other words, it's just as important that a black female manager be aware of how she may be affecting a white male subordinate as it is for the white male to be aware of the impact of his behavior on her.

These observations suggest two strategies. First, audiences should be composed of mixed groups whenever possible. And second, diversity-awareness training should be a priority for all employees.

3. **The programs usually reflect a specific set of values.** Most diversity programs directly or indirectly endorse a particular philosophy of right and wrong. This leads to all sorts of pronouncements: Tolerance is good and bigotry is bad; no group is genetically or culturally superior to any other group; working together is better than working alone; loving is better than hating.

There is nothing overtly wrong with this. In fact, it's difficult to see how any diversity training can be done outside the context of a clearly stated code of values. Things go awry, however, when programs focus on changing people's attitudes, rather than dealing primarily with their behaviors.

It's one thing to opine that one set of attitudes is better than another set of attitudes. It's another to establish a set of "politically correct" views that people had better advocate if they want to do well in the program or be well thought of.

A more pragmatic approach starts with a statement of values, but also includes one crucial precept: All trainees have a right to state how they see things, in complete safety, as long as the boundaries of good taste are reasonably observed.

This precept is aimed largely at participants who hold views that are counter to the values stated at the beginning of the program. To create an environment that subtly or directly punishes a view that deviates from the trainer's or the program's values destroys the credibility of the program. It is difficult to work through diversity issues if people don't feel comfortable stating unpopular opinions.

For instance, a recent series of meetings involving trainers and consultants included a discussion of diversity training. One participant stated that he thought homosexuality was wrong. He did not wish ill upon people who were gay. He merely believed that homosexuality was wrong.

Rather than accepting his view of homosexuality, many participants tried to explain to him that his thinking was wrong and unenlightened. He grew more defensive. All that was accomplished was to make sure that this person never again would state publicly his opinions about homosexuality. There is a saying that summarizes this effect succinctly: "Just because you have silenced a man, do not think that you have converted him."

4. *Diversity awareness is the sole theme of the program.* Generally, these programs deal with nothing but the issue of diversity and/or discrimination. In this they are similar to the T-groups and sensitivity-training sessions of two decades ago, when self-awareness was the sole theme.

An individual would go off to T-Group training, become more aware of himself, then return to an organization that had not changed a bit. The usual result was that as soon as the person re-entered the organization, it was like hitting a brick wall at 35 mph. The trainee quickly adjusted to the old way of doing things.

The problem with diversity training that is focused exclusively on awareness is that it's divorced from real life. To deal with diversity out of context lets you know what is needed but rarely how it can best be accomplished.

Diversity training has the greatest impact when people who work together are trained together. Also, the training may have more impact if it encompasses more than just issues of diversity. That is, it's often more effective to deal with diversity as a component in a training program focused on another organizational need such as team-building or leadership.

This puts the training and performance emphasis on specific behaviors and their effects, rather than on "attitude adjustment." It is much easier to get positive, measurable change working with the former than with the latter.

5. *Programs are frequently guilt-driven.* Many programs try to use guilt to make SWAM managers change their attitudes. Some programs teach white males to think of themselves as "oppressors" or to think of themselves as "recovering" racists, sexists or homophobes simply because they are SWAMs. That is, their own personal attitudes, behaviors and values are of no concern. If one is a straight, white American male, then one is clearly an oppressor, by definition, and needs to change.

Certainly, there are endless examples of grave injustices done by one group to another. If there weren't, there probably would be no need for diversity training. Some of these injustices have been committed because of malice; others stem from ignorance.

These past injustices deserve to be acknowledged and respected. But then they have to be put aside. Although they serve as examples of unacceptable behavior, overemphasizing them blocks the goals of the training program.

The danger of leaving the focus too long on past injustices is that the whole thing turns into a game—a competition involving whose group has suffered the most. It quickly devolves into a whining contest, then moves into a final stage called "Get the SWAMs." This last phase allegedly is not intended to get even with the SWAMs; it's supposedly intended to let them see the effects of their behavior so they will become enlightened and never do it again.

This approach can be highly problematic. On a moral level, nobody in the training program is personally responsible for the Holocaust, the historical subjugation of women, the enslavement of Africans, or any other past injustices. On a functional level, when people assume global responsibility for everything, they don't have to take personal responsibility for anything. That is, what they may be doing that is repressive tends to get blurred or lost.

The second problem is that a historical focus locks people into the past, where nothing can be changed. It can be a frustrating, pointless exercise.

Third, a focus on injustice and guilt tends to polarize the different groups into victims and oppressors. This polarization increases resentment among groups, when the goal of diversity training ought to be to reduce it.

Finally, there will always be a certain number of SWAMs (and others) who correctly say to themselves, "But I have intentionally harmed no one." Any attempt to make these people feel guilty will only make them defensive and resistant to anything that's said.

A better approach is this:

- If salient, acknowledge that past cultural injustice has occurred.

- Recognize that nobody has cornered the pain market. Survivors of any injustice, historical or present, hurt exactly the same.

- Assume that no participant in the program intentionally wishes ill toward anyone else, based on ethnic, sexual or religious characteristics.

- Agree that each person must take full responsibility for her own actions, but for nothing else.

- Work on ways to use individual and group differences to achieve organizational objectives.

6. *How a thing is said gains more importance than what is said or intended.* "Languaging" is one of the primary tools for corrective intervention in today's diversity training. Awareness training often centers on how the misuse of words, even with no intention to cause harm, can create situations of chronic pain and loss of self-esteem.

For instance, these courses might assert that we cause pain to women when we say "chairman" rather than "chairperson," that we hurt an entire race when we use the word "black" rather than the currently preferred term "African-American," or that we insult ethnic minorities by not understanding that "Latino" and "Hispanic" are not synonymous terms. Correcting these language errors and guarding against their recurrence is a key goal of many diversity-training programs.

One of the greatest literary apologies of all time is made by Sweeney, a character created by T. S. Eliot, who says, "I'm sorry, but when I talk to you, I have to use words." It is safe to assume that most problems that are encountered at work and in the home are communicative, not substantive. Certainly it is important to attend to the way in which you say something so that what you intend to say is what is actually being heard.

But attention to language, like anything else, can be overdone. When this happens it tends to create a larger problem, rather than solving one. There are three negative effects of being prickly about language.

First, as the concern about language becomes overemphasized, some members of a minority group tend to become overly sensitive about its use. People start looking for insult or insensitivity where none was intended. If I am cast as the "oppressor" it is entirely up to me to say nothing that could possibly offend you. With the full responsibility on me, all you have to do is wait for me to make a mistake. When I do, you let me know and I try harder to make sure it never happens again—at least in theory. In fact, this kind of game-playing is not only pointless, it's tiring.

Second, when members of a minority group become hypersensitive, they tend to place the entire blame on others for being insensitive, even though they may choose to put the worst possible interpretation on an ambiguous statement. This does little to facilitate rapport among different groups.

Third, and most devastating, when we go so far out of our way to anticipate and correct possible hurtful statements before any harm has occurred, the effect is to neutralize the language itself. It destroys almost all spontaneity if people have to pick their words as though traversing a mine field. The first casualty of this overemphasis on language is usually humor; the second is clarity.

We must understand the pragmatic fact that language is important as a tool, not an objective.

One way of dealing with the language issue. at least in training, is something we picked up in a diversity program. Establish this guideline: "If at any time during the program someone says something that hurts you, interrupt with 'Ouch.' This will give you a chance to correct the situation." This approach works on several levels. First, it puts the responsibility for taking care of oneself exactly where it belongs. . . on each individual. It gives the party who has perhaps inadvertently offended someone a chance to find out why. It allows people to get on with being together, rather than having to engineer every statement. And, finally, it gives the training itself some credibility and internal consistency.

7. *The time orientation is mostly past and future.* In most programs a lot of time is devoted to looking into the historical underpinnings of the diversity problem. This could mean an exploration of the role of women in Victorian England or the Civil Rights movement of the 1960s. The avowed purpose is to study the events so that they will not be repeated and we can learn from them.

As soon as the past is probed, the focus shifts to the future. This often becomes a fantasizing exercise in how things ought to be. Little is done to deal with present reality.

With a pragmatic approach, the orientation for time and place is here and now. If the training program is going to succeed in creating more awareness and willingness by the participants to collaborate, there must be a focus on what is happening currently in the organization.

It is much more realistic to approach the diversity issue by dealing with how people are, and making it safe to work now, than it is to try to make changes from a position of how things were or should be.

A pragmatic approach to diversity training can ensure that people not only confront the sometimes painful issues that can arise during one of these workshops, but confront them in a useful way. If done right, the experience can be a helpful one for everyone. Members of minority groups will be satisfied with the results. And, believe it or not, so will SWAMs.

## About the Author

Dr. Hank B. Karp received his Ph.D. in Industrial and Organizational Psychology from Case Western Reserve University , Cleveland, Ohio. He has conducted seminars for managers in the areas of: First Line Leadership Skill Development; Power; Conflict and Resistance; Delegation; Motivation & Job Enrichment; Leadership Style & Managerial Effectiveness; Career Plateauing and Diversity.

He is a Senior Associate at ODT, Incorporated. Dr. Karp's publications include: *Personal Power: An Unorthodox Guide to Success*, available from ODT at 800-736-1293 ($24.00 includes postage and handling) and, "Handling Career Plateaus," from the *National Business Employment Weekly* (A complimentary copy is available from ODT, Inc.; send a self-addressed stamped envelope to ODT, Inc. Box 134, Amherst, MA 01004).

# The Cult of Ethnicity, Good and Bad: A Historian Argues That Multiculturalism Threatens the Ideal That Binds the U.S.

by Arthur Schlesinger Jr. (*TIME Magazine*)

The history of the world has been in great part the history of the mixing of peoples. Modern communication and transport accelerate mass migrations from one continent to another. Ethnic and racial diversity is more than ever a salient fact of the age.

But what happens when people of different origins, speaking different languages and professing different religions, inhabit the same locality and live under the same political sovereignty? Ethnic and racial conflict—far more than ideological conflict—is the explosive problem of our times.

On every side today ethnicity is breaking up nations. The Soviet Union, India, Yugoslavia, Ethiopia, are all in crisis. Ethnic tensions disturb and divide Sri Lanka, Burma, Indonesia, Iraq, Cyprus, Nigeria, Angola, Lebanon, Guyana, Trinidad—you name it. Even nations as stable and civilized as Britain and France, Belgium and Spain, face growing ethnic troubles. Is there any large multiethnic state that can be made to work?

The answer to that question has been, until recently, the United States. "No other nation," Margaret Thatcher has said, "has so successfully combined people of different races and nations within a single culture." How have Americans succeeded in pulling off this almost unprecedented trick?

We have always been a multiethnic country. Hector St. John de Crèvecoeur, who came from France in the 18th century, marveled at the astonishing diversity of the settlers—"a mixture of English, Scotch, Irish, French, Dutch, Germans, and Swedes . . . this promiscuous breed." He propounded a famous question: "What then is the American, this new man?" And he gave a famous answer: "Here individuals of all nations are melted into a new race of men." *E pluribus unum.*

The U.S. escaped the divisiveness of a multiethnic society by a brilliant solution: the creation of a brand-new national identity. The point of America was not to preserve old cultures but to forge a new, *American* culture. "By an inter-mixture with our people," President George Washington told Vice President John Adams, immigrants will "get assimilated to our customs, measures and laws: in a word, soon become one people." This was the ideal that a century later Israel Zangwill crystallized in the title of his popular 1908 play *The Melting Pot*. And no instituion was more potent in molding Crèvecoeur's "promiscuous breed" into Washington's "one people" than the American public school.

The new American nationality was inescapably English in language, ideas and institutions. The pot did not melt everybody, not even all the white immigrants; deeply bred racism put black Americans, yellow Americans, red Americans and brown Americans well outside the pale. Still, the infusion of other stocks, even of nonwhite stocks, and the experience of the New World reconfigured the British legacy and made the U.S., as we all know, a very different country from Britain.

In the 20th century, new immigration laws altered the composition of the American people, and a cult of ethnicity erupted both among non-Anglo whites and among nonwhite minorities. This had many healthy consequences. The American culture at last began to give shamefully overdue recognition to the achievements of groups subordinated and spurned during the high noon of Anglo dominance, and it began to acknowledge the great swirling world beyond Europe. Americans acquired a more complex and invigorating sense of their world—and of themselves.

But, pressed too far, the cult of ethnicity has unhealthy consequences. It gives rise, for example, to the conception of the U.S. as a nation composed not of individuals making their own choices but of inviolable ethnic and racial groups. It rejects the historic American goals of assimilation and integration. And in an excess of zeal, well-intentioned people seek to transform our system of education from a means of creating "one people" into a means of promoting, celebrating and perpetuating separate ethnic origins and identities. The balance is shifting from unum to pluribus.

That is the issue that lies behind the hullabaloo over "multiculturalism" and "political correctness," the attack on the "Eurocentric" curriculum and the rise of the notion that history and literature should be taught not as disciplines but as therapies whose function is to raise minority self-esteem. Group separatism crystallizes the differences, magnifies tensions, intensifies hostilities. Europe —the unique source of the liberating ideas of democracy, civil liberties and human rights—is portrayed as the root of all evil, and non-European cultures, their own many crimes deleted, are presented as the means of redemption.

I don't want to sound apocalyptic about these developments. Education is always in ferment, and a good thing too. The situation in our universities, I am confident, will soon right itself. But the impact of separatist pressures on our public schools is more troubling. If a Kleagle of the Ku Klux Klan wanted to use the schools to disable and handicap black Americans, he could hardly come up with anything more effective than the "Afrocentric" curriculum. And if separatist tendencies go un-

checked, the result can only be the fragmentation, resegregation and tribalization of American life.

I remain optimistic. My impression is that the historic forces driving toward "one people" have not lost their power. The eruption of ethnicity is, I believe, a rather superficial enthusiasm stirred by romantic ideologues on the one hand and by unscrupulous con men on the other: self-appointed spokesmen whose claim to represent their minority groups is carelessly accepted by the media. Most American-born members of minority groups, white or nonwhite, see themselves primarily as Americans rather than primarily as members of one or another ethnic group. A notable indicator today is the rate of intermarriage across ethnic lines, across religious lines, even (increasingly) across racial lines. "We Americans," said Theodore Roosevelt, "are children of the crucible."

The growing diversity of the American population makes the quest for unifying ideals and a common culture all the more urgent. In a world savagely rent by ethnic and racial antagonisms, the U.S. must continue as an example of how a highly differentiated society holds itself together.

## About the Author

Professor Schlesinger is the author of 14 books, including *The Age of Jackson* and *The Disuniting of America*.

## TAMING POLITICAL CORRECTNESS

It's not just the U.S. government that is made up of a set of checks and balances. The philosophy seems to be resident in the minds of U.S. Americans and their sense of democracy and fair play, whether the tyrant is a foreign dictator or an "ism" run rampant.

The *Investor's Business Daily* newspaper cited this story about the ΦΚΣ fraternity at the University of California, Riverside as a case in point.[1]

- "The house had advertised during September rush week for a 'South of the Border Fiesta' party, distributing T-shirts that a radical nationwide Hispanic student group, MEChA (Chicano Student Movement of Aztlan), claimed offensively stereotyped Hispanics.
- "Though more than one-third of the fraternity's 40 members were Hispanic—including the two who designed the shirts—MEChA complained to the school's administration.
- "In response, school officials required each member of Phi Kappa Sigma to perform at least 16 hours of service in a Latino community, and attend two multicultural seminars. The fraternity also had to write formal letters of apology to MEChA and to all fraternities and sororities on the campus.
- "'But MEChA still wasn't satisfied, and convinced the school's assistant vice chancellor, Vincent Del Pizzo, to dissolve the chapter for at least three years.
- "That's when the fraternity decided to sue. Howard[2] acted decisively on their behalf, informing the university that if it lost, it would owe him about $200,000 in attorney's fees, even though he was handling the case on a pro-bono basis.
- "In an out-of-court settlement, university officials had to attend a First Amendment seminar to be exempt from financial liability."

We hope that both parties of this academic community learned something in the process—the fraternity about valuing diversity, and the administration about respect for constitutional freedoms.

---

[1] Horowitz, Carl, "Taming Political Correctness," *Los Angeles Times,* May 16, 1994.
[2] John Howard is an attorney, and founder of the Individual Rights Foundation, a L.A.-based non-profit.

From the book THATCH...Featuring Politically Correct Person, by Jeff Shesol
(Vintage; April, 1991)

271

# Free Speech Under Assault: Remarks at the University of Michigan Commencement Ceremony

by President George Bush

Ironically, on the 200th anniversary of our Bill of Rights, we find free speech under assault throughout the United States, including on some college campuses. The notion of political correctness has ignited controversy across the land. And although the movement arises from the laudable desire to sweep away the debris of racism and sexism and hatred, it replaces old prejudice with new ones. It declares certain topics off-limits, certain expression off-limits, even certain gestures off-limits.

What began as a crusade for civility has soured into a cause of conflict and even censorship. Disputants treat sheer force—getting their foes punished or expelled, for instance—as a substitute for the power of ideas.

Throughout history, attempts to micromanage casual conversation have only incited distrust. They have invited people to look for an insult in every word, gesture, action. And in their own Orwellian way, crusades that demand correct behavior crush diversity in the name of diversity.

We all should be alarmed at the rise of intolerance in our land and by the growing tendency to use intimidation rather than reason in settling disputes. Neighbors who disagree no longer settle matters over a cup of coffee. They hire lawyers, and they go to court. And political extremists roam the land, abusing the privilege of free speech, setting citizens against one another on the basis of their class or race.

But, you see, such bullying is outrageous. It's not worthy of a great nation grounded in the values of tolerance and respect. So, let us fight back against the boring politics of division and derision. Let's trust our friends and colleagues to respond to reason. As Americans we must use our persuasive powers to conquer bigotry once and for all. And I remind myself a lot of this: We must conquer the temptation to assign bad motives to people who disagree with us.

If we hope to make full use of the optimism I discussed earlier, men and women must feel free to speak their hearts and minds. We must build a society in which people can join in common cause without having to surrender their identities.

You can lead the way. Share your thoughts and your experiences and your hopes and your frustrations. Defend others' rights to speak. And if harmony be our goal, let's pursue harmony, not inquisition.

—University of Michigan, May 4, 1991

George Bush's statements, excerpted from "Remarks at the University of Michigan Commencement Ceremony in Ann Arbor, May 4, 1991," were published in the *Weekly Compilation of Presidential Documents*, vol. 27, no. 19, May 13, 1991.

## PLURALISM

"Pluralism," the American philosopher John Dewey insisted early in this century, "is the greatest philosophical idea of our times." But he recognized that it was also the greatest problem of our times: "How are we going to make the most of the new values we set on variety, difference, and individuality—how are we going to realize their possibilities in every field, and at the same time not sacrifice that plurality to the cooperation we need so much?" It has the feel of a scholastic conundrum: How can we negotiate between the one and the many?

Today, the mindless celebration of difference has proven as untenable as that bygone model of monochrome homogeneity. If there is an equilibrium to be struck, there's no guarantee we will ever arrive at it. The worst mistake we can make, however, is not to try.

Henry Louis Gates, Jr.
Chairman of the Afro-American Studies Department and
Professor of English at Harvard University
(*Boston Globe Magazine* 10/13/91)

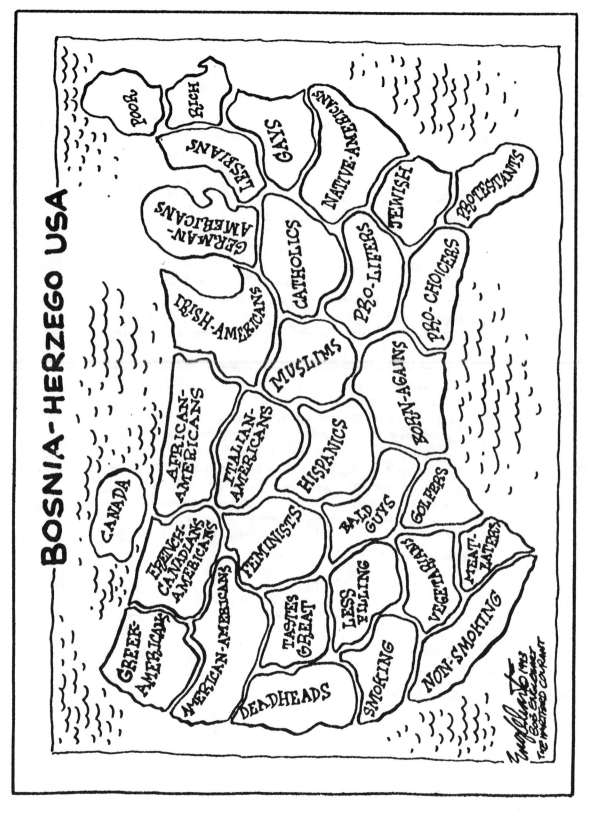

Reprinted with permission of Bob Englehart. *The Hartford Courant.*

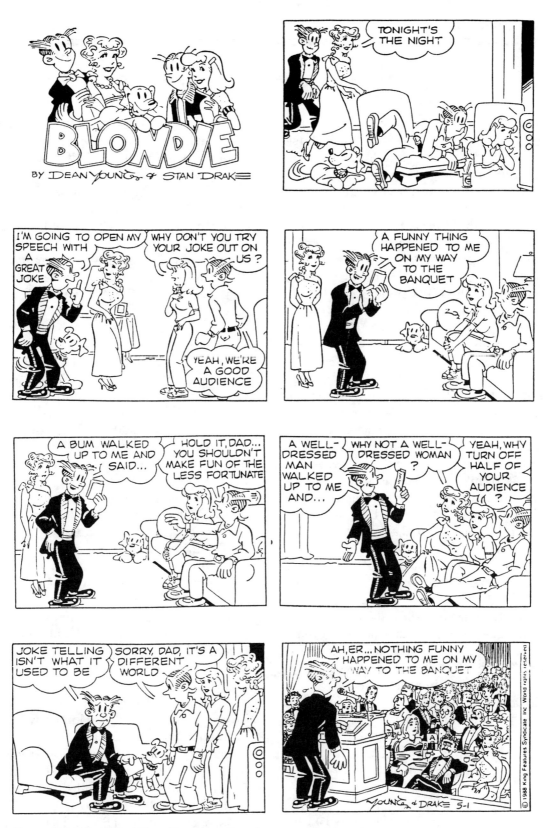

# P.C. in Corporate America

by Leon McKinney (*The Orange County Register*)

*Social Issues: A California firm 'rightsizes' while its 'diversity committee' fiddles.*

"Managing workforce diversity" to prepare for 21st-century competition is a big issue in the business community. However, many liberals see diversity and multiculturalism programs as a way to advance political agendas such as race and gender quotas. Consider the example of McDonnell Douglas Aerospace in Huntington Beach.

For eleven years I worked on advanced space and military systems at McDonnell Douglas. The last two years were rough: The post-Cold War build-down has slashed Pentagon R & D and procurement, with almost no new projects on the horizon; the company's other traditional customer, NASA, is using its funding to keep its people employed, dribbling out a few dollars to contractors.

McDonnell Douglas is suffering a drastic "rightsizing" (management-guru jargon for laying people off). After a great-aunt left a sizeable estate to myself and two cousins, I began thinking about leaving McDonnell Douglas and the aerospace industry to start my own business; McDonnell Douglas pre-empted my decision, giving me a pink slip the Friday before Memorial Day last year. Fortunately, the estate provided a financial cushion for several years.

Those without such luck are a captive audience for the social engineering being practiced by McDonnell Douglas and many other firms.

McDonnell Douglas in California has a "Diversity Subcommittee," run by what one senior manager at Huntington Beach dryly describes as the "glass ceiling" gang—female managers who apparently think the most important issue facing McDonnell Douglas isn't lack of new business but a perceived "glass ceiling" blocking women from promotions.

Last June McDonnell Douglas sent hundreds of employees to a seminar, "Diversity in Corporate America," put on by Gil Scott from Xerox, "diversity consultant," Julie O'Mara, and Dr. Melvin Hall from the University of California, Irvine. I talked to 10 white male engineers who attended the seminar and complained it was egregious white-male bashing, but shied away from confronting upper management—"It wouldn't make a difference," "I can't risk my job."

McDonnell Douglas's "diversity intervention plan" was presented. Near-term goals include managers being "held accountable for achieving diversity objectives" (affirmative-action quotas) and attending "diversity training" on their personal time.

Seminar handouts emphasize that white males "just don't get it," and need to be re-educated; a top priority is recruiting and promoting women and "people of color." When asked how McDonnell Douglas could attain "the right diversity mix" during wholesale layoffs, Dr. Hall replied that once during staff reductions, he laid off more people than necessary, resulting in "slush funds" that gave him flexibility to maintain his "diversity initiative." Evidently laying off qualified people to fulfill quotas was a fine thing.

During my last week at McDonnell Douglas I met with Suzanne Browning, the company's director of general services and one of the leaders of the Diversity Subcommittee. I relayed the engineers' reactions and commented that the seminar's costs probably exceeded $200,000, at a time when company money for proposals to win new work was almost impossible to get. I may as well have talked to a brick wall; Ms. Browning "just didn't get it."

McDonnell Douglas has gone beyond holding diversity seminars. It has joined with the National Women's Political Caucus to "encourage female employees to enter the political arena," according to the Aug. 2, 1993, issue of *Business Week*. The Caucus claims to be "multi-partisan," but 88 percent of candidates it supported in 1992 were Democrats, such as Barbara Boxer, Dianne Feinstein, and Carol Mosely Braun. Support for abortion and the

Reprinted from *The Orange County Register* (February 13, 1994).

Equal Rights Amendment is a litmus test for women seeking endorsement and campaign contributions.

Last July McDonnell Douglas sponsored a NWPC luncheon in Los Angeles for Attorney General Janet Reno. McDonnell Douglas women also attended a political training session.

I called a member of John McDonnell's executive staff in St. Louis and asked whether sponsoring diversity seminars, NWPC luncheons, and political action training sessions was a good use of scarce company resources during tough times. The diversity police had trained him well: "Are you saying diversity is a bad thing?" he asked.

Insisting on being unnamed, he claimed the *Business Week* article was "worth a million bucks" to McDonnell Douglas, but couldn't break that down for me. The Clinton administration now views the company as "a role model for corporations." Ron Dellums, chairman of the House Armed Services Committee—"a black man," Mr. Executive Staff pointed out—also likes McDonnell Douglas. Secretary of Commerce Ron Brown—another "black man"—"leveraged significant business for McDonnell Douglas in Malaysia and Saudi Arabia."

He implied this happy situation has come about thanks to McDonnell Douglas's diversity and women's programs. Dellums is a hard-left liberal, but he's not impressed by kow-towing. Ron Brown's unsavory clientele for his lobbying business indicates the color he cares most about is green.

Mr. Executive Staff said "white male engineers will be a minority in the engineering work place by the next decade." Of course they will if you keep laying them off to pay for sending women and minorities to diversity seminars and Running for Office 101.

Bonnie Soodik, vice president of quality systems and also on the Diversity Subcommittee, responded to my criticism of McDonnell Douglas's policies with "you sound like an angry white male, upset because he lost his job." Well, perhaps.

But women and minorities benefiting from special programs and privileges who dismiss white males' grievances risk setting themselves up for a nasty surprise. If we end up with workplaces where everyone is angry because they perceive they're being treated unfairly, we're in for a series of backlashes as first one group, then another, then still another, gets its pound of flesh. This will cripple American business. Perhaps that's what liberals want.

# Diversity Is Not a Virtue

by Mark Helprin (*Wall Street Journal*)

Of all the divisions in the politics of the Western world the clearest and most consequential are those between corporate or communal rights and the rights of the individual. Though other questions may be all consuming, they are often restatements of this fundamental issue.

Socialists steadfastly champion central planning despite its monotonous failures because they cannot abide individual liberty even if it accomplishes their goals of material advancement. And proponents of the free market who rest their case upon its performance forget that ultimately they are its advocates not because of its operational superiorities but because it is a necessary precondition of free society.

A dispassionate look at the 20th century reveals amid the smoke of distant battles that the great alliances were ultimately what our propagandists held them to be. For all its pathos, the First World War was a struggle between liberal democracy and a state system in which legitimacy flowed merely from the success of executive action. In the Second World War the conflict between raw state power and the idea of individual rights was amplified by fascist enthusiasm for corporate rights, in which group identity was the basis not just of monstrous systems of government but of death warrants for whole peoples. The West then engaged the Soviet Bloc in a half century proxy war, with millions of casualties, over the same division.

Though the Soviet apparatus disintegrated, the communalist ideal escaped. It is still with us, harbored by the old guard in the East and the intellectual elites of the West who, now that their enthusiasms seem no longer a matter of national betrayal, are more fervent than ever.

## A Dangerous Principle

At the founding of the nation, in the Civil War, and in the authentic struggle for civil rights, the corporatist idea was found wanting and the rights of the individual affirmed. Once again we are faced with the same choices but today the churches, the president, the universities and the press endorse rather than condemn the idea that we are most importantly representatives of a class, a tribe, or a race and that we treat others and expect to be treated as such.

They do so to make amends and to "celebrate diversity," without concern that the recipients of their largesse may not themselves have been wronged. As they see it, they need only find people of the same type, and the deed is done. And what amends! To atone for having wrongly judged people by race, they will now rightly judge people by race. To atone for segregated accommodations, they offer separate dormitories. To atone for having said "colored people," they say "people of color." What they do now is as wrong as it once was—not merely because of the effect, but because of the dangerous principle that individuals do not transcend the accidents of birth.

Almost every scholastic body in the country now considers itself a kind of Congress of Vienna with the special mission of making its students aware of race and ethnicity. Though they are forced to dwell on half a dozen categories, told that this is diversity, the reduction of 250 million individuals to a handful of racial and ethnic classifications is not a recognition of differences but their brutal suppression. This is a triumph of the academic impulse to classify, a triumph of the bureaucratic need to categorize, a triumph of reductionism, and a triumph of utilitarianism. But it is a defeat for the human spirit.

A long way from equal justice under law are the debit or credit now furiously assigned to membership in various communities; the federal laws that in requiring complex racial assessments embarrassingly parallel Hitler's Aryan Decree; the virtual *numerus clausus* in the American university, this time directed against Asians; the regrowth of racial segregation; and the computerized homelands of Congressional redistricting.

Many well-meaning liberals now deal carelessly with the stock and trade of Nazism and apartheid, and what they advocate is racism plain and stupid, no different from the laziness of mind and deficiency of spirit of the old-time segregationist—"There goes a white one, there goes a black one, that one's an octoroon."

They are comfortable with what they once abhorred, because it is part of the good work of promoting communal rights, and in the past few years they have expanded their purview with the voraciousness they attribute to corporate raiders. Accelerating far beyond the relatively simple matter of race, they have included absolutely everyone in their systems of grievance, publicity, manipulation, and reward.

The sucking sound (the phrase is Melville's) is that of the entire population disappearing into a communal maelstrom. No longer is the family supposed to be the fundamental unit of society. The wife and female children owe their allegiance to womanhood. The children's loyalties lie not with their oppressive parents, but with the class interests of children. If one of them is adopted he must cleave to his ethnic or racial group, unless she is a girl, whereupon she may be a woman first. Even the dog has a union card, and if he feels abused will summon the people of animal rights.

This damage having been done, the next step is the promotion of diversity as a political value, and the institutional proclamation of ethnic differences ("We're so proud to have Melanie in our class, because she's an Eskimo"). Even were this somehow to further diversity, neither diversity nor unity are virtues, and should be left to find their own balance without stilted prodding. Freezing acculturation to keep each contributing element pristine would have been impossible even in the age of steam, much less now, when things change faster than we can register. Why then the useless, shallow and patronizing acclaim for the great tributaries of this new stream that goes its own way and will not be made to back up? Why the interminable school programs in which parents are forced to listen as their hostage children sing Indonesian Christmas carols? Am I really a European-American? The hell I am.

All the hyphenation and saccharine praise of differences (in which any politically useful subdivision becomes a "culture") is to organize and divide the otherwise unmanageable, unplannable chaos of a society of individuals, and thus augment the power of the state. When you want to control a complex social situation the first thing you do is make categories and award privileges. But, as in any statist system, for every entitlement there is an equal and opposite obligation. When, in the flush of class action, entitlements are compassionately granted to groups, obligations are cruelly drawn from individuals. Over all, the state is the decisive arbiter, its power increasing as it manufactures new rights and new relations, shifting them in an ever changing shell game in which the players have the illusion that they are winning but it is the dealer who goes home with the money.

Those who see individualism as selfishness and narcissism for which the only remedy is state planning and intervention are in full agreement with Mussolini, a bit of a narcissist himself, who said (as if anticipating Ira Magaziner) "The more complicated the forms assumed by civilization, the more restricted the freedom of the individual must become." Bringing rights and powers over the bridge of tribe and class into the hands of government does not diminish world narcissism, it merely concentrates it in the people who think the rest of us should improve our characters by letting them tell us what to do.

## A Portent of Fascism

They always mean well. Communalists, multiculturalists, the politically correct always want to do good, but they always, always require power to do so, and as their appetite for doing good is limitless, so is their capacity for acquiring power. Intent, as history shows, is a poor bulwark against despotism, and as a nation we have never failed to understand this, rightly refusing to accept either a benign despotism or one that is pernicious, for at heart they are the same.

If I have not done so already, let me make myself absolutely clear. The contemporary passion to classify and divide the American people is a portent of fascism both red and black. Where the communal approach rules (Yugoslavia, the Middle East, Northern Ireland, Soviet Central Asia, Hitler's Germany, Stalin's Russia) blood flows and no one is treated fairly. We, on the other hand, have fought many times for the sake of being apprehended not as classes of people but as individual souls.

Six generations ago, my forebears left Russia after the Kishinev Pogrom, left behind the weight of a thousand years, for a future that they thought sparkled and shone like a diamond, because it was fair, because the great, euphoric gift of America—its essential condition, its clarity, its purity, and its decency—was that it took them for what they were, just as God would, looking past the accidents of birth and the complications of history.

I cannot imagine that we would willingly leave this behind, and I, for one, will not.

## About the Author

Mr. Helprin, a novelist, is a contributing editor of the *Wall Street Journal*. This is adapted from a speech he delivered 11/21/94 at the Ethics and Public Policy Center in Washington.

# BLOOM COUNTY

## BY BERKE BREATHED

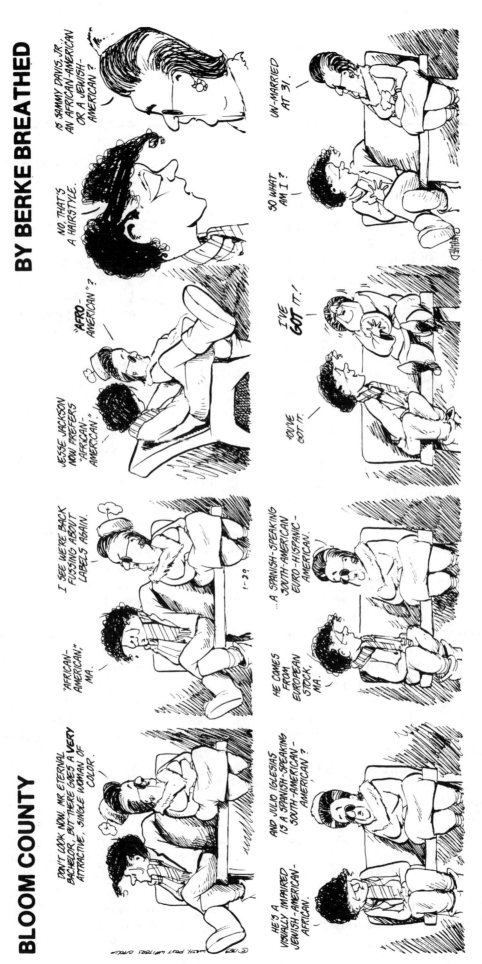

# The Diverse Workforce

by John Cowan (*OD Practitioner*)

*"The first piece of nonsense is that our diverse workforce will create a competitive advantage."*

Nonsense always annoys me. Gramma Cowan used to spit that word out in bold type with triple exclamation points when I would feed her half-baked boyish opinion. And on St. Patrick's Day, the day on which all Irish are to glory in the wonders of the old sod, Liza Feeney Cowan would mutter through the day, her ears assaulted by Irish songs, Irish jokes, Irish green, Irish eloquence, Irish heritage. And to every Irish hyperbole thrust in front of her ancient, but very blue, Irish eyes she would snap, Nonsense! As a true daughter of Erin she had both the understanding of the Irish experience to recognize that the popular snapshot was out of focus, and the license to say what she thought.

I feel in a similar position on the topic of the Diverse Workforce. Because of the way my mind is wired I have never belonged in any group with which I have been associated. Any money I have earned has come to me because people who do belong have had the decency, and I might add, the good sense, to value me for the different thing I had to offer. Therefore, I favor diversity, and understand the experience of being diverse, and have some license to say what I think. Of course, my experience is not the same as that of a person who belongs to an identifiable minority. Perhaps it is comparable. Certainly it is analogous.

What I think is that some royal nonsense is preached in the name of diversity.

The first piece of nonsense is that our diverse workforce will create a competitive advantage. Productivity and quality are improved by conformity, not diversity. Statistical Process Control charts reward conformity and send off alarm bells when they record diversity. The Japanese have taught us this. The quality circle as developed by them is a group of people from the same culture, who think in the same models, who have ferocious loyalty to the same company, whose lives are dependent on one corporation for everything from the paycheck to, in some cases, the dormitory bed they sleep in, whose future is tied to being valued by one ho-mogenous group of executives, who hate diversity. It is a very efficient way to do business. A terrible way to live in my estimate, but a most effective way to beat the pants off a bunch of people concerned about individual differences. The only improvement we will get in productivity by valuing differences is that since our workforce is becoming more diverse we better figure out how to live with it, or we will really be in trouble.

The second piece of nonsense is that an individual should suffer no penalty for being diverse. That is not the way the human race works. I admit I learned this lesson only slowly, but I have discovered that if I am true to my own wiring I will not get a seat on the executive corridor. Gramma used to grin at me, with ironic humor, when I discovered the negative consequences of my decisions. "You pay your money, and you make your choice," she said. If you want a balanced life, the privilege of being feminine, your ethnic habits, you will pay. If you want to achieve corporate power, find out how the game is played by those who are naturally good at it and play it. You won't be the first woman, or person of color, or poet to do so. And I see nothing wrong with doing that. You get a different reward, and you pay a different price. To think that behaving in diverse ways does not have negative consequences is naive. To know that the negative consequences are there and still choose to live out your diversity for the good of your soul or the good of the race is courageous.

The third piece of nonsense is that this centripetal syndrome was invented by the white male business community. Nonsense! It is endemic to the human race. I would rather risk telling a group of white males that I find them dull and uncreative than tell a group of feminists any opinion I have that does not fit their party line. When the day comes that the executive corridors are peopled with color, and whirling skirts, and wheel chairs, I do not know what the new norms will be that the diverse person will be fried for violating, but I do know that these norms will exist. What terrifies me is that some of the groups clamoring for influence in the boardroom seem less open to differences than those they intend to replace. I pray that I am either wrong or that this is a temporary phenomenon brought on by their justifiable anger at being oppressed and impotent.

While I feel a lot of nonsense is spoken in the name of the diverse workforce, I await the day of its coming. Liza Feeney Cowan loved the Irish and I will love color, and dresses, and differences in the corporate hall as I love standing in line at Highland High School, with parents from several races united in the common anxiety of parent-teacher conferences. I hope that some of the new executives will still want to hear a different idea than whatever the new gospel is, because I am fairly sure it will still be on the edge, not quite belonging, hoping to make a buck by lobbing one in there.

## About the Author

John Cowan is an independent organization development consultant living in St. Paul, Minnesota. This article originally appeared in 'A Jotting from John,' a newsletter for John Cowan's clients and friends. It was reprinted in the *OD Practitioner* in June, 1991 along with the following two responses.

# Different Perspectives: A Response to John Cowan's Article

by Jeanne Cherbeneau

I appreciate John Cowan's courage and forthrightness in challenging "popular opinion" and current theses regarding the "value" of a diverse workforce. In fact, in most of his points I find a good measure of truth and consistency with my experience in working with clients in the area of valuing and managing workforce diversity. But as his Gramma Cowan would say, I find his conclusions *Nonsense!*

*John's conclusion #1:* "The first piece of royal nonsense is that our diverse workforce will create a competitive advantage." I believe it is true, as John points out, that what most traditional organizations value *is* conformity and *is* "sameness." It sounds nice, it sounds modern, it sounds liberal and generous to say one values difference. But for the most part, in traditional white male-dominated organizations, the truth is that difference is experienced as threatening, inferior and not conducive to maintaining control over either the workforce or the organization's products or services. Diversity generally is neither welcomed nor enthusiastically embraced.

Most significant efforts or changes in areas of Affirmative Action, Equal Employment opportunity or valuing diversity are primarily the result of legal, regulatory, economic or social pressure. Diversity in the workforce today simply is a fact and a consequent force to be reckoned with, i.e., it is another significant pressure that is impossible to ignore, at least not if an organization wants to survive into the next century. Nonetheless, resistance to diversity does not justify John's conclusion that productivity and quality are improved by conformity, not diversity. Nor is it justified to assume that valuing and managing diversity well means no, or lower, standards, whether they are quality, performance or productivity standards.

Contrary to John's conclusion that managing diversity well is not a competitive advantage, many organizations in fact are discovering a great deal of benefit. The most obvious advantage is that an organization riddled with interpersonal conflicts and embittered, resentful, angry and disenfranchised employees is hardly positioned for success. The organization that manages differences well, i.e., creates an environment where people feel valued and have real opportunities to develop and show their stuff, is certainly in a more competitive position than those organizations who do not utilize their human resources and manage diversity well.

Additionally, it is difficult to support the position that conformity and dependency in the United States are effective means to gain a competitive advantage or, as John states, "to beat the pants off a bunch of people concerned about individual differences." Where is John's evidence for that conclusion? O.D. theory and methodology are based on a significant body of research, as well as experience, that go well beyond one's personal beliefs and values. And there is plenty of evidence that companies who have effectively involved and tapped the knowledge, experience and ideas of all levels of employees in problem-solving and innovation, have, in fact, increased productivity, quality and innovation in products, services and ways of doing business. Clearly it is more than just "learning to live with it." It is learning to benefit and make the best from it. Any production or marketing manager can assure any doubting Thomases (or Cowans) that in today's marketplace it is essential to have the input of a workforce that is knowledgeable about the organization's consumer or client. The increasingly diverse workforce, after all, reflects the swelling numbers and resultant power of the ever-growing diverse consumer/client population.

Options from which consumers can make choices about what they buy or where or with whom they do business also have expanded. Factors which can be utilized as criteria for making choices now include 1) the degree to which one's own preferences or needs are met by an organization's products or services, and 2) one's commitment to patronize organizations which are comprised of diverse employees and/or actively "socially responsible" in one form or another. Indeed, competition has never been more keen or challenging and employee diversity clearly constitutes a significant advantage.

*John's conclusion #2:* "The second piece of nonsense is that an individual should suffer no penalty for being diverse." Since John used the word "should," I understand that to be a value judgment, i.e., what is fair or right, as opposed to

what tends to happen, right or wrong. So if that is nonsense, is John saying people should suffer?

As John's Gramma already pointed out to him, there is a cost or penalty and, presumably, a benefit to any choice one makes. But we each define what is, for us, a cost and a benefit. If you consider it desirable to "get a seat on the executive corridor" then by definition that is your benefit. Not everyone considers that a benefit, so if they don't get it, they suffer no penalty or cost. If you value whatever it is that makes you different, then expressing that difference is your benefit.

In John's case, he implies that whatever it is that makes him different or unacceptable/unbelonging to any group with which he has been associated, is by choice. Many people do not have that luxury—they are who they are by virtue of birth. Their choice is either to be who they are or to attempt to downplay it. To downplay who you are, to feel like you must hide a part of you in order to be acceptable, seems a far more painful choice (penalty) than to go with your difference and optimize its value. Yes, there are tradeoffs and it is admirable and courageous to live out your diversity, especially if you can do it with great aplomb. (Embittered people have rarely gone down in history as leaders of long-lasting effect, which is not to say that some of the things angry or embittered people have done have not made a significant contribution to eventual long-term change for good.)

*John's conclusion #3:* That it is nonsense that penalizing people for being different "was invented by the white male business community." I agree wholeheartedly. The white male business community has just been more visible by virtue of its predominance in business generally. On the other hand I wonder who John's been listening to, as I have not heard anyone—women, people of color, or others who are defined as "different"—make a claim that they are immune from the malady of self-importance and self-interest at the expense of others, or from rejecting others who present a difference that appears threatening in its nonconformance. History itself has demonstrated repeatedly that in the long run, the "downtrodden" who have risen up and taken over eventually become like their oppressors, behaving in much the same self-interested way as those they had overthrown.

Dominance of one (individual, group, organization, nation) over the other, by its very nature, has built into it the assumption that one will protect one's interests at the cost of others. It takes great consciousness, will, courage, and sometimes sacrifice to hold onto a different value set—a value set that strives for "partnership" with others and "win, win" problem resolution. I can't resist at least noting here Riane Eisler's, *The Chalice and the Blade*, and Eisler's and her husband David Loye's book, *The Partnership Way.* Their treatment of the notion, and historical evidence, of a time when "human nature" and human societies were peaceful, equalitarian, non-hierarchial, and were flourishing at high levels of technical and cultural development, presents a dramatically different picture from today's experience and assumptions about what constitutes "human nature" and the natural order of things.

Finally, John attributes any money he has earned to "people who do belong," and who "have had the decency—and good sense to value him for the different thing" he had to offer. Many of us who specifically work in the area of valuing and managing the diverse workforce do so in hopes that some day our work might result in an increase in the number of executives and managers in organizations (be they male or female, white or people of color, or of varying ethnic or religious backgrounds) who are "decent" and do "have the sense" to value "a different idea" as well as different people. Right now, the odds may be against many of us who are considered or consider ourselves different. Why not do what we can to lower those odds?

## About the Author

Jeanne Cherbeneau, Ph.D., is President of Cherbeneau and Associates, a change management organization development and workplace diversity consulting firm located in Berkeley, California. Cherbeneau and Associates specializes in organizational change management and designing successful efforts to enhance the valuing, productivity, and satisfaction of diverse workforces. Organizations served vary in size, stage of development, and industry.

Dr. Cherbeneau's experience includes 30 years as a manager and consultant and 12 years as a National OD Network Board Director. Publications include *The Promise of Diversity*, Irwin Professional Publishing/NTL (1994), and *Values and Ethics in Organization Development*, Jossey-Bass (1990). She can be reached at: Cherbeneau and Associates, 250 Yale Avenue, Berkeley, CA 94708; Phone: (510) 524-3073; Fax: same.

# Different Perspectives: A Response to John Cowan's Article

by Judith Hoy

Diversity, by other names, has been around my whole lifetime.

Thirty-five years ago when I wrote a letter to President Eisenhower telling him I supported the recently passed and controversial civil rights legislation, "diversity" wasn't used to describe our population. We were still a melting pot (although sociologists were starting to think in terms of a stew where flavors mingled but remained distinct, rather than a pot where things melted together into something new).

Twenty years ago, when I left university life for consulting in business, diversity meant differences between men and women at work. But we still weren't calling it diversity (to some it was consciousness raising, feminism, bra burning, and worse).

Ten years ago I began research on women and work. The issue in the workplace and our society was equal opportunity for women, Hispanics, and African-Americans. Somewhere during the past decade, differences became known as diversity and the concept expanded to include all of the things that differentiate groups of people: skin color, age, ethnicity, physical abilities, religious preferences, sexual choice. One can also add socioeconomic class.

A primary flaw in John Cowan's article is that he does not define diversity except by referring to his own personal experience of feeling himself to be an outsider. He claims that because he believes he has never belonged to any group with which he has been associated, diversity belongs to everyone and hence, no one. He's not alone. The recognition that North Americans are not solely of Northern European descent with white skin has come slowly to our public consciousness. But, since Cowan doesn't define diversity, let us, for argument's sake, use the one offered above.

Yes, indeed, we have a diverse workforce. With this definition in mind, Cowan's arguments (or are they Granny Cowan's?) are specious. But, for the sake of inquiry, let's take a look at the arguments he raises.

First, will a diverse workforce create a competitive advantage? No, says John, because conformity, as measured by statistical process control charts and developed in quality circles, is really what creates the competitive advantage. First off, let's agree that a diverse workforce and variance in production or processing are not the same thing. The former has to do with a society of people made up of many different ethnicities, religious beliefs, sexual preferences, skin colors, and, physical abilities; the latter has to do with the anomaly, the odd-ball, the widget that doesn't fit the mold. But, for argument's sake, let's discuss quality and the use of statistical process control in relation to Northern America's diverse workforce.

In describing the quality circle as taught to us by the Japanese, Cowan highlights the homogeneity of the Japanese workforce and their loyalty to common goals as instrumental to their success. These factors, he says, are what have given the competitive advantage to Japan. Let's dispense with homogeneity of the Japanese workforce first. Yes, most of the people working in Japan are Japanese. But that's where the homogeneity ends. There are as many individual differences to be found there as here in North America. Surely we have more skin colors. But when it comes to religious differences, socioeconomic differences, and age differences which lead to value differences, the workforce in Japan has its share of diversity. And, from recent reporting about the changing attitudes of young Japanese workers, it is not safe to assume a strong set of shared values exists and motivates the workforce.

What factors do lead to successful quality programs in the US? They are successful because people from different perspectives hash out the how-to's and design features. They find problems, work out the differences, and suggest solutions. To exclude an African-American chemical engineer, a hearing impaired biochemist, or a female statistician or minimize the significance of their contributions because of skin color, physical ability, or sex certainly puts us at a competitive disadvantage. And, these exclusions take place.

If, in these United States, we are to achieve a competitive advantage, it will certainly come about by wise use of all of the country's resources. Our resources are not inferior and if they are not well used, I believe it is not a matter of individual differences being lauded over group efforts or group goals. Individual perspectives brought to a group, whether representing an ethnic minority or a scientific point of view, can only strengthen decisions and solutions.

In regard to John's second point, it surely is true that from the hallways of our public schools to the boardrooms of our corporations, a price is exacted for being different from the "main stream." Is that fair? No. Should it continue? No. Is society, the labor market, American industry, better for the penalty system? No.

Cowan's third argument is that people believe that the central force in perpetuating sexism, ageism, disability-ism, and any other discrimination, is the white male business community. No, others share in perpetuating discrimination. A recent issue of *Ms. Magazine* included an article on women members of the Ku Klux Klan and other hate groups. Most of us know women who oppose feminism. Most of us know, or know of, African-Americans who hate other African-Americans or Christians who can't tolerate other Christians; the list can go on. Innumerable examples of exclusion are to be found. Groucho Marx added yet another

category of exclusivity when he discussed clubs to which he wanted to belong—only those which wouldn't have him as a member. So, it's not only white male businessmen who fuel the fires of discrimination. But when it comes to having a share in the financial rewards of work, growing professionally, and contributing to the competitive advantage, the gate-keepers of our boardrooms play a major role in doling out the goodies. And, as John notes, there is little diversity.

## About the Author

Dr. Judith Hoy has over twenty years of experience consulting to managers and executives on managing change and in designing and leading management development programs. Her current work focuses on consulting on team development, coaching senior managers, and working with large system change projects. In addition, Judy has developed courses on managing change to help managers and executives deal with the changes involved in mergers, down-sizing, and changes in business strategy.

Among her recent clients are: American Management Association, Bell Labs, Bank LEUMI, Coopers and Lybrand, Episcopal Diocese of New York, Physicians Health Services, Praxair Inc., and NYNEX Science and Technology. Dr. Hoy is an elected member and current Chair of the Board of Trustees of the National Organization Development Network. She can be reached at: 39B Mill Plain Road, Ste. 291, Danbury, CT 06811, Phone: (203) 790-1228, Fax: (203) 790-1228.

# Teach Diversity with a Smile

by Barbara Ehrenreich (*TIME Magazine*)

Something had to replace the threat of communism, and at last a workable substitute is at hand. "Multiculturalism," as the new menace is known, has been denounced in the media recently as the new McCarthyism, the new fundamentalism, even the new totalitarianism—take your choice. According to its critics, who include a flock of tenured conservative scholars, multiculturalism aims to toss out what it sees as the Eurocentric bias in education and replace Plato with Ntozake Shange and traditional math with the Yoruba number system. And that's just the beginning. The Jacobeans of the multiculturalist movement, who are described derisively as P.C., or politically correct, are said to have launched a campus reign of terror against those who slip and innocently say "freshman" instead of "freshperson," "Indian" instead of "Native American" or, may the Goddess forgive them, "disabled" instead of "differently abled."

So you can see what is at stake here: freedom of speech, freedom of thought, Western civilization and a great many professorial egos. But before we get carried away by the mounting backlash against multiculturalism, we ought to reflect for a moment on the system that the P.C. people aim to replace. I know all about it: in fact it's just about all I do know, since I—along with so many educated white people of my generation—was a victim of monoculturalism.

American history, as it was taught to us, began with Columbus' "discovery" of an apparently unnamed, unpeopled America, and moved on to the Pilgrims serving pumpkin pie to a handful of grateful red-skinned folks. College expanded our horizons with courses called Humanities or sometimes Civ, which introduced us to a line of thought that started with Homer, worked its way through Rabelais and reached a poignant climax in the pensees of Matthew Arnold. Graduate students wrote dissertations on what long-dead men had thought of Chaucer's verse or Shakespeare's dramas; foreign languages meant French or German.

If there had been high technology in ancient China, kingdoms in black Africa or women anywhere, at any time, doing anything worth noticing, we did not know it, nor did anyone think to tell us.

Our families and neighborhoods reinforced the dogma of monoculturalism. In our heads, most of us '50s teenagers carried around a social map that was about as useful as the chart that guided Columbus to the "Indies." There were "Negroes," "whites" and "Orientals," the latter meaning Chinese and "Japs." Of religions, only three were known—Protestant, Catholic and Jewish—and not much was known about the last two types. The only remaining human categories were husbands and wives, and that was all the diversity the monocultural world could handle. Gays, lesbians, Buddhists, Muslims, Malaysians, Mormons, etc. were simply off the map.

So I applaud—with one hand, anyway—the multiculturalist goal of preparing us all for a wider world. The other hand is tapping its fingers impatiently, because the critics are right about one thing: when advocates of multiculturalism adopt the haughty stance of political correctness, they quickly descend to silliness or worse. It's obnoxious, for example, to rely on university administrations to enforce P.C. standards of verbal inoffensiveness. Racist, sexist and homophobic thoughts cannot, alas, be abolished by fiat but only by the time-honored methods of persuasion, education and exposure to the other guy's—or, excuse me, woman's—point of view.

And it is silly to mistake verbal purification for genuine social reform. Even after all women are "Ms." and all people are "he or she," women will still earn only 65 cents for every dollar earned by men. Minorities by any other name, such as "people of color," will still bear a hugely disproportionate burden of poverty and discrimination. Disabilities are not just "different abilities" when there are not enough ramps for wheelchairs, signers for the deaf or special classes for the "specially" endowed. With all due respect for the new politesse, actions still speak louder than fashionable phrases.

288

But the worst thing about the P.C. people is that they are such poor advocates for the multicultural cause. No one was ever won over to a broader, more inclusive view of life by being bullied or relentlessly "corrected." Tell a 19-year-old white male that he can't say "girl" when he means "teen-age woman," and he will most likely snicker. This may be the reason why, despite the conservative alarms, P.C.-ness remains a relatively tiny trend. Most campuses have more serious and ancient problems: faculties still top-heavy with white males of the monocultural persuasion; fraternities that harass minorities and women; date rape; alcohol abuse; and tuition that excludes all but the upper fringe of the middle class.

So both sides would be well advised to lighten up. The conservatives ought to realize that criticisms of the great books approach to learning do not amount to totalitarianism. And the advocates of multiculturalism need to regain the sense of humor that enabled their predecessors in the struggle to coin the term P.C. years ago—not in arrogance but in self-mockery.

Beyond that, both sides should realize that the beneficiaries of multiculturalism are not only the "oppressed peoples" on the standard P.C. list (minorities, gays, etc.). The "unenlightened"—the victims of monoculturalism—are oppressed too, or at least deprived. Our educations, whether at Yale or at State U, were narrow and parochial and left us ill-equipped to navigate a society that truly is multicultural and is becoming more so every day. The culture that we studied was, in fact, one culture and, from a world perspective, all too limited and ingrown. Diversity is challenging, but those of us who have seen the alternative know it is also richer, livelier and ultimately more fun.

## About the Author

Barbara Ehrenreich is the author of *The Worst Years of Our Lives: Irreverent Notes from a Decade of Greed* (Pantheon, 1990), *Fear of Falling: the Inner Life of the Middle Class,* and T*he Hearts of Man: American Dreams* and the *Flight from Commitment* (Doubleday, 1983). Ehrenreich's first novel is *Kipper's Game* (HarperCollins, 1994). In addition to her work for *Time Magazine,* Ehrenreich writes a biweekly column for *The Guardian* in the U.K. Her new book, a collection of essays entitled *The Snarling Citizen,* was published in 1995 by Farrar, Straus & Giroux.

# PART 7
# APPLICATIONS

# Dialogue: Applications

*George*—One real test of the success of diversity efforts is that they make a difference where the marketer meets the market, or, for example, where a real estate agent meets the client (see Deena Levine's article on page 305). This section examines how people have applied what we've learned from diversity to various disciplines practiced in the workplace and the marketplace.

*Bob*—We want to identify what's working in a practical and applied way, e.g., where people with disabilities have been hired, enabling them to become productive resources within a workforce. "The Disabled, Ready, Willing and Able" (page 293) is a good example of this.

*George*—And further, have you found a better way for managers to give feedback and performance reviews? Giving feedback successfully must be fine-tuned to the receiver. Different people hear and process information in different ways. That's true even of people from the exact same cultural background. You joked about it the other day after hearing from our first-draft manuscript reviewers. It was a memorable one-liner, "If feedback is a gift, where's the returns desk?"

*Bob*—The bottom line here is to stop making assumptions about what other people need or feel or hear, and start listening. Identify what it is that people respond best to, or even (and here's a radical concept) *ask them* how they'd prefer to proceed with a feedback process. I'm reminded of a study I read back in graduate school. Counselors were introduced to a radical therapeutic strategy: they were encouraged to ask their clients, "What do you think it would take for you to get better?" Rather than requiring the counselor to fish around trying to find the magic strategy for therapeutic healing, *just ask the client!*

*George*—Treating diversity as a endeavor separate from day-to-day operations has too often relegated it to the "nice-to-do" category. As a result, diversity somehow never rises high enough on the priority list to be implemented effectively.

*Bob*—Most of the successful diversity initiatives I've worked on have been integrated with, or built upon, a Total Quality Management (TQM) effort. Diversity in isolation from real tasks and goals is much more liable to fail.

*George*—When linked to bottom-line results diversity efforts become immediately credible. The insights of diversity help us do our jobs and reach our vision more successfully. It's not a new agenda.

*Bob*—It also becomes really clear how costly not understanding the dimensions of diversity can be, for example, the report in the "Muslims Won't Forgive" sidebar (page 310). In this case the offended group spoke up, but how does a company know when it's made a major gaffe, if the victims silently vote with their feet? Or, leave their wallets in pocket or purse?

*George*—"The Power of Cohorts" (page 311) article is useful because it comes at diversity from two angles. First, cohort groups, like any group which begins to have a life of its own, *are* a culturally distinct group. Second, they create a context for understanding how marketing must work in different ways with different groups.

*Bob*—Marlene Rossman (See, "The Importance of Culture in Marketing," page 315) is one of the few people we've seen who articulates this idea very simply and directly. All the politics and philosophy aside, she makes it clear that there are lucrative markets out there for anyone who is willing to make a small investment of time and resources to learn about them. Sometimes sheer profit motivation can do a world of good by recognizing and accepting people.

*George*—All kinds of organizations, not just those with a bottle of something to sell, can apply these concepts to better serving customers. That includes public service agencies, religious groups, and Navy recruiters. Enlightened self-interest can be a very effective motivator.

*Bob*—Right. And at the end of the *Cultural Diversity Sourcebook* we'll show how to avoid purely theoretical diversity. We need the integration of diversity efforts into a curriculum designed to enhance achieving organizational tasks, goals, and objectives. Only then will diversity be widely perceived as valuable in providing the tools for people to do their jobs better.

*George*—Yes. That's about "getting real," too. We're saying "if you've ignored the diversity dimension of your job so far, you haven't gotten real with it yet."

# The Disabled: Ready, Willing and Able

by Beverly Geber (*Training*)

*Relax. The new Americans with Disabilities Act could be the best thing that ever happened to you.*

Late one night your secretary, a petite woman, goes down to the supply room to get the stack of embossed leather binders that will hold all the reports that corporate board members will see during their quarterly meeting in the morning.

She pulls off her high-heeled pumps, steps onto the small stepladder kept in the room and finds that someone has moved the binders to a higher shelf. She stretches mightily but fruitlessly. They're out of her reach.

In the morning, just before you head into the board room carrying the humble cardboard binders she managed to scrounge, you berate her for her inability to perform her job. You fire her on the spot and vow to find a taller secretary.

Absurd? Of course. And it's the kind of reasoning organizations use all the time to justify their decisions not to hire the disabled. Given the chance to hire a qualified paraplegic for a position as, say, a department-store buyer who must travel extensively in the Far East, many managers automatically assume that the applicant won't be able to tolerate the rigor or hassle of the work. They never discuss their concerns during the interview; after all, it's a delicate subject, and—who knows?—it may even be illegal. They go through the motions of seriously considering the paraplegic applicant, but—honestly now—there was never a doubt that this position demands a nondisabled person.

Earlier this year, the United States Congress outlawed such actions. President George Bush signed into law the Americans with Disabilities Act (ADA), which bans discrimination against the disabled by private-sector employers. It describes a disability as a physical or mental impairment, and it's expected to cover some diseases or medical conditions that could constitute an impairment, such as arthritis, cerebral palsy, epilepsy, cancer or acquired immune deficiency syndrome (AIDS). The law requires employers to hire qualified applicants who can perform the essential functions of a job as long as a "reasonable accommodation" will not cause an undue burden to the employer. Beginning in July 1992, the law will apply to all employers with at least 25 employees; two years later, it extends to those with 15 or more employees.

ADA'S passage has caused consternation among employers who are unsure of its demands. Must they fear lawsuits if they don't hire disabled applicants? What's a reasonable accommodation? Will they have to put up with lower productivity and excessive absenteeism from disabled employees? What's the best way to blend the disabled person into the work force?

Jean Mahoney, program manager for the Washington-based President's Committee on the Employment of People with Disabilities, says her organization has been fielding a raft of inquiries from companies ever since Congress passed the ADA. She can't answer them all, since the law carries only the broad brush strokes of Congress' intent. Specific regulations haven't been issued yet.

But she assures employers that this new law is simply an anti-discrimination statute, not an attempt to upend the business world. "The law does not require you to hire anyone who is not qualified for the job," she says.

ADA won't be a foreign concept to all employers. Federal agencies and federal contractors have been complying with its precepts since 1973, when Congress passed the Rehabilitation Act. In addition, 34 states have enacted similar laws covering private employers. The ADA was passed to extend that protection to the disabled in all 50 states.

Private-sector efforts to hire the disabled actually go back several decades. Not all veterans of World War II and the Korean Conflict were able to come marching home, but they needed jobs when they arrived. In the early 1950s, the federal government urged employers to hire disabled vets.

Some companies quietly did just that. Within the last decade, though, many of them have organized and accelerated their efforts to hire the disabled. They were driven in large part by unsentimental business reasons, which many of them found in the pages of *Workforce 2000: Work and Workers for the 21st Century*. That study, written by the Indianapolis-based Hudson Institute and funded by a Department of Labor grant, warned that the U.S. labor pool was shrinking and its complexion changing. Organizations that want to keep their work forces strong had better investigate nontraditional pockets of potential workers that have long been ignored by personnel offices, the study recommended.

The Hudson Institute pointed to underutilized groups such as minorities, women and immigrants, but sharp-eyed organizations also recognized that the disabled represented a promising vein of human gold.

According to the National Institute on Disability and Rehabilitation Research, there are 13.3 million people in the United States with disabilities that affect their ability to work. Of that number, 33.6 percent are in the labor force and 15.6 percent are unemployed, a rate more than twice that of the nondisabled population.

## Exceptional?

It's hard to characterize the types of companies that are already hiring the disabled, but a few generalizations apply. Barbara Judy, manager of the Job Accommodation Network, a resource hot line in Morgantown, WV, says the network gets a fair number of calls from companies in the service sector. Service companies that have a high proportion of low-paying, low-skilled jobs are trying to solve some of their turnover problems by hiring people with mild mental disabilities.

In contrast, high-tech, "knowledge-work" companies generally have more jobs available for those with physical, rather than mental, disabilities. The nature of the business also may limit a company's ability to hire the disabled. At E. I. Du Pont Co., which was named the National Employer of the Year in 1990 by the President's Committee on Employment of People with Disabilities, about 3 per cent of employees are identified as disabled. Richard Drach, manager of disability programs for Du Pont, says some companies employ higher percentages of the disabled. But certain Du Pont divisions, such as coal mining and offshore oil drilling, don't lend themselves well to those with disabilities.

For many years, Du Pont has actively recruited and hired the disabled, believing them to be excellent employees. It has data to support that belief.

In 1957, Du Pont conducted its first survey to assess the performance of people with disabilities in comparison to those without disabilities. Many employers had—and still have—three primary concerns about hiring the disabled: Will they endanger themselves or others at work? Will they miss more work than others because of illness? Will they be able to perform their job duties adequately?

In surveys, Du Pont supervisors generally rated their disabled subordinates as good as or better than nondisabled employees on all three measures.

Those findings dovetail with a 1987 Louis Harris and Associates poll of 920 U.S. employers in which a sizable majority gave disabled employees a good or excellent rating on their overall job performance. Just 5 percent of managers said that disabled employees' job performance was fair and no one said the disabled performed poorly.

These surveys, plus their personal experiences, lead many managers to conclude that their disabled workers are their best employees. Nearly everyone praises their loyalty, dedication and work ethic. Drach tells a story about a Du Pont employee who uses two canes and is always the first one into the office during heavy snowstorms. "She knows her limitations and what she needs to do to get around them," he says.

These kinds of stories are commonplace. Even so, Ethan Loney, senior administrator of equal opportunity programs at Aetna Life & Casualty in Hartford, CT, believes it's erroneous and unfair to stereotype the disabled as extraordinary employees. "Individuals with disabilities run the gamut from deadbeats to exceptional workers, and there's no reason to think that they are any different [from nondisabled workers]," he says. "One [Aetna] manager called and was afraid to discipline a person with a disability. Don't [be]. It's unfair to do anything else. Kick them in the butt when they need it and pat them on the back when they do well."

Susan DeNuccio, vice president of stores and distribution personnel for Target Stores, a division of Minneapolis-based Dayton-Hudson Corp., says managers may think that disabled employees are exceptional because the managers subconsciously expect them to fail. When the disabled employee overcomes a handicap to perform a job as well as anyone else, that seems exceptional.

Mahoney, of the President's Committee, says this is known as the "supercrip syndrome." She considers it one of the barriers to understanding and accepting the disabled in the work force. Even so, she says, there are legitimate reasons why employers might perceive the disabled as superb employees. They must overcome so many obstacles and rejections to get jobs that once they land them, they often work very hard to keep them. They also tend to be quite loyal to an organization, perhaps because they abhor job-hunting.

Dick Monroe, vice president for public relations for Red Lobster Restaurants in Orlando, FL, says one mentally disabled dishwasher has been in one of the stores for 17 years. In that time, he has missed just three days of work and all three times he called a buddy to substitute for him. That kind of dedication is unheard of in the high turnover restaurant business.

## Finding the Right Agency

While some physically and mentally disabled people will walk unannounced through the doors of a personnel office looking for a job, most are placed in a business through a rehabilitation agency. Organizations that decide to make a concerted effort to hire the disabled usually begin working with the local school system or a local agency. For that reason, these efforts rarely are centralized in a large corporation with many locations.

> If the ADA has frightened employers, it's mostly because of these two words: reasonable accommodation.

The number of rehabilitation agencies in a community can be dizzying, especially in large metropolitan areas. So companies just beginning to recruit the disabled sometimes call the Job Accommodation Network to get listings of agencies in their area and the kinds of disabled people with whom the agencies work. Before the company's liaison makes the first contact with a local agency, he or she should be familiar with the kinds of jobs the organization has to offer. That helps to produce a good match of company to agency. For example, a grocery store may have a number of jobs that require physical strength but little decision-making ability; a rehabilitation agency specializing in mild mental retardation might be the best choice.

Du Pont's Drach helped organize a program in Delaware that streamlines the process for employers. A nonprofit organization called the First State Project with Industry Inc., acts as a clearinghouse between Delaware businesses and rehabilitation agencies. "There are dozens and dozens of organizations that do rehabilitation and placement," Drach says. "It's hard to keep all those organizations informed of our needs and also be assured that all those organizations are adequately preparing people." Companies tell First State what kinds of job openings they have and First State tries to find an applicant the company can consider. Last year, Drach says, First State placed 222 disabled people in more than 100 Delaware businesses.

Organizations that hire the mentally retarded often find that they come with job coaches in an arrangement that is called supported employment. The job coach, paid by the agency, will learn the job first, then teach it to the disabled person on the job. Job coaches stick around as long as they're needed.

Sometimes it's a permanent arrangement. Patrick Murphy is president of an Eden Prairie, MN, business called DecoPac, a division of McGlynn's Bakery, which takes in bulk shipments of cake decorations and bakery supplies and repackages them in small assortments for grocery stores and bakeries. The work of repackaging is pivotal to the business, but it's tedious. Murphy originally had a hard time keeping enough people in the positions to fuel his rapidly growing business. He was open to the idea of employing the disabled because he had tutored a mentally handicapped person while in high school. So he contracted with a local rehabilitation agency for the mentally retarded to do the repackaging.

Agency job coaches accompany the nine workers to DecoPac for the part-time jobs and stay with them the entire time. The agency allows its charges to work only part time, so they can spend the rest of the day learning independent living skills.

Target Stores also employs the mentally disabled to do such tasks as stocking shelves, sorting hangers and retrieving shopping carts from the parking lot. Each store makes its own arrangements, but typically they work with school districts in their areas in a work-study arrangement. The school district will send a job coach along with several students. The coach will stay with the students for the six weeks that the typical training program lasts. Then, says DeNuccio, if there is a permanent job available, graduates of the training program can apply for it. Each store employs a minimum of two disabled people.

McDonald's Corp., which has been actively recruiting the disabled since the early 1980s through a program called McJobs, believes that the best job coaches are those who come from within McDonald's. Coaches from agencies, although well-versed in how to work with the disabled, don't know as much about the McDonald's way of doing things as does a company veteran, says Pat Brophy, national special employment manager.

When the program started, disabled employees were trained in a special training store and then placed in the restaurant where they would eventually work. But Brophy found it was disconcerting for the trainees to be moved to a new location after they had just gotten used to the first location. Now, the company trains employees in the store where they will be working.

Each job coach, an experienced McDonald's manager who asks for the assignment and receives special training in working with the disabled, conducts about six two-month classes a year for four or five trainees each time. The company now is extending the program to McDonald's stores in foreign countries.

## Strings on Bathroom Doors

If the ADA has frightened employers, it's mostly because of these two words: reasonable accommodation. Employers that haven't already done so know they must spend the money to make their buildings accessible to the physically disabled. That's sobering enough. But what is meant by a "reasonable accommodation"? Will they be expected to buy mounds of expensive computerized equipment to help the disabled do their jobs?

Those who have a history of employing the disabled say that's a common but baseless fear. "Accommodation is not an overwhelming task," says Kathleen Duffy, Midwest regional manager for community employment and training initiatives for the Marriott Corp. "But as much as we keep telling them, [employers] need to learn it themselves."

> *Quadriplegics graduating from engineering schools can earn starting salaries of $50,000.*

As reassurance, experts keep quoting a 1987 evaluation by the Job Accommodation Network that found that 30 percent of accommodations cost nothing, half cost less than $50 and 70 percent cost less than $500.

Inexpensive accommodations can be simple, commonsensical courtesies. Reserved parking stalls close to doors is a common one. Mahoney says her department put a string on the door of a bathroom stall so that a female employee in a wheelchair could get in and out more easily. Rebecca Osborne, director of compliance, urban affairs and policy for Rockwell International in El Segundo, CA, says the company publishes maps of the interiors of all the buildings in its complex. The map shows physically disabled employees the shortest way to get from one spot to another; it also highlights the widest aisles for those in wheelchairs.

At Aetna headquarters, it can take a nondisabled person about 15 minutes to go from one building to the next, so the company purchased motorized scooters to speed the journey for the disabled. Aetna also installed a $100 TDD teletype phone accessory for the deaf in the office of the company security guard so that deaf employees who can't hear the radio can call in to find out if the Connecticut company is closing because of heavy snows.

Some accommodations intended to make the workplace more comfortable for the disabled also can be conveniences for the nondisabled. The automatic door now common at supermarkets and other businesses is probably the most universal example.

Mahoney also tells of an electric utility that hired a man with limited use of his legs who was determined to become a lineman. The company was able to rig a way for him to stand upright in a cherry picker so he could repair outdoor electrical wires. But because he had little feeling in his legs, the company worried about him catching frostbite on cold days. They installed a heater in his cherry picker, which all the other linemen promptly wanted in theirs. The company complied and found that the workers were able to complete jobs with fewer breaks.

The electric company showed an unusual willingness to accommodate the disabled worker. Many companies would have taken one look at the man and concluded that he could not be a lineman.

The key to complying with the ADA—and figuring out what may be a reasonable accommodation—is to take a fresh look at jobs, ignoring the trivia and focusing on the essential tasks. For instance, says Marriott's Duffy, one of the company's clerical employees is a dwarf who must occasionally file papers in the top drawer of a filing cabinet. A $40 step stool solved his problem. Judy, of the Job Accommodation Network, says one of the Network's clerical employees had the same problem with filing, but a step stool wouldn't solve her problem because she uses a wheelchair. The files were redesigned so that the employee rarely has to file anything in the top drawer. Focusing on the task itself, rather than the manner in which it has always been done, is the crux of accommodation.

Accommodating the disabled sometimes means redesigning jobs slightly, perhaps rearranging or reassigning tasks. Mahoney has a deaf secretary who doesn't answer the phone; others do. Duffy says that one Marriott hotel hired a deaf maid to clean rooms. She's not able to hear a shouted answer when she knocks before entering, so she works closely with the front desk and only cleans rooms whose occupants have checked out.

Suppose, says Loney, you have a very fast typist who is blind. She can't proof her work, which is a problem because proofing constitutes about 20 percent of the job. But why not have that typist concentrate entirely on typing and change one or two other jobs so typists are doing a little less typing and a little more proofing? "It's no different than having a team in which one person is good at one thing but not another," he says. Just be careful, he adds, that you don't give too many unpleasant tasks to another person, making that job less appealing.

Drach illustrates what he believes is the difference between reasonable and unreasonable accommodations. Imagine you want to hire a forklift driver who has a back problem that prevents him from lifting anything over 20 pounds. But a 40-pound weight on the forklift needs to be changed a couple of times a day. If the forklift driver is the only one in an isolated warehouse, it may not be possible to make that accommodation. But if he works in a location with five other forklift drivers, you could rearrange tasks so that the applicant with the bad back needn't lift that load.

## The Impact of Technology

Most accommodations are simple job adjustments or inexpensive adaptations such as the string on the bathroom door. At Sears Roebuck & Co., Paul Scher, manager of selective placement and rehabilitation services, says about 6 percent of Sears' 340,000 merchandising employees have identified themselves as disabled. Yet the company has received just 300 formal requests for some kind of accommodation. Many of those requests are for simple things such as putting a desk on blocks so a wheelchair can fit underneath it.

But some are for more elaborate equipment. Scher, who is blind, has a reading machine that the company bought for him. Printed material is fed into the machine and read back by a synthesized voice. "It's allowed me to be much more effective," he says.

Technology has made an enormous difference in the employability of the disabled over the past 10 years. Mahoney says she knows of quadriplegics who graduate from engineering schools and earn starting salaries of $50,000. If they can use a computer, they are on a par with other engineers. "Technology has made them competitive," Mahoney says.

Some technologies have been developed specifically with the disabled in mind. Phone-receiver amplifiers are inexpensive devices developed for the hearing-impaired. Computers can now be outfitted with special Braille devices or voice synthesizers. For those who are legally blind but still retain some sight, computer screens can be adjusted to magnify the information up to 16 times normal size. Quadriplegics can use computers now by means of a "breath-stick" which they hold in their mouths. There are talking calculators and computerized tape recorders that allow a blind person to "speed-read." Often, employers won't be asked to buy this equipment because the disabled job applicant may have obtained it already through government funding.

Five years ago IBM established the IBM National Support Center for Persons with Disabilities in Atlanta. It's an educational organization that maintains a data base on more than 800 hardware or software adaptive products that can be used with IBM computers.

John Czabala, manager of the center, says the organization fields about 2,500 calls a month from individuals and businesses. Czabala says he knows of no studies focusing on technological devices that establish what the average price of an accommodation might be. But he estimates that the cost ranges from a few dollars (for a piece of Plexiglas attached to a computer keyboard on which a person with cerebral palsy can rest his wrists) to thousands of dollars for the most advanced computers with voice-recognition capability.

Sometimes technology has helped the disabled even when it wasn't designed specifically with them in mind. Electronic mail has been an enormous boon to deaf employees, Drach says.

Technology is not the only concern employers have when they begin to incorporate the disabled into the work force. They also wonder whether they should prepare their current employees.

For instance, some employees may feel uncomfortable around mentally retarded coworkers. DecoPac's Murphy found that one of his subordinate managers resisted Murphy's idea to hire the mentally retarded, even though the manager knew the company needed an unorthodox solution to its business problems.

Employees with severe physical disabilities may cause a different kind of discomfort, because they may remind nondisabled employees of their own vulnerability. A sudden accident could instantly disable anyone.

## Good Advice

Some companies, such as Rockwell, don't conduct special courses but make available informational videotapes that explain particular disabilities. McDonald's, however, sponsors awareness training for its employees. The program, which resembles '60s-era sensitivity training, requires trainees to pretend they have a certain disability and try to perform some tasks. Later on in the session, a facilitator leads a discussion of how the trainees felt and asks them how they intend to welcome the new employee.

David A. Castel, vice president of human resources and enterprise for Abilities Inc. of Florida, a Clearwater company, argues that that approach is all wrong because it brands the incoming disabled employee as different. Castel's company is divided into two parts. One is a rehabilitation agency for people with primarily physical disabilities. The other is a collection of profit-making businesses that hire some of the graduates of the rehabilitation agency—but only if they are the most qualified for the job. Castel believes that the disabled should be responsible for their own acceptance at work.

Drach also believes that is true, up to a point. Du Pont has been employing the disabled for so long that there is no necessity to sponsor special sensitivity courses for existing employees. But departments may need to be prepared for incoming employees in special cases. For instance, he says, if a deaf person will be joining the department, existing employees may want to meet to decide how best to communicate with him.

In a perfect world, Loney says, every disabled person would be as strong as the woman with epilepsy at Aetna, who asked to speak at her first staff meeting with colleagues. She took five minutes to explain to her coworkers about epilepsy, what might happen if she had a seizure and what they should do.

Companies that have a history of employing the disabled have some advice for those who haven't. For one thing, they say, don't try to hire disabled people on your own. Take advantage of the expertise of rehabilitation agencies. "We know how to run restaurants, but we don't know how to hire people with disabilities," says Red Lobster's Monroe.

Perhaps most important is this: Don't prejudge the disabled. Don't take one look at them and decide they can't do the job, as the electric company could have done with the man who wanted to be a line repairman even though he had limited movement in his legs.

"Don't prejudge what that person with a disability can do, because you don't know," Castel says. Give the disabled 90-day probationary periods—just like everyone else—to see if they can do the job.

Also take a look at your preemployment tests and hiring policies to make sure you aren't discriminating against the disabled. Castel tells of one quadriplegic computer programmer he employs who graduated from Castel's rehabilitation program but couldn't find anyone to hire him. It was true that he was slower than other candidates on timed preemployment tests, but Castel doubts that those kinds of tests are really valid for a programmer's job. Nimbleness may be important for fast-food counter clerks, but it's less crucial for a programming job. Castel says the quadriplegic programmer has never missed a deadline and is as productive as any other programmer he employs.

That leads to another bit of advice: Don't coddle the disabled. While it's true that some mentally disabled employees may take longer to learn their jobs and reach the standards you expect of them, don't treat them like glass objects. "They need to stretch and be pushed, just like anyone else," Monroe says.

Companies that employ the disabled find that customers respect them for it. DecoPac's Murphy also found that it helped him in recruiting new employees, especially women, who told him they thought the company must be a particularly caring employer. Murphy sees no drawbacks to hiring the disabled. It makes good business sense. And, he adds, it's the right thing to do.

## About the Author

Beverly Geber is associate editor of *Training*.

## Resources

The Job Accommodation Network: 809 Allen Hall, West Virginia University, Morgantown, WV 26509; (800) 526-7234.

President's Committee on the Employment of People with Disabilities: 1111-20th St. N.W., Washington, DC 20036; (202) 653-5044.

Mainstream: 1030-15th St. N.W., Suite 1010, Washington, DC 20005; (202) 898-1400.

National Organization on Disability: 2100 Pennsylvania Ave. N.W., Suite 232, Washington, DC 20037; (202) 293-5960.

Abledata, Newington Children's Hospital: 181 E. Cedar St., Newington, CT 06111; (800) 344-5405.

IBM National Support Center for Persons with Disabilities: P.O. Box 2150, Atlanta, GA 30301-2150; (800) 426-2133.

# Got the Message?: Giving Feedback in a Diverse Environment

by Lee Gardenswartz and Anita Rowe

- The report just given to you by one of your subordinates misses the mark by a country mile, even though you thought you explained clearly what was needed.

- You overhear a staff member giving inaccurate information to a customer/client. When you quietly correct the employee, he or she blushes and turns away in embarrassment.

- An important step in a procedure is being overlooked by one of your newly hired employees. Each suggestion you make is met with defensiveness.

In each case it is clear you need to give feedback both to help the employee improve performance and to get the results you need for optimum productivity. Yet how do you give it so that it produces the desired results? While the potential risk of hurt feelings, bruised egos and defensive reactions is always present in feedback situations, the risks are even greater in a diverse environment. Miscommunication has a greater chance of happening when differences in background, values, communication styles and perceptions cause misunderstandings on both the giving and receiving ends.

A first step in giving effective feedback in a diverse environment is to understand the impact differences in areas such as age, gender and culture can have on how we send and receive feedback. Finding out how the values and norms of various cultures impact the transmission of the message is a good beginning. Taking a look at the following variables may give you clues about why some of your feedback takes while some does not.

## Diversity Variables Influencing Feedback

### Avoidance of Loss of Face

Employees from some cultural backgrounds will interpret negative feedback as a shameful event that causes loss of face. When this occurs they may attempt to avoid or deflect the information. Embarrassment may be shown by inappropriate smiling and laughter, or by blushing. Avoidance may be attempted by not making eye contact, missing appointments for feedback sessions or unwillingness to participate in discussions about any criticism.

### Emphasis On Harmony

Employees preferring smooth interpersonal interactions often see feedback as disruptive to harmony and good feelings between the giver and receiver. In order to preserve harmony, individuals may agree even when they don't understand or continue to nod in agreement and say "Yes, I understand," then proceed to ignore the feedback or make the same mistake again.

### Respect for Authority

Employees from hierarchical cultures or more traditional upbringings may prefer operating according to a clear "chain of command" and may feel that feedback is an order to be followed without question rather than something to be discussed or debated. In such cases, the employee may be unwilling to ask for clarification, disagree or even to suggest a different approach.

### External Locus of Control

Some cultures place more emphasis on external factors such as fate and chance when attributing the cause of success or failure. On the other hand the culture operating in most organizations in the United States places a greater emphasis on internal factors such as ability, perseverance and hard work. Employees who have a more external locus of control may have difficulty in seeing the consequences of their behavior and in connecting the feedback to their own improved performance, evaluation or compensation.

## Emphasis on Relationship Over Task

"Get to the point." "Don't beat around the bush." "What's the bottom line?" These common expressions heard in American companies are indicators of the task over relationship preference that has little patience for small talk and sees relationship building as a waste of time. Yet some employees may have a different priority, viewing people as taking precedence over the task. Employees with this view may feel that their relationship with the boss, seniority or their status in the group is more critical to success than following the task centered direction given in the feedback.

## Difficulty in Separating Self From Performance

Some individuals see their performance as an inextricable part of themselves so a criticism of behavior is taken as a personal affront rather than as helpful information. When employees have this "I am my performance" view, they may feel betrayed, hurt and embarrassed or respond with defensiveness when given corrective feedback.

## Emphasis on Group Over Individual

Employees from more group oriented cultures may find it awkward and embarrassing to have their individual performance singled out for comment. Whether negative or positive, the individual focus causes discomfort and may be viewed as disloyalty to coworkers on the team.

## Previous Discrimination

Individuals who have been the objects of discriminatory treatment are likely to mistrust any feedback giver of a different group and may tend to discount the value of the message. Sarcasm, sulking silence and withdrawal may be the response when employees doubt the fairness of the feedback.

"So what is a manager supposed to do?" you might ask when you look at all of these variables. The following ten tips may help.

1. *Position the feedback as a benefit to the receiver*

   Feedback has a better chance of being used positively when the receiver sees its benefit in personally relevant terms. Emphasizing these benefits will "hook" the receiver into being open to and utilizing the information given.

2. *Build a relationship first*

   Spending time building a human to human connection with employees will pay off when you need to give constructive criticism. Taking a coffee break or having lunch with different employees each week is a start. Not only will you get to understand your staff members better, but you will have built a foundation that you can rely on at feedback time.

3. *Begin with subtle, and move to more direct, communication*

   Less direct communication can avoid the hurt and loss of face often felt. More implicit rather than explicit statements ("The introduction and conclusion of this report are excellent," rather than "The body of the report needs work.") is one method you can use to be less direct.

4. *Make observations about behaviors and conditions, not judgments about the person*

   The risk of defensiveness is lowered when the focus is on specific behaviors and situations rather than judgments about the person. "These smudges need to be cleaned off," rather than "Your work is sloppy."

5. *Use passive rather than the active voice*

   Passive language can convey your message in a less confrontational manner. Saying "The reports were left unfinished" is softer and a more face-saving way to deliver your message than "You didn't finish these reports yesterday."

**6.** *Be positive, telling what you do want, not what you don't*

Giving positive directions not only takes the sting out of what might feel like a reprimand, it also gives the recipient of the feedback a clearer idea of what to do. You might say, "Please follow the new format this time," rather than "Don't do it that way again."

**7.** *Give feedback to the group rather than individuals*

This suggestion is particularly useful when giving feedback to individuals who come from more group oriented cultures. Talking to the team as a whole avoids the personal blame that might be felt if the feedback were given to one individual. It also may rally the group to help some members "get with the program."

**8.** *Make it low key*

Because of the heightened sensitivity and nervousness that often surrounds feedback interactions, it is helpful to make the discussions as low key as possible. Speaking in a soft tone of voice and meeting privately are two ways to avoid embarrassment and defensiveness.

**9.** *Use an intermediary*

Intermediaries are often used when face saving is valued as well as when difficult negotiations get stalemated. Informal leaders and cultural interpreters can be useful go-betweens who can help gain acceptance of the feedback and avoid embarrassment. Another strategy can be asking a third person for advice, "I'd like to help Luis, but I don't want to offend him. What do you suggest?" or requesting them to pass the message on, "Susan, would you work with Joanna on finding a way to deal with customer complaints about the long waiting time?" for example.

**10.** *Assure the individual of your respect*

Communicating your respect for the individual is critical in getting your feedback listened to. When people feel valued and accepted, they are less defensive and more open to what you have to say. This respect and acceptance can be communicated in many ways. Telling people directly how much you value their contributions, spending time with them, and asking their opinions are just a few ways. The most powerful communicator of all, however, is your attitude. As Emerson said so aptly, "I can't hear what you are saying, because who you are rings so loudly in my ears."

## About the Authors

Lee Gardenswartz, Ph.D. and Anita Rowe, Ph.D. are partners in Gardenswartz and Rowe. They have helped many organizations through their writing on diversity. Among Gardenswartz and Rowe's clients are GTE, Southern California Gas Company, IRS, Society of Consumer Affairs Professionals, DWP, *The Los Angeles Times*, FHP, State of California Department of Health Services, UCLA, South Coast AQMD, First State Bank, VA Medical Center, MCA and The Prudential.

Anita and Lee have lectured widely, giving keynote speeches, facilitating team building retreats and teaching seminars across the country. Gardenswartz and Rowe can be reached at: 12658 W. Washington Boulevard, Suite 105, Los Angeles, CA 90066. Phone: (310) 823-2466; Fax: (310) 823-3923. This article originally appeared in the *Managing Diversity Newsletter*, P.O. Box 819, Jamestown, NY 14702-0819. Phone: (716) 665-3654; Fax: (716) 665-8060.

# Understanding Diversity Blind Spots in the Performance Review

by Lee Gardenswartz and Anita Rowe

If it's true that demographics is destiny, then we are in for some exciting and challenging times. The increasing numbers of women, minorities, immigrants and those with physical disabilities in the work force pose new issues for managers. When individuals from varied backgrounds come together on the job, they can bring new energy and creativity. However, differences in language, norms, and values can also be the source of conflict and misunderstanding. One area of managerial responsibility, where the risk of communication impasse is great, is the performance review.

It is a rare person who does not find the performance evaluation process difficult and tension producing. On both sides of the desk, apprehensions and nervousness are typical reactions. The evaluator worries about being accurate and fair, avoiding hurt feelings and not creating conflict. The evaluatee, however, anticipates potential criticism, judgments and embarrassment. Yet for all its difficulties, evaluating employee performance is the primary tool managers use to maintain accountability and reward employees equitably.

Staff members who are not part of the dominant culture of the institution may have even more apprehensions about the performance evaluation process. Identifying the source of that tension can help supervisors overcome some of the resistance. Think for a moment about how you might feel if you were:

- An older female employee being evaluated by your younger, male boss

- An employee with a temporary work permit awaiting a green card, being evaluated by your American-born manager

- A long term Latino worker being evaluated by your African-American female supervisor

- A paraplegic male engineer being evaluated by your able bodied male manager

- A male Vietnamese immigrant bookkeeper being evaluated by your boss, an Anglo-American female accountant.

What assumptions would you make? What expectations would you have as you approached your evaluation session? Some of the following factors might contribute to the resistance you might be feeling.

## Fear of Repercussions

All of us feel less safe in any organization or culture where we are not the dominant group. Diverse employees, knowing they are not the power wielders, may experience fear when being evaluated by those who are in power. They may perceive they have no recourse to any judgment. They may also fear losing their jobs or their green cards. They may see the evaluation itself as a formalized reprimand, a wrist slapping for past mistakes and hence, be reticent to participate.

*Suggestion for Managers:* Explain the purpose of the evaluation, emphasizing that it is not a disciplinary meeting and that the employee is not going to lose his/her job.

## "Not One of Us" Syndrome

The American judicial system mandates that every person on trial be judged by a jury of his or her peers. It is felt that only those in similar circumstances can make a fair judgment. In diverse organizations, the evaluator is not necessarily of the same group as the evaluatee. The employee may feel that it is not possible to be fairly evaluated by someone who may have little understanding or empathy for the problems of the employee. When individuals do not perceive they will get a fair shake, they are apt to resist.

*Suggestion to Managers:* Sit next to the evaluatee at a table or in chairs rather than across a desk. Show empathy; for example, "People sometimes feel a little nervous at performance evaluation time. I feel that way, too, when I get evaluated."

## Lack of Understanding of the Process

Employees of all stripes often see performance evaluation as a reprimand or dressing down session. When they do not fully understand the reasons behind the evaluation, nor the actual form and process, they may balk. Cultural and language differences can further complicate the issue. Do not assume that a nodding head and a "yes" response indicate understanding. More than likely, these behaviors mean "Yes, I heard," rather than, "Yes, I understand," and are the expected polite responses in many cultures where saying "no" can lead to loss of face for both parties.

*Suggestion for Managers:* Explain the performance evaluation process to the whole staff, telling them the reasons for it, how it can benefit them and how they can help. Explain again briefly at the beginning of each evaluation session.

## It is a Foreign Experience

For employees who are from other cultures, the whole process may be strange and confusing. In many countries, rewards such as promotions and raises are a result of seniority or family connections rather than performance. The employee may have no experience with the notion of individual responsibility, goal setting and monitoring of performance that underlie the evaluation process used by American employers.

*Suggestion for Managers:* Use the evaluation as a teaching opportunity, explaining how individual performance and accomplishing goals lead to rewards.

## All Task and No Relationship

In the more structured setting of an evaluation session, the employee may be taken aback when the task takes precedence over the relationship. Suddenly the evaluation form, with its boxes and categories, seems more important than the person. If the employee has had a comfortable relationship with the boss, he or she may feel betrayed, as though the boss who was so friendly this morning is now cold and all business.

*Suggestion for Managers:* Try to maintain the same tone in the evaluation session that you generally have in relating to the employee. Talk about each section in normal everyday language, making sure to avoid using "legalese."

Both you and your employees will bring your diverse backgrounds, cultures, and experiences into the performance evaluation process. Considering these differences and their potential impact on the appraisal process can help you have more productive performance evaluations with all employees.

## About the Authors

Lee Gardenswartz, Ph.D. and Anita Rowe, Ph.D. are partners in Gardenswartz and Rowe. They began helping organizations with diversity in 1977 when they worked with Los Angeles Unified School District to deal with its diversity challenges at the time of mandatory integration. Since that time they have specialized in the "human side of management" for a variety of regional and national clients, helping them manage change, handle stress, build productive and cohesive work teams and create inter-cultural understanding and harmony in the workplace.

Gardenswartz and Rowe can be reached at: 12658 W. Washington Boulevard, Suite 105, Los Angeles, CA 90066. Phone: (310) 823-2466; Fax: (310) 823-3923. This article originally appeared in the *Managing Diversity Newsletter*, P.O. Box 819, Jamestown, NY 14702-0819. Phone: (716) 665-3654; Fax: (716) 665-8060.

# From Designing to Selling Homes: The Importance of Managing Cultural Diversity

by Deena Levine (*Building Industry Association News*)

Have you experienced any of the following situations involving foreign-born clients?

- clients attempt to negotiate or bargain past the point at which it is still generally acceptable

- clients submit fraudulent information about income or assets in what may be an attempt to "beat the system"

- clients withhold information crucial to the completion of the loan approval process

- male clients have difficulty accepting the professional status of female personnel

- clients do not respond to casual conversation styles

- clients refuse to buy houses with certain house numbers or in certain locations, such as courts or t-intersections

If any of these situations sound familiar, you may have been experiencing incidents of cross-cultural miscommunication and misperception. With increased cultural knowledge, some of your clients' unfamiliar or confusing reactions would become more understandable and sometimes predictable.

Throughout all stages of selling and closing the purchase of a home, skillful communication is of vital importance with foreign-born clients for whom the process of purchasing a home in the U.S. is culturally unfamiliar and completely different than what they may be accustomed to.

The approach, selling techniques and overall style of interaction we use often reflect acceptable "American" expectations of communication, both verbal and non-verbal. Foreign-born clients' styles of communication can differ greatly from those of the Americans with whom they are in contact. The result of such differences and of culturally dissimilar attitudes can range from irritation and frustration to outright withdrawal of business.

At a recent Educational Council seminar, participants were exposed to different styles of communicating through role-playing and analyses of video excerpts exemplifying typical American and non-American modes of interaction.

In one role-play situation involving a salesman and a potential foreign client entering a home for the first time, the salesman demonstrated at least five "American" behaviors, including his type of eye contact, immediate friendliness, conversational tone, line of questioning and use of a particular off-hand type of humor.

When seminar participants were asked "What's 'American' about this interaction?" one of the participants responded with the question, "How do others see us, as Americans?" Seeing oneself in a cultural light makes it possible to demonstrate greater sensitivity to clients from different cultures.

A further challenge of working with home buyers from diverse backgrounds is designing, building and selling homes that reflect cultural differences in home selection. Without knowledge of these differences, builders and their salespeople may lose valuable time trying to sell homes that, while attractive by American standards, would be immediately unacceptable to a buyer from another culture.

As Marsha Golangco explained during the seminar, many people from Asian cultures, whether on a conscious or unconscious level, look for certain features in a home that will enhance the harmony of the house. The individual homeowner, the house and the surroundings are considered to be interrelated and affect the health and prosperity of the owner.

The features considered significant include: location of the house, shape of the lot, orientation of the home, some aspects of the floor plan (e.g., the position of the doors and staircases) and landscaping, to name only a few.

For some Asians, ideas about what constitutes a harmonious environment emanate from an art and philosophy more than ten centuries old called "Feng Shui," literally translated as "wind and water." Feng Shui consists of much more than a collection of superstitions about numbers and colors. It is a Chinese environmental study involving geophysics, aesthetics, common sense and architectural design which aims at promoting the well-being of the owner.

Feng Shui has been interpreted as good and bad luck, such that a house is said to have "good Feng Shui" or "bad Feng Shui." In addition, Golangco explained, the home is an extension of its owner—the roof is like the head (skylights are analogous to holes in the head and are generally not desirable); the front door is like the face, which is why the orientation of the home is of extreme significance. This is a new way for westerners to view the home.

Cultural values and practices can affect builders and real estate professionals beyond preferences for layout and design. In some situations, the question of how far companies should go to accommodate cultural preferences arises.

One company, for example, modified its own policy of allowing only the people on title to go on the walk-through after learning how vital it is for certain cultural groups to rely on their extended families for decision making. Acknowledging the inconvenience of having a large group of family members inspecting hundreds of items in the house, the company management chose to consider cultural background in the formulation of the policy.

Individuals and their cultures are inextricably intertwined. The success and ease with which individuals from totally different backgrounds conduct business depends on the use of cross-cultural communication skills, an ability to establish rapport and demonstrate cultural sensitivity, and an awareness of differences which can become potential sources of miscommunication.

The cultural diversity with which members of the building and real estate professions are faced creates an added dimension to business interactions. Few assumptions can be made about what is "normal" when it comes to conducting cross-cultural business transactions. Suppositions about processing the loan, establishing rapport, negotiating and decision-making must be examined. What is acceptable and normal in one culture may be perceived as strange or even offensive in another.

## About the Author

Deena Levine, M.A. has conducted cross-cultural workplace and business communication training for over fourteen years. She has developed workshops and seminars for a wide variety of corporate clients and for personnel in social services, health care and educational institutions. Ms. Levine has co-authored three texts in cross-cultural communication, all published by Prentice-Hall. She has also recently produced an audio tape training program on sales and rapport-building with clients and customers from other cultures. She can be reached at: Deena R. Levine, President, Cross Cultural Programs, P.O. Box 582, Alamo, CA 94507. Telephone: (510) 947-5627; Fax: (510) 947-5628.

# Quality Through Equality: Working with Total Quality Management Programs to Improve Job Accommodations for People with Disabilities

by Dale S. Brown (*In the Mainstream*)

*How can rehabilitation programs use TQM, not only as a management strategy to guide their own organizations, but as a means of promoting job accommodations? In the following article, Dale S. Brown, Program Manager at the President's Committee, discusses how the current move to "reinvent government" opens windows of opportunities for people with disabilities and their advocates to promote issues of concern to the disability population.*

Many corporations and public agencies are restructuring or "reinventing themselves" to become more productive and competitive. Total Quality Management, a customer-oriented approach to improving quality, is frequently the program of choice. When companies are involved in changing and improving themselves, it can be a good time to assure that issues important to people with disabilities are part of the process.

Accommodations for people with disabilities, often perceived as an expense, can provide benefits beyond the person with a disability and can add to the bottom line of company profits. Job accommodation can create value within a business through improvement of at least three areas: efficiency, innovation, and safety. Let's take each of these in turn:

*Efficiency.* Frequently, accommodations made for one person assist everyone. For example, a man with one arm worked in a company that produced microfiche. A paper cutter was designed especially for him. When he was absent, others used the paper cutter because it was easier for them. To assist a person with quadriplegia, a government agency bought software which allows an individual to use his or her voice to talk to a computer. This made this person's productivity higher than his co-workers'. The agency bought voice-activated computers for everyone.

*Innovation.* Numerous inventions have begun as accommodations for people with disabilities. The telephone's development, for example, was the result of an effort of Alexander Graham Bell to communicate with his deaf niece. The Jacuzzi was invented by the father of a boy who had arthritis who needed warm baths.

*Safety.* Universal design, a concept which is gaining interest, refers to design which allows everyone, tall or short, fat or thin, coordinated or clumsy, disabled or able-bodied, to maneuver with ease through the environment and use products as intended. An accommodation which makes it possible for a person with a disability to move through the environment often makes it easier and safer for nondisabled, mildly disabled, or temporarily disabled people to move. For example, ramps are not as dangerous as stairs, since when people fall, their center of gravity falls a shorter distance than if they fell on stairs. Marking hazards and level changes with flush contrasting visual and tactile marking strips helps people with visual impairments and other individuals to notice dangerous parts of the environment. Improved safety for all has been a welcome by-product of accommodation and accessibility changes.

The linkage of improvements for people with disabilities and improvements for people without disabilities creates a positive argument for including accommodation and disability issues into Total Quality Management programs. When companies improve their procedures, it is a good time to assure that disability issues become part of the process.

Total Quality Management, an integrated system of improving processes, has been the change tool of choice in the majority of private and public entities that have chosen systemic change. Almost every U.S. manager is aware of the process and is somewhat familiar with its terminology. Following are three points that Total Quality Management programs have in common and that give advocates for people with disabilities their best point of entry.

(1) Quality is defined by customers, not the organization.

(2) Total Quality Management programs pay careful attention to every link in the production process and continuously study and improve the entire system.

(3) Continuous improvement requires taking full advantage of the knowledge and skills of all employees.

Each of these points will be covered in turn.

## Quality Is Defined by Customers, Not the Organization

People with disabilities are your customers. As accessibility improves, more people with disabilities are becoming mainstream customers—with potential to profit the companies that serve them. According to June Isaacson Kailes, a disability consultant in California, over 10 percent of the population requires barrier-free design. She explains, "If your average customer sale is $10 and you have 100 customers a day, you may be losing $100 in sales, or $365,000 a year if your business establishment is not barrier-free. Can you afford this lost revenue?"

Companies involved in quality efforts carefully study customer requirements. People with disabilities should be systematically included in these efforts. Two telephone companies give examples of how this can be done. One has a committee of consumers representing various disabilities which reviews the company's products and proposes new products. Another is testing a value-added voice mailbox.

Frequently, customers with disabilities are inadvertently screened out of customer surveys. For example, written surveys do not reach those who cannot read due to visual impairments or dyslexia. A major survey of people with disabilities underrepresented people who were deaf by not including TDDs. Surveys of current customers may miss potential customers. Details of serving people with disabilities should be part of staff training. When staff does not understand the reason for accommodations, the best-meaning results can go awry.

For example, Frank Owe, a well-known advocate for people with disabilities, was staying in a hotel and he requested a TDD because he is deaf. When he returned to the room, he found a note: "We don't know where you want us to put the TDD. Please call the engineering staff at . . . "

Total Quality Management programs go beyond customer "satisfaction" to customer "delight." The company that delights people with disabilities and gains this customer segment today positions itself for profits tomorrow. Many companies go beyond the law to serve their customers with disabilities. Service ideas range from braille on the top of the cups in fast food restaurants to free wheelchairs provided in a major national amusement park.

Sensitivity to people with disabilities often improves service to all customers. A historic site developed a map, with larger print, better contrast, and simpler language, for people with mental retardation and placed it unlabeled next to the ordinary maps. Several weeks later, the staff noticed that the maps developed for people with mental retardation were gone. The box of "normal" maps was full. The map originally designed for people with mental retardation is used for all.

## TQM Programs Pay Careful Attention to Every Link in the Production Process and Continuously Study and Improve the Entire System

When companies study their production processes, it is excellent timing to define essential job functions and to assure that new machinery, new procedures, and educational programs are easy to use for people with disabilities. Several companies have formed focus groups of employees with disabilities to address these issues. One Japanese automobile manufacturing representative explained, "We have no job descriptions, only process descriptions. We work in teams where we match jobs to people's abilities. The person isn't tied to a process. Instead, the process is tied to the person." People with disabilities and people knowledgeable about disabilities should work with engineers and designers in the beginning stages so that there is less need for individual accommodation.

Individual accommodations can be planned using the PDCA Cycle. The PDCA (Plan, Do, Check, Act) Cycle is frequently used to effectively change organizations, processes, and procedures. It is conceptualized as a continuous cycle, rather than something that ends. Here is how it can be applied to an individual's accommodation needs:

*Plan*—The individual with a disability and his or her supervisor locate the problem, choose alternative solutions, and pick the one that appears the best. Both worker and manager participate as team members. They often request assistance from other experts. The President's Committee on Employment of People with Disabilities' Job Accommodation Network (1-800-526-7234) is available to assist in any part of the accommodation process.

For example, a data analyst who was blind started the cycle when his office was computerized. His boss asked him to develop a plan to assure that he had access to the system that his office was using. He studied the products of various vendors and wrote a proposal for a particular voice synthesizer.

*Do*—Implement the accommodation. The data analyst who was blind was trained on his voice synthesizer, using the same software as his co-workers.

*Check*—Assure that the accommodation works. In this, the talking computer was faster than the Perkins brailler and typewriter he had used before. However, some co-workers found the computer voice, which was used in open space, distracting. So the company bought him a headphone.

*Act*—If the accommodation is successful, take steps to assure that the employee does not risk loss of accommodation if he or she is transferred or changes supervisors. If further improvements can be made on the accommodation, start the cycle over. Also, assess if this accommodation can improve the productivity of other employees. One

large company, which won the U.S. Department of Commerce's Baldridge award (the top national citation for quality in management), provides backrests and footrests to any employee who asks, to prevent health problems and to improve productivity.

Employees with disabilities, like all employees, are always looking for ways to improve their productivity. Accommodation should be positioned as part of the company's continuous improvement program.

## Continuous Improvement Requires Taking Full Advantage of the Knowledge and Skill of All Employees

In TQM companies, improvement is seen as a process rather than a sudden and swift leap. Each process is studied, often by the employee who is responsible for doing it, to see how it can be made better. Teams are formed to study specific production problems and propose solutions. The stress on empowerment of the individual worker can assist the individual with a disability to obtain what he or she needs to achieve quality.

Individuals with human resource responsibilities or who represent people with disabilities can work closely with the quality programs of their companies. Employees with disabilities should be included in problem-solving work teams. Accommodation must be built into the various changes as they happen.

A manufacturing plant, for example, changed its assembly line jobs to include statistical process control. Reading and writing became essential job functions. Numerous workers with learning disabilities who had hidden their problems successfully were suddenly forced out of the closet.

Fortunately, the company had an active internal education system which hired several tutors to work with these employees, who formed a mutual support group. All of the plant supervisors were trained in accommodation techniques. The results were a plant-wide improvement in quality.

For example, supervisors went through a simulation of an "auditory figure ground problem" by trying to follow directions being given near a noisy machine. As a result of that exercise, they decided to give directions only in quiet areas of the plant.

In short, Total Quality Management is an opportunity for people with disabilities and their advocates. Companies in the United States are changing to become more competitive. People with disabilities and their advocates can become part of that change and make reasonable accommodation a way of doing business.

## About the Author

Dale S. Brown is a well-known writer and speaker on disability issues and has published the book, *Steps to Independence for People with Learning Disabilities*, and more than 200 articles. Ms. Brown is a program manager for the Work Environment and Technology Committee at the President's Committee on Employment of People with Disabilities, where she has worked since 1979. In addition, she co-chairs her agency's TQM team.

# Muslims won't forgive Chanel's cultural faux pas

■ **FALLOUT FROM** Karl Lagerfeld's use of a verse from the Koran in his spring couture collection for Chanel continues to spread, despite apologies from the designer and the fashion house.

Now Chanel has engaged a bodyguard for Claudia Schiffer, the supermodel who paraded down the runway in a revealing strapless bustier with what Chanel later said were fragments of verses from the Muslim holy book embroidered in gray pearls. Schiffer's mother told *Bild*, a German newspaper, that the model would not set foot on the streets without security because of alleged threats.

The controversy erupted last week after the couture show in Paris, when the Indonesian Muslim Scholars Council, in Jakarta, called for a boycott of Chanel and threatened to file formal protests with the government of Lagerfeld's homeland, Germany. The designer apologized, explaining that he had taken the design from a book about the Taj Mahal, thinking the words came from a love poem.

On Friday, Claude Eliette, president of Chanel, and Dr. Dalil Boubakeur, rector of the Muslim Institute of the Mosque of Paris, met for two hours. In a joint statement, Eliette repeated the apologies and Boubakeur promised to transmit them to Muslims in France and elsewhere.

But that did not end the matter. Reuters reported from Cairo the religious affairs committee of the Egyptian Parliament is urging Muslims to boycott Chanel.

*Santa Cruz Sentinel,* January 26, 1994. Reproduced with permission.

# The Power of Cohorts

by Geoffrey Meredith & Charles Schewe (*American Demographics*)

**Summary: The experiences of youth create habits that can last a lifetime. People who shared powerful experiences in young adulthood can be grouped into lifelong "cohorts" that share certain attitudes and consumer behavior. Americans now fall into six distinct cohorts that affect their attitudes toward savings, sex, a good meal, and the need for hundreds of products and services.**

Imagine that you work for a company named General Beverages. The company has two divisions: the coffee division and the cola division. You know that coffee consumption rises with age, from age 10 through age 60. Even after age 60, consumption remains high. Cola consumption, however, declines with increasing age. Both trends have been the rule for 40 years.

You also know that the first member of the baby-boom generation will soon turn 50. Because of this fact, the AARP will gain a prospective new member every 8 seconds for the next 18 years. The number of 18-to-34-year-olds will decline by 4 million in the 1990s, while the number of older adults will grow by 24 million. Given these facts, which division has the brighter prospect for the future: coffee or cola?

Many would quickly conclude that General Beverage's next CEO should come from the coffee division. Their conclusion would be based on the premise that historic consumption rates by a particular age group will prevail in the future. An aging population should boost the demand for coffee and cut the demand for cola. Unfortunately, it isn't that simple.

Coffee and cola preferences are based more on cohort effects than on aging effects. Webster's Dictionary defines a cohort as "a group of people united in an effort or difficulty," or as "companions or associates." In demographic terms, a birth cohort is a group of people born during a given time period who share the same historic environment and many of the same life experiences, including tastes and preferences.

A cohort analysis of cola and coffee consumption yields the exact opposite outcome from an age analysis of the same problem. Younger, cola-intensive cohorts will continue to consume soft drinks even as they age, according to studies done by Joseph O. Rents of the University of Tennessee. Meanwhile, older, coffee-intensive groups will age and move out of the marketplace. They will be replaced by baby boomers and other lower-consuming cohorts. This would indicate that despite an aging population, General Beverages should look to its cola division for growing profits.

## Shared Experiences

"Men resemble the times more than they do their fathers," according to an ancient Arab proverb. Since 1959, when Norman Ryder published *The Cohort as a Concept in the Study of Social Change*, cohort analysis has been widely recognized and accepted in sociology. Cohort effects are just as important for many marketers, but cohort analysis has been almost totally ignored as a marketing tool.

Ryder spoke of "the demographic metabolism . . . continually receiving raw material by fertility and discharging depleted resources by mortality." He defined each group of people born over a relatively short and contiguous time period as a "generational cohort" that is deeply influenced and bound together by the events of their "formative years." For marketers, many important cohort characteristics are formed during a consumer's "coming-of-age."

In 20th-century America, the passage to adulthood occurs roughly between the ages of 17 and 21. Events that happen when people first become "economic adults" affect their lifelong attitudes toward jobs, money, and savings. Events going on when one is becoming a "sexual adult" influence one's core values about permissiveness, tolerance, and sexual behavior. Psychologists have found that these core values are then carried through life largely unchanged.

The kind of music that is popular when a group first comes of age is likely to be the preferred music format for the rest of the cohort's life. The Rolling Stones have enormous appeal in the 1990s because the baby boom liked the Stones when they were teens. After they turn 50, boomers won't suddenly switch to Mantovani or Glenn Miller. Cohort effects do not change with one's age or stage of life.

The terms "cohort" and "generation" are not exactly the same, although both refer to groups that are age-linked. A generation is usually defined by its years of birth. For example, some researchers use the term "Depression Generation" to describe persons born between 1930 and 1939. But cohorts are better defined by events that occur at various critical points in the group's lifetime. The "Depression Cohort" in this case includes people born between about 1912 and 1921, who became adults between 1930 and 1939.

A generation is usually 20 to 25 years in length, or roughly the time it takes a person to grow up and have children. But a cohort can be as long or as short as the events that define it. The World War II Cohort is only six years long, and the Post-War Cohort is 18 years. Centuries ago, when the pace of events was slower, cohort spans might have been even longer. Imagine a cohort of 14th-century Europeans defined by The Hundred Years War.

# Six Distinct Cohorts

In 1994, American adults can be divided into six distinct cohorts, ranging in age from the Depression Cohort (aged 73 to 82) to what many people are calling Generation X (aged 18 to 29). The roughly 4 million people who are aged 83 and older are not included for two reasons. First, this group is much smaller than other cohorts. Also, much of their consumer behavior is controlled by physical need. There are also over 68 million persons under age 18. No one knows yet how many of them will belong to the Generation X Cohort and how many will create new cohorts in the next two decades.

Understanding cohort effects can improve business decisions in two ways. First, cohort effects help reveal the underlying mindset toward different categories of products and services. This can be an invaluable aid for everything from new-product design to brand positioning. Second, cohort effects can help make advertising aimed at specific age groups without offending those groups.

Age-specific advertising can be deadly to a product, particularly when it is aimed at the mature market. Johnson & Johnson discovered this when it tried to market Affinity shampoo as the product for "over-40 hair." The product quickly went down the drain. So did Campbell's "Senior Singles-Soup for One." Explicitly positioning yourself as an old people's shampoo, soup, bank, or HMO is a dumb move. But with the judicious use of cohort effects, a marketer can zero in on a specific age group without offending its members.

A recent television commercial for Nabisco's Oreos is a good example of how to use cohort cues. Oreo consumption is heaviest among the young, but Nabisco wanted to boost consumption among older adults. The resulting commercial didn't say, "Hey, 60-year-olds, try Oreos!" Instead, it made the same point subtly and emotionally. The company chose actors from the right age group. The music—"Kiss me once again, it's been a long, long time"—was a favorite when this cohort was coming of age. The actors do a slow dance, play gin rummy, and flirt by playing spin-the-bottle with a glass milk bottle. This is age-specific marketing that is also acceptable to the target market.

Cohort effects are not widely understood. You can see this in a recent newspaper story headed, "Generation Gap Narrows on Sexual Attitudes." The story cited an analysis of three decades of national opinion surveys that seemed to show that older people are becoming more tolerant of homosexuals, premarital sex, and other sexual alternatives. According to the surveys, the difference in attitudes between the youngest (18 to 24) and older (35 to 64) age segments has shrunk by more than two-thirds since the mid-1970s. But older people haven't really become more tolerant. It's fairer to say that tolerant people have become older.

Sexual attitudes are the prototypical cohort effect. People don't become less tolerant about sex as they age. It's just that recent surveys of older Americans now include aging boomers whose core values about sex were formed during the permissive 1960s and early 1970s. It will be interesting to see if journalists in 2020 write that the middle-aged are becoming sexually intolerant, as the cohort that came of age in the time of AIDS approaches age 50.

## Savings and Bequests

Cohort effects can explain consumer behavior that confounds other models. "Although factors such as income and family size are likely to affect savings and spending rates, they do not adequately explain the older person's behavior," writes George Moschis in Marketing to Older Consumers. "According to the lifecycle hypothesis, baby boomers are expected to save relatively more, and the elderly to draw down their assets. But an analysis of census and survey data shows exactly the opposite."

Cohort analysis shows that people in the Depression Cohort tend to be compulsive savers. Over 60 percent of this group have outstanding debts of less than $2,000, including mortgages. And even those with low incomes tend to be savers. Many Depression-era consumers are also extremely wary of risk. They prefer "guaranteed" investments such as CDs, even though returns today are a fraction of what they were a decade ago.

To appeal to the wealth and caution of the Depression Cohort, creative marketers are developing new financial products. For example, Bankers Trust New York and other firms now offer a federally insured CD whose yield is tied to the performance of the stock market. This vehicle provides a way to participate in the equity market without fear of losing principal.

The financial attitudes of the Depression Cohort are in sharp contrast to those of baby boomers, and these attitudes will largely determine behavior. Age-based analysis would suggest that baby boomers will save more because their incomes are peaking. But their key formative years coincided with a fiscal boom, as well as a boom in fertility. During those years, the prevailing interest rates rewarded those who went into debt. In the 1950s and early 1960s, the "real" interest rate, measured by Treasury Bond yields minus the annual consumer price index, averaged less than 1 percent. In 1974 and 1979, it hit record lows of minus 4 percent. Under those circumstances, widespread consumer debt was not just a symptom of the "I want it all now" mentality. It actually made economic sense.

Many pundits predict that the current low national savings rate (around 4 percent) will soon turn upwards. The increase should be driven by an aging population and future needs for savings reserves for children's college funds, care for aging parents, and retirement. But if attitudes are truly cohort-driven, boomers' savings behavior will not change much with age. After all, people in the Depression Cohort do not spend freely, regardless of their resources.

Another cohort effect is seen in attitudes toward one's inheritance. The Depression Cohort and the World War II Cohort do not share the same attitudes about their responsibility in this area. People in the Depression Cohort feel an acute need to leave a legacy for their children. They feel that the future is uncertain, and they want to be sure that their heirs never have to go through what they did during the Depression.

The World War II Cohort has childhood memories of the Depression, but they did not have to seek employment or start a family in a near-dead economy. This younger cohort lacks interest in leaving a legacy for their children. They feel that their children are much better off than they were at their age. They see their children buying new cars, fancy dinners, and trips to Florida. Why should they assist these free spenders? The Depression Cohort is a prime target for inheritance-need life insurance. The World War II Cohort couldn't be less interested.

## A Good Meal

Why are older people reluctant to try new foods? Their hesitancy is often attributed to an unwillingness to try new things in general. But eating patterns, like sexual and musical tastes. are strongly influenced by cohort effects. If a "good meal" meant meat and potatoes when you were coming of age in 1935, that's what a "good meal" will mean to a 75-year-old today.

Some eating habits are affected by aging. As people realize that their bodies are not immortal, they become concerned about nutrition. Later in life, medical conditions such as diabetes or hypertension can dictate food choices, and a less tolerant gastrointestinal system can lead to a preference for less spicy foods. Yet basic patterns of food consumption aren't much affected by aging. Baby boomers aren't going to start baking lots of tuna casseroles and listening to Lawrence Welk when they turn 50. They will still eat pizza and listen to Rock & Roll.

The index of ethnic food consumption is 71 for adults aged 50 and older, compared with 100 for the average adult. Like soft-drink consumption, this index declines steadily with advancing age. But boomers were brought up on tacos, pizza, and egg rolls. As a result, the mature market's consumption indexes for these kinds of foods are poised for rapid growth. Fast foods will also benefit. When President Clinton soon turns 50, he will still love McDonald's.

Separating cohort effects from other influences is a complex job for market researchers. Aging effects, like changes in health, must be indexed by chronological age. And period effects, which shape behavior at specific points in time, are often difficult to measure. An example of a strong period effect is the Surgeon General's finding that smoking is harmful, which affected cigarette consumption from that point forward.

For the coffee cohort study, Rentz and colleague Fred Reynolds created a complicated model that took into account both aging and period effects. Using 40 years of consumption data by age decile, this model predicted a decrease in daily coffee drinkers from 57 percent of adults in 1980 to 52 percent in 1990. While an age-based analysis predicted an increase of nearly 60 percent, the cohort model was much closer to the actual 1989 data, which showed a decline to 53 percent.

Cohort analysis is the only way to fully understand how people drink coffee, save money, and buy and use many other products and services.

## About the Authors

Geoffrey Meredith is president of Lifestage Matrix Marketing of Lafayette, California. Charles Schewe is a professor of marketing at the University of Massachusetts, Amherst.

The first references to the cohort as distinct from a "generation" can be found in a paper titled "The Cohort as a Concept in the Study of Social Change" by Norman B. Ryder, which was read at the annual meeting of the American Sociological Association in August 1959 and reprinted in the *American Sociological Review* in 1965. The two referenced marketing-oriented cohort studies by Dr. Rentz appeared in the *Journal of Marketing Research* in February 1983 and August 1991. For more information on applying cohort effect in marketing, contact Lifestage Matrix Marketing, 3517 Eagle Point Road, Suite 500, Lafayette, CA 94549; (510) 283-4806; or 23 Ash Lane, Amherst, MA 01002; (413) 256-0914.

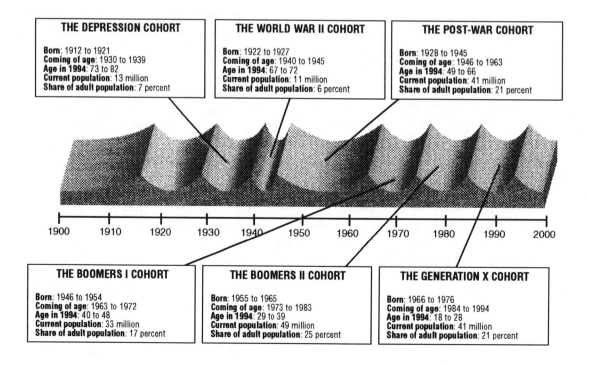

**THE DEPRESSION COHORT**
**Born**: 1912 to 1921
**Coming of age**: 1930 to 1939
**Age in 1994**: 73 to 82
**Current population**: 13 million
**Share of adult population**: 7 percent

**THE WORLD WAR II COHORT**
**Born**: 1922 to 1927
**Coming of age**: 1940 to 1945
**Age in 1994**: 67 to 72
**Current population**: 11 million
**Share of adult population**: 6 percent

**THE POST-WAR COHORT**
**Born**: 1928 to 1945
**Coming of age**: 1946 to 1963
**Age in 1994**: 49 to 66
**Current population**: 41 million
**Share of adult population**: 21 percent

**THE BOOMERS I COHORT**
**Born**: 1946 to 1954
**Coming of age**: 1963 to 1972
**Age in 1994**: 40 to 48
**Current population**: 33 million
**Share of adult population**: 17 percent

**THE BOOMERS II COHORT**
**Born**: 1955 to 1965
**Coming of age**: 1973 to 1983
**Age in 1994**: 29 to 39
**Current population**: 49 million
**Share of adult population**: 25 percent

**THE GENERATION X COHORT**
**Born**: 1966 to 1976
**Coming of age**: 1984 to 1994
**Age in 1994**: 18 to 28
**Current population**: 41 million
**Share of adult population**: 21 percent

1900 1910 1920 1930 1940 1950 1960 1970 1980 1990 2000

# The Importance of Culture in Marketing

by Marlene L. Rossman

With all of the brainwork that goes into developing a strategic marketing plan, you might think that the last thing marketers need to deal with is cross-cultural and ethnicity issues. Wrong! It's the first thing that we need to look at if we want to prosper in the late 1990s and into the next century. Marketers who spend their time and resources learning about the cultural differences (and similarities) among consumers and who use that knowledge to develop products, promotions, and distribution strategies will become industry leaders.

## Culture

What is this thing called culture that we keep hearing about? Culture is what gives us our identity and the code of conduct that we live by. It is learned, shared, and passed on from one generation to the next, by families, by religious institutions, by schools and governments. Culture is learned behavior that distinguishes members of a society and includes what the group thinks, says, and does.

Mainstream U.S. culture stresses the importance of the individual, prizes informal, direct, and open communication, believes that "time is money," sharply delineates the time for work and for play, highly values the concept of self-help, desires change, seeks to get ahead of the competition, believes in the egalitarian ideal, and emphasizes material gain.

Other cultures may be rooted in totally opposite beliefs and behaviors. Our job as marketers is to understand the differences, not to judge them.

## Understanding Minority Segments

How do we begin to unravel the differences so that we can design successful marketing programs for ethnic and minority markets that will give a

satisfactory return on investment? According to Larry Glover, executive vice president of J. Curtis & Co. in Montclair, New Jersey, "If you reach the African-American market with the right mix of product and promotion, the bottom line is a much higher return on investment than you would achieve in the general market. But the key issue here is that of making critical decisions about ethnic marketing without knowledge of ethnics. Companies would not do that in any other phase of business."

Although no one expects every marketer to be an anthropologist, sociologist, or ethnologist, we need to learn how cultural issues of language, religion, family patterns, gender roles, education, and aspirations affect consumer behavior patterns. Whether we obtain this information from books, by taking courses, or by bringing in experts (or by any combination of these) is not the issue. What's important is that the information is obtained with sensitivity through a structured format by qualified managers.

What's needed is the same kind of research that is done for the general market. Only then can we analyze whether to change or adapt the product or service, the promotional mix, or the channels of distribution. But we must take cultural differences into consideration when designing all aspects of the marketing mix.

## High and Low-Context Cultures

Dr. Edward Hall, an anthropologist who has spent many years writing and teaching about intercultural behavioral differences and their applications to business, spoke about how some of his colleagues working on a road project during the Depression of the 1930s had trouble communicating with Native Americans, even though they all spoke English. His colleagues, Dr. Hall explained, held a "deficit model" of the unfamiliar behavior they encountered—that is, they saw Native American patterns of behavior as defective or inferior, rather than as simply different.

315

Dr. Hall, who has spent many years as consultant to major corporations and who wrote about cultural issues in business for the *Harvard Business Review* as early as 1960, divides cultures into high-context and low-context cultures. Communication in a high-context culture depends heavily on the context, or nonverbal aspects of communication; low-context cultures depend more on explicit, verbally expressed communication. According to Hall, the United States is a low-context culture, relying heavily on information communicated explicitly by words. Asian and Hispanic cultures, by contrast, are high-context cultures.

Janet Davis, a Princeton, New Jersey, consultant specializing in minority issues, says, "African-American culture is highly stratified and regionalized. Southern blacks are very traditional and tend to be higher-context than northern blacks. There are also tremendous class differences regionally and generationally."

African-Americans sometimes span two cultures. A black lawyer friend of mine says that during the week he works in the mainstream Anglo-American world wearing pin stripes and speaking highly educated legalese. On weekends he occasionally listens to rap music and speaks "blackspeak" with his friends.

# Nonverbal Communication

In low-context cultures such as the United States and Germany, communication is mostly verbal and written. Very little information about the culture is communicated nonverbally. In high-context cultures, in contrast, a good deal of the communicating process occurs nonverbally. Body language, status, tonality, relationships and family, the use of silence, and many other factors communicate meaning.

But that doesn't mean that American culture doesn't allow for nonverbal communication. Mainstream Americans interpret gestures, silences, eye contact, and facial expressions in ways learned at home or at school. For example, most children in the United States are taught to look at the teacher or parent when they are being scolded. In many Asian, Latin American, Caribbean, and other cultures, in contrast, children are often taught to look down or away as a sign of respect for the person who is scolding them. Adult Americans regard

someone who doesn't look them in the eye as shifty or untrustworthy, but most Asians think that looking someone in the eye is rude or confrontational. Similarly, people in mainstream America learn to smile broadly as a sign of friendliness or openness; in other cultures smiling may be considered false, overbearing, or worse.

A dramatic example of how gestures can be misinterpreted, with a devastating outcome, emerged during the 1992 riot in Los Angeles. Some of the African-Americans interviewed discussed their angry feelings toward Korean-American shop owners. They said they felt poorly treated because the Koreans didn't look them in the eye, smile at them, or put change from a purchase in their hand. The African-Americans interpreted the Korean-Americans' behavior as disrespectful.

Although Koreans are somewhat more outspoken than other Asians, they still consider it rude or aggressive to look deeply into someone's eyes, inappropriate or false to smile at someone they don't know very well, and improper to touch a stranger. If they are to succeed as retailers in the United States, however, they must learn that it's vital to take into account the cultural currency of the community. The Korean shopkeepers will have to adapt to the communication style of the culture of their customers in order to succeed for the long term. In Chicago, to help bridge intercultural gaps, the United Way has hired Karen Gunn, a highly trained black woman, to help African and Korean-Americans understand one another. Gunn works in the community to teach Koreans to smile and to put change directly into a customer's hand, and she mediates minor disputes between the two groups.

My own experience while delivering marketing training to a group of Russian and Korean managers some years ago illustrates the explosive potential of misunderstandings between groups. A Russian manager had knocked over his overstuffed briefcase, which had been perched precariously on the edge of a desk. The Korean manager standing next to him began making a high-pitched, tittering sound that the Russian interpreted as laughing. The Russian turned beet-red and screamed, "You think is funny, is not funny." He pushed the Korean out of his way to begin picking up the pencils and paper that had fallen from the briefcase.

Fortunately, I knew that the Korean was not laughing at the Russian. The tittering with his hand over his mouth indicated that he was embarrassed or distressed at what had happened. I hoped that my negotiating skills would be sufficiently diplomatic, and I told the Russian that the Korean wasn't laughing at him but that he felt badly. The Korean instantly piped up, "Oh yes, badly, very badly."

I bent down and began picking up the pencils and papers, and before the Russian could say another word, the Korean speedily bent and picked up the rest of the papers and handed them to the Russian.

Another flashpoint for nonverbal communication or miscommunication is the concept of space. In some parts of the world the sense of personal space is totally different from the sense of space in the United States. As a result, some Latin Americans, for example, feel that Americans are cold, distant people simply because Americans' "comfort" distance is greater than theirs and Americans don't touch one another.

In one study, conversations in outdoor cafes in different countries were observed. The number of casual touches (of self or of the other party) per hour were counted. A total of 180 touches per hour were recorded in San Juan, Puerto Rico; two per hour were observed in Florida, and none at all in an hour in London.

Understanding these and other differences can be vital in determining the outcome of an ethnic marketing campaign. Unless we are aware of these differences, the messages and intentions can be misunderstood.

## Advertising and Context

In the United States, most advertising is low-context. It traditionally relies on words to explain the product and its features and how the product differs from the competition. By comparison, ads used in high-context countries such as Japan and Mexico rely on nuances and overall differences in the tone, music, style of dress of the actors, scenery, and other nonverbal cues to differentiate the product.

According to Dr. Diane Simpson of Simpson International in New York, "People from low-context cultures are often puzzled by high-context ads and wonder 'What's the point?' Whereas those from high-context cultures are more likely to say the ad taught them something worth remembering and made it easier for them to choose what brand to buy next time." She adds, "People from high-context cultures often find low-context ads pushy and aggressive, whereas those from low-context cultures often find them informative and persuasive."

One attempt to use a high-context ad in a low-context culture caused tremendous confusion in the United States when it was first introduced in 1989. Remember the Zen-like ads for the Infiniti by Nissan, which consisted of rocks and water and hills? Many consumers were frustrated by not seeing the car or hearing about its specifications and kept asking "Where's the beef?" But when they finally saw the cars in later ads, their interest had already been aroused, and some people actively sought out the car.

## Selling in a Foreign Language

One of the most basic cultural considerations is language. In the United States, there are millions of people who either speak no English at all or speak very little of it. If you're advertising in ethnic media, therefore, make sure the translation is correct for the subsegment you want to reach. And make sure your products and services are accessible to the target market.

United Airlines, which expanded its service to Latin America in 1992, operates a Spanish-speaking reservations line. The estimated number of calls on the line is about 450 a day. Imagine losing 450 consumers of your product because it was inaccessible to them! And, just to "let their fingers do the walking," there are Russian, Chinese, Iranian, Spanish, Korean, and other foreign-language yellow pages directories available.

Once you attract non-English speaking customers with your ad, however, you have to follow through. Customers who speak only Spanish or Chinese and who buy your product because of a newspaper ad in their native language will be frustrated and resentful if, when they get the product home, they find that the owner's manual is only in English. In an extreme case, one manufacturer was sued by an injured consumer in Florida because the company heavily advertised the product in Spanish ads aimed at Hispanic buyers but put the label warning of the product's dangers only in English.

## Time

One important cultural difference observed by Edward Hall involves the way people perceive and use time. Some cultures have a much more flexible concept of time than does mainstream American culture. This difference has given rise to stereotypical attitudes about productivity and efficiency. Americans work first, play later; some cultures, however, thread social interaction into the workday instead of putting it at the end. Their work gets done, but the pattern is different.

## Formality

Another cultural variable is formality. In many cultures, formality is taken very seriously. As a marketing consultant, I have gone into many meetings with a senior executive of a company, greeted the individual using Mr. (occasionally Ms.), only to be told, "Call me Bob." By contrast, I will never forget the offended look on my Mexican client's face when a colleague of mine, in a misdirected attempt at friendship, called Guillermo (Spanish for William) Rodriguez, Billy.

In selling or marketing to ethnics and minorities, it's a mistake to use a person's first name until and unless a relationship has been established. Many salespeople and telemarketers are trained to use prospects' first names to create rapport and establish an instantaneous relationship. African-Americans and others, however, are often offended when a white person, especially a white man, calls them by their first name, particularly if the white person uses a title and a last name to identify himself or herself. "That aversion dates from slavery when whites called all slaves by their first name, regardless of their respective age," says Noel A. Day, president of Polaris Research and Development of San Francisco.

## Individualism

Individualism is another cultural issue. Mainstream American culture emphasizes the "I" con-sciousness, in which identity is rooted mostly in the self, compared to the "we" consciousness, in which a person's identity is rooted in groups. Latin American cultures and, to varying degrees, Asian cultures focus more on the group than on the individual.

For example, Chinese names place the family name before the given name; the Chinese name Wong Li Ping translates to Mr. Wong. Many Chinese-Americans, however, Anglicize the order of their names. Sometimes by the first generation, and certainly by the second and third generations, we see names such as Mr. Robert Wong.

More important, in Asian cultures it is inappropriate to call attention to oneself by what mainstream American culture calls blowing one's own horn. Americans may say, "The squeaky wheel gets the grease," but there is an expression in Japanese that says, "The nail that sticks up is the one that gets pounded down." When marketing to Japanese and Chinese consumers, it's a good idea not to show an individual achieving personal gain or performing a feat of heroism by using the product or service but to show how the family or group benefits from its use.

In Latin America, the group is the family or the extended family, and obligation to the family usually supersedes all other responsibilities. Because of the interlocking system of godparentship, families include both those who are blood relations and some who are not.

A few years ago, I rented a condominium in Puerto Rico and asked the housekeeper to buy a one-pound box of rice for the delicious Puerto Rican dish arroz con pollo (chicken with rice). She came back with a three-pound box of rice and apologized, explaining that there were no one-pound boxes.

My marketer's curiosity got the better of me, and I toured supermarkets within a twenty-mile radius of my condo. There were no one-pound boxes of rice to be found. Of course, I realized, rice is the primary staple of the island. Puerto Ricans tend to have large extended families, and members who drop in are always invited to have a plate of food. A one-pound box of rice would be gone in one dinner. Since the larger sizes are more economical, it's not unusual to see twenty and fifty pound sacks of rice at the big mainland-style supermarkets.

When designing packaging to appeal to the Hispanic market, cooking instructions and pictures should show culturally appropriate quantities. Also, when marketing to the Hispanic population, it's smart to avoid ads showing a diner eating alone; such ads would violate the well-known rule of marketing that people are most likely to buy products if they can identify with the individuals in the ads, promotion, or sales situation.

This family or group orientation was the key issue in the failure of a promotional campaign that was offered in Los Angeles, where there are a large number of Hispanics. Radio listeners were urged to enter a contest, with the prize of two expensive tickets to Disneyland. Promoters were astonished that so few people entered the contest. They failed to consider that many Hispanics have large or extended families and wouldn't think of participating in an offering in which they would have to choose only two members.

## Rank, Hierarchy, and Tradition

The issues of rank, place, and hierarchy can affect buying patterns in the traditional Hispanic family. The head of the family is the "patron," or senior male, who is ultimately responsible for everyone in his family. To some degree, this arrangement limits the role of women in the family. Assimilation and acculturation have influenced this tradition, however, and in many Hispanic families buying decisions are now made by both husband and wife.

In traditional Latin American families, if a woman works, it implies that the men in the family cannot take care of her. Therefore, if you want to sell cars to first or second-generation Hispanics, your advertising, promotion, and selling should have a group or family orientation.

Consider, for example, a 1990 ad campaign for a Chevrolet car in a mainstream women's magazine. The ad showed a pretty young woman saying, "What's the rush? Sure, I'd like to get married, but I love my work. And I don't have to answer to anybody."

This type of ad would not work well with Hispanic consumers, except, perhaps, for a third-generation, well-educated, highly assimilated woman of Hispanic ancestry in the Southwest. But softening the message by showing the young woman with friends or out driving with her husband and baby would key into the group or family identity that is so important to Hispanics.

Tradition is an important cultural value for many groups. Tradition plays a big role in the lives of Asian-Americans, who see change as not necessarily desirable. For many Asian-Americans, older is better. The elderly are revered for their knowledge and experience and are respected far more than young people.

Positioning a product as "new and improved," therefore, is not the best way to reach a traditional Asian consumer. A much better way to reach the Asian-American audience is to stress the manufacturer's long-standing reputation for quality and reliability: "We at XYZ Co. have produced quality products for thirty years and look forward to serving your family or company for years to come."

Preserving dignity and saving face are extremely important values for most Asians and many Hispanics. Knocking the competition in any selling campaign is frowned on, because the mud slinger causes the other company to lose face. It also makes the combative company look bad. Instead of comparing your products or services to those of the competition, emphasize the benefits and strengths of your own product or service.

## Religion

Religion plays a big part in the way people perceive and use products and services. When George McGovern was campaigning for president in 1972, he offended traditionally observant Jews by visiting a kosher delicatessen and asking for a kosher hot dog and a glass of milk. Traditionally observant Jews are forbidden to mix dairy and meat products in the same cooking utensils or to eat them in the same meal. McGovern violated not only the kosher law but the marketers' law that reads, "Know thy product, know thy market." His gaffe clearly cost him many votes because negative word-of-mouth spreads like wildfire.

One U.S. company exported its goods to the Middle East with packaging that had stylized designs vaguely resembling crosses and stars on its packaging. In the Middle East, where Islam is the dominant religion, designs with what was interpreted to be Judeo-Christian symbols are unacceptable, and the company was booted out of the market.

## Taste and Diet

Taste and diet play a big part in people's lives. Preferences are rooted partly in religion, partly in the practical question of what foods are available in a group's homeland.

It's easy to make mistakes if you're not tuned into these preferences. For example, some Asians are lactose-intolerant (as are some people of other ethnic groups). Most adults in China do not have dairy foods in their diets and consider cheese to be spoiled milk. Imagine their surprise, then, when a midwestern trade group visiting its sister city in China brought a wheel of (justifiably famous) cheese as a gift to its Chinese hosts.

A study reported in the May 1991 *Atlantic Monthly* magazine mapped areas of the United States where people are more likely than the average American to prefer tartness in their food and drink and areas where they are more likely to prefer sweetness. The map, which was based on market data about the popularity of lemon-lime soft drinks and which was called "The Lemon-Lime Latitudes" revealed that the areas where tart drinks don't sell well tend to have large proportions of black and Hispanic consumers and are clustered in the Southern and coastal parts of the country. The article reported that "food historians say that popularity of sweets among blacks may have its roots, in part, in the plantation system of the South, where sugarcane was a source of cheap calories. Hispanic-American cuisine uses less meat and is more highly seasoned than northern European cuisine and demands a different complement; sweeter (or blander) flavors."

## Colors, Numbers, and Symbols

Aesthetic elements, such as colors, numbers, symbols, and gestures, are important to consider when marketing to ethnics. If a foreign company were to use a black cat slinking through a ladder with thirteen rungs to illustrate the elegance or sleekness of its product, the ad probably wouldn't appeal to the many mainstream Americans who associate those symbols with bad luck.

Before you laugh at that image, consider that one U.S. company offered its products in Japan in lots of four displayed with white packaging. To many Asians, both the number four and white cloth or clothing are associated with death. To a mainstream American, on the other hand, the number four is quite innocuous and white is a symbol of purity.

Remember, too, when former President Ronald Reagan would get off an airplane somewhere in Latin America and give the A-OK sign, with his thumb and forefinger in a closed circle. To most Latin Americans (and to some Europeans and Asians), that gesture is obscene.

## Assimilation and Acculturation

There are many cultural issues that may affect the marketing and sales success of your products and services. But we must also take into account the assimilation level of ethnic consumers in determining the marketing mix strategy for foods and services.

If we are doing our job properly, we'll take the time to research how assimilated our customers are. In addition to using geodemographic databases, we'll take a long look at where our ethnic and minority customers live and listen to how well they speak English.

We'll see what they eat and how they prepare it; find out how long they have lived in the United States; learn how and if their values have changed; see what their personal and professional affiliations are and what their education levels are. The level of assimilation and acculturation must be factored into marketing campaigns. (Assimilation is when an immigrant group adopts mainstream values and behaviors instead of keeping the culture of their heritage; acculturation means adding some elements of the mainstream culture without abandoning the native culture.) This may sound like a big job, but experience has shown that the gunshot method of marketing is more expensive in the long run, because it reaches few and alienates many.

It's interesting to note, however, that in marketing to teenagers and young adults, assimilation and acculturation sometimes work in reverse, that is, the mainstream takes on some aspects of the ethnic or minority culture. Black culture has strongly influenced the music, clothing, and speech of young people in the American mainstream and is considered quite fashionable.

In fact, this phenomenon has not only influenced U.S. teens but has given rise to a global "youth market." Just walk down any street in Tokyo, Munich, Lagos, Tel Aviv, Sao Paulo, or Chicago and, adjusting for regional ethnic differences, you'll see that teens look very much alike. They wear the same jeans, T-shirts, and sneakers, have similar hairstyles, eat and drink the same soda and burgers, and, most important, listen to the same pop music. Global goods, such as soda, jeans, cigarettes, and inexpensive cosmetics, can be sold in the same way with just about the same marketing campaign to any ethnic group anywhere in the world, thanks to the great pressure for conformity among teenagers, at least on the surface.

On the other end of the spectrum, expensive goods, such as diamonds, gold watches, luxury cars, and aged scotch, are also considered global goods and can be sold in much the same way to the very rich of almost any ethnic segment anywhere in the world. The people who regularly buy these goods have one important shared characteristic: money, and lots of it.

Once we move away from these two groups—one in which MTV has become its own subculture and one in which wealth is culturally unifying—we must consider the ways in which we differ in how we use and perceive things. Culture is a powerful and deep part of our lives. Marketers who hope to prosper in the twenty-first century will realize that tastes will never be uniform in the United States or anywhere else and will adapt their product line to reach profitable ethnic segments.

## About the Author

Marlene L. Rossman, president of Rossman, Graham Associates (New York), has helped major U.S. and overseas companies develop sales and marketing strategies, including multicultural programs. This chapter is excerpted from *Multicultural Marketing: Selling to Diverse Markets* (1994) available from AMACOM Books at 518-891-1500.

Ms. Rossman is a trainer for the American Management Association and a frequent speaker and radio/television guest expert. She is also an adjunct professor of marketing at Pace University School of Business and the author of *The International Businesswoman of the 1990s*, as well as numerous articles and sales training films. She can be reached at: Rossman, Graham Associates, 201 E. 17th Street, New York, NY 10003. Phone: 212-533-5981; Fax: call for hook-up.

# The New Spin on Corporate Work Teams

by Cassandra Hayes (*Black Enterprise*)

Are self-directed teams beating the experts at achieving multicultural harmony in the workplace?

Work teams, the darlings of corporate America's reengineering efforts, have taken off. Over the past decade, teaming has become a way of life in virtually all American companies. Why the great appeal? Heightened productivity, improved quality and customer service, fewer layers of management as well as increased employee morale are just a few of the selling points.

As teams come of age in many firms, an interesting, and rather surprising, additional benefit has surfaced as well. Based on the experiences of several firms, it now appears that teams indirectly support an important workplace initiative—diversity. When team members are forced to work closely together toward common goals, the most unlikely alliances can, and do, emerge.

Darrel Ray, Ph.D., is a consultant who has specialized in work team development for the past 12 years. He recalls working with one particularly memorable group: five black men and five white women charged with processing credit card insurance claims for a financial services company. "Sparks were flying the moment they got together," says Ray, who is a Senior Associate with ODT, Inc. in Amherst, MA. Expected to manage themselves, team members found it impossible to work together. Resentment, backstabbing and unresponsiveness on both sides were the order of the day. Cooperation and communication—the hallmarks of successful teamwork—were nonexistent.

After about two months, the team facilitator—a black male—intervened and got the members to air their differences. For three hours, "there was a lot of yelling and crying," says Ray. But once they had expressed the fears, stereotypes and assumptions they had about one another, they were able to get on to the business at hand. After a month, productivity had jumped markedly and several team members were even socializing after work.

Of all the types of work teams, the self-directed, or self-managed, work team is most effective in promoting diversity. In this arrangement, employees are responsible for all phases of a team's operation from hiring to maintaining quality control, from devising strategy to scheduling, from ordering materials and equipment to setting profit targets—and everything in between.

Generally, it's up to the company to define job responsibilities and set up rewards and incentives to motivate workers. But it's the team members' responsibility to figure out, on their own, how to work together to achieve the group's goals. In this sense, self-directed teams are unique. The members have a built-in opportunity to build the intercultural bridges that some companies are paying diversity consultants thousands to install.

"I've seen many diversity processes and workshops, and the truth is, many of them don't work," notes Ray, who co-authored the book *Teaming Up* with ODT's president, Howard Bronstein (McGraw-Hill). Balanced, fruitful relationships across racial and ethnic lines are a real by-product of self-directed work teams. "With other types of teams there is still a manager to use as a go-between, or to run crying to when things go wrong or when you want to complain about somebody or place blame," says Ray. "With self-directed teams, you no longer have that choice. Team members have to come to grips with each other and their differences face-to-face, day to day, in order to get their jobs done."

## Breaking Down Barriers

For years, language barriers among workers at Standard Motor Products (SMP) in Edwardsville, KS, formed an impenetrable block between African-American and white workers (who are actually in the minority there) and the company's Latino and Asian employees. Even the introduction of English language classes five years ago, partially subsidized by the auto supply company, didn't help. Hardly anyone attended them. Then three years ago, in the face of increasing foreign competition, the company implemented self-directed work teams to make operations more cost-efficient. The teams delivered savings—and more.

At SMP, team members take responsibility, on a rotating basis, for various tasks. At some point, each member heads the team. This means that the workers can no longer rely on a bilingual supervisor or claim language ignorance when something doesn't get done. Many workers, some of whom had been with the company for over a decade, were forced to learn English for the first time.

Downtime at SMP has dropped by about 60%, according to Ernest Lewis, chairman of Local 710 of the United Auto Workers, which represents some 300 employees at the plant. "Work teams have allowed the communication lines to open. In the past, employees who didn't speak English would not participate or mingle with those who did," he says. Now, productivity is up, along with camaraderie. There is more dialogue between the groups, says Lewis, so they are learning more about each other.

Generally, they're also earning more. SMP implemented an employee gain-sharing program. Quarterly cash awards are based on the amount of money the company saves on productivity, quality, returned products and safety costs due to team efforts.

For example, if $50,000 was allocated annually for work-related injuries and only $35,000 was used, then SMP splits the $15,000 50-50 with its employees. Other factors such as attendance and customer satisfaction also affect how much an employee receives. In the first year, awards averaged $2,000 each, thanks to gain sharing.

Morale is up at SMP. The number of employee grievances filed against management has dropped from more than 50 in 1993 to 20 last year; employee turnover is also on the decline.

## Management's Role In Teaming

Of course, none of the benefits of a self-directed team—cross-cultural or otherwise—can be achieved without first laying a solid foundation. Many managers underestimate the time and effort it takes to make a team work. According to consultant Ray, it takes an organization at least six

months to measure potential gains and evaluate costs to see if teams will be beneficial.

Companies must create appraisal and compensation systems, like SMP's gain-sharing program, to fairly measure and reward team performance. They can't expect to increase productivity without paying employees to take on additional responsibility. For teams to stay motivated, "companies have to pay 10% or more above the market rate," says Ray. Beyond that, says Glenn Hallam, research associate at the Center for Creative Leadership in Colorado Springs, Colo., "praise and acknowledgment for a team's contributions" are essential.

It takes another three months to design team selection and training sessions. "Anything less," says Ray, "and the organization is fooling itself." Developing a self-directed work team is an exacting process. "Unless there is shared responsibility for the work, shared authority to make decisions and shared ability, there is really no team," says Hallam.

Communication between team members and management is essential. It's impossible for teams to thrive if members are unclear about their roles and responsibilities and management's expectations. Managers must be involved throughout the entire process. They can't just set up the group and then leave it to fend for itself. "They must be committed to getting into the boat with the workforce and crossing the ocean," says Ray. "They can't send them off alone and get in only if the workforce comes back alive."

Ironically, from a manager's viewpoint, the incentive is not always there. A successful self-directed work team ultimately eliminates the need for a manager.

Few know this better than Janie Payne, organization development consultant at Bell Atlantic Corp. in Arlington, Va. In 1988, Payne, who was then an assistant manager in the customer service area, orchestrated Bell Atlantic's most successful self-directed work teams by herself, without any training. Since then, she has experienced firsthand the growing pains associated with setting up a self-directed work team in a hierarchical organization.

Payne's very first team was a hit. In two years, it slashed customer response time from eight days to less than eight hours. Quality of service increased by more than 40%. As they cross-trained and gained additional skills, seven of the team's 15 members were promoted.

Meanwhile, Payne's priorities also shifted. Instead of spending 75% of her time responding to customers, as she had done in the past, she now spent that time developing her team. She also watched them steadily absorb all of her previous responsibilities, as well as those of three other managers.

For Payne, the risks were worthwhile. In 1992, she was promoted to organization development consultant. Today, she and another colleague oversee Bell Atlantic's team initiatives for all of its 70,000 employees, 24% of whom are black. In her experience, the self-directed work team has proven "the epitome of teams for empowering employees and encouraging them to appreciate the differences of the group."

## Not Just a Fad

Over the next five years, Hallam predicts, the hard work and expense associated with the self-directed work team concept will discourage many companies. Nonetheless, many more will take the plunge. Although the main impetus for implementing teams is to heighten productivity, the human incentive is just as significant, says Hallam. True team members can't help but get closer to one another, and as they do, they tend to become like family. "Teams provide a sense of community. With people spending more of their day at work, it makes sense to look to fill that need for family within the context of the organization," Hallam explains.

If corporate America remains true to its diversity initiatives, that family, at all levels, will increasingly be made up of various ethnic groups. Self-directed work teams can improve a company's bottom line. But more importantly, they can also help different groups of people get along, both in—and out of—the office.

## About the Author

Cassandra Hayes is a staff writer for *Black Enterprise Magazine*, where her primary duties include writing and editing the magazine's Powerplay section. An alumna of Columbia University Graduate School of Journalism, Ms. Hayes also writes feature stories on career management and workplace issues and trends, as well as travel articles for the *Black Enterprise Magazine*.

*Black Enterprise Magazine* has 288,000 subscribers and a total readership of over 3.1 million people. It recently celebrated its 25th anniversary. For subscription information, call toll-free 1-800-727-7777. Or write to them at 130 Fifth Avenue, New York, NY 10011-4399 (Fax: 212-886-9610). Subscriptions are 12 issues for $15.95.

# PART 8
# SPIRIT

# Dialogue: On Spirit

*Bob*—This section focuses on the rich spiritual heritage and deep religious traditions of U.S. culture. It contains perspectives from Jewish, Buddhist, Christian, Muslim, and other faiths. Some are explicitly religious, some simply call out from the depths of the human spirit. For example, nothing I have read so eloquently proclaims the inclusiveness at the heart of diversity than the closing piece, Robert Fulghum's essay, "Where Do Mermaids Stand?" As Fulghum observes, it takes humility to recognize when we play the fool, and courage to wake up to the talent, perspectives and contributions of the people around us. These are products of the spirit.

*George*—People nourish themselves as individuals and groups with theology and spirituality. Women, in recent years, have been busy creating theologies, though many might not call it that. Women have been exploring ancient images of the mother goddess, and empowering their daily lives with attention to languaging and imagery that is inclusive of women's experience of reality. Witches, hags and crones are now positive figures in this revitalized mythology of the feminine.

My observation is that the black community has long nourished itself from Christian roots. The African-American community has also created another spiritual resource, the Nation of Islam. Furthermore, Black scholars and others have of late been exploring indigenous African religions that pre-date the invasion of European colonizers. People feel a need to celebrate who they are, and see how what they do is connected with the deeper meaning of their lives.

In this section we want to present how such spiritual resources work. We encourage people to tap into them to inspire and sustain the diversity enterprise. Spirit is the best kept secret in America—we keep it from the public eye, though usually not from ourselves. Much of what we do emerges from our spiritual side.

Separation of church and state in the U.S. makes us keep religion in low profile or at least separate from our workplace endeavors. Additionally, re-sentment and fears about other people's religiosity, of fundamentalism or liberalism, keep U.S. Americans from talking rationally. Religious divisions on issues like school prayer, homosexuality, and abortion often keep people from discussing these issues in a civil fashion.

But, we have some deep inconsistencies in this regard. Despite the wedge we have driven between the spiritual and the secular, we are motivated by values that do not come from the marketplace or politics. Quite the contrary, many are likely to engage in politics and the marketplace for another reason—what our hearts believe is right. What we do at work and how we behave there often takes its cues from things we would call our "faith," "spiritual awareness" or "enlightenment."

*Bob*—When we walk on eggshells around this topic, we fail to make contact with an important dimension of diversity work.

*George*—And we have to remember that the early steps toward diversity in this land resulted from the search for freedom to practice one's religion . . . but when widely differing groups had to live side by side a philosophy of tolerance was necessary and ultimately became a constitutional right. The more recent wave of ecumenical movement of the 60's was not exclusively a North American phenomenon, but it brought at least mainline U.S. religious groups into ongoing dialogue, communities of faith and cooperative efforts both in religious education and social service.

*Bob*— . . . even if groups of settlers and colonists originally claimed freedom only *for their own group,* they established *principles of pluralism* that we can still call on today.

*George*—U.S. mythology includes two key ingredients: freedom of the individual and freedom from state oppression. Freedom of the individual is historically tied to freedom of conscience, i.e., religion. Freedom from state oppression comes in the form of resistance to taxation. We don't have as deep a commitment to a social safety net as many other countries do, because the national myth is founded on not paying taxes, i.e., the Boston Tea

Party. Mostly some people wanted independence—they were doing well and wanted to do better. The myth grew to justify that desire.

*Bob*—That's why the tea went into the harbor. When was the first year the United States had an income tax?

*George*—The first successful tax was enacted by President Woodrow Wilson in 1913 and required a constitutional amendment. Not paying taxes is just about as sacred as not having a state church. I wish the debate about religious values was as public as the noise over taxes.

*Bob*—Aren't we entering somewhat risky territory here? Proclaiming that the diversity dialogue in the U.S. can be enhanced by drawing on the world's religious heritage . . .

*George*—Yes, we could turn off the agnostics and atheists, and annoy those who feel oppressed by their own religious background or come from a very rigid spiritual framework and feel offended before they get a whiff of what other traditions offer. Religion has been tossed into the melting pot, too. People struggle with their religious tradition as part of their cultural background as they become "Americans." In the U.S., they learn that religion is something you personally and individually choose—or reject, not something you are from birth, even though the opposite may be more often true. Strong family structures contribute to this. The macroculture, the dominant values in the U.S. culture, shapes religion, too, and tears at inherited values of religion as well as other values.

*Bob*—In this section we look to religious traditions for practical reasons. First, we believe they help us live out diversity in new ways because they can join people together in intentional and purposeful communities. Secondly, we are convinced (and this is true whether you believe in a higher power or not) that spiritual traditions have some very powerful things to say about the topic of diversity, ways of accepting or reconciling differences . . .

*George*—It occurs to me as you talk about our "practical reasons" for examining spirit and diversity, that perhaps you and I are doing what we talked about earlier . . . We're being pragmatic (a U.S. cultural value) about religion. But, you're right, spiritual community and the mandate of so many religious traditions—to love, to have com-

passion, to serve your brother and sister, the alien and the outcast—are rarely spoken about explicitly in the diversity dialogue.

*Bob*—It's interesting—I mentioned this when we introduced the "Best Practices" section—how spiritual values are often the core belief systems of those most competent in managing diversity in organizations. Religion provides the purest reflection of the societal debate between what we've called "The forces for cohesion" and "The forces for difference" . . .

*George*— . . . or assimilation or acculturation, versus balkanization. The "forces for cohesion" are those elements of the culture that have us emphasize the things we have in common, the ways in which we share a common heritage, ideology, or practice. The "forces for difference" reflect the ways in which we feel separate from others who are not part of the group we most closely identify with.

*Bob*—The debate between "The forces for cohesion" and "The forces for difference" is reflected throughout this *Sourcebook*. On one side we look at individual perspectives like Schlesinger's (page 268) and note how the political right is now talking freedom of speech, etc., while some on the left are encouraging limits (like codes of speech) and restrictive legislation. On the other side, we present articles that examine the group dynamics and cultural forces influencing the American psyche more apparent to outsiders than ourselves ("Innocents Abroad," page 156). So there are forces for cohesion on both the individual and collective levels. We also look at the uniqueness of cultural groups immigrating and living here, and the distinctiveness of their experiences in coming to grips with U.S. culture.

*George*—If we reflected on these "forces for difference," what would we include on the list?

*Bob*—I think it started in my era with black power and black pride in the 60s. Since then, we've had a movement to correct historical omissions and distortions as in Black History—we've even dedicated the month of February to that. I would also list the women's movement, including breakthrough research in psychology by Carol Gilligan and others, the renewed interest in the biological basis for differences between women and men (see page 130—"Gray Matters"), and that very shady area of differences between races and ethnicities, the attempts to have research establish different IQ ranges for whites and blacks, for example.

*George*—It seems like rewriting history books and redefining language are important in the search for dignity and wholeness on the part of so many ethnic groups.

*Bob*—Yes, U.S. American women accomplished this as well. We could also put Political Correctness on our list. Ethnic pride, including European-American ethnic pride are all part of the forces for difference. Sometimes European-American ethnic pride seems healthy and informed as in the Resisting Defamation group or frightening and ignorant as in the Aryan Nation, and other Neo-Nazi groups (see "Keeping Hate Out of the Workplace, page 403).

*George*—It all comes down to where we draw the line between "Self" and "Other," "Individual" and "Group." We may think that Native American religions had a strong sense of collectivism, and in our U.S.-pragmatic way we see this as necessary to support their group nomadic lifestyle or fragile ecological base. But this does not tell us about them, only about how we think about them. It may only be a mental projection of ours. The classical Greek thinkers posed this problem as that of "the one and the many." How do we account for difference and sameness? How do we manage them? What is a bundle of sticks to one person is a chair for another. Our minds and our use of the sticks make them into a chair (a one, a unity) until it is broken up (many) and cast into the fireplace.

*Bob*—Once again, the one vs. the many. If religion's purpose is union with the divine, is it a mystical love-making between two beings, or a mind-melt in which we disappear into the All like a drop of water into the sea? If "charity starts at home," how far out does "family" go (and my actions in its behalf)? To the neighborhood? The nation? All sentient beings . . . ?

*George*—Pondering imponderables is spirit business. It's the realm of theology and philosophy and the struggles between them. Out of it we create the things we call "harmony," "balance," "the middle way." It's the whole enterprise that counts, the holding and ruminating on the paradoxes and

mysteries of life, those that can't be reduced to a scientific formula. As a matter of fact, today the hard sciences don't look so hard any more as we hear of such things as the Tao of Physics being discussed by qualified Ph.D.s. Religion and serious science (even psychology) are much more comfortable bedfellows today than the cynicism of much popular media with its focus on cults, abuse and aberration would lead us to believe.

*Bob*—Religion is not always, despite our U.S. cultural bias, an individual matter. It isn't that way for Latinos, by and large, nor for Hasidic Jews, though the U.S. culture keeps trying to change them.

*George*—The problem that religions face, and we in the West have faced for hundreds of years now, is the temptation to fall into dichotomous thinking. We do too much "either-or" thinking. But when the conflict gets too great to manage—U.S. dominant culture is also conflict-adverse—we become syncretistic, unhappy unless all of our beliefs fall into one happy family and we can say, "Well, there are no real differences . . . " Religions become same-old, same-old, or we assert that there is a *philosophia perennis,* which is one way scholars have asserted that there is an abiding core which makes all religions essentially the same. This does to religious diversity what assimilation does to people.

If you think in right-wrong, black-white terms you come away with empty hands from your encounter with difference. On the other hand, if you think, as Rabbi Stevie Robbins used to put it when he was Hillel chaplain at Berkeley, in terms of "On one hand . . . And then on the other hand . . . " you come away with both hands full. Religions and spiritualities have not "solved" diversity but have developed a lot of wisdom from long efforts at managing it. That bears listening to.

*Bob*—Theology goes crazy when it loses the perspective of history. There is a reason why the pendulum swings from individualism to community and back again in different ages and environments. The U.S.'s keen sense of individualism came already with the Puritans. These early religiously motivated communities planted the first-person singular pronoun on American soil. "Puritans taught Americans to trust the 'I,' to respect and protect individuals against the tyranny of the group," says Richard Rodriguez, editor at Pacific News Service.

*George*— . . . and the frontier called for self-reliance and mostly small group reliance. On the other hand, in Catholicism prayer is deeply communal. If Protestantism gave Christianity an understanding of the "I," then Catholicism promoted the experience of "We." How Americans trade off the balance between the individual and the collective is a good deal of what public policy, politics, and current values debates are about. Perhaps it's time we re-explored the origins of these belief systems.

Catholicism emphasizes liturgy and community, not bible and conscience, though it has been substantially assimilated to these Protestant values in the U.S. The persecution of Catholics in the U.S. throughout the last century and into this has left its mark. Anti-Catholic feelings directed against my father kept him from opening a shop in Chagrin Falls, Ohio as late as 1950. Today a lot of my friends jokingly describe themselves as "recovering Catholics," but I see what they are doing (or a big part of it) as their need to be assimilated to dominant U.S. religious culture with its dominant Protestant flavor. They are looking for self-esteem and acceptance in this individualist society. But, it's a two-edged sword. To the extent that they pull themselves free from the collective warmth of Catholicism which they experience as oppressive, a loneliness starts to develop. Many of them start making psychic space for nostalgia about their once dreaded Catholic past and ruminate about it together.

*Bob*—This struggle has other roots as well. Forces for universality are "Yin" and forces for emphasizing difference are "Yang." In Taoist philosophy these names describe the nature of the opposites within the whole. The pendulum swings back and forth between them. It never reaches the point of complete exclusion of one or the other, before reversing its direction. When you think of the diversity debate as it swings between assimilation and separateness in this context, it seems far less perplexing.

*George*—Even in the Buddhist tradition there are such philosophical splits. Hinayana Buddhism, "the little raft," focuses on personal enlightenment—an approach somewhat comparable to the Protestant spirit of the American psyche. This contrasts with the postponing of one's personal arrival until everyone else is taken care of—as found in Mahayana Buddhism, "the great raft."

Buddhism mirrors the dual nature of the Catholic churches, viz., the Romans, Anglicans and others like them. On one hand, they have orders of contemplative nuns and monks, usually cloistered and in silence, and on the other, priests and religious sisters and brothers who are on mission out in the world helping the sick and needy, or running church-related hospitals, orphanages, schools, etc. Catholic theology says they need each other. The idea that spirituality and social justice are intertwined and support each other is a very old one.

*Bob*—Nearly every religious lineage has major philosophical splits and branches. The only exception I can think of is the Baha'i faith (see the article on page 351), but it was itself the result of one such split. Many sects of the Muslim world are violently opposed to others. It's true in the Christian world as well.

Sometimes it is difficult to sort out the true nature of separatist violence, for example Northern Ireland, the former Yugoslavia, and Cyprus, as well as the causes and remedies. Religious differences and historical relationships only begin to explain, for example, ethnic-cleansing. Inevitably power, economic disparities and their social effects—the broad definition of class we are working on—are key ingredients. This reinforces our assertion throughout this volume that attention to "class" will identify the multiple core of such conflicts a bit better.

*George*—Playing on religious values where they are strong, along ethnic lines, is also a tactic of unscrupulous power seekers. It's a divide-and-conquer strategy which the Hitlers and Milosovics of the world use for their own purposes. Sadly, they also add to the burden of future hatred. It's nearly impossible to break this on-going cycle. Germany is one hopeful sign. But it took bitter defeat to bring that about. Today Germany, despite the amount of press it gets when its skinheads act up, is certainly more conscious and conscientious than most countries in this regard. Racist outbreaks are at least as common in Italy, France and Britain, but they rarely get the exposure in the U.S. press that Germany does. Recent studies by the ILO and others indicate that even The Netherlands, which has always prided itself on not being like the Germans, has a citizenry that is far more likely to act out of bias toward foreigners than the Germans are.

*Bob*—We're talking about hate and hurt now. Religion has caused them but also healed them. Let's look at a few positive values. One can go back to ancient Sanskrit teachings to hear that "all religion is kindness." Ghandi exemplified this and was at the cutting edge of where religion and politics intersect. Ghandi professed that "all religions are true." It's also a Hindu and Buddhist belief that "non-injury is the highest duty." What implications does that have if a culture chooses to emphasize "ahimsa," non-injury and the preciousness of life?

*George*—The problem is that in order to do so you make yourself very vulnerable. You march up to life and take it on the chin. I wonder what would have happened if Ghandi's non-violent protesters had faced Himmler's SS or Mao's Red Guard instead of British regulars? Still this was commitment of spirit to healing. Diversity gives us this richness. How boring life would be if we were all the same. . . . Even when we talk about the common good, or teamwork in business, we're making the assumption that there is difference to draw on for a better result than we could achieve as individuals.

*Bob*—A 14th century sociologist, Ibn Khalbun . . .

*George*—A 14th century sociologist! . . .

*Bob*—I know it's anachronistic, but listen to what he had to say. Ibn Khalbun identified a cultural trait he called "Asabiyah." He saw it as the "team spirit" of a culture, a people's willingness to pull together for the common good, to be a caring, harmonious society. For Ibn Khalbun "Asabiyah overwhelms diversity." If he were alive today, he'd probably put the U.S. on the bottom of the scale if he saw how our emphasis on "diversity" was like acid rain on the cement that binds us together.

*George*—In the U.S. individualism is the supreme value—including my *right* to develop my property any way I see fit, even to the detriment of polluting the community, or damaging ecological diversity . . . all the way to my prerogative to own and carry a semi-automatic weapon. In the light of the Okla-homa bombing, many U.S.-Americans are now discussing this right, but it hasn't been questioned seriously in the popular press before. Geert Hofstede in his now classic study of diversity among managers confirmed this strong trait of individualism for U.S. culture. (See reference [at end of Future section] on page 504.)

*Bob*—The U.S. became a powerful nation founded on an adversarial spirit between us and our neighbors, and even amongst ourselves. What was a driving force for ascendancy to power now seems to be a force for tearing us down.

*George*—I'm not sure we'd want to change the adversarial nature of our society entirely. The U.S. thrives on the possibility of controlled conflict. Witness the design of our constitutionally-based system of checks and balances. Nobody *should* get too much power. The assumption is that if everybody concerned is politically active, this will be impossible. As we know this is not always, if ever, the case. Therefore there is a wide range of power swings. If you strike the phrase "under God" from "one nation, under God" you still have to use spiritual forces to keep us "indivisible" in the pursuit of liberty and justice.

Concern for the underdog in U.S. culture, at least to the degree that the underdog is motivated to fight for his or her share, also helps balance things out. We also have devices like handicapping in a golf game which enables people of different talents to compete with each other and work to better their own game simultaneously by playing with people better than themselves. However, when sports become professional, like boxing, professional golf, or football, where all that counts is raw performance and skill or teamwork, everyone is considered an equal competitor and there are no handicaps. You make it or are sent down to the minor leagues.

Maybe we need an outlook that integrates both perspectives. While pro sports may be a model for business, the truth is you have a very select number of players in the pro game . . . the top half of 1%. In business you need a variety of talents, many of which come from "average" folks. In order to develop everybody, you need a policy that's both competitive and compassionate; one that enables people to develop themselves, with feedback, coaching, role modeling, training and skill practice.

Religious communities have been one of the factors in the environment caring for those too bruised and helpless to play in the game, those excluded or who have decided to opt out. People in need of care and healing have gravitated towards religious communities . . .

*Bob*—On the other hand, religion has also been a subversive force. It often seeks to level power structures in favor of the poor and oppressed. It goes on today in the Liberation Theology of Latin American churches. This is one reason for both the persecution of religious institutions and the attempts to declaw them by, for example, declaring an official religion answerable to the state . . .

*George*— . . . or allotting it too much public money.

*Bob*—Religion and the individual believer are accountable only to God. For those who want to wield power, particularly absolute power, religion is a loose cannon on the ship of state. When Ashoka or Constantine get converted—each of them were heads of state who made a new religion (Buddhism and Christianity, respectively) the state religion—it ultimately bodes ill for the life of the spirit.

*George*—Because of its independence from the influence of the state, religious charity, in the best sense of the word, greatly impacted the history and development of this country. Today this volunteerism of faith and philanthropy is becoming weaker and weaker. There are fewer people involved and fewer resources available. Think of how the costs of health care have driven so many religious groups out of control of the hospitals they created. Women were traditionally powerful forces of volunteerism. Their husbands' salaries could support their being volunteers. Now women either want to work or have to work given the decline in average earning power in the last twenty-five years. Women's work roles have also increased as a function of the dramatic rise in the number of female heads-of-households.

*Bob*—I don't think our women readers will appreciate being seen as the caretakers . . .

*George*— . . . certainly not, and all too many of them are still stuck in low-paying, dead-end and care-taking jobs anyway. But we're simply looking at one real reason why charitable work has shrunk. Peter Drucker in a recent article, "The Age of Social Transformation" (*Atlantic Monthly*, November, 1994, pages 53–80, passim.) points to this decline and argues for the reempowerment and growth of what he calls a "social sector" that would include religious groups.

Drucker argues that government at least since the New Deal has stepped in and become the great social caretaker and its programs are failing. Business, in prosperous and more stable times a provider of social benefits, can no longer offer life-time employment. The nature of work and competition is putting an end to this. Pensions are declining as are most other benefits.

How do we bring about a renewed and effective social force? Who will take care of the rapidly increasing number of powerless in a society where having and using power is an absolute value for success, if there is no social sector? Even the homeless are using what power they have to take care of themselves on the streets, almost as a separate society. Drucker's article is long on challenge and short on solutions.

*Bob*—Ralph G.H. Siu, the contributor of "'Us' Versus 'Them'" (page 342) says, "Diversity in power is necessary to move society." In the context of the "checks and balances" you have mentioned, the question becomes, "What level of inequality of power is reasonable? or unreasonable?" The trend we've observed at various points throughout the *Sourcebook*, and confirmed again here—we are moving at an accelerating pace to greater inequality.

Siu is the founder of the International Society of Panetics, whose objectives are none other than to minimize the unwarranted infliction of suffering in the world. While the scope of Siu's enterprise goes far beyond the covers of this book, it is interesting to note that public policy, foreign policy, as well as business and economic decision-making, would be quite different if minimizing suffering were a criterion. (See "Work and Serenity" by Siu in the *Cultural Diversity Fieldbook*, available from 800-736-1293.)

*George*—Of course, society now uses a "reasonable" infliction of suffering as a tool to get things done. We are more concerned with humaneness to animals than humanity toward humans. This is done on the basis of one single U.S. cultural value:

humans should be able to help themselves. For me this raises the question of the degree to which we are connected to our "fellow Americans." Or for that matter to "fellow Earth-dwellers." How separate are we really? Can I just take care of myself responsibly, and be the best I can be? Or, am I my brother's and sister's keeper? To what degree can I focus, or should I focus, on meeting the needs of my life, or my family, my community and my nation? How about my religious or ethnic group? When does my focus on my self and my home act to the detriment of, or lack of concern for, those outside my circle? These are all dimensions of the diversity question that spirit and religion have the resources to deal with, or at least work with, if they are allowed to be part of the debate.

*Bob*—Sally Walton's "Spiritual Dimensions of Globalization" points out another perspective—how urgently we need to recognize the role that religion and spirit play in other people's cultural traditions. If we are to interact satisfactorily, and to conduct business successfully, we need cultural data. In the U.S., we are inclined to keep religion in the background, and therefore we tend to project this attitude—downplaying the importance of religion—to others, where it is not true at all.

*George*—The "Gospel of Guyhood" from *Newsweek* presents a glimpse at the evangelical men's movement. I've been part of the men's movement for at least fifteen years now, and it was inevitable that it would provide a tool to renew men in religious traditions as well. Father Ray Roh, though we don't publish him in this anthology, is a Franciscan Catholic priest who has successfully done retreats on Christian manhood for years, so it's not surprising to see the evangelical approach to renewal directed at men as well.

Connecting men to their archetypal heritage is difficult. Men's stuff is a hard sell, mostly because both the feminist movement and numerous psychological practitioners of both genders approach men as broken objects to be fixed rather than as a culture to be understood, respected and acknowledged. If you tell men they need to be "fixed," they know exactly what that means and they want nothing to do it. Finding a positive approach is not easy. Finding and enjoying masculinity is complicated by what is today described as patriarchy and dominance. But when it comes to European-

American men, we must start from where we are. Recognizing what things men are doing and feeling, and helping us grow, using masculine resources and approaches, has paid off for the men's movement, both secular and religious.

*Bob*—Terry Dobson's story, "A Soft Answer," takes place in Japan. The piece is a moving one, but it underscores the need to cultivate compassion, even if it's the last thing you are inclined to do in the moment, when faced with someone scary or different. When we see the "other" as foreign, dirty, we often feel a need to control them, to fix them, or even to hurt them.

*George*—Dobson's tale also demonstrates how the principles of spirit need to be used to rein in spiritual hubris, that arrogance that comes from being "saved" as in Western religion or "enlightened" as in some Eastern tradition. On the other hand, Ralph G.H. Siu's article highlights how pervasive the dichotomy of self-versus-other is, and how it gets transmitted to us quite early in life. He reveals how there is a tendency to impute unfavorable, inferior, and fearsome traits to strangers. "Moving from Blame to Dialogue" (page 346) cites further examples of the tendency to project our fears outward in the form of hostility to others.

*Bob*—Moving from how we're different to how we're connected, Ellen Hofheimer Bettmann's contribution, "Jewish Sources of Inspiration in Doing Diversity," is a piece I really resonate with. Even with my own very liberal background of Reformed Judaism, I found that my own family culture and ethnic heritage conveyed the same principles she mentions. I never knew the Hebrew (or Yiddish) sayings that she quotes, but their meaning came across loud and clear to me as a child in the English language.

*George*—And how interesting it is to read about our connection to others from an Islamic perspective. The Muslim stories and sayings in "Islamic Universalism" by Rabia Harris provide a valuable viewpoint from a voice that's not often available in the mainstream U.S. press. We have a contribution from a Christian perspective as well . . .

*Bob*—Yes! Eric H. F. Law is a diversity consultant as well as an ordained Episcopal priest. His "Lessons for Diversity from a Spiritual Realm" (page 353) is provocative and insightful as it applies traditional Christianity to diversity issues. He uses the personal challenges he faced to foster his personal growth and to take his own faith to its next logical level of development.

*George*—You mentioned when we started that Robert Fulghum's "Where Do Mermaids Stand?" closes this section—it's also on the back cover of our *Sourcebook*. What makes it so special?

*Bob*—I think the "Mermaid" piece highlights the key concepts which are important for us to "get." We need to appreciate fully the discussion, debate, and dialogue concerning diversity today. You and I have tried to reflect that position in this book. I have several reasons for asserting this:

First, with the best of intentions, whenever we get in charge we are likely to leave people out of the "games" we play. Even if we think we're including everyone, and that everyone has a fair chance for participation, that's usually just not the case.

Secondly, it takes a good deal of courage to point out to those in power that there are people left out,

especially if you are one of those feeling left out. It takes so much energy to accept the rules as given, that little thought can be given about who might not be included.

*George*—It takes "a prophet," to use religious terms . . .

*Bob*—Yes, and you know what happens to them . . . That leads me to my third point, it takes courage (and humility) for those in charge to admit that the rules *just might* not have been inclusive or fair. It's easier to shoot the messenger.

Finally, once you've "got" numbers 1 through 3, actually remedying the situation may not be at all as hard as it first looks.

Maybe I've made too much of Fulghum's story. A Politically Correct power analysis of its dynamics (the authority figure being a white male, etc.) might rip it to shreds. But after all we've presented in this *Sourcebook*, risking a heart-warming story like that feels like a risk I can easily take. Enjoy the collection we've assembled here . . .

---

*"All creation speaks to us of diversity!"*

Laura Sarino-van der Smissen

---

# Spiritual Dimensions of Globalization

by Sally J. Walton

As we look to the new millennium, business has a global perspective, the environment is in global crisis, and the term globalization seems omnipresent. After discussions of the global aspects of manufacturing or services, management styles or conflict resolution, the next powerful step is the recognition of the spiritual dimension of globalization. Beyond management issues or conflict resolution models, spirituality is a human orientation underlying cultural values and behaviors.

Because the world is no longer defined by national boundaries in a parochial sense, we need new ways of thinking about and relating to our "globalized" reality. The core of human experience has always been an impulse toward the Infinite, whether expressed as religious traditions or personal spiritual seeking. It is natural, then, to use spiritual orientation as pivotal in developing those needed new ways of thinking and relating.

The world's cultures are a dizzying array of values and behaviors. But the outer diversity is only the tip of the iceberg. In recognizing deeper layers of the cultural iceberg, we go beyond the study of gestures or habits, beyond negotiating styles or motivation patterns to what underlies these outer differences. Exploring spirituality in cultural context is to acquire another tool for working within the world's pluralism.

Addressing similarities and differences in spiritual orientations is also a tool for visioning the future of our world. The richness of global spiritual resources offers us many vantage points for visioning the future we will create together. With instant telecommunication, interdependent stock markets, and wide-scale environmental impacts of war or industry, it is a future all the peoples of the world will create together, whether purposefully or inadvertently.

This same richness of spiritual perspectives offers us much on an individual level as well. As we search for a personal reorientation of values after the "greed decade" of the '80's, opening to the breadth and depth of the world's spiritual thought and practices may be the salvation for our psyches.

We have an opportunity to experience on a personal level the world's rich traditions and wisdom. This is not a wholesale adoption of other beliefs, any more than an outright rejection of them. Nor is it simply token mention in our public professional presentations. Rather, globalization offers more access and motivation to explore the world's spirituality, while exploration of this spirituality, in turn, can facilitate the challenges involved in cross-cultural interactions. The exposure to other world views in our era of globalization offers benefits to business, to our clients, to the protection and improvement of the environment, as well as to our personal lives.

## Spiritual Dimensions of Global Business

For most cultures of the world, building a relationship precedes business, and maintaining relationships underlies ongoing business. Understanding the culture in reference to time expectations, appropriate gift-giving, comments, or gestures helps to initiate these relationships and avoid a cultural faux pas. However, an acquaintance with the spirituality that gives birth to these outer behaviors enables deeper understanding than lists of cultural do's and don'ts can provide.

In international business, experiencing the tea ceremony before going to Japan, or learning about the Koran and its teachings before going to the Middle East can be as essential to the success of your negotiations as your market survey or company profile. On a very practical level, if you are doing business with someone who not only believes there is "mañana," but perhaps lifetimes before and after this one, adjusting your time expectations would be wise counsel.

The impact of the spiritual dimension in the culture, and, in turn, on your business, organizational, or political decisions may be assessed by:

(1) How "public" are the spiritual traditions?

(2) Are the spiritual traditions represented by the majority of the population?

The question of how "public" is highlighted by the coronation of the Japanese Emperor Akihito who spent six hours with the Sun Goddess Amaterasu sharing rice, each grain of which had been hand-picked by a select group of priests. Though some of the Japanese population was indifferent or even derided the event, giving question to whether this expression of spiritual tradition represents majority sentiments or is an anachronistic aberration, this awesome event did take place in a country of ultra-modern tastes and accomplishments.

(3) Are many spiritual traditions represented in the same country?

(4) How aggressive or tolerant is the dominant religion?

In parts of the world where Hindus, Moslems, Jains, Christians, and Jews live in close proximity, it is wise to know about the dynamics among the groups. This is especially true if you will be with members of various religious traditions at the same meeting.

Observe how the behaviors and priorities of ourselves and "others" reflect the underlying spiritual values, and in turn, how the spirituality influences the habits and attitudes and actions. Just as in managerial situations or conflict resolution, the goal in exploring the spiritual dimension is not formulas for different cultural groups, but a new mode of encompassing cultural spiritualities and learning from them for our personal lives and our professional interactions, and on a larger scale for the future of our world.

# Other World Views for Our Environment/Earth

For the Cherokee and other Indian people the world view of spirituality and interdependent connectedness was reflected in the White Council, the wise all women's council, and in the Red Council, the wise all men's council. Children were taught to consider acts as affecting the seventh generation. So it was until the mid–1800's when the Bureau of Indian Affairs replaced the Councils with bought-politicians, and the balance between women, the givers of life, and men, the protectors of life, to say nothing of the balance with the Earth, the land, the environment, was disrupted. As we hover in the 90's over the chasm of environmental self-destruction, we could do well to study and understand the spirituality native to this land which we now call the United States of America. It offers valuable insights for the balance of life and the respect of the environment.

# Other World Views for the Workplace

Anyone who has participated in a meditation retreat where the "agenda" is to look within or at a wall for hours, knows that silence, listening, and prayer can be scary, even in a setting where such behavior is accepted and expected. To transfer that radical experience of fecund, receptive moments "without words" to a workplace setting where known and expected behavior is to talk, generate ideas, etc. is usually uncomfortable and for many, unbearable, for more than a few seconds. It's fine (for some of us, at least) during retreats or certain conferences, but allowing that in the day-to-day functioning of our organizations? I'm not talking about a self-conscious or facilitator-imposed silence but the openness in organizations and organizational processes to allow those who don't "jump in" an opportunity to speak within their own time-frame and rhythm to enrich the process and, when applicable, the product.

Allowing for openness where creativity can occur to develop new products, new Standard Operating Procedures, and so on, demands a delicate balance between the known comfortable ways and the unknown "open times." For American corporations it is really the open time which is threatening. In a culture where time-is-money, use of time becomes the critical issue.

In our own lives, we often know that those imposed "open times" are often the most rewarding. They can even be bottom-line-valuable, helping us discover new directions, or giving us energy to produce more. Taking steps to live "open time" demands courage, and, to some extent (do I dare say it to most business organizations?), a healthy sense of fun, or play.

To experience play, delight, and creativity in daily life is not merely a shift of attitude or even behavior, but a change in core perception. There are cultures that are more comfortable with less formal structure, with humor at work and in daily life, cultures that perceive a mixture of work and play not as dilution but enrichment. In India we find gods who dance and play the flute and relax in the cosmic ocean to bring forth creation. Quite a contrast to the Protestant work ethic.

A knowledge of the religious traditions will give you an advantage in your business relationships. Penetrating to the spiritual spark within those outer trappings will enhance your personal journey, which is perhaps the most important journey you can make.

# Role Models for the Personal Journey

In this seeding period toward the Millennium, many individuals are longing for a balance in their personal and professional lives. Through my own exploration of spirituality while living in other cultures and many years of study in comparative religions, two figures have emerged for me as particularly relevant to our current stage of evolution. Though these role models are two goddesses, Durga and Persephone, from the traditions of India and ancient Greece, their examples can be taken by men as well as women.

## Durga and Persephone:

In India, stories of Goddess Durga tell us that the gods asked her to destroy a buffalo demon which was ravishing the countryside. A stone relief at Mahabalipuram in the south of India commemorates her victory over the demon. Exquisitely serene, Durga rides her lion as demons are toppled on all sides. Beautiful and poised and calm, she carries a sword and vanquishes evil. Durga offers us the balance of beauty and strength, tranquillity and might. Here is an example to emulate in the "battle" to balance the personal and professional aspects of our lives, the private journey and the public contribution.

Durga is a current dynamic presence in the lives of the people of India. Her worship has continued for centuries (the Mahabalipuram relief

dates from the 7th century, A.D.), she is still the supreme deity in the Indian state of Bengal. For a week during the month of October, the city of Calcutta celebrates Durgapuja with pageants, fireworks, and night long tours to the numerous temporary pavilions in her honor.

When we turn from India to the Greek pantheon, we find the goddess Persephone at first glance appears almost insipid, easily influenced by others, especially her mother and Hades. As a young maiden with her identity most obviously that of Demeter's daughter, Persephone was abducted to the Underworld by Hades.

Demeter was goddess of crops, and her grief caused the vegetation to wither and die. The gods met in council and decided that a messenger should be sent to the underworld to bring Persephone back to earth. Just as she left him, however, Hades offered Persephone some pomegranate seeds, and she ate them.

Demeter was overjoyed at the return of her daughter, and the fields blossomed with new life. But when the mother learned that her daughter had partaken of seeds of the other world, she knew that Persephone was destined to spend part of the year in the nether reaches as Hades' queen, and part of each year on the earth.

Some may easily relate to the warrior quality and wisdom of Durga, but for those who say, "Oh, I couldn't do that . . . ," Persephone offers an example. Persephone in one aspect personifies the victim: her fate is determined by others. She seems merely a pawn, or at best, a "supporting actress" in a larger drama.

Yet she held within herself the seeds to decide her own destiny, to develop into a queen. Somewhere in the ongoing events, she mastered the mysteries of the underworld and the ability to make the repeated transition between the outer world and the inner.

Somewhere also in the details we don't know, she was able to "prove herself" to be not a compliant pretty thing whom Hades had a whim to place upon a throne, but a power recognized by other gods and goddesses, heroes and heroines, as a keeper of the deepest mysteries. In the Eleusian Mysteries, major religion of the Greeks for 2000 years prior to Christianity, Persephone was the central figure, worshipped both as Queen of the Underworld and bringer of the renewal of life in her annual return to earth.

Most significantly, Persephone spent part of the yearly cycle deep in the mysterious, receiving those who seek beyond the obvious. And the rest of the year, she lived "in the world." More than any other archetype, she personifies the ability to go between—again and again—the deepest spiritual realms and the most outward physical manifestation of abundance. Is this not our own very modern and present challenge?

Whether we look to Durga, who maintains inner calm and serenity while battling amidst the most challenging circumstances, or Persephone, who is mistress of the inner world while still manifesting creatively in the outer, we find guides and mentors for the frenetic demands of contemporary life.

## Discovering the Spiritual Dimension

If you are working on an international project, or with people of another culture, you have a definite starting point to get past the interesting outer details to the spiritual dimension of why people behave as they do in their interactions, why their cultures have evolved as they have. For others not in these situations, a starting point may be inviting your employees or co-workers or students or neighbors to share some of their spiritual traditions.

The process may begin for non-Jews with experiencing the beauty of the opening and closing of the Sabbath in a Jewish gathering. It may begin simply by questioning the source of our festivals and holidays in the United States. Christmas, Easter, Halloween all have their roots in the pre-Christian era, yet how many of us question the "pagan" tradition of the Easter egg, the cats and broomsticks of Halloween, the Christmas tree. Asking and answering how/why the celebration of Birth takes place at the time of the return of the Light at the Winter Solstice, why Easter is called Easter, or why we dress as ghosts at the time of the ancient year when "the Veil between the two worlds is thinnest" can decrease feelings of uniqueness and exclusivity that foster attitudes of "us" and "them." The deep roots of our cultural diversity can be explored in these taken-for-granted celebrations.

Go to bookstores and libraries; ask the knowledgeable people there for help. Look at the people you come in contact with; you may not have thought of them as sources for learning about the spirituality in their culture. Check out seminars in your area on various spiritual traditions; it doesn't have to be "your thing" for you to gain another perspective on the world. The process is vast, but never boring as we move toward the new Millennium focused on the spiritual dimension of globalization.

## About the Author

Sally J. Walton, M.A., author of *Cultural Diversity in the Workplace* (Irwin, 1994) has 14 years international experience in 39 countries including Latin America, Asia, and Europe. Her programs on The Art of Crossing Cultures are in English or Spanish. Often *Marca Polina*, a modern descendent of Marco Polo, makes a guest appearance at her sessions. The challenges of cultural diversity and globalization are taken in stride by this feminine expression of Marco Polo who tells us how anyone can master the Art of Crossing Cultures!

Her work as a professional speaker, consultant and author focuses on maximizing human performance in a multicultural setting. She can be reached at: Global Perspectives, 504 Cliff Street, Santa Cruz, CA 95060; Phone: 408-429-8308; Fax: 408-429-9393.

# The Gospel of Guyhood

by Kenneth L. Woodward with Sherry Keene-Osborn (*Newsweek*)

*Religion: Hugs, sports and righteousness in the evangelical men's movement*

Good-bye, macho man. Kiss off, Sensitive Man. Get lost, Wild Man. Make room, brothers, for the latest icon in the quest for masculine identity: the Godly Man. He is the image offered by evangelical Christians and modeled, of course, on Jesus Christ. Not the androgynous Sunday-school Jesus with the long, penned tresses, pale blue eyes and soft pink lips—the Jesus who turned the other cheek and never married. No, this is the Jesus of the burgeoning Christian Men's Movement and he trumps all the secular archetypes. He's a mighty King and Warrior, a Leader of Men and their Savior, a Wild Man with a redeeming purpose—and absolutely the best buddy a guy could ever have.

The Godly Man also looks a lot like Bill McCartney, the rugged, bronzed, born-again football coach at the University of Colorado. Four years ago McCartney was seized by a vision of stadiums filled with deep-throated men chanting the praises of Jesus. The fruit of that vision is Promise Keepers, a nondenominational, multiracial organization committed to training men how to be responsible to God, to their wives and children, to their churches and to each other. Already this year Promise Keepers has filled six stadiums with a total of 234,000 disciples. In turn, the success of Promise Keepers has inspired a whole new evangelical industry: dozens of books, tapes and videos explaining how Christians can recover their true masculinity. There's even a slick bimonthly magazine, *New Man*, which features advice on safe sex ("it's called 'marriage'") and columns on fitness and finances.

For Promise Keepers, the first step in forming Godly Men is getting them away from women. At their latest weekend rally, 52,000 men—farmers in overalls, bikers with ponytails and black leather jackets, businessmen in Bermuda shorts and 300 Texans wearing fluorescent orange hunting caps—jammed Colorado's Folsom Stadium last month. A Christian rock band set the mood. When the music stopped, the crowd rose to do "the wave," shouting "Jesus, Jesus, Jesus." Preacher followed preacher with messages on how to be a good father and loving husband, expressing emotion and the importance of male bonding. "We're scoring baskets for Jesus," declared emcee Bob Horner, an official with Campus Crusade for Christ. Then, as the band broke out with "Born to Be Wild," evangelist Chuck Swindoll roared onto the platform astride a motorcycle to deliver a sermon on avoiding temptation. Never, he said, has he allowed himself to be alone—even at lunch—with any woman other than his wife. There was some gentle, if clunky gender-based humor: "You know why it takes one million sperm and one egg to make a baby?" another speaker asked. "It's because not one of those stinkers will stop and ask directions."

The hit of the weekend was coach McCartney. Welcomed by wild cheers, he mounted the platform, surrounded by members of his football team. Suddenly the coach called for his wife, Lyndi, in order to "show 'em how the Black and Gold [his team's colors] do it." The crowd roared as he bent his wife over backward in a long kiss.

McCartney then launched into a rambling, Hemingway-esque speech about death, risk-taking, winning and racial harmony—all flavored with anecdotes from the Bible and sports. "We are the brotherhood," McCartney shouted. "We're connected. We're going to look out for each other." A chant filled the stadium, echoing his words. An African-American in the stands began to weep and was hugged by a tattooed white man with no shirt. Nor were they the only pair to embrace. "One guy confessed his addictions to drugs and sex to me," said Larry Dong, 35, a real-estate broker from Phoenix, Ariz. "If my wife were here, I wouldn't have been able to talk about things like sexual impurity." From the podium, McCartney looked out and saw that it was good. "It doesn't get any better than this," he said.

This isn't the first time that evangelicals have used athletics to turn men on to religion. At the turn of the century, evangelist Billy Sunday, a former baseball star, rallied "back-slid" Christians with robust sports metaphors. Billy Graham, who feels equally at home in a stadium and on a golf-course, has assured audiences that "Jesus was the greatest athlete who ever lived." McCartney was inspired by the 4-year-old Fellowship of Christian Athletes.

But the current men's movement is not just another revival of muscular Christianity. As their therapeutic approach makes clear, the movement's leaders are primarily focused on restoring ruptured relationships. "God has dictated that we answer the questions men are asking," says Dan Schaffer, Promise Keepers' Colorado state director. The answer may be Jesus, but the questions concern wounded egos, broken marriages, neglected children, alcohol, drugs and even incest. The movement's rapid growth—some 150,000 local churches have tapped Promise Keepers for information—indicates that evangelicals are no less prone to sin than those they seek to save.

*Male bonding:* Boisterous stadium rallies are only the beginning for men who join the movement. Promise Keepers pledge to form small male-bonding groups when they return to their communities. Each Promise Keeper also designates a "faith partner" with whom he can share his deepest fears and secret sins on a daily basis. The purpose is to make each man "accountable" to another for keeping his promises. It takes a year for most men to develop that trust. And some never do. "I'd like to get an accountability partner but it's hard to find someone with my standards," says Robert Smith, who is head deacon at First Baptist Church in Rawlins, Wyo. Wives, it appears, are the principal promise reapers. "My husband came home with patience, which he never had, listening and understanding," says Madeline Cialella of Waterbury, Conn. "I give God the glory."

Ultimately, the Christian Men's Movement hopes to restore male leadership in the home—and in what some leaders see as increasingly feminized churches. "In Biblical times, men identified with and received their identity from the church," argues Dan Schaffer of Promise Keepers. Jesus had his Apostles and Paul confided in traveling companions like Barnabas and Timothy. But ever since the 19th-centuwry temperance movement, Schaffer believes, "women [have been] looked to for moral leadership" in American churches. No one at the last rally criticized the modern feminist movement. But clergymen there felt so hungry for male affirmation that McCartney called 5,000 pastors to come forward and be blessed by their lay brethren. "My grandmother was a prayin' woman," recalled a tearful Robert Lavala, pastor of a bikers' church in Las Vegas. "But my granddaddy was a fishin' man. It seems like it's been like that forever." The movement's message to men is simple: following Jesus is not for women only, nor is it a spectator sport.

> *In between talking
> we listen to each other
> and sometimes ourselves*
>
> Walt Hopkins

# A Soft Answer

by Terry Dobson

A turning point in my life came one day on a train in the suburbs of Tokyo, in the middle of a drowsy spring afternoon. The old car clanked and rattled over the rails. It was comparatively empty—a few housewives with their kids in tow, some old folks out shopping, a couple of off-duty bartenders studying the racing form. I gazed absently at the drab houses and dusty hedgerows.

At one station the doors opened, and suddenly the quiet afternoon was shattered by a man bellowing at the top of his lungs yelling violent, obscene, incomprehensible curses. Just as the doors closed the man, still yelling, staggered into our car. He was big, drunk, and dirty. He wore laborer's clothing. His front was stiff with dried vomit. His eyes bugged out a demonic, neon red. His hair was crusted with filth. Screaming, he swung at the first person he saw, a woman holding a baby. The blow glanced off her shoulder, sending her spinning into the laps of an elderly couple. It was a miracle that the baby was unharmed.

The couple jumped up and scrambled toward the other end of the car. They were terrified. The laborer aimed a kick at the retreating back of the old lady. *"You old whore!"* he bellowed, *"I'll kick your ass!"* He missed, the old woman scuttled to safety. This so enraged the drunk that he grabbed the metal pole in the center of the car, and tried to wrench it out of its stanchion. I could see that one of his hands was cut and bleeding. The train lurched ahead, the passengers frozen with fear. I stood up.

I was young and in pretty good shape. I stood six feet, weighed 225. I'd been putting in a solid eight hours of Aikido every day for the past three years. I liked to throw and grapple. I thought I was tough. Trouble was, my martial skill was untested in actual combat. As students of Aikido, we were not allowed to fight.

My teacher, the founder of Aikido, taught us each morning that the art was devoted to peace. "Aikido," he said again and again, "is the art of

reconciliation. Whoever has the mind to fight has broken his connection with the universe. If you try to dominate other people, you are already defeated. We study how to resolve conflict, not how to start it."

I listened to his words. I tried hard. I wanted to quit fighting. I even went so far as to cross the street a few times to avoid the chimpira, the pinball punks who lounged around the train stations. They'd have been happy to test my martial ability. My forbearance exalted me. I felt both tough and holy. I wanted a chance, an absolutely legitimate opportunity whereby I might save the innocent by destroying the guilty.

"This is it!" I said to myself as I got to my feet. "This slob, this animal, is drunk and mean and violent. People are in danger. If I don't do something fast, somebody will probably get hurt. I'm gonna take his ass to the cleaners."

Seeing me stand up, the drunk saw a chance to focus his rage. *"Aha!"* he roared, *"A foreigner! You need a lesson in Japanese manners!"* He punched the metal pole once to give weight to his words.

I held on lightly to the commuter-strap overhead. I gave him a slow look of disgust and dismissal. I gave him every bit of piss-ant nastiness I could summon up. I planned to take this turkey apart, but he had to be the one to move first. And I wanted him mad, because the madder he got, the more certain my victory. I pursed my lips and blew him a sneering, insolent kiss. It hit him like a slap in the face. *"All right!"* he hollered, *"You're gonna get a lesson."* He gathered himself for a rush at me. He'd never know what hit him.

A split second before he moved, someone shouted *"Hey!"* It was earsplitting. I remember being struck by the strangely joyous, lilting quality of it as though you and a friend had been searching diligently for something, and he had suddenly stumbled upon it. *"Hey!"*

I wheeled to my left, and the drunk spun to his right. We both stared down at a little old Japanese. He must have been well into his seventies, this tiny gentleman, sitting there immaculate in his kimono and hakama. He took no notice of me, but beamed delightedly at the laborer, as though he had a most important, most welcome secret to share.

"C'mere," the old man said in an easy vernacular, beckoning to the drunk, "C'mere and talk with me." He waved his hand lightly. The big man followed, as if on a string. He planted his feet belligerently in front of the old gentleman, and towered threateningly over him. *"Talk to you,"* he reared above the clacking wheel, *"Why the hell should I talk to you?"* The drunk now had his back to me. If his elbow moved so much as a millimeter, I'd drop him in his socks.

The old man continued to beam at the laborer. There was not a trace of fear or resentment about him. "What'cha been drinkin'?" he asked lightly, his eyes sparkling with interest. *"I been drinkin' sake,"* the laborer bellowed back, *"and it's none of your goddam business!"* Flecks of spittle spattered the old man.

"Oh, that's wonderful," the old man said with delight, "absolutely wonderful! You see, I love sake, too. Every night, me and my wife (she's 76, you know), we warm up a little bottle of sake and take it out into the garden, and we sit on the old wooden bench that my grandfather's first student made for him. We watch the sun go down, and we look to see how our persimmon tree is doing. My great-grandfather planted that tree, you know, and we worry about whether it will recover from those ice-storms we had last winter. Persimmons do not do well after ice-storms, although I must say that ours has done rather better than I expected, especially when you consider the poor quality of the soil. Still, it is most gratifying to watch when we take our sake and go out to enjoy the evening—even when it rains!" He looked up at the laborer, eyes twinkling, happy to share his delightful information.

As he struggled to follow the intricacies of the old man's conversation, the drunk's face began to soften. His fists slowly unclenched. "Yeah," he said slowly, "I love persimmons, too . . . ." His voice trailed off.

"Yes," said the old man, smiling, "and I'm sure you have a wonderful wife."

"No," replied the laborer, "My wife died." He hung his head. Very gently, swaying with the motion of the train, the big man began to sob. "I don't got no wife, I don't got no home, I don't got no job, I don't got no money, I don't got nowhere to go. I'm so ashamed of myself." Tears rolled down his cheeks, a spasm of pure despair rippled through his body. Above the baggage rack a four-color ad trumpeted the virtues of suburban luxury living.

Now it was my turn. Standing there in my well-scrubbed youthful innocence, my make-this-world-safe-for-democracy righteousness, I suddenly felt dirtier than he was.

Just then, the train arrived at my stop. The platform was packed, and the crowd surged into the car as soon as the doors opened. Maneuvering my way out, I heard the old man cluck sympathetically. "My, my," he said with undiminished delight, "that is a very difficult predicament, indeed. Sit down here and tell me about it."

I turned my head for one last look. The laborer was sprawled like a sack on the seat, his head in the old man's lap. The old man looked down on him all compassion and delight, one hand softly stroking the filthy matted head.

As the train pulled away, I sat down on a bench. What I had wanted to accomplish with muscle and meanness had been accomplished with a few kind words. I had seen Aikido tried in combat, and the essence of it was love, as the founder had said. I would have to practice the art with an entirely different spirit. It would be a long time before I could speak about the resolution of conflict.

## About the Author

Terry Dobson, holder of a fourth-degree black belt in Aikido, is co-author of *Giving in to Get Your Way* (Delacorte) and author of *Safe and Sound: How Not to Be a Victim* (Tarcher). He has worked with conflict resolution for 20 years, and now conducts seminars called "When Push Comes to Shove" for business executives.

# "Us" Versus "Them": How We Make It Palatable to Inflict Suffering Upon Strangers

by Ralph G.H. Siu

The discrimination between "them" and "us" is pervasive. During the 1980s, for example, the presiding bishops of the Mormon Church discharged a non-Mormon engineer at a Church-operated gymnasium and six non-Mormon workers at a Church-owned garment factory because they were not Mormons. The ex-employees sued claiming discrimination on the basis of religion in violation of the Civil Rights Act of 1964. The Church claimed exemption as a religious organization in accordance with Section 702 of the Act. The case ended in the Supreme Court. In 1987, it ruled unanimously in favor of the bishops, because it did not feel it should get "excessively entangled" with religious organizations in accordance with the spirit of the constitutional separation of Church and State. The discrimination against "them" by "us" was upheld.

This discriminatory bent begins early in life. Infants develop an affectionate tie with their close caretakers and a dreaded anxiety to strangers. The aversion continues in a lesser degree after that. It has been experimentally demonstrated that the mere use of pronouns like "ours" and "theirs" or "us" and "them" would often bias effective responses to the stimuli. The solidarity in each camp is increased by what I. L. Janis calls "groupthink." Most individuals simply go along with what they think the group wants. In so doing, they enjoy a feeling of security, invulnerability and correctness in their collective wisdom, which often leads them into extreme risks, attitudes and inflictions of suffering on others.

There is a tendency to impute unfavorable, inferior, and fearsome traits to strangers. In past centuries, cannibalism had been a common incrimination. Many people have accused others of

it and have been accused by others in turn. In the 5th century BC, the Greek historian Herodotus spoke of people living beyond a great desert to the east. "The Androphagi have the most savage customs of all men; they pay no regard to justice, nor make use of any established law. They are nomads, and wear a dress like a scythian; they speak a peculiar language; and of these nations are the only people that eat human flesh."

The Romans accused the Christians of drinking blood; the Christians of 15th century Germany condemned the Jews for the same thing. The Koreans had once thought of the Chinese as maneaters and the Chinese had accused the Koreans of the same. During the 16th century, detailed descriptions of cannibalism among the South American Tupinamba Indians were written by the Portuguese seaman Hans Staden, prefaced by the professor of medicine John Drysander, and widely read. The explorer Henry Stanley also published sensational accounts of cannibalism among 19th century Africans. In our own day, the Chamula Indians of Mexico inquired of the visiting anthropologist Gary Gossen whether or not the inhabitants of California are still eating each other. Despite many reports of these kinds, the anthropologist William Arens was unable to find any reliable first-hand account of man-eating.

Once the "them" is clearly distinguished from the "us," then inflictions by "us" on "them" will be that much easier to condone and overlook. In 1833, the economist and logician William Jevons recorded such an attitude among his fellow Britishers regarding the atrocities of their kinsmen in Australia: "When it was stated that the aborigines in the north of Queensland were being shot like kangaroos or poisoned wholesale by strychnine, one solitary member of parliament went so far as to ask the Government whether this was true. The Government replied that they did not know, but would make inquiries, and nothing more has been heard of the matter to the present day."

This article was reproduced with permission from the *Panetics Trilogy*. It is from *Panetics and Dukkha: An Integrated Study of the Infliction of Suffering and the Reduction of Infliction*. This monumental and seminal work is the creation of Ralph G.H. Siu who has founded the International Society of Panetics (the trilogy is available from 202-362-3710).

Any imagined or real distinctive feature that separates "them" from "us" exacerbates the mutual infliction of suffering. It quickens the tendency to think the worst of "them." This can be seen from a dispatch by Jonathan Schell from the South Vietnam battlefield during the 1960s. The American captain was explaining his actions in preventing any Vietnamese moving freely in the so-called "Free Zone" designated by his commander. "From now on anything that moves around here is going to be automatically considered V. C. [enemy Viet Cong] and bombed or fired on. The whole Triangle is going to become a Free Zone. These villagers here are all considered hostile civilians."

When the Captain was asked as to how he was able to tell a hostile civilian from an innocent refugee, he replied, "In a V. C. area like this, there are three categories. First there are the straight V. C. . . . Then there are the V. C. sympathizers. Then there's the . . . There's a third category . . . I can't think of the third just now but . . . There's no middle road in this war." It's either "them" or "us."

So it is that most multinational corporations would expose the people of other countries to a higher risk of industrial safety hazards than the people of their own. Seventy percent of the Americans favored the withholding of unemployment benefits to recent out of state arrivals.

In this connection the systems theorist Will McWhinney has been studying what is called "externalizing." This manifests itself in various forms, such as "sending mass production work overseas, building walled enclaves which keep out social noise [and] projecting blame on to other races." After studying the socioeconomic issues involved, he concluded that "all forms of externalizing cause pain to those places in the world in which the externalized 'bad' is placed."

Decrying this kind of insensitivity to the suffering of "them" the following account was filed by Asghar Ali in June 1987 to the *Indian Express* about the Hindu-Muslim altercation in Meerut and the subsequent killing spree in the Muslim quarter by the state police, who were largely Hindus: "With all that has happened in Meerut I do not think we can call ourselves civilized, let alone citizens of a great nation with a rich heritage. We are simply barbarians who take pleasure in killing each other . . . What is sad, Hindus told me how many Hindus were killed and Muslims how many Muslims were slaughtered. No one was genuinely concerned about human beings as such."

The continuing conflict between the Catholic Irish Republican Army and the Protestant Irish government and majority in Northern Ireland is another case in point. Were it not for the religious fervor behind the civil war, the killings would probably have stopped quite some time ago. In the words of the theologian Paul Badham, "it is inconceivable that the animosities of a displacing settlement nearly 400 years ago could possibly have survived until today." He envisioned that "the two communities of Northern Ireland would have merged through intermarriages within 150 years just as the Anglo-Saxons and Danes merged in ninth and tenth century England, or as the dominating Norman settlers gradually lost their sense of separateness from the conquered English in the eleventh and twelfth centuries."

In late August 1992, German youths staged three nights of violence in the Baltic seaport of Rostok to drive out the aliens. Vietnamese and Romanian gypsy workers were assaulted and their residences firebombed. "Germany for the Germans!" they cried. "Foreigners out!"

This is a representative outburst of the dread of "strangers in our midst," which is infesting the world. Eleonora Masini pointedly referred to "the enormous migration processes which are underway all over the world in search of economic, political, or environmental security. This is leading to a greater and greater confrontation of different value systems and principles guiding behavior. Values and behavior which are different will have to learn to coexist."

## About the Author

Ralph G.H. Siu is a retired executive who devotes his intellectual energy to the synthesis of East-West psycho-philosophical thought. He has published a wide variety of provocative and stimulating papers and books. These include "Work & Serenity" which draws on Taoist and Buddhist principles to achieve harmony and integrate work properly into one's life (included in the Balanced Living Kit from 1-800-736-1293). Other works include: *The Tao of Science*; *The Portable Dragon: The Western Man's Guide to the I Ching*; and *Transcending the Power Game: The Guide to Executive Serenity*.

He has lectured on the topic of Civility on college campuses, and is known for his entertaining use of universal proverbs to illustrate principles and applications of diversity. Siu also has completed an unpublished manuscript entitled, *Management by 3,333 Proverbs*, covering all aspects of management. He can be reached at 4428 Albermarle Street, NW, Washington, DC 20016; Phone: 202-362-3710.

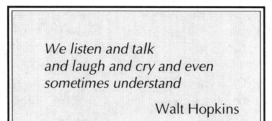

*We listen and talk
and laugh and cry and even
sometimes understand*

Walt Hopkins

# The Foreigner in Each of Us
by Elie Wiesel (*Christian Science Monitor*)

Why are people mistrustful of foreigners? Why do they hold them at arm's length?

A foreigner represents the unexpected, therefore he is a burden. You might say he came out of nowhere, and usurped someone else's place if not his life. He is shrouded in mystery, indefinable in his solitude. He lunges into a world that was there before he was, and which had no need of him. He arouses fear as much as he himself fears.

People are afraid of foreigners; there is no denying it. A foreigner conjures up the unknown, the forbidden. Who knows what he is doing on the sly. Perhaps he is cooking up plots and intrigues.

The foreigner represents something that we are not. He is different. He is an emissary of unknown, hostile powers. He is the vagabond in search of a resting place, the noisy Bohemian with a crowd of ragged children trailing behind him, the fugitive unjustly pursued by the law, the hungry beggar. He is the one nobody loves or welcomes, for whom scarcely any sympathy or compassion is felt. He is someone with whom we will never consent to identify ourselves.

The fear which the foreigner inspires in us causes us to see something in him which calls into question our own role in society. Looking at him I realize that, like him, I am a foreigner in someone else's eyes. To that person, I am someone who arouses fear. On a human scale, this could mean that we are all foreigners. What if the other person were me? The truth is that he is. Or rather, it behooves me to act as if he were.

It is not because I have a home, a job and a family that I am less foreign than the foreigner. It takes little for someone to be uprooted, for the satisfied, happy man to lose his place in the sun. My generation has seen just how unstable everything is and how vulnerable people are.

When destiny winked its eye, in the space of a day, the rich lost their treasures, men of status lost their friends, and thinkers lost their bearings. Suddenly, they found themselves deprived of their most basic rights. France repudiated its Jews just as Hungary did. Military medals, aristocratic titles, social status, nothing counted any more. All it took was a decree, the stroke of a pen, and old families who had been living in supposedly civilized countries for centuries found themselves treated like foreigners and intruders.

It is enough for someone to treat me like a foreigner for me to be one. If I am excluded, it is because someone has pushed me out. Therefore, it is my fault, too, if the other person is excluded, that is to say deprived of a feeling of security and of belonging, of a sense of identity. For it is up to me whether someone feels at home or not in our common world, and whether he feels tranquil or anxious when he looks around him.

Since I am responsible for the other person being alienated or otherwise, just as I am responsible for his freedom, I must do everything in my power not to betray myself by betraying him. I must see in him my likeness, rather than a suspicious-looking stranger, so that our relationship can take on a human character. I live like him and I shall die like him. The same threats hang over us while we sleep. We cry out for rain or for love with the same voice. Despite appearances, despite the differences, the fate of people everywhere is the same.

Our passage on this Earth is part of a picture that transcends us. Is mine any more important than the other person's? Do I have a higher mission than he? No matter where he comes from, the foreigner is close to me. He conjures up visions of a world which offers itself to us as a place to live in, enrich, and make fertile.

I remember that, as a child, I used to wait impatiently and lovingly for the unknown visitor to arrive. I waited for him so that I could make him talk and also so that I could dream. I was grateful for his presence. I shall never forget the hours I spent with strangers during my childhood. Some of them told me happy or sad stories. Others told me about faraway countries, inspired sages, or adventurers looking to put themselves to some sacred test. In my head I followed them, spellbound.

Their lives seemed so much more exciting than mine. I would have given anything to be like them, free as the wind and the night shadows. Yet most of them were beggars with no name and nowhere to go.

What attracted me to them was that they came from somewhere else. This is because, in the Jewish tradition from which I draw my inspiration, any foreigner might be a sage in disguise, perhaps even the prophet Elijah himself. Or he might be a righteous man in exile, and therefore cloaked in anonymity. To offend him would be to risk damnation. That used to be my attitude toward foreigners.

And now? I am older now. Am I any less romantic? Less optimistic perhaps. If I still respect the foreigner, it is for more concrete reasons. It is to let him know my solidarity with him as a human being, and my good faith as a human being. Torn apart from his family, environment, and ethnic or national culture, he has rights over me, for legally he has no rights. I am his hope. To refuse him this hope would be to shirk my obligations as a man. That is why I am in favor of welcoming as many foreigners as generously as possible. Whoever needs a refuge must feel welcome wherever I am. If he is a foreigner in my country, then I will be one too.

## About the Author

Elie Wiesel, recipient of the Nobel Peace Prize and numerous literary awards, writes and lectures on the Holocaust and human rights. A survivor of the concentration camps, he shapes the questions the Holocaust continues to pose in his autobiography, novels and essays. Mr. Wiesel has been an Andrew Mellon Professor in the Humanities at Boston University and Chairman of the United States Holocaust Memorial Council. Reprinted from *The Christian Science Monitor*, August 7, 1991, p. 23.

# Moving From Blame to Dialogue

by Linda Teurfs

I am reading my *LA Times*, shaking my head in disbelief. In the reporting of the riots in South Central Los Angeles, I count what seems like hundreds of references to racism and prejudice. I see pictures of fires, guns, buildings ravaged, people homeless and helpless, death. As never before, it is time to pause and look deeply into how our thoughts and attitudes create so much suffering and agony in the world.

This is hard to do. We would rather put the blame outside ourselves than do our internal housecleaning. Politicians blame the riots on social programs of the 1960s or on the police force. Others blame it on economic conditions. In the *Time's* "World Report" section I read how the British blame the riots on our welfare system; the Japanese on our jury system; the Italians on our indifference to prejudice.

Only what I read from the *Joong Ang Daily* of Seoul gives me pause. It suggests that "the Korean community in the United States should take a close look at its lifestyle and engage in self-reflection . . . What Koreans in America should improve on is their measures to deal with . . . envious feelings. If we accumulate wealth, we must also be prepared to share that wealth with other members of the community."

What an enlightened perspective. Whoever wrote those words wasn't blaming anything or anyone for the senseless destruction of the Korean community's businesses and lives. They were stressing an inward, self-reflective approach.

Andrew Bard Schmookler wrote about how the projection of our unexplored fears onto others is the root of civil strife and war in *Out of Weakness: Healing the Wounds That Drive Us to War*. If we are unwilling to do our own inner work, we project our fears outward in the form of hostility to others. When our fears join with other fears we have the makings of riots and wars.

We need to get a grip on our individual fears and prejudices, and begin a process that David Bohm refers to as "dialogue." This is where we come together and, in an atmosphere of non-judgment, explore how our society's thinking process may be leading us astray.

Bohm learned about dialogue from a French psychoanalyst, Patrick de Mare, who uses dialogue as a form of what he calls "socio-therapy," a way of helping a society or community learn a new way of being together that promotes common understanding and early conflict resolution.

Dialogue is quite distinct from the way most of us have learned to talk to each other. Instead of trying to convince each other who is right or wrong, we bring a "learning attitude" into our conversations. We use a deeper level of listening and place our attention on understanding rather than persuasion. This gets us out of the "us versus them" mentality. We examine assumptions underlying our attitudes and begin to see how our thinking process has many incongruencies, or what Bohm calls "incoherencies."

As we uncover these incoherencies, we find a common ground between us. We focus more and more on commonalties. While we may differ on the surface, we are all very much the same at the root of our being, and very much the same in what we want out of life. Dialogue offers a new way of dealing with the conflicts that inter-racial and multicultural differences bring. If we are willing to reflect and share deeply with each other, to learn from each other and our differences, I think we will see a transformation. Surely it is time, now, to try.

## About the Author

Linda Teurfs has her own consulting practice specializing in managerial team building. She is co-founder of The Dialogue Group, a partnership focused on the research, development and facilitation of Dialogue. Contact her at: 4265 Marina City Dr. #1105, Marina del Rey, CA 90292; Phone: 310-822-4111; Fax: 310-822-8011.

# ANIMAL LOGIC
## by Amy Kahn

So you see
said the monkey to the
kangaroo
things just jump
around until
you climb to the top
of a big tree and
bellow.

But no I don't
see at all said
the kangaroo
I'd prefer to hide
in my pouch where
I can't be misunderstood,
and then hop around.
Thank you for the advice
Though.

But no
screams mister frog
you are both mistaken
when hopping you
should remain
in camouflage.

Camouflage? asked
the bigger creatures
Yes, and hop from lily
to lily and then in the
water. That's what I do.

A meandering rhino
listened nearby and laughed
inside. He knew that
the best thing to do is
just take it in stride.

*In the Name of God, Most Beneficent, Most Merciful*

# Islamic Universalism

by Rabia Terri Harris

The relation of unity to diversity is one of the great Qur'anic themes. The sacred text emphasizes again and again that oneness and manyness must be understood as inseparable dimensions of a global reality. Such a vision is an essential medicine for human ills. It is only by abandoning the exaggerated importance we assign to our special separate identities that peace and truth may be found. To realize that I myself—whoever I may be—am not the center of the universe, but one of its many functions, is both the foundation of social sanity and the beginning of spiritual growth. Only our delusions of grandeur prevent us from claiming the real grandeur of the human state! For Islam teaches that, where God is recognized, human dignity ceases to be an abstract notion and becomes a fact.

Dignity is the result of a life lived with purpose and meaning. It comes from nowhere else. When we live aimlessly we do without dignity altogether, and make ourselves miserable without knowing why. When we try and invent our own meanings for life, something within us knows we are telling ourselves stories. Our made-up dignity is fragile, and that turns us into touchy, defensive, and sometimes even dangerous people.

Real self-respect is independent of winning or losing, and of other people's praise or blame. It is the result of knowing, in an unshakable way, that our existence matters. In the long run, only God can provide that context. It is only by turning to the Creator that we can learn what we have been created for. The alternative is to live one's life as a fraud, a sleepwalker, or a statistic.

Muslims follow the Prophet's guidance, and the Qur'anic revelation that came through him, in order to tie themselves firmly to the Giver of meaning and existence. Of the Five Pillars of religious practice that support every observant Muslim's life, the very first is to explicitly acknowledge this goal. To do this, one recites the profession of faith: "I bear witness that there is no god but God,

and I bear witness that Muhammad is the servant and messenger of God." Making this statement before witnesses is all that is required for a person to enter the community of Islam.

The most fundamental Muslim responsibility, to affirm that there is no god but God, does not mean that we are choosing to back a single player out of a pantheon of heavenly competitors, disqualifying all the others. When monotheism is merely polytheism with fewer options, it justifiably generates skepticism! But Allah, God Itself, is something quite distinct from all this—for the one true God is the ultimate object of worship beyond whatever it is we *think* we love. Grasping this definition changes the terms of a perennial argument.

It is Abraham (peace be upon him), the father of the Western Tradition, who first made this enormous breakthrough of understanding. Abraham is presented to us in the Qur'an as embodying the ideal religious sensibility. This sensibility, which joins a deep awareness of the infinite and eternal with a unique sense of human responsibility to the divine, is what the Qur'an refers to as *islam*.

*Islam*, the surrender to God, is identified by scripture and the Holy Prophet's own comments with *hanifiyyah* or *fitrah*, "natural religion," the essential primary orientation of every human being toward truth. (The Islamic tradition does not subscribe to the notion of original sin.) "Abraham was not a Jew, nor yet a Christian, but a *hanif*, a *muslim*," runs the sacred text (Surah Al-i 'Imran, 67). Abraham (peace be upon him) was the fountainhead of both Judaism and Christianity, but his relation to God existed before either of these traditions entered the world. The great insight into reality he represents, the verse tells us, cannot be claimed as exclusive property by anyone. The islam of Abraham has priority over all later developments, whether in the spiritual history of the planet, or in our private spiritual lives.

Islam as a world religion draws its strength from the principle for which it is named: the Way of Muhammad (peace and blessings be upon him) is designed to guard and transmit the experience of Abraham. Each time Muslims offer prayers, we ask blessings upon the two of them together. For through specific religious observances, a detailed practice of mindfulness, and a course of moral care—all given to us through the Holy Prophet—the sincere Muslim works toward Abraham's original awareness of the unity of God.

What was the experience of Abraham?

The Qur'an tells us that when Abraham (peace be upon him) was a young man, he had a profound and transforming realization, one which was to echo through the millennia. Dedicated to the search for the divine, he identified one thing after another as his soul's beloved, but was forced to discard each in turn as insufficient. He worshipped a star, the moon, the sun . . . only to have to admit that "I love not gods that set" (Surah Al-i 'Imran, 74). He embraced them all, but had to let them go. Something that was sometimes there, and sometimes not, was not God enough for him. No partial divinity could satisfy the universal human need that was at his core.

When he recognized this, he found his being flooded with the intimacy of the Transcendent. He had rediscovered the primal human spiritual heritage. He was simultaneously charged with the mission of awakening others, and immersed in peace.

After he had received the revelation of divine oneness, Abraham grew disgusted with the habits of his tribe. What was this worship of limited and specific things, each contradicting the next? Why should a human being, created for unity, be subordinate to a fragment, or a collection of fragments? (For that is the practical meaning of idolatry.) Didn't people see that the competition for human devotion by so many rival forces, each with its own exclusive demands, led only to chaos, disintegration, and a continual state of fear? That a war for dominance among them would be inevitable, and the precarious triumph of any would rest on the destruction of the rest? And that none of this was necessary, or even real?

To make his point, young Abraham staged an act of theatre. One night he went into the sanctuary of his people and smashed all the idols at their altars, except the largest. Furious, the other tribesmen demanded to know whether Abraham had done this outrageous thing. But Abraham just pointed at the remaining image. "Why don't you ask him?" he inquired. "He's clearly the boss!"

Unsurprisingly, not long after this his people threw him out. And the war of parts for dominance over the whole still continues. But the *islam* of Abraham, the Friend of God, continues too.

"Call upon 'God,' or call upon 'the Beneficent,'" the Qur'an tells us, "by whatever name you call upon Him, His are the most beautiful names" (Surah Bani Isra'il, 110). It is a key insight of Islam that the Divine Oneness is brimming, and touches each of us differently. These varied relationships, termed Names, are at the root of the multiplicity of the world. Ultimate reality, by Its own decree, may be addressed in many ways, and much of human conflict results from the failure—or refusal—to recognize someone else's form of address.

The great saint Jelaluddin Rumi illustrated this with a succinct story. A Turk, a Persian, and an Arab were traveling together. They had pooled their little money, and had only enough for a single purchase. They were all hungry, and each knew exactly what he craved. "I want *uzum*!" said the Turk. "No, no, we must have *angur*!" insisted the Persian. "It's '*inab* or nothing," declared the Arab. They had almost come to blows when a fourth man, a wise man, came down the road and interrupted them. "If you will entrust your money to me," he proposed, "I promise to satisfy you all." With no other resolution in sight, they nervously agreed. And the fourth man, who was a knower of languages, went off to the market and bought them grapes—which is what they all had asked for.

The Muslim community, we believe, was intended to play a universalizing and reconciling role—to take, as it were, the position of the wise man in the story. "Thus have We made you a middle community," God informs us in the Qur'an (Surah Baqarah, 143), and the thoughtful Muslim will consider seriously the requirements of such mediation. There are many episodes in history that reveal its results: the *convivencia* of Southern Spain in the Middle Ages, where Muslims, Christians, and Jews came together in a great cultural flowering, is only the most famous of them. In circumstances where passions rule, the social responsibility ordained for us may all too easily be forgotten. This in no way, however, changes the fact of its institution.

"O People of the Book! Come to what is common among us," the Holy Prophet was told to invite the other religious communities of his time. "That we worship none but God; that we associate no partners with Him; that we do not set up from among ourselves lords other than God" (Surah Al-i 'Imran 64). This call was not a summons to take up his own practice, to receive the immense gift he had been given to distribute; it was a call to the shared understanding of all the children of Abraham. Even so, it was generally refused. Yet Muhammad (peace and blessings be upon him) was never authorized by God to exert any pressure, under any circumstances, upon those who did not respond to his invitations. Fighting was permitted him for the defense of the community, but was never, ever, to be employed for "conversion by the sword." Do not be misled: in all of Muslim history, trying to spread religion through violence has been the rarest of aberrations. For the object of Islam is not to be the one big idol left standing in the temple.

"No compulsion in religion: truth stands out clear from error" (Surah Baqarah, 256) is an exalted doctrine from which the Holy Prophet never in his life departed, and it remains an immovable cornerstone of the Muslim point of view. Unity cannot be imposed by force—nor is there any point in attempting it. Oneness exists, has always existed, and will always exist. But who will be able to see how much of it, and from what perspective, is wholly in the hands of God. "The goal of you all is God: it is He that will show you the truth of the matters in which you dispute" (Surah Ma'idah, 48).

Since individuals differ necessarily in their points of view, so also must groups. The human community is singular, according to Revelation, but human communities are plural, and there is no mistake in that: that is the way it is supposed to be. "We created you all from a male and a female and made you into nations and tribes *so that you may recognize one another*" (Surah Hujurat, 13). Diversity is a divine tool for the furtherance of human consciousness. It ensures that we can never escape some knowledge of the full range of our possibilities, which habit and inertia continually work to confine.

If the fact of you did not challenge me, if the fact of me did not challenge you, what would save either of us from complacency? What would induce us to grow? Were it not for the variety ordained by God, what would become of us here? The divine richness is not served by homogeneity. And we would be so bored!

"If God had so wished, He could have made you all one community, but His plan is to test you in what He has given you. *So vie with each other in good works*" (Surah Ma'idah, 48). The secret of difference, the verse intimates, is that it incites us to display our best, to bring what is unique to each of us into the presence of all. But the full realization of God's wish requires us to agree to what He has done—to accept that He has made all of us, equally, participants in the constant outpouring of creation, recipients of the endless divine gift. If we seek to be fully human, rather than just the biggest bully on the block, then there is no alternative to doing as we are told: we must recognize both the divine unity, and each other. Islam, in this sense, cannot be "just for Muslims." It is desperately needed by us all.

## About the Author

Rabia Terri Harris is coordinator of the Muslim Peace Fellowship and the translator of Ibn 'Arabi's *Journey to the Lord of Power* (Rochester, Vermont: Inner Traditions International, 1981, 1989) and other works of medieval Arabic spirituality. Born in the United States and educated at Princeton and Columbia, she embraced Islam in 1978. She is a member of the Jerrahi Order of America, the major US branch of a three-hundred-year-old Muslim religious and cultural association.

The Muslim Peace Fellowship (Ansar as-Salam) is a gathering of peace and justice-oriented Muslims of all backgrounds who are dedicated to making the beauty of Islam evident in the world. The MPF was formed to help give voice to those currents of Muslim thought and life which receive the least public attention but are of the most central importance. Its newsletter, *As-Salamu 'Alaykum*, is published eight times a year.

The MPF is an affiliate of the Fellowship of Reconciliation (FOR), an international, multireligious, faith-based pacifist organization founded at the outbreak of World War I. FOR runs programs on peace and disarmament, youth training, interfaith and international affairs, racial and economic justice, and Latin America and the Caribbean, and publishes a bimonthly magazine, *Fellowship*. It also serves as an umbrella over sixteen single-faith peace organizations.

For further information, contact: Muslim Peace Fellowship, FOR, PO Box 271, Nyack, New York 10960. (914) 358-4601. Fax: (914) 358-4924.

---

*Strangers are not people, but gods for whom there was no room in the heavens.*

Malagasy saying

---

# The Baha'is—Introduction to a World Community

Office of Public Information, Baha'is of the United States

The Baha'i Faith, founded a century and a half ago, is today among the fastest growing of world religions and has already become the second-most widespread faith, surpassing every religion but Christianity. Its global scope is mirrored in the composition of its membership. With more than five million followers in at least 232 countries and dependent territories, Baha'is come from virtually every ethnic group, culture, profession and social or economic class, mirroring the diversity of humankind itself. Since it also forms a single community, free of schism or factions, sects or subgroups, it comprises what is very likely the most diverse and widespread organized body of people on earth.

The Faith's Founder was Baha'u'llah, a Persian nobleman from Teheran who, in the mid-nineteenth century, gave up a princely existence of comfort and security for a life of persecution and deprivation. Imprisoned and exiled for the last 40 years of his life, he authored the equivalent of more than 100 volumes which form the foundation of the Baha'i community. Baha'u'llah claimed to be nothing less than a new and independent Messenger from God, the most recent in a succession which also includes Abraham, Krishna, Moses, Zoroaster, Buddha, Christ, and Muhammad. The essential message of Baha'u'llah is that of unity. He taught that there is only one God, that there is only one human race, and that all the world's religions have been stages in the revelation of God's will and purpose for humanity. The purpose of life is to know and to worship God and to contribute to an ever-advancing civilization. As humanity has now come of age, the time has arrived for the uniting of all peoples into a peaceful and integrated global society.

In the hundred years since Baha'u'llah lived, the Baha'is have seen the process of global unification advance. Through historical processes, the traditional barriers of race, class, creed and nation have steadily broken down. Baha'u'llah predicted the birth eventually of a universal civilization, in which people accept their oneness. This global society will be based on several fundamental principles: the elimination of all forms of prejudice; full equality between the sexes; recognition of the essential oneness of the world's great religions; the elimination of extremes of poverty and wealth; universal education; the harmony of science and religion; a sustainable balance between nature and technology; and the establishment of a world federal system, based on collective security and the oneness of humanity.

The Baha'i faith is unique in other ways, in addition to its emphasis on unity. It has a global administration, with freely elected governing councils. Its scriptures and activities address virtually every important trend in the world today, from cultural diversity and environmental conservation to a renewed commitment to family life and morality and the call for a "New World Order." Baha'i communities are quite diverse in composition. Yet, they maintain their essential unity through a system of freely elected governing councils, which operate at the local, national, and international levels. At the local level, Baha'is each year elect a nine-member administrative council, which is known as the Spiritual Assembly. They are expected to obey civil law and remain loyal to their respective governments, but are required to refrain from partisan political activity.

> "Let your vision be world-embracing, rather than confined to your own self "—Baha'u'llah

Baha'is around the world express their commitment to these principles chiefly through individual and community transformation, often in small scale, grassroots-based social and economic development projects. Most Baha'i projects emphasize moral development and collective decision-making, with the view that the best way to solve social problems is by unlocking the latent capacities of human beings at the individual level while at the same time better preparing them to work together in groups for common goals.

In the Andes mountains of Bolivia, for example, Primo Pacsi and other Baha'is of Laku Lakuni, have established a small pre-school and promoted use of solar-heated greenhouses which permit families to grow a variety of fruits and vegetables which would not ordinarily survive at such altitudes. Mr. Pacsi is the main teacher in the pre-school, which serves all of the children of the village to prepare them for the government-run primary school.

And in Japan, Kimiko Schwerin, who is married to a non-Japanese, runs an English language school in a Tokyo suburb. Because the family unit is the foundation of human society, according to Baha'u'llah, both Schwerins see their experience as an example of cross-cultural unity, of how international marriage can demonstrate the oneness of all peoples and promote a greater awareness of other cultures.

Stanlake Kukama, a local secretary of the African National Congress in the 1950s, saw the white man as the oppressor when he first began to investigate Baha'u'llah's teachings. He found it difficult to accept the oneness of humanity and the necessity of working to eliminate all racial prejudice that are fundamental principles of the teachings. He came to believe that this path rather than the confrontational world of politics would lead to a better world. Since that time he has worked to build a harmonious and diverse community which could demonstrate to all South Africans that association between people of all races is not only possible—it is joyous and reflective of the reality of human oneness.

The problems faced by so-called "children of the street" in Brazil are helped by a project in the city of Manaus in the Amazon region. A Baha'i center seeks to help these children become healthy, conscientious, and productive members of society by combining an elementary school with a special program of vocational and moral training. In addition, poor women in the neighborhood are provided material and educational assistance.

Baha'u'llah's followers have created a far-flung and diverse worldwide community. It is marked by a distinctive pattern of life and activity which offers an encouraging model for cooperation, harmony and social action. In a world so divided in its loyalties, this is a significant achievement.

## Source Information

Ann Hopkins and the editors of the *Cultural Diversity Sourcebook* compiled this article from documents provided by the Office of Public Information, Baha'is of the United States. They can be contacted at: 866 United Nations Plaza, Suite 120, New York, NY 10017-1811; Phone: 212-756-3500; Fax: 212-756-3566.

> *We struggle to hear*
> *each other and relax to*
> *hear the waves roll in*
>
> Walt Hopkins

# Lessons for Diversity from the Spiritual Realm

by Eric H. F. Law

## Introduction

I was invited to be the music minister of a national Episcopal Church conference. On the opening night of the conference, I led the gathering in singing hymns with different cultural origins. To close the evening celebration, I thought it would be appropriate to sing "Lift Every Voice and Sing," a song which had been tagged as the "African American national anthem." I have heard this song sung by an African American congregation and appreciated the energy and spirit the congregation brought to it. Outside of this context, this energy is often missing when this song was being sung. With the help of the accompanist, I encouraged the gathering to sing "Lift Every Voice and Sing" with more vigor and spirit and invited them to watch my signal to hold and emphasize certain notes. . . . At the end, some people applauded.

While I was enjoying the praises coming my way, an African American woman approached. "I don't know how much you know about this song," she said to me. "Since you're Asian, I don't expect you to know that. So, I'm sure you didn't mean it, but I have to say this: I am deeply offended by the way you did that song."

But I thought I was being very inclusive and authentic. I swallowed my pride and said, "I'm sorry. Can you tell me what I did wrong so that I won't do it again?" "This song came out of the struggle of African Americans. It should be sung with more dignity."

The only response I could muster was, "Thank you for sharing that with me." I thought to myself: what a trite answer. Did I really mean it? Or did I just want to get rid of her?

I did not sleep much that night. I kept replaying the scene over and over again, unwilling to face up to what I had done. From past experience, I knew that whenever I went around in circle, I was surely avoiding something—usually pain. In the middle of the night, I finally admitted that I was hurt. . . . The part that hurt the most was that not only was my effort to be inclusive not recognized but it actually had had the opposite effect.

The next morning, I addressed the gathering. "Before we begin this morning, I would like to explain the principles behind the choice of hymns in this conference. I had tried to be inclusive in picking hymns with various ethnic and cultural origins. Also, in singing and teaching these songs, I attempted to sing them as authentically as possible. However, sometimes I may make mistake in my effort to do that. It's like when someone invited me to dinner and in their effort to include me, they attempted to cook what they believed to be an authentic Chinese meal. It consisted of chop suey and egg fu young." They laughed. "Well, sometimes, I do that too. This is part of the pain of living in a multicultural community. If I commit myself to be inclusive, I must face that danger of making such mistakes. So, I want to make a deal with you.

If at any time during this conference, I abuse a song from a culture with which you are more familiar, I expect you to let me know so that I can continue to learn and grow from my mistakes. In this process, I also invite to you to recognize my intention to be inclusive." Graciously, they agreed.

*Lesson #1—In a culturally diverse environment, what you intend to do is not always the outcome. Sometimes, our effort to be inclusive may be misunderstood, create emotional dispute or even be offensive. When it happens, we must be willing to open our ears to listen, our minds to reflect, our lips to dialogue and our hearts to change if we are to continue to address diversity constructively.*

Through my years of traveling and working with groups, I have asked people of all colors to share their multicultural group experiences with me. Eighty percent of them described the same frustration. Whenever two or three culturally diverse groups come together, the white English-speaking group most likely sets the agenda, does most of the talking and decision making, and, in some cases, feels guilty that the other ethnic groups do not participate in the decision making.

I observed the same scenario over and over again. For a long time, I felt totally powerless about changing the course of these encounters. I call it the "wolf and lamb" scenario. When a wolf is together with other wolves, everything is fine. When a lamb is together with other lambs, everything is safe and sound. But if you put a wolf and a lamb together, inevitably something bad is going to happen. Some people are so disheartened by it that they are giving up the idea of integration all together. Many white English-speaking people enter a multicultural situation with dread and apprehension that the other might accuse them of domination and oppression.

Many people of color stop accepting invitations to multicultural gatherings knowing that they will be ignored and put down one more time and the result will be a waste of their time.

*Lesson #2*—Physical inclusion is not enough.

If we stretch the analogy of the "wolf and lamb" scenario further, one might say that the cultures of the world are as numerous as the kinds of animals inhabiting this earth. Each culture has its own characteristics, values and customs. Some are perceived as strong and some weak. Some are more aggressive and some are considered passive and timid. People in one culture survive as individuals while people in another culture find livelihood in larger groupings. If cultures are analogous to the different animals, then Isaiah 11:6–9 becomes a vision of culturally diverse peoples living together in harmony and peace. This passage is known popularly as the "Peaceable Kingdom." I prefer to call it the "Peaceable Realm." For me, the word Kingdom has too many connotations of the hierarchical human system that the passage challenges. Realm may be a more neutral term. It connotes a state of being. It can also imply a philosophical essence as in "realm" of thoughts.

In order for the animals to coexist in this Peaceable Realm, very "unnatural" behaviors are required from all who are involved. How can a wolf, a leopard or a lion not attack a lamb, a calf or a child for food? At least our fairy tales taught us to believe that. How can a lamb or a calf not run when it sees a lion or a leopard coming close? How can a lion eat straw like an ox when a lion is known to be a meat eater? It goes against their "instinct" to be in this vision of the Peaceable Realm. Perhaps that is what is required of human beings if we are

---

### POWER DYNAMICS AND "PEACEABLE REALM"

The wolf shall dwell with the lamb,
and the leopard shall lie down with the kid,
and the calf and the lion and the fatling together,
and a little child shall lead them.

. . .

and the lion shall eat straw like the ox.
The sucking child shall play over the hole of the asp,
and the weaned child shall put his hand on the adder's den.
They shall not hurt or destroy in all my holy mountain; . . .

(Isaiah 11:6–9) RSV

to live together peacefully with each other. Perhaps we have to go against the "instinct" of our cultures in order for us to stop replaying the fierce-devouring-the-small scenario of intercultural encounter. Perhaps, when all of us have learned how to do that, we may be able to regain our innocence like a child playing over the hole of the asp and putting his or her hand on the adder's den and not be afraid anymore.

In another conference at which I was the music minister, after an African American hymn was introduced, a group of whites complained that the language in the hymn was sexist and demanded that the male references to God (i.e., Lord) be changed. The African Americans did not want to make the change and were on the verge of calling the request racist. The white group was close to calling the African Americans sexists. I did a power analysis of the situation based on the cultural contexts of the group involved. From the context of the African American history and culture, I drew the conclusion that the predominant use of "Lord" to refer to God was very important to the African American. Because of their experience of slavery, they responded to the God of the Hebrew scripture—an all-powerful Lord who would deliver them from the hardship of slavery. The need to see God as strong and powerful was crucial to the survival of the African Americans.

I also evaluated the situation from the context of the white liberal American culture. In this context, a cultural assumption was that all people were equal. With the help of the feminist movement, there was the need to see men and women as equal. Furthermore, since humankind, both male and female, is made in the image of God, to continue to image God in exclusively male terms is unacceptable. Therefore, there was the need to change all male references to God to more gender-neutral terms.

I then analyzed the context of this encounter and realized the African Americans were the minority and were perceived by others as powerless. The white group, even though their concern was valid in their own cultural context, were perceived as powerful. Based on this analysis, I decided to continue singing the African American hymns without any changes, because, in this situation, it might be more important to support the African Americans. However, I tried to counterbalance this decision by intentionally introducing new hymns with feminine images of God to the whole group. I wanted to affirm the importance of inclusive language but not at the expense of taking power away from a group that was already perceived as powerless.

Church leaders, in addition to doing power analysis, must understand and practice the dynamic of giving and retaining/receiving power if we are to be faithful leaders in a multicultural community. This dynamic is also cyclical in nature, moving from being powerful to powerless and then from powerless to powerful again, from death on the cross to the empty tomb of resurrection and from powerful living to choosing the cross again.

When I worked in a small Chinese ministry which worshipped in the cathedral of the diocese, I walked through this cycle within the same day, sometimes several times. For example, I would have a meeting with the diocesan committee representing the Chinese ministry—a time to know I was blessed and resurrected and empowered by the Holy Spirit to challenge the system. In the afternoon, I would visit a Chinese church member—a time to serve, be humble, and empower others by taking up the cross. Then, I would have a meeting with the bishop—time to be resurrected again. That evening, I would have a Chinese Bible study group—time to take up the cross again.

## Giving Power Away

Giving power away is an essential step in this spirituality. I believe this is where we stumble in our work for justice to realize the Peaceable Realm.

There is much fear associated with giving power away. People feel that once they do, they will be powerless forever. But that fear is based on the assumption that people in general like to keep the power that they have. This assumption, which may be true in the world today, is a source of evil.

In our fear of becoming powerless, we hold on to whatever power and material goods that we have. As long as we give in to this fear, we are supporting the evil system where there is no justice—no even distribution of power.

Jesus combats evil by facing the fear of powerlessness. Jesus lets go of power, dies on the cross and triumphs over evil. Much of the Gospel teaches us to give power away and not be afraid of becoming powerless because in our powerlessness, we will become powerful in combating the evil of the world.

Imagine a world where all who have power give their power away to those who have less. Those who give their power away to those who have less will become powerless initially. But this does not happen just once. If everyone has the same value, then the people, who received power earlier and therefore become more powerful, will give their power back to those who have become powerless. So the more we give away, the more we receive. Try the following exercise. Say you have ten people in the room. Give two people ten chips each. The instruction is that when you have more chips than others, you give them away until you have none. This could be a lot of fun. You realize after a while the exercise has become an endless sequence of giving and receiving. No one is ever left without any chip even though you are instructed to give them all away. The more times you give yours away, the more times you will receive.

This is the dynamic of living the Gospel. This is what the Peaceable Realm is about. This is what the Kingdom of God is like. If everyone learns to give power away, the Kingdom of God would be here. "Your Kingdom come . . . " in the Lord's Prayer would be realized."

## About the Author

The Rev. Eric H. F. Law, a partner of Diversity Dynamics, has been a consultant and trainer in multicultural organization development helping educational, health care and religious institutions to deal with issues of cultural diversity for over eight years. He is the author of the book, *The Wolf Shall Dwell with the Lamb—a Spirituality for Leadership in a Multicultural Community* from which much of this article is excerpted. It is available from Chalice Press, Box 179, St. Louis, MO 63166-0179; Phone: 1-800-366-3363.

He is a part-time instructor of courses dealing with cultural diversity for health-care professionals, religious leaders and general studies. He can be reached at: Diversity Dynamics, 3175 South Hoover Street, Box 357, Los Angeles, CA 90007; Phone: 213-656-0436.

---

### STICKS 'N' STONES WILL BREAK MY BONES BUT WORDS WILL BREAK MY HEART
by Arlyne Diamond

Remember the old children's retort, "sticks 'n' stones will break my bones, but words will never hurt me"? Children would chant it in an attempt to deal with the pain of insults, slurs, teasing and other verbal taunts.

Did it work? A little bit.

Acts of bravado do indeed make us feel a little better about ourselves, but, and this is a very important but, they never do erase the pain and humiliation we experience when others call us names or say bad things about "our kind."

In this age of expediency, pragmatism, and political-correctness, we seem to have lost some important social truths! It is hurtful to say things about a person—or parts of their anatomy—or a group of people, that leave them embarrassed, humiliated, or diminished in any way. Although beauty may be in the eye of the *beholder*, insults are in the ear of the *receiver*.

So, if the other person, or group of people, believes a particular word or phrase or symbol to be ugly, demeaning, threatening, or insulting, it is! It is, because it is to them.

The bottom line is: If you don't intend to hurt others, please pay attention to and respect the requests of the groups or individuals who ask us not to use certain descriptors or symbols.

# Jewish Sources of Inspiration in Doing Diversity

by Ellen Hofheimer Bettmann

*"I am always torn between trying to make the world a better place and learning how to be happy in the world in its present form. It makes it very hard to plan my day."*

E.B. White

The most useful advice my mother ever gave me was to always leave the campsite a little cleaner than when I found it. As an adult I have come to realize how big the campsite is, and how hard it is, sometimes, to accomplish this task. The clarity of her expectation has been a guiding force in my life as a human rights activist. My father's counsel, bait your own hook, has also proved to be extremely useful, especially as a counter to the frequent messages about helplessness that I got as a girl. However, for the purposes of this Jewish exploration, I will focus on the "campsite" philosophy, because it illustrates perfectly how Jewish tradition guides my work and all aspects of my life.

I grew up in a suburb of New York, the middle of three sisters. My father's parents had been born in the U.S.; my mother's parents came from Europe at an early age. My mother's mother was so private about "the old country" I didn't know until two years ago where she had been born. When I was growing up, the United States was devoted to the "melting pot" theory, and my family was doing its very best to be American, truly assimilated, still Jewish, of course, thank-God-we-have-religious-freedom-in-the-new-country, but not "too Jewish." I have had to work hard as an adult to reclaim some of my misplaced heritage.

The year I turned twelve my family moved to a new neighborhood in our town. One day, shortly after we moved, one of our new neighbors shouted at my mother, "Get your Jew dog off my lawn!" I remember wondering how that woman knew that my dog Harry was Jewish. From my perspective, Harry was just a dog, and, like my family, well assimilated into mainstream American life; that is to say, Harry was a not-very-observant Jew dog.

My parents' response to the incident was immediately to give Harry away. In protest I ran away from home. I returned with knowledge about my new neighborhood I wished I didn't have, and an understanding that sometimes Jews try very hard to gain acceptance. I knew even then that getting rid of Harry wouldn't make our new neighbor like us, but, in retrospect, it must have, at the very least, given her a satisfying feeling of power. While she couldn't stop our moving into the neighborhood, she could make sure that we didn't feel welcome there.

I missed Harry, but more than that, I missed my lost innocence about what it means to be Jewish. I tied this event up in an invisible knot and swallowed it. It went down but it still sits like a lump inside me waiting to dissolve or explode.

This family background is important to understand, because, while Jewish wisdom guides and sustains me, it has come to me from many directions, like roots taking water from the soil, often undetected during the process of absorption.

Jewish teaching, like all cultural knowledge, is transmitted both formally and informally. Although I didn't know it at the time, my mother's advice about the campsite has a Jewish counterpart: *tikun olam*, Hebrew for (literally) repairing the world. *Tikun olam* is a theme that underlies many rabbinic teachings, but it is not one of the major commandments. It is first found in prayers dating from the third century C.E. As I think about what God wants me to do, I know that *tikun olam* is God's short-hand message to me: just do it! However tempting it might be, I am not free to say, "I didn't make this mess, therefore it has nothing to do with me." My task is to discover what needs "repairing" and use my God-given gifts to set it right. While finding the appropriate tasks may sound a little vague and confusing at first, we Jews are helped in this process by the concept of *mitzvot* (plural for *mitzvah*.) A *mitzvah* is sometimes loosely translated as a "good deed," however it has another component, beyond the meaning of a kindly act. There are 613 *mitzvot* in Judaism. They are Biblical in origin, and as a Jew I don't have a choice about whether or not I want to perform these deeds; I am commanded by God to do them.

Among the 613 *mitzvot* are several commandments that are central to my life. One of these, often translated from the Hebrew as "Do not stand idly by" [Leviticus 19: verse 16] reminds me that it is my job to notice suffering, to care, and to act. The literal English translation is "don't stand on your friend's blood." In the same way that I learned to expand my concept of the "campsite" I have spent my adult life discovering the broadest interpretation of "friend." This sometimes creates problems for me because at any given time there is always more human suffering than any one person can tackle. It is often hard not to feel overwhelmed by the enormity of the task. On one such occasion I called my rabbi during a week-long training-of-trainers workshop. "It's so slow!" I complained. "The workshop is going well, and everyone seems to be 'getting it,' but there is so much more to do, and this is only one group, and I'm only one person, and I don't have enough time . . ." He let me finish my lament before he told me the following saying from *pirkei avot*: [historically translated as "Sayings of Our Fathers;" in modern, less gender-biased language, it is referred to as "Wisdom of Our Ancestors."] "Yours is not to complete the task, but nor are you free to desist from trying." The fact that I cannot possibly end racism and all forms of bigotry by myself in my lifetime should not, in fact, cannot be used as a reason for my not making the attempt. Because the work that I do is often described as trying to do the impossible, it is crucial for my sense of balance to have a statement of faith that acknowledges the enormity of the task and the possibility that I might not be completely successful, but refuses to consider abandoning the attempt.

A key element in Judaism is remembering our history as slaves. Remembering the exodus from Egypt is one of the 613 *mitzvot*. It is so basic it is a part of the *shema*, a daily prayer. *Yom Hashoah*, the Holocaust Day of Remembrance, is a twentieth century version of remembering; we vow never to forget the six million Jews who were murdered by the Nazis, and we say "Never again! Never again!" As a Jew it is important for me to know the Jews' history of oppression, so I can use the experience of the suffering of my people to understand the pain of others. Every year, at Passover, we Jews

read the *Haggadah* in which is recorded the story of our exodus as slaves from Egypt. *Haggadah* means literally "to tell." The Passover celebration includes symbolic rituals, traditional foods, games, and songs that accompany this festival. A catechism of "The Four Questions" is asked by the youngest child at the *Seder*, the Passover meal, and responses are given by everyone at the table. I look forward to and love celebrating Passover every year. In part, the joy in this holiday is connected to the gathering of family and friends. In part, it is a centering experience, a time for me to remember my place and role in Jewish history.

Finally, I am sustained regularly by the words of many Jewish sages and prophets, living and dead. From my mother's aunt Lily, who lived with us when I was growing up, I learned the importance of establishing priorities and learning to deal with the conflict that often accompanies having more than one thing to do at any given time. This wisdom came to me in English, although I am convinced that the original must have been Yiddish: "With one *tuchus*,"(Yiddish for "behind") Lily proclaimed emphatically, "you can't dance at two weddings!" On a daily basis I face more legitimate competing demands for my time and energy than I can possibly respond to, and it is a comfort to me to remember Lily's words as I try, like a circus juggler, to keep all the plates spinning at the same time.

> *"If I am not for myself, who is for me?*
>
> *If I am only for myself, what am I?*
>
> *If not now, when?"*

Rabbi Hillel wrote those words in the first century C.E. When I lose my sense of urgency about this mission of creating a more equitable society, "If not now, when?" is like the sound of the *shofar*, the ram's horn blown in the synagogue at the new year. It is a shrill blast that calls me back to my work on this earth. Jewish work, human work: timeless and timely. The words of my Jewish tradition keep reminding me: this is what God wants me to do. And then no task seems too great.

## About the Author

Ellen Hofheimer Bettmann has been in the field of education for thirty years. She is currently the director of Research and Development for the ADL A WORLD OF DIFFERENCE Institute, a national education and diversity training program of the Anti-Defamation League. Among her proudest moments is her Bat Mitzvah, the Jewish coming-of-age ceremony, traditionally celebrated at age 13, but in her case at age 42. She would like to thank and acknowledge her friend and often-teacher Pearl Mattenson who helped with the research of this piece, her rabbi and friend David Whiman, her husband Michael who always serves as an excellent critical reader, and her children, Will, Joanna, and Rob, whose lives carry Jewish wisdom into the next generation.

For information about the Anti-Defamation League and ADL's A World of Difference Institute: Anti-Defamation League, 823 United Nations Plaza, New York, NY 10017. Telephone: (212) 885-7700; Fax: (212) 867-0779.

---

### THE PROMISE OF AMERICA

We exist on a fragile spacecraft called "Earth" only by the graces of forces much greater than ours . . .

. . . our relative abilities to obtain and use them notwithstanding, the resources of that spacecraft are finite . . . [W]e are all dependent upon its tenuous supply of air and water and soil. And, of necessity, all committed for our own safety to its security and peace, preserved from extinction only by the love and work we give each other and our home. To comprehend that these physical limits dictate that we conceive of ourselves as a "family of man" . . .

Observable to the discerning eye, life is growth in bone and tissue, skills and expertise, awareness and feeling. Living skills, including interpersonal, problem-solving and program development, give us the skills necessary to live with decency and responsibility in the "family of man." Incorporating all of our humanity and reaching out for that of all mankind, and in so doing transcending ours, we live life as fully as we love and have the skills to do so.

Excerpted from "The Promise of America," keynote address given by Dr. Robert R. Carkhuff at the American Personnel and Guidance Association Convention in New Orleans, LA, April 1974.

"Every society on earth needs to step back (in mind) and consider once more who they are, what their deepest loyalties are, what life is for. Of all the memberships we identify ourselves by (racial, ethnic, sexual, national, class, age, religious, occupational), the one that is most forgotten, and that has the greatest potential for healing, is place. We must learn to know, love, and join our place even more than we love our own ideas. People who can agree that they share a commitment to the landscape/cityscape—even if they are otherwise locked in struggle with each other—have at least one deep thing to share. Community values (which include the value of the nonhuman neighbors in the 'hood') come from deliberately, knowledgeably, and affectionately 'living in place'."

Gary Snyder
Pulitzer Prize-winning poet and a proponent of bioregional thinking

# Where Do Mermaids Stand?

by Robert L. Fulghum

Giants, Wizards, and Dwarfs was the game to play.

Being left in charge of about eighty children seven to ten years old, while their parents were off doing parenty things, I mustered my troops in the church social hall and explained the game. It's a large scale game of Rock, Paper, and Scissors, and involves some intellectual decision making. But the real purpose of the game is to make a lot of noise and chase people until nobody knows which side you are on or who won.

Organizing a roomful of charged up gradeschoolers into two teams, explaining the rudiments of the game, achieving a consensus on group identity—all this is no mean accomplishment, but we did it with a right good will and were ready to go.

The excitement of the chase had reached a critical mass. I yelled out: "You have to decide now which you are—a *Giant*, a *Wizard*, or a *Dwarf!*"

While the groups huddled in frenzied, whispered consultation, a tug came at my pants leg. A small child stands there looking up, and asks in a small, concerned voice. "Where do the Mermaids stand?"

Where do the Mermaids stand?

A long pause. A very long pause. "Where do the Mermaids stand?" says I.

"Yes. You see, I am a Mermaid."

"There are no such thing as Mermaids."

"Oh, yes, I am one!"

She did not relate to being a Giant, a Wizard, or a Dwarf. She knew her category. Mermaid. And was not about to leave the game and go over and stand against the wall where a loser would stand. She intended to participate, wherever Mermaids fit into the scheme of things. Without giving up dignity or identity. She took it for granted that there was a place for mermaids and that I would know just where.

Well, where *do* the Mermaids stand? All the "Mermaids"—all those who are different, who do not fit the norm and who do not accept the available boxes and pigeonholes?

Answer that question and you can build a school, a nation, or a world on it.

What was my answer at the moment? Every once in a while I say the right thing. "The Mermaids stand right here by the King of the Sea!" says I. (Yes, right here by the King's Fool, I thought to myself.)

So we stood there hand in hand reviewing the troops of Wizards and Giants and Dwarfs as they roiled by in wild disarray.

It is not true, by the way, that mermaids do not exist. I know at least one personally. I have held her hand.

# PART 9
# ALTERNATIVE MODELS AND VISIONS

# Dialogue: Alternative Models

*George*—It's time for us to look at some other ways to approach diversity. The U.S.-made models we use for studying culture are themselves cultural artifacts. They bear the stamp of our own background and favorite ways of thinking. We want to examine other models or ways that provide alternatives, as well as look at what cultures outside the U.S. may offer to broaden our perspective in the diversity debate and enrich its conduct.

*Bob*—None of the new models here can provide the definitive answer for the diversity dilemmas we face; but looking at familiar issues in new ways can refresh us and can help each of us see beyond some of our filters and cultural biases. Hank Karp's article on Gestalt (page 366) is an example of an alternative psychological approach. It looks at an old problem through a new lens.

*George*—Our section on spirit is also a source of alternative models. In the current section we'll explore more deeply how various cultures see diversity. What paradigms or mental processes do they use to manage or comprehend difference? How do they deal with the outsider, the stranger, the invader, cultural change? In other words, we're looking for the value diversity adds to undertaking diversity initiatives themselves.

*Bob*—Some cultures use storytelling to show how to reconcile differences. On page 369 there is a Native American story of how a great storm devastated the forest and all the tribes had to come together, first to learn to survive and then to learn to live together even on a spiritual level. Other cultures have their own metaphors to deal with diversity questions. In fact, there is a book available[1] which uses metaphors for cultures; for example, the English garden, known for its beauty in the variety of its flowers, its rigid planned structure, stands for Britain. Metaphors are constantly being created. Poetry is full of them. In our own tradition, the freedom songs of the 60s and 70s dealt with the diversity of other cultures . . .

*George*—and their focus then was largely on unity with, and love for, those different from oneself. They were songs of solidarity and freedom designed for escape from oppressive cultural and colonial structures. Many were drawn from black spiritual music, earlier social movements, here and from around the world.

*Bob*—I still hear echoes of "We shall Overcome," "Freedom Train."

*George*—Lately, we've been looking at diversity too much with our heads. We need more. That's one reason my organization develops games that bring people's senses, feelings, and imagination into play. Some diversity professionals like Elsie Cross, who is one of the nation's best, give short shrift to the little cross-cultural things we do together, like ethnic dinners, etc., but in this case I disagree with her. For example, sharing your cuisine and its story can create a bit of comfort and a small bond of togetherness through experiences that enable and encourage people to take one more step toward understanding.

*Bob*—Perhaps Elsie Cross is right, though, in the sense that you can't consume all your energy in these little events, without going to other important efforts. Still, I think, too, that everything we do gives us more to build on.

*George*—There's much we do together that we don't examine from a cultural perspective. We participate together in a global marketplace. We do business across national and ethnic boundaries every day. This is a diversity event, but seldom do we slow down to take a look at the cultural dimensions, the values, the decision making criteria, etc., that affect how we work together and do business with each other. The difficulty of eating with chopsticks, if you've never done it, isn't just a metaphor for entering another culture. It's an object lesson in how "head" solutions for diversity problems need to be supplemented by "hands-on" experience.

*Bob*—Another Western alternative model, the MBTI (Myers-Briggs Type Inventory), deals with dimensions of personality difference that can exist

---

[1]*Understanding Global Cultures: Metaphorical Journeys through Seventeen Countries*, by Martin J. Gannon, Sage Publications, Thousand Oaks, CA, 1994.

within the same ethnic or gender or age group. It's really a different cut. The cross-cultural uses of this instrument are discussed in "What 'Type' of Person are You?" (page 373).

*George*—Tony Hill gives us a similar personality type inventory, simpler and more interactive, that he uses with much success. The technology he describes gets people to accept and deal with each other along lines other than race and ethnicity.

*Bob*—In other words it gets them to show and act out of their "True Colors" (page 379), not just their superficial differences.

*George*—Walt Hopkins and Geof Cox make a modern use of perennial wisdom about personality in their search for "Developing a Whole Organisation Culture" (page 384). The origin of the four personality types seems to be buried in prehistory, but it surfaces again in culture after culture. It seems to have a deep resonance with human experience that can be called upon for interpreting new experiences, as well as old.

*Bob*—Hank Karp's "Working with Resistance to Diversity" (page 381) is a follow-up to his piece on the Gestalt perspective earlier in the section, but it is more closely tied to the issue of why diversity work isn't more successful.

*George*—Actually, he tells us how to use resistance that builds up in individuals and groups as a help rather than a hindrance to learning and change. In this sense, what p.c. people label as "backlash" is an untapped resource.

*Bob*—Billi Lee's "Circles & Triangles" (page 388) shows why some other things don't work. Her reframing is particularly valuable for newcomers or outsiders to an organization. I remember when the film series "Valuing Diversity" by Griggs Productions appeared. It was really the first professional-quality diversity film. It said explicitly . . . "share the rules" if you want to include others. Well, at the most basic level of "political savvy" (those words are the title of Billi Lee's training program), people need to understand both when their input is welcome, and when they're expected to "fall in line" and follow their "marching orders." The Circles and Triangles model is simple and elegant. And when you tell people about it, they light up with recognition!

*George*—Finally, "Ubuntu" is a delight, reframing the values of being human in a social context, but in the plain language and stories of traditional wisdom. Author Lente-Louise Louw mines these stories for insights into how we can do better diversity training. I wish there were more stuff like this making the rounds of diversity work.

# Diversity Training from the Gestalt Perspective

by Hank Karp

Diversity training today is no longer a matter of adhering to a single set of values dictated by any one interest group. Whether out of a genuine concern for people, a fear of running afoul of the law, or a concern for the organization's public image, diversity is a growing concern for almost all organizations. Regardless of the reason, and I hasten to add that there is *no* bad reason for being concerned, a much wider degree of interest has been generated in diversity training. This is shared by both those who design and conduct the training *and* by those who experience it, or in all too many cases, are obligated to *endure* it.

The bottom line objective of all diversity training programs is to better the relationships among people who work together and who are, for the most part, interdependent. Unfortunately, with the best of intentions, some of these diversity training programs are producing results just the opposite of what they were designed to accomplish. That is, people are leaving programs more resistant then when they entered; more confused about what they can and cannot say to others; and, more defensive and guarded in their relationships with anyone who is noticeably different from themselves. One very real reason for this is concern over who is going to sue you for saying what. Previous casual working relationships have become more formal; new people are viewed as potential threats rather than as potential friends; and *this is not what we had in mind!*

To make diversity training something that will take hold in the organization, it has to reflect the values of that organization and the individuals who make it up. In developing a training program, more has to be done than just grabbing the latest training films off the shelf and trying to couple them with a few interactive exercises. Effective diversity training is not conducted by blind adherence to some externally imposed set of values about how people *should* deal with other people; but, rather, it is a matter of making some real choices to accomplish what *you* want to accomplish in terms of creating a more supportive and realistic working environment. Choices have to be made by the initiator and the designers of the program as to what this program needs to stress. This can be started by making a few choices ahead of time.

## The Choices

The interesting thing about the choices below is that you make them whether you are aware of doing so or not. Some of the options you would clearly want to avoid; others you would want to make consciously. My bias is very clear in how I am presenting these choices, and I ask only that you consider them before making your own.

1. **Individual vs. Group.**

   Diversity is much more than minority vs. majority. If we view diversity on a minority vs. majority basis, rather than on an individual basis, we tend to deal with each other based on how we are *similar*, e.g., stereotypically, rather than on how each person is unique. One's **marker**, i.e., that which identifies the individual as a member of an identifiable subgroup, is best responded to as a *background* element, rather than as a figural element.

   More important: we can theorize, we can agonize, we can even conceptualize about diversity as a group; however, we can only *act on it* as individuals. As long as we conceive of diversity as a group or societal issue, rather than as an issue of individual responsibility, the easier it is to just talk about it . . . and, in the end, we don't have to *do* anything about it. Once diversity becomes a matter of personal choice and accountability, we can begin to respond to the realities of it a lot more pragmatically.

2. **Strengthen The Weaker Vs. Weaken The Stronger.**

   By insisting that each person always be on guard about what *might* offend someone else, and then to feel fully responsible for not doing so, the onus is always and *solely* on the speaker and the other person's (TOP's) only function is to be hurt. In this case the speaker takes all the responsibility for TOP's feelings. He has to spend time and energy trying to anticipate what TOP *might* feel and then modify his message to accommodate that assumption. This weakens the speaker.

If, on the other hand, the speaker only takes responsibility for his *actions*, it is then up to TOP to take responsibility for her own feelings. This says that if TOP is offended, she is obligated to say something. This is forcing her to take responsibility for her own welfare, by letting the speaker know and then demanding a change. This strengthens TOP.

### 3. Do Unto Others vs. Do No Harm

There is a problem with making a virtue out of "doing unto others." It presupposes that one person knows what is in the best interest of another. It is much more realistic to assume that there is a wide variation as to what different people would like "done unto them."

Pain, on the other hand, is much more universal and, consequently, there is a much stronger likelihood that what will hurt me would .also be painful for you. That is, if you are under the impression that what you would like, everyone would like, chances are you are going to be wrong. On the other hand, if you think that what would hurt you would hurt others, chances are you are going to be right.

In developing diversity programs it is easier and more effective to concentrate on avoiding doing what is harmful, than it is focusing on doing what seems good. By focusing primarily on avoiding the bad, e.g., *Thou shalt not*, stereotype, assuming what others are feeling, and so forth, *an outer boundary for inappropriate behavior* is established. Once this boundary is clear and agreed upon, the range of choices for appropriate behavior is now virtually limitless. That is, if you have successfully identified and outlawed those things that are painful and destructive, every other possible choice has a *potential* for being effective. It is now much easier to creatively respond to the real and varied preferences of individuals.

When you focus on doing good, you are restricting yourself to those specific choices, and to only those choices. This could easily preclude a lot of other options out there just waiting to be discovered. As a rule of thumb, it seems to me that the *"Thou shalt nots"* are lot less burdensome and easier to work with than are the *"Thou shalts."*

### 4. Behavior vs. Attitudes

People are *always* accountable for everything they say, or don't say; do or don't do. On the other hand, people are *never* accountable to others, under any circumstances, for two things: what they want and what they feel. This says that you are 100% accountable for your behaviors and *never* accountable for your attitudes. You will like whom and what you like; and dislike whom and what you dislike, no matter who says you should or should not . . . and this includes *you*. The easiest and most effective way of dealing with diversity issues is to help people concentrate on what they are *doing* and what the effects of those actions are. People are usually willing to explore their specific actions because there is no implication that there is anything wrong with them personally. Leave the attitudes alone!

The irony in this is that prejudice is appropriate whereas discrimination is not. If you tell people that they shouldn't feel what they feel, they will defend that feeling to the death. On the other hand, if you make it safe for people to honor their feelings, *no matter what they are*, you increase the probability that they will be willing to surface these feelings and explore them.

### 5. Respect vs. Patronage

There is no question that the current move toward softening the language is well intended, and may even be well received by the minority person. Being referred to as being "visually challenged," rather than "blind" might be preferable for some people (The truth is this is usually *not* the case). However, the fact remains that what is respectful for one person may be patronizing for another. When euphemisms are employed, there is a subtle

367

message that says, "Poor baby, you just can't take it."

One option in designing diversity programs is to have people honor their markers, rather than blur them. A person's marker, like most other human characteristics, has a potential for positive *and* negative results. That is, whatever my marker is, it is a part of the whole me. Along with the possible problems associated with one's marker, people also need to address: What does this marker contribute that is positive or strengthening? How has it provided me with a unique perspective? What has it forced me to come to grips with and overcome? What does this allow me to teach others?

### 6. Guilt vs. Empathy

The reason that diversity training is even considered necessary is because there has been a history of discrimination, unfairness and even brutality of the many towards the few. Racism, anti-Semitism, and gay bashing are just a few of the more institutionalized forms of this, but no less painful are the subtler forms of exclusion that are leveled at those who are physically handicapped by size, weight, or deformity.

All human characteristics operate in polarities, e.g., strong-weak, good-bad, introvert-extrovert, and so forth. Everyone has *some* capacity and *some* experience on both sides of every polarity. This is so with the polarity of oppressor-oppressed, as well. Almost *everyone* at some point has experienced discrimination in some form or another. It could be exclusion from a neighborhood because of race, a place in school because of religion, or it could be not making the basketball team because you were too short when compared to the other competitors.

The point is that, regardless of ethnicity, religion, gender, or any other marker, *nobody has the pain market cornered!* In designing a diversity program, you will be better off if your focus is on creating empathy rather than guilt. To do so, it makes more sense to help the straight, white, American, male (SWAM), *since he is the intended target of most diversity training*

*programs*, get in touch with his personal role or experience with being oppressed rather than trying to get him to feel guilty and own a generalized and amorphous role of oppressor . . . particularly when he has not personally oppressed anyone. Asking him questions like, Were you ever discriminated against? On what basis? How did you react? will go a lot farther in eliciting his awareness and support for the pain of others, than will trying to "sign him up for the next guilt trip."

In a like vein, it makes sense to help the minority members get in touch with their capacity, experience, or role as an oppressor. Some of the key questions here are: Have you ever intentionally dealt with someone unfairly? What was it like being in the majority? What good did you get out of this? How did it feel? This process, if done willingly, should help the minority individuals understand the majority individuals from their own experience. The key is to have *all* participants in a diversity program be able to touch *both sides* of the polarity, regardless of their primary orientation. Empathy is essential on *both* sides if we are going to make things better permanently.

### 7. Victim vs. Survivor

How people see themselves has a lot to do with how well they respond to prejudice and discrimination. Reinforcing the role of *victim of discrimination* tends to focus on pain and weakness. The message is "see how I have suffered." When this occurs in a training program, "suffering contests" can frequently emerge among the various subgroups to determine who has suffered the most. As this perspective continues to be reinforced, the outcome is that people leave the program feeling more vulnerable, victimized, and weak as a function of it, than when they came in. The worst possible outcome of this progression is that the individual or group can end up wallowing in self-pity. If that happens, all communication stops, positions are set in concrete, and there is very little chance of any positive outcome occurring. This is hardly the desired outcome for *any* training effort.

While acknowledging that victimization has occurred is important, it is far better to develop a program that reinforces the role of *survivor of discrimination*, rather than victim of it. The role of survivor tends to reinforce the strength of the individual with the message now being, "listen to how I have conquered."

Having people identify the discriminatory behavior, honoring how it felt, and then unearthing what they did to overcome it, or could do to overcome it the next time, puts a whole new perspective to the diversity issue. It reinforces people's responsibility for, and their *ability* to, take care of themselves. Like the old saying goes, "That which doesn't kill you makes you stronger."

## Conclusion

There is no question that, as individuals, each one of us is far more different from anyone else than similar. This individuation is just as distinct *within each identifiable sub-group*, as it is in randomly selecting two people and comparing them. That is, the *only* similarity I might share with anyone who has the same marker as I do, *is the marker itself.*

The only place where being similar really matters is in identifying what we want to accomplish together. Paradoxically, by focusing on how we are individually unique as sub-group members, we can more easily identify our common customs, values, and objectives, and more readily share these with, and learn from, others.

## About the Author

Dr. Hank B. Karp received his Ph.D. in Industrial and Organizational Psychology from Case Western Reserve University, Cleveland, Ohio. He completed his post doctoral work in Gestalt Therapy through the intensive Postgraduate Program at the Gestalt Institute of Cleveland. In addition, he is a licensed Professional Counselor in the State of Virginia. He has conducted seminars for managers in the areas of: First Line Leadership Skill Development; Power; Conflict and Resistance; Delegation; Motivation & Job Enrichment; Leadership Style & Managerial Effectiveness; Gestalt Organization Development, and Career Plateauing.

He is a Senior Associate at ODT, Incorporated. Dr. Karp's publications include: *Personal Power: An Unorthodox Guide to Success*, available from ODT at 800-736-1293 ($24.00 includes postage and handling) and, "Handling Career Plateaus," from the *National Business Employment Weekly* (A complimentary copy of the last article is available from ODT, Inc.; send a self-addressed stamped envelope to ODT, Inc., Box 134, Amherst, MA 01004). He has just completed *Change Leadership from a Gestalt Perspective* (1995, Pfeiffer).

---

### DIVERSITY TRAINING IN ANOTHER VOICE

*"When I was a child, my grandfather decided to move from the Reserve where we all lived and find a home in the city. He said he wanted to see how the white man lived. We were all nervous about living with white people, so to prepare us, Grandfather told us this story.*

*"'In the ancient time,' he said, 'when our people were still living in separate communities in the forests, one day there was a great storm. During the storm, the people of many tribes were scattered and mixed in together. After the storm, many wandered into foreign villages and camps, and had to learn to live together, work together, and even pray together.'"*

---

This quotation spoken by the character Jacob Lightborn is taken from the videotape, "Hidden Conversations," a co-production of Panoply Productions, Ltd., and George Simons International. For information about these materials, call GSI at 408-426-9608, or in Canada, Panoply Productions, at 613-225-4568.

# Leadership: Sulaiman's Dilemma

by George F. Simons

---

*"My youngest daughter is twenty-four. She has just finished school. Not only has she found a well-paying job in her field, but she has become engaged to a young man, both handsome and well-to-do. She told me that they want to marry in September, only a few months from now. My daughter is very headstrong, and I know that while she wants my blessing, she will go ahead with the marriage one way or the other.*

*"Her elder sister is very upset. She is twenty-seven and does not yet have a boy friend. She is very worried about losing face, if her younger sister marries before she does. To make matters even more complicated for me, her mother is taking her side.*

*"I would like to persuade my younger daughter to go slowly, to wait, but also to help her sister accept that times are changing and to go along with the marriage."*

---

This story is from another culture, from Indonesia, from a different hemisphere, from a high level corporate manager whom we will call Sulaiman. Yet there is a familiar ring to it. It reflects what many U.S. managers experience in their workforce today. Part of their workforce has been around for a long time. It is upset with newcomers who are different and want to do things differently. This elder daughter has real fears about her honor and her value. She can be loving, faithful, hard working, but also bullheaded and petulant in her claim to be acknowledged as eldest and first.

The younger daughter is another part of the workforce; different, less like you, more separate in time and experience, hard to understand. While you love her too, she is for you unpredictable. And, she is becoming strong enough to go off in her own direction. She eventually will do this, with or without your blessing. You also know that you all have much to offer each other if you can keep the family together. Mother, the "provider of comfort" is there too, in the form of the traditional organizational culture. She always seems to support the eldest daughter, who "fits in."

This diverse workforce is with us. It is an undeniable and irreversible fact. The Indonesians say for such a situation, *Nasi sudah menjadi bubur,* "The rice has become porridge." You can't change it.

Perhaps you are in the Sulaiman's dilemma. You may have deep affinity and respect for the elder daughter, the more traditional workforce, perhaps you even have felt more comfortable with her. She may be more predictable, more like you. On the other hand you may be a manager who feels more akin to the younger workforce, the powerful and impatient newcomer, in love with the energy and frustrated with the structures which hamstring its progress.

To lead effectively, you need both daughters to understand, respect and work with each other to get the bottom-line productivity, creativity and agility you need to survive and thrive. Your fears of losing what either or both daughters bring to your organization are real. They are like two halves of a 5,000 rupiah note. Unless you have both halves they are worthless—you cannot buy lunch. *Bersatu kita teguh, bercerai kita runtuh!* "As one we are strong, apart we collapse!" As Benjamin Franklin put it, perhaps even more poignantly to those who would be leaders in difficult times, "Either we all hang together, or we shall each hang separately." Without embracing the two daughters, without addressing the predicament of diversity, it makes little sense to get on with business as usual.

---

# Using Values to Manage Diversity

by George Simons, Carmen Vazquez, and Philip R. Harris

Most managers would agree that they have a set of values by which they lead others. Sometimes these values are consciously and powerfully expressed in an organization's mission or goals statement. At other times they are simply the unconscious driving forces of an individual manager's decisions and actions, deriving from experience in the organization and culture in which she or he grew up.

Today's successful organization is motivated by a common set of images and values which includes diversity. Valuing diversity also means that we respect the values of others when they differ from ours. For example, I as a manager from one culture may not value family or group ties in the same way as my co-worker from another group does, but I can accept that he or she values it in that way. I can then consciously incorporate that value into how I communicate with, motivate, and collaborate with him or her. There are several steps to this process.

First, discover the other person's values. Begin by watching how others behave. When someone makes a choice or behaves consistently in similar circumstances, it suggests that a value is at work there. Because culture and experience set us apart, however, the same value might not motivate me to behave in the same way, or, both of us might behave in the same way out of two entirely different values. To make a new worker comfortable, for example, coworkers from one culture may express curiosity and interest by asking frequent personal questions, whereas others would find that intrusive and would try to make the newcomer comfortable by being available, but not intruding on her or his privacy. The more you know about a culture, the easier it is to behave appropriately.

Filipino management expert Tomas Andres (see his book, *Management by Filipino Values*, New Day Publishers, Quezon City, RP, 1985) insists that knowing another's values becomes most useful to us when we identify precisely which value or

values are at play in a given situation. The art of Values Clarification developed in the 1960's and '70's can be valuable here. It is one thing to know that an individual values family ties more than you do. It is quite another to recognize that that is the value at stake when that individual is absent from work for what would seem like an inconsequential family event to you. Your tendency is to judge the person negatively by your standards about responsibility or consistent attendance at work rather than positively in line with his or her standards of obligation.

Because other people's values tend to be interpreted as negative when they conflict with our own, we fail to see how they could be useful in our system. The next step to managing by values, Andres says, is to look for the positive side of the other person's values. This means not only seeing how the value functions beneficially in his or her cultural system, but how that same value could be applied in ways consistent with your values or the objectives of the organization in which you both work. Group-oriented values, for example, can be more functional than high individual motivation, e.g., when a manager needs a team to accomplish something previously done by individuals. Similarly in a more traditional organization, an individual with highly individualistic tendencies may be chosen for an assignment requiring more isolation and independence. Or someone may be needed who can deal more comfortably with personal confrontation than others in the group can.

Once this positive side of the value is identified, Andres tells us how to apply the value to the issue at hand. Here is an example. Many U.S. trainers, when they work with individuals from more traditional cultures, are often seen as authorities. They are not to be interrupted and not to be questioned. The U.S. trainers, coming from a highly individualistic culture, thrive on a high degree of participant involvement. The result is frustrating for both sides, the trainer demanding engagement and the participants feeling pressured and holding back. One U.S. trainer deals with this situation by pointing out to the group how important it is for her not to lose face with the manager who set up the program, and that this would happen if the group did not participate with their personal questions and opinions. The values conflict created by this step is usually resolved by the trainer getting more of what she wanted from the participants, while the participants feel empowered to behave in terms of a value that is important to them. Were the trainer to insist on or openly preach her own values of individualism, directness, and openness, resistance and passivity would simply build in the group.

When people begin to use values in new ways, the nervousness this causes can be overcome and turned into a sense of satisfaction, Andres says, if you reinforce the new behavior. Choose reinforcers, recognition, and rewards that the recipients value as such. Culturally inappropriate rewards are actually punishments.

The critical difference between managing by values and traditional motivation techniques lies in recognizing how differently values function from one cultural group to another. Once we get beyond our ethnocentric disbelief and disdain for how others actually think and feel, we can explore how those values, different as they are, can be called upon to make relationships work and get the job done.

## Managing Prejudice with American Values

A colleague recently did an organizational culture survey in the midst of what seemed to be a powerful hate campaign against women and minorities promoted to first-line supervision in a federal government agency. The new supervisors were being harassed by having the air let out of their tires, offensive phone calls to their spouses, and other forms of direct and indirect intimidation.

The survey revealed that less than 3% of the other employees were behind the hate campaign. This made it rather easy to challenge the majority with American pluralistic values of fair play and respect for the individual. The majority could then use their sense of outrage to set informal but powerful organizational norms that said that such abusive behavior would no longer be accepted. Having 3% of one's employees bigoted enough to

create sabotage is still intolerable, but it is possible to manage by values so that such behavior becomes socially unacceptable and, in fact, stops.

What are some ways of sounding out value differences? The challenge is to get to the level of difference in people's interpretation of the values themselves. One technique that we have found useful for multicultural, multigender teams is to take a value that people agree upon as important, "honesty," for example. Then, instead of asking people to define the value in abstract terms, ask that each person tell a story from their culture which illustrates this value best for them. Or, you may ask that each person simply make up a story about honesty and tell it to the rest of the group. Then use appreciative inquiry techniques, i.e., raise questions that do not challenge, but explore the story more deeply. The participants come to a greater understanding of each other's behavior. They will also begin to discover how other cultural values, say, responsibility to blood relatives, or the weight given to one's word versus written contracts, etc. come to play in what is seen as "being honest." Two individuals from two different backgrounds may be willing to die for "absolute honesty," but differ radically in what honesty means and when it should be important.

## About the Authors

Carmen Vazquez, a native of Puerto Rico and fluent in English and Spanish, has fifteen years of consulting experience specializing in diversity and cross-cultural management training issues. She designs, develops and implements programs on the topics of customer service, time management, leadership, motivation, team-building, supervisory and management skills, and outplacement. Ms. Vazquez is a Senior Associate with ODT, Inc., a management consulting and publishing firm committed to organizational effectiveness and diversity management training. She can be reached at The Paradigm Group, 15914B Shady Grove Road, #300, Gaithersburg, MD 20877, (301) 424-3675.

Philip R. Harris, Ph.D., is a senior scientist for NETROLOGIC, Inc., in San Diego. As an international consultant in management and executive development, he has assisted more than 185 multinational corporations and associations, government and military agencies, and educational institutions. He has written or edited more than 40 volumes and 200 journal articles. He can be reached at: Harris International, 2702 Costebelle Drive, La Jolla, CA 92037; Phone: 619-453-2271; Fax: 619-454-4712.

George F. Simons is co-editor of this Sourcebook (see biography on page 505).

This piece is adapted from, George F. Simons, Carmen Vazquez, and Philip R. Harris, *Transcultural Leadership: Empowering the Diverse Workforce*, published by Gulf Publishing Company, and available from GSI at 408-426-9608.

# What "Type" of Person are You?: Psychological Type—A Key Dimension of Diversity

by Helen Pelikan and Barbara Deane

> David:    "You drive me crazy!"
> Maria:    "You can't make a decision!"
> David:    "How can you lay off all these people and be so insensitive to their situations?"
> Maria:    "Stick to the facts—you can't make decisions based on your feelings."

Does this conversation sound familiar? You can hear the strong undertone in both David's and Maria's statements; each believes he or she is right and the other's way of thinking is faulty or just plain wrong. How might we explain these differences? One of the best explanations arises from a dimension of human diversity that we often ignore—psychological type.

Over the last several years, we have come to include in diversity such differences as age, ethnicity, gender, national origin, physical ability, race, and sexual orientation, but not psychological type. As we progress in this field, we can no longer ignore the basic psychological differences that exist at the individual level.

Each of us develops a world view based on the mental strategies we prefer. We easily assume that others think as we do. When they don't, we may quickly judge them to be inadequate because they are not like us. If we are not aware that different types of mental strategies exist across individuals, we may view our psychological preferences as right and appropriate and those of our opposite as wrong and inadequate.

## How Do You Discover Your Psychological Type?

The most widely-used tool for determining the individual differences of psychological type is the Myers-Briggs Type Indicator (MBTI)™. When appropriately applied, this tool explains some basic ways human beings differ in terms that are easy to understand and non-threatening; it quickens respect and appreciation for other kinds of diversity.

The MBTI was developed in the 1940s by a mother-daughter team, Katherine Briggs and Isabel Myers. Building on Carl Jung's theories about normal personality differences among people, the mother/daughter team moved beyond just observation and created a seemingly simple, yet subtly complex, instrument for assessing psychological type.

Its popularity is based on how profoundly it offers a self description. It is not uncommon to hear someone say, "At last, there is an instrument that describes me!" It shows individual differences both within and across groups, occupations, interests, professions, and genders. The instrument has

---

## Figure 1
## What is "Psychological Type"?
## The Four Preference Scales of the Myers Briggs Type Indicator

1. **Extraversion (E) vs. Introversion (I)**—how you focus mental energy

2. **Sensing (S) vs. iNtuition (N)[2]**—how you gather data

3. **Thinking (T) vs. Feeling (F)**—how you make decisions

4. **Judging (J) vs. Perceiving (P)**—how you organize your life and get things done

A person's psychological "type" includes one element from each of the four scales listed above. After answering the indicator's questions, the user is assigned four letters, one from each of the scales, as in ESTJ or INTP. There are a total of 16 "types."

---

demonstrated an 85–93 percent validity and reliability for the U.S. populations that have used it over the last 50 years.[1]

The MBTI is a questionnaire that helps people identify preferences along four scales: 1) how mental energy is focused, 2) how data are gathered, 3) how decisions are made, and 4) how one organizes one's life. The MBTI does not measure whether or not you are mentally healthy. Rather, it is a tool for learning more about yourself and how you may be similar to and different from others.

Users report that the measurement "fits" for them at least 90% of the time, so we know that people find the results to be meaningful. However, psychological type is still a hypothesis. You can't see someone's type, but you can observe the style that seems to emanate from it. People who take the instrument are often relieved to find that their differences are really based on preferences, not on some kind of irreconcilable problem. Too often variations in the behavior of others are seen as flaws or afflictions rather than as style differences.

The MBTI is used extensively in business, educational, and religious settings to deal with communication issues, team building, and conflict resolution. Increasingly, it is being used by organizations of all kinds as an entrée into the topic of diversity, to help people deal constructively with their differences.

## What Does the MBTI Measure?

The MBTI distinguishes people along four scales; each scale represents two opposite preferences for performing mental tasks. [See Figure 1]

According to Jung, each of us is more comfortable with one of the two preferences even though we use all of them every day. Over time, we prefer the mental strategy that is more comfortable, since it takes less effort, uses less mental energy, and feels more natural. This results in habits of thinking and behaving that we come to see as right and appropriate. Now, let's examine each scale.

## Extraversion (E) vs. Introversion (I)

This scale measures one's comfort with the two psychological worlds we all inhabit—the world outside, of people, places and events, and the inner world of thoughts, feelings, and sensations. Extraverts focus their awareness on and obtain their mental stimulation primarily from the world around them, while Introverts focus their awareness on and obtain their mental stimulation primarily from within.

Extraverts tend to be gregarious, enjoy being in groups, and like a lot of verbal action. They also like to think out loud, and typically have a large network of friends. Introverts, on the other hand, prefer intimate, one-on-one relationships, are typically reserved, prefer to think through ideas alone, and tend to feel drained by too much interaction.

Because Extraverts in the U.S. outnumber Introverts, they often fail to recognize Introversion as valid; for example: An Extraverted teacher may chastise Introverted students because they do not "talk" or "speak up" in class.

How can you use these distinctions to improve your own abilities? If you have a strong Extravert preference, find a colleague whom you admire who seems to have a strong Introvert preference. Observe the thoughtful way he or she handles situations. You may even want to ask how it's done.

*Strategies:* Introverts may need to become more assertive or take a public speaking class. Extraverts can try writing more often when communicating with Introverts so that the Introverts can have more time to absorb information. Strategies like these allow each person to appreciate and respect the other's type.

## Sensing (S) vs. iNtuition (N)

Jung postulated that there are two different ways to gather data from the world around us—Sensing and iNtuition. Those who prefer the sensing mode pay more attention to the tangible world, focus on facts, and seek data to minimize ambiguity. iNtuitives, on the other hand, are more comfortable paying attention to the abstract impressions they perceive in the meaning behind data and to the relationships among the various facts.

Ask a Sensor to describe spring, and you hear "Spring: starts on March 21st. More rainfall, warmer temperatures. Green grass. Baseball season." An iNtuitive might say, "Oh, spring is a time of rebirth, of renewal. It's a greening of the spirit."

The Sensing/iNtuitive dimension is strongly related to job choice. Sensors like occupations in which they can achieve practical results with tangible things. More Sensors than iNtuitives become bankers, accountants, military commanders, and chemists. iNtuitives are attracted to fields where they can operate at a more abstract level. They are often the strategic planners, psychotherapists, and poets. About 70% of the U.S. population prefers Sensing over iNtuition.

Meetings often bog down because of a failure to understand the different needs of Sensors and iNtuitives. Sensors try to gather as many facts as possible to make a decision. iNtuitives may find this tedious, preferring instead to deal with the issue at a more conceptual level. The iNtuitives strive for the "big picture" while the Sensors seek the details.

Communication problems could be avoided if both Sensors and iNtuitives were recognized for their valuable, unique contributions and if the meeting were structured to allow for both factual input and conceptual discussion, labeled as such.

*Strategies:* Pick a topic and ask someone, with the opposite MBTI style, what comes to mind. Listen to what that person says, then share what comes to your mind about the topic. Notice the richness when you combine the two sets of responses. Ask someone with the opposite preference what drives them crazy about the way you describe things. Then ask what would help. Offer to switch and share your view.

## Thinking (T) vs. Feeling (F)

This scale is perhaps the most critical for understanding interpersonal relationships within an organization. The Thinking vs. Feeling scale measures two different ways of making decisions. Jung did not mean feeling in an emotional sense, but more as "valuing," i.e., what a person considers important when making a decision.

Thinkers make decisions in a detached, logical, and objective way. They employ deductive thinking and make a conscious effort not to let their personal issues get in the way of making a "right" decision. Feelers, on the other hand, prefer to base their decisions on subjective factors like harmony in relationships or appreciation of emotions. Thinkers tend not to take conflict personally and may actually look forward to a good argument. Feelers, though, are typically uncomfortable with conflict, take it personally, and try to promote harmony. Thinkers tend to be attracted to work for its intellectual challenge, whereas Feelers often enjoy work whose primary focus is helping people.

When Thinkers encounter their opposite, they do not commonly say "Oh, I see. My colleague (or client or spouse) is using a different strategy from me and prefers to evaluate things on the basis of how people will be personally affected." Instead, the Thinker is likely to assume that her or his logic applies to everyone, and that the colleague is simply using it poorly. Feelers may conclude that Thinkers are insensitive and out of touch with the people.

This explains much of the miscommunication in our organizations and relationships today. With diversity issues so complex, Thinkers often advocate a quick, decisive, and businesslike set of answers, while many Feelers urge a more gradual, individualized, and personal approach. The Feeler may be criticized for being inefficient, impractical, and unrealistic; the Thinker for being hard and insensitive.

*Strategies:* Both sides need to be more aware that their preference is complemented by an opposite style. Both can learn to recognize which of their colleagues or family members have similar or opposite preferences and investigate the merit of what that opposite style is paying attention to. Feelers can speak their truth and become more adept at arguing for their values. Thinkers can pause before they make an objective criticism and acknowledge the Feelers' concern with subjective values.

# Judging (J) vs. Perceiving (P)

The final area of the MBTI addresses which process—making decisions or gathering information—you most naturally use as you relate to the outer world. Those who prefer Judging focus on planning, decisiveness, and order. (The word judging is not necessarily associated with the idea of being judgmental.) In contrast, those who prefer Perceiving focus on flexibility, adaptability, and spontaneity. Judgers like to have control of the environment and tend to act methodically. They make contingency plans "just in case." They tend to arrive at meetings on time and have a strong sense of closure, i.e., they want to "get it done" or "have it finished" as soon as possible. They manage work assignments in a systematic way and make lists of things to do, which they tend to use as agendas for action, checking off items when they complete the tasks.

Perceivers, in contrast with Judgers, prefer to "go with the flow" and appear to be spontaneous. They like to keep their options open and try not to decide until the last possible moment. Perceivers may also make lists, but instead of containing a few

do-able items per day, they often contain dozens of items—an unending list of options—that will get done "one day." Perceivers may forget to follow their lists because what's happening around them captures their attention.

In the general population in the United States, 55% of the people have a Judging preference; 45% prefer Perceiving.

*Strategies:* Both Judgers and Perceivers need ample notice of deadlines and events, but for different reasons. Judgers need to know the end point to prepare for it in an orderly and timely way. Perceivers need advance notice of a deadline so they can collect all the information they need before completing the task. Both Judgers and Perceivers can announce their plans and intentions and identify what's negotiable and what isn't. Having done that, the Perceiver, who is continually gathering new information with the desire to have it included in the decision-making process, can drop a few new ideas on the Judger then leave, allowing the Judger to mull it over. The Perceiver can return later to discuss with the Judger the possible inclusion of the new ideas.

When one's preferences on each of the four MBTI scales are combined, the resulting set of four letters refers to one's "psychological type." Co-author Helen Pelikan's type, for example, is ENFP (Extravert, Intuitive, Feeler, Perceiver). Co-author Barbara Deane is an ENTP (Extravert, Intuitive, Thinker, Perceiver). By combining two possible choices on each of the four scales, a total of 16 type combinations are possible. These types do not occur with equal frequency. For example people in middle and upper management in American business organizations overwhelmingly fall into four types (ISTJ, INTJ, ESTJ, ENTJ). In other words, management is dominated by the presence of the Thinker/Judger combination. In contrast, IN preferences (Introvert, iNtuitive) make up only 4% of the U.S. population and each type separately accounts for only 1% of the population.

# Psychological Type and Diversity

Although the preferences exist within all cultures, the behavior used to express a preference varies from culture to culture. For example, the dominant culture in Japan supports the preference of Introversion; the culture doesn't encourage people sharing all their thoughts verbally. Co-author Pelikan noticed, when she lived in Japan, that the Japanese seemed to be able to express Extraversion best via ritualized events such as organized parties attended by co-workers after work. Japan seems to have a cultural norm for Introversion in contrast to the U.S. where Extraversion via constant verbal sharing of ideas is the norm.[3]

It is now believed that cultures and co-cultures (a term used by anthropologists to refer to cultural groups within a larger society) demonstrate a bias for certain preferences based on gender. For example, MBTI data in the United States show that 70–75% of women prefer to make decisions based on subjective values (Feelers), whereas 70% of men make decisions on objective data (Thinkers). We believe these percentages not only represent individual differences, but also indicate cultural norms for how women and men should be. If a woman shows a preference for objective decision making, she may be seen as cold-hearted, arrogant, or "a bitch." A man who relies on subjective information may be seen as "a wimp" and not strong enough for the business world.

When Ed Muskie, a presidential candidate in 1972, cried in front of national television, he was viewed as not strong enough to be President. He lost his popularity and eventually dropped out of the race. More currently, First Lady Hillary Rodham Clinton has an objective thinking style that is seen as out of sync by a good number of American people. It is not acceptable for a woman to be so rational, even in these progressive times. These two examples show how a culture is actually biased toward certain styles for men and for women and is not very forgiving when a man or woman does not fit the cultural norm. Individuals whose types differ from their culture's ideal for their gender must work harder to be accepted. They are more likely to develop skills and behaviors in their non-preferred areas. As with other dimensions of diversity, people who do not fit the dominant culture have to adapt, accommodate, and develop skills that don't come easily or naturally, and they experience greater stress.

The standard answer sheet sold with the instrument, provides information about occupation, gender, educational status, age, and academic likes or dislikes, but has never included information about ethnicity or cultural background. However, many professionals who use the MBTI have collected their own data about the national origin and ethnicity of the people who take it. Data is available on Japanese middle managers from Tokyo, Australian aborigines in the outback, and African Americans, Hispanics, and Whites in a southern college in the USA. Such data represent only a mosaic of information that is in the process of becoming more complete.[4]

We have many connections between type and occupation. The MBTI is not meant to be a career predictor but is one of many tools used to make career decisions. All over the globe, people in similar occupations seem to have similar MBTI types. For example, people in management positions in organizations around the world prefer objective thinking and have a need for orderly completion of tasks. Substantial data exist to show that foreign service officers all over the world cluster around certain type patterns. Upper rank military officers also cluster, as do international managers, career counselors, artists, science professors, bankers, and police officers. The same occupational roles often attract individuals with the same kinds of psychological type.[5]

Knowing more about psychological type can help people deal better with stereotypes, judgment, and blame by helping us realize that people may act in quite different yet legitimate ways.

Thinking of psychological type as a dimension of diversity allows you to step back and observe how another person's type preferences may be different from your own. You can adjust your expectations and communication accordingly or add to your filters and assumptions so that you can hear, appreciate, and work effectively with those who prefer different mental strategies.

Let's return to the conversation between Maria and David. At a quick glance, you might attribute the difficulty in this conversation to such differences as gender, ethnicity, age, or national origin, or just plain orneriness. In fact, the difficulty may be linked to psychological type. David seems to be making decisions based on subjective values (a Feeler) while Maria relies on objective data (a Thinker). The clash seems to be based on type differences in the way the two make decisions. Interestingly, Maria and David's styles reflect the reverse of what you might expect from members

377

of their genders. Your expectations are reinforced by what U.S. culture prefers.

What if Maria and David could communicate with each other respecting the differences between their styles? Here is a possible conversation:

*Maria:* David, I think we've gotten stuck here. Look, this is how I work. I make decisions based on facts and fairness.

*David:* Hmm. I'm concerned with how the people are going to be affected by this lay-off decision. I'm taking time to find out what those effects are going to be.

*Maria:* We can't avoid this lay-off David. We don't have sales to justify keeping these employees. We have to cut 50 jobs.

*David:* But these aren't just jobs—these are people. These people have family obligations, and also, some of these people are very talented; they could help us.

*Maria:* Look David, I do want to be fair. What are you suggesting?

*David:* Well, let's come up with some criteria that will help us think about both our need to increase sales and about our employees' needs. We may be able to invent some creative options.

Knowing their psychological types opens the door for Maria and David to expand their dialogue. By recognizing their styles as legitimate ways of being, they can honor the different gifts each brings to their communication. Such recognition of different gifts needs to be encouraged in other areas of diversity like race, ethnicity, gender, and sexual orientation. Seeing these differences as gifts, people can benefit from listening to each other and looking for ways to integrate their styles for better results.

# How to Get More Information

If you are interested in taking the MBTI, contact the Association for Psychological Type for assistance in locating qualified professionals who administer the instrument. You can reach them at 9140 Ward Parkway, Kansas City, Missouri 64114. Tel. 816/444-3500, Fax 816/444-0330. For more information about the training program using MBTI in multicultural settings, contact Helen Pelikan at the address below.

# About the Authors

Helen L. Pelikan is President of Pelikan Associates in Washington, DC, a consulting and training firm providing national and international human resources services. Her work has ranged from creating an international counseling center in Rome, coaching financial leaders in Japan, and producing her own TV show in Tokyo, to consulting with UNESCO and designing programs for the U.S. State Department in Paris. She can be reached at Pelikan Associates, 6501 Bannockburn Drive, Bethesda, Maryland 20817-5431; Phone: 301-229-8550; Fax: 301-229-6609.

Barbara Deane is Editor-in Chief and Co-founder of *Cultural Diversity at Work* newsletter and *The Diversity Training Bulletin*, the first national publications to examine how diverse people can work together and conduct business effectively. She is also Vice President of the Seattle-based consulting and training firm The GilDeane Group, the publisher of the newsletter. She can be reached at: The GilDeane Group, 13751 Lake City Way N.E., Suite 106, Seattle, WA 98125-3615; Phone: 206-362-0336; Fax: 206-363-5028.

## Footnotes

1. The statistics in this article come from the data gathered over the 52 years of the use of the MBTI. The two key resources are *Manual: A Guide to the Development and Use of the Myers Briggs Type Indicator* by Isabel Briggs Myers and Mary H. McCaulley, Consulting Psychologists Press, Inc., Palo Alto, California, 1985. The Center for the Application of Psychological Type is the source for research information on the MBTI, Mary H. McCaulley, President, Gainesville, Florida, USA.

2. The letter "N" is used to designate "iNtuition" to distinguish it from "Introversion," which uses the letter "I."

3. Data from Takeshi Ohsawa, President of HRR, Tokyo, Japan, who has administered the MBTI to several million Japanese workers since 1969.

4. Helen Pelikan developed the first, and at this point, the only training program ("Successfully Applying the MBTI in Multicultural Settings") that connects the MBTI with cultural differences.

5. This data has recently been collected from both published and unpublished research studies.

# True Colors: 21st Century Human Technology

by Tony Hill

According to business reform experts, doing "more with less" is the definition of productivity. It requires that organizations and leaders maximize the potential of all of their resources. Human resources are essential to this process. Individuals working for organizations where both the environment and the leadership generate self-worth, respect, dignity, esteem and self-confidence are motivated to perform at much higher and more productive levels.

One of the learning processes I like to use in exploring ways to maximize our human potential is called "True Colors," which has been developed by my colleague Don Lowry of Laguna Beach. This valuable learning tool is organized into program delivery systems for virtually every context, whether it be families, schools, advertising, work place, entertainment, seminars or anywhere else people gather into groups.

The True Colors methodology utilizes a simple process that any individual can understand—regardless of age, gender, cultural, religious or ethnic differences. By selecting a spectrum of color-coded cards—blue, green, orange and gold—that are correlated to personality and character traits (for example, "curiosity," "competitiveness," etc.), an individual comes to recognize and appreciate their "true colors."

This recognition gets us beyond the historic conditioning of responding to each other and ourselves based on the color of our skin and other superficial physical stereotypes. It empowers us to look at our true selves. Because it is experienced through the individual's participation in the communication processes that promote a "positive state of mind," information retention in this learning process is dramatic. More importantly, I have found that new skills are developed for facilitating successful relationships and establishing climates that allow everyone to experience esteem.

Self-esteem grows in each of us when we feel good about ourselves—when we can tell ourselves we are capable and believe it; when we have the confidence to face life and the many situations in it; when we believe that we are important to ourselves and to others. Most importantly, self-esteem flourishes when we feel a sense of personal power—often called empowerment.

- We know that although we don't control all events in our lives, we have the ability to influence the outcome of many of them.

- What do you do to feel good about yourself?

- Can you say, "I feel capable of meeting life's changes head on and coming out a winner?"

- Do you believe that you have the personal power to influence what happens to you?

Self-esteem is an inside job. While others can create environments and opportunities which encourage or discourage the growth of self-esteem, we ultimately have to do it for ourselves. Each of us has the keys, and those keys are to be found in our own "true colors." Through the True Colors technology, we develop a better understanding of the values, joys, needs, and strengths that contribute to our self-esteem.

Here are some of the characteristics of the four colors:

- *Blue:* People in this group esteem themselves when they are authentic. They seek harmony in life with both people and things. Making a difference in the world comes naturally and is important to them. They work hard to cultivate the potential in themselves and in others.

- *Green:* People in this group esteem themselves when they see themselves as competent. They want to understand and control the realities of life. People in the Green group feel best about themselves when they are solving problems. They feel appreciated when their ideas are recognized. While they do not express their emotions openly, they do experience deep feelings.

- *Gold:* People in this group esteem themselves when they feel responsibly involved in groups and organizations. They must earn their way through hard work and being useful. Finding comfort in structure, responsibility is a blessing for the golds. They cling to and uphold the traditions.

- *Orange:* People in this group esteem themselves when they are free to act on a moment's notice. They are action oriented and choose to be impulsive. They take pride in being highly skilled in a variety of fields.

If you recognize some of yourself in all of the color keys, it's true! We are all enriched with diversity! When we recognize and appreciate the diversity inside of us, we'll be less threatened by diversity outside ourselves. What if we could start over and recognize each other's unique spectrum of true colors?

## About the Author

Tony Hill is the founder of the Alliance for Improving Race Relations (AIRR) and a community consultant on issues of affirmative action, multiculturalism and leadership. He is a member of the Santa Cruz Sentinel's Board of Contributors. Tony Hill can be reached at: 429 Continental, Santa Cruz, CA 95060; Phone: 408-454-0168.

One approach is to couple the need for diversity training with implied threat, e.g., "Attendance

# The Company as a Diverse Ecosystem
by Tom Chappell

In his wonderful book *The Diversity of Life*, which has been key to catalyzing my commitment to diversity, Edward O. Wilson illustrates the ecosystem of the rain forest by describing what happens when loggers cut down so many trees that they leave a gaping hole in dense, leafy, green cover—the canopy—of the forest. The new light shining on the floor of the forest soon changes the ecosystem dramatically. Insects or a species of animal in the area who were dependent upon the moist ground or darkness may now be damaged or wiped out by the intense sun; other species that depend on the presence of those life-forms will be soon affected too. The entire ecosystem, simply because of the disappearance of a few trees, is thrown into disarray; shifts are made; ways of restoring the balance and replenishing what is missing have to be found. The nature of things is changed, perhaps forever.

Just as scientists like Wilson teach us about how ecosystems live in balance with one another, we have to learn how companies, too, can work to balance their own internal and external diverse "ecosystems" of human interrelationships, gifts, talents, abilities, and complaints.

I am convinced that a company cannot be too diverse. There is no human or spiritual limit. We have not yet even seen the horizon. We have certainly not learned everything there is to know about fairness and justice. Nor have we mastered combining the complexity of power on the one hand with humility on the other—the paradoxical traits embodied in the great figures of Christ and Buddha. Diversity is a complex beauty, but it is also the affirmation of the different gifts we all bring to the table. Diversity is part of our interdependence, broadening our tolerance and our understanding that we are not in a larger sense powerful and indispensable. Just as we need other people in our personal lives, we need others in business too. We are like the denizens of one vast rain forest, dependent on every tiny insect and leaf for our lives. Therein lies the balance to the system.

Unlike life in the rain forest, however, we CEOs have a choice about how we survive in the jungles of business. Our diversity is not forced upon us by nature; we can manage our diversity and set goals. We can take the initiative to change the way we are, to choose to be different. What holds all these differences together is the way in which we, like life in the rain forest, learn to adjust and live in balance with one another.

In 1992 I actually spent a few days walking through a Brazilian rain forest. It is like nothing else you've ever experienced. You see green upon green, brown trunks and brown limbs—and then suddenly you come upon one beautiful, rare flower, tall, pointing straight toward heaven, stunning in its vibrant, natural, and isolated beauty.

My dream is for Tom's of Maine to be that rare beauty standing in the midst of diversity, part of it, feeding off it, growing from it, seeding it, and shining forth as an example of what can be.

## About the Author

Tom Chappell is president of Tom's of Maine, Inc., a leading manufacturer of natural personal care products.

# Working with Resistance to Diversity

by Hank Karp

In designing and delivering diversity training almost all, if not all, programs focus on making changes in the awareness and the attitudes of the participants. The strategy is to create changes that will have a long term positive impact on the organizational culture, with the objective of creating a safer and more productive working environment for all organizational members.

Most of these diversity programs are value driven, rather than skill driven, so that there is a clear message being sent out as to how things "should be." The nature of the value doesn't really matter much. What does matter is that the moment that one person tells others how they should think or feel, a certain amount of resistance is automatically created. This resistance has nothing to do with the nature of the demand, itself, but rather serves to protect the integrity of the individual. That is, no matter how positive the message or how much I may support it, a certain part of me is going to simultaneously resist an uninvited outside effort to change who I am. And, make no mistake, any attempt to change someone else's attitudes, beliefs, or values is exactly that, an attempt to change who they are. In some cases this might be a very good thing to do. Just realize that it's going to be met with a certain amount of natural resistance that has nothing to do with the demand for change itself, and it is best that you are aware of this potential from the outset. This resistance may not always be operating on the conscious level, but I contend, aware or not, your safest bet is to assume it is there, with the possibility of growing stronger.

## The Nature of Resistance

People will resist what others want them to think or feel for one of two basic reasons; either the demand is not perceived to be in their best self-interest, or the demand is experienced as an attack on their self-image. Quite often, the demand for change is being made very powerfully so that the message is being delivered with some very compelling reasons for people to conform to it.

to this program is a company policy and all personnel will conform." Another approach is to couple the need for diversity training with guilt, e.g., "We, the Straight, White, American, Male, majority have traditionally been racists, whether we intended to be so or not. We have to change our ways and attitudes." Still another way is to sell the values of diversity with the hope of generating enthusiasm for the up-coming training programs, e.g., "We need to be more responsive to the unique capabilities of others so as to maximize our potential for effectiveness."

Regardless of whether the attempt is to break down the resistance to diversity training, or to minimize it, or to avoid it all together, it is still going to exist. The resistance needs to be recognized, honored and worked with.

It is very important that designers and deliverers of diversity training be aware of the positive aspects of participant resistance. First, resistance is absolutely unavoidable. Since that is the reality, you are much better off focusing on, and working with, the positive aspects of resistance than you are wasting time bemoaning the negative ones.

Second, resistance provides protection. It is as beneficial for the participant to avoid what is not wanted in the program, as it is in embracing what is wanted. The more you provide a safe environment that is non-threatening to all participants, the less unintended resistance you are going to have to deal with.

Third, resistance is a source of energy, and anything that provides energy in a training program is an asset. If you can provide a safe forum for some of the resistance to be expressed, you are likely to have a more involved group of participants.

Fourth, resistance provides boundary. It is where someone's "Yes" changes into a "No." Surfacing that information and finding out what participants are resisting in the program provides the opportunity for some real reality testing. It allows you to address specific concerns that may be blocking the implementing of the training back on the job.

# Working with the Resistance

There are several things you can do to avoid unnecessary resistance or to work productively with the resistance that is there.

1. *Provide a Contract.**

As the very first step of any diversity training program, negotiate a contract with the group. The contract sets the guidelines for appropriate behavior for the length of the training session. Elements in the contract can include things like: "No 'shoulds' from me." ; "I make mistakes too. If I inadvertently step on someone's toe, you are obligated to let me know. Yell, 'Ouch' and I'll ask you what I did wrong."; and, "Everyone has a right to their own opinion and to state it responsibly."

The key to contracting is to allow the group to respond to each idea separately and get agreement on that item before moving on. In addition, ask them for additional ideas that would make the training safer, more relevant, or more enjoyable. The contracting process allows the group to take responsibility for itself, increase their buy-in, and see you as a trainer, rather than as a preacher.

2. *Deal Only in Behaviors and Awareness, Never in Attitudes.*

The more you state or imply that someone's attitude, belief, or value is not as good as yours, or is outright wrong, the more defensiveness and resistance you are going to create. (Check out your own reaction to that message.) On the other hand, the more you show people a better thing to do or a new way of seeing things that is to their advantage, the higher the probability you will get a positive change in attitude as a result.

Rather than telling people how you would like them to feel about what you have to say, show them what you would like them to do, or see, instead. Explain what the behavior or awareness is, e.g., diverse cultural concepts of time,

*For more on how to set up and use a training contract see: H. B. Karp, "The Use of The Training Contract," *The 1985 Annual: Developing Human Resources.* Goodman & Pfeiffer, Pfeiffer and Co., San Diego, 1985.

and how come it is important for them to be aware of these. You end up with a more involved group.

3. **Work with the Resistance.**

As we have said, since participant resistance is unavoidable, there is a way to work with it to your, and the group's, advantage. First, I would suggest that you have a statement in the contract that spells out your view of resistance. For example, "This is intended as training, not indoctrination. We are dealing with 'diversity' and diverse opinions are certainly welcomed."

When resistance begins to arise in the group, try the following strategy:

A. **First, make your points clearly.**

The clearer and more unequivocal your point, the clearer will be the resistance that rises up against it and, the easier it will be to work with.

B. **Surface the resistance.**

When someone says that they disagree with a point you made, thank them and ask them to say more. Ask them to state the resistance in behavioral terms, if possible. The more specific detail you get describing the resistance, the more you can respond to it constructively.

C. **Honor the resistance.**

Listen to what the person is saying about the problem they are having with what you are saying. Honoring their position does not mean agreeing with it. For example, some honoring statements include: "I understand how this could be a problem for you."; "I know that there are many out there who might agree with you."; or, "I can certainly see where you are coming from." Honored resistance does not increase. Honoring the resistance lets the resistor know that he or she has been heard and their position acknowledged. This will put the other person in a more receptive mood without you being seen as patronizing.

4. **Explore the resistance.**

After the resistance has been surfaced and honored, you can let it go at that, or you can explore it. For instance, you can say something like: "Given your situation as you just described it, is there some way that what I have just said could be of use?" or, "If you got support from you boss, would this idea then be worth considering?" The best way to create positive change is to help the participants to adapt your input to their situation, rather than you doing it for them.

One additional small, but important consideration. When probing someone's resistance, never ask then "Why do you feel that way?" Asking "why" tends to put people on the defensive and demands that they justify their position. This will increase the resistance. Try asking, "What is your objection?" instead.

5. **Recheck**

When you have responded to the participant's resistance it is a good idea to summarize the work before moving on to the next point or participant. There are three benefits to doing this:

A. It condenses the cognitive learning coming out of the interaction so that the other participants can see the points made more clearly.

B. It allows the participant, with whom you were working, the opportunity to put the whole learning encounter into a brief and clear context.

C. It encourages other participants to state their concerns and then to have the opportunity for you to cast your input into their unique situation. This goes a long way toward encouraging the individual application of the program material back in the work environment.

## Conclusion

Resistance is just as natural a phenomenon in diversity training as it is in any other training context. It is seen as being more potentially volatile here because cultural diversity is purely subjective and people go into this a little afraid of what "might" happen.

The first thing to do is to view resistance as an asset, rather than as a liability. The second is to recognize your own ability to deal with it competently. From this position, resistance can be used to enhance a diversity training program, just as readily as it can any other.

## About the Author

Dr. Hank B. Karp received his Ph.D. in Industrial and Organizational Psychology from Case Western Reserve University, Cleveland, Ohio. He has conducted seminars for managers in the areas of: First Line Leadership Skill Development; Power; Conflict and Resistance; Delegation; Motivation & Job Enrichment; Leadership Style & Managerial Effectiveness; Career Plateauing and Diversity.

He is a Senior Associate at ODT, Incorporated. Dr. Karp's publications include: *Personal Power: An Unorthodox Guide to Success*, available from ODT at 800-736-1293 ($24.00 includes postage and handling) and, "Handling Career Plateaus," from the *National Business Employment Weekly* (A complimentary copy is available from ODT, Inc.; send a self-addressed stamped envelope to ODT, Inc., Box 134, Amherst, MA 01004).

# Developing a Whole Organisation Culture
by Geof Cox and Walt Hopkins

What is an organisation culture? Why is changing organisation culture so difficult? Is there an alternative to changing the culture?

"How we do things round here" is based on a set of assumptions that underlie our actions. That set of assumptions is our organisation culture. It attracts people who like to do things the same way while it repels those who do things differently.

As an organisation grows and develops, the organisation culture that originally proved so helpful may begin to get in the way. The functional structure that enables a large corporation to manage diverse interests efficiently becomes a series of bureaucratic committees that prevent the company from responding to changes in its environment. A young company racing along a visionary track can discover that the track becomes a rut which excludes outside information.

When we understand the set of values, beliefs and actions that make up our organisation culture, we can then use that understanding to create an organisation in which people want to give their best. This will be an organisation that is flexible enough to respond to the rapidly changing environment and the demands of the marketplace.

So let's look at organisation culture by considering four different kinds of organisation culture. The idea of four different approaches to life has been around for more than two thousand years. The ancient Greeks described people as Sanguine, Phlegmatic, Melancholic, or Choleric. Later theorists and researchers have seen the same traits in organisations. Charles Handy[1] in the UK and Roger Harrison[2] in the USA developed a four-culture model in the mid-seventies and each has since developed the model further. Our own version of the four cultures emerges from the work we did with Roger Harrison in 1990.

We call the four cultures Control, Role, Goal, and Soul. Our simplified definitions of each culture are summarised in Table 1. Each culture has its own distinct characteristics. Although each culture is present to some extent in any organisation, usually one or two cultures predominate.

## Table 1: A Summary of the Four Organisation Cultures

|  | Control | Role | Goal | Soul |
|---|---|---|---|---|
| My priority is my | Boss | Duty | Task | People |
| Decisions come from the | Boss | Policy | Goal | Consensus |
| Authority comes from | Power | Seniority | Expertise | Wisdom |
| The system is | Autocratic | Bureaucratic | Charismatic | Democratic |
| People are | Stratified | Interchangeable | Unique | Equal |
| Myths are about the | Boss | Organization | Champions | Team |
| The world is a | Jungle | System | Opportunity | Community |
| As a boss I expect | Obedience | Reliability | Competence | Cooperation |
| As an employee I expect | Reward | Security | Challenge | Support |
| Interaction between people is based on | Exchange | Reason | Values | Sharing |
| Interaction between organisations is based on | Conquest | Function | Competition | Networking |
| People succeed by knowing the | Boss | System | Resources | People |
| We go out in the world prepared for | Battle | Debate | Game | Learning |
| People work for | Reward | Contract | Achievement | Enjoyment |
| Instinctive reaction to a customer | Deal | Explain | Connect | Listen |

The Control culture begins and ends with the boss who makes all the decisions. If an organisation is large enough, the Control culture becomes a hierarchy, with a series of bosses.

When the Control culture works well, a good boss decides quickly and accurately, adjusts to the changing environment, and takes good care of the people in exchange for solid loyalty. When the Control culture works less effectively, the boss makes decisions slowly or inaccurately, refuses to adjust to change, and does not take good care of the people.

## Table 2: Features of the Control Culture

| Effective | Ineffective |
|---|---|
| · Unites effort | · Limited by leader |
| · Moves quickly | · Politics |
| · Strong leader | · Isolated from bad news |
| · Clear direction | · Overworked leaders |
| · Clear expectation | · Information as power |
| · Loyalty | · Short range thinking |

385

The Role culture often develops in response to the excesses of the Control culture. The culture uses rules and procedures to prevent any one person from wielding too much power.

When the Role culture works well, the systems are well-designed and regularly adapted, everyone knows what to do in order for the system to function, and specialisation enables individuals or units to develop expertise. When the Role culture works less effectively, the systems don't get updated, the communication slows down so that no one knows what anyone else is doing, and people stick to their own jobs even when the organisation needs something else.

## Table 3: Features of the Role Culture

| Effective | Ineffective |
|---|---|
| • Well designed systems | • Change is slow |
| • Clear lines of authority | • Low trust |
| • Structure | • Following the rules |
| • Limit to personal power | • People as parts not human |
| • Efficient operations | • Under-utilize talent |
| • Specialist expertise | • Boundaries |

The Goal culture wants to achieve something. This culture may emerge in response to an ineffective Role culture that has lost its direction.

When the Goal culture works well, it is generating enthusiasm, decentralising structure, motivating people, and getting things done faster and better. When the Goal culture works less effectively, it goes too far too fast, ignores structure

## Table 4: Features of the Goal Culture

| Effective | Ineffective |
|---|---|
| • High motivation | • Burnout |
| • Maximum use of talent | • Waste resources |
| • Rapid learning | • End justifies the means |
| • Unity of effort | • Isolated from reality |
| • Reduced controls | • Inward focus |
| • Mutually valued goals | • Arrogant |

completely, burns out people, and arrogantly ignores reality in pursuit of its goal.

The Soul culture values people. This culture may emerge to deal with the burned out people of an overdone Goal culture.

When the Soul culture works well, people communicate well, cooperate with each other, and provide lots of support for each other. When the Soul culture works less effectively, people communicate with each other about everything except the task, every single decision requires consensus, and people no longer challenge each other.

## Table 5: Features of the Soul Culture

| Effective | Ineffective |
|---|---|
| • Good communication | • Task neglect |
| • Commitment | • People before organisation |
| • High trust | • Slow decision making |
| • Cooperation | • Loses direction |
| • Caring and listening | • Slow to change |
| • Sense of belonging | • Frustrates ambition |

When we use this model with people in organisations, two things often happen. Both are confirmed by our colleague Roger Harrison, who has gathered such reactions from organisations around the world.[3] First, many people describe the organisation they work for as dominated by Control or Role culture and say that they would prefer to work in a Goal or Soul culture. So they are working in a culture that does not motivate them.

Second, people higher up an organisation are more likely to see the culture as Goal or Soul, while those at lower levels tend to see the culture as Control or Role. So the top managers—when they first hear that people want Goal or Soul culture—believe that nothing needs to be done.

But when the message does sink in, the immediate reaction of many organisations, and many consultants, is to promote a "culture change" programme. This is reinforced when some older companies think that their bureaucracies are being out-paced by the newer entrepreneurial companies. Since those companies seem to have visions instead of rules, that must be the answer.

Most of these "culture change" attempts do not work. When an organisation throws out the excesses of Control and Role, it also throws out the successful features. People still want to know the rules and still want someone to make decisions. People are confused when told that shifting to a new culture means the old culture is suddenly taboo. Despite its shortcomings, it must have had some positive benefits for it to have fostered earlier success. So people resist. After all, you know what you are doing in the old culture, while the new one requires effort to learn.

We believe that "culture change" is doomed to failure because what people need is not a conversion to a new culture, but a balancing of all four cultures.

This belief has been reinforced by our experience in designing and leading training courses in influencing and negotiation skills. We use a model that focuses on obtaining four different results. Each result—not coincidentally—matches the beliefs and actions of one of the four cultures.[4] As we work with participants on these courses, we see that the most effective communicators are those who develop skills in obtaining each of the four results and who move easily among them depending on the demands of the situation.

In the same way, we believe that effective organisations focus attention not on one culture, but on an appropriate balance of the four cultures so that the best attributes of each enable the organisation to thrive. This may mean that there is a need to do some re-balancing. This may mean that just as our course participants focus on one result for a while to improve their skills, an organisation may need to focus on one culture for a while to improve the organisation's skills.

But the long-term goal with both communication skills and organisation culture is to achieve a balance. This balance is what we call the *Whole* culture. In one version of a Whole culture, people make quick and accurate decisions (Control); everyone functions smoothly within clear systems (Role); everyone is aligned with common values and aims (Goal); and there is a high level of communication, support, and cooperation (Soul).

Balancing cultures is easier if we look at the effective side of each culture. When we think of cultures in their ineffective state, they seem very different from each other. Roger Harrison suggests that it is like standing at the base of a pyramid—with each of the four sides being one of the cultures. At the base of the pyramid, the distance to walk to another side is great. As we climb the pyramid and increase our effectiveness in any one of the cultures, we get closer to the others. Toward the top of the pyramid, you can move around the pyramid much more easily. And at the top itself, the cultures are balanced in the Whole culture.

We take the pyramid analogy a step further. The sun shines on only two sides of the pyramid; these are the cultures that we see most. The other two are definitely there, but they are in shadow. What we need to do is bring them into the light and value all four sides equally.

Do such balanced organisations exist? The answer is yes, but they are rare. And even the balanced organisation needs to monitor itself carefully. It is very difficult to keep your balance on top of a pyramid!

Historically, some of the most balanced organisations were the ones set up in the UK and the USA by Quakers. As Anita Roddick says, "I am still looking for the modern-day equivalent of those Quakers who ran successful businesses, made money because they offered honest products and treated their people decently, worked hard, spent honestly, saved honestly, gave honest value for money, put more back than they took out and told no lies. This business creed, sadly, seems long forgotten."[5]

Other examples of balance come from the East. The Japanese business culture is noted for its vision and commitment (Goal), and its consensus style and employee support (Soul). Many Western observers see only those two sides of the pyramid and miss the high degree of autocratic decision making (Control) and the stratification into functions (Role).

Anita Roddick's Body Shop organisation is a UK based organisation that comes close to balancing the four cultures. The Goal and Soul cultures are very evident to anyone who has entered a Body Shop. The staff share values that extend beyond the immediate work into the values of conservation and environmentalism. At the same time, the success of the organisation is also based on a Role culture of specific systems and a functional split into manufacturing and sales as well as the Control culture strongly exerted over the world-wide operation by the founders. Anita Roddick's book, *Body and Soul*, provides many stories of the four cultures working harmoniously together.[6]

Or think of a theatre company. In a recent television programme on the Royal Shakespeare Company at work, the Whole culture blended the Control culture of the powerful director with the Role culture of clear job descriptions for the actors and stage crew, the Goal culture of a shared vision of excellence, and the Soul culture of supporting and coaching. The magnificence of their performance revealed the effective organisation at work.

We all know that the real work is done in rehearsal and behind the scenes. When things go wrong, it is usually because the balance of cultures has been upset—the director is too dominant, the responsibilities are not clearly defined, there is no shared vision, or there is conflict among the players.

In all organisations there are times when the cultures are in balance, but unfortunately these are all too rare. We need to look at the imbalance in our organisation and train ourselves in the appropriate behaviours to redress the balance. Then our organisation will also be like a theatre company at its best—producing a magnificent performance.

## About the Author

Walt Hopkins is President and Geof Cox an Associate of Castle Consultants International, a management consulting firm with UK offices in London and Edinburgh, and other European offices in France, Switzerland and The Netherlands. They can be reached at Castle Consultants, 27 Thames House, 140 Battersea Park Road, London SW11V 4NB UK, Phone: 011-44-171-798-5688, Fax: 011-44-171-498-6769, e-mail: CastleLondon@AppleLink.Apple.COM

### Footnotes

1. Charles Handy, *The Gods of Management,* Souvenir Press, 1978

2. Roger Harrison, "Understanding Your Organisation's Character," *Harvard Business Review,* 1972

3. Roger Harrison, "Introduction to Managing Culture Change," Harrison Associates Inc., 1987, 1988, 1990

4. Walt Hopkins, "Influencing for Results" and "Negotiating Internationally for Results," Castle Consultants International, 1990, 1992

5. Anita Roddick, *Body and Soul,* Ebury Press, 1991

6. Anita Roddick, *Body and Soul,* Ebury Press, 1991

# Circles & Triangles: A Primer On Savvy Team Play
by Billi Lee

## Success Is a Joint Venture

Most of us are brought up to believe that hard work and talent are the keys to success. If we just keep our nose to the grindstone and persistently pull ourselves up by our own bootstraps, we will eventually succeed. While this Horatio Alger model of success may be inspiring, it is not very practical.

In the real world, hard work and talent only open the door to success a crack. Keeping our nose to the grindstone keeps us in the dark about the ever-changing environment.

Success is a joint venture. We need the help and collaboration of many other people to succeed. Hard working and talented low income college graduates who "pull themselves up by their own bootstraps," are assisted by government loans and grants, employers who hire part-time help, and roommates who share expenses. Still many such students believe they are self-made, that they "worked their way through college" alone. They expect that future success will also come by their own hand.

In today's increasingly complex jobs, the determined individual, the Horatio Alger, is replaced by the "Team Approach." As with many good, simple, practical ideas, the concept of collaborative effort has become a complex new organizational religion. High priests and gurus preach the new doctrine, workers are initiated through team building and bonding rituals and everyone must speak the gospel. If you suggest that a particular job might be better done by an individual, you will be called "heretic," "not a team player."

Some organizations eliminate standard business titles in an attempt to foster the team approach. Managers across the board in some companies are now referred to as "coaches." Ironically, in this non-hierarchical structures these coaches invariably report to a "head coach."

Often the terms of team play are not clearly defined, the assumption being that all of us must have played team sports, so all of us must know about "end runs" and "bench strength," and understand that a "Hail Mary pass" is not a penance. Not so. A "tight end" means something different to me than it does to sports fans.

The rules of team play are rarely articulated clearly or listed for all to see. It is assumed that all of us know that: you don't argue with the coach in public, you give credit for success to your team mates, if you are benched you have to earn your way back on the team, and above all, you play to win.

A walk down the halls of corporate America makes you wonder if you are in a locker room at half time. You will hear: "Team Player." "Coach." "Dropped the ball." "Carried the ball forward." "Out in left field." "Touchdown." "Scored." "Monday morning quarterbacking." "Goal." "Tackled." "Offense." "Defense." "In the ball park." "The ball's in your court." "Hit a home run." "Three strikes and you're out."

As comfortable as sports metaphors are to veterans of the playing fields, they are confusing to countless others. When organizations urge their managers to become "coaches," I think they have a nurturing model in mind. No corporate coach orders his people to run twenty laps around the building, or to drop to the floor for twenty push-ups. The football coach is not the desired archetype for the corporate coach.

Football teams do not practice affirmative action hiring, giving women, or physically challenged people, an equal opportunity. There are no off-site bonding rituals for getting to know each other, no attempts to build trusting relationships by climbing ropes together. Football club owners certainly don't practice participative management with the players.

"Well," you argue, "a football team is not the same as a corporate team." Exactly my point!

You could probably learn as much, if not more, from the army about good team development as from team sports, but the military, hierarchical model is out of fashion. Trend setting corporations don't encourage first line managers to be drill instructors, and they certainly don't preach the value of hierarchy anymore. Yet hard boot camp lessons can provide invaluable insights into savvy corporate team play. You still need to recognize a "marching order," even when "coach" is issuing it. You still need to be able to work and observe the chain of command, even in a flattened organization, and accomplishing the mission in today's competitive marketplace is still more important than a nice try.

During boot camp a friend of mine was assigned to a squad of nine hale and hearty fellows and one unfortunate weakling who lacked the upper body strength to even hang from a bar. Boot camp is the quintessential team building experience; its purpose is to meld individuals into a fighting unit. In my friend's squad, the hale and hearty soon figured out that they had to help their weakest link through the obstacle course before they could return to the barracks. I naively asked my friend if this team experience eventually helped the strong members bond with the weak one. He scoffed, "Bond with him!? We didn't like him any more after boot camp than we did at the start. We just learned that all of us would succeed or fail together. Liking him had nothing to do with it!"

That is an important lesson for corporate team training! You don't have to like everyone to be able to work with them. You don't have to be able to "relate" to everyone to accomplish the mission effectively. Good relationships among team members are certainly more desirable and comfortable than strained ones, but personal bonding is not a prerequisite for team play. A respect for, and a willingness to utilize the talents and abilities that someone brings to, the team is.

In today's diverse work force, fewer and fewer managers and workers share team sports and the military service as common background. Enlightened managers, who do have such experience on hierarchical teams, have gone on to explore new and different team skills: consensus building, improved interpersonal communication, respect and sensitivity to individual differences. But earlier lessons from the drill instructor and the football coach provide a context from which to view the newer forms of team activity. While the hierarchical team may have lost its former prominence, it still provides one foundation for effective team play.

As more workers enter the work force without the early hierarchical team imprinting they are immediately trained into today's new consensus model. Naive about workplace realities, and lacking the context for interpreting company jargon, many of them try to be good team players in the new organizational game. With blessings and encouragement from upper management, they express their creative ideas openly, expect to have their input heard and implemented, and vigorously use the open door policy.

Inadvertently, they also step on toes, get their boss in trouble, and express contrary views at inopportune times. When their ideas are not immediately implemented, or when the boss makes a snap decision without consulting them, they become disillusioned and cynical and suspect that this "team stuff" is just another management ruse. To add insult to injury, they are told that they are not "team players."

Without a "boot camp for business," with no drill instructor to imprint organizational basics, and with no hierarchical team experience, newer members to the corporate world hear the new team rhetoric and misinterpret the jargon. It sounds like the organization is some new form of democracy! Without the fundamentals of basic team play, they are being asked to play a more sophisticated game. No wonder countless employees turn a deaf ear to their "coach" when he or she espouses the latest team gospel.

Many good workers need only a simple explanation of team rules and plays from their coach. Yet a person does not automatically know how to manage people just because she is promoted, nor does a coach acquire coaching skills just because management changes his title. To coach effectively, the manager must be able to articulate the game and the rules clearly and model the right behaviors.

# A Simple Model

For the last eight years, I have used the following simple model of circles and triangles to explain team form and function. Because it is so simple, many managers use it themselves to coach their people into savvy team play. It helps individuals read the signals and know which team form is being used and what behaviors are appropriate. They can quickly clarify this by asking, "Are we still in the circle, or is it triangle time?"

## The Circle Team

*Egalitarian:* A circle team is an egalitarian

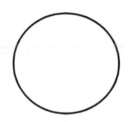

group. Members are peers and pay little regard to rank or seniority.

*Process:* The team is process-oriented. It spends its time in "ing" activities: creating, deliberating, inventing, discussing, dissenting, brainstorming, etc.

*Interpersonal Skills:* Time and effort is spent helping members develop personal relationships, bonding, team building. These help foster the easy give and take of a circle team.

*Personal Power:* The team leader earns and uses personal power to inspire and encourage the team.

*Consensus:* The team leader's main job is to facilitate group consensus.

*Value:* The value of the circle team is its creativity, its freedom to explore, the richness that comes from many different viewpoints.

*Downside:* It takes time to reach consensus.

*Best Use:* The circle team is best used when the goal is a process, e.g., to invent or explore.

The circle team has many advantages and virtues. Sometimes it is the only model advocated by companies who encourage participative management. Without denying the benefits of circle team training, there always has been and always will be another team in organizations: the triangle team.

## The Triangle Team

*Hierarchical:* A triangle team is a hierarchical

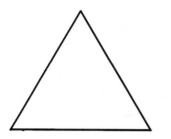

team. Its members are assigned rank in a chain of command.

*Task:* It is a task-oriented group, often with little tolerance for process. Triangle teams would prefer to be given the mission and the mandate to get it done.

*Job Skills:* Interpersonal relationship skills are less necessary for this group to function. Often the task is divided amongst the members with individuals working alone.

*Position Power:* While it never hurts a leader to have personal power, the leader of a triangle team must have and exercise position power. His or her main job is to make decisions and issue commands.

*Value:* The value of the triangle team is its speed.

*Downside:* Triangle teams can lack the variety of viewpoints that bring quality to decisions. There is often resistance to "marching orders" in today's participatory workplace culture.

*Best Use:* When "the bear comes over the hill."

The triangle team's focus on decision making and goal accomplishment is an essential part of a high performance team's repertoire.

## The Confusion

Circles and triangles. A simple concept. Yet confusing to those who don't recognize the forms or recognize the signals.

When a manager says to the team, "What do you think?" it sounds like an invitation to circle. The team proceeds to spend the next forty minutes discussing, dissenting and dissecting the proposal. Suppose the manager intercedes and says, "Thanks. That was a great session! I've decided to proceed with the original proposal." If a team member doesn't recognize the shift from circle to triangle and interjects, "But I still don't buy this!", a manager who doesn't realize the team's ignorance of circles and triangles could walk out of the room muttering about what a difficult person the interjector is, how he is "not a team player."

There are other problems. A manager may say it is circle time, but really not mean it. He or she goes through the motions only because current company culture requires it. A manager may need to get into triangle to make a decision but stays stuck in circle.

Sometimes employees complain that management asks for their input and then makes its own decisions anyway, unaware that a request for input does not a decision make.

All of the above scenarios show confusion produced by the singular emphasis on circle teams in recent corporate training. Many companies have forgotten to mention the triangle, or only talk about it in whispers. Team gurus who espouse empowering employees forget to talk about how followers need to empower leaders. And executives who fall in love with the latest advanced theory of enlightened management forget that many of their people haven't had Organizational Savvy 101.

Organizations, even flattened ones, are triangles. Companies are not democracies. They are enterprises designed to accomplish tasks. Decisions must be made and followed, strategies devised and implemented.

Good decisions require some circle time. But some people seem to forget the ultimate goal in putting together a circle is to get to a decision, and once the decision is made the shape of the team changes. It's triangle time.

The circle is spontaneous, inventive. The only rules that need apply are common communication courtesies. You want people to "get out of the box," to see things differently. Imposing too much structure defeats the purpose of the circle.

## Team Rules

The triangle is structured. There is a chain of command and a list of generally understood, albeit unwritten, rules:

1. *Obey the Coach.* Argue behind closed doors. Share your opinion, but when you're given a marching order, march. If you cannot consistently back and support the coach, the mission or the rest of the team, get out of the way, leave.

2. *Never Tackle Your Own Team Members in public.* Save it for the circle.

3. *Know the Mission.* Be clear on the objective and the price the company is willing to pay to accomplish it.

4. *Sublimate Your Personal Goal to the Team Goal.* When your goal conflicts with the team goal, sublimate it. Helping the team win should eventually help you win. If not, you're on the wrong team.

5. *Know Your Role and Your Position.* You may be the front person, the "point man," the cheerleader, the spy or the scapegoat, or any other role assigned. You may play forward or behind the scenes. You may get credit or give it away.

## High Performance Teams

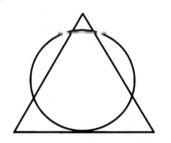

With the growing need for productivity, every team needs to be a high performance team; skilled at facilitating creative solutions and approaches and skilled in decision making and implementation. Every team member needs to be capable and willing to circle and to triangle.

Every organization needs to utilize the new participatory team approach with more savvy. Every organization also needs to bring the hidden hierarchy out of the shadows and train people into the smart use of this powerful team tool.

## About the Author

Billi Lee is an international speaker, author, columnist and commentator on workplace issues. Her unique perspective challenges conventional wisdom, leaving no "sacred cow" untouched. Believing there aren't any "Ten Guaranteed Steps" or "Seven Best Habits" to success, Billi helps individuals and organizations get in touch with reality, and get savvy. She is the author of "Savvy: Thirty Days to a Different Perspective," and her book on savvy team play will be available soon. Billi's columns are read in business journals nationwide.

Organizations as diverse as Apple Computer, Bank of America, the CIA, NCR, ANZ Bank of Australia, Sun Micro Systems, Coors, AT&T, West Point Academy, NASA, the TVA, Blue Cross-Blue Shield, and the Pentagon have all used Billi's common sense materials to prepare their people for the changing realities of the workplace. She can be reached at: Billi Lee & Company, Inc., P.O. Box 50400, Colorado Springs, CO 80960; Phone: 719-520-5051; Fax: 719-475-9331.

# Ubuntu: Applying African Philosophy to Diversity Training

by Lente-Louise Louw

*You might have much of the world's riches, and you might hold a portion of authority,*
*but if you have no ubuntu, you do not amount to much.*

Archbishop Desmond Tutu

buntu is a subtle and not easily translated concept. As a white Afrikaner whose family fought alongside black farmworkers in the Boer War, I grew up being called *Puleng* (Rain) in a rural province with black children as my constant playmates. And so, it was my good fortune to *experience ubuntu* long before I knew the word. Certainly, it was decades before I sought to define it for others so that its richness could be understood, its precepts learned and valued, and its practice extended beyond black Africa.

## The Philosophy of *Ubuntu*

A Nguni word, *ubuntu* simply means "the quality of being human." *Ubuntu* manifests itself through various human acts, clearly visible in social, political, and economic situations as well as among family. According to sociolinguist Buntu Mfenyana, it "runs through the veins of all Africans." Elaborated, the quality of being human, for Africans, is embodied in the oft-repeated: *"Umuntu ngumtu ngabanye abantu"* ("A person is a person through other people"). While this African proverb reveals a world view—that we owe our selfhood to others, that we are first and foremost social beings, that, if you will, no man is an island, or, as the African would have it, "One finger cannot pick up a grain"—*ubuntu* is, at the same time, a deeply personal philosophy that calls on us to mirror our humanity for each other. To the observer, *ubuntu* can be seen and felt in the spirit of willing participation, unquestioning cooperation, warmth, openness, and personal dignity demonstrated by the indigenous black population. From the cradle, every black child inculcates these qualities so that by the time adulthood is reached, the *ubuntu* philosophy has become a way of being.

The word used to capture this elusive concept varies from one regional dialect to another. In Shangaan, we say *munhu*; in Zulu, *umuntu*; in Xhoza, *umntu*; in Se-Sotho, *motho*; in Venda, *muthu*, and in Tswana, *motho*. Whatever the term used, the philosophy embodied in *ubuntu* is one that honors a trusting, interdependent, reciprocal relationship delicately balanced with individual needs for autonomy and self-expression.

## The Consequences of *Ubuntu*

It is understandable that when we act upon a deeply felt sense of being connected to others by our common humanity, when we truly regard self and other as one, when we cherish human dignity, all of our relationships and the level of our behaviors and actions are raised to a higher plane. By contrast, it should be evident that, without such a binding ethos—and scores of societies, particularly in the West, are notably lacking in such shared values—human relationships deteriorate, remain instrumental, or are thwarted at superficial ritualistic behavior.

Willis Harman, founder of the Institute of Noetic Sciences and author of *Global Mind Change* (Knowledge Systems, Inc., Indianapolis, IN, 1988) is not alone in expressing the need for a coming together of three prevailing views if the world is to survive and prosper: the manipulation of the external world that is characteristic of Western traditions; the focus on inner experience and reflection that is important in Eastern thinking; and connectedness to nature valued by indigenous peoples the world over. Each has a vital role to play, but they must be held in balance, no one dominating the other.

# Building and Fostering Relationship

*In a multicultural context, we need to leave behind cultural dictates for what constitutes relationship: . . . codes of appropriate behavior . . . sex roles . . . codes of diplomacy and the strictly delineated institutional forms that we have used to define what is and what is not relationship.*

Charles Johnson, *The Creative Imperative*
(*Celestial Arts*, Berkeley, 1984/1986)

Relationship—that which connects one person to another, bridges differences, and, in some real way, creates the future—is vital to our personal, professional, and organizational lives. As individuals, we enjoy a network of relationships with family and friends; as members of our community, we form relationships with teachers, civic leaders, and a host of other public employees and commercial enterprises; as workers we are the managers and the managed who spend significant portions of our daily lives in close interaction with coworkers, colleagues, customers, clients, partners, and those to whom we report.

When it comes to institutional life, the reaches of relationship are even greater. For example, just as hospitals rely on a continuing influx of patients, banks rely on adequate numbers of depositors and loan seekers, service organizations and commercial establishments demand our patronage if they are to stay in business, and the list goes on. All institutions, by their very existence, are in relationship with us. Beyond that primary relationship of provider to consumer, every organization is obliged to manage relationships within their walls, setting forth institutional goals and seeking accountability from all who work for the organization. It is not difficult to agree, then, that relationships, whether personal, civic, or organizational, serve as the basis of our growth and development, our expression of warmth and creativity, our support and strength, in everything we do. Indeed, for renowned philosopher-theologian Martin Buber, "In the beginning is relationship" (*I and Thou*, Charles Scribner's & Sons, NY, 1970).

Consultants who look at dynamics in small and large organizations continue to note that synergistic relationships, those in which all workers feel that their contribution to the whole is vital to an organization's success, not only boost worker participation and productivity but constitute the difference between organizations that falter and fail and those that flourish. Much of the advice such consultants offer to CEOs, consequently, is aimed at fostering the kinds of relationships necessary, within the context of a given organization, to assure policies and procedures that do more than ask workers to come into alignment with organizational goals and, rather, make it possible for them to have a real say in defining those goals. One of the common occurrences in organizations that invite this level of participation and trust is that workers, on their own, begin to set increasingly higher stakes for themselves, individually and as members of a group or team. Asa Joe Ndlela, a black human resources manager, remarked to me, "Trust is one-ness. It is being you, watching yourself in a mirror; that's what trust is."

The pioneering collaboration in the eighties between Toyota and GM was as demanding as it was daring; for American automotive workers, the Japanese way of working was counter to everything they knew. For whatever it did and did not accomplish (the outcomes went well beyond the production of the Chevy Nova), the experiment calls up the admonition of Charles Johnson that we must walk away from all that we have known and felt safe with in working relationships where diversity, when it did exist, was confined to simple differences in gender, or age, or skill level. As he suggests, in a multicultural workforce, the demands on relationship are far greater than in relatively homogeneous settings, for the "space" between the managers and the managed, and between and among coworkers in such an environment sometimes looms as an unbridgeable chasm. Norms of behavior specific to each cultural, ethnic, or racial group—largely invisible in groupings where few are perceived as "outsiders"—are suddenly up for grabs in work environments with an ethnically or racially diverse staff. (We have discovered already, and continue to discover, the disruption that occurs when women are brought into professions or trades or power positions traditionally regarded as the exclusive provinces of men.)

On finding themselves a part of a diverse working team, the natural tendency on the part of most workers is to establish camaraderie with those who are *like* rather than unlike them, whether in race, class, gender, age, or country of origin.

Among managers faced with a diverse workforce, the temptation for some is to gloss over "people" differences and focus on the *task*, hoping to avoid potential clashes of individual style, temperament, and relationship patterns that they feel ill-equipped to resolve and that they fear will have repercussions on productivity, and, of course, undermine them as managers.

Much the same situation is occurring now in our public school system, especially in populated urban areas where immigrant children are changing the face of the classroom. Not having a ready solution, teachers, administrators, and educational researchers find themselves to be part of the problem. Teachers, most of whom already feel underpaid, unacknowledged, and overburdened, are becoming increasingly frustrated, angry, and defensive about their inability to teach ever larger classes filled with children at wildly different levels of competence and language proficiency.

In the case of businesses and corporations, calling in outside experts and consultants is an accepted response when internal resources are strained and inadequate to the task. With the kind of coaching those trained and experienced in valuing and managing diversity can provide, CEOs and middle management are gradually made aware of the heightened potential their company has *because* of the diversity in their workforce. With this recognition, they begin to shed their reactive and defensive stance (how am I going to make do?) and adopt—even take pleasure in—striving to assure that, in their firm, *no potential is lost*. ("No Potential Lost" is the name of a core strategy I have implemented in my work with large corporations in South Africa, and it has been very successful.) From my perspective, and from the vantage point of all those working with multicultural organizations, the opportunity provided by the burgeoning global economy of the nineties is one of unprecedented breakthrough, creativity, and bottom-line profit that will be translated into but go beyond dollars.

As psychotherapists know very well from their clinical practices, and sociologists from years of field studies, most of us—regardless of our cultural, racial, or ethnic group or our gender, age, or occupation—are trapped by our belief systems, our unexamined values, our past experiences, and all of the associated emotions—fear, anger, and mistrust—that have been frozen along with them over a lifetime. This "baggage" from the past, combined with often unrealistic expectations of the future, is astonishingly effective in keeping us from being fully present to what is happening here and now. What does that mean? It means, for one thing, that a terrible deception is going on: We are allowing our preconceptions, past associations, and judgments made rigid over time to color and distort most if not all of our present interactions—without our recognizing it. The inconsequential judgments we all make in the presence of another ("She reminds me of my sister." "He smiles a lot.") reside quietly next to far more insidious judgments we make (indeed, that we made long ago) about entire races or ethnic groups or people from a certain part of the world or a different socioeconomic class—and all of this on top of the more consciously held assumptions women hold about men and men about women, and both about dress, appearance, mannerisms, age, disabilities, and other differences we encounter every day.

Until we can see our unexamined biases as opportunities lost—opportunities for friendship, for learning, for broadening our perspectives, for reenergizing our creative impulses—we will remain locked into decisions we signed and sealed in childhood. Many, by the time they reach high school, are already unable to hear what those different from them are saying. They have settled into a pattern of evaluating rather than listening for understanding and are becoming well versed in the energy-wasting, Western practice of polarizing and labeling: right-wrong, black-white, good-bad.

Portions of "Ubuntu" have been excerpted from the book *Valuing Diversity: New Tools for a New Reality*, 1995, McGraw-Hill, co-edited by Lewis Brown Griggs (Griggs Productions, San Francisco) and Lente-Louise Louw (Career Resource Development Strategies/Johannesburg, South Africa). To order the book contact Griggs Productions, 2046 Clement Street, San Francisco, CA 94121. Phone: 800-210-4200; Fax: 415-668-6004.

## About the Author

Lente-Louise Louw is a clinical psychologist who has worked in the fields of education and human resource development over the past 20 years. She has received a number of awards in South Africa, in particular, for her work in career and educational development of Black students and employees. With the assistance of disadvantaged communities in South Africa, she pioneered a broad-based holistic, human resource development model, focusing on career progress in technology fields.

She is currently Director of Product Development and Training for Griggs Productions in San Francisco with whom she has been associated since 1992. She can be reached at the address to the left.

# PART 10
# KEY DILEMMAS: ASSIMILATION, ACCULTURATION & SUBTLE DISCRIMINATION

# Dialogue: Key Dilemmas

*Bob*—We've covered a lot of ground in our survey of the "state of diversity." We've listened to many voices, old and new, with fresh and powerful perspectives. Soon we'll be wrapping up our insights and findings in the closing Section, "The Future." Before closing, however, we would like to review the key dilemmas we continue to face.

*George*—So the stories, issues, and perspectives we share here simply don't have easy answers. Or the answer may be easy. Yet, other forces keep it from being actionable. It's then important for us to be willing to engage in conversation and strategize about those answers. We are taking our cue from Teurf's comments in "Moving from Blame to Dialogue" (page 346).

*Bob*—Let's list the key dilemmas as we see them. First, I would put the persistence of the "malignant disease" of racism. Bigotry is not going away; and as conflict-averse Americans we tend to look away when it makes us too uncomfortable.

Charlene Solomon's article, "Keeping Hate Out of the Workplace" (page 403), covers the first Key Dilemma well. I remember when she interviewed me for the story, I had a really hard time helping her find organizations (even those that had done good work in diversity) who were willing to go on public record.

*George*—In fact, we assert that racist incidents are likely to increase in hard economic times as Bill Day's cartoon on page 18 suggests. My vote for Key Dilemma number two would go to the tension between Assimilation and Acculturation. What does one need to do to fit in? How much acculturation is bona fide job requirement? How much is a demand for change simply in an organization's or its managers' limited perspectives or just pushiness about their preferred way of doing business?

*Bob*—Third, I see the issue of the persistence of subtle discrimination. No one has done more work in this area than Dr. John Dovidio of Colgate University. His research documents that, despite the substantial progress in reducing the prejudice we admit to, we are racist in countless ways that we are not even conscious about. These effects play themselves out in results like those we heard from Ed Jones (pages 53 and 61), Ellis Cose (page 72), and Anthony Walton (page 105). They occur day-in and day-out to people of difference in your organization. Just acknowledging this is the first major hurdle.

*George*—Perhaps related to subtle discrimination, is a fourth Key Dilemma which we'll call "Monocultural Drift"—referred to in the article from Kaleel Jamison Associates (page 432). What do you do, when despite best efforts in the direction of valuing diversity, people continually drift back into monocultural groupings?

*Bob*—So those are the four Key Dilemmas we see: (1) racism, (2) assimilation vs. acculturation, (3) subtle discrimination and (4) monocultural drift.

We kid ourselves if we fail to see the truth about the persistence and prevalence of old-fashioned raw forms of prejudice. In a society where gender roles are changing, it's even a little tougher to see the insidious nature of sexism. We still see patterns of male dominance and female subordination. There are rock albums and posters with abusive scenarios of men dominating women that we would now find intolerable if they were white people demeaning people of color . . .

*George*—but not if women were demeaning men. Warren Farrell, whose work we have anthologized in *The Cultural Diversity Fieldbook*, has done important research that highlights how men can be portrayed in abusive ways in ads. They are also "the expendable sex," dying in battle by the droves (see *The Myth of Male Power*, NY 1993, Simon & Schuster). Did you ever notice how humanitarian concern in wartime and other disasters is almost exclusively focused on "innocent women and children" while the men are at best "body count"—and presumed not "innocent"? The value of men's lives is a key cultural issue as well . . . Until we face it squarely, all life is at risk.

*Bob*—This is rarely addressed, as is another issue some call "Lookism," which says that the fairest-looking get more than their fair share of the goodies in life. We look at this and how to respond to it in the article on "Beauty Pays" (page 422).

*George*—"Only English Spoken Here" highlights the assimilation vs. acculturation issue. How much does one want to get into the mainstream culture and how can one? What are "the forces for cohesion" here, and what pulls us apart? We've referred to this theme in earlier sections (Diversity Under Fire, Spirit, etc.). This article takes to task some ethnically proud stances against assimilation. Perhaps this theme is more current now because of the economic stress we are experiencing.

On the one hand, people fear losing their own culture ("The Fear of Losing a Culture," page 410), while on the other they need to learn at least enough of the mainstream culture to economically succeed in it. In his article Richard Rodriguez reiterates themes woven throughout this *Sourcebook* and links them to specific features of Latino culture.

*Bob*—Lee Gardenswartz and Anita Rowe also offer some practical tips on solving assimilation and acculturation dilemmas in their short piece, "When Language Causes a Barrier" (page 414).

*George*—These issues become more acute when we talk about profit-making and public service organizations where people need language tools to perform the functions of the organization. It's often an important part of their job description.

I want to assert that the language debate is often a red herring, or at best a symptom of deeper acculturation or bias issues. When we look at bilingual education as carried out today, we see people coming out of our school systems without having learned any language well at all. I would be very happy if every child in California could speak both English and Spanish. California would be a better and richer place for it. But our system is conforming people to a lowest common denominator, not teaching them what they need to learn.

*Bob*—Can you insist that people become educated, whatever their background? Or is this politically incorrect?

*George*—This is an assimilation vs. acculturation issue too, for everybody. How will the nation pass on its common, as well as its diverse, cultural values without education that works both at home and in school? Remember, learning is a major survival strategy. Without a core amount of common culture, there is no nation.

In the educational system as it works today, the negative side of the melting pot is at work again. Now both the minorities and the macroculture are being thrown in the soup together. One of the reasons people—and not just young people—resist learning is the sense that it's not okay to be different. In U.S. culture being different inevitably means better or worse than someone else. While it's true for everyone, it's especially true for men. Knowing something someone else doesn't know or value makes you different. So we resist learning other about cultures, our own included. We become the ugly American at home as well as abroad.

*Bob*—It's certainly been the U.S. way. It's cultural arrogance that takes a peculiar form here but is common to many other parts of the world.

*George*—Our particular ethnocentricity may have been inherited from the British and their island mentality. This is decreasing in Britain itself today due to trade, telecommunications and now the "chunnel," the new underwater tunnel between the UK and the rest of Europe. In the U.S. we have a tradition of isolation, too, at first because of our continent's remoteness from the rest of the world . . .

*Bob*— . . . then with the Monroe Doctrine which said "leave us alone—the Western Hemisphere is our sphere of influence."

*George*—The settlement patterns in the vast geographical expanse of the United States then, and now, contribute to our isolationism. Thousands of communities in this country are extremely monocultural. Despite the national trend of mobility, a surprising number of people still do not wander far from where they were born. As an international consultant, I can be called on to speak four languages in a single day on the streets of most major European cities.

*Bob*—You might be able to do that in Los Angeles, too, if you felt as safe as you do in Amsterdam, Paris or even London.

*George*—Learning languages can teach Americans not only to live with each other but to compete and succeed in a global environment. Fairness and bias reduction do not accomplish this per se—sometimes they are carried out in ways that are inimical to cultural competence. If you know something about blacks, or Latinos, or women, then you're stereotyping! Some time ago major talks with Poland broke down because President Carter did not have an adequately skilled translator. Not that such person didn't exist in the U.S., but he or she wasn't found. There was no way to access that person in our system. We are talking about cultural competence and skills which are not generally seen as a part of most corporate and educational diversity programs here.

*Bob*—The acculturation issue is played out on a symbolic level, for example, in how people conform to dress codes and norms. The excerpts we have from the *Review of Public Personnel Administration* grapple with some of these issues (see "A Case for Moving from Tolerance to Valuing Diversity: The Issue of Religiously Distinctive Dress and Appearance," page 419). We don't say that one position is more productive than another, but discussing them should lead us to greater awareness and resolve.

*George*—Our intentions may be good, but our skills fall short. I remember how JFK stood at the Berlin Wall and announced to the world in a Boston German accent, "Ich bin ein Berliner," "I am a jelly donut."

*Bob*—That's really how he pronounced it?!

*George*—It's not pronunciation. To say you are a citizen of someplace, German doesn't use the definite article. "Ich bin Berliner; ich bin Hamburger." No "ein." If I say, "ich bin ein Berliner," "ein Berliner" is a jelly donut. Of course, everybody knew what Kennedy meant, but in retrospect you chuckle a little over such avoidable, and as Europeans would say, "typically American" gaffes.

*Bob*—Can you say more about the non-assimilation issue? We have disenfranchised youth, African-Americans and others, who rebel against the system and identify with those who don't succeed.

*George*—This is about power and class again. If having to learn another language and another culture is oppression rather than a source of power,

we have a real dilemma in a multicultural society. On one hand, people don't want to feel they need to give up who they are in order to be accepted. On the other hand, you need to know how to function successfully in an environment, especially if it's not your own.

*Bob*—As consultants we have said, You don't have to assimilate, but you do have to acculturate. You have to learn how to function, to speak the language, to work with the tools.

*George*—Then, you are able to use this learning to bring your own resources to bear and may even ultimately transform the environment. To do that you have to communicate, make enough contact to make something different happen. Savvy people in the dominant culture do this all the time unconsciously . . . or sometimes consciously.

*Bob*—Black youth, on the other hand, has been so long disenfranchised that non-participation in the perceived dominant culture is chic. Whereas Asian-American students commonly use peer pressure to support each other in accomplishment, many blacks use it to discourage academic effort as uncool.

I am not blaming black inner-city youth in these circumstances. The level they'd have to aspire to make them successful is way beyond the resources that the system (teachers, resources, discipline, etc.) provides. You can't study when you are in a life-threatening situation day after day. When the gap is so huge, it's easy to be resigned. But since you have to feel good about yourself, you make it chic.

At the same time it is hard it to tell Asian-American parents that their children (with excellent SAT scores) can't get into Berkeley for example, because places are reserved for other minorities.

*George*—We are clear about our good intentions here, but we lack strategies to level the playing field in ways that don't diminish us by perpetuating the racism and resentment we are trying to eliminate.

*Bob*—There is another problem that occurs in acculturation. It may seem to the cultural majority that only the person of difference has the job of accommodating to the mainstream, but isn't everybody involved?

*George*—Right. Culture is not static. So both the newcomer and the culture always change in the process of acculturation. Everybody acculturates when acculturation is taking place. Also, acculturation happens whether a person resists or accommodates. For example, black culture today is not what it was thirty years ago. Some common threads run through it, some preserved values. But a major cultural revolution has occurred among black people with black consciousness, black power, and, more recently, the dismantling of the Great Society. The black value system has been shaken and settled down in new patterns, with more variety, wider class distinctions. Whether one succeeds or not in a culture depends on having the tools of acculturation.

*Bob*—I guess it's not politically correct, but I'll suggest that it's also the responsibility of the "outsider" to find out how the system works, rather than say, "I could never be a white man, so why bother to understand the white male system."

*George*—"To survive," is the easy answer, but, it's a two-way street. If you are joining my organization, and the goal of my organization is to survive with you in it, it's going to be my responsibility to explain to you how things work.

*Bob*—Which the mainstream culture has been woefully inadequate in doing.

*George*—The tools exist for it. Some corporations, ones that have very powerful cultures, make use of a deliberate acculturation process. And people really identify . . .

*Bob*—Give me a concrete example . . .

*George*—Several of my clients are Fortune 50 companies. I have been to their installations around the world and have met people who call themselves, somewhat tongue-in-cheek, "company clones." When I enter one of their buildings and start meeting people, the first thing I notice is that they reflect the culture of that company, and *then* I also see that the people are shorter and darker or taller and fairer than I am.

*Bob*—So you feel the organizational culture first?

*George*—Even when they speak with a different accent, I get an overwhelming sense that they're company folk. I walk into a training session in Geneva or Cincinnati or Amsterdam, and a native

Japanese employee walks up to me and says, "Hi, George," (reading my name tag), "I'm Taro, and I'm really pleased to see you (ear-to-ear grin)." This is not the way most Japanese easily meet strangers, even when they've had a cross-cultural communications course. Strong company culture makes this happen.

*Bob*—Walt Hopkins, who co-authored a piece for this *Sourcebook* (page 384) often muses about the situation: where two executives, one from the U.S. and one from Japan, meet for the first time. The U.S. executive bows at appropriate depth; the Japanese sticks out his hand for a shake. Both recognize the humor and delight that the other has reached out to his or her culture. They laugh together and go on to do business.

*George*—Both appreciate. The problem in the U.S. is that we have made diversity largely an issue of power not culture, which means we're back to dealing with justice and prejudice. Transcultural skills, the abilities that lead to value added are still waiting in the wings. We can't stop and appreciate when we're always conscious of being in a zero-sum game.

*Bob*—With the power issues not addressed, in other words, the rest is superficial. Nothing's going to work.

Let's move our discussion to the chart included in this section which shows the decline of negative stereotyping in professed opinions and attitudes towards African-Americans (page 430). Notice *(Bob points)* there's a marked reduction.

At the same time, we can also see a rise in subtle or "aversive" racism, as John Dovidio calls it. People are making discriminatory choices unconsciously when these choices can be rationalized by some other reason. It seems when people know what is the right thing to do, they not only do it, but treat people of difference better than they treat people from their own cultural background. They do this, apparently, because they know they're in the spotlight. Some very strong unconscious racism still needs to be dealt with, it seems. This must be considered simultaneously with some of the substantive issues of social justice and class.

*George*—There are ways of dealing with this! Organizations have systematic ways for countering perceptual errors in their Performance Management and Performance Appraisal training programs. Why can't averse racism be addressed in the same fashion?

*Bob*—Our resistance to admitting racism is pervasive and prevents us from dealing with the problem. We know how to counter subtle perceptual distortions like halo effect, latency, data-collection errors, and closure through skill training.* It's time we turned our efforts to the issue of pervasive subtle discrimination as well. It's a matter of using what we know about human performance and organizational development—diversity does not stand on its own.

*George*—Judith Katz and Fred Miller's contribution is a case in point. Entitled "Teaming High Performance with Inclusion" it provides an interesting "snapshot" of what organizations can face on the road to achieving diversity. The "monocultural drift" that led diverse teams to become more monocultural was an enigma. Is it subtle racism?

---

*See "How to Avoid Stereotyping and Nine Other Pitfalls of Person Perception," an audiocassette training module available from ODT: 1-800-736-1293.

*Bob*—Not necessarily. The management at "Transcontinental Camshafts" paid attention to more than just establishing the teams as mixed-culture groups. By Organization Development interventions and close attention to supporting empowered teams, they brought about an overall more inclusive work culture. With this in place, they determined that they didn't have to worry so much about teams reconfiguring themselves in more monocultural patterns.

*George*—This could be a dangerous assumption if there was not also a clear link to performance and performance measures, one of the points we've been emphasizing throughout this *Sourcebook.* Some kind of intervention, a la Affirmative Action, may get the ball rolling. Over time, if systems are put in place to really support diversity, the need for some diversity-specific interventions may wither away somewhat naturally. This provides a good link to our next section on "Dismantling Affirmative Action" which seems to be a reflection of a changing political and social climate in the U.S.

# Keeping Hate Out of the Workplace

by Charlene Marmer Solomon (*Personnel Journal*)

*Despite recent efforts to promote diversity, HR professionals are finding that the workplace isn't immune to the racism that exists in society.*

An African-American employee at an East Coast company took the day off to celebrate Martin Luther King Jr. Day. Upon returning to work, he discovered a note that had been scribbled on his desk calendar. It read: "Kill four more, get four more days off."

An elderly Jewish employee in an East Coast electronics firm was told face-to-face by another employee that the new boss was about to design microwave ovens large enough for people to walk into.

A group of 15 employees from a West Coast public utilities corporation marched in a gay pride parade with the company's logo. When they returned to work on Monday, they were greeted by hundreds of letters on their E-mail, one of which read, "If I had been anywhere near the gay pride march and had had an axe, I would have axed those people."

> *There's a direct relationship between the racism that exists in society and in the workplace. Because one spills into the other, human resources professionals have realized the need to find new ways to deal with this ugly underbelly of the diversity equation.*

Hostility in the workplace. It's an ugly subject. People still make racial slurs and perform such dramatic acts as hate mail and hate faxes, graffiti scrawled on desks and lockers, computer data scrambled and destroyed or a cross burned on a pick-up truck.

These incidents seem to lead to one simple question: Why does hostility still exist in the workplace, given the recent attention placed on welcoming diversity in companies large and small throughout the U.S.?

According to Howard J. Ehrlich, director of research for the National Institute Against Prejudice and Violence, a nonprofit organization in Baltimore, societal problems have found their way into the workplace through such external issues as rapid immigration, socio-economic difficulties and unemployment levels. "The workplace probably is going to be the major site of ethnoviolent conflict throughout the 1990s," says Ehrlich.

Recent events, such as the Los Angeles riots, testify to the fact that the effects of changing demographics have the potential to be explosive. Increased polarization about ethnic issues causes inter-group tension. Increasing diversity—on and off the job—brings some discomfort and anxiety. Fears of an unknown economic future, competition for jobs and housing, and even desperate conditions for some, are other reasons for greater animosity. When people are fearful about survival issues, they look for scapegoats.

"The racism that exists in the community exists in the workplace," says David Barclay, vice president of work force diversity at Hughes Aircraft Co. in Los Angeles and a founder of the Los Angeles Human Relations Commission Corporate Advisory Committee. "It's nothing more than a reflection of the community at large. We [Hughes Aircraft] don't have those kinds of dramatic incidents, but it would be unrealistic for people to think that their work force is different from the general community."

Crime in general is on the rise, as are crimes of hate. From 1990 to 1991, there was a 31% increase in attacks on gay people in five major U.S. cities. Anti-Semitic incidents reached the highest level since the Anti-Defamation League started its annual audit—an 11% increase from 1990. In Los Angeles County alone, where the first human relations commission was established in 1944 to promote understanding among ethnic groups, hate crimes (which are classified legally as violations of the law based on the victim's background—ethnicity, gender, sexual orientation, and so on) increased 22% from 1990. Gay men, African-Americans and Jews were the targets in the majority of cases. There's been a significant increase in hate-related incidents in colleges.

Hate crimes are just the tip of the iceberg, though. "People who act it out reflect the feelings of a much larger group of individuals who aren't going to commit a crime," says Eugene Mornell, executive director of the Los Angeles County Human Relations Commission. "We can assume there's a much larger number who share the same feeling. We really don't know what's out there, but companies just can't get away from the problems of their communities."

When hostility spills over from the streets into the office, the factory or the showroom, it becomes the concern of HR professionals, as well as other members of senior management. When it appears, what to do? And, even more importantly, can it be averted? How can HR professionals deal with this ugly underbelly of the diversity equation?

For starters, they have to begin talking about it and sharing experiences. That was part of the reason the Los Angeles Human Relations Commission initiated a Corporate Advisory Committee.

"The thought that your firm has had hate crimes and no one else has is troubling," says Mornell. "When you share information, you begin to find out that other companies have similar

---

## HOW TO AVOID HOSTILITY IN THE WORKPLACE

When all of the societal factors that are present today coalesce, the frustration level increases geometrically, says Los Angeles psychologist Kevin Flynn. "When people are under that degree of tension, they tend to act out their discomfort in an aggressive manner," he says.

When people see violence modeled for them in society, those people who are maladapted are more inclined to engage in blind violent anger. They don't see alternatives. Flynn, who's often brought in to evaluate the seriousness of verbalized threats in the workplace, believes there's greater likelihood today for hostility and violent action in the workplace.

Some factors may be poor selection—hiring people who may be somewhat unstable. Promotion practices may contribute if they don't promote the best people. So do mediocre or incompetent supervisors at higher levels of management that tolerate abuse. Or a tremendously high level of stress in the individual who perceives there's no way out, perhaps, is another contributing factor.

What can you do? As the people who are charged with maintaining the good mental health of the organization, human resources managers must measure the tension in the workplace.

*Monitor the culture.* In some parts of the workplace, for example, fooling around may entail pushing and other forms of physical *macho* behavior. Human resources people must intervene and tell the group it's unacceptable. It's a short step from shoving to more hostile or violent action. HR people must create boundaries. There must be clear standards for acceptable behavior and consequences when those are violated.

*Ask for management's help.* Supervisors need to call in a management team at the first inkling of discomfort with regard to their own safety. This team might be made up of HR people, security, employee-assistance or medical staff.

*Consult psychologists.* Companies may want to have a well-trained consulting psychologist available to assess these questions.

*Provide help for supervisors.* Watch for toxic supervisors who engender high levels of frustration and hostility in their subordinates. Get that supervisor counseling or additional training.

One final piece of advice is: Always look at the *gestalt*, the whole picture, and the part each component plays. It's rare that one person is a jerk; it's usually a combination, in which some people are destructive and others are reacting to it.

problems. The next step is to find out to what extent someone else has started to deal with these problems—what kinds of programs and materials they have developed, what has been successful and what hasn't."

Bob Abramms, senior associate of ODT Inc., an Amherst, Massachusetts based management consulting firm specializing in diversity, was shocked to discover how few people—even those in proactive organizations—are willing to talk about overt acts of prejudice. "Looking at the problem is a beginning," he says. But that isn't enough. An effort needs to take place on multiple levels.

There must be vision and commitment to the ideal of valuing diversity demonstrated by an underlying respect toward everyone in the organization. It can't be lip service. For example, the CEO whose gay employees faced verbal intimidation on their electronic mail called in consultants from Equity Institute (in Emeryville, California), who offered workshops to eliminate homophobia.

At the Federal Bureau of Investigation (FBI), the director has explained his position in no uncertain terms on issues of diversity and equal employment—there's no place for discrimination in the organization. "There's enough influence from the director on down that a person would have to be a fool or have a death wish regarding his or her career if he or she were to exhibit racist or bigoted behavior," says James A. Kavina, supervisory special agent and EEO training officer at the FBI in Quantico, Virginia.

At another level, businesses must root out the more subtle forms of discrimination, the ways in which racism and sexism are implicit and built-in. For example, where does denial of opportunity exist? Is there bias, so that certain kinds of people don't get into the pipeline? Abramms believes that this requires a collaborative effort, including senior management, human resources, industrial relations and EEO—an integration across many different functions. And finally, instances of outright bigotry and ethnoviolence must be examined. Abramms offers two contrasting examples.

Scene 1: The loading dock in a manufacturing setting. There were two employees who couldn't see each other but needed to work together, communicating via radio. One was driving a truck. picking up materials. The other was a radio dispatcher, receiving and giving information. The two didn't know each other. The truck driver informed the dispatcher that the loading dock appeared to be empty; that the materials weren't ready to be picked up.

The response from the dispatcher over the radio so that anyone in range could hear, "Even a one-eyed nigger can see that! They certainly don't have the materials ready to go."

The event was unreported and wasn't reprimanded. It festered for more than four years until the truck driver, an African-American, reported it in a diversity training workshop. "The heartfelt way he reported it made it obvious how painful it is to live with that kind of ethnic slur," says Abramms. "The remark wasn't directly targeted at anyone, but was just a flippant, pejorative expression that was extremely hurtful." It wasn't addressed and resolved.

Scene 2: Emergency services in an urban setting. In this situation, the two employees knew each other well, interacted daily and, to function as a team, had to have trust and confidence in each other.

The Caucasian worker was in a patrol-dispatcher situation. The African-American employee was doing rounds. They were bantering back and forth on their walkie-talkies. The African-American had finished his rounds and told his partner that he was coming in.

"Look forward to having you back here, Buckwheat," was the reply. Buckwheat was a term of endearment that he used when he was being smart-alecky. (Buckwheat refers to the dull-witted African-American child in the *Little Rascals* films.)

"What did you say?" the African-American employee asked. He immediately went back to headquarters and sat down with his partner. He was extremely hurt by the remark and told him so. His partner, who hadn't intended malice and still couldn't understand why it was hurtful, was willing to listen and immediately apologized.

"These were people who didn't have training in diversity skills, but had the good sense to realize you can't let this stuff slide, because it impairs team ability to function," says Abramms. "If you don't have a willingness to address these problems, you'll have serious problems in a team, working together."

This is where training enters. Most workers behave the way the employees did in the first example. When negative instances occur, they often fester until they're expressed in diversity training, discrimination complaints, exit interviews or lawsuits.

"However, you take a significant risk doing diversity training without first taking a few days to access the situation, talking with a diagonal slice of the work force—women, senior managers, minorities, white males," says Abramms, who often uses focus groups. "You can get data that's explosive . . . stories that would chill you but don't get repeated beyond the target populations they affect."

He feels passionately that the more you delve into situations in which there are diversity problems, the more you find that the diversity issues are compounded severely by a lack of effective management practices.

Witness the example of a business organization that had trouble with people who didn't clean up the kitchen area. Someone in the department had posted a sign that read, "Please clean up after using this area."

Someone else had come along and scrawled below it in felt marker, "Dirty nigger." The fact that one bigoted person had defaced the sign was offensive. This alone, however, wasn't really an indicator of how bad things were in the company. What was an indication was that this sign stayed posted for almost two weeks.

The manager of the group was perceived as unsupportive of diversity efforts. She was out of touch with her people, so they experienced a vast psychological distance from her. They felt they couldn't approach her. No one had the courage to tell her about the sign.

"An event such as this breeds a climate of intolerance," says Abramms. "It encouraged the person who wrote it, and because it stayed up so long, may have influenced some and embarrassed others."

It's important to combine any diversity effort with sound management practices, he says. A poor supervisor may be inconvenient and irritating to a white male, but to a woman, or a person of color, the lack of management skill can easily turn into a career calamity, because it's compounded with the psychological distance of the difference of race or gender. If the supervisor can't do effective coaching and counseling or performance appraisals, or provide an effective, intelligent reprimand when called for, it looks as if it's outright racism.

These are the kinds of situations that lead people to call the Anti-Defamation League. The ADL is a human rights organization formed in 1913 and based in New York City. Its mission is to combat prejudice and bigotry. Although its primary target is anti-Semitism, it also serves to attempt to build understanding among other racial, religious and ethnic groups.

Most often complaints of discrimination are a result of ignorance on the part of the employer. For instance, a Seventh Day Adventist was told he would have to take an entrance examination on Saturday (which is the group's Sabbath); an Orthodox Jew was told he couldn't wear a *kepah* (skullcap). In these cases, as most frequently happens, an explanation from the ADL is all that's needed for the employer to find alternative solutions and avoid the problem.

Many times, businesses call in the ADL to provide cultural bias (or diversity awareness) training, which is perhaps the most logical way for companies to confront and diffuse any hostility that may exist in the workplace. One of the ADL's education projects, *Workplace of Difference*, is designed to teach people to examine stereotypes and cultural assumptions, combat various forms of discrimination and divisiveness, explore the idea of culture and its effects on perceptions of differences, and examine the value of diversity by expanding cultural awareness.

It's a tall order, and the ADL does it in stages. As with ODT, Inc. and Equity Institute, the first step is an assessment of needs and exploration by the consultant to tailor the program to the business's needs.

"We operate under the assumption that most people are well-intentioned and really don't mean to offend," says Angela Antenore, the Western States Director of the ADL's department of special training. If we're going to embrace diversity, we have to realize that we don't have all the answers, she says. Therefore many of the exercises model the sharing of information and expressing the idea, "I don't know." To accomplish this, the program trainers try to create a safe environment in which people can explore their areas of bias and ignorance, and then build empathy.

One of the warm-up exercises is called *A Taste of Home*. It exemplifies the changes in diversity in the workplace and capitalizes on the idea that

## UNEXPECTED EFFECTS OF WORKPLACE HOSTILITY

When a hate crime occurs in the workplace, the victim isn't the only person who knows about the crime. Most often coworkers become aware of the information by rumors.

Consequently, there's a whole set of secondary victims—people who share the same background as the victim. "It doesn't affect merely the person who's directly victimized, but also many of the other African-American workers who know that this event happened and that it just as well could have happened to them," says Howard J. Ehrlich, director of research for the National Institute Against Prejudice and Violence, a nonprofit organization in Baltimore. The term used to refer to this phenomenon is covictimization.

This finding is a result of research conducted by the Institute that involved African-American and white employees and supervisors from corporations of all sizes. Ehrlich says another important finding is that employees who are victims of ethnoviolence experience stress and psychosomatic symptoms.

For example, some individuals report beginning to smoke again, having trouble sleeping, reliving the incident or being extremely angry. Hate crimes also can affect an employee's job performance. Victims talk about not wanting to go to work in the morning, especially if a supervisor was the perpetrator, and about no longer being enthusiastic about their jobs.

In addition, victims of hate crimes experience twice the number of symptoms as someone who's victimized for other reasons, such as having a purse stolen from a desk.

people are more at home with people who are similar to themselves.

The trainer tells people to line up based on seniority. They make a giant horseshoe and look at the line. Typically, the white males are at the front of the line (with some white females who are

support staff). Then, there is a burst of diversity that reflects the hiring practices in the 1970s, when women and people of color were hired in. Then, back to white males up to the mid '80s, and the last five years are more diverse again. (Obviously, some companies have greater diversity throughout the years.)

Throughout the day, they seat veterans with newer people. The title *A Taste of Home*, reflects the idea that everyone gravitates toward those people they know best and feel most comfortable with. This exercise is to expand that taste of home. "There are many unwritten rules in a corporate culture," says Antenore. "When you sit these people together, they all learn something new about the environment."

Another experience is the Four Questions Exercise. Participants describe themselves in terms of their heritage or their background—whatever classifications are important to them. For example, one may say, "I am a white male, Anglo-Saxon Protestant." Another may be a white male, single father professional.

"In the past, the workplace hasn't been a place in which to speak about differences," says Antenore. "You find that, for some people, this is the first time they have been able to bring up their differences in the workplace." For many, this is the first time they have defined themselves in ways other than what exists on a census card. It isn't only race, religion, ethnicity, gender and sexual orientation, it's age, education level, socioeconomic class, disabilities, which part of the city you come from and so on. These differences predict different perceptions.

Next, people talk about their experiences around these differences, and around the labels. The goal is to develop empathy—that people may have similar experiences, even though they're different. "We examine the question, 'Aren't we all the same?'" says Antenore. "We all have the same human needs, but how we meet them can be very different."

Another exercise is called *Name Five*.

Participants name five prominent people, then five prominent Americans, five prominent American males (most people will find that they've named males for the five prominent Americans), five prominent people in their field, and so on. This exercise helps people discover where they draw their knowledge from, and where they have knowledge gaps about who their powerful role models are.

The *Workplace of Difference* trainers come into an organization and state that they aren't going to presume how to do the day-to-day job. They aren't going to change people into thinking in the politically correct way. Their goal is to offer information that will make doing the daily job more efficient.

The ADL isn't out to eradicate bigotry and prejudice, either. "Realistically, prejudice of some kind always is going to exist," says Janet Himler, associate director of the ADL. "Everyone has his or her own internal belief systems that are very difficult to change. Our workshops are designed to change behavior. In the workplace it's vital to change behavior to create an environment of mutual respect and dignity."

Ehrlich agrees with this approach. "Although there's a great deal of talk about diversity training, what we're talking about here is old-fashioned prejudice," he says. "There's no talk about prejudice-reduction programs, which really is the direction in which we ought to be moving. We need cross-cultural training, but we also need to deal with prejudice directly."

It's Ehrlich's belief that hate crimes and hostility will continue to occur in the workplace unless direct intervention on the part of human resources professionals takes place. And if that intervention doesn't involve some type of prejudice-reduction training, Ehrlich says the employer is running the risk of such incidents "exploding."

Consideration and respect for all individuals is an admirable goal. It sounds simple. To achieve it in a pluralistic environment, though, takes great effort. McDonnell Douglas Aircraft Co. in Long Beach, California, has had cultural diversity training for many years. It's now taking another step in anti-bias training. The company has an anti-discrimination policy based on sexual orientation. But that isn't enough. It will start with specific sensitivity awareness for HR managers.

The program uses resources from several legal, gay and lesbian organizations. It starts with a 20-minute film in which the audience (presumably heterosexual) experiences what life is like when you're one of few, i.e., what it would be like to be heterosexual in a homosexual world. It's followed

## WHERE TO GET HELP FOR WORKPLACE HOSTILITY

Anti-Defamation League
823 United Nations Plaza
New York, NY 10017
212/490-2525
Contact: Jill Kahn
310/446-8000 (In Los Angeles)
Contact: David Lehrer

County of Los Angeles
Commission on Human Relations
1184 Hall of Records
320 West Temple St.
Los Angeles, CA 90012
213/ 974-7611
Contact: Cella Zager

Equity Institute
6400 Hollis St., Ste. 15
Emeryville, CA 94608
510/658-4577
Contact: Joan Lester

NAACP
4805 Mt. Hope Dr.
Baltimore, MD 21215
410/358-8900
Contact: John Johnson

National Gay & Lesbian Task Force
1734 Fourteenth St., N.W.
Washington, DC 20009-4309
202/332-6483
Contact: Robin Kane

The Prejudice Institute
Stephens Hall Annex
Towson State University
Towson, MD 21204-7097
410/830-2435
Contact: Howard J. Ehrlich

ODT, Inc.
PO Box 134
Amherst, MA 01004
413/549-1293
Contact: Bob Abramms

by a panel of experts who address the panoply of questions that arise around sexual-orientation issues. The panel allows participants the opportunity to ask questions, examine their biases and stereotypes, and engage in conversation about their fears and moral beliefs about the subject.

"We're trying to do more than just sensitize people," says Timothy Saner, who is the senior administrator of the Equal Opportunity Program in Affirmative Action and the co-chairman of Los Angeles County Human Relation's Corporate Advisory Committee.

As Annelle Lerner, Saner's counterpart at McDonnell Douglas, explains, "We're hoping they'll be able to identify their biases clearly, and go back to the workplace having a different perspective, so they can start making decisions that are progressive and beneficial to the employees in the company." Saner and Lerner say they'll follow up with questionnaires to assess additional information HR people require to pull together programs on these aspects of diversity.

Aspects of these projects are extremely challenging to human resources professionals and others who must handle the emotions and possible conflicts that emerge. "Anytime you make a presentation in which you talk about issues that haven't been vocalized before, you heighten the expectation that something will happen," says Saner. "Most often people go along to get along. It's easier for them to let things go."

Although training may be the most comprehensive way in which human resource managers can address hostility in the workplace, it isn't the only way. There are smaller-scale approaches to be taken that also will yield results.

For example, Saner suggests getting out of the office, wandering around and attending staff meetings to find out what's happening within the company and what issues are on the minds of the people you're representing. Barclay agrees, saying this kind of interaction will allow line human resources people to hear about problems before they fester and become more serious. It's essential to solve these problems at the lowest levels. Otherwise attitudes harden, problems escalate, and resolutions become more difficult.

When employees bring a problem to your attention, don't classify them as troublemakers, says Barclay. They're the ones who are bringing these problems to your attention. Instead, he says, HR professionals must learn to understand fully the process of problem resolution.

In addition, opinion surveys are extremely valuable in helping to identify feelings and perceptions about the workplace. Hughes also uses network groups as a source of information in this area. The network leaders meet with senior executives to discuss the strengths and weaknesses of the company. They express their concerns and offer recommendations for ways to alleviate problems in the organization.

Perhaps the most important role human resources professionals can play in preventing employees from becoming victims of hostility and hate crimes in their places of work isn't in the workplace at all. As Barclay points out, it may be in their local communities.

"I'm not very optimistic," says Barclay, who's passionate about community leadership. "I worry about our losing control of this thing. We may end up with a lot of civil disturbances, such as we had 20 to 25 years ago. We can't just sit here and expect everything to be OK. We have to play a more active role in making sure we have peace in our community.

"There's a direct relationship between what's going on in the community and what could go on in our plants. Violence in the community means potential problems for us."

# The Fear of Losing a Culture

by Richard Rodriguez (*TIME Magazine*)

What is culture, after all? The immigrant shrugs. Latin Americans initially come to the U.S. with only the things they need in mind—not abstractions like culture. They need dollars. They need food. Maybe they need to get out of the way of bullets. Most of us who concern ourselves with Hispanic-American culture, as painters, musicians, writers—or as sons and daughters—are the children of immigrants. We have grown up on this side of the border, in the land of Elvis Presley and Thomas Edison. Our lives are prescribed by the mall, by the 7-Eleven, by the Internal Revenue Service. Our imaginations vacillate between our parents, and the repellent plate-glass doors of a real American city, which has been good to us.

Hispanic-American culture stands where the past meets the future. The cultural meeting represents not just a Hispanic milestone, not simply a celebration at the crossroads. America transforms into pleasure what it cannot avoid. Hispanic-American culture of the sort that is now in evidence (the teen movie, the rock song) may exist in an hourglass, may in fact be irrelevant. The U.S. Border Patrol works through the night to arrest the flow of illegal immigrants over the border, even as Americans stand patiently in line for *La Bamba*. While Americans vote to declare, once and for all, that English shall be the official language of the U.S., Madonna starts recording in Spanish.

Before a national TV audience, Rita Moreno tells Geraldo Rivera that her dream as an actress is to play a character rather like herself: "I speak English perfectly well . . . I'm not dying from poverty . . . I want to play *that* kind of Hispanic woman, which is to say, an American citizen." This is an actress talking; these are show-biz pieties. But Moreno expresses as well a general Hispanic-American predicament. Hispanics want to belong to America without betraying the past. Yet we fear losing ground in any negotiation with America. Our fear, most of all, is of losing our culture.

We come from an expansive, an intimate, culture that has long been judged second-rate by the U.S. Out of pride as much as affection, we are reluctant to give up our past. Our notoriety in the U.S. has been our resistance to assimilation. The guarded symbol of Hispanic-American culture has been the tongue of flame: Spanish. But the remarkable legacy Hispanics carry from Latin America is not language—an inflatable skin—but breath itself, capacity of soul, an inclination to live. The genius of Latin America is the habit of synthesis. We assimilate.

What Latin America knows is that people create one another when they meet. In the music of Latin America you will hear the litany of bloodlines: the African drum, the German accordion, the cry from the minaret. The U.S. stands as the opposing New World experiment. In North America the Indian and the European stood separate. Whereas Latin America was formed by a Catholic dream of one world, of meltdown conversion, the U.S. was shaped by Protestant individualism. America has believed its national strength derives from separateness, from diversity. The glamour of the U.S. is the Easter promise: you can be born again in your lifetime. You can separate yourself from your past. You can get a divorce, lose weight, touch up your roots.

Immigrants still come for that promise, but the U.S. has wavered in its faith. America is no longer sure that economic strength derives from individualism. And America is no longer sure that there is space enough, sky enough, to sustain the cabin on the prairie. Now, as we near the end of the American Century, two alternative cultures beckon the American imagination: the Asian and the Latin American. Both are highly communal cultures, in contrast to the literalness of American culture. Americans devour what they might otherwise fear to become. Sushi will make them lean, subtle corporate warriors. Combination Plate No. 3, smothered in mestizo gravy, will burn a hole in their hearts.

Latin America offers passion. Latin America has a life—big clouds, unambiguous themes, tragedy, epic—that the U.S., for all its quality of life, yearns to have. Latin America offers an undistressed leisure, a crowded kitchen table, even a full sorrow. Such is the urgency of America's need that it reaches right past a fledgling, homegrown Hispanic-American culture for the darker bottle of Mexican beer, for the denser novel of a Latin American master.

For a long time, Hispanics in the U.S. felt hostility. Perhaps because we were preoccupied by nostalgia, we withheld our Latin American gift. We denied the value of assimilation. But as our presence is judged less foreign in America, we will produce a more generous art, less timid, less parochial. Hispanic Americans do not have a pure Latin American art to offer. Expect bastard themes. Expect winking ironies, comic conclusions. For Hispanics live on this side of the border, where Kraft manufactures Mexican-style Velveeta, and where Jack in the Box serves Fajita Pita. Expect marriage. We will change America even as we will be changed. We will disappear with you into a new miscegenation.

Along and across the border there remain real conflicts, real fears. But the ancient tear separating Europe from itself—the Catholic Mediterranean from the Protestant north—may yet heal itself in the New World. For generations, Latin America has been the place, the bed, of a confluence of so many races and cultures that Protestant North America shuddered to imagine it.

The time has come to imagine it.

## About the Author

Richard Rodriguez, a free-lance writer, editor and expert on Hispanic affairs, is the author of *Hunger of Memory: The Education of Richard Rodriguez.* This article was edited by *Time* from an original piece entitled "Children of a Marriage" and permission to reproduce it is available exclusively through the author's agent. Contact Georges Borchardt, Inc. at (212) 753-5785; Fax: (212) 838-6518.

---

### BIAS BY DEFAULT
by James Fallows

The world is full of "close-enough" judgments, which are also known as "prejudice." Statistically, the average American is five hundred times more likely to be infected with Acquired Immune Deficiency Syndrome than is the average Japanese, and American male homosexuals are many times more likely than anyone else. Therefore, because I'm American, people in Tokyo might be justified, on close-enough grounds, in avoiding touching the commuter strap I'd held in a subway for instance, and heterosexual Americans might be justified in shunning homosexuals altogether. This policy would be "close enough," but it would be ugly and unfair. Statistically, the average black American man is more likely to be a criminal, a drug abuser, and a credit risk than the average white American. Therefore, employers would be "close enough" if they refused to hire any blacks.

Excerpted from *More Like Us: Making America Great Again,* by James Fallows, Houghton Mifflin Co., 1989.
Reprinted with permission.

# Only English Spoken Here: Language as Politics Spawns a Backlash Against Immigrants

by Margaret Carlson. Reported by Careth Ellingson and Cristina Garcia (*TIME Magazine*)

At a Los Angeles Hospital, the head nurse forbade workers to speak anything but English and urged employees to report anyone overheard using another language. The city council in Monterey Park, a suburb of L.A., ousted the trustees of the library for buying foreign-language books and magazines. The manager of an insurance company in Los Angeles ordered Chinese-American staffers to speak only English unless they were dealing with a Chinese-speaking customer.

These incidents and others like them occurred in the wake of California's adoption two years ago of an initiative declaring English the official language. Until recently language, which has sparked wars and altered national boundaries abroad, was not a political issue in this country. Now a growing number of Americans seem to feel their mother tongue needs protection. Voters in Florida, Arizona and Colorado have approved similar initiatives, bringing to 17 the number of states with such laws.

These victories have made U.S. English, the group that sponsored the initiatives, a formidable political force. Founded with the guidance of linguist S. I. Hayakawa, a former U.S. Senator from California, the 350,000-member organization is seeking a constitutional amendment making English the official language of the U.S. Says Steve Workings, the group's director of government affairs: "Language is one of the very few things we have in common in the U.S." U.S. English urges a written English-proficiency test for naturalization. It also advocates an end to bilingual ballots and an increase in funds for bilingual education, though only for short-term, transitional programs. Current bilingual courses, the group claims, fail students by weaning them from their mother tongues too slowly. "It is cultural maintenance, not language acquisition," says Workings.

> **Seventeen states have reaffirmed English as their official language. Advocacy groups urge:**
>
> ■ Printing ballots only in English. They plan to challenge multilingual provisions of the federal Voting Rights Act.
>
> ■ Limiting bilingual education to "transitional" status. Current programs can last four to six years before students are ready for regular classes.
>
> ■ Tightening standards that measure English-language proficiency for would-be citizens.

Opponents of the official-English movement consider it to be no more than a socially acceptable way of tapping into xenophobic fears: fear of being outnumbered by immigrants, fear that jobs are in jeopardy from cheap labor, just plain fear of anyone different. Stewart Kwoh, executive director of the Asian Pacific American Legal Center of Southern California, charges the initiatives are partly responsible for unleashing a backlash against foreign-language minorities. Colleen O'Connor, spokeswoman of the American Civil Liberties Union, says the initiatives shout, "You're here but we would like to make it difficult for you." Even conservatives like Arizona Senator John McCain oppose initiatives like the one just passed in his state. Says McCain: "Our nation and the English language have done quite well with Chinese spoken in California, German in Pennsylvania, Italian in New York, Swedish in Minnesota and Spanish in the Southwest. I fail to see the cause for alarm now."

But others do. The sheer numbers of Hispanic immigrants, their cohesiveness and their growing political power set these immigrants apart from earlier groups who had to assimilate or fail. In the Miami area, for example, Spanish-language versions of everything from lottery tickets to televised game shows, as well as bilingual shops and restaurants and even jobs where only Spanish is acceptable, make it possible to live a full life without ever learning English. So widespread had Spanish become in Miami that in 1978 Emmy Shafer started the English-only movement when she could not find a clerk in the Dade County municipal offices who could speak English to her.

Those who believe that the movement inflames nativist resentments got some ammunition this fall. The ethnocentric views of U.S. English's co-founder and former chairman John Tanton came to light when initiative opponents uncovered a 1986 memo in which he expressed worry that low white birthrates and high Hispanic birthrates would endanger American society. Wrote Tanton: "Perhaps this is the first instance in which those with their pants up are going to get caught by those with their pants down." Board member Linda Chavez, former staff director of the Civil Rights Commission and later candidate for the U.S. Senate from Maryland, quit in disgust, as did Walter Cronkite, and Tanton was forced to leave the organization.

Tanton aside, the English-language movement is something of a political hybrid, resisting categorization. Former and current members of the board of directors of U.S. English like Chavez and Cronkite, Bruno Bettelheim, Saul Bellow and Alistair Cooke are hardly xenophobes. They believe that, in a land that was founded by immigrants, English is the essential unifying force. The propositions they support may be little more than useless clutter, a reassurance that the U.S. is not vulnerable to a Quebec-style bilingualism with all its attendant bitterness. Ironically, it is the debate over the ballot initiatives themselves that has created so much rancor.

◆

---

## IS ASSIMILATION SIMPLY WHITE MALE DOMINATION?

How do we deal with these changes [of ethnic, cultural, and gender differences in the workplace]? Who accommodates to whom? Should employees continue to assimilate into organizational cultures premised on Western values? Or should we "celebrate differences" and critique organizational cultures allegedly created by and for white males in order to make other people more comfortable?

Sondra Thiederman and Tom Kochman are fairly non-ideological PhD pros who offer sensible cross-cultural instruction about the thoughtways and habits of black, minority-immigrant, and female employees and customers. (They're careful to talk about diversity within cultural groups and not to create new stereotypes—an admitted problem in the diversity biz.)

But the more ambitious gurus of diversity management—such as Elsie Cross, R. Roosevelt Thomas (*Beyond Race and Gender*), and Ann Morrison (*The Glass Ceiling, The New Leaders*)—see assimilation as a cover for white male domination.

Frederick R. Lynch
An excerpt from "Workforce Diversity: PC's Final Frontier?"
National Review (2/21/94)

# When Language Causes a Barrier

by Lee Gardenswartz and Anita Rowe

- *You overhear a couple of colleagues speaking together in their native language. You feel left out and wonder if they are talking about you.*
- *You have a difficult time understanding the heavily accented English of some of your co-workers. You hesitate to keep asking them to repeat what they've said as you don't want to offend them.*
- *You speak fluent though accented English. You feel that you are understood, but often you have the feeling that what you say is discounted because of your accent.*

Language, one of the main tools for controlling our world can also produce obstacles that limit our ability to communicate. In today's workplace where it is not uncommon for employees of 10 or more ethnic groups to work together, differences in language often add another hurdle to the communication process. As an employee in such an environment, how can you prevent language differences from hindering your interactions and blocking your work relationships?

1. **Understand the reasons why people speak another language on the job.**

   Non-native speakers of English say they lapse into their native languages for a number of reasons. First, and probably most obvious, it is easier to communicate in a language that is second nature rather than to struggle with an adopted one. Some even say it is a stress reliever to relax in the comfort of their mother tongue. Second, communicating in one's native language may also make for a more accurate exchange of information. Third, some employees are unsure of their skills in English and may be afraid of making embarrassing mistakes.

2. **Recognize and question your assumptions.**

   Could the employees you overheard be talking about a work problem, their families or the weather, rather than about you? Would your co-workers who speak with an accent prefer you ask them to repeat rather than have you walk away confused? Could you be unknowingly discounting another employee? One employee recently commented that he was confronted with his own incorrect assumption, when he was surprised to learn that his newcomer colleague could speak five languages and had an advanced degree from his native country. Recognizing and questioning your own knee jerk assumptions when you encounter language impasses is critical to overcoming them.

3. **Create options and alternatives.**

   Ask yourself what you can do to overcome the obstacle. Finding ways to deal with the blocks you are experiencing can reduce frustration and help you gain control. Letting people know how you feel, "When you speak together in another language, I feel left out," is one possibility. Another is asking for a translation, "I'd like to hear your idea. Could you say it in English, too?" Asking for help from your colleague is another option, "How can I let you know I don't understand without offending you?" Still another suggestion is to spend time with people of the different language background learning the most common sound patterns and substitutions. For example, Spanish speakers often substitute "ch" for "sh". Having interpreters on call, such as with ATT's language line, is yet another alternative. Finally, using diagrams, sign language and other non-verbal methods may also help.

4. **Build relationships.**

   It's often amazing to see that language becomes less and less of an issue when people begin to get to know and care about one another. The more time you spend with co-workers of different language backgrounds the easier you will find it is to understand each other. The language of caring and respect knows no nationality.

## About the Authors

Lee Gardenswartz, Ph.D. and Anita Rowe, Ph.D. have authored *Managing Diversity: A Com-* *plete Desk Reference and Planning Guide* (Business One Irwin, 1993). They can be reached at: 12658 W. Washington Boulevard, Suite 105, Los Angeles, CA 90066. Phone: (310) 823-2466; Fax: (310) 823-3923. This article originally appeared in the *Managing Diversity Newsletter*, P.O. Box 819, Jamestown, NY 14702-0819. Phone: (716) 665-3654; Fax: (716) 665-8060.

# Skills for Future Success

by Everett T. Robinson

Besides the skills related to personal style development, there are some specific skills you need to develop if you want to be in high demand in the future. Future predictions indicate that there will be many major shifts within the world of work in the next decade. The beginning of such shifts is rapidly appearing in the economies of the world.

For example, the center of the financial world is now located in Tokyo rather than in Europe or America. It is also noteworthy that more North American trade crosses the Pacific Ocean than the Atlantic. In addition, many of yesterday's major manufacturing services are now located in underdeveloped countries where labor is less expensive. These and other trends have many futurists claiming most employment in the future will fall into the following five career areas:

1. Services

2. Information

3. Tourism

4. Entertainment/Recreation

5. Space-and ocean-related technology

---

## HOW MUCH DO YOU NEED TO KNOW?

Diversity in U.S. organizations is about difference as it affects getting, holding, and succeeding at a job. These are very concrete objectives that take place in a cultural context. If culture is a set of rules about the way of doing things developed by a group of people, this way of doing things always corresponds to what needs to be done for the success and survival of the group. Success is defined as performing in the world or the part of it in which one places him or herself. Thus, going to work in the U.S. means either becoming an entrepreneur who must succeed in a specific market niche or setting, or joining a group of people in a organization or company where a specific mission and objectives already exist (whether they are written down or not).

The newcomer, though she or he may (hopefully) bring fresh ideas, resources, outlooks and creativity to the job and even, in some cases, eventually transform or come to own the company, must at the outset interact with the existing culture enough to be a part of its successful functioning toward its objectives. This implies varying degrees of communicative ability (language and interaction skills) and an ability to do the work assigned (technical knowledge and skills). In some cases this will mean speaking enough Eng-

*continued on next page*

## HOW MUCH DO YOU NEED TO KNOW?
### (continued)

lish or Spanish or Creole to serve the customer and make change for a twenty. In other cases it will mean mastery of a computer programming language in order to create a customized spreadsheet.

The workplace, the market, and the existing culture of specific organizations all demand a degree of acculturation in those who would enter them. "Getting real," for most people, means engaging this world of work in a productive and constructive way, even if one intends to change it. There will of course, always be some drop-outs, critics and prophets who will proclaim and live out an alternative reality. These are important citizens, too, because they keep us from being possessed and destroyed by our own culture's reinforcement of itself. They help the rest of us to think about what we do and make it more appropriate, thus preventing widespread alienation.

By and large, however, we do what needs to be done (work) with the tools that we shape for the task (culture). The culture that we have created, however, in turn dictates the work to be done. This means that the future success of diverse populations depends on their ability to bring their cultural resources to bear on the work to be done. The nature of that challenge will depend on what the work itself is like. The accompanying article, "Skills for Future Success," discusses what's required in the future in the U.S. workplace culture. It's really just another way of describing what much of the work is going to be like in the future. Use it as a starting point for asking how the resources of your diverse workforce can be brought to bear, not only on how to accomplish the tasks, but to decide on what the tasks should be.

—Ed.

Those individuals who want to be employed in a high salary position will need to have the knowledge and skills required for the job. Those individuals without the necessary education will run a greater risk of working for less money or being unemployed. A higher education is now positively correlated with higher earnings. It is essential that effective skills be developed if career-seekers want to be competitive in their career search. Regardless of what your personal style is, you will need skills to succeed in the world of work. The following is a quick list of 15 skill areas that are presently highly valued within the work world. I anticipate that they will continue to be needed in the work world of the future.

1. *Self-Management Skills*

   Self-management involves all skills that are related to self-control. Having these skills increases your effectiveness when interacting with others. Examples of this type of skill would be telling the truth, controlling your temper, being polite, dressing appropriately, and having patience. While these skills will not get you work, not having them can keep you from being hired.

2. *Coping Skills*

   These skills are behaviors that help you deal with pressure and stress. Situations in life often leave individuals feeling overwhelmed. Successfully managing stressful life situations requires skills such as developing support relationships, knowing where to get help if needed, not overreacting to problem situations, and being resourceful. Coping skills help you keep the pressure at "arm's length" so that you have a chance to problem-solve and make decisions.

3. *Assertiveness Skills*

   Assertiveness is often equated with aggressiveness, which is far from the truth. Aggressiveness occurs when you get what you need or want at the expense of others. Assertiveness is the ability to get what you need or want without disrespecting or hurting others. Skills in this area would include speaking appropriately when telling others how you are feeling and what is important to you, saying no to people who are pressuring you into doing something you don't want to do, and asking for what you need.

**4.** *Problem-Solving Skills*

Knowing how to solve daily problems takes skill. People who can work through difficult dilemmas and situations tend to be more successful and happy in life than those who can't. A major factor in problem-solving is long-range planning. Many problems arise from short-sighted planning and could be avoided with more follow-through. Skills like editing, estimating, analyzing, calculating, and investigating can help you solve problems and lower the chances of creating situations in the future that will lead to additional problems.

**5.** *Decision-Making Skills*

One thing which is certain about the present age we live in, and which will probably hold true in the future, is that life is more complex than ever before. Technology has exacerbated the pressures in daily living. If you have trouble making decisions now, you may experience more stress as time goes on because you will be required to make more decisions in less time. These daily decisions must be made if you are to interact effectively within society. Decision-making skills such as accurately assessing situations, weighing information, evaluating alternatives, considering short-and long-range costs and gains, and making a commitment are some examples of decision-making skills.

**6.** *Communication Skills—Written and Oral*

Over the last generation, written and oral skills have become increasingly important, yet it is increasingly difficult to find employees with these skills. Skills such as reading, spelling, writing, word usage, editing, and public speaking are valuable in many work settings. With the information age coming to power within the marketplace, the ability to communicate effectively will become a more valuable skill and a more common requirement for employment.

**7.** *Interpersonal Communication Skills*

With jobs getting harder to obtain, the ability to impress others will be of greater importance. Having good interpersonal communication skills is one way of showing others that

you are ready and willing to be a productive part of their work team. Such skills also help you develop relationships with customers, co-workers and supervisors. Such skills can be of even bigger benefit in other areas of life such as marriage, parenting, and doing public or community service. Centering, attending, checking for accuracy, active listening, confrontation, and responding with understanding are a few skills of this type.

**8.** *Job Search Skills*

Finding work and convincing others that you are the best person for the job has never been easy, but in the future it will become even more difficult. Having the skills necessary for obtaining work can be a real plus for you, as many people lack skills of this type. Writing resumes and cover letters, identifying job prospects, initiating contact with potential employers, and successful interviewing would be examples of job search skills.

**9.** *Job Maintenance Skills*

Obtaining work is one thing; not getting fired is another. With more and more people wanting to work, employers do not have to settle for less than the best, and as the number of workers increases in the future, they will become even more demanding and evaluative. Skills such as time management, consistent work performance, being trustworthy, being trainable and other skills like these will often determine which employee stays and which one goes.

**10.** *Computer Skills*

Most jobs in the future will have something to do with computers. Having a basic working knowledge and skill level will even be mandatory for many low-skilled jobs. Programming, word processing, analyzing data, taking inventory, and many other computer-related skills will be needed in the work force, and individuals with skills of this type will be given preference in hiring.

**11.** *Research Skills*

Since information and knowledge will be of primary value in the future, all jobs that involve inquiries of any kind will require research skills. These skills will help you learn how to locate up-to-date information and how to utilize it in a manner that will be valuable to others. Research skills include investigating, studying, compiling, organizing and presenting information; conducting statistical analysis; and knowing how to use a library.

### 12. *Leadership Skills*

It can sometimes be difficult to find individuals who have the requirements necessary to be effective leaders. It takes both personal characteristics and knowledge to guide others successfully. Leaders must have many of the skill areas that have been previously mentioned, such as decision-making skills and communication skills. In addition, they also need to demonstrate administrative skills, the ability to delegate, group process skills for team meetings, and organizational skills.

### 13. *Instructional/Training/Facilitation Skills*

The ability to teach others what you know will be a very marketable skill in the future. To do this with success, skills such as lesson planning, presenting information, using educational aids, testing, modeling, giving feedback, and evaluating will be needed. While many workers are proficient in their jobs, they don't always have the skills to help train new employees. Having group process skills to facilitate classroom learning will make you a valuable asset to any employer.

### 14. *Cross-Cultural Skills*

As previously mentioned, more and more business is being conducted in international markets. Individuals with knowledge and skills related to different cultures will be sought after. Having skills such as speaking and writing in different languages, understanding different customs and religions, and establishing a network of contacts in foreign countries can be to your advantage in finding work.

### 15. *Entrepreneurial Skills*

While not everyone is capable of going out and starting their own business, this type of employment is currently on the increase. Many jobs in the future will be service-oriented. Success in your own business will require most of the skills previously mentioned and others such as selling yourself and your ideas, acquiring working capital, accurate market analysis, production and promotion of services, and accounting and financial planning.

## About the Author

Everett T. Robinson, M.A., has over a decade of experience as an author, seminar leader, trainer and professional counselor. He has led personal and professional development workshops and courses for over 4,000 people. He has co-authored the Personal Style Indicator (PSI), the Job Style Indicator (JSI), and *Why Aren't You More Like Me?* (available from HRD Press at 800-822-2801; Fax 413-253-3490).

Everett T. Robinson is internationally recognized as an authority on the subject of personal style differences. He can be reached at Consulting Resource Group International, Inc., 386-200 West Third St., Sumas, WA 98295-8000; Phone: 604-852-0566; Fax: 604-850-3003.

# A Case for Moving from Tolerance to Valuing Diversity: The Issue of Religiously Distinctive Dress and Appearance

by Hindy Lauer Schachter (*Review of Public Personnel Administration*)

What are the administrative implications of public agency dress codes that have the effect of barring an employee from maintaining a personal appearance mandated by his or her religion? I assert that the issue should be reconceptualized as one centering on workforce diversity.

Absent specific state or agency dress regulations, public-sector employees can wear religiously distinctive clothing (such as a nun's habit) in governmental functions. Restrictive codes exist in many jurisdictions, however, and they have engendered many conflicts that have escalated into court cases in federal, state and local settings—including the military, police and fire, education and the judicial system. The debate is presented as one between the right of a public organization to promote uniformity or religious neutrality versus the employee's right to free exercise of his or her religion. This style of presentation allows the agency to claim that it maximizes its own goals by prohibiting employees from wearing religiously-mandated garb.

The argument of this article is that public managers should take a broader orientation to religious appearance issues and should not see allowing religiously-mandated dress as simply a question of toleration (important as that may be). The question should be viewed as a key human resource management issue that speaks directly to the extent to which political leaders and agency executives prize workforce diversity. The stakeholders in dress disputes are not limited to the agency personnel directly involved; they include the entire political community.

People wear distinctive clothing for many reasons. The issue of allowing religiously-mandated dress is part of the question of whether public employees should be able to wear any clothing that does not interfere with getting a job done (e.g.,

does not produce a safety hazard or depart from universally recognized professional standards such as cleanliness). This article concentrates on increasing latitude for religiously mandated clothing because current bans on such attire have the effect of excluding members of minority religions from certain branches of the public service. This indirect outcome of dress codes may be managerially problematic when those agencies are supposed to serve the entire community without favoring or disfavoring any particular religious group.

A representative workforce communicates an important impression of social fairness in public institutions and provides role models for minority group members. Religious representativeness differs in two significant ways from participation by race and gender.

First, current questions of religious diversity involve the treatment of behavior (e.g., wearing distinctive dress, refusing to work on the Sabbath) rather than ascriptive status. The questions of making it easier for people from minority religions to work in public agencies is always a question of degree; even those who argue for much more latitude than the current situation allows might still say that some restrictions may have to remain.

Second, a state could not promulgate goals for religious representativeness as it does for racial or gender participation. The first amendment both prohibits the government from interfering with an individual's free exercise of religion and from making laws that establish a given faith. Yet, it is wrong to suggest that this means the government is prohibited from doing anything to promote religious diversity among its employees.

Dress codes diminish the atmosphere of hospitality if they restrict public-sector workforce participation of people from minority religions.

The public service equity issue of the 1990s will be how agencies react to behavioral diversity in a multicultural workforce. To some commentators increased diversity means that organizations will face a problem in acculturating employees. But an agency that respects the uniqueness of its minority cultures will find that members of traditionally under-represented groups can bring new ways of looking at problems that increase the organization's ability to deal creatively with its environment.

Do employees have the right to a personal appearance that is mandated by their faith but that contravenes organizational dress codes? Much can be learned about a society's cultural climate by seeing how decision makers respond to minority requests to wear religiously distinctive clothing; a different climate prevails when agencies refuse such requests than when they see them as an advantageous opening to encouraging a more diverse workforce.

The legal record is pretty dismal for sustaining a public employee's right to wear religiously distinctive clothing in the face of dress codes prohibiting this behavior. Courts generally defer to legislative and bureaucratic arguments that diverse dress inhibits agency performance even though public agencies have brought scant evidence at best to show a negative outcome attributed to greater tolerance.

The courts allow agencies to limit employee action stemming from religious convictions in ways they would never tolerate in matters relating to race or gender. Not so many years ago, military and police units might have argued that they needed racial and gender uniformity to create instinctive obedience and esprit de corps. Which court would tolerate such rhetoric now? The unit commander would be told to train the officers to feel a sense of solidarity across racial and gender boundaries.

In my own lifetime a police department might have refused to hire African Americans or women on the grounds that the public would be hostile to such officers. Which judge would listen to this argument today? The department would be told that the community's prejudices cannot affect Affirmative Action hiring. Why then does a court accept rhetoric about community hostility in the case of religious attire or religiously mandated beards?

For many people the animosity to religiously motivated dress stems from a belief that this is a distinctive form of behavior that the employee can

(and thus should) change at will. The clothing that lands public employees in court is not simply dress with a religious origin, but more precisely garments that appear odd to the majority at a given time and which key decision makers do not want to see on people who perform respected, visible public actions. It should be recalled in this connection that throughout the nineteenth century some teachers taught in Protestant clerical garb without objections being raised; when immigrant Catholic groups wanted to teach in clothing distinctive of their faith, however, state laws were passed (and upheld by courts) to prevent it.

The court argued that since religious liberty is a fundamental value, the government must satisfy a considerable burden before it can put pressure on a person to forego a tenet of his or her faith. Through factual evidence (not speculation), the government must demonstrate that a compelling state interest is at stake and the restriction on religious liberty is the least burdensome way of protecting that important state interest.

Agencies have bolstered their claims of state interest through speculation rather than facts (e.g., people might not respect officers with beards, students might believe the state of Oregon favored the Sikh religion, etc.). The public agencies in question have not considered whether less restrictive statutes could protect laudable goals such as maintaining religious neutrality in schools. Far from treating religious liberty as needing special protection, some agencies give greater deference to secular reasons for avoiding dress regulations by permitting beards on officers with medical problems but not on men with sincere religious motivations.

To imagine how these conflicts would look if approached from a diversity-centered viewpoint, let us examine the arguments made in the case of Janet Cooper, a Sikh convert. Using conventional neutrality-centered arguments, the school district asserted that Cooper could not teach in religiously-distinctive clothing because this might convince children who were not Sikhs that the state favored Cooper's faith. This perspective sets up a conflict between the first amendment's no establishment and free exercise clauses—and the no establishment clause wins (without much contest).

A diversity-centered approach would begin by acknowledging that the power relations of American society are such that it is extremely unlikely that a few teachers in turbans could convince any child that the government favors the Sikh religion. What actually happens is that the policy hurts the school's ability to deal with Sikh children because the dress code says to such pupils that the most loyal and conscientious members of their own religion are not wanted as public school teachers. It also harms the school's ability to foster tolerance within majority-group children because the policy teaches them that diversity is unimportant. It shows them that the school district only recognizes one style of dress—that of centrist Christians. Constitutionally, the dress code can be shown to trample on both the free exercise and no establishment provisions of the Bill of Rights.

In all the conflicts I have researched, agencies are embarrassing and alienating minority religious groups (whose members these public organizations are supposed to serve) while teaching citizens from mainstream Protestant backgrounds that symbols of rival faiths are divisive for the polity. The clothes that both the majority and minority administrators wear to work inevitably send powerful nonverbal messages; restrictive dress codes allow only one message to get through.

A diversity-centered approach would also note that organizations suffer when they must dismiss otherwise competent employees because their dress differs from that of the majority. As far as public records show, all of the people who brought suits were performing satisfactorily when religiously mandated dress cost them their jobs. The number of potential civil servants affected by dress codes is much larger than the court record indicates. While our cities need additional police and teachers, are we prepared to bypass all those candidates with beards or headscarfs? Such exclusion is particularly vexing when these people may have special talent in dealing with clients from their own communities or those of other religious minorities.

The time has come to be proactive in encouraging diverse behavior among public employees, a celebration of difference mirroring the actual heterogeneity occurring in our country. One place to start is by encouraging public-sector workers to dress in conformity with their own cultural and religious convictions as long as these do not pose health or safety hazards. In most of these cases I have investigated, safety considerations are irrelevant.

Increasingly, public agencies say they want to be representative and responsive to diversity. Yet some organizations maintain dress and appearance codes that preclude employing members of religious minorities even though no hard evidence exists that these appearance regulations are necessary for job performance. These codes are relics of a time when ascriptive and behavioral uniformity were considered organizational advantages. Today, scholars and practitioners are more likely to state that representativeness and diversity of personnel constitute assets to an organization in meeting its goals—particularly if one of these goals is to offer services to a multicultural population. When worn by public administrators, religiously distinctive dress could constitute a visible confirmation of an agency's desire to serve diverse populations with dignity; such confirmation is long overdue.

## About the Author

Hindy Lauer Schachter is a management professor at the New Jersey Institute of Technology and the author of *Public Agency Communications*. She has had articles published in *Public Administration Review*, *Administration and Society*, and other journals. She can be contacted at: N.J.I.T., Newark, NJ 07102; Phone: (201) 596-3251; Fax: (201) 596-3074

# Beauty Pays—Thank Goodness You've Got It≠

by George F. Simons & Sally J. Walton

Hiring and displaying people of good looks has been part of both the implicit and explicit image and advertising strategy of many organizations. Many of us can remember favoritism based on looks in our own families, at school or in our own work life. Studies now prove beyond a reasonable doubt that, all things being equal (and sometimes when they are not), the good-looking get the job, the sale, the raise, or the promotion, in preference to their less attractive counterparts. Researchers can even identify the facial proportions which result in cuteness.

But beauty is fickle and cultural in its definition. What was handsome or beautiful in one age or place may be perceived as ugly in a later one. Today the mature and substantial figures of successful and beautiful men and women, admired in past centuries, have stepped aside for the lean and lithe. In the more loosely knit North American culture, where the future counts more than the past, age is not valued for wisdom and experience. Youth is preferred for its vitality, its flexibility and its future potential. We have stopped burning witches, but there is still substantial discrimination against older women and women who do not fit the categories of being young and single, or belonging to a traditional family.

The American Society of Plastic and Reconstructive Surgery recently reported that 25% of its patients were male, up from 5% a decade ago. Many are executives and businessmen reshaping their faces and removing fat at considerable (non-insured) expense, fully conscious that success follows the appearance of youth and energy in American culture. Moreover in a culture where identity is unsure, good looks pay off in confidence and self-esteem for those who have them or can get them. Not surprisingly, image making has become a lucrative profession, since having beautiful people on the front lines creates a competitive edge.

Discrimination on the basis of age and weight, like race, sex, and disability, is beginning to have legal recourse. Recently our town debated an ordinance forbidding employers to discriminate in hiring on the basis of looks. Can one define and enforce something so culture bound? In the meanwhile, most of us must make fair, ethical, and sound business decisions in the face of the payoffs of glamour. We do need to learn how to look at each other better, because the fact is that we have already been educated to perceive others in ways that are painful and discriminatory.

For the moment, we can begin to address the countless injustices that occur daily, by training our own sensitivities to catch our prejudices before they result in discriminatory behavior. Why we like or dislike, choose or reject people, often has little to do with our conscious selection process. Subtle cultural biases sway our minds even when we follow fair procedures for interviewing and assessing others. Criminals who don't look right or are the wrong color, for example, spend more time behind bars than others. Though we've long recognized that ethnic and racial traits provide easy triggers for discrimination our minds still do it. Arab Americans can attest to this, now that their looks form the latest bad guy stereotype in movies and on TV.

Looks and class are associated in U.S. culture. Being slender is perceived as an upper class trait. Americans, who eschew class distinctions, bow to a hidden class system in much of what they do and appearances trigger such classifications.

One image-conscious organization employed female models instead of women peers and employees to stand in next to its male executives in the photographs used in its 10K report. Blatant sexism? Certainly, but we cannot successfully address gender as a cultural factor without seeing how intimately people's perceptions of beauty, success, and even their sense of safety is related to looks. Organizations can improve this situation, by presenting their real people to each other. Internal media (posters, demo and training tapes, etc.) can help us value diversity by power broadening our perception of what is beautiful. A well acknowledged and fairly treated workforce will outperform one which relies on superficial glamour.

---

**BOTTOM LINE #1**

Become aware of how personal appearances may create unfairness to individuals and damage productivity in your organization.

---

Of the two authors of this article, one is beautiful and the other handsome. Valuing diversity taught us how to be so. Perhaps the most important factor in feeling and being beautiful is recognition by others and the self-esteem which it creates. Here is the story of how it happened to one of us. "In the early days of my childhood, blond, curly hair and straight, turned-up noses were the ideal image of a little girl. As I grew, I knew that I did not meet that ideal. Before I traveled abroad, I was self-conscious about my "Roman nose," aware that some even used surgery to correct such a profile.

"I emerged from a small town in Pennsylvania to launch my international career, and discovered after two years in Chile, that I looked Chilena. As I traveled throughout Latin America, other Latinos usually thought I was Chilena, in part from my increasingly fluent Spanish which bore the flavor of Chile, and in part from my appearance, which was considered attractive!

"I traveled among Europeans and other internationals who often gave favorable comments about my appearance. I was often asked if I were French. (Not, however, because of my fluent French!) In Egypt and the Middle East, I finally realized that I may not have been an American beauty, but my beauty was much more universal.

"The most memorable incident came in India where I was a dinner guest of U.S. American missionaries. The husband, a Lutheran minister, suddenly blurted out at the dinner table with a tone of admiration, even awe, in his voice as he studied my profile, "You look just like Queen Nefertiti." I don't know exactly why his wife was so flustered and embarrassed, and asked him to stop saying such things immediately, but I was never asked to dinner there again. It greatly enhanced my self image to know that my beauty was admired even by a fellow countryman, albeit a well traveled one.

So the next time you think you are:

- too fat or too thin,
- too dark or too light,
- too curly or too straight,
- too bosomy or too flat-chested,

remember there is a cultural beauty ideal somewhere in the world that just matches YOU.

---

**BOTTOM LINE #2**

Seeing beauty as diverse can help us see ourselves as beautiful

---

Travel the globe, or just look around you. The richness of cultural diversity offers many gifts—and enhanced self image is one of them.

Admiring others for who they are and how they look is not out-of-style nor is it sexual harassment, if you do it with full appreciation and without the desire to manipulate. It also calls the attention of others in earshot to beauty they may have missed about the people they see every day. They won't be jealous, of course, because you'll be admiring them as well. Therefore, always keep in mind

---

**THE WALTON-SIMONS COROLLARY**

Don't be so politically correct that you fail to tell the people you work with the many ways in which they are beautiful.

---

## About the Authors

George Simons is President of George Simons International, a diversity training and consulting firm located in Santa Cruz, CA. See full biography and contact information on page 505.

Sally Walton, also based in Santa Cruz, CA is a professional speaker, author, and consultant on maximizing human performance with a global perspective. She can be reached at: Global Perspectives, 504 Cliff Street, Santa Cruz, CA 95060; Phone: 408-429-8308; Fax: 408-429-9393.

# Recognizing the "New" Racism: Its Causes and Consequences

by John Dovidio

Race relations in the United States are better now than ever before. Or are they? On the one hand, the dramatic positive impact of the Civil Rights Legislation of the 1960s is undeniable. Before this legislation, in many parts of the country it was customary for whites to limit the freedom of blacks (e.g., limiting blacks to the back of buses), to demand deference from blacks (e.g., requiring blacks to give up their seats to whites on buses), and to restrict residential, educational, and employment opportunities for blacks. Under the Civil Rights Legislation, discrimination and segregation became no longer simply immoral, but also illegal. As a consequence, black Americans currently possess greater political, social, and economic power than ever before in our history. On the other hand, there are new signals of deteriorating race rela-

tions. Symptoms of racial tension, which emerged in the 1960s, are reappearing. Over the past five years, over 300 colleges have reported significant racial incidents and protests. As the 1990s began, riots in Miami, Tampa, New Jersey, Washington, DC, and Los Angeles reflected large-scale and violent racial unrest. Over two-thirds of hate crimes today are race-related. This article looks at one factor that contributes to the current frustrations of black Americans: the development of a new, subtle form of racism that is less overt but just as insidious as old-fashioned racism.

## Racial Attitudes in America

Across time, the attitudes of whites toward minorities in general, and blacks in particular, are becoming less negative and more accepting. Negative stereotypes are declining. For example, in

1933, 75% of the white respondents to a survey described blacks as lazy; in 1995, that figure was less than 5%. In addition, current attitudes toward equal opportunity are favorable. In a recent nation-wide Gallup Poll, 97% of white Americans said that they felt that blacks and whites deserve equal employment opportunities, and 76% said that they explicitly supported equal opportunity programs. White America is also becoming more accepting of black leaders. In 1958, the majority of whites reported that they would not be willing to vote for a well-qualified black presidential candidate; in 1991, over 90% said that they would. In addition, the increase in racial tolerance of white Americans extends beyond African Americans. For example, in a 1987 poll, more Americans than ever before were accepting of Hispanic and Jewish neighbors.

Despite these encouraging trends in the racial attitudes of white Americans, there are still reasons for concern. One reason is that, across a variety of surveys and polls, 10–20% of white population still expresses the old-fashioned, overt form of bigotry. These respondents consistently describe African Americans as innately less intelligent than whites, say that they will not vote for a well-qualified presidential candidate simply because that person is African American, and oppose programs designed to insure integration and equal opportunity. Another reason for concern, which is the focus of this article, is that there is also evidence that many of the people who are part of the 80–90% of the white population who say and probably believe that they are not prejudiced may nonetheless be exhibiting a modern, subtle form of bias.

The existence of this subtle form of bias helps to account for the persistence of racism in our society. In a 1988 Gallup Poll, 25% of the African American respondents said that they believed that white people want to hold black people down; 44% of all respondents said that they believed that society is holding blacks down. Furthermore, despite dramatic improvements in whites' expressed racial attitudes over time, racial disparities persist in the United States. Gaps between African Americans and white Americans in the areas of physical health (e.g., infant mortality, life expectancy) and economic well-being (e.g., employment, income, poverty) have continued to exist, and in many cases have actually increased, over the past thirty years.

Subtle bias may also be involved in the complicated reactions that many white Americans have toward programs designed to eliminate racial disparities. White Americans, for example, have very mixed feelings about affirmative action. On the one hand, 76% of whites agree that "affirmative action programs that help Blacks and other minorities get ahead should be supported." On the other hand, there is resistance to the implementation of affirmative action programs. Approximately 80% of whites oppose giving preference to a black worker over a white worker of equal ability. Furthermore, among those whites who report that they endorse preferential treatment in principle, only about one-third will support specific programs reflecting this principle. The pattern of discrepancy between what people say and what they actually do is thus another reason for concern, and it suggests the existence of a more modern, subtle form of prejudice.

## Subtle Prejudice: Aversive Racism

Aversive racism is a subtle form of bias. It characterizes many white Americans who have strong commitments to racial equality and who believe that they are nonprejudiced. Many of these people also possess negative racial feelings and beliefs which they are unaware of or which they try to distance from their nonprejudiced self-images. Because aversive racists truly want to be fair and just people, they will not discriminate against blacks in situations in which discrimination would be obvious to others and themselves. Wrongdoing, which would directly threaten one's nonprejudiced self-image, would be too obvious. However, because aversive racists harbor negative feelings toward blacks, these negative feelings will eventually be expressed, but they will be expressed in subtle, indirect, and rationalizable ways. When an aversive racist can justify or rationalize a negative response on the basis of some factor other than race, discrimination will occur. Under these circumstances, aversive racists may discriminate but in a way that is not obvious and thus protects them from ever having to believe that their behavior was racially motivated.

There are six characteristics that distinguish aversive racists from overt racists. First, aversive racists, compared to old-fashioned racists, argue for fair and just treatment of all groups, at least in principle. Second, despite these good intentions, aversive racists have unconscious negative feelings towards blacks, and thus they try to avoid interracial interaction. Third, when interracial interaction is unavoidable, aversive racists experience anxiety and discomfort in these situations. They try to escape from interracial situations as quickly as possible, not because of anger or racial hatred but because they are nervous and uncomfortable. Fourth, because part of aversive racists' discomfort is based on a concern about appearing prejudiced, when they cannot avoid interracial situations they strictly obey established rules and standards of behavior. Fifth, aversive racists frequently assert that they are colorblind; if they do not see race, then no one can accuse them of being racist. Finally, their negative feelings will get expressed, but in subtle, rationalizable ways that ultimately harm minorities, often by failing to help them.

## The Kitty Genovese Incident

An incident that occurred in New York City in 1964 shows the importance of taking personal responsibility for helping others. Kitty Genovese was returning home one evening. As she entered the parking lot of her building, a man drove up, jumped out of his car, and began to stab her. She screamed. Lights went on in her building. The brutal attack continued for 45 minutes, but no one intervened or even called the police. After he was sure she was dead, the assailant calmly got into his car and drove away.

We know so much about this case because when the police arrived a short time later, they found that there were 38 witnesses who watched the event from beginning to end. How could it happen that none of these people helped, either directly or indirectly? One explanation that psychologists have developed concerns the bystander's sense of responsibility. When a person is the only witness to an emergency, that bystander bears 100% responsibility for helping and 100% of the guilt and blame for not helping. The appropriate behavior in this situation, helping, is clearly defined. If, however, a person witnesses an emergency but believes that somebody else is around who can help or will help, then that bystander's personal responsibility is less clearly defined. Un-

der these circumstances, the bystander could rationalize not helping by coming to believe that someone else will intervene. Of course, if everyone believes that someone else will help, no one will intervene. That presumably was what occurred in the Kitty Genovese incident.

## In the Laboratory

We created a situation like the Kitty Genovese incident, but involving a serious accident rather than a stabbing, to see when whites would help black victims. We led some people to believe that they would be the only witness to this emergency, while we led others to believe that there would be two other people present in this situation who heard the emergency as well. We also varied the race of the victim. In half of the cases the victim was white; in the other half of the cases the victim was black. The participants in the study were white, as were the other two people who were sometimes presumed to be present.

We found that when people were the only witness to the emergency, whites did not discriminate against the black victim. They helped both the black and white victim virtually every time. In this situation, appropriate behavior was clearly defined. To not help a black victim could easily be interpreted, by oneself or others, as racial bias. We also found, however, that whites did discriminate when they believed that two other people witnessed the accident. Here they helped the black victim half as often as they helped the white victim (38% vs. 75%). If this situation were real, the white victim would have died 25% of the time; the black victim would have died 62% of the time. In this situation, whites could justify their failure to help on the basis of some factor other than race—the belief that someone else could help the victim. The nature of the situation therefore determined whether discrimination did or did not occur.

## Evaluating Blacks and Whites

Aversive racism also relates to the way that whites express their attitudes about blacks. For instance, whites typically evaluated blacks and whites equally well when we asked them to rate both groups in general—a situation in which a biased response would be obvious. However, we also found that bias exists in a more subtle form. Although whites' ratings of blacks and whites on negative scales (such as bad or cruel) showed no racial bias, their ratings on positive scales (good and kind) showed a significant difference. In other words, it is not that they say that blacks are worse than whites; this remark could easily be interpreted as racial bias. Instead, they say that whites are better than blacks—a more subtle form of bias. This is not the old-fashioned, overt type of racism associated with the belief about black inferiority. Rather, it is a modern, subtle form of bias that reflects a belief about white superiority.

## Lingering Negative Feelings

Aversive racists may consciously try to suppress their negative feelings about blacks, but these feelings may still linger unconsciously. How can we test for unconscious thoughts and feelings? We have found that by presenting a picture of a black or white face very rapidly (literally in a fraction of a second) and then covering it with a word, the image of the face will register on people's minds even though they are not aware that they had actually seen it. The face becomes a subliminal cue that brings to mind related thoughts and beliefs. Since people are not even consciously aware that they have seen a picture of a black or a white face, these are unconsciously held beliefs that occur automatically and unintentionally. These thoughts and associations are different for black and white faces. Positive traits (e.g., good) come to mind more readily for images of white than for black faces, whereas negative characteristics (e.g., bad) come to mind first for black than for white faces. That is, when we go below the level of consciousness, we now find that there are negative feelings. Not only do whites have more positive feelings about whites than about blacks, but unconsciously they also have more negative associations about blacks than about whites.

What does all this have to do with behavior? If the decisions that people make are biased in systematic ways, they will have biased outcomes for minorities and non-minorities. Attitudes translate into the way people think, and the way people think translates into the way people behave, sometimes in terms of discrimination.

## Higher Status, Greater Bias

We recruited white college students to help us make admissions decisions for their university. They were presented with information about an applicant whose qualifications were systematically varied. Some evaluated a poorly qualified applicant, some rated a moderately qualified candidate, and others judged a highly qualified applicant. In addition, the race of the applicant was varied by a photograph attached to the file. The central question concerned how this picture would affect people's admissions decisions.

Discrimination against the African American applicant occurred, but, as expected, it did not occur equally in all conditions (see Figure 1). Whites rated the poorly qualified African American and white applicants equally low. They showed some bias when they evaluated the moderately qualified white applicant slightly higher than the comparable African American candidate. Discrimination against the black applicant was most apparent, however, when the applicants were highly qualified. Consistent with our other studies, there was no bias on the negative end: Poorly qualified African American applicants were not rated as worse than poorly qualified white applicants. As in the previous studies, discrimination occurred at the positive end. Although whites evaluated the highly qualified African American applicant very positively, they judged the highly qualified white applicant—with exactly the same credentials—as even better.

Although the expression of aversive racism may be subtle, the consequences may be profound. Aversive racism, like more blatant forms, may limit opportunities for blacks and other minorities. Affirmative action, for example, was originally designed to insure fair treatment to historically disadvantaged minorities. Consistent with the idea of aversive racism, resistance to affirmative action is not commonly expressed directly but rather mainly as concerns about individual freedom or about unfair distribution of rewards. Nevertheless, although common protests by whites regarding affirmative action seem to express mainly the concern that qualified whites will be disadvantaged relative to less qualified blacks, it is possible that the reversal of the traditional role relationship, in which whites occupied positions of superior status,

## Figure 1

### Evaluations of Black and White Applicants with Weak, Moderate, and Strong Qualifications

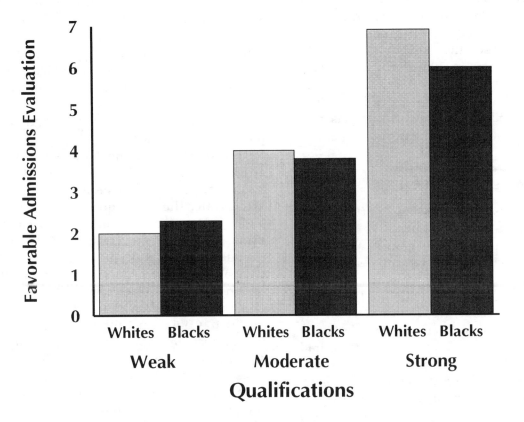

represents the primary threat to whites. We have discovered laboratory evidence that supports this idea that whites react more negatively to higher status blacks. Black supervisors, regardless of how qualified they were for their position, were helped less than both black subordinates and white supervisors. Status, not ability, was the major factor determining reactions to blacks. In general, the higher the status of blacks, the greater the bias expressed by whites.

Aversive racism is difficult to identify definitively in organizations because it is subtle and other explanations are normally possible. We cannot say that simply because disparities exist in organizations, racism is the cause. But, where racism exists, disparities will exist. These disparities reflect the patterns we have discovered in the laboratory. Across organizations as diverse as the armed forces, federal government, and Fortune 1000 companies, greater racial disparities exist at higher status levels. In addition, these patterns have per-

sisted over the past decade. Within the Navy, for example, African Americans represent 13% of the force, but only 5% of the officers and 1.5% of the admirals. Furthermore, these differences cannot be accounted for by vastly different backgrounds. The success rate of African Americans who qualified for officer promotions in 1988 was consistently below the rate of whites in the Navy and across all of the services in 1988. Consistent with our laboratory demonstrations, disparities in promotion rates tended to increase with higher ranks. We have also examined patterns of disparities for various segments of federal employees and found consistent evidence: Blacks are generally less well represented in higher grades (e.g., GS 16–18) than in lower grades. Furthermore, these disparities have remained relatively stable across time.

A recent Department of Labor survey of Fortune 1000 companies provides independent evidence of the "glass ceiling effect" for blacks and other minorities in industry. Representations of

## Figure 2
### Representation of African Americans by Occupational Level

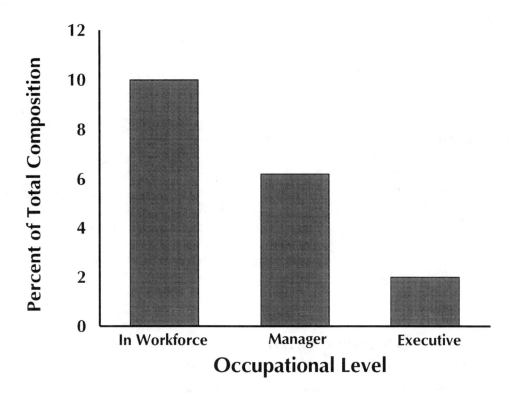

minorities consistently declined with higher occupational status (see Figure 2). A Department of Commerce survey further confirmed substantial income disparities between African American and white men. In 1989, African American men with a high school education earned $6,230 less per year than white men with comparable education ($20,280 vs. $26,510). The gap was even larger ($9,710) between college educated African American and white men ($31,380 vs. $41,090).

Thus, across a range of settings we see consistent patterns of disparities in occupational advancement and income. We know that the "glass ceiling effect" can occur for a wide range of reasons and that the leap from the laboratory to organizations is a large one. Nevertheless, the pattern of disparities that we see in organizations conforms to what we find in the laboratory. Furthermore, we suggest that by understanding some of the fundamental causes of these disparities, individuals and organizations will be better equipped to combat bias.

## Conclusion

In summary, despite consistent improvements in the expressed racial attitudes of whites over time, aversive racism continues to exert a subtle but pervasive influence on the lives of black Americans. This bias is expressed in indirect and rationalizable ways that restrict opportunities for blacks while protecting aversive racists from ever having to confront their prejudices. It is an elusive phenomenon: When aversive racists monitor their interracial behaviors, they do not discriminate. In fact, they may respond even more favorably to blacks than to whites as a way of reaffirming their nonprejudiced self-images. When they are not conscious of their actions, however, bias is subtly expressed, usually in ways that can be justified on the basis of some factor other than race.

Like a virus that has mutated, racism has evolved into a new form that is more difficult not only to recognize but also to combat. The traditional techniques for eliminating bias that emphasized the immorality of prejudice and illegality of discrimination are not effective for combating aversive racism. Aversive racists recognize prejudice is bad, but they do not recognize that they are prejudiced. Nevertheless, the impact of aversive racism is the same as old-fashioned racism: restriction of opportunity to other groups and support for a system that is believed to be fair in principle but that reinforces the social and economic advantages of the majority group over minority groups.

Racism is costly to both blacks and whites—in terms of the unfulfilled potential of human lives as well as the expense of violence and other crimes that arise out of rejection of the system and personal despair. Thus, recognition of this "new" racism may be an essential step in moving a significant segment of white America from feeling nonprejudiced to actually being nonprejudiced.

## About the Author

Dr. John Dovidio, Professor of Psychology at Colgate University, has authored over 50 books, chapters, articles, and technical reports; a major portion of these publications has focused on contemporary forms of racism and sexism. His book, *Prejudice, Discrimination, and Racism* (co-authored with S. L. Gaertner), is an edited collection of recent work on the dynamics of racism. It is available from Academic Press (Orlando, FL) at 407-345-4100.

Dr. Dovidio regularly makes presentations and conducts seminars on the topic of modern racism for professional and general audiences. He has conducted workshops for the Department of Defense, the Pentagon, the Anti-Defamation League, and numerous colleges. He can be reached at Colgate University, 13 Oak Drive (Psychology Dept.), Hamilton, NY 13346-1398; Phone 315-824-7349; Fax: 315-824-7942.

## Percentage of Subjects Selecting a Trait to Describe African Americans (formerly "Negroes" or "Blacks") in 1933, 1951, 1967, 1982, 1988, and 1990

|  | 1933 | 1951 | 1967 | 1982 | 1988 | 1990 |
|---|---|---|---|---|---|---|
| Superstitious | 84 | 41 | 13 | 6 | 2 | 3 |
| Lazy | 75 | 31 | 26 | 13 | 6 | 4 |
| Happy-Go-Lucky | 38 | 17 | 27 | 15 | 4 | 1 |
| Ignorant | 38 | 24 | 11 | 10 | 6 | 5 |
| Musical | 26 | 33 | 47 | 29 | 13 | 27 |
| Ostentatious | 26 | 11 | 25 | 5 | 0 | 1 |
| Stupid | 22 | 10 | 4 | 1 | 1 | 3 |
| Physically Dirty | 17 | —— | 3 | 0 | 1 | 0 |
| Naive | 14 | —— | 4 | 4 | 2 | 3 |
| Unreliable | 12 | —— | 6 | 2 | 1 | 4 |

**As the above table indicates, negative stereotypes of African-Americans have generally decreased over the last 50 years. Despite this trend, research on white attitudes continues to reveal significant bias in terms of subtle discrimination or aversive racism (see Dovidio, page 424).**

Table is excerpted from: "New Technologies for the Direct and Indirect Assessment of Attitudes" by John Dovidio and Russell H. Fazio, p. 212 of *Questions About Questions*, edited by Judith M. Tanur, Russell Sage Foundation. Reprinted with permission.

# DEALING WITH SUBTLE DISCRIMINATION
## by Dianne M. LaMountain

Discrimination (real or imagined) is still a very significant barrier in the career development of women and minorities. Blatant discrimination is easy to identify and much has been written about alternatives available in responding to such behavior. However, detecting and responding to subtle discrimination is more difficult. Yet, the effects of these less conspicuous acts can be highly detrimental to individuals and the organizations in which they work.

There are four key tenets that must be understood in order to deal effectively with subtle discrimination:

**Intent vs. Effect**—We probably have all been "guilty" at some point of hurting someone, despite having good (or, at least, neutral) intentions. Being willing to examine the effects of our actions, separate from our intent, can help us be less defensive and more apt to change our behavior if we find that it is having an adverse impact on others. If we are "victims" of such actions, separating intent from effect can prevent us from giving the "guilty party" the benefit of the doubt.

**Perception is Reality**—Each person's perception is that person's reality. The way we see the world and interpret its meaning is shaped by all our experiences and learnings. Life is rather like an on-going Rorschach ink blot—what we know or believe affects what we see. (An excellent example of this, for many people, is to compare the "new view" of the world presented on the Peter's Projection Map which we generally see as our "point of reference."*) When in conflict, realizing that others may be operating from a different perception (or different point of view) can help us "reframe" the discussion by asking "what would cause this person to see things this way." The key here is to remember that different is not right or wrong, it's just different!

**Comfort vs. Competence**—Technical competence is necessary but often not sufficient for success in business! Those in power will tend to surround themselves with those they know & trust, those whose behavior they can predict, those with whom they feel a level of comfort. The more one is perceived as different, the more uncomfortable people feel around you. Overcoming this obstacle means bringing it out from the unconscious and dealing with it on a conscious level. It can also mean making some hard choices about how far one is willing to go to "fit into the corporate culture."

**Outsiders**—Those who are perceived as different are often treated as outsiders. They are not included in the informal socializing or formal decision-making process of the organization. When people feel like outsiders they tend to act defensively and sometimes do foolish things that are self-destructive. The spiral can be self-perpetuating.

Obviously, all four tenets are closely related. If I see myself as an outsider (or perceive myself as being treated as an outsider) I am more apt to attribute malicious intent to others' actions and react with defensiveness or hostility. That, in turn, is apt to make others uncomfortable around me and, despite my technical abilities, I am apt to find I can make less and less contribution to the organization. Understanding these four tenets and overcoming the obstacles they present are but a first step in dealing with subtle discrimination, but they are prerequisites for any effective strategy.

Dianne M. LaMountain
Senior Associate, ODT Inc.
(Diversity Consulting Firm)
Richmond, VA (phone: 804-355-3874)

* Peters Projection maps and training materials are available from 1-800-736-1293

# Teaming High Performance with Inclusion: A Case in Progress

by Judith H. Katz & Frederick A. Miller

To improve productivity, quality and performance, a growing number of organizations have organized their workforces into self-managed teams. Many have simultaneously "addressed" the diversity issue by establishing the teams with diverse populations. The results have not always been as expected, as the following example illustrates.

When Transcontinental Camshafts* analyzed why its productivity levels were falling behind industry norms, the analysis showed that the company's workforce was far less diverse than the competition. To keep up, it began aggressively recruiting more white women, women of color and men of color. But the company was disappointed when its more diverse workforce seemed no more productive than its original monocultural one. In fact, it seemed less productive because there were more conflicts and more complaints of unfair treatment. As a result, the company implemented a new initiative specifically to address performance.

The company's productivity program involved grouping the workforce into diverse self-managed teams. The company spent a great deal of time and resources in the preparations, which included training in teamwork. Productivity increased dramatically at first, then leveled off. Management would have been satisfied with the gains, if not for some unexpected feedback from the teams.

Over time, the teams were evolving along racial and gender lines. Initially, they simply made decisions along these lines, with majority viewpoints holding sway. But through turnover and replacement, the teams were actually becoming more monocultural. Turnover was greatest among those who weren't part of the majority cultural groups. Openings were filled by people who looked and acted like each team's majority cultural group.

Managers were concerned, yet reluctant to interfere. They didn't want to appear to be "taking back" the decision-making power they had entrusted to the teams. And productivity didn't seem to be suffering. Maybe, after all, the highest performing solution would prove to be monocultural teams representing different ethnic, racial and gender groups.

But Transcontinental Camshaft's management saw the fundamental deficiencies that would limit the productivity of monocultural teams. They chose to work toward achieving the potentially greater benefits of fostering diversity within the teams. They decided to approach diversity as a means to thrive, not as something to endure.

To achieve a higher level of performance and productivity, company leaders committed themselves to support a total organizational culture change. They began a long-term initiative to create an inclusive culture—one that does more than tolerate and seek conformance from people of different gender, race, age, nationality, and other identity groups. Instead, they wanted to embrace and encourage people's individual and group differences as a source of added value.

The initiative was designed to maximize the self-managed team structure: by providing team members with the skills to work effectively with differences; by making a clear commitment to a diverse, inclusive work culture; and by rooting out the bias in the company's structures, management practices, benefits and incentive programs.

And what about the results? Are the benefits of inclusion for real?

The hard data shows that productivity is up and turnover, particularly among people of color, is down. But that's not all that matters. There are also some other encouraging indicators. People are engaging with each other more. All people are feeling more included. And management feels more comfortable with a unified approach to performance and diversity.

---

* The company's name has been changed.

432

Just as important as the commitment to inclusion, perhaps, is the organization's acceptance of the need for change and its recognition that change will be constant. Together, these factors are positioning the company to make the constant adaptations necessary to achieve long-term success in a constantly changing world.

## Case Study Follow-up: Two Years Later

As a result of working on high performance and inclusion, the people and teams of Transcontinental Camshafts have not only enjoyed greater productivity and success but undergone much change as well. Though outsiders might see this as a result of successfully focusing on "diversity," the people of the organization are more likely to speak about:

"Focused leadership."
"Motivated work force."
"Smart strategic management."
"Sound business execution."

A prime characteristic of a successful "diversity" effort—it looks like just plain good business!

In fact, an effective strategic culture change intervention *must* address *all* of the above. Unfortunately, too many efforts stop at addressing work force motivation, or leadership skills, or *awareness*, before arriving at the organization's real needs—the structural and functional changes it needs to maximize its resources and achieve sustainable success.

The key word here is *sustainable*. If an organization fails to survive, whatever environment—humanistic or oppressive—it creates for its people will be gone as well. That is why combining High Performance and Inclusion is crucial.

In a world where continuous improvement is the only means to remain competitive, a flat performance record like that of Transcontinental Camshafts' teams will eventually be unsatisfactory—and therefore not sustainable. But it took more than the addition of inclusive norms and values to put T.C.'s teams on the path to continuous improvement. It also took new skills and attitudes like:

- Accepting constant change as the only constant.

- Seeing people for who they are, and viewing their differences as assets, not deficits.

- Making the organization's commitment to diversity their own.

- Creating the safety needed to communicate honestly, discuss intelligently, face conflicts, take risks and learn.

- Not avoiding differences, assimilating them, or "agreeing to disagree," but actively exploring them for better solutions to problems and getting closer to 360° vision.

Transcontinental Camshafts knows that this is an ongoing challenge and is moving forward with its diversity and inclusion efforts:

- 300 champions of diversity and inclusion have participated in multi-day educational events.

- Leadership forums have brought together the top 100 senior executives with 100 champions to develop strategies for seeing people as an asset.

- With 300-plus champions of diversity and inclusion throughout the organization, and with senior executives modeling inclusive behaviors and values, the rest of the organization is regularly learning about diversity and the barriers to inclusion in staff meetings and day-to-day work interactions.

- These thousands of employees understand the organization's commitment to leveraging diversity as well as learn and practice inclusive norms and behaviors at work.

- T.C. has reviewed and strengthened its "people policies"—a.k.a. HR policies—to reflect inclusive values and practices.

- T.C. is working toward creating an economically literate work force, i.e., training all the people of the organization to read and understand the balance sheet and finances of the organization, and to appreciate the part each person plays in its overall financial success.

- Programs actively supported by the organization work to carry inclusive, people-as-assets practices outside its walls. Since many members of the organization are leaders in the community, they are leveraging their influence to create a better environment for their families and neighbors as well as for the organization. Some results are:

- New partnerships with suppliers and customers.

- Community housing, health and recreation programs.

- Ongoing training of public safety and police departments.

- Redesign of the school system and ongoing teacher training.

## When Diversity Is an Asset, Action Is Required to Sustain It

A basic culture change is needed for most teams and organizations to see difference as an asset. The old view has been that differences cause conflict, and conflict is bad; that differences take more energy and time because people need to assimilate and learn to conform and "fit in"; that differences are a deficit.

What T.C. discovered was that differences bring fresh eyes to look at situations in new ways; that different sets of skills, styles and perspectives help find new solutions; that honest disagreement, in a safe and respectful environment, leads to greater engagement and closeness among team members as well as more balanced problem solving.

They are finding that, in an inclusive environment, diversity actually costs less energy than conformity. People need only learn that it's okay to be themselves. They don't have to lie low and figure out which talents to hide and which are safe to expose; they can bring 100% of themselves to the job.

Even teams that are diverse in terms of race, gender and ethnicity tend to develop a unified point of view when they are together long enough. They can become *too* agreeable and fail to constantly question *what is*, limiting their vision of *what can be*. Like the oyster, they need an internal irritant to produce a pearl. To stay on the path of continuous improvement, these teams must proactively recruit new members who bring fresh perspectives, talents *and disagreements* to the team.

Affirmative *Action* with a traditional focus on men and women of color and white women, has been the traditional means to address this need,

but it does not do enough. To create 360° vision and continuous improvement, inclusion will have to go beyond race and gender, bringing aboard gays and lesbians; people with disabilities; people of different generations, educational backgrounds, family situations, nationalities and language groups; and other dimensions of difference. It cannot be a "one shot" deal.

*Sustained* action is required for organizations to accomplish their mission over the long haul. Taking steps to create the team and overall organizational population that will best accomplish the organization's work isn't one of those dreaded "social programs." It's just good leadership, and good business.

## About the Authors

Frederick A. Miller is President and CEO of The Kaleel Jamison Consulting Group, Inc. Fred has devoted his career to implementing sustainable strategic cultural change within organizations. His experience has included groundbreaking work in many large systems change initiatives within Fortune 100 companies and with other clients throughout the United States, Europe, Asia and the former Soviet Union.

Judith H. Katz, Ed. D. is Executive Vice President of The Kaleel Jamison Consulting Group. Currently Judith is focusing on helping organizations integrate strategic initiatives such as quality, leadership, empowerment and teamwork to create sustainable positive change. Her book, *White Awareness: A Handbook for Anti-Racism Training* (1978) remains a landmark in the field, and her courageous autobiographical work, *No Fairy Godmothers, No Magic Wands: The Healing Process After Rape* (1984), is in wide use in the recovery process for rape survivors. Judith and Fred were co-editors of the noted anthology, *The Promise of Diversity*.

The Kaleel Jamison Consulting Group, Inc. has been helping build High Performing Inclusive(SM) organizations nationwide since 1970. They can be contacted at: The Kaleel Jamison Consulting Group, Inc., Patricia A. Volk, Administrative Manager, 1731 Robinway Drive, Cincinnati, OH 45230-2236; Phone: (513) 231-1007; Fax: (513) 231-0890.

# PART 11
# DISMANTLING
# AFFIRMATIVE ACTION

# Dialogue: Dismantling Affirmative Action

*George*—We open our discussion of this section with an article by Roosevelt Thomas who speaks of Affirmative Action (AA) dying a natural death. While his analysis is penetrating, given all the vested interests in it, I think that AA will do anything but die a natural death. We have titled this section "Dismantling Affirmative Action" not because of a firm belief that it will be taken apart piece by piece, but simply to reflect the discussion we are listening to right now about it.

*Bob*—The question we want to address in this *Sourcebook*, of course, is "What do we want to do next?" Where will we get the most "bang" for our social buck in the U.S.? It is Thomas's contention that we've already got most of the bang from Affirmative Action based on race. We agree with him and therefore have chosen class as the factor to redirect our social energies.

*George*—Some people will disagree. Some will disagree with us, because we're white men over forty-five. Some will disagree with Roosevelt Thomas because he's a successful, educated, credentialed African-American and is assumed to be remote from the underclass experience. I feel that Affirmative Action is most vulnerable because in order to function it requires economic prosperity. As far as most people are concerned, we are currently in a declining economy. AA came about in a spirit of leveling the playing field for the historically disadvantaged player—the underdog. However, this U.S. value (one type of fairness) is running afoul of another value of fairness: Specifically, in cases where it confers advantage on one underdog over another on the basis of race, ethnicity or gender.

*Bob*—"Black Pride for White People" by Adrian Piper (subtitled: "Are You Sure You Didn't Have an African Ancestor?"; page 453) is a radical and provocative article in our discussion on the dismantling of Affirmative Action. It looks at the absurdity of racial division and identifies race as an artifice originally designed solely to reassert power and political privilege. The issue developed in colonial times over who owned whom and what and how property should be recorded. Racial distinctions were created to determine who received privileges and who didn't. Race was adopted as a class screening device during the formative stages of our country.

*George*—To me, the article doesn't sound so radical at all. If I understand you and the author correctly, race and other visible factors are the most expedient methods to slot people into class distinctions: It sounds like an all too enduring human tendency. If the factors are not visible, humans will invent ways to create distinctions. Think of all the absurdity that was concocted in Hitler's Third Reich to find a scientific set of measurements for who was Aryan and who was not.

*Bob*—There are innumerable examples of this racist dynamic. In the history of U.S. immigration, a newly arrived group is relegated to the bottom of the class ladder. They become the most disparaged or most exploited. Their physical traits are caricatured. Once someone holds the bottom rung, the mainstream allows inclusiveness toward that group who previously held the lower position. The Germans, the Irish, the Jews, the Italians—all occupied the bottom rung for a while. Once we arrive at the middle levels of the social ladder we don't have to have such rigid boundaries. These other levels have been more accessible, once it's clear who's on the bottom. It only becomes tight again at the top.

*George*—I've enjoyed that little sidebar (page 166) about watching how in successive years the kids fighting in the golden gloves boxing matches tend to be the most recently arrived. It's almost a metaphor. The young men start at the bottom of the social ladder, fight their way up, and as soon as someone gets to be world heavyweight champion, the next ethnicity comes along to unseat them. But there are always black contenders, and that continues to worry me. It's been an easy out for everybody else to have a readily identifiable group permanently at the bottom level.

*Bob*—Because of the economic situation today, racism is on the rise. As income levels fall for many people the fear of landing at the bottom is ever present.

*George*—Everyone's confidence in the future is eroding. You and I think of ourselves as having been lucky, privileged individuals in this country. Yet we know full well, given the vagaries of the economy, the breakdown of the family, the lack of an adequate social security system and the failure of health care to provide for all citizens, we could well be street people before we die. While this sobering thought gives me compassion for the homeless, it can lead, if I am not careful, to invidious competition with others for increasingly scarce resources. How much do I have to acquire to feel safe? With an unraveling safety net, people are in greater fear and feel less generous towards others.

*Bob*—In "Who's What?" we go from a demographic viewpoint (page 455) to concrete genetic data from Richard Lewontin's findings reported in *Human Diversity* (page 459).

In this section the sidebars are as revealing as the articles—at the same time that racial classifications are hopelessly senseless, there is real discrimination. Billi Lee articulates that "Life and Work Aren't Fair" (page 458) but we are still convinced that it is important to make them both as fair as possible. Affirmative Action was created to make things more fair. It's had substantial success and also some failures. If AA is dismantled (based on race and gender), it will no doubt be replaced by an effort that will also get mixed reviews.

*George*—Even on a simple economic level fairness is not easy to define, let alone achieve. This is illustrated in the story of the Filipino and Norwegian sailors argument with one another over whose wages mean more. Perhaps we should recognize that "fair," as we use it in everyday politics, is usually about how we make claims on each other. "It's not fair," could often best be translated into, "I want more" or, "You're hurting me." It is rarely a formula for how to distribute the common good.

*Bob*—In such a context it shouldn't surprise us that people who consider themselves victims can easily justify using what power and ruses they can muster to improve their situation.

*George*—I am old enough to remember immigrants who lived in my neighborhood or were part of my family. While they valued the American Dream, it was clear to them that many of the rules in the U.S. were made for the benefit of somebody else, and not them. The immigrant generation cut what corners they could. My grandfather built his own still, and other relatives managed to slip onto the Social Security rolls when their eligibility was questionable. It would surprise me greatly if other generations working their way up the social ladder, or at least trying to improve their economic standing, did not take advantage of the government wherever they could.

*Bob*—"Masks of Minority Terrorism" (page 460) explores this theme and looks at the uses of power for the achievement of group goals. Many feminists have strongly insisted that their struggle is all about power. The language of Political Correctness is about the leveraging of power. In many instances Affirmative Action has become focused on the leveraging of power. As those who have had power continuously begin to feel the brunt of power from those previously excluded, they are beginning to react. When attacked, they defend themselves.

*George*—So the discussion about dismantling Affirmative Action is about dismantling a power structure which has grown up around an equity effort, or . . .

*Bob*—Or simply using other resources to level the playing field. The history of the police department recounted in "Black and Blue" is a hopeful one despite being a story full of conflicts and dilemmas. It also indicates to me that historically we have gone through an evolutionary process in the development of social policy. We had to work through the issues of Affirmative Action before we can begin to define new and more appropriate policies.

*George*—There's one more issue to discuss about Affirmative Action, and it's reflected in the report about Kara Hultgreen, the ill-fated Navy fighter pilot whose demise would be tainted by debate over her qualifications as an "Affirmative Action" pilot candidate. In this case, it seems to me, Affirmative Action, which on one hand was designed to protect and promote competent women, provided the excuse for gender bias to run rampant.

This occurred even though investigation showed that Hultgreen was eminently qualified and proficient as a air combat pilot. And further investigations by Navy brass concluded it was an engine problem. But her subsequent exoneration doesn't alter the initial flack this stirred up about Affirmative Action.

A similar effect has been experienced by African-Americans who have frequently complained that the stigma of Affirmative Action can consistently get in the way of their being seen and dealt with as fully professional . . .

*Bob*— . . . so Affirmative Action can also be seen as an excuse for promoting racism as well as sexism.

*George*—All the more reason for us to take another approach to the search for justice in diversity. Richard Kahlenberg will be an eloquent spokesperson for this in his article from the *New Republic*, "Class, Not Race" (page 469). Many readers will find a surprise in reading this piece. Kahlenberg documents the fact that the massive social initiatives of the '60s were primarily a war on poverty and only in that context an attack on bias. President Lyndon Johnson's Great Society programs focused on dismantling class inequities, and this, it was hoped, rather than highlighting racial distinctions, would enable the country to make significant steps in eradicating prejudice as well. We will never know whether or not this optimism was well founded since the political shift changed the focus to racial and ethnic identities instead of class identities. The economic climate is less supportive today than it was in the decades of the '60s and '70s, but this has made class an even more acute issue than it was before the fragmentation of energies into racial and ethnic divisiveness.

*Bob*— . . . shall we begin again?

# From Affirmative Action to Affirming Diversity

by R. Roosevelt Thomas, Jr. (*Harvard Business Review*)

*Diversity is what makes America different. Why don't we turn it to our advantage?*

Sooner or later, affirmative action will die a natural death. Its achievements have been stupendous, but if we look at the premises that underlie it, we find assumptions and priorities that look increasingly shopworn. Thirty years ago, affirmative action was invented on the basis of these five appropriate premises:

1. Adult, white males make up something called the U.S. business mainstream.

2. The U.S. economic edifice is a solid, unchanging institution with more than enough space for everyone.

3. Women, blacks, immigrants, and other minorities should be allowed in as a matter of public policy and common decency.

4. Widespread racial, ethnic, and sexual prejudice keeps them out.

5. Legal and social coercion are necessary to bring about the change.

Today all five of these premises need revising. Over the past six years, I have tried to help some 15 companies learn how to achieve and manage diversity, and I have seen that the realities facing us are no longer the realities affirmative action was designed to fix.

To begin with, more than half the U.S. work force now consists of minorities, immigrants, and women, so white, native-born males, though undoubtedly still dominant, are themselves a statistical minority. In addition, white males will make up only 15% of the increase in the work force over the next ten years. The so-called mainstream is now almost as diverse as the society at large.

Second, while the edifice is still big enough for all, it no longer seems stable, massive, and invulnerable.

In fact, American corporations are scrambling, doing their best to become more adaptable, to compete more successfully for markets and labor, foreign and domestic, and to attract all the talent they can find. (See the inserts for what a number of U.S. companies are doing to manage diversity.)

Third, women and minorities no longer need a boarding pass, they need an upgrade. The problem is not getting them in at the entry level; the problem is making better use of their potential at every level, especially in middle-management and leadership positions. This is no longer simply a question of common decency, it is a question of business survival.

Fourth, although prejudice is hardly dead, it has suffered some wounds that may eventually prove fatal. In the meantime, American businesses are now filled with progressive people—many of them minorities and women themselves—whose prejudices, where they still exist, are much too deeply suppressed to interfere with recruitment. The reason many companies are still wary of minorities and women has much more to do with education and perceived qualifications than with color or gender. Companies are worried about productivity and well aware that minorities and women represent a disproportionate share of the undertrained and undereducated.

Fifth, coercion is rarely needed at the recruitment stage. There are very few places in the United States today where you could dip a recruitment net and come up with nothing but white males. Getting hired is not the problem—women and blacks who are seen as having the necessary skills and energy can get into the work force relatively easily. It's later on that many of them plateau and lose their drive and quit or get fired. It's later on that their managers' inability to manage diversity hobbles them and the companies they work for.

In creating these changes, affirmative action had an essential role to play and played it very well. In many companies and communities it still plays that role. But affirmative action is an artificial, transitional intervention intended to give managers a chance to correct an imbalance, an injustice, a mistake. Once the numbers mistake has been corrected, I don't think affirmative action alone can cope with the remaining long-term task of creating a work setting geared to the upward mobility of all kinds of people, including white males. It is difficult for affirmative action to influence upward mobility even in the short run, primarily because it is perceived to conflict with the meritocracy we favor. For this reason, affirmative action is a red flag to every individual who feels unfairly passed over and a stigma for those who appear to be its beneficiaries.

Moreover, I doubt very much that individuals who reach top positions through affirmative action are effective models for younger members of their race or sex. What, after all, do they model? A black vice president who got her job through affirmative action is not necessarily a model of how to rise through the corporate meritocracy. She may be a model of how affirmative action can work for the people who find or put themselves in the right place at the right time. If affirmative action in upward mobility meant that no person's competence and character would ever be overlooked or undervalued on account of race, sex, ethnicity, origins, or physical disability, then affirmative action would be the very thing we need to let every corporate talent find its niche. But what affirmative action means in practice is an unnatural focus on one group, and what it means too often to too many employees is that someone is playing fast and loose with standards in order to favor that

## OUT OF THE NUMBERS GAME AND INTO DECISION MAKING

Like many other companies, Avon practiced affirmative action in the 1970s and was not pleased with the results. The company worked with employment agencies that specialized in finding qualified minority hires, and it cultivated contacts with black and minority organizations on college campuses. Avon wanted to see its customer base reflected in its work force, especially at the decision-making level. But while women moved up the corporate ladder fairly briskly—not so surprising in a company whose work force is mostly female—minorities did not. So in 1984, the company began to change its policies and practices.

"We really wanted to get out of the numbers game," says Marcia Worthing, the corporate vice president for human resources. "We felt it was more important to have five minority people tied into the decision-making process than ten who were just heads to count."

First, Avon initiated awareness training at all levels. "The key to recruiting, retaining, and promoting minorities is not the human resource department," says Worthing. "It's getting line management to buy into the idea. We had to do more than change behavior. We had to change attitudes."

Second, the company formed a Multicultural Participation Council that meets regularly to oversee the process of managing diversity. The group includes Avon's CEO and high-level employees from throughout the company.

Third, in conjunction with the American Institute for Managing Diversity, Avon developed a diversity training program. For several years, the company has sent racially and ethnically diverse groups of 25 managers at a time to Institute headquarters at Morehouse College in Atlanta, where they spend three weeks confronting their differences and learning to hear and avail themselves of viewpoints they initially disagreed with. "We came away disciples of diversity," says one company executive.

Fourth, the company helped three minority groups—blacks, Hispanics, and Asians—form networks that crisscrossed the corporation in all 50 states. Each network elects its own leaders and has an adviser from senior management. In addition, the networks have representatives on the Multicultural Participation Council, where they serve as a conduit for employee views on diversity issues facing management.

group. Unless we are to compromise our standards, a thing no competitive company can even contemplate, upward mobility for minorities and women should always be a question of pure competence and character unmuddled by accidents of birth.

And that is precisely why we have to learn to manage diversity—to move beyond affirmative action, not to repudiate it. Some of what I have to say may strike some readers—mostly those with an ax to grind—as directed at the majority white males who hold most of the decision-making posts in our economy. But I am speaking to all managers, not just white males, and I certainly don't mean to suggest that white males somehow stand outside diversity. White males are as odd and as normal as anyone else.

## The Affirmative Action Cycle

If you are managing diverse employees, you should ask yourself this question: Am I fully tapping the potential capacities of everyone in my department? If the answer is no, you should ask yourself this follow-up: Is this failure hampering my ability to meet performance standards? The answer to this question will undoubtedly be yes.

Think of corporate management for a moment as an engine burning pure gasoline. What's now going into the tank is no longer just gas, it has an increasing percentage of, let's say, methanol. In the beginning the engine will still work pretty well, but by and by it will start to sputter, and eventually it will stall. Unless we rebuild the engine, it will no longer burn the fuel we're feeding it. As the work force grows more and more diverse at the intake level, the talent pool we have to draw on for supervision and management will also grow increasingly diverse. So the question is: Can we burn this fuel? Can we get maximum corporate power from the diverse work force we're now drawing into the system?

Affirmative action gets blamed for failing to do things it never could do. Affirmative action gets the new fuel into the tank, the new people through the front door. Something else will have to get them into the driver's seat. That something else consists of enabling people, in this case minorities and women, to perform to their potential. This is what we now call managing diversity. Not appreciating or leveraging diversity, not even necessarily understanding it. Just managing diversity in such a way as to get from a heterogeneous work force the same productivity, commitment, quality, and profit that we got from the old homogeneous work force.

The correct question today is not "How are we doing on race relations?" or "Are we promoting enough minority people and women?" but rather "Given the diverse work force I've got, am I getting the productivity, does it work as smoothly, is morale as high, as if every person in the company was the same sex and race and nationality?" Most answers will be, "Well, no, of course not!" But why shouldn't the answer be, "You bet!"?

When we ask how we're doing on race relations, we inadvertently put our finger on what's wrong with the question and with the attitude that underlies affirmative action. So long as racial and gender equality is something we grant to minorities and women, there will be no racial and gender equality. What we must do is create an environment where no one is advantaged or disadvantaged, an environment where "we" is everyone. What the traditional approach to diversity did was to create a cycle of crisis, action, relaxation, and disappointment that companies repeated over and over again without ever achieving more than the barest particle of what they were after.

Affirmative action pictures the work force as a pipeline and reasons as follows: "If we can fill the pipeline with qualified minorities and women, we can solve our upward mobility problem. Once recruited, they will perform in accordance with our promotional criteria and move naturally up our regular developmental ladder. In the past, where minorities and women have failed to progress, they were simply unable to meet our performance standards. Recruiting qualified people will enable us to avoid special programs and reverse discrimination."

> *The wrong question: "How are we doing on race relations?"*
> *The right question: "Is this a workplace where 'we' is everyone?"*

441

This pipeline perspective generates a self-perpetuating, self-defeating, recruitment-oriented cycle with six stages:

1. *Problem Recognition.* The first time through the cycle, the problem takes this form—We need more minorities and women in the pipeline. In later iterations, the problem is more likely to be defined as a need to retain and promote minorities and women.

2. *Intervention.* Management puts the company into what we may call an Affirmative Action Recruitment Mode. During the first cycle, the goal is to recruit minorities and women. Later, when the cycle is repeated a second or third time and the challenge has shifted to retention, development, and promotion, the goal is to recruit qualified minorities and women. Sometimes, managers indifferent or blind to possi-

---

### "IT SIMPLY MAKES GOOD BUSINESS SENSE."

Corning characterizes its 1970s affirmative action program as a form of legal compliance. The law dictated affirmative action and morality required it, so the company did its best to hire minorities and women.

The ensuing cycle was classic: recruitment, confidence, disappointment, embarrassment, crisis, more recruitment. Talented women and blacks joined the company only to plateau or resign. Few reached upper management levels, and no one could say exactly why.

Then James R. Houghton took over CORNING as CEO in 1983 and made the diverse work force one of Corning's three top priorities, alongside Total Quality and a higher return on equity. His logic was twofold:

First of all, the company had higher attrition rates for minorities and women than for white males which meant that investments in training and development were being wasted. Second, he believed that the Corning work force should more closely mirror the Corning customer base.

In order to break the cycle of recruitment and subsequent frustration, the company established two quality improvement teams headed by senior executives, one for black progress and one for women's progress. Mandatory awareness training was introduced for some 7,000 salaried employees—a day and a half for gender awareness, two-and-a-half days for racial awareness. One goal of the training is to identify unconscious company values that work against minorities and women. For example, a number of awareness groups reached the conclusion that working late had so much symbolic value that managers tended to look more at the quantity than at the quality of time spent on the job, with predictably negative effects on employees with dependent-care responsibilities.

The company also made an effort to improve communications by printing regular stories and articles about the diverse workforce in its in-house newspaper and by publicizing employee success stories that emphasize diversity. It worked hard to identify and publicize promotion criteria. Career planning systems were introduced for all employees.

With regard to recruitment, Corning set up a nationwide scholarship program that provides renewable grants of $5,000 per year of college in exchange for a summer of paid work at some Corning installation. A majority of program participants have come to work for Corning full-time after graduation, and very few have left the company so far, though the program has been in place only four years.

The company also expanded its summer intern program, with an emphasis on minorities and women, and established formal recruiting contacts with campus groups like the Society of Women Engineers and the National Black MBA Association.

Corning sees its efforts to manage diversity not only as a social and moral issue but also as a question of efficiency and competitiveness. In the words of Mr. Houghton, "It simply makes good business sense."

ble accusations of reverse discrimination will institute special training, tracking, incentive, mentoring, or sponsoring programs for minorities and women.

3. *Great Expectations.* Large numbers of minorities and women have been recruited, and a select group has been promoted or recruited at a higher level to serve as highly visible role models for the newly recruited masses. The stage seems set for the natural progression of minorities and women up through the pipeline. Management leans back to enjoy the fruits of its labor.

4. *Frustration.* The anticipated natural progression fails to occur. Minorities and women see themselves plateauing prematurely. Management is upset (and embarrassed) by the failure of its affirmative action initiative and begins to resent the impatience of the new recruits and their unwillingness to give the company credit for trying to do the right thing. Depending on how high in the hierarchy they have plateaued, alienated minorities and women either leave the company or stagnate.

5. *Dormancy.* All remaining participants conspire tacitly to present a silent front to the outside world. Executives say nothing because

---

## TURNING SOCIAL PRESSURES INTO COMPETITIVE ADVANTAGE

Like most other companies trying to respond to the federal legislation of the 1970s, Digital started off by focusing on numbers. By the early 1980s, however, company leaders could see it would take more than recruitment to make Digital the diverse workplace they wanted it to be. Equal Employment Opportunity (EEO) and affirmative action seemed too exclusive—too much "white males doing good deeds for minorities and women." The company wanted to move beyond these programs to the kind of environment where every employee could realize his or her potential, and Digital decided that meant an environment where individual differences were not tolerated but valued, even celebrated.

The resulting program and philosophy, called Valuing Differences, has two components:

First, the company helps people get in touch with their stereotypes and false assumptions through what Digital calls Core Groups. These voluntary groupings of eight to ten people work with company-trained facilitators whose job is to encourage discussion and self-development and, in the company's words, "to keep people safe" as they struggle with their prejudices. Digital also runs a voluntary two-day training program called "Understanding the Dynamics of Diversity," which thousands of Digital employees have now taken.

Second, the company has named a number of senior managers to various Cultural Boards of Directors and Valuing Differences Boards of Directors. These bodies promote openness to individual differences, encourage younger managers committed to the goal of diversity, and sponsor frequent celebrations of racial, gender, and ethnic differences such as Hispanic Heritage Week and Black History Month.

In addition to the Valuing Differences program, the company preserved its EEO and affirmative action functions. Valuing Differences focuses on personal and group development, EEO on legal issues, and affirmative action on systemic change. According to Alan Zimmerle, head of the Valuing Differences program, EEO and Valuing Differences are like two circles that touch but don't overlap—the first representing the legal need for diversity, the second the corporate desire for diversity. Affirmative action is a third circle that overlaps the other two and holds them together with policies and procedures.

Together, these three circles can transform legal and social pressures into the competitive advantage of a more effective work force, higher morale, and the reputation of being a better place to work. As Zimmerle puts it, "Digital wants to be the employer of choice. We want our pick of the talent that's out there."

443

they have no solutions. As for those women and minorities who stayed on, calling attention to affirmative action's failures might raise doubts about their qualifications. Do they deserve their jobs, or did they just happen to be in the right place at the time of an affirmative action push? So no one complains, and if the company has a good public relations department, it may even wind up with a reputation as a good place for women and minorities to work.

If questioned publicly, management will say things like "Frankly, affirmative action is not currently an issue, " or "Our numbers are okay," or "With respect to minority representation at the upper levels, management is aware of this remaining challenge."

In private and off the record, however, people say things like "Premature plateauing is a problem, and we don't know what to do" and "Our top people don't seem to be interested in finding a solution," and "There's plenty of racism and sexism around this place—whatever you may hear."

6. *Crisis.* Dormancy can continue indefinitely, but it is usually broken by a crisis of competitive pressure, governmental intervention, external pressure from a special interest group, or internal unrest. One company found that its pursuit of a Total Quality program was hampered by the alienation of minorities and women. Senior management at another corporation saw the growing importance of minorities in their customer base and decided they needed minority participation in their managerial ranks. In another case, growing expressions of discontent forced a break in the conspiracy of silence even after the company had received national recognition as a good place for minorities and women to work.

Whatever its cause, the crisis fosters a return to the Problem Recognition phase, and the cycle begins again. This time, management seeks to explain the shortcomings of the previous affirmative action push and usually concludes that the problem is recruitment. This assessment by a top executive is typical: "The managers I know are decent people. While they give priority to performance, I do not

believe any of them deliberately block minorities or women who are qualified for promotion. On the contrary, I suspect they bend over backward to promote women and minorities who give some indication of being qualified.

"However, they believe we simply do not have the necessary talent within those groups, but because of the constant complaints they have heard about their deficiencies in affirmative action, they feel they face a no-win situation. If they do not promote, they are obstructionists. But if they promote people who are unqualified, they hurt performance and deny promotion to other employees unfairly. They can't win. The answer, in my mind, must be an ambitious new recruitment effort to bring in quality people."

And so the cycle repeats. Once again blacks, Hispanics, women, and immigrants are dropped into a previously homogeneous, all-white, all-Anglo, all male, all native-born environment, and the burden of cultural change is placed on the newcomers. There will be new expectations and a new round of frustration, dormancy, crisis, and recruitment.

# Ten Guidelines for Learning to Manage Diversity

The traditional American image of diversity has been assimilation: the melting pot, where ethnic and racial differences were standardized into a kind of American puree. Of course, the melting pot is only a metaphor. In real life, many ethnic and most racial groups retain their individuality and express it energetically. What we have is perhaps some kind of American mulligan stew; it is certainly no puree.

At the workplace, however, the melting pot has been more than a metaphor. Corporate success has demanded a good deal of conformity, and employees have voluntarily abandoned most of their ethnic distinctions at the company door.

Now those days are over. Today the melting pot is the wrong metaphor even in business, for three good reasons. First, if it ever was possible to melt down Scotsmen and Dutchmen and Frenchmen into an indistinguishable broth, you can't do the same with blacks, Asians, and women. Their differences don't melt so easily. Second, most people are no longer willing to be melted down, not even for eight hours a day—and it's a seller's market for skills. Third, the thrust of today's non-hierarchical, flexible, collaborative management requires a ten or twentyfold increase in our tolerance for individuality.

So companies are faced with the problem of surviving in a fiercely competitive world with a work force that consists and will continue to consist of unassimilated diversity. And the engine will take a great deal of tinkering to burn that fuel.

What managers fear from diversity is a lowering of standards, a sense that "anything goes." Of course, standards must not suffer. In fact, competence counts more than ever. The goal is to manage diversity in such a way as to get from a diverse work force the same productivity we once got from a homogeneous work force, and to do it without artificial programs, standards—or barriers.

Managing diversity does not mean controlling or containing diversity, it means enabling every member of your work force to perform to his or her potential. It means getting from employees, first, everything we have a right to expect, and, second—if we do it well—everything they have to give. If the old homogeneous work force performed dependably at 80% of its capacity, then the first result means getting 80% from the new heterogeneous work force too. But the second result, the icing on the cake, the unexpected upside that diversity can perhaps give as a bonus, means 85% to 90% from everyone in the organization.

For the moment, however, let's concentrate on the basics of how to get satisfactory performance from the new diverse work force. There are few

## DISCOVERING COMPLEXITY AND VALUE IN P&G'S DIVERSITY

Because Procter & Gamble fills its upper level management positions only from within the company, it places a premium on recruiting the best available entry-level employees. Campus recruiting is pursued nationwide and year-round by line managers from all levels of the company. Among other things, the company has made a concerted—and successful—effort to find and hire talented minorities and women.

Finding first-rate hires is only one piece of the effort, however. There is still the challenge of moving diversity upward. As one top executive put it, "We know that we can only succeed as a company if we have an environment that makes it easy for all of us; not just some of us, to work to our potential."

In May 1988, P&G formed a Corporate Diversity Strategy Task Force to clarify the concept of diversity, define its importance for the company, and identify strategies for making progress toward successfully managing a diverse work force.

The task force, composed of men and women from every corner of the company, made two discoveries: First, diversity at P&G was far more complex than most people had supposed. In addition to race and gender, it included factors such as cultural heritage, personal background, and functional experience. Second, the company needed to expand its view of the value of differences.

The task force helped the company to see that learning to manage diversity would be a long-term process of organizational change. For example, P&G has offered voluntary diversity training at all levels since the 1970s, but the program has gradually broadened its emphasis on race and gender awareness to include the value of self-realization in a diverse environment. As retiring board chairman John Smale put it, "If we can tap the total contribution that everybody in our company has to offer, we will be better and more competitive in every thing we do."

P&G is now conducting a thorough, continuing evaluation of all management programs to be sure that systems are working well for everyone. It has also carried out a corporate survey to get a better picture of the problems facing P&G employees who are balancing work and family responsibilities and to improve company programs in such areas as dependent care.

adequate models. So far, no large company I know of has succeeded in managing diversity to its own satisfaction. But any number have begun to try.

On the basis of their experience, here are my ten guidelines:

1. *Clarify Your Motivation.* A lot of executives are not sure why they should want to learn to manage diversity. Legal compliance seems like a good reason. So does community relations. Many executives believe they have a social and moral responsibility to employ minorities and women. Others want to placate an internal group or pacify an outside organization. None of these are bad reasons, but none of them are business reasons, and given the nature and scope of today's competitive challenges, I believe only business reasons will supply the necessary long-term motivation. In any case, it is the business reasons I want to focus on here.

   In business terms, a diverse work force is not something your company ought to have; it's something your company does have, or soon will have. Learning to manage that diversity will make you more competitive.

2. *Clarify Your Vision.* When managers think about a diverse work force, what do they picture? Not publicly, but in the privacy of their minds?

   One popular image is of minorities and women clustering on a relatively low plateau, with a few of them trickling up as they become assimilated into the prevailing culture. Of course, they enjoy good salaries and benefits, and most of them accept their status, appreciate the fact that they are doing better than they could do somewhere else, and are proud of the achievements of their race or sex. This is reactionary thinking, but it's a lot more common than you might suppose.

   Another image is what we might call "heightened sensitivity." Members of the majority culture are sensitive to the demands of minorities and women for upward mobility and recognize the advantages of fully utilizing them. Minorities and women work at all levels of the corporation, but they are the recipients of generosity and know it. A few years of this

second-class status drives most of them away and compromises the effectiveness of those that remain. Turnover is high.

Then there is the coexistence-compromise image. In the interests of corporate viability, white males agree to recognize minorities and women as equals. They bargain and negotiate their differences. But the win-lose aspect of the relationship preserves tensions, and the compromises reached are not always to the company's competitive advantage.

"Diversity and equal opportunity" is a big step up. It presupposes that the white male culture has given way to one that respects difference and individuality. The problem is that minorities and women will accept it readily as their operating image, but many white males, consciously or unconsciously, are likely to cling to a vision that leaves them in the driver's seat. A vision gap of this kind can be a difficulty. In my view, the vision to hold in your own imagination and to try to communicate to all your managers and employees is an image of fully tapping the human resource potential of every member of the work force. This vision sidesteps the question of equality, ignores the tensions of coexistence, plays down the uncomfortable realities of difference, and focuses instead on individual enablement. It doesn't say, "Let us give them a chance." It assumes a diverse work force that includes us and them. It says, "Let's create an environment where everyone will do their best work." Several years ago, an industrial plant in Atlanta with a highly diverse work force was threatened with closing unless productivity improved. To save their jobs, everyone put their shoulders to the wheel and achieved the results they needed to stay open. The senior operating manager was amazed.

For years he had seen minorities and women plateauing disproportionately at the lower levels of the organization, and he explained that fact away with two rationalizations. "They haven't been here that long" he told himself. And "This is the price we pay for being in compliance with the law."

When the threat of closure energized this whole group of people into a level of performance he had not imagined possible, he got one fleeting glimpse of people working up to their capacity. Once the crisis was over, everyone went back to the earlier status quo—white males driving and everyone else sitting back, looking on—but now there was a difference. Now, as he put it himself, he had been to the mountaintop. He knew that what he was getting from minorities and women was nowhere near what they were capable of giving. And he wanted it, crisis or no crisis, all the time.

3. *Expand Your Focus.* Managers usually see affirmative action and equal employment opportunity as centering on minorities and women, with very little to offer white males. The diversity I'm talking about includes not only race, gender, creed, and ethnicity but also age, background, education, function, and personality differences. The objective is not to assimilate minorities and women into a dominant white male culture but to create a dominant heterogeneous culture.

The culture that dominates the United States socially and politically is heterogeneous, and it works by giving its citizens the liberty to achieve their potential. Channeling that potential, once achieved, is an individual right but still a national concern. Something similar applies in the workplace, where the keys to success are individual ability and a corporate destination. Managing disparate talents to achieve common goals is what companies learned to do when they set their sights on, say, Total Quality. The secrets of managing diversity are much the same.

4. *Audit Your Corporate Culture.* If the goal is not to assimilate diversity into the dominant culture but rather to build a culture that can digest unassimilated diversity, then you had better start by figuring out what your present culture looks like. Since what we're talking about here is the body of unspoken and unexamined assumptions, values, and mythologies that make your world go round, this kind of cultural audit is impossible to conduct without outside help. It's a research activity, done mostly with in-depth interviews and a lot of listening at the water cooler. The operative corporate assumptions you have to identify and deal with are often inherited from the company's founder. "If we treat everyone as a member of the family, we will be successful" is not uncommon. Nor is its corollary "Father Knows Best." Another widespread assumption, probably absorbed from American culture in general, is that cream will rise to the top. In most companies, what passes for cream rising to the top is actually cream being pulled or pushed to the top by an informal system of mentoring and sponsorship.

Corporate culture is a kind of tree. Its roots are assumptions about the company and about the world. Its branches, leaves, and seeds are behavior. You can't change the leaves without changing the roots, and you can't grow peaches on an oak. Or rather, with the proper grafting, you can grow peaches on an oak, but they come out an awful lot like acorns—small and hard and not much fun to eat. So if you want to grow peaches, you have to make sure the tree's roots are peach friendly.

5. *Modify Your Assumptions.* The real problem with this corporate culture tree is that every time you go to make changes in the roots, you run into terrible opposition. Every culture, including corporate culture, has root guards that turn out in force every time you threaten a basic assumption.

Take the family assumption as an example. Viewing the corporation as a family suggests not only that father knows best; it also suggests that sons will inherit the business, that daughters should stick to doing the company dishes, and that if Uncle Deadwood doesn't perform, we'll put him in the chimney corner and feed him for another 30 years regardless. Each assumption has its constituency and its defenders. If we say to Uncle Deadwood, "Yes, you did good work for 10 years, but years 11 and 12 look pretty bleak; we think it's time we helped you find another chimney," shock waves will travel through the company as every family-oriented employee draws a sword to defend the sacred concept of guaranteed jobs.

But you have to try. A corporation that wants to create an environment with no advantages or disadvantages for any group cannot allow the family assumption to remain in place. It must be labeled dishonest mythology. Sometimes the dishonesties are more blatant. When I asked a white male middle manager how promotions were handled in his company, he said, "You need leadership capability, bottom-line results, the ability to work with people, and compassion." Then he paused and smiled. "That's what they say. But down the hall there's a guy we call Captain Kickass. He's ruthless, mean-spirited, and he steps on people. That's the behavior they really value. Forget what they say. "

In addition to the obvious issue of hypocrisy, this example also raises a question of equal opportunity. When I asked this young middle manager if he thought minorities and women could meet the Captain Kickass standard, he said he thought they probably could. But the opposite argument can certainly be made. Whether we're talking about blacks in an environment that is predominantly white, whites in one predominantly black, or women in one predominantly male, the majority culture will not readily condone such tactics from a member of a minority. So the corporation with the unspoken kickass performance standard has

## THE DAILY EXPERIENCE OF GENUINE WORKPLACE DIVERSITY

Chairman David T. Kearns believes that a firm and resolute commitment to affirmative action is the first and most important step to work force diversity. "Xerox is committed to affirmative action," he says. "It is a corporate value, a management priority, and a formal business objective."

Xerox began recruiting minorities and women systematically as far back as the mid–1960s, and it pioneered such concepts as pivotal jobs (described later). The company's approach emphasizes behavior expectations as opposed to formal consciousness-raising programs because, as one Xerox executive put it, "It's just not realistic to think that a day and a half of training will change a person's thinking after 30 or 40 years."

On the assumption that attitude changes will grow from the daily experience of genuine workplace diversity, the Xerox Balanced Work Force Strategy sets goals for the number of minorities and women in each division and at every level. For example, the goal for the top 300 executive-level jobs in one large division is 35% women by 1995, compared with 15% today. "You must have a laboratory to work in," says Ted Payne, head of Xerox's Office of Affirmative Action and Equal Opportunity.

Minority and women's employee support groups have grown up in more than a dozen locations with the company's encouragement. But

Xerox depends mainly on the three pieces of its balanced strategy to make diversity work.

First are the goals. Xerox sets recruitment and representation goals in accordance with federal guidelines and reviews them constantly to make sure they reflect work force demographics. Any company with a federal contract is required to make this effort. But Xerox then extends the guidelines by setting diversity goals for its upper level jobs and holding division and group managers accountable for reaching them.

The second piece is a focus on pivotal jobs, a policy Xerox adopted in the 1970s when it first noticed that minorities and women did not have the upward mobility the company wanted to see. By examining the backgrounds of top executives, Xerox was able to identify the key positions that all successful managers had held at lower levels and to set goals for getting minorities and women assigned to such jobs.

The third piece is an effort to concentrate managerial training not so much on managing diversity as on just plain managing people. What the company discovered when it began looking at managerial behavior toward minorities and women was that all too many managers didn't know enough about how to manage anyone, let alone people quite different from themselves.

at least one criterion that will hamper the upward mobility of minorities and women.

Another destructive assumption is the melting pot I referred to earlier. The organization I'm arguing for respects differences rather than seeking to smooth them out. It is multicultural rather than culture blind, which has an important consequence: When we no longer force people to "belong" to a common ethnicity or culture, then the organization's leaders must work all the harder to define belonging in terms of a set of values and a sense of purpose that transcend the interests, desires, and preferences of any one group.

6. *Modify Your Systems.* The first purpose of examining and modifying assumptions is to modify systems. Promotion, mentoring, and sponsorship comprise one such system, and the unexamined cream-to-the-top assumption I mentioned earlier can tend to keep minorities and women from climbing the corporate ladder. After all, in many companies it is difficult to secure a promotion above a certain level without a personal advocate or sponsor. In the context of managing diversity, the question is not whether this system is maximally efficient but whether it works for all employees. Executives who only sponsor people like themselves are not making much of a contribution to the cause of getting the best from every employee.

Performance appraisal is another system where unexamined practices and patterns can have pernicious effects. For example, there are companies where official performance appraisals differ substantially from what is said informally, with the result that employees get their most accurate performance feedback through the grapevine. So if the grapevine is closed to minorities and women, they are left at a severe disadvantage. As one white manager observed, "If the blacks around here knew how they were really perceived, there would be a revolt." Maybe so. More important to your business, however, is the fact that without an accurate appraisal of performance, minority and women employees will find it difficult to correct or defend their alleged shortcomings.

7. *Modify Your Models.* The second purpose of modifying assumptions is to modify models of managerial and employee behavior. My own personal hobgoblin is one I call the Doer Model, often an outgrowth of the family assumption and of unchallenged paternalism. I have found the Doer Model alive and thriving in a dozen companies. It works like this: Since father knows best, managers seek subordinates who will follow their lead and do as they do. If they can't find people exactly like themselves, they try to find people who aspire to be exactly like themselves. The goal is predictability and immediate responsiveness because the doer manager is not there to manage people but to do the business. In accounting departments, for example, doer managers do accounting, and subordinates are simply extensions of their hands and minds, sensitive to every signal and suggestion of managerial intent.

Doer managers take pride in this identity of purpose. "I wouldn't ask my people to do anything I wouldn't do myself," they say. "I roll up my sleeves and get in the trenches." Doer managers love to be in the trenches. It keeps them out of the line of fire.

But managers aren't supposed to be in the trenches, and accounting managers aren't supposed to do accounting. What they are supposed to do is create systems and a climate that allow accountants to do accounting, a climate that enables people to do what they've been charged to do. The right goal is doer subordinates, supported and empowered by managers who manage.

8. *Help Your People Pioneer.* Learning to manage diversity is a change process, and the managers involved are change agents. There is no single tried and tested "solution" to diversity and no fixed right way to manage it. Assuming the existence of a single or even a dominant barrier undervalues the importance of all the other barriers that face any company, including, potentially, prejudice, personality, community dynamics, culture, and the ups and downs of business itself.

While top executives articulate the new company policy and their commitment to it, middle managers—most or all of them still white males, remember—are placed in the tough position of having to cope with a forest of problems and simultaneously develop the minorities and women who represent their own competition for an increasingly limited number of promotions. What's more, every time they stumble they will themselves be labeled the major barriers to progress. These managers need help, they need a certain amount of sympathy, and, most of all, perhaps, they need to be told that they are pioneers and judged accordingly.

In one case, an ambitious young black woman was assigned to a white male manager, at his request, on the basis of her excellent company record. They looked forward to working together, and for the first three months, everything went well. But then their relationship began to deteriorate, and the harder they worked at patching it up, the worse it got. Both of them, along with their superiors, were surprised by the conflict and seemed puzzled as to its causes. Eventually, the black woman requested and obtained reassignment. But even though they escaped each other, both suffered a sense of failure severe enough to threaten their careers. What could have been done to assist them? Well, empathy would not have hurt. But perspective would have been better yet. In their particular company and situation, these two people had placed themselves at the cutting edge of race and gender relations. They needed to know that mistakes at the cutting edge are different—and potentially more valuable—than mistakes elsewhere. Maybe they needed some kind of pioneer training. But at the very least they needed to be told that they were pioneers, that conflicts and failures come with the territory, and that they would be judged accordingly.

9. *Apply the Special Consideration Test.* I said earlier that affirmative action was an artificial, transitional, but necessary stage on the road to a truly diverse work force. Because of its artificial nature, affirmative action requires constant attention and drive to make it work. The point of learning once and for all how to manage diversity is that all that energy can be focused somewhere else.

There is a simple test to help you spot the diversity programs that are going to eat up enormous quantities of time and effort. Surprisingly, perhaps, it is the same test you might use to identify the programs and policies that created your problem in the first place. The test consists of one question: Does this program, policy, or principle give special consideration to one group? Will it contribute to everyone's success, or will it only produce an advantage for blacks or whites or women or men? Is it designed for them as opposed to us? Whenever the answer is yes, you're not yet on the road to managing diversity.

This does not rule out the possibility of addressing issues that relate to a single group. It only underlines the importance of determining that the issue you're addressing does not relate to other groups as well. For example, management in one company noticed that blacks were not moving up in the organization. Before instituting a special program to bring them along, managers conducted interviews to see if they could find the reason for the impasse. What blacks themselves reported was a problem with the quality of supervision. Further interviews showed that other employees too—including white males—were concerned about the quality of supervision and felt that little was being done to foster professional development. Correcting the situation eliminated a problem that affected everyone. In this case, a solution that focused only on blacks would have been out of place.

Had the problem consisted of prejudice, on the other hand, or some other barrier to blacks or minorities alone, a solution based on affirmative action would have been perfectly appropriate.

10. *Continue Affirmative Action.* Let me come full circle. The ability to manage diversity is the ability to manage your company without unnatural advantage or disadvantage for any member of your diverse work force. The fact remains that you must first have a work force that is diverse at every level, and if you don't, you're going to need affirmative action to get from here to there.

450

The reason you then want to move beyond affirmative action to managing diversity is because affirmative action fails to deal with the root causes of prejudice and inequality and does little to develop the full potential of every man and woman in the company. In a country seeking competitive advantage in a global economy, the goal of managing diversity is to develop our capacity to accept, incorporate, and empower the diverse human talents of the most diverse nation on earth. It's our reality. We need to make it our strength.

## About the Author

Formerly an assistant professor at the Harvard Business School, R. Roosevelt Thomas Jr. is executive director of the American Institute for Managing Diversity, Inc., at Atlanta's Morehouse College, where he also serves as secretary of the college.

# 'Affirmative Action': Never-Ending Folly

by Paul Craig Roberts (*Wall Street Journal*)

Job quotas are gradually turning white males into second-class citizens with second-class rights and undermining their traditional role as principal breadwinners. They are now routinely sent to the back of the lines for employment and promotion by "affirmative action" programs.

Indeed, white males have been dispossessed to the extent they now claim to be black in order to get jobs. In a recent case reported by *The New York Times*, two fair-complected brothers, claiming a black great-grandmother, listed their race as black in order to qualify for jobs with the Boston Fire Department. They were later dismissed—thus raising the question of the definition of black (and Hispanic) for "affirmative action" purposes.

Since "affirmative action" has created new privileged rights based on race, the definition of who qualifies for special treatment has become a critical legal matter. Before long Congress or the judiciary will have to define black, Hispanic and other legally privileged classifications. Does half-black qualify for "affirmative action"? What about a person with 1/32 black ancestry? A great deal is at stake.

In addition to jobs and promotion, minority-owned businesses have a right to 10 percent of the federal contracts—a lot of money. Here are various programs that allocate funds to minority groups, and minorities qualify for protection under civil rights laws that do not protect others.

There is absolutely no doubt that the United States is in the process of creating a new aristocracy of race and sex. It is a unique event in history for a dominant group—in this instance, educated white males who hold economic and political power—to institute legal privileges based on race and sex that will disadvantage their sons and grandsons.

Well-meaning whites think of "affirmative action" as a way of compensating for past prejudice, real and imagined, and for speeding up integration. They no doubt intend for "affirmative action" to end once blacks are proportionately represented in every occupation and neighborhood. However, the real world doesn't work that way and never has. Once minorities are legally endowed with special privileges, how do you take them back? The feudal aristocracy held on to its special legal status for centuries beyond the point of its functional contribution as agents of the king and protectors of society. The new racial employment preferences began at the bottom of the job ladder where they do not disturb the educated white males who are imposing them. But the same logic that imposes quotas on fire and police departments holds for the corporate hierarchy and board room. Moreover, as the new privilege is racial, it is hard to oppose it on grounds of qualifications.

The new property rights based on racial and sexual classification will radically transform American society. White women are gaining superior legal status to white men, and this will lead society in a matriarchal direction.

*The same logic that imposes quotas on fire and police departments holds for the corporate hierarchy and board room.*

Aggressive white males who resist this direction will intermarry with racially privileged minorities in order to qualify their children for legal preferences. It is easy to say it can't happen, but that is what medieval kings thought when they created counts and other lowly agents of the crown. Before long the valuable privileges were hereditary.

Moreover, it is pointless to dispute that "affirmative action" creates legal privileges when those in the lower job rungs already are maneuvering to claim them. In New York city recently, for example, two white policemen eyeing promotions sought reclassification to Hispanic status, and one Hispanic demanded to be redefined as a black.

The creation of a highly racially sensitive society and the new politics of privilege will Balkanize Americans by forcing everyone to organize in groups for protection against the special privileges of others. This will cost the economy as more effort is spent in political action and less in producing goods and services. As our productivity falls, so will our ability to compete in world markets.

## About the Author

Paul Craig Roberts is the William E. Simon professor of political economy at the Center for Strategic & International Studies in Washington and is a former assistant secretary of the U. S. Treasury.

# Doonesbury

BY GARRY TRUDEAU

# Black Pride for White People

by Adrian Piper (*Transition*)

*Are you sure you don't have an African ancestor?*

*She's heard the arguments, most astonishingly that, statistically . . . the average white American is 6 percent black. Or, put another way, 95 percent of white Americans are 5 to 80 percent black. Her Aunt Tyler has told her stories about these whites researching their roots in the National Archives and finding they've got an African-American or two in the family, some becoming so hysterical they have to be carried out by paramedics.*

Elaine Perry, *Another Present Era*

*Estimates ranging up to 5 percent, and suggestions that up to one-fifth of the white population have some genes from black ancestors, are probably far too high. If these last figures were correct, the majority of Americans with some black ancestry would be known and counted as whites!*

F. James Davis, *Who Is Black?*

The fact is that the longer a person's family has lived in this country, the higher the probable percentage of African ancestry that person's family is likely to have—bad news for the Daughters of the American Revolution, I'm afraid. And the proximity to the continent of Africa of the country of origin from which one's forebears emigrated, as well as the colonization of a part of Africa by that country, are two further variables that increase the probability of African ancestry within that family. It would appear only the Lapps of Norway are safe.

A number of years ago I was doing research on a video installation on the subject of racial identity and miscegenation, and came across the Phipps case of Louisiana in the early 1980s. Susie Guillory

Phipps had identified herself as white and, according to her own testimony (but not that of some of her black relatives), had believed that she was white, until she applied for a passport, when she discovered that she was identified on her birth records as black by virtue of having one thirty-second African ancestry. She brought suit against the state of Louisiana to have her racial classification changed. She lost the suit but effected the overthrow of the law identifying individuals as black if they had one thirty-second African ancestry, leaving on the books a prior law identifying as black an individual who had any African ancestry—the "one drop" rule that uniquely characterizes the classification of blacks in the United States in fact though no longer in law. So according to this long-standing convention of racial classification, a white who acknowledges any African ancestry implicitly acknowledges being black—a social condition, more than an identity, that no white person would voluntarily assume, even in imagination. This is one reason that whites, educated and uneducated alike, are so resistant to considering the probable extent of racial miscegenation.

No reflective and well-intentioned white person who is consciously concerned to end racism wants to admit to instinctively recoiling at the thought of being identified as black herself. But if you want to see such a white person do this, just peer at the person's facial features and tell her, in a complimentary tone of voice, that she looks as though she might have some black ancestry, and watch her reaction. It's not a test I find or any black person finds particularly pleasant to apply (that is, unless one dislikes the person and wants to inflict pain deliberately), and having once done so inadvertently, I will never do it again. The ultimate test of a person's repudiation of racism is not what she can contemplate doing for or on behalf of black people, but whether she herself can contemplate calmly the likelihood of being black. If racial hatred has not manifested itself in any other context, it will do so here if it exists, in hatred of the self as identified with the other—that is, as self-hatred projected onto the other.

When I was an undergraduate minoring in medieval and Renaissance musicology, I worked with a fellow music student—white—in the music library. I remember his reaction when I relayed to him an article I'd recently read arguing that Beethoven had African ancestry. Beethoven was one of his heroes, and his vehement derision was completely out of proportion to the scholarly worth of the hypothesis. But when I suggested that he wouldn't be so skeptical if the claim were that Beethoven had some Danish ancestry, he fell silent. In those days we were very conscious of covert racism, as our campus was exploding all around us because of it. More recently I premiered at a gallery a video installation exploring the issue of African ancestry among white Americans. A white male viewer commenced to kick the furniture, mutter audibly that he was white and was going to stay that way, and started a fistfight with my dealer. Either we are less conscious of covert racism twenty years later, or we care less to contain it.

Among politically committed and enlightened whites the inability to acknowledge their probable African ancestry is the last outpost of racism. It is the litmus test that separates those who have the courage of their convictions from those who merely subscribe to them and that measures the depth of our dependence on a presumed superiority (of any kind, anything will do) to other human beings—anyone anywhere—to bolster our fragile self-worth.

When I turned 40 a few years ago, I gave myself the present of rereading the personal journals I have been keeping since age 11. I was astounded at the chasm between my present conception of my own past, which is being continually revised and updated to suit present circumstances, and the actual past events, behavior and emotions I recorded as faithfully as I could as they happened. My derelictions, mistakes, and failures of responsibility are much more evident in those journals than they are in my present, sanitized, and virtually blameless image of my past behavior. It was quite a shock to encounter in those pages the person I actually have been rather than the person I now conceive myself to have been. My memory is always under the control of the person I now want and strive to be, and so rarely under the control of the facts. If the personal facts of one's past are this difficult for other people to face too, then perhaps it is no wonder that we must cast about outside ourselves for someone to feel superior to, even though there are so many blunders and misdeeds in our own personal histories that might serve that function.

For whites to acknowledge their blackness is, then, much the same as for men to acknowledge their femininity and for Christians to acknowledge their Judaic heritage. It is to reinternalize the external scapegoat through which they have sought to escape their own sense of inferiority.

## WHY WE SORT PEOPLE BY RACE

In a 1942 book, anthropologist Ashley Montagu called race "Man's Most Dangerous Myth." If it is, then our most ingenuous myth must be that we sort humankind into groups in order to understand the meaning and origin of humankind's diversity. That isn't the reason at all; a greater number of smaller groupings, like ethnicities, does a better job. The obsession with broad categories is so powerful as to seem a neurological imperative. Changing our thinking about race will require a revolution in thought as profound, and profoundly unsettling, as anything science has ever demanded. What these researchers are talking about is changing the way in which we see the world—and each other. But before that can happen, we must do more than understand the biologist's suspicions about race. We must ask science, also, why it is that we are so intent on sorting humanity into so few groups—us and Other—in the first place.

*Newsweek*, February 13, 1995, p. 69.

# Who's What?: The crazy world of racial identification

by Lawrence Wright (*The New Yorker*)

Whatever the word *race* may mean elsewhere in the world, or to the world of science, it is clear that in America the categories are arbitrary, confused, and hopelessly intermingled. In many cases, Americans don't know who they are, racially speaking. They are confused both about how they assess themselves, and how they assess others. A National Center for Health Statistics study found that 5.8 percent of the people who called themselves black were seen as white by a census interviewer. Clearly a third of the people identifying themselves as Asian were classified as white or black by independent observers. That was also true of 70 percent of people who identified themselves as American Indians.

Robert A. Hahn, an epidemiologist at the Centers for Disease Control and Prevention, analyzed deaths of infants born from 1983 through 1985. In an astounding number of cases, the infant had a different race on its death certificate from the one on its birth certificate, and this finding led to staggering increases in the infant mortality rate for minority populations—46.9 percent greater for American Indians, 48.8 percent greater for Japanese-Americans, 78.7 percent greater for Filipinos—over what had been previously recorded. Such disparities cast doubt on the dependability of race as a criterion for any statistical survey.

"It seems to me that we have to go back and reevaluate the whole system," Hahn says. "We have to ask, 'What do these categories mean?' We are not talking about race in the way that geneticists might use the term, because we're not making any kind of biological assessment. It's closer to self-perceived membership in a population—which is essentially what ethnicity is."

Racial statistics do serve an important purpose in the monitoring and enforcement of civil rights laws; indeed, that has become the main justification for such data. Hiring practices, jury selection, discriminatory housing patterns, apportionment of political power—in all these areas, and more, the government patrols society, armed with little more than statistical information to attempt to ensure equal and fair treatment. "We need these categories essentially to get rid of them," Hahn says.

The unwanted corollary of slotting people by race is that such officially sanctioned classifications may actually worsen racial strife. By creating social welfare programs based on race rather than on need, the government sets citizens against one another precisely because of perceived racial differences. "It is not 'race' but a *practice* of racial classification that bedevils the society," writes Yehudi Webster, an African-American sociologist at California State University, Los Angeles, and the author of *The Racialization of America*. The use of racial statistics, he and others have argued, creates a reality of racial divisions, which then require solutions, such as busing, affirmative action, and multicultural education, all of which are bound to fail, because they heighten the racial awareness that leads to contention. Webster believes that adding a "multiracial" box to the Native American, Asian-Pacific, black, and white racial options and Hispanic ethnic option—in the racial self-identification section of the U.S. census, as some advocate, would be "another leap into absurdity," because it reinforces the concept of race. "In a way, it's a continuation of the one-drop principle. Anybody can say, 'I've got one drop of *something*. I must be multiracial. It may finally convince Americans of the absurdity of racial classification."

"The one-drop rule is racist," G. Reginald Daniel of UCLA says. "There's no way you can get away from the fact that it was historically implemented to create as many slaves as possible. No one leaped over to the white community—that was simply the mentality of the nation, and people of African descent internalized it. What this current discourse is about is lifting the lid of racial oppression in our institutions and letting people identify with the totality of their heritage. We have created a nightmare for human dignity. Multiracialism has the potential for undermining the very basis of racism, which is its categories." Such a category would introduce nightmares of its own. How would the entire civil-rights regulatory program concerning housing, employment, and education be reassessed? How would affirmative action programs be implemented? What would happen to desegregation plans? Meant to solve anomalies, the category of "multiracial" creates more anomalies of its own.

Representative Thomas Sawyer of Ohio, Chair of the House Subcommittee on Census, Statistics, and Postal Personnel, agrees that the one drop rule, while embedded in perception and policy, does not allow for the racial blurring that is the reality. He notes that a deluge of new Americans from every part of the world is overwhelming our traditional racial distinctions. While interracial marriages have increased enormously, they have occurred between people who themselves do not have a clearly defined ethnic or racial base.

Representative Sawyer, whose subcommittee reviews the executive branch's policy about which racial and ethnic groups should be officially recognized by the United States Government, argues that racial categories are important to correct clear injustices under the law. "The dilemma we face is trying to assure the fundamental guarantees of equality of opportunity while at the same time recognizing that populations themselves are changing as we seek to categorize them. It reaches the point where it becomes an absurd counting game. Part of the difficulty is that we are dealing with the illusion of precision. We wind up with precise counts of everybody in the country, and they are precisely wrong. They don't reflect who we are as a people. To be effective, the concepts of individual and group identity need to reflect not only who we have been but who we are becoming. The more these categories distort our perception of reality, the less useful they are. We act as if we knew what we're talking about when we talk about race, and we don't."

Jon Michael Spencer, a professor in the African and Afro-American Studies Curriculum at the University of North Carolina at Chapel Hill, believes that race is a useful metaphor for cultural and historic difference, because it permits a level of social cohesion among oppressed classes. "To relinquish the notion of race even though it's a cruel hoax at this particular time is to relinquish our fortress against the powers and principalities that still try to undermine us." he says. He sees a multiracial box as politically damaging to "those who need to galvanize peoples around the racial idea of black. If you had who knows how many thousands or tens of thousands or millions of people claiming to be multiracial, you would lessen the number who are black," Spencer says. "There's no end in sight. There's no limit to which one can go in claiming to be multiracial. For instance, I happen to be very brown in complexion, but when I go to the continent of Africa, blacks and whites there claim that I would be 'colored' rather than black, which means that somewhere in my distant past—probably during the era of slavery—I could have one or more white ancestors. So does that mean that I, too, could check multiracial? Certainly light-skinned black people might perhaps see this as a way out of being included among a despised racial group. The result could be the creation of another class of people, who are betwixt and between black and white."

An equally problematic issue in classification concerns Hispanics. In the 1960 census, people whose ancestry was Latin-American were counted as white. Then people of Spanish origin became a protected group, requiring the census to gather data in order to monitor their civil rights. But how to define them? People who spoke Spanish? Defining the population that way would have included millions of Americans who spoke the language but had no actual roots in Hispanic culture, and it excluded Brazilians and children of immigrants who were not taught Spanish in their homes. One approach was to count persons with Spanish surnames, but that created a number of difficulties: marriage made some non-Hispanic women into instant minorities, while stripping other women of their Hispanic status. The 1970 census inquired about people from "Central or South America," and more than a million people checked the box who were not Hispanic; they were from Kansas, Alabama, Mississippi—the central and southern United States, in other words.

The greatest dilemma was that there was no conceivable justification for calling Hispanics a race. There were black Hispanics from the Dominican Republic, Argentines who were almost entirely

European whites, Mexicans who would have been counted as American Indians if they had been born north of the Rio Grande. The great preponderance of Hispanics are mestizos—a continuum of many different genetic backgrounds. Moreover, the fluid Latin-American concept of race differs from the rigid United States idea of biologically determined and highly distinct human divisions. In most Latin cultures, skin color is an individual variable—not a group marker—so that within the same family one sibling might be considered white and another black. By 1960, the United States census, which counts the population of Puerto Rico, gave up asking the race question on the island, because race did not carry the same distinction there that it did on the mainland. The ad-hoc committee decided to dodge riddles like these by calling Hispanics an ethnic group, not a race.

The discussion over such classifications and their implications is likely to result in the most profound debate of racial questions to be seen in decades.

## About the Author

Lawrence Wright grew up in Dallas, graduated from Tulane University, and spent a year at the American University in Cairo, Egypt. He is a staff writer for *The New Yorker* and is the author of four books: *City Children, Country Summer; In the New World; Saints and Sinners;* and *Remembering Satan.* He lives with his wife and two children in Austin, Texas.

---

### SMALL COMPENSATION
A Drama of Diversity

Scene:    A ship's mess aboard the freighter *Pride of the Celebes* somewhere in the mid-Atlantic.

Dramatis
Personae:    A handful of Filipino (F) sailors squared off against their Northern European (NE) mates.

F:    You get paid almost twice as much as we do. It's unfair. We should be given a raise to equal your salary.

NE:    It costs you nothing to live in the Philippines compared to us in Europe. When it comes to spending power, we should get the raise. You are making more real money than we are . . .

F:    We have families to support. We deserve to be paid equally.

NE:    You spend your money on everybody. You waste it. That's why you are always complaining and asking the Captain for advances on your pay.

F:    We are just making ends meet. We have mouths to feed. How many children and relatives do you take care of? You have more money than you need.

NE:    You just don't need so much to live where you live. We could go there and live on half what you spend. Things are so cheap.

F:    Cheap for you, maybe. Not for us!

*and so on . . .*

# Life and Work Aren't Fair

by Billi Lee

Jimmy Carter got into serious political trouble when he dared to declare that "life isn't fair." Fairness is one of our most cherished American values, perhaps our most sought after Golden Fleece. We create government agencies just to guarantee it. Businesses sell it in their commercials and declare to live by it in their value statements. Both sides of the NAFTA debate claimed it. And perhaps the most confusing use of the concept is when people say that they don't want special treatment, they just want to be treated fairly. A reasonable request, but just ask someone what fair means and you suddenly step into thin air.

Some say that fairness is giving every person equal opportunity. But does the 5'3" athlete have equal opportunity to play basketball as the guy two feet taller? Not in our sport systems. Well, that's not fair, but how do we make it right? Outlaw basketball? 5'3" athletes? Tall players? Do we make every team have one short player for every one over six feet? Should we impose racial quotas on every sports team to insure equal representation?

Another view is that fair means taking turns, so that everyone gets their fair share. Does this mean that the customer can't choose her own counselor, lawyer, insurance agent, or surgeon? If one professional outshines all his competition and gets the greater number of calls, what should we do? Spread them around to the less accomplished so everyone has an equal client load? Make the busiest turn down work so her calendar is only as full as the person's next door? None of this seems fair.

And yet another perspective on fair play is that the same rule applies to everyone, no matter what. No one gets special treatment. But that's hardly fair either. The rules are pretty rigid about no animals in the apartment building: including the seeing-eye dog? What about the school rule that says all children must drink a pint of milk a day? Does that include children who are allergic to milk?

The parking lot committee assigns spaces according to seniority. The newest employees walk the furthest: even if they have a heavy box to carry or a broken leg? Doesn't the concept of fairness require exceptions to every rule at some time or another?

In horse racing the animals are handicapped by ability, experience, and weight to get as close as you can to a race among equals. But with human beings the concept won't work. We don't handicap the college graduate to make it fair for the high school dropout. Or maybe we do. Lowering the standards to include those who previously have been excluded is fair to some but not to others. Having three minorities, one disabled worker, one wealthy heir, one genius and one senior citizen on the company team for the sake of equality isn't fair to the business, the stockholders, or the customers.

Fairness is an elusive concept, defined and experienced differently by each participant in any situation. To be fair to one, is to be unfair to another.

Business in a free market system is by design unfair. The consumer being king determines who wins and who loses. The reward does not always go to the hardest working or best product. I owned a successful restaurant in the ski resort Aspen, which I built on hard work and good food for moderate prices. The next season I still worked hard and had good food, but the unforeseen Sushi fad seduced many of my customers away. Fair or unfair? Fair to the consumer, not fair to me.

Every qualified professional, at least at one time in their career, has lost a promotion to one of many other equally qualified candidates because there was only one promotion available. By whatever criteria you choose the winning candidate, you will be unfair to another qualified candidate.

The changing needs of the organization, as it tries to adapt to the changing demands of its customers, will require changes in company structure, policy and culture that will be unfair to many workers who won't have the skills or experience to meet those needs.

The workplace is unfair, will always be unfair, and needs to be unfair. We only have to remember the failure of communism to understand that fairness really can't be legislated, guaranteed or even universally defined.

So why do we continue to sell, promote, and attempt to guarantee lofty, well intentioned, yet impossible, goals? Does management understand that the use of warm touchy-feely words that promise, but can't deliver to everyone's satisfaction, eventually backfire? Words and phrases like "fair," "empower," "corporate family," or even "world class" can be interpreted so many different ways, can build up so many unrealistic expectations, that the naive usage of such phrases will cause misunderstanding, create cynicism, and decrease trust, instead of inspiring teamwork and increasing morale.

I urge my clients, to be fair, that they use the word "fair" carefully, to define exactly what they mean and to be absolutely certain they can deliver. Jimmy Carter was right after all! Life, certainly work, isn't fair!

---

## About the Author

Billi Lee is an international speaker, author, columnist and commentator on workplace issues. This article was syndicated and appeared in newspapers, magazines, and journals nationwide. She can be reached at: Billi Lee & Company, Inc., P.O. Box 50400, Colorado Springs, CO 80960; Phone: 719-520-5051; Fax: 719-475-9331.

---

## RESEARCHERS FIND THAT ONLY 6.3% OF ALL HUMAN DIVERSITY IS A FUNCTION OF TRADITIONALLY DEFINED RACIAL GROUPS

The four blood types (A, B, AB, and O) are found in all human populations. An Irishman with type A blood can receive a transfusion from a Ugandan with type A blood. In fact, the "races" of humanity do not differ in terms of the presence or absence of certain genes, but only in their frequencies of occurrence. This statement about genetic diversity can be quantitatively validated. One can measure the amount of genetic diversity in a population by answering the question, "If two individuals are picked at random from this population, what is the probability that they will differ in some inherited characteristic, such as blood type?" Lewontin reports a study of genetic diversity using inherited blood groups. The study indicated that of the diversity that exists in the global gene pool, only 6.3% is due to differences between traditionally defined major races (Caucasoid, Negroid, etc.), only 8.3% comes from the differences between nations and tribes within the major races, and 85.4% is contributed by differences between individuals within a nation or tribe. He summarizes quite instructively,

"To put the matter crudely, if, after a great cataclysm, only Africans were left alive, the human species would have retained 93% of its total genetic variation, although the species as a whole would be darker skinned. If the cataclysm were even more extreme and only the Xhosa people of the southern tip of Africa survived, the human species would still retain 80% of its genetic variation. Considered in the context of the evolution of our species, this would be a trivial reduction."

Richard C. Lewontin, *Human Diversity*, Scientific American Books, New York, 1982, p. 123.

# The Masks of Minority Terrorism

by Pico Iyer (*TIME Magazine*)

When Actors' Equity briefly decided three weeks ago that the part of a Eurasian in the play Miss Saigon could not be taken by a European, its board members provided some of the best entertainment seen on Broadway recently. It was not just that they were asserting an Orwellian principle: All races are equal, but some are more equal than others. Nor even that they were threatening to deprive thousands of playgoers of a drama that promised to shed some light on precisely such cross-cultural nuances; nor even that they were more or less ensuring—if the principle were to be applied fairly—that most Asian-American actors would have to sit around in limbo and wait for the next production of *The Mikado*. They were also raising some highly intriguing questions. How can John Gielgud play Prospero when Doug Henning is at hand? Should future Shakespeares—even future August Wilsons—stock their plays with middle-class whites so as to have the largest pool of actors from which to choose? And next time we stage *Moby Dick*, will there be cries that the title part be taken by a card-carrying leviathan?

The quickly reversed decision, which effectively proclaimed that actors should do everything but act, was a short-running farce. But when the same kind of minority terrorism is launched offstage, as is more and more the case, the consequences are less comical. Jimmy Breslin, long famous as a champion of the dispossessed, speaks thoughtlessly and finds himself vilified as a "racist." Spike Lee, an uncommonly intelligent filmmaker whenever he remains behind the camera, maintains that films about blacks should be directed by blacks (what does this mean for *The Bear*, one wonders, or for *Snow White and the Seven Dwarfs*?). Lee in turn becomes an irresistible target for charges of anti-Semitism. And others contend that Marion Barry is being hounded because he is black, as if to suggest that he be excused because he is black.

The problem with people who keep raising the cry of "racism" is that they would have us see everything in terms of race. They treat minorities as emblems, and everyone as typecast. And in suggesting that a white cannot put himself in the shoes, or soul, of a half-white, or a black, they would impose on us the most stifling form of apartheid, condemning us all to a hopeless rift of mutual incomprehension. Taken to an extreme, this can lead to a litigious nation's equivalent of the tribal vendetta: You did my people wrong, so now I am entitled to do you wrong. A plague on every house.

Almost nobody, one suspects, would deny that equal rights are a laudable goal and that extending a hand to the needy is one of the worthiest things we can do. Reserving some places in schools, or companies, or even plays for those who are less privileged seems an admirable way of redressing imbalances. But privilege cannot be interpreted in terms of race without making some damningly racist assumptions. And rectifying the injustices of our grandfathers is no easy task, least of all in a country made up of refugees and immigrants and minorities of one, many of whom have lived through the Holocaust, the Khmer Rouge, the unending atrocities of El Salvador. Sympathy cannot be legislated any more than kindness can.

The whole issue, in fact, seems to betray a peculiarly American conundrum: the enjoyment of one freedom means encroachment on another; you can't school all of the people all of the time. Older, and less earnest, countries like Britain or Japan live relatively easily with racial inequalities. But America, with its evergreen eagerness to do the right thing, tries to remedy the world with an innocence that can become more dangerous than cruelty. All of us, when we make decisions—which is to say, discriminations—judge in part on appearances. All of us treat Savile Row-suited lawyers differently from kids in T shirts, give preference to the people that we like—or to the people that are most like us—and make differing assumptions about a Texan and a Yankee. To wish this were not so is natural; to claim it is not so is hypocrisy.

But state-sponsored favoritism is something different. As an Asian minority myself, I know of nothing more demeaning than being chosen for a job, or even a role, on the basis of my race. Nor is the accompanying assumption—that I need a helping hand because my ancestors were born outside Europe—very comforting. Are those of us lucky enough to be born minorities to be forgiven our transgressions, protected from insults and encouraged to act as if we cannot take responsibility for our actions (it wasn't my fault I failed the exam; society made me do it)? Are we, in fact, to cling to a state of childlike dependency? As an alien from India, I choose to live in America precisely because it is a place where aliens from India are, in principle, treated no better (and no worse) than anyone else. Selecting an Asian actor, say, over a better-qualified white one (or, for that matter, a white over a better-qualified Asian, as is alleged to happen with certain university admissions) does nobody a service: not the Asian, whose lack of qualifications will be rapidly shown up; not the white, whose sense of racial brotherhood is hardly likely to be quickened by being the victim of discrimination himself; not the company, or audience, which may understandably resent losing quality to quotas.

Affirmative action, in fact—so noble in intention—is mostly a denial: a denial of the fact that we are all born different; a denial of a person's right to get the position he deserves; a denial of everyone's ability to transcend, or live apart from, the conditions of his birth. Most of all, it is a denial of the very virtues of opportunity and self-determination that are the morning stars of this democracy. People around the world still long to migrate to America because it is a place, traditionally and ideally, where people can say what they think, become what they dream and succeed—or fail—on the basis of their merits. Now, though, with more and more people telling us not to say what we think and to support everyone except the majority of Americans, the country is in danger of becoming something else: the land of the free, with an asterisk.

---

## NEWSWEEK POLL

Should there be special consideration for each of the following groups to increase their opportunities for getting into college and getting jobs or promotions?
(percent saying yes)

| GROUP | BLACKS | WHITES |
| --- | --- | --- |
| Blacks | 62% | 25% |
| Women | 62% | 26% |
| Hispanics | 57% | 22% |
| Asians | 48% | 18% |
| Native Americans | 65% | 34% |

THE NEWSWEEK POLL, FEB. 1–3, 1995

## NEWSWEEK POLL

Race relations in the U.S. are:

| | BLACKS | WHITES |
| --- | --- | --- |
| Excellent | 2% | 1% |
| Good | 10% | 22% |
| Fair | 45% | 44% |
| Poor | 41% | 31% |

THE NEWSWEEK POLL, FEB. 1–3, 1995

# Affirmative Action on the Edge

by Steven V. Roberts (*U.S. World & News Report*)

*A divisive debate begins over whether women and minorities still deserve favored treatment*

Affirmative action is a time bomb primed to detonate in the middle of the American political marketplace. Federal courts are pondering cases that challenge racial preferences in laying off teachers, awarding contracts and admitting students. On Capitol Hill, the new Republican majority is taking aim at the Clinton administration's civil rights record. On the campaign trail, several Republican presidential hopefuls are already running against affirmative action. And in California, organizers are trying to put an initiative on [the upcoming] ballot banning state-sanctioned "preferential treatment" based on race or gender.

This increasingly angry and divisive debate about the role of race and gender in modern America could help the Republicans . . . change the way many institutions allot jobs, business and benefits. A recent *Wall Street Journal*/NBC News survey found that 2 out of 3 Americans, including half of those who voted for President Clinton in 1992, oppose affirmative action. The *Los Angeles Times* found 73 percent of Californians back the ballot initiative. "The political implications are enormous," says Will Marshall of the democratic Leadership Council, a moderate group. "Obviously, a lot of Republicans look at affirmative action as the ultimate wedge issue."

The assault on affirmative action is gathering strength from a slow-growth economy, stagnant middle-class incomes and corporate downsizing, all of which make the question of who gets hired—or fired—more volatile. Facing attacks on such a broad front, women's groups, civil rights organizations and other defenders of affirmative action are circling their wagons. Women and minorities still need preferential treatment, they argue, because discrimination still exists, causing blacks and other minorities to lag far behind whites in terms of economic status. "If African-Americans are taking all these jobs," asks Barbara Arnwine of the Lawyers Committee for Civil Rights Under Law, "why is there double-digit unemployment in the African-American community?" Adds Patricia Williams, a professor at Columbia Law School: "There is this misplaced sound and fury about nothing. Access is still very limited, and the numbers are still very low."

But the sound and fury are real. Affirmative action poses a conflict between two cherished American principles: the belief that all Americans deserve equal opportunities and the idea that hard work and merit, not race or religion or gender or birthright, should determine who prospers and who does not. In 1965, Lyndon Johnson defended affirmative action by arguing that people hobbled by generations of bias could not be expected to compete equally. That made sense to most Americans 30 years ago, but today many argue that the government is not simply ensuring that the race starts fairly but trying to decide who wins it.

Moreover, many women and racial minorities are no longer disadvantaged simply because of their race or gender. Indeed, most of the young people applying for jobs and to colleges today were not even born when legal segregation ended. "I'll be goddamned why the son of a wealthy black businessman should have a slot reserved for that race when the son of a white auto-assembly worker is excluded," says a liberal democratic lawmaker. "That's just not right."

***Disheartening.*** The critics of affirmative action include some conservative minority and women's leaders who believe it has a destructive effect on their own communities. Thomas Sowell, the black

> In 1990, 62,100 charges were filed with the EEOC. In 1994, the number was 91,200.

economist, argues that affirmative action has created a process of "mismatching," in which competition for talented minorities is so fierce that many are pushed into colleges for which they are not ready. "You can't fool kids," says Linda Chavez, a Hispanic activist. "They come into a university, they haven't had the preparation, and it's a very disheartening experience for some of them."

Others say affirmative action causes co-workers to view them with suspicion. "White skepticism leads to African-American defensiveness," says Sharon Brooks Hodge, a black writer and broadcaster. "Combined, they make toxic race relations in the workplace." Glenn Loury, an economics professor at Boston University, says proponents of affirmative action have an inferiority complex "When blacks say we have to have affirmative action, please don't take it away from us, it's almost like saying, 'You're right, we can't compete on merit.' But I know that we can compete."

William Bennett, former education secretary and a leading GOP strategist, says that "toxic" race relations, aggravated by affirmative action, have led to a damaging form of re-segregation: "Affirmative action has not brought us what we want—a colorblind society. It has brought us an extremely color-conscious society. In our universities we have separate dorms, separate social centers. What's next—water fountains? That's not good, and everybody knows it."

But supporters of affirmative action maintain that arguments like Bennett's are unrealistic—even naive. "We tried colorblind 30 years ago, and that system is naturally and artificially rigged for white males," says Connie Rice of the NAACP Legal Defense and Education Fund. "If we abandon affirmative action, we return to the old-boy network."

Voices on both sides of the debate are starting to discuss a possible compromise that would focus eligibility on class, instead of on race or gender. For example, the son of a poor white coal miner from West Virginia would be eligible for special help, but the daughter of a black doctor from Beverly Hills would not. "Some of the conventional remedies don't work as one might have hoped," says University of Pennsylvania law professor Lani Guinier, whose ill-fated nomination as Clinton's chief civil rights enforcer sparked a storm of protest from conservatives. "Perhaps there is an approach that does not suggest that only people who have been treated unfairly because of race or gender or ethnicity have a legitimate case."

No one questions the sensitivity of the subject. For years, the civil rights lobby, backed by Democrats in Congress, was so strong that critics often felt intimidated. Even today, Democrats who disagree with affirmative action are reluctant to voice their doubts. "The problem is political correctness—you can't talk openly," says a member of Congress.

Democrats are talking privately, however, urging the White House to formulate a response to the anti-affirmative-action wave before it swamps the president and the party. At the Justice Department, chief civil rights enforcer Duval Patrick is ready: "We have to engage; we can't sit to one side."

But—[even with the looming California initiative,] the administration seems sluggish, even paralyzed. Laments a senior adviser, "We're going to wait until it's a crisis before reacting." White House political strategists admit one reason for the inaction: The issue is a sure loser.

*Referee?* Caught between angry white males and the party's traditional liberal base, White House advisers think the best they can do is position the president as an arbiter between two extremes. In a recent interview with *U.S. News,* the president voiced his aim this way: "What I hope we don't have here, and what I hope they don't have in California, is a vote that's structured in such a way as to be highly divisive, where there have to be winners and losers and no alternatives can be easily considered." Asked his views on affirmative action, the president tried—as he often does—to please both sides: "There's no question that a lot of people have been helped by it. Have others been hurt by it? What is the degree of that harm? What are the alternatives? That's a discussion we ought to have."

But a senior administration official admits that the middle ground will be an uncomfortable place: "The civil rights groups are going to say we're caving in if we make any compromises. And the

> Thirty years ago, 18 percent of black families were middle-class. Today: 40%.

463

Republicans are going to shout, 'Quotas.' " That same tension is already developing within the White House. U.S. News has learned that Chief of Staff Leon Panetta is quietly asking friends on Capitol Hill whether the president should simply endorse the California initiative—a position sure to trigger outrage among the president's more-liberal advisers.

Unsure how resolute the White House will be, civil rights groups are looking for their own strategy to defend affirmative action. One of their main jobs, they say, is to debunk the "myth" that unqualified women and minorities are being hired in large numbers. And some of the best salesmen for affirmative action are big corporations that adjusted long ago to the demands for a more-diverse work force, dread bad publicity and fear the uncertainty change would produce. James Wall, national director of human resources for Deloitte & Touche LLP, a management consulting firm, says diversity is good business: "If you don't use the best of all talent, you don't make money."

Even so, the combination of old resentments, new economic hardships and shifting political winds threatens to explode. "There's a great deal of pent-up anger beneath the surface of American politics that's looking for an outlet," says conservative strategist Clint Bolick of the Institute for Justice. It's the same anxiety that helped pass Proposition 187 in California, which sharply restricts public assistance to the children of illegal immigrants, and thwarted Clinton's plan to push a Mexican aid plan through Congress. "If there is a squeeze on the middle class," says GOP pollster Linda Divall, "people get very vociferous if they think their ability to advance is being limited."

Some African-American leaders insist that this white-male anger is being stirred up by demagogues who make blacks and women into scapegoats. Says Derrick Bell, professor of law at New York University: "There is a fixation among so many in this country that their anxieties will go away if we can just get these black folks in their place." But the anxieties are strong and are coupled with a growing belief that affirmative action is another aspect of intrusive and inefficient big gov-

ernment. "The real back-to-basics movement is not in education but in politics," says William Bennett. "We're rethinking basic assumptions—about government."

Accordingly, the fight over affirmative action is playing out in four arenas:

■ **California.** The real question is [how] the civil rights initiative will [fare and what the results will be] . . .

The initiative is the brainchild of two academics, Tom Wood and Glynn Custred, who say they were alarmed by the prevalence of "widespread reverse discrimination" in the state's college system. The initiative has already attracted some unlikely support: Ward Connerly, a black member of the University of California Board of Regents, said last month that he favors an end to racial and gender preferences. "What we're doing is inequitable to certain people. I want something in its place that is fair." And Hispanic columnist Roger Hernandez wrote: "I've never understood why Hispanic liberals, so sensitive to slights from the racist right, don't also take offense at the patronizing racists of the left who say that being Hispanic makes you an idiot."

California Assembly Speaker Willie Brown, who is black, opposes the initiative as an attempt "to maintain white America in total control." But other Democrats are scurrying for cover. "The wedge potential is absolutely scary," says Ron Wakabayashi, director of the Los Angeles County Human Rights Commission. "The confrontation of interests looks like blacks and Latinos on one side and Asians and Jews on the other."

■ **The courts.** The Supreme Court has generally supported race and gender preferences to remedy past discrimination, but an increasingly conservative bench has moved to limit the doctrine. In 1989, the court struck down a program in Richmond, Va., that set aside 30 percent of municipal contracts for racial minorities and that decision set off a flurry of litigation . . . The court already has heard arguments in a key case: A white-owned construction company is claiming that it failed to get a federal contract in Colorado because of bonuses given to contractors that hire minority firms.

> *Fifty-one percent of whites say equal rights have been pushed too far in the U. S.*

In another case making its way toward the high court, a black teacher in Piscataway, NJ, was retained while an equally qualified white teacher was fired, in the name of diversity. The Bush administration sided with the white teacher after she sued the school board. The Clinton administration backs the board. Two other cases relating to education are also moving forward. In one, white students at the University of Maryland are challenging a scholarship program reserved for minorities. In the other, the University of Texas law school is being sued for an admissions policy that lowers standards for blacks and Hispanics.

While most court watchers do not expect sweeping changes in current doctrine, the high court is closely divided on racial-preference questions, and the deciding votes could be cast by Justice Sandra Day O'Connor. Legal analysts cite her opinion in a 1993 case challenging voting districts that were drawn to guarantee a black winner: "racial gerrymandering, even for remedial purposes, may balkanize us into competing racial factions." The court's most likely move: require programs to be more narrowly tailored to remedy past discrimination.

■ **Congress.** Republican victories last year mean that critics of affirmative action now control the key committees and the congressional calendar. A strategy session was held last Friday at the Heritage Foundation, a conservative think tank, bringing together about two dozen Hill staffers, lawyers and conservative activists. Already, Rep. Charles Canady, the Florida Republican who heads the key House subcommittee, has written to the Justice Department requesting every document relating to affirmative action cases. His goal: oversight hearings that try to demonstrate that the administration's civil rights policies far exceed the original intent of Congress.

Conservatives are considering amendments to appropriations bills that would restrict the administration's flexibility. There also is talk of a measure banning racial and gender preferences altogether. Civil rights proponents remain confident that Clinton would veto any measure that eviscerates affirmative action and that his veto would survive.

■ **Campaign [Politics].** The affirmative action issue will be test-marketed . . . by . . . [a number of ] Republican candidates . . . [It will be debated in elections, in congress, and in community organizations.]

The danger for Republicans lies in going too far in attacking affirmative action and courting resentful white males. If the anti-affirmative-action campaign "turns into mean-spirited racial crap, to hell with it," William Bennett warned fellow Republicans.

But the questions at the core of the affirmative action debate remain unanswered. How much discrimination still exists in America? And what remedies are still necessary to aid its victims?

## About the Authors

By Steven V. Roberts with Jeannye Thornton, Ted Gest, Matthew Cooper, Robin M. Bennefield, Katia Hetter, Jennifer Seter, Scott Minerbrook in New York and Mike Tharp in Los Angeles.

# Black and Blue: A Top Cop's Painful Rethinking of Race-Based Preferences

by Paul Glastris (*U.S. News & World Report*)

St. Louis Police Chief Clarence Harmon never dreamed he'd be fighting against the forces of affirmative action. But that was before last December, when the police department announced the results of an exam taken by officers vying to become sergeants. Though blacks made up about 30 percent of the test takers, they had only 16 percent of the top scores.

In a city that is roughly half African-American, the test results put Harmon, St. Louis's first black police chief, in an awkward political position. Things grew worse when the head of a local black police organization, Dennis McLin, presented reporters with copies of the confidential sergeants exam. The exams, McLin contended, had been mailed to him after being circulated among white officers before the test was given. "That's why we tend to score lower than whites," McLin said.

At the behest of the Board of Police Commissioners, Harmon launched an inquiry and found that the theft had occurred after the officers took the exam. Because the test results had not been compromised, Harmon argued, the scores should stand. That position earned him the gratitude of white officers, especially those who scored well on the exam, but the derision of some African-Americans. One letter in a black newspaper from a retired police officer called, the chief "a disgrace to your race." St. Louis's black mayor, Freeman Bosley Jr. (who has feuded with Harmon over control of the department), called, without success, for an independent investigation.

Ironically, it was Harmon who, in 1980, pushed the police department to adopt its first-ever affirmative action plan, which resulted in the hiring and promotion of hundreds of black and female police officers. Today, sitting in his corner office with a view of the Gateway Arch, Harmon muses on how he arrived at a position on race and gender preferences that is "almost 180 degrees from where I was."

His doubts first arose in the mid–1980s. Then commander of internal affairs. Harmon began noticing that in its haste to meet affirmative action goals, the department was hiring black recruits who scored relatively poorly on entrance exams. In discussions with other high-ranking black officers, Harmon worried that the new recruits would have trouble competing with their white counterparts for promotions. "It got to the point where we were wondering if this was being done by design," the chief recalls.

Like many blacks who joined the force in the 1960s and early 1970s, Harmon and his contemporaries had taken pride in competing head-to-head with whites even as they fought for affirmative action goals. Yet in the 1980s he and his colleagues were noticing that too many younger black officers were using affirmative action as a kind of crutch. "Some of my younger colleagues will be loath to admit this," says the chief delicately, "but for many of them affirmative action has meant that they didn't have to do some of the things they should have done to compete."

The main mechanism of affirmative action in most big-city police departments was something called "race norming," reworking test results to achieve racial balance. In St. Louis, race norming worked like this: Some blacks who scored in lower "clusters" (groups of candidates who achieved approximately the same scores) would be advanced ahead of some whites who scored in higher clusters.

*Mixed emotions.* Harmon saw this "cluster dipping" as a justified means of compensating blacks for years of being systematically held back by white commanders. But he also had "mixed emotions" about the practice, specifically the way it angered whites who were passed over for promotions. So did Congress, which outlawed race norming in the 1991 Civil Rights Act. After reading the statute, Harmon persuaded the St. Louis police board to stop cluster dipping. That didn't stop some white officers who had been passed over from suing for—and winning—their sergeant's stripes.

In the past, what angered police officers, black and white, more than affirmative action was that an officer generally needed "steam" (political clout) in the form of an "ace" (a political patron) to advance in the St. Louis Police Department. Under Harmon's regime, most officers agree, politics is much less important than test scores.

Next week, the police board will vote on whether to accept or throw out the latest test results. Either decision could spark a lengthy court battle. Meanwhile, race relations within the depart-

ment, says one headquarters staffer, are "real friggin' tense."

Yet as old-style affirmative action dies in St. Louis, a new and perhaps healthier variety is being born. Two years ago, Harmon began beefing up efforts to recruit higher-quality minority cadets. Today, disparities between black and white cadet test scores are a third of what they were in the late 1980s. With any luck, that narrowing of scores should translate into more promotions for minorities five years from now, when today's cadets are eligible to take the sergeants exam.

# Kara Hultgreen and the Codes of Prejudice

by Ellen Goodman (*Boston Globe*)

*Affirmative action: The Navy has vindicated its first woman fighter pilot, who was hounded even in death by the ubiquitous slur of double standards.*

So it was the engine after all. Not the pilot. Lt. Kara Hultgreen did not die on the altar of "political correctness," or "preferential treatment" or "reverse discrimination." She died because the F-14A Tomcat stalled as it approached the aircraft carrier. The Navy brass played the videotape of the crash over and over again last week. The officers relayed the findings of their investigation succinctly: It wasn't her fault. It wasn't her sex.

Kara Hultgreen had grown up fearless, a daredevil who believed she could do anything. At 10, she deliberately ran through a glass door. At 28, she broke the glass ceiling. When the Navy finally lifted its ban against women fighter pilots in 1993, this gung-ho pilot who knew all the lines from "Top Gun" was the first to join an air combat squadron. Last October she became the first to die.

But before Kara Hultgreen's body had even been recovered from the sea, 4,000 feet deep, strapped to her ejection seat, the anonymous phone calls, the fax attacks, the rumors had all begun. She was a pilot only because the Navy was

trying to be "politically correct" in the wake of the Tailhook scandal. She was unqualified. She was given preferential treatment. She was, in the modern slang, an affirmative-action baby.

In her too-brief career, Kara Hultgreen had flown across the whole trajectory of prejudice. At the beginning, she was banned from her job because she was a woman. At the end, it was said that she got the job only because she was a woman. One double standard was twisted into another. Even Ted Koppel on "Nightline," probing her qualifications, asked if she had received a "kind of affirmative action." And a reporter, automatically responding in the same shorthand, said no, the Navy didn't lower its standards.

Maybe this is Lt. Hultgreen's last, unwitting service. The people who cast a shadow on her reputation have thrown some light on the debate about discrimination and affirmative action.

In today's language and climate, affirmative action has become synonymous in the public mind with lowering standards. The remedy for discrimination has become a code word for it. Those who oppose affirmative action will say Kara Hultgreen's story proves how much these programs tarnish every successful woman or minority. Even one who rose by the most rigorous of single standards. Those who favor affirmative action will say the story proves how far we still are from a race-blind, gender-neutral society. The people who want to keep the outsiders where they belong—down— have found a new way of expressing an old prejudice. But either way you look at it, affirmative action is now tainted. It's become a fighting term. Politicians who want to appease those legendary angry white men promise to strike it from the policy vocabulary. California is putting the issue on the ballot. The President has vowed a top-to-bottom review of federal programs. We are in for change and we don't have a new language for it.

Affirmative-action plans, the goals and goads designed to remedy past discrimination, have made a difference in the lives of women and minorities. The statistics can tell you that. The plans have also created antagonism between men and women, whites and blacks. The anecdotes can tell you that. This antagonism is stirred every time an employer tries to let a white man down, falsely but easily, by saying, "We have to hire a woman." It's stirred every time a politician wants people to believe that a black American has taken "their" job, not a Sri Lankan or a Mexican.

Those who have favored affirmative action—as I have—have been too busy fighting opponents to confront our own conflicts. We haven't squarely faced the dilemma of fostering group rights to promote individual rights. Nor have we fairly computed the competing disadvantages of race and class, gender and poverty.

It's late in the day and we haven't laid out our own end game. We haven't decided when the time is up for this temporary policy. If not now, when? How will we know? It's no wonder that the country believes the temporary is permanent.

But the opponents of affirmative action also have their work cut out. As the mood of the country shifts, so does the burden. Those who would end programs that have given women and minorities a chance are now obliged to describe the tools they would use on the still-rocky road to equality. Without such a plan we can only assume that the goal is to go backward.

While this debate goes on, it's worth remembering how much prejudice there still is in this world. Enough prejudice to follow a young pilot into her grave.

## About the Author

Ellen Goodman is a syndicated columnist based in Boston.

# Class, Not Race

by Richard Kahlenberg (*The New Republic*)

For many years, the left argued not only that class was important, but also that it was more important than race. This argument was practical, ideological and politic. An emphasis on class inequality meant Robert Kennedy riding in a motorcade through cheering white and black sections of racially torn Gary, Indiana in 1968, with black Mayor Richard Hatcher on one side, and white working-class boxing hero Tony Zale on the other.

Ideologically, it was clear that with the passage of the Civil Rights Act of 1964, class replaced caste as the central impediment to equal opportunity. Martin Luther King Jr. moved from the Montgomery Boycott to the Poor People's Campaign, which he described as "his last, greatest dream," and "something bigger than just a Civil rights movement for Negroes." RFK told David Halberstam that "it was pointless to talk about the real problem in America being black and white, it was really rich and poor, which was a much more complex subject."

Finally, the left emphasized class because to confuse class and race was seen not only as wrong but as dangerous. This notion was at the heart of the protest over Daniel Patrick Moynihan's 1965 report, *The Negro Family: The Case for National Action*, in which Moynihan depicted the rising rates of illegitimacy among poor blacks. While Moynihan's critics were wrong to silence discussion of illegitimacy among blacks, they rightly noted that the title of the report, which implicated all blacks, was misleading, and that fairly high rates of illegitimacy also were present among poor whites—a point which Moynihan readily endorses today. (In the wake of the second set of L.A. riots in 1992, Moynihan rose on the Senate floor to reaffirm that family structure "is not an issue of race but of class . . . . It is dass behavior.")

The irony is that affirmative action based on race violates these three liberal insights. It provides the ultimate wedge to destroy Robert Kennedy's coalition. It says that despite civil rights protec-

tions, the wealthiest African-American is more deserving of preference than the poorest white. It relentlessly focuses all attention on race.

In contrast, Lyndon Johnson's June 1965 address to Howard University, in which the concept of affirmative action was first unveiled, did not ignore class. In a speech drafted by Moynihan, Johnson spoke of the bifurcation of the black community, and, in his celebrated metaphor, said we needed to aid those "hobbled" in life's race by past discrimination. This suggested special help for disadvantaged blacks, not all blacks; for the young Clarence Thomas, but not for Clarence Thomas's son. Johnson balked at implementing the thematic language of his speech. His Executive Order 11246, calling for "affirmative action" among federal contractors, initially meant greater outreach and required hiring without respect to race. In fact, LBJ rescinded his Labor Department's proposal to provide for racial quotas in the construction industry in Philadelphia. It fell to Richard Nixon to implement the "Philadelphia Plan," in what Nixon's aides say was a conscious effort to drive a wedge between blacks and labor. (Once he placed racial preferences on the table, Nixon adroitly extricated himself, and by 1972 was campaigning against racial quotas.)

The ironies were compounded by the Supreme Court. In the 1974 case *DeFunis v. Odegaard*, in which a system of racial preferences in law school admissions was at issue, it was the Court's liberal giant, William O. Douglas, who argued that racial preferences were unconstitutional, and suggested instead that preferences be based on disadvantage. Four years later, in the *Bakke* case, the great proponent of affirmative action as a means to achieve "diversity" was Nixon appointee Lewis F. Powell Jr. Somewhere along the line, the right wing embraced Douglas and Critical Race Theory embraced Powell.

Today, the left pushes racial preferences, even for the most advantaged minorities, in order to promote diversity and provide role models for disadvantaged blacks—an argument which, if it came from Ronald Reagan, the left would rightly dismiss as trickle-down social theory. Today, when William Julius Wilson argues the opposite of the Moynihan report—that the problems facing the black community are rooted more in class than race—it is Wilson who is excoriated by civil rights groups. The left can barely utter the word "class," instead resorting to euphemisms such as "income groups," "wage earners" and "people who play by the rules."

For all of this, the left has paid a tremendous price. On a political level, with a few notable exceptions, the history of the past twenty-five years is a history of white, working-class Robert Kennedy Democrats turning first into Wallace Democrats, then into Nixon and Reagan Democrats and ultimately into today's Angry White Males. Time and again, the white working class votes its race rather than its class, and Republicans win. The failure of the left to embrace class also helps turn poor blacks, for whom racial preferences are, in Stephen Carter's words, "stunningly irrelevant," toward Louis Farrakhan.

On the merits, the left has committed itself to a goal—equality of group results—which seems highly radical, when it is in fact rather unambitious. To the extent that affirmative action, at its ultimate moment of success, merely creates a self-perpetuating black elite along with a white one, its goal is modest—certainly more conservative than real equality of opportunity, which gives blacks and whites and other Americans of all economic strata a fair chance at success.

The priority given to race over class has inevitably exacerbated white racism. Today, both liberals and conservatives conflate race and class because it serves both of their purposes to do so. Every year, when SAT scores are released, the breakdown by race shows enormous gaps between blacks on the one hand and whites and Asians on the other. The NAACP cites these figures as evidence that we need to do more. Charles Murray cites the same statistics as evidence of intractable racial differences. We rarely see a breakdown of scores by class, which would show enormous gaps between rich and poor, gaps that would help explain the differences in scores by race.

On the legal front, it once made some strategic sense to emphasize race over class. But when states moved to the remedial phase—and began trying to address past discrimination—the racial focus became a liability. The strict scrutiny that struck down Jim Crow is now used, to varying degrees, to curtail racial preferences. Class, on the other hand, is not one of the suspect categories under the Fourteenth Amendment, which leaves class-based remedies much less assailable.

If class-based affirmative action is a theory that liberals should take seriously, how would it work in practice? In this magazine, Michael Kinsley has asked, "Does Clarence Thomas, the sharecropper's kid, get more or fewer preference points than the unemployed miner's son from Appalachia?" Most conservative proponents of class-based affirmative action have failed to explain their idea with any degree of specificity. Either they're insincere—offering the alternative only for tactical reasons—or they're stumped.

The former is more likely. While the questions of implementation are serious and difficult, they are not impossible to answer. At the university level, admissions committees deal every day with precisely the type of apples-and-oranges question that Kinsley poses. Should a law school admit an applicant with a 3.2 GPA from Yale or a 3.3 from Georgetown? How do you compare those two if one applicant worked for the Peace Corps but the other had slightly higher LSATs?

In fact, a number of universities already give preferences for disadvantaged students in addition to racial minorities. Since 1989 Berkeley has granted special consideration to applicants "from socioeconomically disadvantaged backgrounds . . . regardless of race or ethnicity." Temple University Law School has, since the 1970s, given preference to "applicants who have overcome exceptional and continuous economic deprivation." And at Hastings College of Law, 20 percent of the class is set aside for disadvantaged students through the Legal Equal Opportunity Program. Even the U.C.-Davis medical program challenged by Allan Bakke was limited to "disadvantaged" minorities, a system which Davis apparently did not find impossible to administer.

Similar class-based preference programs could be provided by public employers and federal contractors for high school graduates not pursuing college, on the theory that at that age their class-based handicaps hide their true potential and are not at all of their own making. In public contracting, government agencies could follow the model of New York City's old class-based program, which provided preferences based not on the ethnicity or gender of the contractor, but to small firms located in New York City which did part of their business in depressed areas or employed economically disadvantaged workers.

The definition of class or disadvantage may vary according to context, but if, for example, the government chose to require class-based affirmative action from universities receiving federal funds, it is possible to devise an enforceable set of objective standards for deprivation. If the aim of class-based affirmative action is to provide a system of genuine equality of opportunity, a leg up to promising students who have done well despite the odds, we have a wealth of sociological data to devise an obstacles test. While some might balk at the very idea of reducing disadvantage to a number, we currently reduce intellectual promise to numbers—SATS and GPAs—and adding a number for disadvantage into the calculus just makes deciding who gets ahead and who does not a little fairer.

There are three basic ways to proceed: with a simple, moderate or complex definition. The simple method is to ask college applicants their family's income and measure disadvantage by that factor alone, on the theory that income is a good proxy for a whole host of economic disadvantages (such as bad schools or a difficult learning environment). This oversimplified approach is essentially the tack we've taken with respect to compensatory race-based affirmative action. For example, most affirmative action programs ask applicants to check a racial box and sweep all the ambiguities under the rug. Even though African Americans have, as Justice Thurgood Marshall said in Bakke, suffered a history "different in kind, not just degree, from that of other ethnic groups," universities don't calibrate preferences based on comparative group disadvantage (and, in the Davis system challenged by Bakke, two-thirds of the preferences went to Mexican-Americans and Asians, not blacks). We also ignore the question of when an individual's family immigrated in order to determine whether the family was even theoretically subject to the official discrimination in this country on which preferences are predicated.

"Diversity" was supposed to solve all this by saying we don't care about compensation, only viewpoint. But, again, if universities are genuinely seeking diversity of viewpoints, they should inquire whether a minority applicant really does have

the "minority viewpoint" being sought. Derrick Bell's famous statement—"the ends of diversity are not served by people who look black and think white"—is at once repellent and a relevant critique of the assumption that all minority members think alike. In theory, we need some assurance from the applicant that he or she will in fact interact with students of different backgrounds, lest the cosmetic diversity of the freshman yearbook be lost to the reality of ethnic theme houses.

The second way to proceed, the moderately complicated calculus of class, would look at what sociologists believe to be the Big Three determinants of life chances: parental income, education and occupation. Parents' education, which is highly correlated with a child's academic achievement, can be measured in number of years. And while ranking occupations might seem hopelessly complex, various attempts to do so objectively have yielded remarkably consistent results—from the Barr Scale of the early 1920s to Alba Edwards' Census rankings of the 1940s to the Duncan Scores of the 1960s.

The third alternative, the complex calculus of disadvantage, would count all the factors mentioned, but might also look at net worth, the quality of secondary education, neighborhood influences and family structure. An applicant's family wealth is readily available from financial aid forms, and provides a long-term view of relative disadvantage, to supplement the "snap shot" picture that income provides. We also know that schooling opportunities are crucial to a student's life chances, even controlling for home environment. Some data suggest that a disadvantaged student at a middle-class school does better on average than a middle-class student at a school with high concentrations of poverty. Objective figures are available to measure secondary school quality—from per student expenditure, to the percentage of students receiving free or reduced-price lunches, to a school's median score on standardized achievement tests. Neighborhood influences, measured by the concentration of poverty within Census tracts or zip codes, could also be factored in, since numerous studies have found that living in a low-income community can adversely affect an individual's life chances above and beyond family income. Finally, everyone from Dan Quayle to Donna Shalala agrees that children growing up in single-parent homes have a tougher time. This factor could be taken into account as well.

The point is not that this list is the perfect one, but that it is possible to devise a series of fairly objective and verifiable factors that measure the degree to which a teenager's true potential has been hidden. (As it happens, the complex definition is the one that disproportionately benefits African Americans. Even among similar income groups, blacks are more likely than whites to live in concentrated poverty, go to bad schools and live in single-parent homes.) It's just not true that a system of class preferences is inherently harder to administer than a system based on race. Race only seems simpler because we have ignored the ambiguities. And racial preferences are just as easy to ridicule. To paraphrase Kinsley, does a new Indian immigrant get fewer or more points than a third-generation Latino whose mother is Anglo?

Who should Benefit? Mickey Kaus, in "Class Is In," argued that class preferences should be reserved for the underclass. But the injuries of class extend beyond the poorest. The offspring of the working poor and the working class lack advantages, too, and indeed SAT scores correlate lockstep with income at every increment. Unless you believe in genetic inferiority, these statistics suggest unfairness is not confined to the underclass. As a practical matter, a teenager who emerges from the underclass has little chance of surviving at an elite college. At Berkeley, administrators found that using a definition of disadvantaged, under which neither parent attended a four-year college and the family could not afford to pay $1,000 in education expenses, failed to bring in enough students who were likely to pass.

Still, there are several serious objections to class-based preferences that must be addressed.

**1. We're not ready to be color-blind because racial discrimination continues to afflict our society.** Ron Brown says affirmative action "continues to be needed not to redress grievances of the past, but the current discrimination that continues to exist." This is a relatively new theory, which conveniently elides the fact that preferences were supposed to be temporary. It also stands logic on its head. While racial discrimination undoubtedly still exists, the Civil Rights Act of 1964 was meant to address prospective discrimination. Affirmative action—discrimination in itself—makes sense only

to the extent that there is a current-day legacy of past discrimination which new prospective laws cannot reach back and remedy.

In the contexts of education and employment the Civil Rights Act already contains powerful tools to address intentional and unintentional discrimination. The Civil Rights Act of 1991 reaffirmed the need to address unintentional discrimination—by requiring employers to justify employment practices that are statistically more likely to hurt minorities—but it did so without crossing the line to required preferences. This principle also applies to Title VI of the Civil Rights Act, so that if, for example, it can be shown that the SAT produces an unjustified disparate impact, a university can be barred from using it. In addition, "soft" forms of affirmative action, which require employers and universities to broaden the net and interview people from all races, are good ways of ensuring positions are not filled by word of mouth, through wealthy white networks.

We have weaker tools to deal with discrimination in other areas of life—say, taxi drivers who refuse to pick up black businessmen—but how does a preference in education or employment remedy that wrong? By contrast, there is nothing illegal about bad schools, bad housing and grossly stunted opportunities for the poor. A class preference is perfectly appropriate.

**2. Class preferences will be just as stigmatizing as racial preferences.** Kinsley argues that "any debilitating self-doubt that exists because of affirmative action is not going to be mitigated by being told you got into Harvard because of your 'socioeconomic disadvantage' rather than your race."

But class preferences are different from racial preferences in at least two important respects. First, stigma—in one's own eyes and the eyes of others—is bound up with the question of whether an admissions criterion is accepted as legitimate. Students with good grades aren't seen as getting in "just because they're smart." And there appears to be a societal consensus—from Douglas to Scalia—that kids from poor backgrounds deserve a leg up. Such a consensus has never existed for class-blind racial preferences.

Second, there is no myth of inferiority in this country about the abilities of poor people comparable to that about African Americans. Now, if racial preferences are purely a matter of compensatory justice, then the question of whether preferences exacerbate white racism is not relevant. But today racial preferences are often justified by social utility (bringing different racial groups together helps dispel stereotypes) in which case the social consequences are highly relevant. The general argument made by proponents of racial preferences—that policies need to be grounded in social reality, not a historical theory—cuts in favor of the class category. Why? Precisely because there is no stubborn historical myth for it to reinforce.

Kaus makes a related argument when he says that class preferences "will still reward those who play the victim." But if objective criteria are used to define the disadvantaged, there is no way to "play" the victim. Poor and working-class teenagers are the victims of class inequality not of their own making. Preferences unlike, say, a welfare check, tell poor teenagers not that they are helpless victims, but that we think their long run potential is great, and we're going to give them a chance—if they work their tails off—to prove themselves.

**3. Class preferences continue to treat people as members of groups as opposed to individuals.** Yes. But so do university admissions policies that summarily reject students below a certain SAT level. It's hard to know what treating people as individuals means. (Perhaps if university admissions committees interviewed the teachers of each applicant back to kindergarten to get a better picture of their academic potential, we'd be treating them more as individuals.) The question is not whether we treat people as members of groups—that's inevitable—but whether the group is a relevant one. And in measuring disadvantage (and hidden potential) class is surely a much better proxy than race.

**4. Class-based affirmative action will not yield a diverse student body in elite colleges.** Actually, there is reason to believe that class preferences will disproportionately benefit people of color in most contexts—since minorities are disproportionately poor. In the university context, however, class-based preferences were rejected during the 1970s in part because of fear that they would produce inadequate numbers of minority students. The problem is that when you control for income, African-American students do worse than white and Asian students on the SAT—due in part to differences in culture and linguistic patterns, and in part to the way income alone as a measurement

hides other class-based differences among ethnic groups.

The concern is a serious and complicated one. Briefly, there are four responses. First, even Murray and Richard Herrnstein agree that the residual racial gap in scores has declined significantly in the past two decades, so the concern, though real, is not as great as it once was. Second, if we use the sophisticated definition of class discussed earlier which reflects the relative disadvantage of blacks vis-à-vis whites of the same income level, the racial gap should close further. Third, we can improve racial diversity by getting rid of unjustified preferences—for alumni kids or students from underrepresented geographic regions—which disproportionately hurt people of color. Finally, if the goal is to provide genuine equal opportunity, not equality of group result, and if we are satisfied that a meritocratic system which corrects for class inequality is the best possible approximation of that equality, then we have achieved our goal.

**5. Class-based affirmative action will cause as much resentment among those left out as race-based affirmative action.** Kinsley argues that the rejected applicant in the infamous Jesse Helms commercial from 1990 would feel just as angry for losing out on a class-based as a race-based preference, since both involve "making up for past injustice." The difference, of course, is that class preferences go to the actual victims of class injury, mooting the whole question of intergenerational justice. In the racial context, this was called "victim specificity." Even the Reagan administration was in favor of compensating actual victims of racial discrimination.

The larger point implicit in Kinsley's question is a more serious one: that any preference system, whether race- or class-based, is "still a form of zero-sum social engineering." Why should liberals push for class preferences at all? Why not just provide more funding for education, safer schools, better nutrition? The answer is that liberals should do these things; but we cannot hold our breath for it to happen. In 1993, when all the planets were aligned—a populist Democratic president, Democratic control of both Houses of Congress—they produced what *The New York Times* called "A BUDGET WORTHY OF MR. BUSH." Cheaper alternatives, such as preferences, must supplement more expensive strategies of social spending. Besides, to the extent that class preferences help change the focus of public discourse from race to class, they help reforge the coalition needed to sustain the social programs liberals want.

Class preferences could restore the successful formula on which the early civil rights movement rested: morally unassailable underpinnings and a relatively inexpensive agenda. It's crucial to remember that Martin Luther King Jr. called for special consideration based on class, not race. After laying out a forceful argument for the special debt owed to blacks, King rejected the call for a Negro Bill of Rights in favor of a Bill of Rights for the Disadvantaged. It was King's insight that there were nonracial ways to remedy racial wrongs, and that the injuries of class deserve attention along with the injuries of race.

None of this is to argue that King would have opposed affirmative action if the alternative were to do nothing. For Jesse Helms to invoke King's color-blind rhetoric now that it is in the interests of white people to do so is the worst kind of hypocrisy. Some form of compensation is necessary, and I think affirmative action, though deeply flawed, is better than nothing.

## About the Author

Richard Kahlenberg is the author of a the newly released book on class-based affirmative action, entitled *The Remedy: Class, Not Race—An Affirmative Action That's Fair*. Available from Basic Books, 10 East 53rd Street, New York, NY 10022 (Order from 1-800-331-3761).

# PART 12
# THE FUTURE

# Dialogue: The Future

*Bob*—This last section works to identify the next evolutionary steps in the diversity dialogue from our perspective as professional consultants. In looking to the future we focus on key issues only, without attempting to include everything. We've deliberately avoided any traditional breakdown into gender, ethnic or other legally targeted groups, but we do have pieces that, by their very nature, will bridge gaps not specifically discussed.

Given the last section, we hope our readers are convinced (or at least willing to entertain the notion) that race is a convoluted, fabricated concept which means only what we project onto it. It's time the concept of race died.

*George*—As two middle-aged U.S. white men our view, like everyone else's, is limited. We are just part of the dialogue. But, besides bringing our own passion and enthusiasm to this project ourselves, our commitment led us to ask many people different from ourselves to contribute. Our phone, fax, e-mail and personal contact networks were very busy with the feedback that has made this a richer discussion. We are sure there are many other perspectives to be heard.

*Bob*—I can't remember how often you and I would have a conversation, put it in writing, and feel that it made complete sense. Then one of our reviewers would read it and call attention to our own cultural limitations. I'll still hear Diane Johnson's voice, saying, *"Excuse* me!! I don't think so!", as she pointed out ways in which we gave people of color short-shrift. Or how Susan Beth Bronstein, Amy Zuckerman or Nanci Luna Jimenez would point out "When you say it this way, *I feel left out!*" So we're not nearly as broadly enlightened as the dialogues might suggest. We should probably admit to the reader now that while these dialogue sections were first recorded during our week-long brainstorming session in Santa Cruz, the words have been carefully refined and polished.

*George*—Do we have to admit that . . . ?

*Bob*—Well, only because we were sensitive enough to know we weren't sensitive enough to do a really good job on our own. We get to look better (or smarter) because we've got value added from the diversity available to us! We have to acknowledge that.

*George*—So, we invite our readers to go and do likewise, to continue the dialogue with each other and with us if they like. This is, after all, how U.S. Americans get real with each other! [*contact information for the editors is provided at the end of their biographies on page 505*]

*Bob*—It's how we get in touch with each others' truth. Still, in retrospect, some omissions strike me forcefully. We didn't consider developmental disabilities (such as mental retardation) or look at issues of people who suffer from chronic pain or environmental disabilities in this *Sourcebook.* Just as this book was going to press, I received a flier on "Guidelines for Supervising Employees with Learning Disabilities"*—another "difference" we failed to include.

Some of these could be reframed as class issues, or simply seen as groups unjustly barred from contributing or participating in society. Too many people are still too easily excluded from opportunity in life. These are omissions I can't remedy now, but I hope that the spirit of this collection will encourage as many diverse groups as possible to share in the discussion.

Just as blacks or women were not seen as an obvious resource some years back, groups now invisible to us will certainly be identified as contributors some years from now. Things change and we see them anew over time.

*George*—That's why Gary Trudeau's Doonesbury cartoon (page 479) hits home for me. "Normal" changes over time and includes a far wider range than we might have imagined twenty or thirty years ago.

*Bob*—The sidebar from Ann Landers (page 484) is about a group that most of us wouldn't even think of. Many forms of difference stretch our minds "off the map."

---

*Available for $10 from Elaine S. Reisman, Threshold Program, Leslie College, 29 Everett St., Cambridge, MA 02138-2790.

*George*—We've focused on the workplace, but most of us take our work home with us emotionally if not literally. We can also hear the domestic diversity struggle, in, as Leonard Cohen so aptly puts it:

" . . . the homicidal bitchin'
that goes down in every kitchen
to determine who will serve and who will eat."

*Bob*—True. About a third of all visits by women to emergency rooms result from domestic assaults. This is an epidemic! Neither sex, it so often seems, has the skills to deal with the other. How we interact respectfully and lovingly with our spouses, lovers, friends, children, and neighbors is really another bottom line of diversity. It counts every bit as much as the bottom-lines of productivity and return on investment.

*George*—We need to get real about how we ought to act around each other, too. U.S. political correctness prescribes that no one should ever say or do anything that offends anybody else (unless, of course, the somebody else is a white European-American, particularly a man). I certainly don't argue that we should insult each other or play with each other's sensitivities. Nor do I want to react by conjuring up freedom of speech as a weapon. I simply want to say that attempts to over-protect diversity can be counterproductive.

For example, we now define some sexual harassment in terms of the feelings and sensitivities of the injured party. This is very close to saying that wrong is what feels wrong to somebody else. In law, a semblance of objectivity is guaranteed by the proviso that the offended person must think as "a rational woman or man" would. In the popular mind this fine point is easily overlooked . . . never enters the debate. What we get is the forceful imposition of one person's cultural values on another, argued as a right by both parties, and backed up by force of law or policy.

*Bob*—You mean that, practically speaking, we place no limit on taking offense to what others say or do?

*George*—Yes. It's sometimes easier for those in the so-called dominant culture not to take offense, partly because they have the power. But a diversity competency we all must develop is our ability to choose *not to take offense*.

Taking offense blocks our option to understand and negotiate something workable. In the U.S. we take offense quickly and go for redress to the legal system. It's available to take even the smallest disputes to court. This has unfortunately eroded the neutral ground on which we could stand to arbitrate, negotiate, apologize, discuss and become more effective at knowing and working with each other. Now we automatically turn to the legal system and indulge the desire to prove each other wrong and punish each other for it, rather than making peace.

*Bob*—This ability to move beyond impasse and come to an accommodation is not a U.S. skill. Our common law tradition decides who is right and who is wrong. Our machismo wants us to fight. We would rather be right, be winners, instead of looking for settlements that would make us friends, or at least respectful neighbors with good fences once again. It's our adversarial outlook again. We are embedded in it and probably can't recognize it because, as we have noted elsewhere, it's so much a part of our U.S. culture.

*George*—Yes. The very structures we created to achieve justice polarize us and get in the way of resolving so many conflicts. They hinder creative dialogue on an interpersonal basis (perhaps a more "feminine" approach). So the same conflicts come up over and again. Stuck in policies and procedures and being at legal risk him or herself, the person investigating a harassment complaint in an organization will behave in a self-protective way. The letter of the law gets followed rather than its spirit.

*Bob*—The system's set up to take the issue straight into the adversarial domain, the queue toward litigation. Does this simply mean that we've lost patience with each other?

*George*—Perhaps, but I think that this is another case of runaway culture, reinforcing its strongest principles by over-applying them. Our adversarial attitude is traditional—union and management are one of its oldest and most obvious expressions. Both sides can use diversity as a stick to beat on the other.

*Bob*—Bill Clinton's remarks (page 480) underscore the need to address issues of opportunity and class. These issues will neither resolve themselves or go away anytime soon. It will take visionary, yet pragmatic, leadership from both political parties, from both the left and right, and from all diverse segments of our society in order to pursue a new direction.

*George*—Yet, it's simplistic to think that a wholesale effort to dismantle government will improve everyone's lot. The sidebar by Richard Moran about "Cutting Regulatory Agencies" (page 485) makes a significant point: Our frustration does us no good if we simply lash out at convenient targets. Moran is a Professor of Sociology and Criminology at Mount Holyoke College.

*Bob*—We'd call his a "contrarian" view, like so many of the voices we've heard in this *Sourcebook*—he is willing to name the truth he sees and engage in public discourse to find new solutions. Those who fall back into "party line" positions, whether they're p.c.—or any other kind of flag-waver—don't create much real dialogue, though sometimes they make the need for discussion very apparent.

*George*—In the U.S. we seem to have lost patience with, and the ability to engage in dialogue with, our neighbors and fellow-workers. Maybe this book can restart some of those conversations. We need, in Bill Clinton's words, . . . to "stop seeing each other as enemies . . . and work together to find a common ground."

*Bob*—"Welfare Hell" by John Callahan (page 482) is a touching and poignant story of a creative professional with a disability trying to break free from the oppressive rules and regulations of the welfare system. The system he describes must be changed to be effective. Clearly, the alternative is not cutting out all support but learning how to deliver it well.

*George*—Plus we need to look at things with creativity and curiosity as Price Pritchett recommends in "Act Like a Child" (page 486). Both our heads and our hearts are guides out of the complex maze of social and economic dilemmas we face.

*Bob*—For example, we must, in Cornel West's words (page 487), "learn to talk of race." This dialogue can be painful and frustrating, but there is no other way out. We can no longer deny that the divide is not there if we want to cross it. West prophesies, "we [shall] learn a new language of empathy and compassion, or the fire this time will consume us all."

*George*—Our closing, "'Getting Real!': Where are we? Where are we going?" (page 491), attempts to pull this journey together. It summarizes the state of the diversity in the USA and, more importantly, presents a model (page 492) to understand the diversity tasks or challenges we face.*

*Bob*—If readers could look at only one page in this book (after reading the "Mermaids" piece on the back cover), we'd like it to be Figure 1 on page 495. This, more than any other analysis, serves to explain why diversity programs as they currently exist so often fail.

*George*—After hearing the eloquent voices of our 100+ contributors, this summary ties it all together and asks our readers to become involved in whatever tasks they can. Do it alone, or with your communities, organizations, churches, mosques or synagogues, even with your family, neighbors, and friends.

*Bob*—Diversity is about how we deal with the "other." Remember the quote from Rabbi Hillel, "If I am not for myself, who am I? If I am only for myself, who will be for me? The time is now."

---

*This model is the basis for *The Cultural Diversity Fieldbook* (p. 288) which contains a collection of visions and strategies based on our work here. For further information call 800-736-1293.

# DOONESBURY

## by Garry Trudeau

# State of the Union Address

President William Jefferson Clinton, January 24, 1995 (excerpts from *Congressional Record*)

. . . While our nation is enjoying peace and prosperity, too many of our people are still working harder and harder for less and less. While our businesses are restructuring and growing more competitive, too many of our people can't be sure of even having a job next year or even next month. And far more than our material riches are threatened: Things far more precious—our children, our families, our values . . .

. . . Let us put aside partisanship, pettiness and pride. As we embark on a new course, let us put our country first, remembering that regardless of our party labels, we are all Americans. Let the final test of any action we take be a simple one: is it good for the American people? We cannot ask Americans to be better citizens if we are not better servants. We've made a start this week by enacting a law applying to Congress the laws you apply to the private sector. But we have a lot more to do.

. . . This is a nation of immigrants. But it is also a nation of law. And it is wrong, and ultimately self-defeating, for a nation of immigrants to permit the kind of abuse of our immigration laws we have seen in recent years.

The most important job of government is to empower people to succeed in the new global economy. America has always been the land of opportunity, a land where if you work hard you can get ahead. We are a middle class country. Middle class values sustain us. We must expand the middle class and shrink the underclass, while supporting the millions who are already successful in the new economy.

America is once again the world's strongest economy. Almost six million jobs in two years. Exports booming. Inflation down. High wage jobs coming back. A record number of American entrepreneurs living the American dream. If we want to stay that way, those who work and lift our nation must have more of its benefits.

Today too many of those people are being left out. They are working harder for less security, less income, less certainty they can even afford a vacation, much less college for their children or retirement for themselves. We cannot let this continue.

If we don't act, our economy will probably do what it's done since 1978: Provide high income growth to those at the top, give very little to everyone in the middle, and leave the people at the bottom to fall even farther behind, no matter how hard they work.

We must have a government that can be a partner in making this new economy work for all Americans—a government that helps each and every one of us get an education and have the opportunity to renew our skills . . .

My test for any proposal is: Will it create jobs and raise incomes? Will it strengthen families and support children? Will it build the middle class and shrink the underclass? Is it paid for? If it does, I will support it. If it doesn't, I will oppose it.

That's why I will ask you to support raising the minimum wage. It rewards work. Two and a half million Americans, often women with children, work for $4.25 an hour. In terms of real buying power, by next year, that minimum wage will be at a 40 year low.

I have studied the arguments and evidence for and against a minimum wage increase. The weight of evidence is that a modest increase does not cost jobs, and may even lure people into the job market. But the plain fact is you can't make a living on $4.25 an hour, especially if you have kids to support.

In the past, the minimum wage has been a bipartisan issue. It should be again. I challenge you to get together and find a way to make the minimum wage a living wage.

Members of Congress have been on the job less than a month. But by the end of the week, 28 days into the new year, each Congressman has already earned as much in Congressional salary as people who work under minimum wage make in an entire year . . .

I know it is hard when you are working harder for less money and you are under great stress to do these things. I also know it's hard to do the work of citizenship when for years, politicians in both parties have treated you like consumers and

Excerpts reprinted from the *Congressional Record*.

spectators, promising you something for nothing and playing on your fears and frustrations. And more and more of the information you get comes in very negative ways, not conducive to real conversation. But the truth is, we have got to stop seeing each other as enemies, even when we have different views. If you go back to the very beginning of this country, the great strength of America has always been our ability to associate with people who were different from ourselves and to work together to find common ground. And in the present day, everybody has a responsibility to do more of that.

We all gain when we give. We reap whatever we sow. That's at the heart of the New Covenant: Responsibility. Citizenship. Opportunity. They are more than stale chapter headings in some remote civics book. They are the virtues by which we can fulfill ourselves and our God-given potential—the virtues by which we can live out the eternal promise of America, the enduring dream of that first and most sacred covenant: That we hold these truths to be self-evident, that all men are created equal. That they are endowed by their Creator with certain inalienable rights. And that among these are Life, Liberty and the Pursuit of Happiness.

This is a very great country. And our best days are yet to come. God bless you, and God bless the United States of America.

---

"The failure of our political system is driving me crazy. It is clear that the role of politicians is to serve the monied elite that puts them into office. Continued $250+ billion military budgets after "the enemy" has vanished are a travesty. Propping up our economy through the sale of arms around the world is immoral. Refusing to deal with the root causes of poverty and economic oppression domestically and internationally is unjustifiable and will ultimately prove to be our undoing. We have the people, the resources, and the technology to deal successfully with all these problems and we would create more jobs and a stronger economy by doing so than by our continued military madness."

Ben Cohen
Co-founder of Ben and Jerry's Homemade Ice Cream

# Welfare Hell: Welfare Rules Make It Hard for Disabled People to Work

by John Callahan (*Mother Jones*)

A welfare client is supposed to cheat. Everybody expects it. Faced with sharing a dinner of Tender Vittles with the cat, many quadriplegics I know bleed the system for a few extra dollars. They tell their attendants that they are getting two hundred dollars less than the real entitlement and pocket the difference. They tell the caseworker that they are paying a hundred dollars more for rent. Or they say they are broke and get a voucher for government cheese.

I am a recovering alcoholic. I have opted to live a life of rigorous honesty. So instead, I go out and drum up some business and draw cartoons. I even tell welfare how much I make! Oh, I'm tempted to get paid under the table. But even if I yielded to that temptation, outfits like *The New Yorker* and *Penthouse* are not going to get involved in some sticky situation. They keep my records according to my Social Security number, and that information goes right into the IRS computer. Very high-profile and unpauperlike. As a welfare client I'm expected to genuflect before the caseworker. Deep down, caseworkers know that they are being shined on and made fools of by many of their clients, and they expect to be kowtowed to as compensation.

I'm not being contemptuous. Most caseworkers begin as college-educated liberals with high ideals. But after a few years in a system that practically mandates dishonesty, they become like the one I shall call "Suzanne," a slightly overweight cop in Birkenstocks.

Not long after Christmas last year, Suzanne came to my apartment on one of her bimonthly inspections and saw some new posters on the wall. "Where'd you get the money for those?" she wanted to know.

"Friends and family."

"Well, you better write it down, by god. You better report it. You have to report any donations or gifts."

This was my cue to grovel. Instead, I talked back. "I bummed a cigarette from someone on the street the other day. Do I have to report that?"

"Well I'm sorry, but I don't make the rules, Mr. Callahan."

Suzanne tries to guilt-trip me about repairs to my wheelchair, which is always breaking down because welfare won't spend the money to maintain it properly. "You know, Mr. Callahan, I've heard that you put a lot more miles on that wheelchair than the average quadriplegic."

Of course I do. I'm an active worker, not a nursing-home vegetable. I live near downtown so I can get around in a wheelchair. I wonder what she'd think if her legs suddenly gave out and she had to crawl to work.

Spending cuts during the Reagan administration dealt malnutrition and misery to a lot of people, not just me. But people with spinal cord injuries felt the cuts in a unique way: The government stopped taking care of our chairs.

My last chair never fit. I was forced to sit in a twisted position that led to lots of medical complications. But they refused to replace it. Each time it broke down and I called Suzanne, I had to endure a little lecture. Finally she'd say, "Well, if I can find time today, I'll call the medical worker."

Suzanne then started the red tape flowing. She was supposed to notify the medical worker, who made an assessment. Then the medical worker called the wheelchair repair companies to get the cheapest bid. Then the medical worker alerted the main welfare office at the Oregon state capital. They pondered the matter for days while I lay in bed, immobilized. Finally, if I was lucky, they called back and approved the repair.

When welfare learned I was making money on my cartoons, Suzanne started "visiting" every other week instead of every other month. She poked into every corner in search of contraband

Cuisinarts, unregistered girlfriends, or illegal aliens serving as butlers and maids. She never found anything, but there was always a thick pile of forms and affidavits to fill out at the end of each visit, accounting for every penny.

"Mr. Callahan, you've simply got to understand the gravity of the situation. Your cartoon earnings could cause your benefits to be terminated!"

"How do I avoid that?"

"I'm not sure . . . but it doesn't look good for you."

"Well, who do I speak to about the regulations on this?"

Suzanne didn't know. One day I simply called her superior and asked if he could tell me where to start. "Well, Mr. Callahan, we have reason to believe that you are a bit of a shady character. I'm fairly certain your benefits will be terminated."

There is no provision in the law for a gradual shift away from welfare. I am a free-lancer who is slowly building up his market. It's impossible to jump off welfare and suddenly be making two thousand dollars a month, even if I could solve the health insurance problem. But I would love to be able to pay for some of my services and not have to go through a humiliating rigmarole every time I need a spare pan.

Like any bureaucracy with complicated rules, welfare constantly creates and eliminates "exceptions" to those rules. Quads often have strained kidneys and need extra protein. So an exception allowed me to keep a little more money to supplement my diet. Then came a note that the exception had been cut off retroactively. I owed welfare for meat and cheese I'd bought with my own money and already eaten. I volunteered to come over to the office and throw up, but they wanted cash.

One day after those benefits were cut off, Suzanne pinched the spare tire around my middle and said, "Well, it sure looks like your attendant's feeding you pretty well. You don't look like you're starving to death." My diet is mainly cheap carbohydrates because that's all I can afford, plus it is very hard for a quadriplegic, especially in his 30s or older, to find ways to burn calories and stay trim. Such insensitivity is typical.

Absurd as it may seem, my success as a cartoonist makes me feel like a renegade, a culprit. When a check comes in from a magazine I look at

it, and part of me says, "Way to go, Callahan! You're getting published!" But the other half of me says, "Watch out, motherfucker! You're cheating the system. You're cheating welfare. You shouldn't have this money. Better put it in an envelope and run it right down to Suzanne."

I know I am lucky to live in a country where I do get some help from the government. I want to distinguish sharply between the professional and courteous treatment I have always received from Social Security and my problems with the inadequately funded and state administered welfare program. The plain fact is, though, that until quite recently, when I began to be perceived as something of a minor media threat, welfare treated me like a bum.

So I have had to make conscious efforts to build up my self-esteem, to tell myself that I am a good person, that I am trying, that I am as good as the average guy working down at the 7-Eleven or over at IBM. I want to get ahead. I have the talent, the desire, and the moxie to do it. I have twice the drive of the average able-bodied person I know. What I am being told by the welfare system is no, we won't let you do it.

There needs to be some ombudsman or legal resource for all welfare clients, because the system so easily lends itself to abuse by the givers as well as by the recipients. Welfare sent Suzanne to snoop around in my apartment the other day because I was using a larger than usual amount of urological supplies. I was, indeed: The hole that has been surgically cut in the wall of my abdomen had

Don't be afraid to ask questions -
Children are spontaneous and uninhibited
in their curiosity. Take a lesson from them...

© 1995, John Callahan (LEVIN REPRESENTS)

483

changed size and the connection to my urine bag was leaking.

The implication of her visit was that I was cheating. What did they think I was up to, selling urine bags to Greeks as wineskins?

While she was taking notes, my phone rang and Suzanne answered it. The caller was a state senator, which rattled Suzanne a little. Would I sit on the governor's advisory board and try to do something about the thousands of welfare clients who, like me, could earn part or all of their own livings if they were allowed to do so, one step at a time?

Hell, yes, I would! I'd sit on an emery board if I could help change some of these medieval rules that have given me gray hair and a heart murmur! Someday quadriplegics will thrive under a new system based on incentive and encouragement. They will be free to develop their talents without guilt or fear—or just hold a good, steady job.

## About the Author

John Callahan, a widely published cartoonist and writer, became a quadriplegic in an auto accident when he was 21. This is an excerpt from his 1989 autobiography, *Don't Worry, He Won't Get Far on Foot: The Autobiography of a Dangerous Man*. In addition to this *New York Times* bestseller, his collections of cartoons include *Do Not Disturb Any Further, Digesting the Child Within,* and *Do What He Says! He's Crazy!!!* He can be reached through his agent, Levin Presents at 310-392-5146.

# Ann Landers

## By ANN LANDERS

Dear Ann Landers: I was dismayed when you referred to an unkind woman recently as a "four-door, brass-plated witch." In the future, Ann, please call her a sadist or a tormentor, but never a witch.

I am one of more than 150,000 Witches in this country. Our religion celebrates life in harmony with the earth and teaches personal responsibility. We are gentle and sincere people who want only to serve mankind. Most Witches believe that whatever one says or does comes back threefold. Because of fear of persecution, however, few Witches let their beliefs be known.

Genuine witchcraft does not embrace the concept of Satan, let alone the worship of it, yet Witches are constantly being slandered and viewed as evil.

If you print this letter, call me:
—A Witch from the Pacific Northwest.
(And always capitalize Witch.)

Dear Witch: I believe the portrayal of Witches in fairy tales as wicked and evil is largely responsible for your poor image. Also, Salem didn't help. Thanks for an enlightening letter.

# The Assumptions that Underlie Social Problems

by Richard Moran

Although Americans are accustomed to thinking in terms of race, social scientists have long known that social class is the actual basis for inequality. Race is important, but much of what we credit to race is actually attributable to social class. To be sure, social class is confounded by race, but in determining life chances, social class is a more powerful influence. Indeed, if you want to make predictions about how a person will behave, or even where he or she will end up in life, all you have to know is the parent's social class. A famous sociologist once remarked: "tell me what hospital a person was born into, whether in a private room or a ward, and I will tell you where and what his life will look like in twenty years."

As a nation we are all prisoners of the past. Outdated ideas dominate our current thinking about social and political problems. Solutions often elude us because we keep searching in the same directions. Very rarely do we attack the assumptions that underlie social problems. I believe that a good teacher leads a student to her own mind. In the classroom a teacher has an entire semester to get his ideas across—and a long reading list. On the radio I have between two and three minutes. I have to shake loose years of thinking in a very short time. The best way to do this is to consider the direct opposite of the so-called conventional wisdom. It is amazing how often crucial assumptions go unchallenged; how often policy makers have gotten it backwards, or, at the very least, how often the opposite argument is equally feasible. For example, is it punishment that deters crime, or crime that deters punishment? Is organized crime preferable to disorganized crime? Is diversity North America's greatest strength or its major weakness? While I've heard that the diversity effort in the U.S. is meant to be inclusive, why do I (a white male) feel left out every time someone mentions "inclusiveness"?

In the sidebar of text to the left is a commentary I prepared for National Public Radio. In it I explore the idea that regulatory agencies are more important to our personal and financial well-being than is traditional law enforcement.

A few statistics illustrate my point. In 1993, there were 24,526 homicides. Property crimes cost Americans about 15 billion dollars. The statistics for work-related deaths, injuries, and financial loss are more difficult to calculate. Taking the most conservative government figures, it is estimated that each year there are at least 115,000 job-related deaths and more than 2 million injuries.

This may sound startling, but the average American is five times more likely to have his life taken by the everyday operation of the industrial system, than he is to be the victim of a criminal homicide. He will lose three times the amount of

## CUTTING REGULATORY AGENCIES

The other night, I watched my neighbor do a most curious thing. After leaving his house, he checked to see that the front door was locked. Then he got into his car and drove away without fastening his seatbelt. What could he possibly be thinking?

Like most Americans my neighbor has a distorted image of the danger he faces. He thinks that the major threat to his life and property comes from individual criminal predators who might attack him on the street or break into his house at night. He doesn't seem to realize that most danger now comes from the everyday operation of our modern industrial system.

My neighbor is the kind of person who checks to see that his bottle of Tylenol has not been tampered with, but thinks that the Food and Drug Administration is a waste of taxpayer's money. Apparently he doesn't know that about 4,500 people die each year from adverse reaction to lawful drugs and that only seven people died by ingesting Tylenol laced with cyanide.

Richard Moran
Professor of Sociology & Criminology
Mount Holyoke College
South Hadley, MA

money to work-related disabling injuries than he will to the thieves who threaten the security of his home. Fraudulent or unnecessary automobile repair will cost him twice as much as crimes committed by conventional criminals.

Since the most serious dangers we encounter in modern society cannot be attributed to conventional criminal activities, the criminal justice system should no longer be regarded as the primary guardian of public safety. Today this responsibility falls upon regulatory agencies. It is ironic in the extreme, that congress has recently voted to scale back regulatory agencies while at the same time greatly expanding the criminal justice system with more police and prisons. Like my neighbor in the sidebar on the previous page, the 104th Congress does not seem to have a realistic view of the danger we face.

◆

---

## ACT LIKE A CHILD
### By Price Pritchett

Kids have a reputation for handling change a lot better than adults do. Children enjoy it and take it in stride. It's their nature to flex, to adapt. They readily bend, while grownups get set in their ways. Instead of resenting the difficulties of change the way older people do, kids just treat problems like another plaything.

Adults also bog down in routine and habit, but children won't settle for the boredom of "sameness." Kids insist on variety. Change is what keeps them from getting sleepy. They crave surprises and seek novel experiences. They love to learn. Youngsters are explorers at heart, and they're open to the unexpected. As a result, their life is a constant stream of "breakthroughs."

We need to approach the "new" the way we did when we were just a few years old. With curiosity, rather than worry. Willing to fumble our way along in the process of figuring out what works best. Quick to abandon any behavior in favor of more efficient new-found solutions. Relentless in our determination to learn. Consumed with our search for mastery, for continuous improvement, intent on finding a better way every day.

Adults try to cope with the challenge of change by "using their heads," trusting in logic, and drawing on experience. But as kids we followed our hearts as much as our heads. We trusted our creative instincts, our intuition, because our logical thinking skills had not yet developed. And since we had not been around long enough to learn much from the past, we did not get trapped by our old solutions. We did not get hung up on tradition.

As kids we did not dread the future, even though it was unpredictable, challenging, and full of problems we were unprepared for. We had fun with change. And we learned more, faster, than we ever have as adults.

We need to act like children again—create a culture that knows how to learn and we can give the organization the keys to the kingdom.

---

# Learning to Talk of Race

by Cornel West

*The Los Angeles riots exposed an 'us versus them' mentality, the author argues, in a country plagued by contempt for the common good.*

What happened in Los Angeles in April of 1992 was neither a race riot nor a class rebellion. Rather, this monumental upheaval was a multiracial, trans-class, and largely male display of justified social rage. For all its ugly, xenophobic resentment, its air of adolescent carnival, and its downright barbaric behavior, it signified the sense of powerlessness in American society. Glib attempts to reduce its meaning to the pathologies of the black underclass, the criminal actions of hoodlums, or the political revolt of the oppressed urban masses miss the mark. Of those arrested, only 36 percent were black, more than a third had full-time jobs, and most claimed to shun political affiliation. What we witnessed in Los Angeles was the consequence of a lethal linkage of economic decline, cultural decay, and political lethargy in American life. Race was the visible catalyst, not the underlying cause.

The meaning of the earthshaking events in Los Angeles is difficult to grasp because most of us remain trapped in the narrow framework of the dominant liberal and conservative views of race in America, which with its worn-out vocabulary leaves us intellectually debilitated, morally disempowered, and personally depressed. The astonishing disappearance of the event from public dialogue is testimony to just how painful and distressing a serious engagement with race is. Our truncated public discussions of race suppress the best of who and what we are as a people because they fail to confront the complexity of the issue in a candid and critical manner. The predictable pitting of liberals against conservatives, Great Society Democrats against self-help Republicans, reinforces intellectual parochialism and political paralysis.

The liberal notion that more government programs can solve racial problems is simplistic—precisely because it focuses *solely* on the economic dimension. And the conservative idea that what is needed is a change in the moral behavior of poor black urban dwellers (especially poor black men, who, they say, should stay married, support their children, and stop committing so much crime) highlights immoral actions while ignoring public responsibility for the immoral circumstances that haunt our fellow citizens.

The common denominator of these views of race is that each still sees black people as a "problem people," in the words of Dorothy I. Height, president of the National Council of Negro Women, rather than as fellow American citizens with problems. Her words echo the poignant "unasked question" of W. E. B. Du Bois, who, in *The Souls of Black Folk* (1903), wrote:

> *"They approach me in a half-hesitant sort of way, eye me curiously or compassionately, and then instead of saying directly, How does it feel to be a problem? they say, I know an excellent colored man in my town . . . . Do not these Southern outrages make your blood boil? At these I smile, or am interested, or reduce the boiling to a simmer, as the occasion may require. To the real question, How does it feel to be a problem? I answer seldom a word."*

Nearly a century later, we confine discussions about race in America to the "problems" black people pose for whites rather than consider what this way of viewing black people reveals about us as a nation.

This paralyzing framework encourages liberals to relieve their guilty consciences by supporting public funds directed at "the problems"; but at the same time, reluctant to exercise principled criticism of black people, liberals deny them the freedom to err. Similarly, conservatives blame the "problems" on black people themselves—and thereby render black social misery invisible or unworthy of public attention.

Hence, for liberals, black people are to be "included" and "integrated" into "our" society and culture, while for conservatives they are to be "well behaved" and "worthy of acceptance" by "our" way of life. Both fail to see that the presence and predicaments of black people are neither additions to nor defections from American life, but rather *constitutive elements of that life.*

To engage in a serious discussion of race in America, we must begin not with the problems of black people but with the flaws of American society—flaws rooted in historic inequalities and long-standing cultural stereotypes. How we set up the terms for discussing racial issues shapes our perception and response to these issues. As long as black people are viewed as a "them," the burden falls on blacks to do all the "cultural" and "moral" work necessary for healthy race relations. The implication is that only certain Americans can define what it means to be American—and the rest must simply "fit in."

The emergence of strong black-nationalist sentiments among blacks, especially among young people, is a revolt against this sense of having to "fit in." The variety of black-nationalist ideologies, from the moderate views of Supreme Court Justice Clarence Thomas in his youth to those of Louis Farrakhan today, rest upon a fundamental truth: white America has been historically weak-willed in ensuring racial justice and has continued to resist fully accepting the humanity of blacks. As long as double standards and differential treatment abound—as long as the rap performer Ice-T is harshly condemned while former Los Angeles Police Chief Daryl F. Gates's antiblack comments are received in polite silence, as long as Dr. Leonard Jeffries's anti-Semitic statements are met with vitriolic outrage while presidential candidate Patrick J. Buchanan's anti-Semitism receives a genteel response—black nationalisms will thrive.

Afrocentrism, a contemporary species of black nationalism, is a gallant yet misguided attempt to define an African identity in a white society perceived to be hostile. It is gallant because it puts black doings and sufferings, not white anxieties and fears, at the center of discussion. It is misguided because—out of fear of cultural hybridization and through silence on the issue of class, retrograde views on black women, gay men, and lesbians, and a reluctance to link race to the common good—it reinforces the narrow discussions about race.

To establish a new framework, we need to begin with a frank acknowledgment of the basic humanness and Americanness of each of us. And we must acknowledge that as a people—*E Pluribus Unum*—we are on a slippery slope toward economic strife, social turmoil, and cultural chaos. If we go down, we go down together. The Los Angeles upheaval forced us to see not only that we are not connected in ways we would like to be but also, in a more profound sense, that this failure to connect binds us even more tightly together. The paradox of race in America is that our common destiny is more pronounced and imperiled precisely when our divisions are deeper. The Civil War and its legacy speak loudly here. And our divisions are growing deeper. Today, eighty-six percent of white suburban Americans live in neighborhoods that are less than 1 percent black, meaning that the prospects for the country depend largely on how its cities fare in the hands of a suburban electorate. There is no escape from our interracial interdependence, yet enforced racial hierarchy dooms us as a nation to collective paranoia and hysteria—the unmaking of any democratic order.

The verdict in the Rodney King case which sparked the incidents in Los Angeles was perceived to be wrong by the vast majority of Americans. But whites have often failed to acknowledge the widespread mistreatment of black people, especially black men, by law enforcement agencies, which helped ignite the spark. The verdict was merely the occasion for deep-seated rage to come to the surface. This rage is fed by the "silent" depression ravaging the country—in which real weekly wages of all American workers since 1973 have declined nearly 20 percent, while at the same time wealth has been upwardly distributed.

The exodus of stable industrial jobs from urban centers to cheaper labor markets here and abroad, housing policies that have created "chocolate cities and vanilla suburbs" (to use the popular musical artist George Clinton's memorable phrase), white fear of black crime, and the urban influx of poor Spanish-speaking and Asian immigrants—all have helped erode the tax base of American cities just as the federal government has cut its supports and programs. The result is unemployment, hunger, homelessness, and sickness for millions.

And a pervasive spiritual impoverishment grows. The collapse of meaning in life—the eclipse of hope and absence of love of self and others, the breakdown of family and neighborhood bonds—leads to the social deracination and cultural denudement of urban dwellers, especially children. We have created rootless, dangling people with little link to the supportive networks—family, friends, school—that sustain some sense of purpose in life. We have witnessed the collapse of the spiritual communities that in the past helped Americans face despair, disease, and death and that transmit through the generations dignity and decency, excellence and elegance.

The result is lives of what we might call "random nows," of fortuitous and fleeting moments preoccupied with "getting over"—with acquiring pleasure, property, and power by any means necessary. (This is not what Malcolm X meant by this famous phrase.) Post-modern culture is more and more a market culture dominated by gangster mentalities and self-destructive wantonness. This culture engulfs all of us—yet its impact on the disadvantaged is devastating, resulting in extreme violence in everyday life. Sexual violence against women and homicidal assaults by young black men on one another are only the most obvious signs of this empty quest for pleasure, property, and power.

Last, this rage is fueled by a political atmosphere in which images, not ideas, dominate, where politicians spend more time raising money than debating issues. The functions of parties have been displaced by public polls, and politicians behave less as thermostats that determine the climate of opinion than as thermometers registering the public mood. American politics has been rocked by an unleashing of greed among opportunistic public officials—who have followed the lead of their counterparts in the private sphere, where, as of 1989, 1 percent of the population owned 37 percent of the wealth and 10 percent of the population owned 86 percent of the wealth—leading to a profound cynicism and pessimism among the citizenry.

And given the way in which the Republican Party since 1968 has appealed to popular xenophobic images—playing the black, female, and homophobic cards to realign the electorate along race, sex, and sexual-orientation lines—it is no surprise

that the notion that we are all part of one garment of destiny is discredited. Appeals to special interests rather than to public interests reinforce this polarization. The Los Angeles upheaval was an expression of utter fragmentation by a powerless citizenry that includes not just the poor but all of us.

WHAT is to be done? How do we capture a new spirit and vision to meet the challenges of the post-industrial city, post-modern culture, and post-party politics?

First, we must admit that the most valuable sources for help, hope, and power consist of ourselves and our common history. As in the ages of Lincoln, Roosevelt, and King, we must look to new frameworks and languages to understand our multilayered crisis and overcome our deep malaise.

Second, we must focus our attention on the public square—the common good that undergirds our national and global destinies. The vitality of any public square ultimately depends on how much we *care* about the quality of our lives together. The neglect of our public infrastructure, for example—our water and sewage systems, bridges, tunnels, highways, subways, and streets—reflects not only our myopic economic policies, which impede productivity, but also the low priority we place on our common life

The tragic plight of our children clearly reveals our deep disregard for public well-being. About one out of every five children in this country lives in poverty, including one out of every two black children and two out of every five Hispanic children. Most of our children—neglected by overburdened parents and bombarded by the market values of profit-hungry corporations—are ill-equipped to live lives of spiritual and cultural quality. Faced with these facts, how do we expect ever to constitute a vibrant society?

One essential step is some form of large-scale public intervention to ensure access to basic social goods—housing, food, health care, education, child care, and jobs. We must invigorate the common good with a mixture of government, business, and labor that does not follow any existing blueprint. After a period in which the private sphere has been sacralized and the public square gutted, the temptation is to make a fetish of the public square. We need to resist such dogmatic swings.

Last, the major challenge is to meet the need to generate new leadership. The paucity of courageous leaders—so apparent in the response to the events in Los Angeles—requires that we look beyond the same elites and voices that recycle the older frameworks. We need leaders—neither saints nor sparkling television personalities—who can situate themselves within a larger historical narrative of this country and our world, who can grasp the complex dynamics of our peoplehood and imagine a future grounded in the best of our past, yet who are attuned to the frightening obstacles that now perplex us. Our ideals of freedom, democracy, and equality must be invoked to invigorate all of us, especially the landless, propertyless, and luckless. Only a visionary leadership that can motivate "the better angels of our nature," as Lincoln said, and activate possibilities for a freer, more efficient, and stable America—only that leadership deserves cultivation and support.

This new leadership must be grounded in grass-roots organizing that highlights democratic accountability. Whoever *our* leaders will be as we approach the twenty-first century, their challenge will be to help Americans determine whether a genuine multiracial democracy can be created and sustained in an era of global economy and a moment of xenophobic frenzy.

Let us hope and pray that the vast intelligence, imagination, humor, and courage of Americans will not fail us. Either we learn a new language of empathy and compassion, or the fire this time will consume us all.

## About the Author

Cornel West has been Professor of Religion and Director of Afro-American Studies at Princeton University since 1988, and was recently appointed Professor of Afro-American Studies and the Philosophy of Religion at Harvard University. He is the author of many books, including *Keeping Faith*, *Prophetic Fragments*, and with bell hooks, *Breaking Bread*.

---

"The average working couple spends 20 minutes a day together. The average father talks to his child for 10 minutes a week. To call this "the sharing of lives" is ludicrous. It is, instead, a collective state of being caught in a maze—a maze in which great and brave effort produces little result, where there's little time to reflect and less to be free.

The discourse of America is done largely by a very few who, by luck or work or privilege, aren't caught in this maze. Too much of our time and thought is spent on saving and/or reforming an economic and political system that has constructed, and cannot live without, the maze. Patchwork reform won't help; violent revolution is madness; and most Americans feel so bound to the wastage that they have to defend it, and are increasingly hostile to its critics.

Michael Ventura
Writer and columnist for the *Austin Chronicle*

# Diversity—"Getting Real": Where Are We? Where Are We Going?

by Bob Abramms and George F. Simons

Today most of us have much clearer ideas of what we mean by "diversity" than we had a few years ago. We are also clearer about the difference between organizationally inspired diversity efforts and what many today are calling their "predecessors," Affirmative Action and Equal Opportunity efforts. It is the purpose of this final article to raise questions, make projections and speculate about where the present situation will lead.

## The Present Situation

A distinct diversity industry with an established technology has emerged and matured in the USA. What are some of its characteristics?

- There is an abundance of practitioners and a stratification of services. Prices for external diversity services and products are going down or at least not rising. This is due:

    — partly to the sheer numbers of people who have entered the field, including large numbers of academicians, clergy, therapists, social workers, management consultants, plus an assortment of part-timers with additional sources of income, etc.

    — partly to the number of professionals who have moved from internal to external status as a result of downsizing. They can use their expertise, connections in the industry and financial resources of their "golden handshake" to enter the field very competitively.

    — partly to the consolidation and maturation of the work itself. The technology of well-tested interventions can be transferred and delivered by junior professionals with lesser skills than the originators of the work.

    — partly to a decreased demand in the climate of uncertainty created by downsizing and the new political climate emerging from the 1994 elections.

- Quality is extremely mixed at the moment and a shakeout is already taking place. Camp followers will move on to the next fad while professionals deepen and specialize their applications. The result? On one hand, there is an abundance of lower-end products and services while the other end is increasingly dominated by a few elite diversity gurus.

- In most places, the old "victim vs. oppressor" terminology has disappeared in actual diversity training. Professionals now define "diversity" as pertaining to everyone, including European-American men. All the mindsets and assumptions associated with the old accusatory words are not yet gone, but there is clearly an emerging bias for interventions that do not "name, blame, or shame" anyone. This may also be the result of a shift in the market. As diversity becomes a mainstream commodity it must appeal to everyone. Most people will not buy services which they feel abuse them or accuse them. European-American liberals once reputed to have a knee-jerk response to guilt are certainly no longer motivated to action or to taking responsibility in this way.

- Today's diversity technology is increasingly cultural, not legal, despite the weighty legislation that has driven its development. People want to know how to work successfully with each other, not simply know what they can and cannot do in the work place to avoid lawsuits over employment, sexual harassment, promotion, etc. Unfortunately, the legal tone so dominates the climate in many organizations, particularly around such issues as sexual harassment, that common-sense solutions to problems are actively discouraged as management protects its back side from legal sanctions, the threat of the courtroom and expensive settlements. This fixation with the legal may keep the organization from benefiting from higher levels of diversity development. (See the model below, pages 495–497.) It is also generating a reaction in the form of initiatives to set limits to liability in lawsuits.

- Training approaches arising from Affirmative Action and entitlements are now viewed by leaders in many organizations as out-of-date. This is no longer the field of choice on which to create cultural competence or play out the management of difference despite the real justice issues that remain. If we want to create more productive work relationships, new ways of leveling the playing field, political and economic solutions, will have to be found. Looking at "valuing" or "managing" diversity, or, as we prefer to call it, "diversity as value added" will play a part in making these understandable and palatable but this new viewpoint alone cannot be expected to do this fundamental justice work.

On the other hand, bias and prejudice have not disappeared, either. Yet, an emphasis on fixing racism or sexism in individuals and organizations will be futile as well without approaches that reduce these very real economic and class hurdles. This is particularly true because much of the training and change technology used in bias reduction efforts are also dominated by content coming from Affirmative Action and EEO priorities that are now under fire.

African-American critics, in particular, were right to be concerned several years back when they perceived that the emergence of a new discipline of "diversity" would siphon off energy needed to complete the agenda that created Affirmative Action. Now it should be openly admitted that while seeing diversity as value added will contribute to fairness at work, justice is not its primary objective. It is also being admitted that Affirmative Action legislation and programs require revamping or replacement if the justice agenda is to proceed.

# Models for Cultural Competence

There is today an established and growing cultural general technology, which originated in the models of Hall (1981) and Hofstede (1984). Another generation of author-practitioners including Fons Trompenaars (1993) as well as our own colleagues (Simons, Vázquez and Harris, 1993; Simons and Hopkins, 1994) have built and extended these models of culture into practical tools of analysis and action for individuals and organizations.

These models provide the tools required for individuals, and as a result, organizations, to become culturally competent in dealing with diverse people in both their internal and external environments. In fact, not everyone needs to know the deeper levels of theory to benefit from the strategies and practices that emerge from these models. Line managers can benefit from their everyday use, relying on knowledgeable diversity experts only when they get stuck.

Most models of this nature seek out a number of dimensions or polarities along which cultural values and behaviors can be distinguished from each other, e.g., how well developed their context may be, masculinity vs. femininity, the level of affinity which group members have with each other, and the degree to which outsiders are excluded. They are then supplemented with culturally specific information about how people in a specific group *tend* to behave in certain situations.

These models are interpretative tools that are applied to how we use and manage our minds. They help us to dismiss old *stereotypes* and generate new ones. We use the word "stereotypes" here in a neutral sense indicating how the human mind simplifies information to understand it, store it and act on it. Stereotypes are our "best theories" about what we perceive about others when we meet or plan to interact with them in some way.

New and richer stereotypes can be used to replace older, sometimes negative or inaccurate ones or simply to add new, fresh dimensions to our understanding. This must be done because many stereotypes either a) come from a lack of accurate information, b) emerge from the native ethnocentrism with which we all are introduced to the world, or c) result from specific negative personal experiences or sad intergroup histories. Using cultural general models also encourages us to introduce these new stereotypes in more tentative terms and regularly review them for their viability. They are to be used as clues to explore and understand our environment and the people in it, not certitudes about how people are, or should be dealt with.

*Can* such models of culture come into more widespread popular use? We think so, not because they are particularly elegant theories, but because they are capable of producing the tangible and visible results that businesses and public organizations need, especially as they more and more deal with new and different customers and clientele.

*Will* such models come into more general use? This is a different question. U.S. culture encourages us to see ourselves as individuals, first and foremost. As a result, U.S. diversity practitioners are disinclined to make models of group cultures or seek out common characteristics of our demographic groups. Psychological profiles such as Meyers-Briggs Type Indicator (see the article on page 373) or True Colors (page 379) on the other hand are very popular. Efforts to describe our characteristics along the lines of ethnic or gender background, on the contrary, have been fiercely resisted and resented by many. The results of both research and training work that does this is discounted in the U.S. environment. There seems to be little middle ground.

When Leonard Cohen sings about the U.S. role in creating *democracy*, i.e., diversity that works, it is a mixture of fact and ethnocentric pride. The U.S. is in fact the largest multicultural experiment that the world knows. It has necessarily developed with both in individuals and organizations tools for dealing difference with some success:

*It's coming to America first,*
*the cradle of the best and of the worst.*
*It's here they got the range*
*and the machinery for change*
*and it's here they got the spiritual thirst.*

*It's here the family's broken*
*and it's here the lonely say*
*that the heart has got to open in a fundamental way:*
*Democracy is coming to the U.S.A.*

If democracy is a way of talking about diversity that works, developing cultural competence will mean both using the U.S. strengths and identifying its blind spots. The power of Cohen's poetry is that he embraces both as part of the same process. Strengths and blind spots are too often trade-offs, as when U.S. culture itself pushes diversity work strongly away from the use of culture-specific information and in the direction of psychological and self-development models. A strength is gained and one is lost.

Part of the resentment, it must be admitted, toward culture-specific information comes from the simplistic application of the models on the part of consultants, trainers and teachers. Trainees may be given research data about the family values of Latinos, but are not rehearsed in the kinds of questions needed to determine how true or important these values are to the individual Latina with whom they work or the specific family who are their customers. As a result, trainees may leave the learning intervention with updated stereotypes and assumptions, but without the skills for determining how these can be useful when they must be applied.

None of us is purely monocultural, i.e., have one single overwhelming cultural influence in our lives that overrides all others. So too, a good model tells us about complex combinations of cultural behavior we find in people, not just one. "Feminine" gender traits, for example, that encourage a woman from a specific ethnic group to be a nurturer, could be modified by her belonging to a feminist subculture with a strong emphasis on taking care of oneself. As a result, her cultural layers enrich her with a number of possible responses to the challenges she is called upon to face in the different environments in which she finds herself, despite the fact that she may interpret this culture clash negatively for a long period of time. The "stereotypes" found in a good analytical model can point us to combinations and possible interpretations of these diverse layers in ourselves and others.

Another source of resistance to models of culture and culture specific information comes from the need to maintain or gain power on the part of non-dominant groups. This phenomenon is not peculiar to the United States though there are many examples of it here because of our intense involvement with diversity issues. For example, it has become politically incorrect for European-Americans to know cultural characteristics or understand some of the experiences of African-

Americans or for men to presume to know about women.

We suggest that these power dynamics are related to class and we have referred to them in passing throughout this book. To advance cultural competence and benefit from the value added that diversity promises, we need to shift from the refrain, "You just don't get it," to a climate of mutual disclosure. However, this can only occur in the context of a real power shift, e.g., real economic and social opportunities for marginalized people.

It is the role of visionary business and political leaders to initiate and respond constructively to, rather than react to, efforts to better distribute resources and opportunities. Until then, marginalized groups and individuals will be wary, and perhaps rightfully so, of admitting to the accuracy of culturally specific information about themselves.

A typical example of this is the rejection in recent years of the work of Thomas Kochman (1982). Kochman remains one of the few culture-specific sources of practical insight into a wide range of behavior and interactions between blacks and whites. He is out of favor primarily because he provides ongoing research into the behaviors of the population he describes. He is also an European-American strangely positioned on African-American turf.

Applications of data such as Kochman's by careless practitioners encourages its rejection when, for example, conclusions about the population under study are indiscriminately applied to all African-Americans. Kochman's seminal work needs to be supplemented and updated, e.g., with information about the now sizable black middle-class. Behaviors he describes may have passed into an unconscious sub-text for many that is then actively repudiated, as the analysis of the black elite by bell hooks suggests (pages 80–85) so that such behaviors may show up only under stress, if at all, instead of accurately reflecting their daily experience. This new middle class is often indignant when others identify them with the culture of lower class African-Americans with their street-smart forms of expression.

Society and organizations need culture-specific information such as Kochman provides if European-Americans and African-Americans are to succeed on each other's cultural turf. This would give us an effective antidote to the two common outcomes of social subordination—marginalization or assimilation. (One could also replace "African-Americans" and "European-Americans" in this analysis with "women" and "men," etc.)

Resistance to culture-specific knowledge is less noticeable when the intergroup power differences are either less relevant or non-existent, i.e., when we are not afraid that our relationship with the other group is going to "melt down" our own cultural heritage or diminish our recent political gains. We are free to mix it up, at least joke about ourselves to each other and test out our stereotypes . . . if only to break/discard them as we really come to know each other. They can even help us to do this.

When U.S. corporate trainers bring up specific cultural differences that show us how to negotiate in Japan or in the European Union, they get much less resistance than when providing culture-specific information about blacks, women, Asians, or Native Americans. Women learning to do business overseas can accept being asked to defer and show respect to their male Japanese business contacts in ways that make their average U.S. male colleagues downright envious.

When the prospect of the loss or alteration of the trainee's culture is remote, it is possible to indulge in models of culture and culture-specific information because such information is exactly what people need to know to succeed at what they are doing. If our society learns to distinguish the issues of power from those of cultural difference, we might be able to develop more sophisticated culture-general models and more accurate culture-specific information. We would do this not because psychological and self-development models in service now are essentially flawed (though they can be quite ethnocentric), but because their exclusive use limits the value-added which organizations might enjoy.

## Leveraging Our Spiritual Heritage

To what degree can we get beyond stereotyping, both negative and positive, to reduce bias and achieve cultural competence? How dependent are we on stereotypes as starting points for learning about others? Many U.S. Americans aspire to a state of spiritual enlightenment about difference. For example, they imagine a sort of diversity consciousness modeled on the state of the selflessness and emptiness that Zen Buddhism cultivates. To a person in such a spiritual state everyone and everything would be perceived as itself, nothing more, nothing less.

This Zen approach and similar ones from other traditions can be very valuable, but they do not succeed well alone and must be coupled with a recognition of the process of how the mind uses stereotypes to know and to act in the everyday world. Appropriately used, spiritual disciplines shower benefits on everyday living in the form of flexibility, peace, and detachment from the products of one's mind and heart, including our fixed ideas about others. Spiritual practice can keep us from being locked into stereotypes even when we are using them. But, use them we must as we function on an everyday basis as householders, workers, artisans, service-givers and managers.

This spiritual approach also has limitations in that it is possible to believe one is enlightened beyond seeing gender and color differences, when in fact the implications and richness of such differences is being avoided and suppressed. We cannot conduct our lives without the constant flow of the interpretative mental images and inner conversations that, in fact, are what we call our stereotypes. They offer us choices about how to understand what is going on about us and what we can or ought to do about it.

Spiritual diversity that draws from both Eastern and Western Traditions serves U.S. social diversity. As Cohen sings, "it's here they got the spiritual thirst." On one hand it is important to provide ourselves and others with the fruits of meditation and contemplation as well as focus ourselves with prophetic mandates from our religious and spiritual traditions. Likewise, we must be able to communicate and act with each other to produce, protect, distribute and consume what we need to survive and to flourish.

We believe that managing diversity in the future will be more holistic. It will blend both old traditions and new spiritualities, the spiritual resources of individuals and groups, with the knowledge of cultures and the practical strategies and management tools required for getting along with each other and getting our tasks done more effectively.

## A Comprehensive Model for Addressing Diversity

The model described below is an attempt to come to grips with the currents of U.S. diversity we have been discussing, and more specifically, to learn why many attempts to export U.S. diversity efforts to organizations abroad fail so miserably. It was elaborated by an international team consisting of the authors of this anthology along with joint venture partners Baudouin Knaapen, Dr. Guurt Kok of SYNACT (Nieuwegein, the Netherlands). We call the model *The ABCD's of Diversity: A Comprehensive Model to Achieve Diversity as Value Added*.

First our team agreed that our underlying premise for managing diversity is:

---

**The organization that benefits from the value that diversity adds will be:**

- **least susceptible to disintegration from within,**
- **best equipped to meet challenges from without, and,**
- **most fully adapted to succeed in the emerging global marketplace.**

---

Managing diversity well consists of meeting the four challenges labeled **A, B, C,** and **D** shown in Figure 1.

### Figure 1
### A Hierarchy of U.S. Diversity Challenges

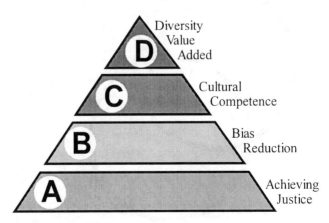

495

These four challenges are distinct from each other because each requires a different set of methods and activities for it to be successfully met. The technologies of one level cannot do the tasks of the other levels.

This means that although work done on levels **A, B, C,** and **D** can contribute to and support the work done on other levels, there is little point in attempting to meet the higher level needs if the lower level needs on which they are based are not being addressed.

This model can be used as an analysis tool to assist organizations to prioritize their diversity efforts. While all parts of an organization may not be at the same level, it is ineffective to invest resources in a division or department where more basic groundwork does not yet exist.

The chart on page 497 contains a schematic description of each the four challenges. It lists some of the specific methods needed to meet each of them, as well as some of the outcomes that can be expected as progress is made at each level.

The pyramidal model so far described reflects the U.S. Diversity experience and responds to the historical unfolding of U.S. society and the nature of U.S. workplace. For use in other cultural contexts, we modify the model from its original pyramidal form to the set of "wheels" as seen in Figure 2, to address different histories and social developments. Addressing non-U.S. contexts also helps us to see our own domestic context much better.

## Figure 2

### The Model Designed for Analyzing Non-U.S. Diversity Situations

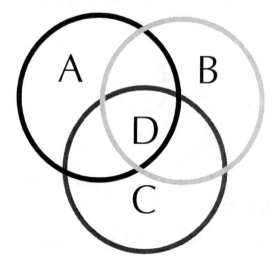

## Figure 3
## Rotating the Wheel

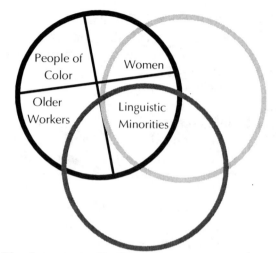

The letters **A, B, C,** and **D** still represent the same challenges as before, i.e., Achieving Justice, Bias Reduction, Cultural Competence, and Diversity Value Added, but the U.S. hierarchy of priorities is no longer assumed. Once again **A, B,** and **C** each support and contribute to the fullness of each other and when all three challenges are being addressed, **D** becomes possible. However, this configuration allows for the fact that, for example, in some situations **A** may be well handled, and **C** is the primary challenge to be addressed.

Picturing the challenges this way also enables us to attend to the specific content of each challenge as it exists in the new social group or organization. For example, "people of color" may be a strong focus for justice efforts in the U.S., but this may not be so in another country, where minorities speaking another language or dialect might be the principal target of inequities. This means that wheel **A** which represents the challenges of Achieving Justice on all levels, needs to be "rotated" (as in Figure 3) so that energy is brought to bear on the critical target group. Only in this way will we have the right basis for achieving **D,** Diversity Value Added.

While this may seem obvious, failing to distinguish U.S. priorities from those of organizations abroad happens all too easily and often. Diversity initiatives originating in the U.S. are rejected by the overseas organization because they do not fit the realities there. U.S. sponsors of the diversity effort then judge the overseas group as even more

| CHALLENGE | DESCRIPTION | METHODOLOGY | POSSIBLE OUTCOMES |
|---|---|---|---|
| **Achieving Justice** | Uses society's legal system or the organization's policies and procedures to assure that all members of the group contribute to, and participate fully and fairly in, the common good, e.g., protection, safety, economic and job opportunity, etc. Restructures groups and organizations to create and preserve fairness. Ensures that justice and fairness are not only real but are seen as such by all stakeholders. | Investigate and learn to use economic, legislative and legal processes; political action, e.g., through campaigning, lobbying, social initiatives. OD strategies to create or modify structures needed to achieve justice. Review of policies, e.g., hiring, firing, promotion, pay equity, for class and other disparities. Public relations to help all stakeholders understand these efforts. *These methodologies lead to fair structures and systems.* | • Fair laws, policies, procedures, e.g., hiring, promotion, mentoring, benefits, etc., that increase diversity and reduce turnover and deal with harassment.<br>• The organization makes its people and structures responsible for fair practices.<br>• People create interest and affinity groups. The organization constructively responds to them.<br>• The organization is and is seen from within and without as fair and equitable. |
| **Bias Reduction** | Helps individuals and, through them, groups to recognize and deal with their personal prejudice mechanisms so that these do not lead to biased behavior against other individuals or groups. Recognizes and deals with historical animosities between peoples and groups. Encourages social contacts and transactions among differing groups. | Cultural, psychological, spiritual interventions that change inappropriate stereotypes, values, beliefs and the internal mechanisms which perpetuate them. Seminars, video documentaries, simulation games, peer counseling skills, promoting intercultural contact, etc. *These methodologies produce self-aware and tolerant individuals.* | • Members of the organization are, and are perceived by their fellows as fair and unbiased.<br>• Reduced cost from polarization in and between groups, less waste from interpersonal and intergroup conflict and fear of avoidance of others.<br>• Increased understanding of each other's racial, gender, cultural issues and better cooperation to resolve them. Fewer incidents of harassment.<br>• A safer, more comfortable workplace. |
| **Cultural Competence** | Gain a multicultural and transcultural view of the world. Becoming aware of one's own culture and cultural "blind spots," and hence of the limitations one brings to interactions with others. Learn specific information about other cultures' beliefs, values, behaviors and preferences, and learn how to put this information into practice to function successfully in other cultures, or with persons from them. | Cross- and transcultural living, learning and skill development, global management skills, applied to communicating, negotiating, teamwork, etiquette, through training, culture specific videos, workbooks, learning games, etc. *These methodologies produce culturally knowledgeable and effective individuals and groups.* | • Ability to recognize, understand, manage, and work effectively with differences in values, beliefs, behaviors, communication styles, etc.<br>• Cultural skill in dealing with customers, marketing and selling, advertising and promotion. Fewer false starts, mistakes, etc.<br>• Individuals (and hence the organization) become locally and globally competent and effective. |
| **Diversity Value Added** | Learn how to habitually and creatively look at differences as social or organizational strengths, using and managing them as resources that contribute to the survival and success of the society or organization. Learn how to leverage this competence in the marketplace or to achieve the objectives of the organization. | Assessment tools, benchmarking, best practices, appreciative inquiry, open space technology. Technologies for creative visioning, thinking and marketing. *These methodologies enable diverse resources to become known and used well.* | • The diverse range of the skills, perceptions, ideas, etc., in the organization's system and environment are profitably employed.<br>• Diversity is part of the organization's competitive edge. Quality products and services succeed in its diverse environments and markets.<br>• The organization is seen and known as a fine place to work and excellent to do business with. |

biased than expected and redouble their efforts to "convert" the "foreigners."

To overcome their own ethnocentrism, U.S. sponsors of diversity efforts abroad, and those they are working with in the new context, must ask and answer certain critical questions about each challenge, e.g.:

- How is the U.S. diversity effort seen by the non-U.S. group or culture? What obstacles or challenges does this create? Using the model can diffuse concerns about U.S. "imperialism" in promoting diversity, and encourage discussion.

- Which challenges are already addressed or given emphasis in the non-US organization or group culture? Which are not? Which are easiest or most difficult to do? Why? The model can be used to chart these.

- What are the best practices already existing in each "wheel" that can be utilized to enjoy Diversity as Value Added? This validates local efforts, rather than imposing U.S. approaches.

- How these challenges are perceived and prioritized abroad in comparison with how they are seen in the U.S., i.e., how must each wheel be rotated to be on target for local conditions?

- How can the overseas diversity effort become a local initiative? How will the U.S. sponsors contribute to, but not dominate these efforts?

- How are the non-U.S. cultures, groups, organizations, etc., stronger or weaker in meeting these challenges?

- Using U.S. experiences not as norms, but as examples , what do they suggest about possible cultural blind spots in the new environment?

- What does the local group need to do or what resources do they need to meet the challenges that are difficult for them?

The answers to all of these questions are not only needed for a successful transfer of diversity technology, they are important for getting a perspective on the U.S. domestic efforts as well.

# Culture Change Efforts

More and more people are seeing that systems interventions, under titles such as "corporate culture change," "reinventing the organization," "reengineering," etc., must be "transcultural" and not the result of ethnocentric OD models if work place diversity objectives are truly reached. What is aimed at in legislation, policy development, and training programs needs to become a part of the everyday life of enterprises and agencies. The challenge is to bring the organizational development professionals and the diversity specialists together in a productive way early enough in the process.

Because the disciplines are often separate, it is not uncommon for OD people to unconsciously perpetrate ethnocentric models while suspecting that the diversity enterprise is faddish and insubstantial. They fear that opening the diversity can of worms could cause them to fail or be sidetracked from their critical concerns. Diversity practitioners who could provide valuable perspectives about the limitations of OD models and efforts often lack organizational expertise to do so effectively. Both diversity and OD consultants rightfully insist on the long-term nature of what they do and its effect on individuals and organizations. Collaboration of both sets of practitioners can lead to the development of focused diversity interventions with more immediate and measurable goals. Despite their differences and mutual fear of each other, both share common perspectives and need each other.

# Embedding Diversity in the Culture

What Leonard Cohen sings about democracy describes many diversity efforts as well:

*It's coming from the feel that it ain't exactly real,*
*or it's real, but it ain't exactly there.*

It is clear that concern for diversity needs to be embedded in the corporate culture itself, in the organization's mainstream processes. This means, for example, that quality efforts, team building and leadership training will be infused by an understanding that the organization and its efforts are inevitably transcultural and that attending to this dimension is a natural and automatic behavior.

498

Cultural competence and the skills of developing diversity as value added that today are objectives of the organization's diversity offerings will penetrate the entire curriculum tomorrow. They will become matter-of-fact assumptions of "how we do things around here," and accepted wisdom about "here's how to succeed in this organization."

Where the organizational culture provides the safety, differences between groups (previously buried for political reasons) begin to surface again and be taken more seriously. For example, male-female differences are receiving wider acceptance as true and functional cultural distinctions. These differences were until recently too dangerous to discuss. They have in the past led to second-class roles for those who were out of the mainstream. To arrive at diversity as value added, we must view previously excluded groups and their characteristics as part of a "cultural gene pool" capable of providing us with strains of imagination, understanding and behavior that will allow us to live and succeed in global and changing environments.

## Diversity & the Bottom Line

Finally, in recent years, diversity has been touted, understood and accepted as a measurable part of the bottom line in many organizations. The challenge, of course, is how to make sure that it appears in black ink and not in red. Valuing diversity must show up as not just something nice or fair to do, but as an investment and a cost-effective step in managing U.S. organizations, if it is to come, for example:

*from the brave, the bold, the battered heart of Chevrolet.*

The desire of both the internal and external champions of diversity to find acceptance and support, as well as fiscal resources, for their efforts has encouraged this focus. Nonetheless, insisting on the importance of the bottom line in both the short and long term should serve as a discipline for diversity efforts, not as a reason to gut them of any other dimensions of meaning.

Doing diversity has had, and continues to have, diverse sources of inspiration, e.g., respect, fairness, desire for justice, peace, harmony, spiritual integration, creative exchange, productivity, reaching global markets, etc. Seeing this rich and diverse motivation as validated only by certain numbers in the ledger is a falsehood, a suppression of diversity and waste of resources.

The bottom line in most organizations may be a number, but if one cannot see the many dimensions of human and social activity in this number, the bottom line is too small, no matter how many commas it contains. Those addicted to a purely dollar definition of the bottom line need to be reminded to "get real." So do diversity practitioners who forget that being cost-effective and profitable is the organization's duty to its stakeholders, customers and society at large.

This is an international as well as domestic issue. Multiculturalism as a bottom-line strategy for organizational success is being taken seriously as well as debated by many organizations both in the United States and in Western Europe. Eastern Europe and Asia are much more problematic in this regard—the discussion has hardly started. Values in these parts of the world are often widely different from our own and too few of us have enough information to discuss them intelligently. Tapping know-how of immigrants and expatriates already in the U.S. is one form of diversity as value added already available to us.

## How Do We Count Ourselves

How shall the census of the year 2000 number the people of this nation? Should the choices offer such things as "Black," "White," "Hispanic," "Pacific Islander," "Other"? This is not just an abstract technical question for statisticians, but an intensely acute social and political question for everyone. Enormous social and economic consequences for the new millennium will result from how we decide to add up who we are. Battle lines will be drawn as benefits are extended to, or withdrawn from, various groups on the basis of the categories in which the census places the population.

If it has become a diversity dogma that people should be allowed to define and name themselves, how should we look on government efforts to define who is what? Will the same government that created "Hispanics," now banish them into other categories? Debating and defining these categories invites us to ask what we intend to accomplish by the laws and discourse that will flow from them.

Will we keep "blacks" black and "whites" white, or will we learn

> . . . from the sorrow on the street,
> the holy places where the races meet

to adequately respond to the mixed racial reality of the United States? Will we create pride in diversity or the kind of false cultural pride that tears us apart?

Should we who are the government, continue to define people along ethnic and racial lines, or should we take an entirely different approach to sharing the common good more fairly in a diverse population? We believe that we will achieve distributive justice and serve the nation's interests better by moving to a system that allocates resources and opportunities to people who lack them, regardless of their other demographic characteristics.

Early in this book we suggested that, now that the threat of Marxism is dead, we might begin to take an unencumbered and practical look at the realities of class in this country as a potentially fresh way of addressing our social problems.

If, as Piper on page 453 of this anthology suggests, more people considered "white" have African-American blood than there are African-Americans in the country, who can hold to the "one drop" theory? Will marginalized African-Americans be any more marginalized if we focus on them as marginalized rather than as a race? If the African-American middle class is invisible, as suggested by Cose on pages 72–80, is this not because lower class African-Americans are overexposed?

## Indicators of a Need for Change

If categories change, how many people will rush to define themselves as members of new targeted groups once existing entitlements have been removed and new ones created? There are also people, who belong to targeted groups as the government defines them, who find their assigned category inaccurate or demeaning and insist that they do not belong there. Mixed race people both deserve and want to be something more than "other."

More people, even from "targeted groups," are growing to accept their mixed background, e.g.,

people who now speak of themselves as "African-Irish-American." This, of course, raises the vexing question, "If I'm multicultural, will the real me please stand up?" and "Whose side should I be on anyway?" The answer, of course, is that any "real me" that is less than the sum of my parts and the fullness of my heritage is a confining caricature whether I so define myself or others do it for me. I have more freedom rather than less if I feel I have a choice of operating out of my Irish-American side as well as my African-American side without feeling guilty for betraying my race.

"White" people, and in particular European-American men, are speaking up in the diversity dialogue. One form of this is resistance to defamation described on page 181. They will no longer tolerate the double standard which protects women and people of color but allows racial slurs against European-American people and gender slurs against men. Attempts to label their insistence on respect as simply "backlash" is insulting. Failing to listen to, and understand the needs of those so accused, simply adds fuel to the fire. It is increasingly far-fetched to explain "white privilege" to those who make up the largest group of unemployed in the nation. Even if the reality is that they are at some moments privileged, they are not about to perceive this anytime soon given their present condition.

Some U.S. systems are simply not working or are out of control and the people know it. Take the growing resistance to our porous immigration system as an example. Those who voted for and overwhelmingly passed California's Proposition 187 in the congressional elections of 1994 were labeled by its opponents as racist and fascist before, on and after election day. Once passed, the implementation of this popular mandate is being blocked and obfuscated by vested interests with the same persistence as Proposition 103 which sought to regulate excesses in the insurance industry. Something is not working in the management of these important social issues and a majority has said so in no uncertain terms. What will this electorate do next if this mandate results only in defiance, accusations and name-calling?

The 13th Generation is coming on line and "telling it like it is" for them. They are not presently invested in the language or values of their parents' Boomer generation. They will find practical, instead of "politically correct" solutions to their problems. These "latchkey kids" are more street-smart than their parents and used to taking care of themselves. They will both accept and reject people who are different from themselves, but on the basis of utility not ideology. They will be dividing the people of their world into categories different from those of their parents and their legislators. Beneath it all we suspect that they resonate not with their parents but, skipping a generation, with Cohen's cohorts who

> . . . love the country but . . . can't stand the scene.

and are

> . . . neither left or right . . . just staying home tonight, getting lost in that hopeless little screen.
> . . . stubborn as those garbage bags that Time cannot decay,
> . . . junk [as perhaps too many parental critics describe them] but . . . still holding up, this little wild bouquet: Democracy is coming to the U.S.A.

The diversity business is under severe criticism and ready for downsizing. This is one more indicator that it has come of age as a mature industry. At its moment of triumph, however, there are signs of changing directions in how it will be done. Consider the following:

1) As Boomers age, the political Center and Right become stronger and are entering into diversity policy and training, fields until recently seen as the turf of liberals, social activists, and the Left. While the new political climate acknowledges common problems, it interprets them differently and suggests other solutions. It is too early to see the entire agenda, but at the policy level it will certainly entail:

   • higher emphasis on the common good of the nation or the organization, e.g., demanding that individuals learn the skills needed to participate effectively in the community, workplace and economy.

   • alternatives to affirmative action and other programs that focused on group membership rather than individual performance.

   • fewer entitlements with "more strings attached," i.e., a demand for more personal responsibility and stewardship on the part of those who distribute and those who receive government assistance programs.

2) Within the field of management and human resources itself we are likely to see a variety of approaches that are less ideological and more practical:

   • less support for efforts aimed simply at the appreciation of the social deprivation or cultural richness of specific groups, and more emphasis on learning how others see and do things.

   • more empowerment through acculturation training, i.e., efforts to bring newcomers into an understanding of the values system of the organization and teaching them the skills they need to be effective in it. It will show them how to function better, in line with the culture of the organization, as well as how to bring their unique perspectives, creativity, and skills effectively into play.

   • changes in organizational values systems will occur both upward and downward through articulate empowered individuals, quality action teams and task forces, as well as through management-led organizational culture change efforts, reinvention, etc.

   • an end to the coercive melting pot mentality of political correctness. "Tolerance" which admits only lowest common denominator values and suppresses the European-American cultural heritage will be recognized as destructive. None of us can afford to lose touch with the roots that bring us understanding about our present structures and strength to face our dilemmas.

   • stronger defense of freedom of speech and insistence on public debate. A reassessment of the role of humor, irony, criticism, caricature, etc., in the social discourse. Perhaps we will actually train people in how to use these tools powerfully and well.

   • more emphasis on acquiring intergroup and cross-cultural skills. Europeans, for example, tend to address diversity in business less as removing oppression than as understanding and taking advantage of ethnic and regional styles. In Europe the roles of

501

---

## FASCISM ON THE LEFT AND THE RIGHT

Fascism lives on **the left** as well as **the right**. It comes from those who adopt a *holier-than-thou* attitude. Whether their passions arise from a philosophy of "eliminate corporate greed" or "eliminate taxation," wherever they come from, these people believe they have the enlightenment you lack. Fascists want you to stop thinking for yourself and simply think as they do!

As a public official of a small town, I've seen authoritarian attitudes spring from both ends of the political spectrum. Fascists seek to limit dialogue and impose their views of "what's correct" on everyone else. I believe the Direct Town Meeting form of government is the last bastion of pure democracy. There, the conversations can be loud and long, but in the end it's one-person-one vote on the town meeting floor.

We need more of a dialogue on diversity issues as well. Once any party believes they have found the singular truth, real exchange of ideas ends. It's my hope that the dialogues between Abramms & Simons can serve us as a model for how to engage each other.

Howard Bronstein
President
ODT, Incorporated
Amherst, MA

---

business and government social services are more clearly separated. As U.S. corporate diversity is increasingly exported to affiliates and partners abroad, it will return to us refined by the experience of others who perceive what we are doing in ways significantly different from our own.

Both a perception and a critique of the very culture of diversity practice is emerging. Those who "do" diversity, like any other professional group, have a culture of their own that impacts on what they do and how they do it. Becoming conscious of this culture raises the possibility of more insightful critique and the adoption of new and different approaches for achieving the challenges of diversity and particularly finding its promised value added that lies outside of current dogma.

## What Do We Need Now?

Unquestionably, what we have discussed suggests a new agenda. On it we would place the following items:

1) **Exploration of worldwide spiritual resources for the acceptance of self and others.** We need to draw, *from the staggering account of the Sermon on the Mount which,* at least publicly, few diversity efforts *pretend to understand at all.* Religions and philosophies frequently encourage openness and acceptance of others despite the often contrary behavior of their membership and leadership. There is room in the diversity endeavor to discuss and apply a Christian principle of universal love or a Buddhist compassion for all sentient beings.

These resources for benevolence and commitment to others need to be tapped, rather than stigmatized and marginalized as they often have been. Somehow in protecting the rights of the individual conscience we have disqualified the many traditions of one of the most religious nations in the world. The U.S. tolerance for religious diversity and its ecumenical dialogue have a far older and richer history than the present diversity movement. They deserve respect along with an opportunity to take part in the public dialogue.

2) **More person-to-person skills and technologies; training in the "how-to" of intercultural and transcultural behavior.** Most diversity in

the future will be taught as a dimension of the other management, teamwork, quality, etc. skills that organizations require. Successful valuing and managing diversity does not take place in a vacuum but in the everyday activities which bring people together in an organization. We want to direct our expertise now at enhancing our work and its outputs by adding value in the form of cultural perception and competence.

3) **A more solid understanding and critique of U.S. culture, and the role of diversity and political correctness within it.** We need a helicopter view of what is going on in order to understand the impact, culture, and products of the diversity revolution. This *Sourcebook* has deliberately scanned the horizon to find points of view that are generally not placed on the map of standard diversity practice.

This means understanding U.S. culture as a culture. We should know how and why our particular approaches to diversity and the cult of political correctness developed here. We need to quiz outsiders and listen to them because from their vantage points they see things that we cannot. U.S. corporations are starting to instill their diversity values in overseas installations. They need to recognize how unconscious ethnocentricity turns into cultural imperialism before saying things like, "If *these people* would only catch up to us in sensitivity and respect for the individual . . ." The Gulf War alerted us to the need *for the grace of God in the desert here and the desert far away*, and also showed us how shallow our self-understanding and diversity skills actually were.

4) **More exploration of gender issues in a cross-cultural context.** Our research suggests that "male" and "female" are the critical primary distinctions being made in every culture. How should we think about this? One thing is sure, we cannot uncritically export or impose the European-American dialogue about sex roles on other groups whether in the U.S. or abroad.

Cohen's earthy vision of the future of women and men holds out hope but in the same breath shows us how frighteningly far apart the sexes have separated in the U.S. How much we have buried our yearning for each other while at-

tempting to equalize our roles and escape from co-dependency, addiction and other "diseases" whose naming is the creation of the past decade or two!

*It's coming from the women and the men.*
*O baby, we'll be making love again.*
*We'll be going down so deep*
*that the river's going to weep,*
*and the mountain's going to shout Amen!*
*It's coming like the tidal flood beneath the*
  *lunar sway,*
*imperial, mysterious, in amorous array:*
*Democracy is coming to the U.S.A.*

5) **More research about successful African-Americans, as well studies about groups who have recently immigrated to the U.S.**

Much energy has been expended on African American people in working-class and inner-city environments. Similarly, too much has been made of the successful integration of European immigrants of the first half of this century and too little said of similar successes on the part of Latinos, Asians, and even new European immigrants who might provide more current models.

6) **Diversity training for all who need it.** Recent surveys (Bureau of National Affairs, in the *BNAC Communicator*, Winter 1995) indicate that diversity training is likely to be offered in organizations where there are less non-traditional workers employed rather than more. Still, European-American men are targeted for more than their share of diversity training. This leads us to speculate. Does it mean that managers who need to "make their numbers" in hiring and promotions are getting the training they need? Does it indicate a prevailing mind-set that the dominant culture is, after all, the real target of such training? Does it reinforce our perception that a disproportionate amount of training resources is still spent on the better-paid or those considered to be at higher organizational levels or of a higher social class? Does it harbor the false assumption that people from targeted or outsider groups have adequate diversity skills simply as a result of their having lived some form of "minority" experience?

The list of questions could go on. Perhaps you will add to it or change it even as a result of reading the materials that we have assembled in this *Sourcebook*. What counts is not only the answers we have given to older questions of diversity, but the process of periodic reexamination that helps us "get real" in our work and with each other and motivate us to believe in and continue to shape this great and diverse democracy.

*Sail on, sail on O mighty Ship of State!*
*To the Shores of Need Past the Reefs of Greed*
*Through the Squalls of Hate*
*Sail on, sail on, sail on.*

## References:

Bureau of National Affairs, in the *BNAC Communicator*, Winter 1995. page 1

Hall, Edward T., *Beyond Culture*, Doubleday Anchor Books, NY, 1981

Hill, Richard, *We Europeans*, Europublications, Bruxelles, 1992

Hofstede, Geert, *Culture's Consequences, International Differences in Work-Related Values*, Sage Newbury Park, CA, 1984

————, *Cultures and Organizations: Software of the Mind*, McGraw-Hill, NY, 1993

Kochman, Thomas, *Black and White Styles in Conflict*, University of Chicago Press, 1982

Miller, Richard, *Understanding Europeans*, John Muir Publications, Santa Fe, NM, 1990. (First edition in 1987 was titled *Painted in Blood*)

Simons, George, Carmen Vázquez and Philip Harris, *Transcultural Leadership*, Gulf Publishing Co., Houston, TX, 1993

Simons, George, and Walt Hopkins, *The Transcultural Communicator*, International Partners Press, Santa Cruz, CA, 1994

Simons, George and Bob Abramms, *Cultural Diversity Fieldbook*, ODT Inc., Amherst, MA, 1996

Trompenaars, Fons, *Riding the Waves of Culture*, 1993

---

### MULTICULTURALISM, NO PANACEA

Granted, multiculturalism is no panacea for our social ills. We're worried when Johnny can't read. We're worried when Johnny can't add. But shouldn't we be worried, too, when Johnny tramples gravestones in a Jewish cemetery or scrawls racial epithets on a dormitory wall?

Henry Louis Gates, Jr.
Chairman of the Afro-American Studies Department and Professor of English at Harvard University
(*Boston Globe Magazine* 10/13/91)

# ABOUT THE EDITORS

**DR. BOB ABRAMMS** is an international expert on designing, conducting and evaluating management training and executive development programs. Bob's background includes a B.S. in industrial engineering, Master's degrees in both business administration and counseling, and a doctorate in applied behavioral science. He has published over fifty articles on leadership, motivation, human relations training, prejudice, stereotyping, and cultural differences.

He is currently Chair of the Board of ODT, Inc., an employee-owned Massachusetts-based management consulting and publishing company. Bob is a certified Human Relations Trainer and Consultant and has been a registered Organizational Development Professional Consultant. He has conducted his seminar on "Managing Cultural Differences" for a wide variety of corporate and association clients.

In 1990, he edited and produced ODT's *Complete Cultural Diversity Library* which won an award as one of the year's "20 hottest Human Resource products." He has pioneered the use of the Peters Projection Map materials in large corporations and been involved in a variety of diversity diagnostic projects. He authored (with Dianne LaMountain) *Cultural Diversity: A Workshop for Trainers*, a best-selling module for empowering organizations to initiate their own in-house diversity efforts.

He has just finished (with George Simons, Ann Hopkins, and Diane J. Johnson) creating *The Cultural Diversity Fieldbook*, a collection of fresh visions and breakthrough strategies for revitalizing the U.S. workforce.

Avocationally, he is a Contact Improvisation dancer, who has worked with mixed dance companies (and classes) of able-bodied dancers and dancers with physical disabilities. This work has enhanced and enriched his perspective as a diversity consultant.

He can be reached at ODT, P.O. Box 134, Amherst, MA 01004; Toll-free: 800-736-1293; Phone: 413-549-1293; Fax: 413-549-3503; E-mail: 347-5157 @mcimail.com.

**DR. GEORGE F. SIMONS** is President of George Simons International, an organization specializing in gender and cultural diversity management, and a Senior Associate with ODT Inc. As an educator, counselor and writer he helps organizations know and achieve their purposes, working with both corporate culture and individual skills.

George is a Doctor of Psychology & Theology (Claremont 1977) and Diplomat of the Gestalt Center, San Diego. He did master's work in the history and psychology of human rituals at Notre Dame and in anthropology at Oberlin.

He has authored: *Working Together: How to Become More Effective in a Multicultural Organization, Men & Women: Partners at Work* (with Deborah G. Weissman), *Transcultural Leadership* (with Carmen Vazquez and Phil Harris) and *Sexual Orientation in the Workplace* with Amy Zuckerman. He is principal designer of the DIVERSOPHY® training game.

He has worked as a clergyman and adult education consultant, creating and editing multimedia training materials. For many years, Dr. Simons also directed Hidden Valley Center for Men, an organization whose purpose is to educate men to meet the stresses of contemporary living.

Speaking English, German, Spanish and French, he has worked in over thirty countries, serving such clients as: The Bank of Montreal (Canada), Chase Manhattan Bank, Colgate (Latin America), The Department of National Defense (Canada), Management Centre Europe (Belgium), Mobil Plastics (Luxembourg), Procter & Gamble (USA, Switzerland and the Rep. of the Philippines), PT Arun (Indonesia), Shell Canada, Silicon Graphics, The Universities of Warsaw and Cracow (Poland), Varian Associates, Whirlpool Corporation, and the General Services Administration of the U.S. government.

He can be reached at: George Simons International, **P.O.** Box 7360, Santa Cruz, CA 95061-7360; Phone: 408-426-9608; Fax: 408-457-8590; E-mail gsintgs@aol.com

# Multicultural Workplace Skills

1-800-736-1293
Fax: 1-413-549-3503

1990's "Best New Human Resource Product" awarded by *Human Resource Executive* magazine has been updated and revised!

## The Diversity Resource Kit

The **Diversity Resource Kit** is the perfect starter set for exploring the impact of the changing workforce on today's organization. The kit includes books, articles, assessment tools, and a reference list. The resources cover issues for legally protected classes (gender, race, etc.), and also include a broader perspective on issues such as sexual preference and class.

Instrumentation and questionnaires in the **Questions of Diversity** assessment tools are **fully reproducible.**

The **Diversity Resource Kit** will provide HRD practitioners with valuable insights on issues of diversity and awareness of the skills needed to help make employees sensitive to cultural differences in the workplace.

The **Diversity Resource Kit** includes:

Two books—**Breaking Into the Boardroom,** and
      **Working Together**
Self-Esteem Passport
Audiotape—**Dealing with Subtle Discrimination**
Peters Projection Mini-Map—a new map of the world
      correcting historically ethnocentric
      perspectives (guidebook & training tips
      included)
Twelve tipsheets and articles
**The Questions of Diversity** assessment tools (6th Edition)
Copyright-free questionnaires!
Cultural Diversity Reference List

Diversity Resource Kit            **$125.00**

## Complete Cultural Diversity Library

The **Complete Cultural Diversity** Library is a comprehensive set of resources for an organization committed to initiating diversity programs. The complete library includes all the materials from the Diversity Resource Kit, plus six additional books, seven audiotapes, a video on people with disabilities that can be reproduced (copyright-free!), and several more timely articles.

Included is a special "USER'S GUIDE" audiotape which provides a guided tour of all the resources including: (1) how to best use them, (2) what their strengths and weaknesses are, (3) how to contact the key diversity consulting organizations and (4) a detailed explanation of each of the four training modules including: "How to Avoid Stereotyping and Other Pitfalls of Perception," "Gender Hostility in the Workforce: An EEO/AA backlash role-play," and "The Internal SELLING of a Cultural Diversity Training Program."

The **Complete Cultural Diversity Library** includes:

Everything from the **Diversity Resource Kit** plus:
Six Books–**A People's History of the United States** •
      **Black and White Styles in Conflict** •
      **Male & Female Realities** • **Indian Givers** •
      **Men and Women: Partners at Work** •
      **Class** •
USER's GUIDE audiotape
Seven additional audiotapes
Twelve additional articles and tipsheets
Four training modules (two are **fully reproducible**)
Diversity videotape—**"Part of the Team"**
      Videotape is **reproducible & copyright-free!**

Complete Cultural Diversity Library        **$525.00**

# Resources from

## GEORGE SIMONS INTERNATIONAL
### TEL: 408-426-9608  FAX: 408-457-8590  E-Mail: GSINTGS@AOL.COM

## BOOKS

*Working Together II: Succeeding in a Multicultural Organization* by George Simons. A workbook teaching the basic principles of working in a multicultural environment. $9.95

*Men and Women: Partners at Work* by George Simons and G. Deborah Weissman. A workbook addressing the basic principles of working with the other gender. $9.95

*Transcultural Leadership: Empowering the Diverse Workforce* by George Simons, Carmen Vázquez, and Philip Harris. A collection of cutting-edge ideas and tools for managing today's diverse workforce in a global business environment. $28.95

*Dynamics of Diversity: Strategic Programs for Your Organization* by Odette Pollar & Rafael González. A workbook on the whys and hows of effective diversity management. $9.95

*Cultural Diversity in the Workplace* by Sally J. Walton. A crash course in how cultural diversity affects the individual and the enterprise. $10.00

*Sexual Orientation in the Workplace: Gay Men, Lesbians, Bisexuals and Heterosexuals Working Together* by Amy J. Zuckerman & George Simons. A workbook for individuals and organizations on how to handle the issue positively and proactively. $17.95

## VIDEO TRAINING PROGRAMS

*Working Together II: Videobook Training Kit.* A complete cultural diversity training program. Contains 25-minute videotape, Leader's guide, 5 copies of workbook. Purchase: $495.00 / 5-day Rental: $95.00

*Men and Women: Videobook Training Kit.* A complete gender diversity training program. Contains 25-minute videotape, Leaders' Guide, 5 copies of workbook. Purchase: $495.00 / 5-day Rental: $95.00

*Achieving & Managing Diversity Series.* A four-part video series with discussion guide: 1) The Executive Vision; 2) Communicating Across Cultures; 3) Developing Diverse Employees; 4) Building the Diverse Team. Available in English and French. Complete series: Purchase: $1,495.00/5-day Rental: $195.00. Per segment: Purchase: $395.00 / 5-day Rental: $95.00

## INSTRUMENTS

*The Transcultural Communicator*™. Prepares the user(s) for critical cross-cultural communication situations. Instruction, six surveys and interpretative instrument included per package. $45.00

## TRAINING GAMES
### DIVERSOPHY™ An innovative board game for all levels of your organization, covering a broad range of cultural issues! $375.00

4–6 players or partner teams roll the dice and move around the board seeking to avoid the Bias, Assimilation, Stereotypes and Ethnocentricity Traps.

In the course of the game they will be tested on their factual knowledge about various cultural groups, and asked to choose an appropriate course of action in face-to-face situations. They will also get a chance to share aspects of their own backgrounds and experiences, and will experience the risks & benefits of working in a multicultural environment.

DIVERSOPHY™ engages players at their own learning level. Its entertaining format enables the exploration of sensitive materials in a non-threatening way, and provides a new learning experience each time.

**CONFERENCE DIVERSOPHY**™ Based upon the professional board game, this new conference format for up to 72 participants livens up any conference or special event! Stimulates interaction within and between the teams taking part. $139.00

**ADVANCED OPTION DECKS for both formats**
- ☐ The Gender Deck
- ☐ Sexual Orientation & The Workplace Deck
- ☐ The Roleplay Deck
- ☐ The U.S. Latinos Deck
- ☐ Doing Business with Canada
- ☐ Doing Business with Mexico
- ☐ Euro*Diversophy*™
- ☐ Custom*Diversophy*™—Tailored for your organization

# ODT, Inc.

For further information contact:
Kate Larson at 413-549-1293

For Immediate Release

Corporate Office: Box 134, Amherst, MA 01004 • 413-549-1293

# Award Winning Cultural Diversity Library Expanded!

ODT, Inc.'s "Complete Cultural Diversity Library" was selected as one of 1990's "20 Hottest Human Resource Products" by *Human Resource Executive* magazine. This collection of diversity awareness resources includes 8 audiotapes, 8 books, a diversity assessment tool, 5 booklets, 24+ articles and tip-sheets, a Peters Projection Mini-Map and full size Wall Map, and 4 complete training modules. The revised and expanded    version will include a reproducible videotape (on people with disabilities) that organizations can copy for all their locations!

From its publishing headquarters in Amherst MA, ODT compiled, published and arranged every detail of this unique resource collection including a "User's Guide" audiocassette. This "user-friendly" feature provides a guided tour of the Library including (1) how to best use the materials (pre-, during-, or post-training), (2) the strengths and limitations of each item, (3) the names, addresses, and phone numbers of the copyright holders of items included in the Library, (4) contact information for key diversity consulting organizations, and (5) a detailed explanation of each of the 4 training modules.

Training professionals challenged by managing diversity — diversity consultants, trainers, EEO and Human Resource specialists — will find practical and effective value in the Library's recently released training modules. The modules include "Gender Hostility in the Workplace: An EEO/AA backlash role play" and "The internal selling of a cultural diversity training program." Both provide a copyright release to reproduce materials for in-house training on a royalty-free basis.

Recent releases for this Library include an audiocassette on "Dealing with subtle discrimination" by senior ODT partner, Dianne LaMountain. Her ground-breaking program offers information for both majority-culture groups as well as those targeted by discrimination. Four critical concepts are discussed: (1) the impact of feeling like an outsider, (2) distinctions between INTENT versus EFFECT, (3) the importance of COMFORT versus COMPETENCE in a person's career success, and (4) understanding that perception IS reality.

A diversity assessment tool, *The Questions of Diversity* edited by Dr. George F. Simons is a best-selling collection of instruments, checklists, and questionnaires that are fully-reproducible for in-house administration. It enables an organization to ask the right questions to determine it's readiness to undertake diversity training. Some section titles are: Cultural Audit, Managing the Dominant Culture, Critical Issues, Effort Level, and Activities. Dr. Simons explains, "This collection of sixteen instruments represents the best of our thinking, as well as 40 years of collective experience doing diversity training and consulting."

Also included are the classic articles on "What it's like to be a black manager" from the *Harvard Business Review* as well as ODT's best-selling tip-sheet, "Working With People from Diverse Backgrounds" by Carmen Colin and Diane Johns which discusses values in other cultures, racial and ethnic identity tips, phases of acculturation, and "How to Begin" suggestions. The Library is available for $525 from ODT, Incorporated, P.O. Box 134, Amherst MA 01004 (413-549-1293). Credit card orders may call 800-736-1293.

# EMPOWER YOUR WORK FORCE
## WITH THESE HIGH-IMPACT, LOW-COST TIPSHEETS!

**1. HOW TO RECEIVE A PERFORMANCE APPRAISAL:**
Provide your employees with quick tips on receiving performance appraisals. This tipsheet instructs employees how to "partner" with their managers to make the performance appraisal process a conversation about shared job expectations. It encourages employees to pre-plan for their appraisal session now and throughout the year.

**2. HOW TO RECEIVE A DELEGATED ASSIGNMENT:**
Saying "yes" to an assignment you have trouble accomplishing does not help anyone. This tipsheet teaches you how to take responsibility for knowing what you can deliver. Skills and strategies for receiving delegated tasks are explained so that you have the confidence you need to effectively discuss—and tackle—new assignments.

**3. WORKING WITH RESISTANCE IN AN ORGANIZATION:**
Resistance to change is a reality of organizational life. Instead of viewing it negatively, you can use it to create a more cooperative and dynamic work-place. This tipsheet takes a clear look at the phenomenon of resistance and some of the myths surrounding it. Your employees will learn how to accept resistance, overcome others' resistance, and implement a five-step strategy for keeping the problems created by resistance under control.

**4. WORKING WITH PEOPLE FROM DIVERSE BACKGROUNDS:** Are you realizing all the benefits from diversity, or are you finding it hard to cope with the variety of styles, ethnic and cultural backgrounds of your employees and customers? This tipsheet includes information on differences in cultural values; racial vs. ethnic identity; stress of immigration and acculturation; plus how to succeed when working with people from diverse backgrounds.

**5. HOW TO HANDLE THE CAREER PLATEAU:** Combat the problems created by flatter organizational charts and less access to promotions. Your employees can find new creative ways to enrich their current jobs. This tipsheet gives you a practical road-map to improve job satisfaction with such strategies as acceptance, developing new opportunities and creating a new action plan.

**6. HOW TO INCREASE YOUR PERSONAL POWER:** Power is the ability to get all of what you want from the environment, given what is available. And, the more that you are able to get what you want from your people, the easier it will be for your organization to achieve its goals and objectives. This tipsheet encourages managers to take charge and increase their impact, while fostering support by empowering their employees.

## ORDER FORM

| | Single copy price | Price per 10-pack | Quantity Ordered | Amount |
|---|---|---|---|---|
| 1. HOW TO RECEIVE A PERFORMANCE APPRAISAL | $2.50 | $20 | ___ | ___ |
| 2. HOW TO RECEIVE A DELEGATED ASSIGNMENT | $2.50 | $20 | ___ | ___ |
| 3. WORKING WITH RESISTANCE IN AN ORGANIZATION | $2.50 | $20 | ___ | ___ |
| 4. WORKING WITH PEOPLE FROM DIVERSE BACKGROUNDS | | | | |
| * $1.00 additional for "Diverse Backgrounds" tip sheets | $3.50 | $30 | ___ | ___ |
| 5. HOW TO HANDLE THE CAREER PLATEAU | $2.50 | $20 | ___ | ___ |
| 6. HOW TO INCREASE YOUR PERSONAL POWER | $2.50 | $20 | ___ | ___ |

**Mix and match to take advantage of quantity discounts:**

50-200 copies .. $1.80 ea.*

200+ copies ..... $1.60 ea.*

International Orders Shipping & Handling:
Canada & Mexico Add 15%
Other International Add 40% for A.O. AirMail

MA residents add 5% Tax _____
Shipping & Handling (U.S.)  $3.50

**TOTAL** _____

❑ Confirmation Of Telephone/FAX Order    ❑ Bill My Organization

❑ Check Enclosed (Prepayment requested for all orders under $25.00.)

❑ Charge To My:  ❑ VISA  ❑ MasterCard  ❑ American Express

Signature _____

Card Number _____  Expires _____

Name _____  Phone ( ) - _____

Organization _____

Street/Address _____

City _____  State _____  Zip _____

### 3 EASY WAYS TO ORDER:

1. **MAIL** completed form to:
   **ODT, Inc.**
   P.O. Box 134
   Amherst, MA  01004

2. **FAX** your order to (413) 549-3503

3. **CALL Toll-Free** 1-800-736-1293

# The First and Only Workshop that Prepares and Empowers Prospective Trainers for the *Process* of Diversity Training!

# Cultural Diversity: A Workshop For Trainers

*by Dianne LaMountain & Bob Abramms*

Maximize productivity by drawing on the talents of a diverse workforce with **Cultural Diversity: A Workshop For Trainers**. This timely new train-the-trainer program will enhance your training staff's awareness of, and ability to deal with, multicultural issues throughout your organization.

Written for private and public sector organizations, the **Workshop** consists of activities, exercises, and self-study assignments. The **Workshop** takes a rigorous approach to the self-qualification process, allowing participants the opportunity to work with their own diversity as a beginning model. This unique training process will reveal the trainees' level of readiness to undertake subsequent diversity training for the rest of the organization.

The **Workshop** offers detailed information on "basic building blocks" of diversity training. It provides the resources for evaluating the content that the organization chooses to select, customize, and teach, although it does not detail the specific content of what organizations should teach. Appendices containing the most comprehensive list of resources from which to draw diversity content include: films, packaged training programs, print, public seminars, and consulting firms, along with information on the capabilities, prices, fees, and target audiences for these resources.

# THE QUESTIONS OF DIVERSITY - 6th Edition

Ten experienced diversity consultants share their best thinking with you about the assessment process of diversity initiatives.  A comprehensive, easy to use collection of:
- techniques
- tips
- instruments
- quizzes
- case studies
- articles   and
- a high-powered in-basket activity

THE QUESTIONS OF DIVERSITY began as a modest collection of diversity diagnostic assessment tools -- a way for an organization to determine its readiness to undertake diversity training. The 6th edition is 130% BIGGER. It contains a whopping 227 pages -- fifty-five percent is new material from a variety of disciplines and perspectives. This has become a best selling classic for organizations to learn how to ask the right questions to begin to implement diversity efforts.

*Whether you're doing business internationally, dealing with a diverse workforce within your organization, or just want to reach new and different markets for your products or services ... this book will provide valuable insights and directions. It includes:*

**Part A:** "Choices and Directions." This portion addresses "Where do I go for help?" as well as nine key questions for a diversity diagnosis. It provides a framework for deciding what your options are and helps to determine how to decide on a focus.

**Part B:** "How to use the surveys" and "How NOT to use the surveys." As diversity consultants will attest, an ounce of prevention here is well worth a pound of cure later.

**Part C:** Nineteen survey instruments. The first nine are useful in an introductory exploration of diversity issues, the remaining ten are most useful for organizations already along the road to fostering, valuing, and supporting a multicultural climate.

**Part D:** new Activities section: a dynamite in-basket activity for group or individual training, "Gender DIVERSOPHY" and a reverse questionnaire (broadening awareness of gay/lesbian/bisexual issues), as well as an activity on assessing the costs of homophobia. This section ends with an activity around the diversity wheel to further legitimize the conversation about diversity.

**PLUS** two great appendices: one explores the classic MBTI personality test and diversity; the second brings the provocative "racism inventory" from the 1960's into the 1990's.

"We don't even know where or how to begin to deal with this touchy topic" diversity consultants often hear clients say. While this valuable resource is no substitute for the counsel of a seasoned consultant, it provides a framework for the organization to undertake a readiness check on where it is, and where it might like to go. Individuals and organizations committed to diversity and multicultural issues cannot afford to be without this valuable collection of tools. Permission to reproduce instruments for internal consulting/diagnostic work is included in the price of the package. **SPECIAL BONUS:** also enclosed with the bound collection is a six-page card-stock tipsheet, "Working With People from Diverse Backgrounds."

236 pages.  $99.  Spiral-bound w. laminated cover        From:   ODT, Box 134, Amherst MA  01004
1-800-736-1293; fax: 413-549- 3503

# EXPAND YOUR WORLD VIEW!

*Which is bigger—Africa or Greenland?*      *Up is which way?*

## Teachers—Trainers—Clergy—Mentors—Educators
## How do these questions GRAB YOU? Your students? Your Organization?

### Maps send messages! We have tools that communicate messages of fairness towards all peoples, and about the pitfalls of ethnocentric bias.

**Peters Map Trainer's Packages** provide innovative resources for inspiring new perspectives and "unfreezing" learners of all ages.

The **Standard Peters Map Trainer's Package** (@ **$39**) includes one each of the following:
- Laminated Peters Projection Wall Map (35"x51")
- Laminated Peters Mini-map (11"x17")
- *A New View of the World* (which explains a variety of cartographic approaches and principles, along with the key message of fairness in the Peters Map; 42 page paperback)
- Peters Postcard
- assorted article reprints

The **Deluxe Peters Map Trainer's Package** (@ **$89**) includes:
- The standard Trainer's Package
- two additional laminated wall maps for comparison purposes:
  — the standard Mercator Projection (34" x 52")
  — the Upside Down World Map—Van der Grinten Projection (29" x 40")

These packages have already brought multiple points of view to wide audiences. For organizations wishing A/V resources we also provide a set of fifteen 35-mm slides or overhead transparencies. The A/V Peters Projection Resource Package comes with a lifetime license for internal use for a $250 one-time fee. These high-quality resources are made available by special arrangement between Akademische Verlagsanstalt, Friendship Press and ODT, Inc.

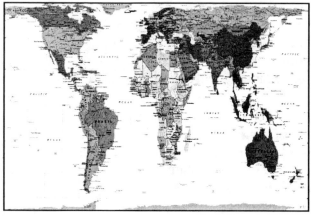

*The* **Peters Projection Map** *clearly shows Africa as it is — 14 times larger than Greenland. It is available in several formats, including 35" X 51" laminated edition @ $25.*

*The* **Upside Down World Map** *is an exciting addition to your teaching resources. It challenges basic notions of "up" and "down". The Upside Down World Map is available in 29" X 40" laminated edition @ $25.*

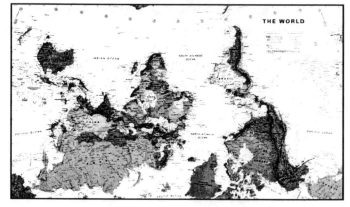

Maps provide more than geographical information. Each map conveys subtle or hidden messages drawn from its assumptions. These resources are the perfect teaching tools for exploring the assumptions about life we all take for granted. They provide an expanded perspective...and a new world-view.

Peters Projection Map Resources: ODT, Inc.
## 1-800-736-1293
P.O. Box 134; Amherst, MA 01004
fax: 413-549-3503 phone: 413-549-1293
*For more info: visit http:// www.diversophy.com*

# New Map...
# New View

Greenland: **0.8** mill.sq.miles

Africa: **11.6** mill.sq.miles

All your life you have looked at OUR WORLD one way. Mercator's map is still used in boardrooms and classrooms everywhere. This view of the world from 1569 has led to centuries of distortion. Ask yourself which is bigger, Greenland or Africa? On the Mercator map they appear equal in size. But **Africa is 14 times larger than Greenland.**

Dr. Arno Peters, historian and cartographer, saw the Mercator map's inaccuracies and created the **Peters Projection Map** which adjusted the Earth's land masses to accurately reflect their relative size. People's perceptions have been shaped by the biases of out-of-date mental maps. How many other concepts have been as misleading as the traditional map? Management Consultant Dr. Bob Abramms reports, "When folks first see the map they are shocked by the limiting assumptions of their old world view. *If all I thought to be true about the Earth is distorted in shape and size, what other mistaken assumptions am I carrying?"*

Now that more than 83 million Peters Projection Maps are in circulation, ODT, Inc. has just released a fully laminated Peters Wall Map (35" X 51"), complete with comparisons and explanatory information panels @ $25 each. The map is available from local book and travel stores, or by calling 1-800-736-1293.

● ● ● ● ● ● ● ● ● ● ● ● ● ● ● ● ● ● ● ● ● ● ● ● ● ● ● ● ● ● ● ● ● ● ● ● ● ● ●

## More Peters Map Products!! Two innovative educational packets...

...will help everyone learn more about the Peters Map approach. At $15 each, the **New Mental Map Packet** and the **Peters Geo-Learning Pack** both include the panel *Why this new world map?* and the comparison panels from the borders of actual wall maps. The **Geo-Learning Pack** includes stationary made from recycled wall maps! <u>BOTH</u> packets also include a Peters mini-map, 11"x 17". (The Geo-Pack's is a Soviet Union-era map and the New Mental Map Packet's is current!) <u>BOTH</u> include *A New View of the World*, a 44-page easy-to-read booklet comparing the Peters map, and answering the most frequently asked questions. The book is also loaded with teaching tips and suggestions for classroom use. *Another tip for teachers...call our Teacher Support Hot-line: 800-736-1293!!!*

The **New Mental Map Packet** also includes the 34-page *Self-Esteem Passport,* a unique and useful resource:"Notice To Passport Holders: This United States of America Self-Esteem Passport -- issued to all persons regardless of age, race or creed -- will permit the bearer to experience a new sense of self after honestly completing all visa entry sections." (Kaiser Permanente used this in diversity training for 5,000 employees.)

*Please turn over for more details on these and other Peters Map Products...*

## Peters Packet Product Summary

| | Peters Geo-Learning Pack | New Mental Map Packet |
|---|---|---|
| Retail Price: | $15 | $15 |
| *New View of the World* booklet | YES | YES |
| "Why This New World Map" panel | YES | YES |
| 7 additional map panels | YES | YES |
| Peters mini-map (old) | YES | no |
| Peters mini-map (current) | no | YES |
| Stationery, Envelopes & labels | YES | no |
| Earth Stickers | 16 small | 4 large |
| Peters Map Postcards | 1 | 6 |
| *Self-Esteem Passport* | no | YES |

### Here is the full list of Peters Map products, available at your map or bookstore or from us at 1-800-736-1293!

**PETERS PROJECTION WALL MAP:** *35" by 50" full-color wall-map with informational panels describing the map and its principle of equality of scale and area.*
| | |
|---|---|
| *Folds to 8-1/2"by 11-1/2"* | **$15.00** |
| *Also available rolled in a tube.* | **$16.50** |
| *Also available fully laminated.* | **$25.00** |

**PETERS PROJECTION MINI-MAP:** *Full-color 11" by 17" version of the map. (Just the map, informational panels not included.) Folds to 8 1/2" by 11"* **$5.00**

**PETERS PROJECTION MINI-MAP, LAMINATED:** *The same version of the map above with a laminated coating. Makes a great placemat for those who want to bring the world to their dinner table. With wipe-away markers, it also makes a great teaching instrument.*
| | |
|---|---|
| *Shipped flat, 11" x 17"* | **$7.00** |
| *Also available with rounded corners* | **$7.50** |

**A NEW VIEW OF THE WORLD:** *Original handbook explains the principles behind the Peters Projection in detail. (42 pages, perfect bound)* **$7.00**

**PETERS POSTCARDS:** *Correspond with full-color Peters Projection map postcards or use as low-cost classroom handouts!* **10-pack @ $6.00**

**PETERS GEO-LEARNING PACKS:** *Stationery and envelopes made from recycled 1990 Peters wall maps, 16 high-resolution Earth stickers, 36 pastel colored mailing labels,* **New View** *booklet, a Soviet Union-era mini-map, plus tips for use in the classroom...a total of more than 90 items.* **$15.00**

**NEW MENTAL MAP PACKET:** *One mini-map: New View booklet: eight data-panels cut from past editions of the wall maps (includes key Why This New World Map panel): stickers viewing Earth from space: six Peters Projection Map post cards and the unique SELF-ESTEEM PASSPORT (32 pages of great inspiration in a U.S. passport format).* **$15.00**

**PETERS MAP REFRIGERATOR MAGNET:** *A 4" x 6" oversized magnet with sturdy 10 mil lamination. Intrigue your guests with this great visual aid.* **$5.00**

**Peters Projection Map Resources: ODT, Inc., P.O. Box 134, Amherst, MA  01004**
**fax: 413-549-3503    phone: 413-549-1293**

# 1-800-736-1293

### For more info: visit http://www.diversophy.com

An important companion resource for owners of the *Cultural Diversity Fieldbook* and the *Cultural Diversity Sourcebook*

## CULTURAL DIVERSITY SUPPLEMENT

### NUMBER ONE

$17.50

- Additional Exciting Material!

- Twelve New Exercises!

- Contributing Authors Include:
  *Gloria Steinem, Kathleen Tyau,*
  *Ward Churchill, William Upski Wimsatt*
  *Zalman Schachter-Shalomi, Connie Hale,*
  *Richard Rodriguez,* and others!

- Reprints From:
  *Mother Jones, Story, Z Magazine,*
  *The American Enterprise,* and many more!

- Large Format (8½" x 11")!

- Low Price: $17.50!

> "These editors keep mining the diversity landscape for provocative and exciting views, many of which lead us far off the trodden path of typical diversity resources. People who found the **Fieldbook** and **Sourcebook** valuable will want **Supplement: Number One** now!"

## WARNING!

The *CULTURAL DIVERSITY SUPPLEMENT: NUMBER ONE* contains raw language, including profanity and racial epithets. We have decided to let contributors speak frankly in their own uncensored language on issues they feel passionately about. Some selections may offend the sensibilities of readers.

## Available from ODT:
## 1-800-736-1293

S&H $3 per copy U.S.,
$5 Canada & Mexico, $9.00 Int'l

## Order Form

❑ Yes! Please send me _____ copy(ies) of the Cultural Diversity Supplement: Number One at $20.50 each (includes shipping + handling)

❑ Prepaid order. Check enclosed, Check # _____ (MA residents, please add 5% sales tax, or provide tax-exempt number)

❑ Charge to my MC/Visa/AMEX account # _____ Exp. Date _____

❑ Bill me (minimum order is 3 copies for billing. Purchase order or request on company letterhead required.) Purchase order # _____

Name _____  Organization _____
        (Please Print)
                                            Title _____

Street Address (No P. O. Boxes) _____

City _____ State _____ ZIP (Postal Code) _____ Phone (Required)  (____) _____

ODT, Inc. • P. O. Box 134 • Amherst, MA 01004 • 1-800-736-1293 (U.S. and Canada)  • 1-413-549-1293 • FAX 1-413-549-3503

# A **Must-Read** for *All* Managers, Human Resource Practitioners & Small-Business Owners

- More than 100 articles, interactive exercises, interviews, and essays from the mainstream, business, and nontraditional press, including: *Business Ethics, National Review, New York Times, Chicago Tribune, Time, Z Magazine, The American Enterprise, Wired, Ms.*

    **Conservative Views** from: Thomas Sowell, Doug Bandow, Charles Krauthammer, Lance Morrow, and Walter E. Williams

    **Progressive Views** from: Jeremy Rifkin, bell hooks, Peter Gabel, Katha Pollitt, Lani Guinier, Barbara Ehrenreich, and Lindsy Van Gelder

    **New Interviews** with: Roosevelt Thomas, Thomas Kochman, and Merlin Pope

    **Compelling First-Person Accounts** from: Colin Powell, Robert Fulghum, and Rita Henley Jensen

- Examples of leading thought and best practices from a wide array of practitioners and thinkers

- Challenges popular assumptions about:

    —The affirmative action debate

    —Sensitizing our workforce to "differences"

    —**Class as a key dimension** of diversity

    —Corporate diversity programs—how realistic are they?

- Clarifies both "**pro**" and "**con**" positions

- Complete with analysis and incisive commentary from the editors, **icons to guide you** through the text, and contact information for over 50 practitioners

"A goldmine of resources, contacts, opinions, and activities. Current political realities, especially around the appropriate role of government, are discussed by commentators all across the political spectrum."

Available from ODT:
**1-800-736-1293**

*Edited by Dr. George F. Simons, Dr. Bob Abramms, and L. Ann Hopkins, with Diane J. Johnson*

**ISBN 1-56079-602-2**
**273 pages, 8 x 8, $26.95 pb, May 1996**

The book that **truly bridges** the spectrum of opinion— conservative to progressive—about diversity.

# New Workbook and Seminar Briefings

## Introducing ODT's Special Seminar Workbook on Empowerment!

✓ What is empowerment?

✓ How do you link it to profitability?

✓ What are the pitfalls and how do I avoid them?

✓ Where can an organization begin?

✓ Learn how to capitalize on workforce diversity!

*Empowering Your Diverse Workforce*

◇

ODT, Incorporated

### *Briefings and Round Table Discussions*

ODT Showcase Seminars are available at major cities throughout the U.S. Our management consulting, training and diagnostic services are available on all these topics and sessions can be conducted for companies on an in-house basis. Call for our latest schedule and request a free information packet. Howard Bronstein or Bob Abramms will be happy to give you the information you need.

If you cannot participate in a session now, order our 180 page showcase workbook pictured above for $139.00 and receive a free pass to attend the next up-coming seminar in your area. To place your order for this outstanding resource call 1-800-736-1293.

## *Upward Feedback and Appraisal for Managers*

◆ Build powerful boss-employee teams
◆ Encourage meaningful feedback conversations
◆ Establish priorities for 50 management skills
◆ Learn about specific feedback tools you can use
◆ Encourage a diversity of management styles
◆ Teach employees how to manage their bosses
◆ Investigate certification for classroom delivery
◆ Explore customized approaches to 360 degree feedback

## *Self-Directed Work Teams/ Organizational Empowerment*

◆ Diagnose organizational readiness
◆ Establish realistic time lines
◆ Coach senior managers to "walk-the-walk"
◆ Provide quality training for team developers
◆ Discuss results achieved in related industries
◆ Learn the "CRAY" feedback system for teams
◆ Create dramatic gains in efficiency, quality and productivity
◆ Explore structured peer feedback systems

## *Cultural Diversity/ Managing A Diverse Workforce*

◆ Assess organizational readiness
◆ Identify key resources to facilitate change
◆ "Selling" diversity internally
◆ Integrate diversity within management training
◆ Identify critical issues of team training
◆ Encourage open dialogue around differences
◆ Move beyond legal mandates to value diversity

## *Performance Appraisal/ Performance Management & Coaching*

◆ Teach employees how to **receive** a Performance Appraisal
◆ Empower employees with Performance Management
◆ Eliminate frustration and defensiveness on both sides
◆ Avoid unproductive communication "games"
◆ Create shared responsibility for the process
◆ Prevent surprises and clarify expectations
◆ Avoid changing the Performance Appraisal forms unnecessarily

ODT, Inc. • P.O. Box 134 • Amherst, MA 01004 • (413) 549-1293 • Fax: (413) 549-3503

❏ Please respond to my comments.

❏ You have my permission to quote my comments.

Name_____

Title_____

Organization_____ # of Employees_____

Address_____

City_____

State/Prov._____Zip/Postal Code_____ Country_____

Phone #_____ Fax#_____